THEODORE DREISER

Theodore Dreiser, 1928

(UP)

THEODORE DREISER

AN AMERICAN JOURNEY
1908–1945

RICHARD LINGEMAN

G. P. PUTNAM'S SONS   NEW YORK

Published by G. P. Putnam's Sons,
200 Madison Avenue, New York, NY 10016.
Published simultaneously in Canada

Photo credits will be found on pages 484-85
The text of this book is set in Janson.
Designed by Anthea Lingeman

Library of Congress Cataloging-in-Publication Data
(Revised for volume 2)
Lingeman, Richard R.
Theodore Dreiser.
Includes index.
Includes bibliographical references.
Contents: v. 1. At the gates of the city, 1871-1907
—v. 2. An American journey, 1908-1945.
1. Dreiser, Theodore, 1871-1945—Biography.
2. Novelists, American—20th century—Biography.
I. Title.
PS3507.R55Z664   1986   813'.52   86-9380
ISBN 0-399-13147-7 (v. 1)
ISBN 0-399-13520-0 (v. 2)

Printed in the United States of America

1 2 3 4 5 6 7 8 9 10

This book is printed on acid-free paper

To the Memory of

My Father,

Dr. Byron N. Lingeman

Contents

THEODORE DREISER

Listen: I will be honest with you; I do not offer the old, smooth prizes, but offer rough new prizes.

—WALT WHITMAN

No facts are to me sacred, none are profane; I simply experiment, an endless seeker, with no Past at my back.

—RALPH WALDO EMERSON

Part One

THE EDITOR

1908–1910

The Bohemian Within

> "Are you writing anything else?"
> "I have another book partly finished, but I don't know when I shall get it done. I have not the time to work on it, much as I want to."
> —Interview in *The New York Times Saturday Book Review* (1907)

In his January 1908 issue Theodore Dreiser, editor-in-chief, proudly announced the birth of the "NEW DELINEATOR," which had added "the idea of a household and literary supremacy" to its "usefulness to women in the matter of clothes." The reader turning to the front of the book might wonder what the fuss was about. She still found eighty or so pages of full-color drawings of the latest fashions, which she could make on her own sewing machine from a Butterick pattern.

But Dreiser's expanded features and more serious articles on current affairs had raised circulation since he arrived in July 1907. Now he was editor-in-chief of Butterick publications, presiding over *The Delineator* (popularly known as "the Del"), its English, French, Italian, and Spanish editions, and two other women's fashion magazines, *The Designer* and *The New Idea*, which, though nominally independent, were scaled-down versions of the Del and ran much the same material. The three magazines, known as "the Trio," had by 1909 soared from 400,000 to 1.2 million readers. In October 1908 newsstand orders for *The New Idea* were up an astonishing 43,000 copies over the previous year for that month.

The new editor's changes infused red corpuscles into the Del's tired blood. Before he came, editors had assumed that the women who read it never bothered their heads over anything that happened outside their backyards. George Warren Wilder, the president of the company, wanted a change. Wilder, known as "G.W." to distinguish him from his brother, Charles, a colorless man who was parked in the treasurer's slot, hired only "stars" to run his publications. He gave them a free rein, but if they didn't produce circulation miracles they would "hit the bricks," as he liked to put it. Magazines interested Wilder more than fashion patterns, Butterick's bread and butter, and although he was an aggressive, tough businessman—in the tradition of a company that had undercut, then bought out its main rivals—he hankered to carry on some modest crusades for the betterment of humanity. And so G.W. hired Theodore Dreiser, former novelist, author of *Sister Carrie*, called by its publisher in 1900 an "immoral book," who after a nervous breakdown that left him unable to finish his second novel, had turned to editing.

When Dreiser took over, managing editor Arthur Hoffman recalled, the Del was still "a fashion sheet with an omelet of magazine material poured loosely on and around it." Dreiser fought for more editorial space; created new departments on cooking, entertaining, and other aspects of women's lives; purchased more sophisticated short stories; and commissioned articles on social problems. In his monthly editorials he exhorted the magazine's housewife readers to take an interest in the world around them and do something about such problems as contaminated milk, ugly towns, and backward public education. He brought in famous names like Woodrow Wilson, Mrs. William Howard Taft, William Jennings Bryan, and Jack London to tell their personal stories.

When Wilder, father of four children, wanted a series on child care, Dreiser snapped to and engaged Dr. Leonard Hirshberg, of Baltimore, to write it. And when Hirshberg's style turned out to be too prolix and technical for the average Del reader, he found him a ghostwriter—a young Baltimore newspaperman named Henry Louis Mencken—and urged him to put Hirshberg's admonitions into simple English. Where Hirshberg had written in an article on diphtheria, "unluckily, there still lingers in the United States a superstitious dread of antitoxin," Dreiser instructed Mencken to speak directly to mothers: "You probably know a great deal about doctoring your children and someone has told you that antitoxin is a deadly poison or a filthy drug. It is nothing of the sort; if you are a wise mother you will listen closely to the wonderful facts in connection with the discovery."

Wilder's biggest idea was the Child Rescue Campaign. While walking through the slums near the Butterick Building in New York, he had noticed large numbers of ragamuffins and asked himself, "What homes have these children?" And so he proposed that the magazine publish pictures and short descriptions of two orphan children in every issue. Readers who wished to adopt them could write in, and their names would be forwarded to the social agency that had custody of the child, and it would choose the most suitable parents and arrange for the adoption. In all, more than 2000 children were placed.

A Butterick executive later downgraded Dreiser's role in this effort. "G.W. had the ideas and Dreiser just happened to be the editor when he got them," he wrote. But Dreiser gave the campaign a strong editorial push, launching it with the publication of an article on city waifs by one of his best writers, Mabel Potter Daggett. The following month he announced in his column of editorial musings, "Concerning Us All," that the magazine would bring together "the child that needs a home and the home that needs a child."

After a year, Dreiser seemed assured of success, but sometimes his subordinates caught him gazing out the window, lost in thought. When William C. Lengel, one of Dreiser's secretaries, asked him why a man who could write such a great book as *Sister Carrie* wasted his time editing a ladies' magazine, Dreiser shrugged. "One must live." Only the year before he had told a reporter from *The New York Times* that he had a book "partly finished" but had no time to work on it. He said he wanted to write about "life as it is."

He had started that unfinished novel, called *The Transgressor,* in 1902, and completed thirty-odd chapters, but because of "an error in character analysis" he virtually abandoned it in 1903. In 1905, while he was editing *Smith's,* Grant Richards, a British publisher who on one of his scouting trips to New York had heard about *Sister Carrie* from the novelist Frank Norris, sent a complimentary note, which arrived just when Dreiser's morale was at a low ebb. Richards asked if he might be the British publisher of his next novel and urged Dreiser to send him a copy of the manuscript as soon as it was finished: "I don't want to wait a day longer than I can help before I read it."

No manuscript was forthcoming, but Richards kept writing Dreiser from time to time. At last, in March 1908, Dreiser sent the British publisher twenty chapters of the manuscript. Richards offered some stylistic advice (the words " 'pronunciamento' and 'affectional' seem to me quite out of place"); he also expressed his "keen pleasure that the promise of 'Sister Carrie' is being fulfilled. . . ." He closed with a lighthearted aside: "I believe the book will healthily depress every one of its intelligent readers."

Richards' jesting remark almost put Dreiser off the novel for good. He replied that maybe he had "better drop that yarn and take up something else. Perhaps my later mood will not be so sombre. . . ." Richards quickly soothed him: "All I can say is that if I did not convince you that I thought 'Jennie' was a very fine piece of work, indeed, a fit and worthy successor to 'Sister

Carrie,' then I must have expressed myself very clumsily and inadequately. It is my 'absolute conviction that the thing is really worth while.' I should publish it with enthusiasm and pride." But a fear that the story was too grim and "immoral" gnawed at Dreiser.

Indeed, although he dreamed of returning to full-time writing, a sense of failure haunted him, even though *Sister Carrie* had received good notices and sold well after it was reissued in 1907. Deep insecurities stemming from his boyhood poverty made the ample pay, not to mention the power and prestige, of his present job addictive. Although he later told biographer Dorothy Dudley that he was "a very simple person with no money to spend on luxuries," he liked fashionable clothes, enjoyed travel, and demanded a well-endowed table. Sartorially, his tastes ran to heavy tweeds—"quality" stuffs, Johnston & Murphy shoes, and Knox hats. "The label gives you a certain standing," he explained to Lengel. Ludwig Lewisohn, an aspiring novelist who had become one of his protégés, saw him wearing an elegant overcoat with a nipped-in waist that looked bizarre on his bulky, six-foot one-inch frame. Lewisohn was surprised to hear that this literary radical was a regular in the Sunday fashion parade on Riverside Drive, resplendent in a top hat and Prince Albert coat, like his brother Paul Dresser, the song-writer, wore during his prosperous days. His correspondence with Richards betrays a creeping Anglophilia.

Still, he lived modestly enough with his wife of ten years, Sara, universally known as "Jug," who kept a tight rein on the budget. They still resided in the apartment at 439 West 123rd Street, to which they had moved in 1906. They vacationed at Mackinac Island, gave dinner parties (at which Jug would allow no alcohol to be served), and spent weekends on Long Island's North Shore as guests at the mansions of J. G. Robin, a Gatsbyan financier, and the fashionable architect William Neil (Billy) Smith. Otherwise they led a quiet bourgeois existence. A friend who called one evening found Dreiser correcting proofs on one end of the dining-room table and Jug ironing on the other.

After two years with Butterick, Dreiser made some modest investments in real estate—a $1000 option on two lots in a 150-acre tract near Nanuet, New York, on which a bungalow colony called Grand View was to be built, and a down payment on a ten-acre apple orchard in Washington State worth $3000.

In 1907 Dreiser had also purchased $1000 worth of B. W. Dodge and Company stock, in effect subsidizing the reissue of *Sister Carrie*. As a member of the firm's board of directors, he played an active editorial role in scouting literary talent. He concentrated mainly on unknowns, men like Lewisohn; H. L. Mencken, whom he initially approached to do a short book on Schopenhauer; Fritz Krog, an eccentric genius and, like Lengel and Homer Croy, one of the young men from Missouri he hired because he had met Jug while working as a reporter in St. Louis; Charles Fort, a novelist and philosopher; and Upton Sinclair, who after *The Jungle* had touched the stomach but not the heart of the American people, had written two socialistic novels, *The Metropolis* and *The Money-Changers,* which attacked Wall Street and Newport society and which no other publisher would handle. Dreiser also brought in Peter McCord, an artist whom he had known since their days together on the St. Louis *Globe-Democrat,* whose novel, *The Wolf,* the firm published. (When McCord died suddenly of pneumonia in 1908, Dreiser was severely shaken.) All of these literary aspirants were more drawn to the author of *Sister Carrie* than to the editor of *The Delineator.*

Dreiser kept his ties with Dodge a secret from the Butterick hierarchy, reading manuscripts in his spare time or delegating the task to Jug. He was also forced to deal with the company's increasingly snarled financial affairs, though he had no head for business. Receiving a financial statement from Dodge, he passed it on to his assistant, Fremont Rider, with a penciled notation: "Can you make any sense out of this?"

Possibly no one could have made sense of the books, not even Dodge, who was a brilliant promoter but a disorderly businessman, forced constantly to search for a "doughbags" to bail him out. Later, Dodge admitted to Dreiser that he had gambled $3000 of the firm's funds on the Grand View venture. With pathetic pride, he said he had pledged his own stock in the firm—which could hardly have been worth much, given the impending bankruptcy—as restitution. The gesture typified Ben Dodge's life. He was an alcoholic and his benders grew more frequent as the company sank deeper into debt. In October 1910 the firm was reorganized with William Rickey as president and a new board of directors, composed of major creditors, installed.

In July 1909 Dreiser purchased for $1000 a disreputable and bankrupt magazine called the *Bohemian.* In a letter to Mencken he explained that he hoped to "have some fun with the project." He seemed to regard it as an editorial pasture, a place to kick up his heels against the restraints at the Del. He assured Mencken, however, that he was not about to relinquish control of Butterick publications. Mencken, ever ready to oblige his New York mentor, replied that he was "in with both feet." Dreiser dispatched a more detailed editorial prospectus. First of all, he wanted to make the *Bohemian* "the broadest, most genial little publication in the field." While he wanted no "tainted fiction" or "sex struck articles," he aimed at "a big catholic point of view, a sense of humor grim or gay, and articles on any conceivable subject. . . . I want bright stuff. I want humor. And above all I want knowledge of life *as it is.* . . . "

Perhaps Dreiser hadn't noticed that the young Baltimorean had become an important figure in his city's press corps. At age twenty-nine, Mencken was holding down the jobs of editorial writer, editor of the Sunday section, and assistant managing editor of the daily *Sun*. He submitted a number of ideas for a department called "At the Sign of the Lead Pencil," which Dreiser had described vaguely as "broad interesting shots at current conditions from any point of view so long as it is clever." Mencken's first contribution, "A Plea for Profanity," suited Dreiser to a T, and he begged for more. When the first issue, dated October, was in the works, Dreiser bombarded his Baltimore genius at the eleventh hour with requests for copy: "Need three funny editorials bad. Can I get them Monday." Mencken's stuff was in hand on Monday—a weekend's fast work—and it was good. Dreiser positively doted on his find, an editor's dream. Their friendship had flourished in the shared recognition that neither was doing the work he wanted to do. Although Mencken loved journalism, he was in a hurry to make his mark in a literary way. As he wrote Dreiser: "I am getting along toward thirty and it is time for me to be planning for the future. Specifically, I want to write a couple of books for you within the next few years. Specifically again, I want to write a play that now encumbers and tortures my system. You will understand what a stew I am in."

Dreiser understood. Discussing fees for the baby-care series, Dreiser had said, "I suppose the low ebb of the literary life in Baltimore has something to do with" his resorting to hackwork.

Although ten years younger, Mencken was a fellow alumnus of the newsroom university and an early admirer of *Sister Carrie*. When they met face to face in the late spring of 1908, Dreiser's initial impression was of the playboy son of a prosperous brewer dressed in a loud suit and yellow shoes for a night on the town. Unawed by Dreiser's cavernous office or his large chair designed to intimidate visitors, the 5′ 8″ Mencken lolled back insouciantly, a cocky, snub-nosed, jug-eared young man, his hair parted in the middle, and beamed at the great editor "with the confidence of a smirking fox about to devour a chicken."

On Mencken's subsequent visits to New York City he and Dreiser quaffed steins of lager at Lüchow's and argued boisterously about literature, science, God, religion, and myriad other topics. Dreiser did not share Mencken's near worship of Nietzsche, calling the German philosopher "Schopenhauer confused and warmed over." Mencken inscribed his third book, *The Philosophy of Friedrich Nietzsche*, to his friend, "In memory of furious disputations on sorcery & the art of letters."

Their differences erupted when Mencken contributed a short essay called "The Decay of the Churches" to the *Bohemian*. In it he praised science and deplored reliance on a higher power. Dreiser, who was still a disciple of Herbert Spencer, contended that the universe functioned in harmony with fixed scientific laws, that the religious instinct was inherent in human nature, and that scientists and philosophers were "truly reverential" in that they prayed for more knowledge. He concluded, "The truth is men are not less religious—they are religious in a different way—and that's a fact."

This dispute was quickly smoothed over. It was only a hairline fracture in their growing friendship, and Mencken repaired it by telling Dreiser to change the editorial any way he wished. Their affinities ran deep despite their disparate backgrounds. Mencken had been raised in solid bourgeois comfort by a freethinking father, while Dreiser had grown up in deepest poverty in a large family ruled by a strict, dogmatic Catholic father. Dreiser had rebelled against the Church and the stern God and fiery hell conjured up by his father but tended to believe that the universe was guided by an intelligent, if not intelligible, purpose. When he wrote in his editorial column, "Back of all this show . . . back of the numberlessness of things, and the difference of things, is the *same* thing. . . . What is it? Laws, will you say? Higher laws? . . . And who sets the laws in motion? Who keeps us?"—he was expressing his own agnosticism, complete to the question mark.

Dreiser's most important intervention in Mencken's life was to help launch him as a book critic. In the spring of 1908, Dreiser learned that a former Butterick employee, Fred Splint, was seeking a reviewer for the *Smart Set,* of which he had recently become editor. Dreiser recommended Mencken, and he was hired "with the rank and pay of a sergeant of artillery" and handed a pile of books. By fall he was reviewing at a furious pace—twenty-five volumes a month—praising realistic American literature and damning publishers' timidity and the genteel best sellers of the day. The following year he was joined on the staff by a kindred spirit, George Jean Nathan, a drama critic.

The *Bohemian* lasted four issues and died unmourned, save by Mencken. The magazine was a hodgepodge of fiction and articles on such subjects as spiritualism, Russian spies, and "How [Oscar] Hammerstein Chooses a Chorus." In December 1909 Dreiser told Mencken he had decided to close the magazine and would pay him for several editorials and a satirical playlet called *The Artist.* When Dreiser couldn't get the money from Smith, he sent his personal check for eighty dollars, and when Mencken refused to cash it insisted he at least take fifty dollars for the play because "I feel a sense of responsibility beyond your kind feelings."

After nearly ten years of marriage, Dreiser's marriage, like Hurstwood's in *Sister Carrie,* was like dry tinder, waiting the spark. It came when he joined a group of ballroom dancing devotees called the Fantastic Toe Club and met an eighteen-year-old beauty named Thelma Cudlipp. As Dreiser wrote in his autobiographical novel, *The "Genius,"* "Nothing could equal the beauty of a young woman in her eighteenth or nineteenth year."

Thelma was studying at the Artists League and was the daughter of Annie Ericsson Cudlipp, a formidable widow from Virginia who was in charge of the stenographic pool at the Butterick Company. Hired by

Dreiser, who had a soft spot for widows with families to support, she had been befriended by Jug, who invited Thelma and her mother to dinner and sometimes invited the young woman to sleep over after a night's dancing. Jug seemed to encourage her husband's outings with the younger crowd as a way of taking his mind off his Butterick responsibilities. She would call Mrs. Cudlipp and say, "Theo wants a party. Can you manage it, dear Mrs. Cudlipp? Bring your gayest young people."

Thelma's first intimation of Dreiser's interest in her came during a ball at the Staten Island Yacht Club. They had walked out on the veranda. "Do you like to dance with me as much as those younger men?" Dreiser suddenly asked her. Stirred, Thelma replied, "You must know I do, Mr. Dreiser." He told her to call him Theo and assured her that Mrs. Dreiser approved of their friendship.

"Then he kissed me," Thelma wrote in "October's Child," her unpublished memoirs. Throughout their friendship that was the only time he kissed her. His most amorous memories of her consisted of "your soft little pats on my cheek, your murmured sweet words, your snuggling body. The day . . . you drew so close to me rubbing your shoulder against mine. . . ." Thelma was so innocent that she could not imagine anything more, in a physical way, in their relationship. She was as much in awe as in love. There were other meetings, dances, rendezvous at Long Island house parties, long walks, even meetings at a Butterick employee's apartment. He called her "Little Blue Bird," "Flower Face," "Divine Fire" and "Honeypot," a twist on Jug's pet name for him, "Honeybugs." He talked baby talk to her, and together they composed silly jingles that he proposed to make into a children's book that Thelma would illustrate.

Mrs. Cudlipp did nothing to discourage what seemed an innocent friendship, and when Jug fell ill with rheumatic fever in the spring of 1910, she counted on the Cudlipps more than ever to provide amusement and companionship for her neglected Theo. It was at that point that the relationship between Dreiser and Thelma entered a dangerous phase.

He was making a grab for the brass ring of youth. Acutely, even neurotically conscious of the passage of time, he felt the cold blasts of forty bearing down on him. Even before Jug's illness his sexual desire for her had cooled. It was now a marriage of convenience—his from the standpoint of comfort and hers from that of convention and social position. Jug was that paragon of "practical home-craft," that "one great humanizing force of humanity" he extolled in a *Delineator* editorial. She trimmed her own hats and ran off dresses on the sewing machine (presumably following a Butterick pattern). Nearly two years older than her husband, she turned forty in 1909. To Dreiser, that seemed practically middle-aged.

But she provided the home and mothering he both craved and subconsciously resented. As his niece Vera Dreiser, a psychologist, wrote in her biography, *My Uncle Theodore*, he was still inseparably bound to his much-adored mother, who had died twenty years before but who had "dwarfed his capacity to love, leaving him forever in a state of arrested emotional development. Consequently, he transferred to his young wife . . . the latent hostilities that rightly belonged to his mother." Poor Jug had unwittingly assumed the role of maternal superego in his life. Or as he once told her, *she made him mind, and he hated having to mind.*

As though asserting her hold over him, she insisted on calling him Honeybugs in public, in a way that made Dreiser's friends wince. She constantly fussed over him, as witness this communiqué dispatched while visiting her brother and sister-in-law in Schenectady: "I wish you were coming tonight. I don't know what you'll do for underwear. Better get a new suit. You have clean sox and shirt, etc. Your sox are on the towels in the window box. Change your towels too."

One spouse was shocked by Dreiser's "shabby" treatment of Jug when they came to dinner. Many Butterick colleagues wondered what he saw in her; she seemed nice but small-townish. Dreiser felt that she had not kept pace intellectually with his rapid rise in the magazine world. In an editorial in *The Delineator* he was surely describing her: "In case a man has married a woman in one state or plane of his life and finds at forty or fifty that he has risen above that state, supposing the woman that he married at twenty no longer represents the spirit or interests of his larger existence—that she is neither beautiful nor intellectual—has not kept pace with him in his upward progress—what does that man owe that woman?"

As for her, she gloried in her role as consort to the editor of *The Delineator*. Sharing in his success was her rightful due, she thought. She had, after all, nursed him through the dark days following the failure of *Sister Carrie* (actually she had returned to her family when his fortunes and spirits were at their lowest ebb). She even took some credit for the subsequent literary success of that book—or so he declared. Some of their friends suspected she harbored literary ambitions.

When Dreiser took over, *The Delineator* was running a lengthy series of articles on "Marital Unrest," but he concealed his own from the staff. Most assumed he was happily married.

But Dreiser had begun some furtive roving, and Jug was mortified by his "uncontrollable urge when near a woman to lay his hand upon her and stroke her or otherwise come into contact with her." Yet despite—or perhaps because of—his own vagrant drives he was extremely jealous: He "had no confidence in the fidelity of any woman or man—not even me," she said. "He thought himself typical."

Jug begged him to let her have a child, thinking that fatherhood would steady him. But he adamantly refused, as he had throughout their marriage. He liked children well enough and could sincerely pity the orphans featured in *The Delineator*'s Child Rescue Campaign—they too had been abandoned. But having a child of his own would mean the end of his monopoly of Jug's maternal instincts. He did not tell her this, of course, instead saying that giving birth would ruin her figure, the implication being that she would become unattractive to him. And, obviously, having a child would strengthen her hold over him. (Much later, he told a woman friend that he used to have a recurrent dream of Jug chasing him with a perambulator.)

The tinder was dry, and Thelma set it aflame. Their initial platonic friendship gave way to the pressure of his strong sexual desires. He pursued her in total obliviousness to Jug. As Thelma later put it, "He must have hypnotized himself." She was the glittering prize that would make his success complete. As he wrote her, "I NEED you. You are the breath of life to me. All my life I have longed for this."

One evening in the spring of 1910, after an excursion to the Palisades amusement park with a group of young Butterick employees, Thelma and Dreiser were sitting alone in the living room of the 123rd Street apartment. He told her that their love had reached a stage when his "man's desire" must be satisfied. Suddenly Thelma glimpsed a slender figure framed in the doorway, her copper hair in braids that seemed to reach to the floor, her eyes flashing, her body trembling with a profound emotion. Jug called Thelma a foolish girl and threatened to tell her mother about the entire affair. Later, there was a horrendous quarrel between Dreiser and Jug—or so he wrote in *The "Genius."* The real-life outcome was the same as the one in the book: he refused to stop seeing Thelma.

Despite her illness, Jug fought ferociously to save her marriage. She wrote Thelma reproachful letters, ordering her to forget Dreiser. Aghast at the prospect of her daughter's becoming involved with a married man twice her age, the distraught Annie Cudlipp began playing a double game, trying to buy time in hopes that Thelma would tire of the romance.

In late July 1910 Dreiser wrote Mencken, "Mrs. Dreiser was quite bad but is better and looks as though she will be all right in the course of 10 days or two weeks." Beneath those bland words flowed an undercurrent of guilt. The thought that Jug might die and free him to marry Thelma had surely crossed his mind. He later wrote a story called "Free," about an unhappily married man who waited too long. His wife's death liberates him, but he is too old to enjoy his freedom. Bitterly, he tells himself he is "free—free to die." Dreiser evoked the stifling sense of entrapment he felt in his own marriage. His creative powers were deeply implicated in his erotic drives: the blind force of love was inseparable from the life urge itself—it represented desire, danger, conquest, beauty.

CHAPTER 2 *Amid the Ruins*

> Here was all the solid foundation knocked from under him.
> . . . His shimmering world of dreams was beginning to fade
> like an evening sky. It might be that he had been chasing
> a will-o'-the-wisp, after all.
>
> —*The "Genius"* (1915)

hat was already a bad melodrama took a farcical turn when Fritz Krog, himself infatuated with Thelma, heard of Dreiser's involvement. He became wildly jealous, telling Croy he intended to kill his rival, but then decided he didn't want to kill Dreiser after all.

Meanwhile, Annie Cudlipp revealed the full story to George Wilder and issued an ultimatum: if Wilder did not put a stop to the romance, she would take the story to the newspapers. Not only would she tell them that the editor of *The Delineator* was carrying on with an eighteen-year-old girl, she would also reveal that Erman J. Ridgway, publisher of *Everybody's* magazine, which had recently merged with the Butterick publishing group, was doing the same with one of *his* assistants. Faced with that double-barreled threat, Wilder was forced to act. In late September 1910, a delegation from the fourteenth floor —the Butterick executive suite—consisting of Birmingham, Ridgway, and Wilder, marched into Dreiser's sanctum. Wilder offered Dreiser a choice: Thelma or his job. Dreiser refused to give her up.

. . .

In fact, the Thelma scandal was only the proximate cause of Dreiser's downfall. As Arthur Hoffman, managing editor at the time, recalled, "Though the young lady afforded occasion and might have been sufficient warrant, office politics was out for his scalp long before that came up." Lengel thought the advertising department was miffed because Dreiser had increased circulation faster than they could legitimately raise their rates; as a result, the costs of the expanded readership had outstripped revenues, making the advertising salesmen look bad.

All the fights with what Dreiser called "the God damned hyenas on the eighth floor" had left suppurating wounds. He had enemies in the advertising and the pattern departments. In his simmering quarrel with Lewis Dempsey of the former, tensions ran so high that they stopped speaking, and Hoffman had to carry messages between them. Another Dreiser foe was James F. Birmingham, a tough, self-made man who ran the pattern department. They frequently clashed over the amount of space in the front of the book devoted to fashion reporting and lavishly illustrated descriptions of the latest Butterick patterns.

"Butterick . . . was notorious for its office politics and the difficulties of its many editors," Hoffman recalled. Office politics had heated up in the fall of 1909 after Butterick purchased *Everybody's* magazine, owned by the Ridgway Company, and Erman J. Ridgway became a director of Butterick publications. Inevitably, Dreiser locked horns with Ridgway over budgets and editorial content. A trace of their infighting survives in a memorandum that Dreiser wrote about a year after the merger, complaining about Ridgway's order that *The Delineator* staff work on Labor Day and reminding him that he had promised not to interfere with "the working arrangements of Butterick Company employees."

Success may have made Dreiser overconfident. His first misstep was a six-part series on spiritualism in 1908, "Are the Dead Alive?" It was considered blasphemous by Bible Belt readers, generating a wave of angry letters, to which Dreiser was forced to reply in the magazine. Admitting that the articles "have raised a storm around our editorial head," he assured readers that he had not intended to proselytize for spiritualism, "only to give an unbiased, impartial presentation."

In an interview with a Boston *Globe* reporter who had inquired about *The Delineator*'s "prospectus" for the coming year, Wilder was jocular, as was his style, but there was an edge in his voice: "Our editor is a wonder,— he changes his mind so fast there ain't no Prospectus." One thing Wilder is sure of: the magazine is going to discontinue the "Are the Dead Alive?" series and "a few other circulation destroyers, but even then I won't guarantee the editor from attacking the church—any old church—but I am going to try to keep him good."

Thereafter Dreiser trod softly when religion was the subject. He announced in the Christmas issue an upcoming series of articles on "the spirit of the new Christianity," the first being "Why One Hundred Sunday-Schools Have Succeeded." In 1910 he asked H. G. Wells to tone down a novel submitted to the Del for serialization. While Wells's theme "might delight the highly intellectual women," he said, "it would possibly offend the rank and file." He asked Wells "to modify or eliminate in the remainder of the book the keen thrusts against morality and society. . . ."

Dreiser's personality was also an issue. He himself admitted he was hard to get along with. He seems to have respected Wilder, and vice versa, but socially they had little in common beyond an interest in the success of *The Delineator*. As the son of an immigrant and a "Westerner," Dreiser lacked the Eastern establishment credentials of Wilder and Ridgway, both of whom were graduates of Ivy League schools, fraternity men, Congregationalists, and Republicans. Wilder was a strong family man, while Dreiser had a shaky marriage and no desire for offspring.

With the advent of Ridgway, who was friendly with the Butterick president, Dreiser became increasingly isolated and vulnerable. He had little talent for corporate infighting. He was a creative editor who preferred generating ideas and working with writers to empire building. His style was to delegate authority to talented people, and after he became obsessed with Thelma Cudlipp, he let the reins on his department heads go slack. He withdrew from the battle at the wrong moment: just as his rival was busily forging alliances and installing his own people. Dreiser's protégés could sense the power shift, and some of them defected to Ridgway's camp to protect their jobs.

And so *l'affaire Thelma* was the pretext for drawing the knives. All that remained was for Wilder to set the day. Unwilling to give up Thelma, Dreiser renounced his throne. He agreed to a face-saving resignation as of October 15, 1910.

Only Croy was there to bid him farewell and hand him a briefcase stuffed with his personal things. His departure came as a surprise to most of the staff. Few knew the real reason for his going, and even Lengel was in the dark for a long time. Fremont Rider, who had been intimately involved in Dreiser's extracurricular business interests, was also unaware of his amorous affairs and sent a letter expressing his regrets. In his reply, Dreiser implied that he had resigned on a matter of principle: "I do not consider my resignation in the light of a loss. The big work was done there. . . . I had been fighting interference for sometime & finally stood the whole thing out."

He let slip his true feelings to Mencken in a hasty, unsigned memo: "I have just discovered that this is a very sad world." Later he explained,

"Nothing's up save a big row. It's all over now though & I am considering several good things. My conscience hurts me a little though for first-off I should finish my book. And I may."

Temporarily separated from Jug, who was being nursed by her sister, he moved to a Park Avenue hotel to pine for Thelma in lonely splendor. His room overlooked the courtyard restaurant, and, in the evening when the sounds of an orchestra wafted up and the little red lamps on each table glowed like fireflies, he felt unutterably sad. One day Lengel dropped in and found his former boss sitting disconsolately on his bed, endlessly folding his handkerchief, the picture of a broken man. Yet Dreiser insisted that he was all right and spoke optimistically of his prospects. He might buy into a publishing house or manage a literary syndicate or edit a newspaper. He dickered for an interest in the Wildman Magazine and News Service, but negotiations broke down when he insisted on an equal partnership and refused to invest his own money.

He was, as he told Mencken, inclining toward finishing "The Transgressor" and so was hanging on to his savings. He told Thelma, who had been spirited by her mother to North Carolina to stay with relatives, that he was "not at all anxious" about his future and that Jug was "taking it all much better than I thought she would and I fancy things are going to come out nicely." As for the loss of his job—"You are worth it all—my worry, my position, the danger of publicity—everything—I gladly pay the price & would pay it again. Strange isn't it and wonderful. But it is exactly so—"

Meanwhile Annie Cudlipp was playing her last hand—double or nothing. She told Dreiser he could marry her daughter on two conditions: that he obtain a divorce and that he agree not to see Thelma for one year. He agreed, but the prospect of a long separation plunged him deeper into gloom.

Actually Annie's offer was a bluff—another attempt to buy time in hopes her daughter's interest would cool. Even the self-hypnotized Dreiser now suspected that Annie was leading him on.

Fearing that he might do something desperate, Mrs. Cudlipp refused to accompany him to North Carolina for a meeting on neutral ground. In a letter to Thelma written before he left, he begs her not to go away; he would accept "even a mere sight of you once in two weeks." He closes with an abject plea: "Oh, Honeypot be kind—be kind to me. You said once you would be mother & sister and sweetheart to me. I am a little pleading boy now in need of your love, your mother love. Won't you help me. Please do Honeypot—please do. I beg of you—oh, I beg of you! I will make it up to you in a thousand ways all my life. Don't leave me to stay here alone. Please don't."

The meeting would have changed nothing. If Thelma had once loved him, a love that was part hero-worship and part schoolgirl crush, she was now having doubts; she had blundered into a terrifying grown-ups' world with lurking monsters of convention and sexuality. The man who had once been her idol was now begging her to be a mother to him. She was a very inexperienced and mixed-up young woman, and it was years before she realized that Dreiser "had counted on me with all his man's passion for final liberation. I didn't know what passion was. I was such a stupid thing." Perhaps Dreiser could have won her if he had swept aside Annie's protestations and forced Thelma to come back with him to New York. But tattered remnants of the decorum with which he had conducted his courtship remained, and he hadn't the courage to face down the tiger-mother.

Then, to make sure that Thelma did not elope with Dreiser on her own, as Thelma recounts it in her unpublished memoir, her mother had a friend tell her all about sex and "man's desire." It was evidently a graphic lesson, laced with Victorian horrors, for it left Thelma disgusted and angry at Dreiser for wanting to subject her to such a nasty business. She agreed to go to London, where she would live with her uncle and study art at the Royal Academy.

Inwardly Dreiser was shattered, but unlike Hurstwood, he was not without resources. He had saved money; he had friends, editorial contacts, a literary reputation—and an unfinished novel on his desk. Richards, Mencken, his literary agent, Flora Mai Holly, among others, urged him to return to writing. The influential critic James Gibbons Huneker had written him only recently: "I'm sorry for the Delineator's sake that you are leaving it and I hope you have something better. *But*—if you, Theodore Dreiser, could or would return to your old field, the gain for our literature would be something worthwhile. We have but one *Sister Carrie*, despite the army of imitators."

But how much easier it was to be a well-paid purveyor of Human Betterment to housewives than to subject himself to what he had called "the lonely tortures of writing." In what he saw as a country without culture, where the businessman called the tune, the serious artist was ignored or condescended to. As he would write in *The "Genius,"* "Why follow a profession or craft in which . . . all your days you were tolerated for your genius with a kindly smile, used as an ornament at receptions but never taken seriously as a factor in the commercial affairs of the world?" Why not be a sort of businessman-artist—somehow melding power and affluence with the artist's selfless aspiration for beauty?

But there was a price for the power and affluence he had enjoyed. Much later he candidly assessed the *Delineator* years:

> It was pathetic, as I look at it now, the things we were trying to do and the conditions under which we were trying to do them—the raw commercial force and theory which underlay the whole thing, the necessity

of explaining and fighting for so much that one should not, as I saw it then, have to argue over at all. . . . My own experience with *Sister Carrie*, as well as the fierce opposition or chilling indifference which, as I saw, overtook all those who attempted anything even partially serious in America, was enough to make me believe that the world took anything even slightly approximating the truth as one of the rankest and most criminal offenses possible. One dared not talk out loud, one dared not report life as it was, as one lived it.

CHAPTER 3

Jennie Redivivus

> I have just finished one book—Jennie Gerhardt—and am half through with another. I expect to try out this book game for about four or five books after which unless I am enjoying a good income from them I will quit.
>
> —Dreiser to Mencken (1914)

Worried about whether Dreiser would continue to provide for her, Jug consulted Thomas H. McKee, the lawyer who had tried to untangle Paul Dresser's song copyrights in 1906.

When McKee called on her in the fall of 1910, he found her ill but anxious to confide in someone. As the lawyer recalled to Dreiser biographer Robert H. Elias, "Little by little she unfolded a tale of marital distress, giving details which were strange even to my accustomed ears and of which I cannot speak." When he asked her if she was willing to take legal action to force Dreiser to support her, she demurred. Theo must not even know that she had spoken with McKee; the publicity of a court proceeding would hurt his "standing" and she did not want that. His hands tied, McKee advised her to work out a reconciliation and left.

Dreiser continued to send her money and paid a conciliatory visit, for he felt sorry for her and did not intend to abandon her. But their separation continued, and Jug went off to Missouri to recuperate, and Dreiser moved from his hotel to a rented room in the large apartment of Elias Rosenthal at 608 Riverside Drive. The cultivated Rosenthal, an attorney, and his wife,

Emma, a writer, frequently entertained people from the artistic and business worlds. They also provided a cover of respectability, for Dreiser was still worried about appearances.

Like other defectors from middle-class conventions, he sometimes fled to Greenwich Village, a burgeoning Bohemian quarter. On Christmas Eve, he attended the Anarchists' Ball, where he was spotted by a lanky, red-haired Minnesota exile named Sinclair Lewis, who had three years before written an item for *Life* about Dreiser's accession to the top job at Butterick. In that squib, Lewis compares Dreiser to a wholesale hardware merchant with a well-filled waistcoat, but he also suggests that he admired *Sister Carrie.* In a letter describing the anarchists' fete he calls Dreiser "about the biggest realist in America . . . in spite of the fact that he's done only one book so far."

Lewis was more awed by the star guest—Emma Goldman, whom Dreiser engaged in a heated discussion of anarchism. He "waggled his scrawny forefinger, and looked superiority [sic] through his heavy, gold rimmed, scholastic eye glasses; but Emma sent back hot shot." She proclaimed that "a complete emancipation of individuality from all the old bonds of religion and government and prejudice and ignorance is at hand." Dreiser considered her the most important American woman of her time, and had commissioned a profile of her for *The Delineator,* instructing the writer to pretend to denounce her while smuggling across her ideas.

Later, Lewis reports, Dreiser turned his attention to a more glamorous woman, and the three of them repaired to a café called Joel's and "watched the actresses celebrate Xmas at 4 in the morning."

Dreiser was exploring the charms of Greenwich Village in a tentative way, and he met such Bohemians as the anarchist Hippolyte Havel, cook and live-in lover at Polly Holladay's restaurant, where *le tout Bohème* dined. His artist friends Robert Amick and Percy Cowan shared digs in the Village, and he invited Mencken to a "dandy lobster blowout" at their place at 63 Washington Square.

But he had little time for play. None of his halfhearted efforts to launch a new career had panned out, so he turned to the job of finishing the story of Jennie Gerhardt. He had no publisher as yet, but he had received nibbles from several editors, including Ripley Hitchcock at Harper & Brothers, an admirer of *Sister Carrie* who had discussed the second novel with Dreiser as long ago as 1903. As soon as Hitchcock heard that Dreiser had departed from Butterick, he wrote to congratulate him on being "fortunate enough to be released from the strain of office work" and asked if he had a novel on the hob. Dreiser replied that he expected to finish one by December 1 and had engaged Flora Mai Holly, who had handled the republication of *Sister Carrie,* as his agent. Send along the manuscript, Hitchcock cried—in time to make the spring list.

. . .

Dreiser's prediction that he would finish by December was unrealistic. Nevertheless, he worked furiously and actually completed a version by early January, picking up where he left off as long ago as 1904, the point in the story when the sister of Lester Kane, Jennie's wealthy lover, barges in on the apartment where the two are living together. Once he reached the place where Lester faces the disapproval of his family, he had been beset by doubts about how to handle the outcome of the story. Should the couple continue to live in sin or should they marry? And if the latter, wouldn't the moralists protest that he was "rewarding" her?

He solved the problem by the Victorian device of a will. Lester's father dies, leaving a testament stipulating that if he abandons Jenny he will receive his full inheritance worth an estimated $1.5 million; if he marries her, he will receive $10,000 a year for life, but he will lose his share of the family fortune. Dreiser thus writes the moralists' choices into Archibald Kane's will, enforcing them with a pecuniary sanction. If Lester does the "right thing"— observes the convention—he will collect his full monetary reward and return to the good graces of his family. But he will also grievously hurt Jennie, a devoted woman, and destroy the only loving relationship in his aimless life. Conventional morality is ironically reduced to a financial calculation, opposed to human feelings.

Lester has three years to decide. Loath to hurt Jennie, he procrastinates and almost weds Lettie Gerald, a beautiful, wealthy widow and an old admirer. Marriage to Lettie would be a most attractive solution to Lester's dilemma, but in the end he realizes that Jennie's love is the only happiness he will ever know in a life that he finds increasingly meaningless, and so he returns to her for good.

Dreiser had toned down the rakish side of Lester's character (in 1902 it had been a projection of his own fantasies, which he was now living). He also made Jennie more sexually magnetic and womanly. These are improvements: Lester is no longer a Machiavellian seducer but a complex man who sees through social sham; Jennie is a life force rather than merely a seduced and abandoned waif.

In Dreiser's revised plot, marriage "rewarded" Jennie, but at least it gave her respectability. Perhaps that compromise would satisfy the prudes. Still, he was uneasy and circulated copies of the manuscript among friends for advice and criticism.

Among the first readers was Lillian Rosenthal, the twenty-year-old daughter of Elias and Emma, a plump and pretty young woman with a musical bent. Her literary background consisted mainly of reading some of the more "advanced" European authors, but that was enough to tell her that the optimistic ending rang false. The Tolstoy who wrote *Anna Karenina,* the Hardy of *Tess of the D'Urbervilles* (a book Dreiser had long admired that traces the cruelty society visits on a young woman who has an illegitimate child), or the George Moore of *Esther Waters* would not have so diluted their realism. Too shy to tell this to Dreiser face to face, she sent him her critique in a letter. The novel "establishes a standard for American fiction," she said, but "if Lester had not married Lettie, the tragedy of Jennie would have been greater. Poignancy is a necessity in this story, and it can only be maintained by persistent want on the part of Jennie. The loss of Lester would insure this." She timidly added that maybe such a change was unnecessary, for the novel was so strong that it "compels one to recognize the truth about life."

Dreiser teased her about claiming to know so much about life at her age, but inwardly he agreed with Lillian. As he had previously written Fremont Rider, who had also read the manuscript, "I am convinced that one of the reasons of lack of poignancy is the fact that Lester marries Jennie. In the revision I don't intend to let him do it. And I may use your version for the rest. . . ."

He told Rider the changes involved "very little work," though in fact they took him another month. In his revision, Lester marries Lettie. Dreiser added further poignancy by having Jennie's illegitimate daughter, Vesta, die of typhoid fever. Lettie elbows her way into New York's "400" and keeps a mansion staffed by liveried servants while her husband devotes himself to the pleasures of the table. Eventually his gourmandizing ruins his health, and he is struck by a fatal illness. Realizing he is dying, he sends for Jennie (Lettie is abroad) and tells her that she is the only woman he ever loved. Jennie stays by him until he dies, attends his funeral heavily veiled, and watches at the railroad station as his coffin is loaded on a train, thinking of the empty, lonely life ahead—"Days and days in endless reiteration, and then—?"

The book should have ended on that dangling question, but Dreiser tacked on a meditative coda, as he had done with *Sister Carrie*, summarizing the meaning of his heroine's life and, not incidentally, justifying her. The moving evocation of death amid life in that final scene of Jennie at the station was epilogue enough—the holiday travelers bustling about their journeys, the train announcer's litany of distant cities, the baggage handler bawling, "Hey, Jack! Give us a hand here. There's a stiff outside!"—and Jennie a still figure in the center of it all, her eyes fixed on "the great box that was so soon to disappear" bearing all the happiness she ever had or ever would know. The moral was that there was no moral. Human lives are subject to inscrutable purposes. As Lester tells Jennie, "All of us are more or less pawns. We're moved about like chessmen by circumstances over which we have no control." The hurrying crowds of the city: "So shadows march in a dream."

· · ·

On February 24 Dreiser wrote Mencken that he had "full-finished" his novel and reiterated his intention to write several more if there was any money in it. Mencken urged him "to give the game a fair trial." He had the goods and *Sister Carrie* was beginning to "soak in," creating anticipation for his next novel. He scoffed at Dreiser's financial worries: "The money be damned. You will not grow as rich as [George Barr] McCutcheon . . . but there's a good living in it." Mencken was already boosting *Sister Carrie* in his columns in the *Sun* and *Smart Set:* "I seize every opportunity to ram in the idea that it must be read."

Holly sent the revised manuscript first to Edward G. Marsh, a Macmillan editor, who rendered a quick negative verdict. He predicted commercial success, but added, "There are some things about it . . . which I do not like." He did not elaborate, but Dreiser later learned that he felt it was too "broad," i.e., explicit. The following day Dreiser wrote Mencken, "I sometimes think my desire is for expression that is entirely too frank for this time—hence that I must pay the price of being unpalatable. The next book will tell." And he told Grant Richards, "I had better be careful. My turn comes later."

That next book, which, he told Mencken with excessive optimism, was "half-finished," was called *The Genius,* the story of a young artist harried by sexual desires, mesmerized by feminine beauty, and torn between art and commerce. Some of the surface details of the hero's career were drawn from that of Everett Shinn, one of the "Eight," a group of young painters who shocked the New York art world with a show in 1907 that featured cityscapes painted in a gritty realistic style. Shinn was also a successful commercial artist, specializing in glib drawings of handsome tuxedoed young men and soignée young women, and Dreiser had used his work in the *Broadway Magazine* in 1906. Most fascinating to Dreiser was the gossip about his amorous escapades. Shinn, who would go through a string of wives, had a boyish quality that made women want to mother him, it was said. He epitomized the Bohemian sexual freedom that Dreiser, trapped in an unhappy marriage, had envied.

He had conceived the idea of *The Genius* while he was still at *The Delineator.* John Sloan, another member of the Eight, remembered Dreiser visiting his studio in search of "color" for the novel. Sloan, a political radical and a dedicated Bohemian, was not impressed by Dreiser, regarding him as an "ex-novelist" who had sold out to Mammon. And Dreiser was disappointed by Sloan's atelier, finding it too austere. It didn't fit his romantic preconceptions of the artist's life—a chi-chi studio decorated with fish nets and antique furniture.

But Dreiser was not only telling Shinn's story; he was attempting to trace his own rough path to success, and to come to terms with his fall from Butterick, his dead marriage, and his unrequited love for Thelma. Some of the grief he felt had added a somber music to the passages on love and sorrow in *Jennie Gerhardt.*

Meanwhile, Dreiser's agent, Flora Mai Holly, had sent that manuscript to Hitchcock at Harper & Brothers. The response was favorable, which was fortunate, since next on Holly's list was Frederick A. Stokes, a conservative house. Sinclair Lewis, an editor at Stokes, had urged his boss, William Morrow, to sign up Dreiser. But Morrow demurred, on the ground that Dreiser's books were immoral. He was by no means the only editor of that opinion along Publishers Row.

Hitchcock, however, thought he could tame the barbarian. After all, in the 1890s he had bowdlerized Stephen Crane's *The Red Badge of Courage* for Appleton, and it had become a best seller. Founded in 1817, Harper & Brothers had fallen on hard times at the turn of the century and been rescued by J. P. Morgan. Dreiser told Richards that he wanted the prestige of "a dignified American house" behind his novel because it was more controversial than *Sister Carrie.* He demanded favorable terms but found himself in a weak bargaining position. He told Richards, who badly wanted to publish it in England, "They were nervous about [the book]—practically dictating their own terms. . . . I tried to hold out [British rights] & did so almost to the breaking point." But Harper had "agreed to advertise it heavily & to do much to put my attitude properly before Americans," so he thought it best "to make a few sacrifices now" and bide his time until there was a more liberal climate in America.

The contract gave the publisher an option on Dreiser's next book, which was now shaping up to be *The Genius.* On April 17 he reported to Mencken that "the 3d book draws to a close. It's grim, I'm sorry to state but life-like." Too grim for Harper's, he thought, confiding to Richards. "They may not take number three."

He could take heart from Mencken's advance judgment on *Jennie.* Toward the end of April, his Baltimore correspondent tossed his hat in the air:

> I have just finished reading the ms.—every word of it, from first to last—and I put it down with a clear notion that it could remain as it stands. The story comes upon me with great force; it touches my own experience of life in a hundred places; it preaches (or perhaps I had better say exhibits) a philosophy of life that seems to me to be sound; altogether I get a powerful effect of reality, stark and unashamed. It is drab and gloomy, but so is the struggle for existence. It is without humor, but so are the jests of that great comedian who shoots at our heels and makes us do our grotesque dancing.

Dreiser replied that this praise sounded "too good to be true" but it was a great comfort. He added that Charles De Camp, an editor, and Huneker, "as grim critically as any I know," had agreed with Mencken's opinion. Huneker, who had done more than any single writer to introduce modernist European art and literature to American intellectuals, and whose colorful, racy prose Mencken had taken as a model, wrote Dreiser that he had read *Jennie* through without stopping from 11:30 in the morning until ten at night. Though he had qualms about the style ("You write like a Dutch uncle—of the Gerhardts—the older branch"), the "bookishness" of the dialogue, and the repetitions, he thought *Jennie* "the best fiction I have read since Frank Norris."

By the time he heard from Huneker, Dreiser had moved to 225 Central Park West. His literarily inclined landlady, awed by his work habits, later recalled that he was at his desk from "rosy dawn to dewy eve." He had put himself on a schedule of completing a novel every six months. Since he was drawing on deeply personal material, the memories gushed forth. Some of them were painful, yet when William Lengel asked if the book wasn't, for that reason, difficult to write, Dreiser told him, "You don't know how practically I went about it, or how cheerfully it was executed."

Distracted by *The Genius*, Dreiser had turned the initial cutting of *Jennie* over to Jug. He had gone back to her, as she no doubt hoped, and she was probably eager to be of use, seeking to revive those troubled yet hopeful days when she helped edit *Sister Carrie*. She took the script with her to a Virginia spa, where she could work on it while recuperating from her recent siege. In late April she sent an edited version to Dreiser in New York. When he went through it, he must have exploded. On *Sister Carrie* she had confined herself largely to stylistic changes, though she managed to insert some genteelisms. Much of her work on *Jennie* echoed the job she did on *Carrie*, but often her changes were obviously intended to tone down physiological or sexual references.

For example, Dreiser wrote a rather daring scene in which Jennie and Lester discuss her becoming his mistress, in exchange for which he will provide for her family. In Dreiser's version she timidly raises the question of pregnancy, and Lester assures her she needn't worry about having a child because "I understand a number of things that you don't yet. It can be arranged." That veiled reference to contraceptives was too much for Jug, and she cut it.

Dreiser's claim in later years that Jug had wanted "to cut what she called the 'bad parts' " stemmed from that spring in Virginia, though he retroactively applied the charge to *Sister Carrie* as well. Nevertheless, he apparently accepted some of her changes, including the removal of references to contraceptives, for in the published version Jennie says, simply, "I couldn't have a baby," and Lester replies, "You don't need to have a child unless you want to, and I don't want you to." Dreiser sent the script to Hitchcock as a guide for his cutting. Hitchcock, whose own editing was "fairly well advanced" by that time, had told Dreiser that the manuscript would have to be heavily edited and retyped, at a charge of $600 to the author.

It is really not clear how much Jug cut from *Jennie Gerhardt* and how much Hitchcock did, since the final version of the manuscript was lost, but a comparison of the book with the script that Jug worked on indicates that most of the cuts were by Hitchcock and other Harper editors. Probably about 25,000 words were excised. Hitchcock had also made some adds, Dreiser told the novelist W. B. Trites, who after reading the novel said he could detect Hitchcock's hand in it.

Dreiser had inserted a clause in the contract that allowed him to withdraw the novel if he was dissatisfied with the editing. In his resistance he was backed up by Mencken, who wrote him: "If anyone urges you to cut down the book bid that one be damned. And if anyone argues that it is over-gloomy call the police."

At one point Dreiser complained that Harper's had not let him see the edited script. To which Hitchcock replied jauntily, "Why you should abuse me I do not quite know, but I take it the harsh terms you use are really an expression of affection." In June, when galleys were being run, Dreiser asked to see the original manuscript to compare with the proofs. Hitchcock told him to wait until he had it retyped, probably hoping that on a clean copy his cuts and changes would not be noticeable. Dreiser did notice, however, for in July Hitchcock writes that he had "put back pages and pages of MS. in accordance with your request."

One has to wonder how much was actually restored. In fact, Hitchcock (and his literary assistants) did more than eliminate verbosity and untangle syntax; they rewrote sentences and slashed controversial matter. For example, in a description of Jennie's father, Dreiser implies that he neglected the Church "during the ruddiest period of his youth," returning to it only when he decided to marry. That was excised, probably because it hinted that as a young man Gerhardt had sowed some wild oats. When Dreiser describes the wife's conversion from the Mennonite faith and her embrace of Lutheranism, he injects a mild touch of impiety. Hitchcock, a religious man who was active in church affairs, cut this, as he did a clause reading, "there was scarcely a Sunday in which [Pastor Wundt] did not refer to the iniquitous license which was observable among American young men and women." The paragraph that follows, which describes Wundt's fulminations against lax parents, "whose daughters walked the streets after seven at night" and whose sons spent their time "loafing about the street corners," also was dropped. Dreiser's mild allusions to the restlessness of modern youth were perhaps regarded as too daring.

Later, Dreiser asked Mencken to read through the bound book to ascertain if it had been hurt or helped by the editing. Mencken replied that at first the cuts "irritated me a good deal," but on further thought, he had decided that they had not damaged the novel. That was not the whole truth; while Dreiser was sweating out the reviews, Mencken was reluctant to say anything that might discourage him. He expressed his real opinion to his friend Harry Leon Wilson, former editor of *Puck*: ". . . the Harpers cut about 25,000 words out of the ms. . . . Such ruthless slashing is alarming. The chief virtue of Dreiser is his skill at piling up detail. The story he tells, reduced to a mere story is nothing."

Yet Dreiser had earlier written Huneker that the manuscript was being "carefully edited" and the repetitions and moralizing the critic had complained of had been eliminated. Apparently, Dreiser was in the end satisfied with (or resigned to) the editing, for Hitchcock wrote Holly in September: "We can congratulate ourselves that Mr. Dreiser's book is now in print and it has gone through with practically no demur on his part. He seems to have accepted my final work on the manuscript without any changes of consequence."

By July Dreiser had finished a draft of *The Genius* and while it was being typed, relentlessly moved on to the fourth book on his literary schedule. This was a novel called *The Financier*, which was based on the life of traction magnate Charles T. Yerkes, Robber Baron and connoisseur of fine art and beautiful women. He spent all of July on research, reporting to Mencken on August 8 that the data for *The Financier* were "practically gathered." (As usual he was exaggerating; at most he had compiled a history of Yerkes' early career.)

That same day, a literary column in the Chicago *Evening Post* carried a detailed story on *Jennie Gerhardt*, which quoted Mencken's letter praising the novel and rehashed the familiar legend of the "suppression" of *Carrie*. Dreiser's efforts to orchestrate prepublication publicity earned him a cautionary letter from Frederick A. Duneka, Harper's general manager, who warned that other journals might be offended by the *Evening Post*'s scoop. Dreiser was sorry it happened, he told Mencken, who was panting for advance galleys so that he could write his encomium in time to make the November *Smart Set*. Just to be sure, Dreiser sent his Baltimore correspondent the typescript that Jug had worked on, "marked for cutting but it was not cut in that fashion."

Working from what was essentially an unedited version, Mencken delivered a lengthy review in which he hailed *Jennie Gerhardt* as "the best American novel I have ever read, with the lonesome but Himalayan exception of 'Huckleberry Finn.' " He called the book "assertively American in its scene and its human material, and yet so European in its method, its point of view, its almost reverential seriousness that one can scarcely imagine an American writing it."

His anxiety at a high pitch now that the book was in the stores, Dreiser asked the critic Edna Kenton to find out what Floyd Dell, editor of *The Chicago Evening Post Literary Review,* intended to do with the book. Kenton, a devotee of *Carrie* in its first incarnation, informed him that Dell intended to blazon *Jennie* to the world. He promptly forwarded Mencken's notice to Dell's wife, Margery Curry, cautioning, disingenuously, "but don't let Mr. Dell read it for I don't want his opinion crossed by the least thought for or against. . . ."

Dell not only read the *Smart Set* notice, he cited it approvingly in his review. But he sincerely conveyed his own reactions, and tried to divine the source of the book's power. A great part of the effect, he decided, "must be due to the long-sustained simplicity of the narrative, rather than to the quality of any certain passage. Quiet sympathy, it seems, can be prolonged until it reaches the breaking point of poignancy. . . ." Like Mencken, he was attuned to the book's somber music, the contrapuntal themes of life and death, that coalesce in the final scene of Jennie at the station.

Those two reviews (Dell's appeared about two weeks after Mencken's) set the terms of the critical debate. Resolved, the two young critics had said, that *Jennie Gerhardt* is a great novel. Most of the subsequent reviewers sided with the affirmative, greeting Dreiser as a major writer. *Contra* were the moralists such as the poet Edwin Markham, author of "The Man With a Hoe," a stark picture of the American peasantry, who was naturally sympathetic to the parts of the book that etch "with power the dark side of poverty with all its cares and despairs." But he condemned Jennie's decision to become Kane's mistress in part because he promises to help her impoverished family: "Is a woman ever justified in smirching her womanhood, in staining her virtue, in order to help her relatives—even to save them from starvation? This must be answered with an iron 'No' by all who take a deep look into life. The wise are aware that there are some misfortunes that are worse than starvation."

Even more damning was the reviewer for the Lexington, Kentucky, *Herald,* who wrote that the novel "is a long, full and unreserved statement of the lower motives and base instincts of the worst order of human animals. . . . There is . . . not one chapter that is not unutterably base; every line is upon such a low plane it is hard to believe that this is all."

Fearing such a reaction, Duneka had sent an advance copy to the influential critic Hamilton Wright Mabie of the Christian *Outlook.* The Harper's executive expended most of his cover letter in apologizing for the novel's "rather unpleasant" theme and noting, "it is a fair question whether any really good end is subserved." He added that Dreiser's novel had "provoked more discussion before we decided to publish it than any book since *Jude the Obscure.*" There were more disclaimers and apologies in that vein, ending with the lukewarm certification that in spite of its having been "written in almost violent sincerity, and in spite of its heroine being outside the pale, it is about as suggestive as a Patent Office Report or Kent's Commentary."

Mabie replied that he had liked *Jennie* more than he expected. The general tone was "reverential" and the portrait of Jennie "very winning." Indeed, "One had no sense of moral dirt except with regard to the men." He thought Dreiser showed considerable promise—if he could be "kept from getting obsessed by the general sex theme which has made so many writers insane."

Dreiser was offended that Duneka had sought out the prim Mabie's views, and he urged the Harper's executive to read Mencken's notice in the *Smart Set* as an antidote.

As a reviewer for the New York *Tribune* later wrote, Theodore Dreiser *imposed* himself on American literature. That incursion began with *Jennie Gerhardt*. *Sister Carrie* was a greater book, but its publication in 1900 had been the tree falling in the empty forest. Even its successful reissue in 1907 had left Dreiser, as Sinclair Lewis had noted, a great American realist who had written only one book. Now, with *Jennie* out, *The Genius* seemingly completed, and *The Financier* in the stocks, the invasion was fully launched. And leading it was Mencken, who for the next five years would remain in the van.

Dreiser was quite aware that his friend occupied an exposed salient, writing him in November, "It looks to me from the drift of things as though your stand on Jennie would either make or break you. . . . They are tying you up pretty close to it." But Mencken saw his *Smart Set* review as the beginning of a grand fight and an opening to glory. He believed in what Dreiser was doing; his praise had been given with a full heart. But he was also ambitious and eager to push his own notions of a "European" literature in America. As he later said, "Dreiser simply gave me a good chance to unload my own ideas, which were identical with his." And so a literary alliance was forged, but it was still to be tested in battle.

Part Two

ANNI

MIRABILES

1911–1914

CHAPTER 4

Grand Tour

Sunday Nov. 5th G.R. [Grant Richards] calls. . . . His chief
characteristic, I should say, which I have long noticed is not
an uncommon trait in Englishmen, is a strong sense of
individual and racial superiority. . . . I am a very peculiar
person. I like being managed at times—only at times.
Sometimes it is a great convenience . . . to have someone
step forward and take from your weary shoulders the burden of responsibility. . . . G.R. admires my work greatly.
At this time he fancies I am a great writer. He likes my
personality. Time will tell what becomes of all this. . . . I
do not know. I hope it lasts.

—Dreiser (1911)

The favorable reviews by Mencken, Dell, and others were welcome but Dreiser had been out of a regular job for a year now,
and no money was coming in. And he also had a wife to support
in her accustomed style. Despite his differences with Jug over
her editing of the manuscript (which he had resolved, at least
in his own mind, by a determination henceforth to keep his literary and
marital affairs separate), in June 1911 he had taken a smaller apartment at the
Riverview Court, 3609 Broadway. It was a middle-class building, with a
middle-class rent of fifty dollars a month.

Suppressing his money worries, he let Jug fix up the apartment as she
liked. What Dreiser's long-term intentions were is unclear, but he felt guilty
and so let her assemble the stage settings of a normal home life. But now
they had a tacit arrangement which allowed him to go his way.

His relationship with Lillian Rosenthal had progressed to greater intimacy, and Jug tolerated his infidelities with gritted teeth. One evening in
September while Mencken was visiting the apartment, Dreiser suddenly
excused himself, pleading unspecified business, and was away for more than

an hour. As soon as he left, Jug said bitterly, "He's gone around to that Jewish girl."

Mencken was a staunch advocate of the bourgeois proprieties (he classified adultery as "hitting below the belt") and treated Jug courteously. Yet privately he suspected she was jealous of her husband's literary fame. Also, he had seen Christian Science magazines in the house, and wrote her off as a deluded believer. To him, Mary Baker Eddyism was the worst kind of pious snake-oil.

Dreiser apparently hadn't told Mencken of his own interest in Christian Science, or else passed it off as mere scientific curiosity, knowing the other's violent dislike of any sort of "spiritualism." Not that Dreiser could be a convert; he once wrote, "I think I know as much about metaphysics as Mrs. Eddy & can read my God direct." Still, he had been much taken by Eddy's ideas of mind as the only reality. He believed: "So-called life is an illusion. There is a larger life which is the only reality." Eugene Witla, his alter ego in *The Genius,* submits to the ministrations of a Christian Science healer during a spiritual crisis, and Dreiser and Jug had consulted with practitioners in the manner of contemporary couples visiting a shrink. His sister Sylvia became a practitioner. "There is no question about C.S. healing every known disease of man," she once wrote him, "for it is all a lie that man must die—his beliefs must die."

Haunted by a fear of death, Dreiser half-agreed. He had investigated spiritualism by proxy in the "Are the Dead Alive?" series and assigned an article on "The New Healing" which discussed CS, New Thought, and psychotherapy. Describing Jennie's grief after the death of her daughter, Vesta, he interjects, "If only some counselor of eternal wisdom could have whispered to her that obvious and convincing truth—there are no dead." Jug trotted along behind him on this and other notions, but it was sometimes a strain for her to keep up. She once wrote of his "great power to make people believe almost what they do not believe." Raised a Methodist, she found his deterministic view of the universe hard to swallow, and she found spiritualism, as Dreiser interpreted it, bleak consolation for the tragedy of death—an end after life without Heaven or Hell.

A promising 5000 copies of the novel were sold in the first month after publication, thanks to the wave of favorable reviews, and throughout October Dreiser bombarded Harper's with letters suggesting stunts to promote the book (selling it in hotels, for one) and complaining about the dearth of advertising. Bypassing Hitchcock, Dreiser took his complaints directly to Major Leigh, treasurer of the firm, a big, genial man who patiently explained to the nervous author that Harper's wanted *Jennie* to be a commercial success almost as badly as he did.

As more reviews assailing the novel on moral grounds appeared, religious groups were alerted and there were isolated instances of censorship—a book dealer refusing to stock it, a condemnation of the novel as unsuitable on moral grounds by the National Library Association. Leigh wrote Dreiser that the experience of *Sister Carrie* "was not helpful to the sale of *Jennie Gerbardt*. I am not arguing about whether it is right or not,—I am simply stating you a fact." He insisted that Harper's didn't consider *Jennie* immoral; if it did, the firm wouldn't have published it. Dreiser no doubt feared another Doubleday-style "suppression," but Harper's spent more than $1500 on advertising in the book's first month, a fair sum.

Floyd Dell, who had grown increasingly unhappy with interference with the *Literary Review* by the publisher of the Chicago *Evening Post*, came to New York in November and attended a press conference for Arnold Bennett sponsored by Harper's. Annoyed because no mention had been made of *Jennie Gerbardt*, Dell asked the guest of honor: "What do you think of Theodore Dreiser?" Bennett responded: "*Sister Carrie* is the best realistic American novel ever written."

There was more praise from Great Britain, and Grant Richards arrived in New York in early November with some good news. As Dreiser relayed it to Mencken, "I have a good chance of getting the next Nobel prize for literature following Maeterlinck, if it's worked right." Richards was willing "to organize the sentiment in England where he says I am a strong favorite, through Frank Harris, & others. . . . He thought some American critic of prominence ought to make the suggestion somewhere in which he could call attention & I spoke of you." Harris had ranked *Carrie* among the twenty greatest novels of all time.

Although the Nobel Prize boomlet went nowhere, Richards' visit to the States was a turning point in Dreiser's life. On November 4 he called at the publisher's hotel while Richards was out, and left a copy of his new novel with a doleful note: "I hope if you are interviewed you will say something definite about me and Jennie. It seems almost impossible to make my fellow Americans understand that I am alive. I am thinking of moving to London. Once there I will get at least an equal run with . . . Arnold Bennett over here."

Dreiser invited the Englishman over for breakfast the next morning and there he summed up his troubles in a word: "Money." He was well along with *The Financier*, he said (actually about one-third done), but the real-life inspiration for his hero, Charles T. Yerkes, had spent the last years of his life in Europe, engineering a takeover of the London Underground and dallying romantically in Paris and on the Riviera. To see the things that Yerkes had seen would take money, and he saw no way of obtaining it. He had $400 in the bank and a life insurance premium of $244.44 coming due in two weeks, a $175 payment for the Grand View lots shortly thereafter, as well as one on the Washington State apple orchard. He was, in effect, broke.

Richards, a tall, charming man who was about Dreiser's age, eyed the American sternly through his monocle and, as was his wont, took charge. Ridiculous, he said. Why couldn't Harper's advance him the money? Dreiser explained they might be reluctant to go beyond the original advance in order to finance a Yerkes-style grand tour. Richards told Dreiser he had overestimated the cost of touring Europe. Richards could show him how to do it economically and would put him up at his own home while he was in England. As for funds, he would arrange that too. Tomorrow he was calling on executives of the Century Company, with whom he was on good terms, and he would talk them into parting with an advance for some articles on Europe for the *Century* magazine and possibly on Dreiser's next book after *The Financier*. In return, Dreiser would give him the English rights to his books. Dreiser was skeptical. Under the *Jennie Gerhardt* contract Harper's had an option on his next novel. Moreover, he doubted that the *Century*, a last bastion of the genteel tradition under its editor, Robert Underwood Johnson, would want him as an author.

When Richards met the next day with Frank H. Scott, president of the Century Company, he encountered some resistance. Dreiser was considered "risky" and a "difficult fellow," Scott told him. Richards argued that with proper handling Dreiser could be a valuable asset to Century, which needed new blood; he was probably aware that the genteel *Century* was losing its loyal readers through natural attrition while newer, livelier journals attracted younger people. Scott agreed to read *Jennie* and copies were supplied to five other principal editors.

Events moved rapidly after that. On November 10, at a luncheon at the Century offices in Union Square, Dreiser found himself reminiscing pleasantly with Johnson about their disagreement over a story he had submitted in 1900. With everyone in a genial mood, a preliminary agreement was drawn up providing a $1500 advance for three travel articles for the *Century* and a payment of $1500 for a future novel should Dreiser eventually decide to defect from Harper's.

Then Richards put into motion the next phase of his plan. According to Dreiser, on Richards' advice he sent Harper's an ultimatum: advance him $2500 on *The Financier* immediately and $2500 more on completion. A yes-or-no answer must arrive by Friday, November 17, and the money by the following Monday or else Dreiser would consider "other propositions before him," as he put it in a letter to Hitchcock. Those were stiff demands, and Dreiser characterizes them as a "bluff" devised by Richards to provoke Harper's into dropping him. The day after the Century lunch, he wrote Mencken, "Strictly between you & myself [the Century Company] would like me to move with my books to Union Square, but theres nothing definite about that. . . ." In his memoirs, Richards insists he had no ulterior plans to undermine Dreiser's relationship with Harper's.

Three days later Harper's called Richards' bluff, if that's what it was, agreeing to pay Dreiser $2500—$2000 of that for *The Financier* and the remainder as an advance against royalties from *Jennie*. Major Leigh chided Dreiser for apparently forgetting "the fact that you have already agreed to deliver us a manuscript on terms set forth in your contract of April 29, 1911." Nevertheless, he said, Harper's recognized his need for European research on *The Financier* and would be happy to provide him some money. The check arrived the next day. The conditions were that Dreiser show Harper's the thirty-nine chapters of *The Financier* he had completed; if the publisher didn't like them, the money must be returned.

In fact, he preferred Harper & Brothers, despite his complaints about their niggardly advertising. Leigh had been kind to him, and he sensed the house was as good a publisher as he could get. Richards' claim—long after the fact—that he had no desire to come between Dreiser and Harper's was not entirely candid. He knew that Harper's had an active London office and expected to sell the British editions of Dreiser's books. That was written into the contract. Therefore, the only way Richards could get Dreiser's books was to decouple him from Harper's. The Englishman was a gambler— literally, for he was a regular patron of the casinos at Monte Carlo. He had the virtue of loving literature and the sin of being a poor businessman and a high liver, going bankrupt several times over the course of his career. But he published George Bernard Shaw (who chided him for being too literary), A. E. Housman, John Masefield, and James Joyce, among others.

They booked passage on the *Mauretania*, sailing November 22, and Dreiser scurried about putting his affairs in order. On his last day ashore, he was interviewed by a reporter for the New York *Sun*. Dreiser deplored the paucity of novels in the American grain, particularly set in his own Middle West—"that stretch of country which is universally called to mind by the term 'American,' in which a real and a throbbing life exists, has been allowed no literary expression." He said that newspapers and magazines were "so far ahead of all the novels that have been published that there is no comparison. For they are vital, dramatic, true presentations of the life that is being lived today." The novels of William Dean Howells, whose critical endorsement he had once courted, were a prime example of the prevailing reticence. They reminded him of a family he had visited. "I mentioned a certain episode. 'We don't talk of that,' I was told." So it was in Howells' novels, and those of others like him; the authors did not talk about certain phases of life. Later in his stateroom he wrote of his hopes that America would someday "love its realists . . . as it now loves its patriots—Nathan Hale and Ulyssess [sic] S. Grant, and Abraham Lincoln, and it will have the same noble basis for doing so."

In another interview, with critic Baldwin Macy, he explained his reasons for going to Europe. First, to research Yerkes' career. He predicted that in *The Financier* he would interpret "the American man of affairs and millionaire as he has never yet been interpreted. . . . It's a big theme, too big for a little handling, too big to look at from any one angle. . . . All I'm after is the source of his inevitability—why he is what he is." But he also wanted to see how his country measured up in the world. "I've got an idea about America," he said, "that over here we've got a monopoly on the biggest ideals, and the largest amount of raw material energy by which to execute them than any people on earth. . . . I'm going over to find out . . . how we rank really in our chances for the future among the rest of the nations."

Aboard ship, Dreiser experienced a heady sense of freedom. Richards introduced him to two pretty actresses, Sarah Burke, who was British, and her American friend, Malvina Longfellow. With the latter he sat in the fantail, watching the pitching green waves and singing "coon songs," of which he had a large repertoire picked up from his brother Paul. Malvina was a type new to his experience—an adventuress who freely admitted she would barter sex for wealth and luxury.

Richards assumed the roles of host and guide. For Dreiser's hotel in London he chose the Capitol, a Victorian pile with a somewhat louche reputation but now supposedly respectable. But sounds of laughter and flirtation in the hall prompted Dreiser to observe in his diary, perhaps wishfully, that hotels had become modern-day sites of sexual license comparable to "Greek Arcadian days." He was less impressed by the elegant Carlton, where Richards took him to lunch in the Grill. Dreiser thought it a bit dowdy and inferior to the Waldorf-Astoria.

When he checked out of the Capitol for a weekend in the country with an admirer, Gilbert Christie, Richards provided detailed instructions on what to tip the hotel maid, valet, porter, outside man, and the "gold-braided boy."

But Richards did not content himself with playing preceptor to his guest; he also pressed him to sign over the English rights to his books. On December 6, when Dreiser called at Richards' Dickensian offices in Henrietta Street near Covent Garden, the publisher had drawn up a preliminary agreement giving him the English rights to *The Financier*, the travel book, and *Sister Carrie*. In his diary Dreiser says he refused to sign, but Richards wrote him: "We made last night . . . an arrangement by which this house is to have the publication of 'The Financier.' . . ." He asserted that this letter would be a "sufficient agreement" between them; a "more formal contract" would be drawn up later.

That was not Dreiser's intention, and he probably felt under obligation to Harper's. But he seems not to have given Richards a definite no, in order to keep his options open for a better offer from Century. Thus far Richards had produced nothing from that particular hat, but he still held out hopes of a long-term arrangement that would end Dreiser's financial worries. It was not on a whim that Richards later titled his autobiography *Author Hunting: By an Old Literary Sportsman.* "No publisher worthy of his job will, if he can help it, allow an author whose work he respects and admires to go elsewhere," he wrote.

During one of his first days in London Dreiser visited the British Museum, probably intending to research Yerkes' London operations. But he spent most of his time copying a list of ancient omens. That evening in Piccadilly Circus he picked up a prostitute named Lilly Edwards, accompanied her to her room, and questioned her about her life. She undressed and he examined her body with clinical detachment (she told him she was six months pregnant). He approved of Europe's tacit acceptance of the "social evil." As he later wrote Mencken: "The prostitute is as necessary as a lawyer & more so. She is the worlds sex safety valve," a preventive of rape and other sex crimes.

But he yearned for the lost Thelma, who was no longer in London. Forewarned of Dreiser's visit by his letters, she had fled to America. He saw her face everywhere—a woman on the street reminded him of her, then a dancer onstage. When he found a horseshoe on a walk through the East End, his first thought was of "luck with Thelma . . . I dream of what I would do if she was to come to me."

Mingled with his longing for her was a panicky sense of growing old. In August he had turned forty, and everywhere, it seemed, he encountered reminders that he had crossed that great divide into middle age.

Outfitting himself in Savile Row suits and haberdashery, he made his debut in London society. But his Anglophilia was fast disappearing. He argued with the American-born wife of his British agent, Hughes Massie. Her Anglophilia provoked him to launch "a steady attack" on the British, and he crowed in his diary, "Defeated them all. Very brilliant." Not surprisingly, however, his indictment touched off a "stir of general antagonism I think." The appearance of a negative review of *Jennie* in the London *Nation* had shaken his faith in the British critics. While he admired British traditions and "civility," he thought the national character too conservative and stodgy, and the condition of the poor more hopeless than in America. Most repugnant was the rigid class system, the gulf between rich and poor.

Then the New York *International* published a long, sneering review of *Jennie* sarcastically titled "The Lyrical Mr. Dreiser." The notice hurt. He had expected a triumphant reception from the British intelligentsia, but now every review seemed to be a slam. When he met John Masefield, not until they parted did the seaman poet mention Dreiser's books: he said he had liked *Carrie.*

Back in his hotel room that evening, he experienced spells of homesickness, loneliness, and depression. One seizure was so painful that he wrote in his diary, "If I were of a suicidal turn these things would end me. Try to reason myself out of it by counting all my blessings. Not possible. My principle [sic] difficulty is a longing for loving companionship. I have had so little of loving understanding on the part of a big woman."

Fortunately, Paris was next on his itinerary. After settling in at the Normandy Hotel, he and Richards cut a swath through Montmartre, ending up at the wicked Abbaye de Thélème bar, where Richards caught this word picture (printed in his novel *Caviare*) of Dreiser hurling small white pasteboard balls, lightly weighted with shot, at his fellow patrons: "With one foot on the ground, and another on his chair, he flung his missiles with a vigour that meant execution when they struck; his coat half off his back, his hair tousled, his face red, his eyes asparkle. He . . . had forgotten the United States!"

During the day they had met the painters Anne Rice and J. D. Ferguson, whom Dreiser was intrigued to learn were not only man and mistress but maintained separate studios—an ideal living arrangement, he thought. He was trying something along those lines with Jug but could not afford separate domiciles. He filed his impressions away for future use in describing Eugene Witla's Paris sojourn in *The Genius*.

Aware of his affectional/research needs, Richards introduced him to a sometime actress, a Mme de Villiers, who, it turned out, supported herself by talents other than acting. She later invited Dreiser to her flat, and, after practicing on him the "French" technique, graphically described her heterodox sexual experiences, which included lesbianism. Dreiser found Paris a haven of sexual freedom and approved of the openly displayed pornographic books in the Rue St. Honoré.

His nocturnal rounds acquired the cachet of science with the arrival of Abraham Flexner, the playwright and social investigator who had done a study of prostitution in America for John D. Rockefeller Jr.'s Bureau of Social Hygiene, and was now researching the subject in Europe. Also in the party was W. W. Ellsworth, vice president of the Century Company, who was in Europe on an author-hunting expedition and had recommended Richards to Flexner as a guide to the underside of Paris. The four of them spent an evening of research at Palmyre's, a notorious *boite* run by the woman in whose arms Toulouse-Lautrec was said to have died.

Then came news from Duneka about *Jennie:* 7720 copies sold through January 1, 1912, with total orders of 10,000. Also, the Harper's executive said, the firm would not let Richards have the English rights to *The Financier* without a sizable payment in return. Dreiser complained to Richards about the sales figures, concluding gloomily: "If I were you I wouldn't be so concerned about me. I am not going to be a best seller or even a half seller.

My satisfaction is to be purely critical if even that. . . . I haven't the drag with the public—that's all." He'd never be a moneymaker, he said, probably seeking to put off Richards. But the latter was undeterred.

"Tush" he responded, "I think you're very easily discouraged." To him 10,000 orders seemed a capital showing. Though *Jennie* might not be a best seller, it "can be a big seller." He reminded Dreiser that ten weeks ago he was deeply depressed about his future; now he was touring Europe. He must not be "so damned mercurial."

At the end of January they left for the Riviera, accompanied by Richards' friend Sir Hugh Lane, a collector, dealer and connoisseur of art. At Monte Carlo, Richards introduced Dreiser to the Municipal Casino. Filling out an admission form, Dreiser, still troubled about turning forty, gave his age as "39." Under profession he penned "*Rentier.*" In the company of the dapper, monocled Richards and the cultivated, elegantly bearded Lane, he transformed himself into a gentleman of means.

His evenings were devoted to a cocotte named Marcelle. Staying at the luxurious Grand Hotel in Nice, the expenses mounted up, and Dreiser accused Richards, to whom he had turned over a fair sum, of spending too freely. When Richards asked him for another "loan" (as Dreiser terms it in his diary) of £120—over $600—and proposed allotting him £100 for the rest of his trip, Dreiser demanded a full accounting, which insulted Richards.

On that sour note, Dreiser departed for Italy, leaving Richards and Lane fuming at his accusations. Modern-day Rome he dismissed as an "eighth-rate city," although "as a collection of ruins and art objects it cannot be surpassed." After four days, though, the antiquities had begun to seem "endless" and it would "take a lifetime to decipher them." He was also worried about expenses.

Yet he lingered, probably because he met Rella Abell Armstrong, an attractive American woman separated from her writer husband and living with her children in the Grand Continental. She proved a catalytic influence, recounting the lurid history of the Borgias, which so fascinated him that he made her write it all down. She insisted that America's history was, in its way, as glorious as Rome's. One can sense between the lines of his diary his subconscious mind forging a link between the Robber Barons of post–Civil War America and the pagan emperors who conquered the world and built such architectural splendors as the Baths of Caracalla, about which he comments, "Christianity is supposed to have healed the evil which produced all this."

He had found the key to Cowperwood and titans like Rockefeller, Jay Gould, E. H. Harriman, and others of that "race of giants" who used finance as "the one direct avenue to power and magnificence" as ruthlessly as the Borgias in their day had pursued the same ends. One must not judge them by Christian morality; they must be seen in the context of the "pagan" morality of ancient Rome, the grandeur of which whispered to him from these great ruins. Such a perspective, striking him at this peculiar time, was liberating.

Perhaps inspired by the same pagan spirit, he was emboldened to propose to Mrs. Armstrong, while they were strolling in the gardens of the Villa d'Este, that they "come together." She smiled archly, but when he pressed her to accompany him to Florence, she refused, saying she could not leave her children. And so he prepared to go on alone.

Meanwhile there was news about his affairs in America. On the debit side, a $1000 payment was due on the apple orchard in Washington. Duneka got him the money, but Holly extracted her 10 percent commission, and since he had no funds in his bank at home, she sent him $900, to which he added $100 from his letter of credit in London and forwarded. Also, there was his continuing disappointment with the small sale of *Jennie*. He expressed his astonishment to Duneka, and later remarked bitterly about the "munificent returns" of authorship. In a letter to Richards, he mentions hearing that Erman J. Ridgway might leave Butterick (his old rival was ousted because *Everybody's* was losing money) and adds casually, "I may go back there." This betrayal of his vocation threw Richards into a high dudgeon. He remonstrated that such an idea was "disloyal . . . to yourself and your qualities. The trouble with you is that you do really you know, get cold feet. You are in streaks." As for the fate of *Jennie*: "I've been seeing a lot of American publishers and I have been struck by the extent to which you have put it across there. . . . You have made a dent in the national conscience, all right." And in an earlier letter, he put his finger on one reason for Dreiser's lack of confidence: "Such things not having been done before from your country you have nothing to compare yourself with. . . ."

Dreiser did not tell Richards that Duneka's letter contained a positive note. After reading the first thirty-nine chapters of *The Financier*, Duneka said he was "trembling" for the rest—"Not that I doubt you but because of the greatness of it all." He urged Dreiser to turn in the manuscript by the latter part of July, because Harper's was anxious to publish—*had* to publish the book by September 19. They were hemming him in further, cutting off his escape to Richards and the Century Company.

By now Richards had become sufficiently accustomed to his charge's moodiness to shrug off the assault on his financial integrity in Cannes; he never would grasp the depth of the poverty-haunted Dreiser's worries about money.

The latter continued to complain about being pinched financially and wanted to cut his trip short. "No more Europe on a worry basis for me," he wrote while still in Rome, to which Richards riposted that he was "glad . . . that you have been stopping in the best and most expensive" hotels. The next day Dreiser adds that Duneka was still optimistic about *Jennie,* and "If the Century Company isn't interested, it is very likely that Harper's will do something further when I get back. . . ." Richards began to sense that the fox was going to ground and spoke of a wonderful new plan, devised with Ellsworth, whereby the Century Company would give Dreiser a ten-year contract.

With time and money slipping away, Dreiser departed Rome on February 26 for Florence and Venice with stopovers in Spello, Assisi, and Perugia on the way. And then it was on to Germany and the heart of his journey—the village of Mayen, his father's birthplace. After being mistakenly diverted to the town of Mayence, miles out of his way (possibly his rudimentary German was misunderstood), he boarded a milk train in Cologne that took him to his destination. The medieval walls still stood, as did the ancient castle and the twisted spire of St. Clements Catholic church, where his father was baptized. Although it was late in the day, he went straightaway to the graveyard in search of the tombs of his ancestors. He was shocked to read the inscription on the first family marker he happened upon:

THEODOR DREISER
GEB'N 16 FEB 1820
GEST'N 28 FEB 1882

In his notebook he describes the "dear old graveyard all wet now with a spring rain & odourous of mold," and then writes: "I am the 13th grave in the 5th row beyond the first wall. . . ." He had gone back to his beginnings to discover his own end. The spectacle of his fate profoundly unnerved him, as though all his worries about time slipping away had culminated here.

The next day, while Dreiser strolled about the little town, a fancy struck him: "If there is any of my father in me it is now looking at his home town through my eyes." He had a vision of generations of Mayeners reproducing themselves so that "my father's life is still here. I have gone in & out of his very gates."

After a chat with the innkeeper, who seems to have told him there were no living Dreisers around (if he had consulted parish records, he would have discovered that he had numerous cousins residing in the area), he paid a farewell visit to the old graveyard and caught a train to Frankfurt. There he made himself known to Julia Culp, a singer friend of Richards' who was giving a concert. She had expressed admiration for *Jennie Gerhardt,* and after her performance they shared a late supper. Dreiser accompanied her to her hotel, where, after insisting she must not be unfaithful to Richards, she allowed him to kiss her. She led him to believe there might be even more love play in Berlin, where he was to stay at her home and she was to join him when her concert tour was finished.

Ensconced in Mme Culp's comfortable suburban villa, he tried to puzzle out the relationship between his absent hostess and her nominal husband, Herr Merton, a rather pompous gentleman who lectured Dreiser on German superiority. Walking about Berlin, Dreiser was moved to meditate on his various romantic liaisons back home. He decided that love was an explosive force, capable of wrecking lives—as his passion for Thelma had done his. Yet it was central to human existence: "the great fact is that love—complete chemical responsiveness to the universe—is the greatest thing in the world and as such is the most astounding, the most dignified & the most artistic . . . no individual sees what life really is emotionally and otherwise until he is in love. He is not complete. When he becomes so, the astonishing chemical reaction which takes place may result in anything."

He floated a theory: "I am coming gradually to believe that sex enthusiasm of some sort—abnormal or otherwise—is the true basis of great art."

Another day he saw a hunchback, a sign of good luck in his personal catalogue of omens. He refers in the diary to the "genius" who watched over him and warned him by signs or omens of impending favorable or unfavorable changes in his life.

On another excursion he happened upon a cemetery where a funeral was in progress. The mourners threw handfuls of dirt into the open grave, like a gaping wound in the earth, and a woman, who appeared to be the mother of the deceased, wept uncontrollably. Suddenly he was crying too: "I fancy my tears are for the whole world—for grief such as this cannot be healed."

These sometimes distraught jottings in his diary were reflections of an inner journey, parallel to the outer one, which would have future reverberations in his novels. His ruminations about the ancient Romans confirmed his amoral interpretation of Frank Cowperwood in *The Financier.* The thoughts on the explosive power of love, all too painfully evidenced by his lingering obsession with Thelma and its consequences, would find its way into *An American Tragedy.* And the sentiment he expressed at the funeral would become, in slightly different phrasing, the summation of *The Bulwark,* a novel that he would conceive after meeting a young bluestocking admirer named Anna Tatum, whose first letter to him had been forwarded to Berlin.

Mme Culp returned, but he soon discovered she was a tease, and when later she casually canceled a promised rendezvous in Amsterdam, he was infuriated. By then he was tired of cocottes and prima donnas and homesick for America. His venture into Europe had left him believing more strongly than ever "that America is the greatest country in the world & that New York City is incomparable for real grandeur."

Back in London, Dreiser was told by Richards that his funds were low, reviving the suspicions he had on the Riviera. He decided that Richards either had pocketed some of the money entrusted to him or else squandered it so that Dreiser would be forced to "hypothecate" his future books with the Century Company. He was, of course, being unreasonable, but his fear of not having enough to carry him through the writing of *The Financier* was real. The upshot was that he cabled Harper's for an additional $500.

But then Richards suggested he invite Marcelle to England for a final fling. That he should propose this added expense astounded Dreiser—the man was "a true advocate of the devil." But Richards argued that it would cost him only ten pounds, and he acquiesced without further resistance. His *petite amie* arrived on the boat train at five in the morning, and they immediately repaired to his hotel room, where the porter had laid a fire.

Dreiser had originally wanted to sail on the *Titanic*, a modern, "smart" ship, which departed from Liverpool April 9, 1912, on its maiden voyage to New York, but Richards persuaded him to spend a few more days in Paris. Thanks to the intervention of Richards' colleague Mitchell Kennerley, the British-born New York publisher, Dreiser was able to book a reasonably priced stateroom on the slower *Kroonland*, departing on April 13.

On his last night in London, Dreiser had a farewell dinner with Marcelle and Richards. Dreiser spent the evening wrapped in a sullen cloud of jealousy as Richards and Marcelle merrily conversed in French. When the party returned to the hotel, he ordered Richards to leave and spent a cool night with Marcelle, though in the morning, after his bath, he reports, "find myself passionate and the usual sex relation follows."

Later, Richards called, acting as though the previous evening's quarrel had not taken place, to report that the money from Harper's had arrived. They went to Cook's to draw the remainder of his letter of credit, finding only a few pounds left. Nonetheless, he presented Marcelle with a *pourboire* of 800 francs ($160) and a new hat, which Richards had chosen, and after saying an ambivalent goodbye to the publisher, accompanied his *petite amie* to Dover, where he saw her off, and then boarded the *Kroonland*.

The return voyage was quiet. A purser confided the news of the *Titanic*'s sinking, but in his diary Dreiser refers to the ill-fated ship as the "Teutonic" and writes he had thought it was *returning* to London. He read an article about Dostoevsky and strongly approved of the Russian's "compassion for the tragedy of the obscure & the submerged."

As they drew near to New York, he stood on deck, watching the sea and thinking about the transience of life: "Youth is gone. With it the possible fulfillment of the dreams of youth. . . . I think of Thelma—but that is all over. Nothing but work now—and it makes no difference anyhow."

He disembarked on April 22, 1912, and called on the Rosenthals that evening. Lillian played for him Irving Berlin's new hit song "Everybody's Doin' It."

Europe was the past, America the future, the new Colossus of trade and industry, with its conquering capitalists and financiers (such as Yerkes). In Europe he had clearly realized that he was irrevocably an American writer. His subject was the energy and change of its cities, where achieving, not living, was the watchword, where life was attuned to a jagged ragtime beat.

He had clipped Edwin Markham's book review that day in the New York *American,* along with the story of the sinking of the *Titanic,* the technological marvel that seemed to carry with it to the bottom the Victorian hopes of Science and Progress. Declared the poet-critic: "America today is in a somber, self-questioning mood. We are in a period of clamor, of bewilderment, of an almost tremulous unrest."

CHAPTER 5

The Financier

> Like a wolf prowling under glittering, bitter stars in the
> night, he was looking down into the humble folds of simple
> men and seeing what their ignorance and their unsophisti-
> cation would cost them.
>
> —*The Financier*

His apartment having been sublet, Dreiser moved into temporary quarters at the St. Paul Hotel. He obviously hadn't rushed to Jug, who was staying at the Brevoort on lower Fifth Avenue, a raffish but not inexpensive establishment. He had written her from Rome, apparently pleading financial hardship and asking that she support herself or live with friends or relatives for a while; perhaps he asked for a divorce. At any rate, she replied: "I cannot grant your request, Theo—you know why." He had probably pleaded poverty, as a result of his trip and the lackluster sales of *Jennie,* in hopes that she would relieve him of his financial responsibility for her. She seems to have been as interested in the returns from *Jennie* as he was, for in her letter she reported the theory of Thomas B. Wells, associate editor of *Harper's Magazine,* that the book appealed to men but they did not want it in their homes—presumably because of its kept-woman theme—and noted innocently: "I tho't wives and children did the buying and reading of novels not men." There was a hint of reproach in her words: why couldn't Theo write books that wives and children might buy?

Though the marriage bond still publicly held, its frayed state was becoming apparent to Dreiser's sisters, and they began taking sides. Mame and Sylvia gave Jug to understand that she was no longer welcome in their homes, while his brother Ed's wife, Mai, and Claire Gormley, Theodore's youngest sister, both devout Catholics, swung into Jug's camp.

But she must have been lonely. Mencken called on her during Dreiser's absence; he had been "so nice to me this winter." In late January 1912 she visited her sister Rose and spouse in Missouri. Her nerves were still frayed from the Thelma crisis, and when she returned to New York, troubled by insomnia, she took refuge in the Our Lady of Peace convent, ignoring her Christian Science practitioner's warning that the nuns would unleash Malicious Animal Magnetism on her. On the contrary, the sisters had been kind, and she had been happy "—and slept." She moved back into the Broadway flat in May, but Dreiser did not join her, instead taking a room at 605 West 111th Street, presumably explaining that he could work better living alone.

His publishers were pressing him for a completed manuscript by the end of July, but in a concession to him had agreed to publish *The Financier* in three volumes. That was a load off Dreiser's mind, for he calculated that at the rate he was going a single volume would have run to more than 500,000 words (he was being conservative as it turned out). But, as he explained to Richards, the breaks between volumes occurred naturally, since Yerkes' career had three phases, the first in Philadelphia, the second in Chicago, and the last in London. He also told Richards that he had no quarrel with Harper's, who "are civil & fairly decent as publishers." Four days later, on May 30, he wrote that "by a private arrangement . . . which does not mean hypothecating either my future work or my time" he had reduced his debt to Harper's from $5000 to $2000. But he had kept the door ajar, telling Richards, "I have preferred to reduce the obligation in this way in order that in case I wish to leave there will be no great difficulties on this score." And he pointed out that the trilogy plan would enable him to take a break between Volumes I and II to write the travel book for the Century Company.

Yet, two weeks after his return, he told the Englishman, "I am profoundly glad that I am on my home ground and out of your clutches." Richards was not amused; he was miffed at Dreiser's discourtesy in not writing him until two weeks after his arrival, what is more making no mention of what Richards conceived to be his pivotal role in saving him from going down with the *Titanic*. He protested: "One day you press me to your bosom and tell me you are not going to take any step in regard to your literary affairs without my approval and sanction . . . and the next you go allowing Harper to 'plan' your future." Four days later he refers to the "agreement" they had entered into on December 15 giving his firm the English rights to all Dreiser's books.

Under the circumstances, Dreiser needed Mencken, who had departed on his own to the Continent. Mencken returned in June, and Dreiser wrote, "For heaven [sic] sake keep in touch with me by mail for I'm rather lonely & I have to work like the devil." In addition to winding up the book, he was cutting and rewriting earlier parts. His first draft was overloaded with details of Cowperwood's financial manipulations. By extensive reading he had mastered the essentials of his subject, but had trouble folding the raw facts into the narrative batter.

He had immersed himself in Yerkes' world, reading numerous financial histories, inventories of his art collection, and press accounts of the decor and furnishings of his New York mansion at Sixty-fourth Street and Fifth Avenue. Dreiser's chief source, however, was the files of the Philadelphia *Public Ledger*, which provided voluminous detail on Yerkes' financial manipulations and subsequent conviction for larceny and wrongful conversion of municipal funds.

Dreiser went about his research methodically, recording each important event of Yerkes' life on a separate sheet of yellow paper, either by handwritten note or in the form of a clipping pasted to the paper. He then arranged the sheets in chronological order to speed composition, and he followed the historical record in his narrative. In his obsession with getting the facts right, he corresponded with Joseph Hornor Coates, a Philadelphia editor he had met in 1902. Coates helped him gain access to the relevant newspaper files and served as technical adviser on Philadelphia history, customs, business practices, politics, and much else. In one letter Coates counsels Dreiser that "your young couple [Cowperwood and his first wife] would probably belong to the Merion Cricket Club and the Philadelphia Country Club." In another, he supplies a lengthy description of the stock exchange in Yerkes' time, pointing out that each broker had his own chair, which he sat in when he bid on stocks, like an auction. When Dreiser wrote back that this intelligence had ruined one of his scenes, Coates advised him to let the anachronism stand. Since he wasn't writing a biography or a history, he shouldn't "let an *unimportant* fact spoil a good fiction scene." Dreiser was thinking of his climactic scene, the panic that convulsed the Philadelphia exchange when news of the failure of Jay Cooke's firm came chattering over the telegraph. Such a scene demanded crowds of shouting brokers—not rows of men in chairs sedately murmuring "Sell Northern Pacific!" which was what Coates' description conjured up. And so he fudged a bit, perhaps drawing on other accounts, but nevertheless inserted a sentence early in the book explaining that "later in the history of the exchange" the chair system had given way to a setup in which the brokers moved about to various points, marked by signs, where different stocks were sold. Mencken noted Dreiser's passion for accuracy, once observing, "It was seldom that he departed from what he understood to be the record, and he never did so willingly."

Facts or factual accuracy do not make a novel, as Coates pointed out. And there were many places where the record was incomplete, especially relating to his hero's personal life—Yerkes' boyhood; his marriage to Susanna Gamble, a wealthy widow several years older than he; his adulterous affair with Mary Adelaide Moore, the daughter of a well-to-do pharmacist. Here Dreiser's imagination took over. He freely created scenes or altered or compressed events that were in the public record.

He also changed historical figures, sometimes in drastic ways. For example, Yerkes acted in league with other prominent Philadelphia financiers, but in the book, and to serve Dreiser's heroic conception of him, he is a lone wolf. Mary Adelaide Moore becomes the rebellious, passionate Aileen Butler, and her tame pharmacist father is transformed into Edward Malia Butler, a canny Irish political boss whose monopoly of city garbage collections, gained through bribes and favors, has made him a wealthy man. The character is closely modeled on a politico of that name and background whom Dreiser had interviewed and admired as a reporter in St. Louis. And he often manipulates the chronology of Yerkes' life, contracting his time in Philadelphia after his release from prison to speed up the narrative.

Dreiser had first heard of Yerkes as a boy in Chicago in the 1880s when the traction magnate's grossly underpaid employees went out on a long, bitter strike. When Yerkes died of Bright's disease in late 1905, Dreiser had clipped an editorial saying that the financier's career contained the materials for a great novel—by an "American Balzac." In 1907 Charles Edward Russell wrote about him in a series on financial chicanery that ran in *Everybody's* and was later published as a book by B. W. Dodge under the title *Lawless Wealth.* An article by Edwin Lefèvre on Yerkes titled "What Availeth It?" in the June 1911 *Everybody's* conveyed Yerkes' insouciant, public-be-damned philosophy, which was crucial in forming Dreiser's interpretation of him as a man who scorned conventional morality. As Lefèvre concluded, "He was not worse than so many other captains of industry. He merely was less hypocritical." That suggestion of defiance of the conventions appealed to Dreiser, as did one of Yerkes' maxims quoted in a newspaper interview: "Whatever I do, I do not from a sense of duty, but to satisfy myself." He did not need to overstrain his imagination to concoct Cowperwood's motto: "I satisfy myself."

Such statements were congenial to Dreiser's idea of Cowperwood as a kind of Nietzschean superman, a concept in vogue among intellectuals in the early 1900s. Dreiser had read Mencken's book on the German philosopher, and although he told his friend that he preferred Schopenhauer, he must have been impressed by Nietzsche's ideas on the superman's transcendence of conventional morality. He was determined to suppress the feminine side of his nature, and in an interview with *The New York Times Book Review,* which was published in June 1912, Dreiser announced that he was through writing books about women. "Jennie's temperament does not appeal to me any longer," he said, "in the new novel, the note of the plot will come from the man, and the man shall be the centre of the next three or four novels." He may even have thought that with a "business man's novel" (as the second volume of the Cowperwood saga was later advertised), he could reach a new, more broad-minded audience and escape the clutches of the largely feminine book-buying public, whom the antivice forces were dedicated to protecting from "immoral" books.

In writing the chapters on Frank Cowperwood's boyhood, Dreiser drew on his own experiences, Yerkes' sparse autobiographical statements, and a biography of Jay Cooke, a near contemporary of Yerkes in Philadelphia. There are two pivotal events in the shaping of Frank's character. The first is a fight with a bully. Cowperwood cuts the other boy's face with a ring he is wearing (the reverse of what had happened to Dreiser as a boy in Chicago in a similar fracas), learning that he must use craft and guile to become stronger than his enemies. The second occurs during a visit to an aquarium, where Frank watches a lobster and a squid cohabiting a tank. Eventually the lobster eats the squid, and the boy has a revelation: "How was life organized? Things lived on each other—that was it." Dreiser had touched indirectly on this idea in the 1906 essay "A Lesson From the Aquarium," in which he tried to draw a series of analogies between animals and predatory capitalists, and also in a sketch about a butcher in a slaughterhouse, "Our Red Slayer." In the latter, he presents the carnage of the stockyard as a metaphor of life living on life. (The slaughterhouse image traced back to his boyhood in Sullivan, Indiana, when he lived near a farm butcher named Spilky and had nightmares about the animals herded to their deaths.) The title comes from a line in Emerson's antideath poem, "Brahma"—"If the red slayer think he slays. . . ."

And so young Cowperwood comprehends that he must live off— use—others: "A real man—a financier—was never a tool. He used tools. He created. He led." (So G. W. Wilder used his editor-in-chief.) Though not inherently dishonest, he regards laws and conventions as fetters, like the net of tiny ropes with which the Lilliputians subdued Gulliver. The great man takes care to observe the proprieties when it is in his interest to do so and to avoid getting caught at something illegal (the same thoughts are ascribed to Hurstwood in *Sister Carrie*), but he must never let small men tether him, prevent him from pursuing his interests. (In a note scrawled alongside one of the clippings he pasted up, Dreiser wrote, "The strong man wants to be allow[ed] to do. The little man wants to stop him.") Cowperwood's cold eyes penetrate the veil of hypocrisy to the naked self-interest or desire underneath. Religion and morality are merely "toys of the clerics, by which they made money." The strong man manipulates the rules to his own advantage. (Watching a soccer game in Germany, Dreiser was inspired to write in his diary: "Morality and ethics are nothing but footballs wherewith people—strong people—play to win points.")

With such touches Dreiser transformed the historical Yerkes into Cowperwood, a projection of his own psyche. The cool, self-contained, supremely confident Cowperwood was the *beau ideal* of his anxiety-ridden, sometimes gauche creator. Yerkes was indeed a philanderer and an art collector, but his philosophy was "Wealth does not buy happiness; it buys luxuries." He was a man who had no illusions about what he was purchasing. Dreiser, however, sublimates his own strong yet guilt-hobbled sexual drive into the suave Cowperwood and transforms it into a quest for beauty, for the ideal. In a passage cut from the published version of *The Financier,* Dreiser writes that beautiful women "were like wondrous objects of art but to get the full value of their artistry [Cowperwood] had to be in close individual relationship with them and that could only be achieved through the affections"—sexual relations, a condition Dreiser set in his own love life.

Cowperwood also embodied a conflict within Dreiser. On the one hand he admired and envied the famous rogue builders of American capitalism, reflecting his own boyhood ambitions (it's no accident that Cowperwood's middle name is "Algernon"—after Horatio Alger) and his strong lust for power. On the other, his acute sense of social justice condemned them as exploiters of the common people.

The philosophy of Herbert Spencer, as adapted by Dreiser, suggested a resolution to this conflict between the great individual and the masses. Analogizing from the laws of physics to the laws of sociology, the British savant taught that every force produced a counterforce, every action a reaction, resulting in constant change until an ultimate balance—"suspended equation"—was reached. Dreiser borrowed this idea, gave it a personal meaning and eventually a name—the Equation Inevitable. He saw society as a Darwinian jungle; but he also saw it as ruled by Spencerian laws, which imposed a pattern on the endless struggle between the haves and have-nots, resulting in an eventual balance whenever one side became too powerful. As Dreiser explained to a reader of *The Delineator* who in 1910 asked him to state his views on protective tariffs and other issues of the day:

> We who feel that justice is not being done have but one thing to do and that is—fight, by argument, by example, by insistence on fair play where ever we have the power to compel such. The rest is in the hands of the Lord or nature which swings like a pendulum from one extreme apparently to another. Depend on it, that from every condition of distress

or evil there is a great reaction, and the greater the evil or distress, the greater the reaction.

By July Dreiser was deep into revisions. Hoping to avoid arguments over cuts, Hitchcock had written him that "I want to have the book made with the fullest understanding between us." Nevertheless, Dreiser reacted so angrily to one of his critiques that Hitchcock had to telephone him and then write a letter the same day assuring him that the overall story was strong and that it was now a matter of pruning excessive financial detail.

With this criticism Dreiser agreed, and he labored to dramatize Cowperwood's fight for survival after the Panic of 1871, triggered by the Chicago fire. In a series of rapidly shifting scenes he details Cowperwood's coolly brilliant maneuvers, which are nonetheless doomed by the workings of chance and the greater power of his enemies, led by old Butler, who wants revenge on the man who seduced his daughter. Dreiser transposed the scene of Butler's discovery of Cowperwood and Aileen *in flagrante* at their house of assignation to a point earlier in the narrative to break up a technical discussion of Cowperwood's financial and legal troubles.

Hitchcock had another worry. He suggested playing down the fact that this was only the first volume of a trilogy, citing the precedent of the American Winston Churchill's bestselling trio of historical novels, *Richard Carvel, The Crisis,* and *The Crossing.* The initial book must be presented to the public as complete of itself, and then, as with Churchill, "the rumor allowed to percolate" that the author would write another volume dealing with the characters introduced in the first. In furtherance of this plan, each volume of Dreiser's trilogy would have a separate title, rather than being titled *The Financier,* Volumes I, II, and III, as Dreiser suggested.

Dreiser was willing to go along with Harper's scheme if it would increase sales, but the problem with it was that reviewers and readers might think *The Financier* incomplete. And, in fact, several oblivious reviewers did remark that the novel seemed to end abruptly.

Living on a tight margin, Dreiser was also eager to have a book in the stores as soon as possible. Harper's had been keeping him afloat with periodic $500 advances, plus a payment of $1000 in February. Counting the money he had received in 1911 prior to his trip, he collected more than $5800 between October 1911 and December 1912. Deducting at least $1500 for his European trip, an unknown allowance to Jug while he was away, $1000 for the payment on the apple orchard, and $183 to his agent, Flora Mai Holly, it could be seen that he was not living in luxury.

Working furiously, Dreiser sent Hitchcock the concluding chapters of *The Financier* in mid-July. He had met his deadline, but it had been a brutal task, and he was not entirely happy with the results. He rejoined Jug at 3609 Broadway and presumably she helped him read proofs. After the *Jennie* experience, he had not let her work on the manuscript, dealing directly with Hitchcock, whom, rightly or wrongly, he did not trust. But there was no time to reconvene the literary jury that had vetted *Jennie* and *The Genius*. Mencken was his only remaining sounding board. In late August he flashed a broad hint to Baltimore: "It looks to be a book of 700 pages or more unless I can cut it. Alas, alas." Could he send a set of galleys to his friend?

The sergeant of artillery snapped to. "Let me have those proofs by all means. . . . Don't let the damnable Harpers cut the story! A pox on all such butchery." But Dreiser too was worried about length, estimating that the manuscript contained 270,000 words—probably an understatement—and he was frantically revising. As a result Mencken did not receive proofs until October 3—too late to write a review for the November *Smart Set*. Three days later he conveyed his personal reaction to Dreiser: "No better picture of a political-financial camorra has ever been done. It is wholly accurate and wholly American." Yes, it was too long; whole scenes of irrelevant description could go, but the massive documentation was one of the chief virtues.

Dreiser wrote him gratefully, "I am glad you like it fairly well only I suspect your good nature is getting the better of your judgment." Mencken had pulled his punches a little, for he wrote a more objective opinion to his friend Harry Leon Wilson, a writer and editor. Dreiser had "got drunk on his story" and piled on too many financial details. At the same time, he had said too little about Cowperwood's relationship with Aileen Butler, a point Mencken had made to Dreiser, suggesting that he should deal with "the girl's initiation and the constant menace . . . of pregnancy."

That suggestion must have seemed rather naive to Dreiser, given all the blows he had taken from moralistic editors and critics. Otherwise Dreiser took his resident critic's suggestions and made many cuts on page proofs, incurring a huge charge of $726.90 for author's alterations. He had excised 77 pages in all, wrote Mencken that he wished it had been 200, and asked him to suggest any chapters that could come out or be dropped in toto. "You always see a thing as a whole which is a Gods blessing."

Grant Richards' patience and forbearance finally ran out. A letter Dreiser wrote in July was the last straw. "Do you really think you ought to have it?" he teasingly asked, referring to *The Financier*. "Personally I get very dubious when I think that the one financial thing I really wanted you to do you did not do and rather wilfully and inconsiderately I think." By "the one financial thing" Dreiser was referring to Richards' alleged mismanagement of his money in Europe so that he had nothing left when it came time to return. Coming at this late date, the remark was a low blow, and Dreiser compounded the cruelty by adding in a subsequent letter that the reason he had not signed the agreement in Richards' office in April was that he "did not care to be rushed into any understanding I might regret." Now he was glad he hadn't.

Richards was deeply offended. On August 8 he wrote with chilling condescension: "My poor friend: When I read your letter I confess that I had a rather bad half hour." Now he understood what Dreiser had meant when he warned of his "suspiciousness," he said. "I should perhaps have known that there are men who can't believe that one is friendly, disinterested or enthusiastic from conviction. You searched for a motive for all the trouble I took . . . & you found one after your own kind. Well, I wish you joy of it."

Dreiser had indeed warned Richards: "There's something strange in my makeup. I quarrel with my friends." He had let that quality poison their friendship; moreover, wanting the trip to Europe and hoping for a better offer than Harper's had given him, he had let Richards develop expectations of a future association. And yet, Richards should have realized that Harper's would not give up Dreiser, with whom the firm had a perfectly valid contract. And he had offered Dreiser little but promises.

Months went by; then, on December 16, when the publisher was about to sail for England after completing his annual visit to New York, Dreiser wrote him a note asking permission to call at the Hotel Knickerbocker. "Quite deliberately," he said, "I am giving you a chance to 'cut' me." Richards replied that he couldn't imagine what reasons there were for a meeting, but he would be in his hotel room between 2:30 and 3:45, should Dreiser care to turn up.

We have only Richards' account of the meeting, but it is probably accurate enough: "After some salutation we each waited, like nervous dogs, for the other to begin, I folding my clothes and putting them away, he leaning back in his chair, interminably folding and unfolding his handkerchief. In effect, I believe, we neither of us spoke and, after a space he departed."

Much later Dreiser would say, "I would give anything not to have quarreled with him, and over money too! I owe him so much; that trip to Europe! It was like a tonic that lasted me for years; it was a new life to me."

What Dreiser did not know was that Richards now had an additional grievance: he had read in the first draft of *A Traveler at Forty*, as the travel book was called, Dreiser's indiscreet account of his relations with the cocottes to whom Richards had introduced him and with Mme Culp, not to mention blunt comments on some of Richards' friends. On December 5 Douglas Doty, who was editing the book at the Century Company, had sent Richards a revised script out of concern that, having read the "unexpurgated" first draft, he might not have gotten a "clear impression of the material I had dug out."

But Doty's editing did not mollify Richards. On December 12 he dispatched a scorching protest. Dreiser had slanderously portrayed him as "a go between and a continual patron of . . . ladies of bad character. . . . Half of Dreiser's facts are wrong; and if right they are generally wrongly seen and lead to wrong deductions." He vowed to "come down on the Century Company with all the power of the law" if the offending matter was not removed.

Doty could not be considered Dreiser's staunch ally, having told Richards in an earlier letter, "What you have to say confidentially about T.D. does not surprise me. He's a curious combination of real man and *mucker.*" But he said he preferred not to show Dreiser Richards' objections while he was still working on the book lest it discourage him. And he feared that if they cut too much, Dreiser might "take his book and go elsewhere with it and print it as he likes." Still, with the threat of a lawsuit hanging over him, he was willing to accommodate Richards.

The Financier was published on October 24, 1912, to generally favorable reviews. Their effect was to assure Dreiser's literary stature. As Mencken later wrote, "You are gaining a definite place . . . as the leading American novelist. . . . New serious novels are no longer compared to 'Silas Lapham' or to 'McTeague' but to 'Sister Carrie' & 'Jennie Gerhardt.' " Dreiser was regarded as an independent force, by far the most compelling writer on the American literary scene.

In addition to seeing his friend through the accouchement, Mencken tirelessly pounded out reviews, opening with a major article in *The New York Times Book Review.* He recited Dreiser's now familiar weaknesses as a novelist, but by subtle twists, turned each of them into a virtue. Possibly to Harper's consternation, he noted that *The Financier* was but a prologue to "the more important second volume [in which] the real drama of Frank Cowperwood's life will be played out." He also held forth in the Los Angeles *Times,* in the *Smart Set,* and in "The Free Lance" column in the Baltimore *Sun.*

"Dreiser is a real fellow and deserves all the help he can get," Mencken later wrote Willard Huntington Wright. "Some day, I believe, we will be glad to think that we gave him a hand. He is bound to win out." The good reception of *The Financier* seemed to indicate that a sea change in literary taste was taking place. Indeed, in 1912, the year of the rise of ragtime, Woodrow Wilson's election to the presidency, and the defeat of William Howard Taft and Theodore Roosevelt, who represented the politics of the past—the old order seemed to be fading. A youthful minority was searching for new forms of expression, new values, new experiences—new freedoms. Historians would call this premature cultural spring the American Renaissance, and Dreiser was its chief harbinger in the novel. *The Financier* demonstrated that now a preponderance of the critics were sympathetically disposed to his efforts to critique, in Cowperwood's story, the rise of American finance capitalism in the post–Civil War era.

There had been novels aplenty about business in recent years, but until *The Financier* the business novel had been reformist or moralistic in impulse. Dreiser had approached the world of high finance in a radically new way. The business-political elite that really runs Philadelphia is pitted against Cowperwood in a test of superior strength, not progressive ideals. Cowperwood emerges from prison wiser but not sadder. "I have had my lesson," he says. "They caught me once but they will not catch me again." Be a lobster, not a squid. The antagonists in the story are not the representatives of religion's good and evil or of reform's decency and corruption; they are emissaries of natural forces, and they bring Cowperwood down not because his kind must be stopped, but out of countervailing selfishness, greed, jealousy. "We live in a stony universe whose hard, brilliant forces rage fiercely," Dreiser writes in the novel. "Life moves in an ordered hierarchy of forces of which the lesser is as nothing to the greater."

Cowperwood is not presented as an immoralist who is humbled by conscience (as in Howells' *The Rise of Silas Lapham*) or reformist zeal (as in Churchill's best sellers). He is an admirable fellow in many ways—highly intelligent, charming, even honorable. He takes no sadistic or evil pleasure in ruining his rivals. Ideally, he would like a world in which a cabal of the strong peaceably divides up the spoils, but he quite understands that another's self-interest may conflict with his. But he also loves a fight, and employs all the means at his command, fair or foul. And he takes his defeats with the stoical courage of a warrior. His nemesis, the grizzled Irish boss, Edward Malia Butler, is driven by a fierce paternal love of his daughter, but in the process of saving her honor he loses her and dies of a broken heart. Butler is as compelling a portrait as old Gerhardt, with whom he shares a deep religious faith.

Dreiser's vision of man—"his feet are in the trap of circumstance, his eyes are on an illusion"—gives his book a deeper tragic resonance than its predecessors. And the historic scope of his theme, the monumental architecture of his story, and the exhaustiveness of his documentation make *The Financier* the greatest business novel written in America of its time—and probably of all time.

Before beginning the second volume, which he had decided to call *The Titan*, Dreiser took time off to write a short story, "The Lost Phoebe." It tells of a devoted old couple, Phoebe and Henry, grown gnarled with the years, like the twisted, lichen-encrusted apple trees in their orchard. Estranged from their children, they have only each other and their ramshackle farm. Then Phoebe, the wife, dies. Henry is lost without her and he begins to catch glimpses of her ghost, looking like she did when he was courting her. The delusion grows stronger as the years pass; he wanders about the county, searching for her. In the end, standing on the edge of a ravine, he thinks he sees her down among a bed of apple tree blossoms and leaps to his death.

"The Lost Phoebe" is a moving, harshly realistic story of a deluded quest for the unattainable (resembling in that respect Maeterlinck's play *The Blue Bird*). It is about how dreams lead to destruction, a theme Dreiser first broached in *Sister Carrie*. Illusion is, in a different way, a strong theme in *The Financier*. In the coda the three witches from *Macbeth* apostrophize Cowperwood—"master and no master, prince of a world of dreams whose reality was disillusion!" We need dreams to lure us into achievement, Dreiser says, but once we attain them we inevitably find disillusionment—or death.

"The Lost Phoebe" may also be read as a symbolic version of Dreiser's love for Thelma, his "little Blue Bird" of happiness. He sought through her to recapture youth—and fell to his destruction. The subconscious title of the story was "The Lost Thelma."

He sent "Phoebe" to a new agent, Paul Reynolds, for what would be a long journey, and turned to real youth in the person of Anna Tatum, who had written him admiring, disputatious letters while he was in Europe and had arrived in New York. When they met in the dining room of the Brevoort, she blurted out, "I didn't know you were so homely." Dreiser stalked out the door. Anna was apparently not really dissatisfied with what she saw, for Dreiser later wrote in his diary that they lived together from May 1, 1912, to January 1, 1913; at least part of that time he was nominally living with Jug at 3609 Broadway.

When Anna met Dreiser she was no innocent, though she was a virgin. According to his diary, she had a lesbian affair with a doctor at the Woman's Hospital in New York, but when she met Dreiser, she was spoiling for a liaison with a great writer and urged him to take her, which he did. She was slight, blond, and attractive, and also brilliant and well read. A graduate of Wellesley, she came from an old and wealthy Pennsylvania Quaker family. During their affair, she related to Dreiser the story of her family and he found it so compelling that he decided he would make a novel of it. What attracted him to it was the figure of the father, a stern, pious man like John Paul Dreiser. In Anna's version, her father's severity and domineering ways drove the children to rebellion. Anna was a case in point. She defiantly puffed cigarettes in public, began drinking after she met Dreiser, and read Verlaine, then little known in the United States.

Her family's story hit Dreiser hard. Hadn't his own father's fanaticism driven his sisters to leave home and rush into illicit affairs with older men? His brother Paul had run off to join a medicine show rather than face further beatings by his father, while two other brothers, Rome and Al, had also taken to the road at an early age. Out of those associations was born *The Bulwark,* a novel he would work on intermittently for the next thirty years.

CHAPTER 6   *Chicago*

Chicago is my love; I don't believe any one could be crazier
over a girl than I am over that city.
                                                        —Dreiser (1912)

After being released from prison, Yerkes went to Chicago. In December 1912, Dreiser followed him. The city had changed since he was last there, in the 1890s; it had grown and acquired a veneer of culture, though the wind off Lake Michigan was just as raw in the winter, and the smell of the stockyards just as rank in the summer. As a young boy he had stood at the door of their flat on Madison and Throop dazzled by the sounds and bright lights. His memories of this city had been distilled into *Sister Carrie,* of which Floyd Dell had recently written in the *Evening Post,* "The poetry of Chicago has been adequately rendered, so far, by only one writer, and that in only one book."

Dreiser was well known among the city's literati, thanks in part to his champion Dell, whose *Friday Literary Supplement* had become an influential voice for the new writing. And as one who had begun his literary career in the 1890s, he had ties to the generation of Hamlin Garland and Henry B. Fuller, two of the city's most prominent writers-in-residence. Although Garland had found Dreiser cynical and uncouth at their last meeting, in early 1904, he respected *Sister Carrie* as a work of realism. Dreiser in turn respected Garland's earlier books, particularly *Main-Travelled Roads* and *Rose of Dutcher's Coolley,* a more moral precursor of *Carrie,* which was nevertheless attacked by the censors in the 1890s. As for Fuller, he had sent Dreiser a rather stiff but friendly letter about *Jennie Gerhardt,* praising his "consistent and persistent employment of the approved latter-day method" of realism.

Garland invited Dreiser to a gathering at the Little Club, which convened in the Fine Arts Building: "Do you like to stand on your hind legs, and talk? If so, I think the members of this Club would like to hear from you before you go East." Dreiser abhorred public speaking, but he came for conversation. Both Garland and Fuller had abandoned "the approved latter-day method," and he asked them why. Fuller had been embittered by local criticism of his satirical novels about the city's New England establishment, but he may also have simply exhausted his material. Garland had given up writing his grim stories of the Middle Border because they weren't commercial and he had a family to support. He had fallen by economic necessity into the hands of Richard Watson Gilder, then editor of the *Century,* who convinced him that truth was not beautiful. Dreiser found Garland conservative to the point of timidity. When Garland recounted some scandalous activities in his Wisconsin hometown, Dreiser urged him to make a novel out of the material. "Oh, no," Garland said. "That wouldn't do for me. It's something that should interest you."

The defeatism of these veteran realists did not infect Dreiser. He was at the peak of his powers, recognized as a literary force, riding a historical wave. It was sweet to walk the Chicago streets again and encounter at odd corners and moments memories of his youth and his improbable dreams of literary fame.

He zestfully pursued his researches at the Newberry Library, within walking distance of his boardinghouse, filling hundreds of pages with abstracts from newspapers and municipal records on Yerkes. When he tired, he could stroll over to nearby Bughouse Square and listen to the open-air philosophers. He also called on Edgar Lee Masters, a lawyer who wrote poetry on the side and who had praised *The Financier.* He had practiced law during Yerkes' last years and gave Dreiser a letter of introduction to Carter H. Harrison, former mayor of Chicago and leader of the opposition to the traction magnate's attempt to bribe the state legislature and the city council into granting him a fifty-year monopoly of the city's street railways. Dreiser had letters to others who knew Yerkes, including one of the battery of attorneys he had kept on retainer solely to deal with heartbalm suits by discarded mistresses, who were paid off handsomely if they cooperated. Dreiser's relish for his story grew, as plum after juicy plum fell into his lap.

The two men hit it off. Lee Masters was also trapped in an empty marriage and hated the necessity of doing work he loathed to support his family. He had written several volumes of poetry, which he had published with his own money. He was a friend of William Reedy, the St. Louis editor of the *Mirror* and an eloquent champion of new writing, including *Sister Carrie*. Reedy had published articles by Masters on law and politics and tried to discourage his friend's poetic ambitions, without much success. The conventional odes to autumn and Helen of Troy kept coming, and out of friendship Reedy published a few of them under a pseudonym.

A stocky, scholarly city lawyer with a commanding chin and shrewd twinkling eyes behind rimless spectacles, Masters had made a lot of money (most of it, he said, lost on bad investments) as the "inside" man in a firm headed by Clarence Darrow. Masters ran the office, drew up pleas, and handled the boring paperwork for bread-and-butter civil cases. Finally, deciding that Darrow had been withholding fees that he should have paid into the firm, Masters struck out on his own. But after twenty years' practice in Chicago, he was weary of the law and longed to accumulate enough money to be able to write full time.

Dreiser visited Masters' home and met his wife, Helen, who came from an old Chicago family. She would play mood music on the piano in the parlor while Lee worked on his poetry in his study—really abandoning her, he later said. There were three children from the marriage, and they were the main reason Masters plodded to his office every day and squinted at the fine print in title abstracts and wills. As he said of himself, "The horse on the treadmill starts the machine that keeps him from stopping." Dreiser's visit proved a godsend, and the two men walked the streets in animated conversation. Masters was impressed by the fecundity of the visitor's mind, bursting with literary projects, and heard the story of the religious Quaker father and his rebellious brood.

In addition to his talks with Masters, his researches, and spells of writing on *The Titan*, Dreiser found time to play. He seemed bent on researching firsthand Yerkes' amorous career as well. On New Year's Eve, he bunny-hugged and turkey-trotted the old year out with Lengel's date.

Having a rule that went, "Never take a girl away from an old friend," Dreiser was reasonably restrained that night, but he soon found other flowers to pluck: a garden of lively, "advanced" young womanhood was in bloom at the Little Theater, founded by Maurice Browne, a wandering Englishman who had landed in Chicago. The Little Theater was a popular gathering place for the cultural set where Bohemia and new money rubbed shoulders. Every weekday, subscribers could take refreshments at the tearoom adjacent to the tiny auditorium, where a samovar bubbled and cakes and sandwiches were dispensed by the fashionable catering establishment run by the widow of Chicago University professor and poet William Vaughn Moody. On Sundays an open house was held in honor of some

visiting celebrity, and Dreiser was guest of honor at one of these gatherings
and thereafter a frequent visitor.

Fanny Butcher, newly appointed secretary of the Little Theater and
later doyenne of the Chicago *Tribune*'s book page, watched him flirt with
her predecessor, an aspiring poet. Although Butcher, like many contemporaries, remembered Dreiser as unattractive, he was presentable enough in his
forties, as the pictures show. What he had was an animal magnetism, and
also an intense sincerity and *interest* in women: he listened to what they had
to say, was sympathetic to their troubles, probably a trait he acquired growing up with four older sisters who had more than their share of troubles. The
British novelist John Cowper Powys, then a lecturer, who occasionally held
forth on the Little Theater stage, described him as approaching a woman
"like a botanist examining a plant at his leisure." He would "seek to draw
out—sympathetically, you must understand . . . yet with a kind of soul-
ravishing violence, the deepest life-secrets of her essential being. Nothing
that the girl might say . . . would pass disregarded, no affectation, no
narcissism, no feminine weakness, no feminine subterfuge." He was interested in women's minds, what they thought, and so liked intelligent, though
preferably young and impressionable, ones.

He was inevitably dazzled by the lovely Margaret Anderson, but she
had no interest in flirtations; besides she had a boyfriend, who had promised
to finance the literary magazine *(The Little Review)* she was dreaming up.
She froze him, even though she had written a favorable review of *Sister
Carrie* in the *Continent*.

In contrast to Anderson's withering reaction, the poet Mary Elizabeth
Barry was flattered by the attentions of the literary lion from New York.
They fell into a deep conversation and met again at breakfast the next day
to continue it, and when she returned to the Little Theater, she composed
a poem called "Dead Sea Apples." The title did not augur well for Dreiser's
courtship, but it did show she had been impressed. The first lines went:

> *You, whom I do not love*
> *Have taught me what love is.*

After Dreiser read it, he promptly invited Barry to come to New York,
but she was engaged.

Enter Elaine Hyman, at a Little Theater open house. She was with
Floyd Dell, a considerable figure in his own right with his small mustache,
a cigarette perpetually dangling from his lips, his soft hat and flowing tie,
the image of a dashing Latin Quarter poet. Elaine had been the star of
Browne's production of *The Trojan Women*. At her first meeting with
Dreiser, she was put off by the famous novelist's Hoosier twang, and she
soon swept out of the room, accompanied by Dell and an equally flamboy-

antly clad friend, the poet Michael Carmichael Carr. But Dreiser was drawn to Elaine's unconventional beauty. With her olive complexion and coal-black hair, she was Grecian-looking. Her father was Jewish and her mother of New England stock, and the two heritages warred within her. At this stage in her life she was rebelling against the New England side and had made what she called her "half-baked entry into Jewish society" in New York. Her father doted on her and wanted her to be a professor of literature. She was intelligent and well read; she sang, wrote poetry, and painted. But she was also restless and unable to settle down to hard study, and her education had mainly consisted of tutoring by her father and courses at the Art Institute.

It was perhaps inevitable that a girl so close to her father would choose the older man. Dreiser, it should be said, had a way of broadcasting his helplessness and need for mothering, and these qualities were attractive to Elaine, young as she was. When Dell asked her why she chose Dreiser over him, she said, "He needs me. You don't."

After a rapid, intense courtship, Elaine "gave herself " to him, Dreiser later wrote in his diary. She determined to join him in New York and become an actress, and Dreiser had encouraged her.

He left Chicago on February 10, 1913, and stopped off in Baltimore for dinner with Mencken on the way. They had much to talk over. Dreiser faced another busy year, with deadlines for *The Titan* and the travel book looming up. But he was full of extraneous causes and enthusiasms. The Little Theater for one. It was going on tour, and he asked Mencken to arrange an engagement in Baltimore, and urged him to write a "radical" one-act play for Browne, whom Dreiser extolled as "the real thing."

The antivice crusaders for another. His talks with Masters and other Chicago freethinkers had awakened him to the bane of censorship. Mencken had been tilting with the Baltimore Society for the Suppression of Vice in his "Free Lance" column, and as a follow-up to their meeting Dreiser asked Mencken to send him six sets of his columns attacking the literary moralists, saying he was "going to place them where they will do real good."

Back in New York, Dreiser sent a financial-distress call to Major Leigh. Royalties from his books, he pointed out in a letter dated February 19, had totaled about $4500 since the publication of *Jennie* in October 1911. "I have drawn, as you know considerable more than that," he admitted. Over the past ten months, however, his advances had averaged only about $230 a month—good pay for a clerk, say, but about a quarter of what he had been drawing at *The Delineator*. He swore he had "led the simple life," but asked Leigh for $200 a month to see him through the writing of *The Titan*. Leigh was amenable, but Dreiser was required to turn over the manuscript of *The Genius* as a security; Harper's would have the right to publish it, if by

October 1914 his other books hadn't earned back their advances. In effect, he was on a drawing account, pledging the royalties on past, present, and now, possibly, future works as security for the debt.

But one manuscript of *The Genius* was in Chicago, being circulated among Lengel, Dell, Masters and Lucian Cary, a newspaper critic, and another copy was being read in the East. Dreiser was worried not only about the merits of the novel but its moral acceptability.

He might have been even more distressed to learn that Harper's was already uneasy about *The Titan.* In a confidential letter to Flora Mai Holly, written in the fall of 1911, Hitchcock told the agent that he must see the "last part" of *The Financier* (which at that point was still envisioned as a one-volume work) because of "certain delicate conditions involved. There may be something in the latter part which, from our point of view, would be wholly inadvisable. . . ." What Harper was worried about was the reaction of J. Pierpont Morgan. In 1901 he and Yerkes had tangled over who would handle the financing of the consolidated London underground transit system, and Morgan had lost—something J.P. was highly unaccustomed to doing. The "last part" of Dreiser's novel would deal with Yerkes' London operations. Surely this was the meaning of Hitchcock's cryptic reference: it would not be wise to reopen old wounds of the chief financial backer of the House of Harper.

Meanwhile *The Genius* manuscript was encountering objections of another kind. Dell found it "badly written" and said no amount of cutting would improve it. Lengel told Dreiser that publication of it now "would do more to damage your career than to help it." He recognized many of the figures and incidents from the Butterick days and felt that Dreiser had "clung too closely to life . . . to give a calm portrayal." Nevertheless, at Dreiser's request he cut the script for possible serialization and showed it to Ray Long, editor of *Red Book,* which was based in Chicago. Long thought the writing was too diffuse. The story "could not possibly grip the reader."

Dreiser was not visibly disheartened by these reactions. He told Lengel that the book couldn't be published for two or three years, anyhow, and that he had been thinking of revising it. Still, he had "six or seven" other opinions that were favorable. As for Dell, "You know I never have been sure of Dell's inmost convictions about anything and I am not now." Regarding a reservation of Lengel's that Eugene Witla was not a sympathetic character, he wrote, "The whole test of a book—to me—is—is it true, revealing, at once a picture and a criticism of life. If it measures up in those respects we can dismiss sympathy, decency, even the utmost shame and pain of it all." Those words stated the credo of his realism, which no criticisms could shake.

After journeying safely through many hands, the Chicago manuscript was lost by the Post Office. Dreiser's theory was that it had been delivered, but Jug had got hold of it and after reading the portrayal of herself as the character Angela Blue, destroyed it in a fit of anger. That seems improbable, for she surely would have told him about her reactions, since they were still living together at 3609 Broadway. (In later letters to him she implies she never read the book, even after it was published.) At any rate, Dreiser was forced to have another copy typed at a cost of $135.

He was juggling too many other projects to devote much thought to *The Genius.* He was working furiously on *A Traveler at Forty,* and an early chapter, the one describing his meeting with the London prostitute called Lilly Edwards, appeared in the June *Smart Set.* In the latter part of May, Dreiser wrote Elaine Hyman that he had finished fifty-two chapters and was finding the work taxing. He wound up the travel book by mid-July (he had written some of it in England), turning in a 500,000-word manuscript, by Doty's estimate. That seems incredible, and a surviving typescript is less than half that length.

Between times working on *Traveler,* he managed to compose a one-act play called *The Girl in the Coffin,* inspired by "Big Bill" Haywood, the Wobbly leader, who was then leading the silkworkers' strike in Paterson, New Jersey. The strike had galvanized Greenwich Village Bohemians, and Dreiser may have attended support meetings or even the great pageant on June 7 in Madison Square Garden directed by John Reed, which powerfully dramatized the workers' cause and inspired dreams of a new revolutionary theater among the intelligentsia. (These hopes were shaken when it turned out that the pageant, a fund-raising event, actually lost money. Its failure hurt the morale of the hard-pressed silkworkers, who had counted on it to provide money for food and clothes, and by August the strike was broken.)

The Girl in the Coffin is implicitly pro-strike, but the underlying ideology is Dreiser's. A labor leader, Magnet, is grieving for his daughter, the girl of the title, who died during an abortion. A conventional father, he wants to find the man who made her pregnant and avenge her death. Ferguson, the organizer of the strike, talks him into returning to the picket line and forgetting his obsession with vengeance. At the end it is revealed that Ferguson was the girl's lover. And so the play is a critique of conventional morality: Magnet was wrong to place his daughter's honor above the greater cause of the workers he leads. He belongs in the struggle, in the maelstrom of conflict between the masses and those who exploit them. Labor needs its supermen too. And so a play about a labor leader was not so far removed from a novel about a financier after all.

Although somewhat static and talky, *The Girl in the Coffin* is a powerful play within its limited frame—one of the best theater pieces Dreiser ever wrote (he had technical help on it). Somewhat deferentially, he sent it to Mencken for possible publication in the *Smart Set.* Mencken praised it, and the new editor, Willard Huntington Wright, whom George Jean Nathan and Mencken had installed in a palace coup, bought it immediately.

Dreiser worked steadily on *The Titan* from July into December, when his publisher was still badgering him for copy for the printer. Despite Hitch-cock's advice to make the second volume "relatively concise. . . . Pray let the reader infer something for himself," it was growing into another behe-moth. For cutting he depended on Hitchcock and another editor, W. G. van Tassell Sutphen, who approached the task with some trepidation and later thanked Dreiser for "the forbearance with which you have accepted my literary surgery." As with *The Financier,* Dreiser was distressed about exces-sive length, even as he hated to see the book cut.

He was working too fast and he knew it. Necessity, of course, was goading him, but he was also in a hurry to get down on paper the ideas and characters that were seething in his brain. As he later told a biographer, Dorothy Dudley: "The country is big: you can't write about it in a small peckish way; there's not time to polish. Later on I intend to rewrite my books, condense them. I have too much to do, too much to put forth. People need it. They need to know things."

He believed in the long novel, he told Anna Tatum, "because it is more life like. It gives both author and reader a better opportunity to grow into a deep sympathetic understanding with the characters." In keeping with this philosophy, the physical act of writing for him was akin to opening a valve, as one of his literary assistants once said. He had iron concentration, and the words flowed forth, steadily, the protruding wire on his stylographic pen whirling like a dervish as it stirred up the ink in the barrel. He could sit completely immobile. He kept a stack of typewriter paper on his desk, filling one sheet after another, placing the finished ones on another steadily grow-ing pile or letting them drift to the floor to be put in order later.

All the while, Elaine was sending him frequent, yearning letters. In March the Little Theater made a tour of several cities on the Eastern Seaboard, and Dreiser took a room in a boardinghouse in Boston. Elaine slipped away from the others for clandestine meetings.

As immersed in work as he was, Dreiser urged her to come to New York. Her letters show she was eager to join her "lover husband" but her parents were a problem; they knew nothing about the affair and she had to write him secretly. But she managed to cajole her father into subsidizing a try at a stage career on the condition that if she didn't find work after a reasonable time, she must come home. She adopted the stage name Kirah Markham.

At the end of May she took a room on East Fifty-ninth Street, where

Dreiser undoubtedly was a frequent visitor; he may even have told Jug that he had taken a studio there. Kirah believed that he had broken with Jug; it was not that simple. The situation was confused, and confusion was compounded when Dell arrived in the city in late summer. When he called at what he took to be "their" apartment, Dreiser greeted him genially and said he would leave so Floyd and Kirah could talk things over. "I suppose when I come back I'll see you disappearing around the corner," he joked, "Dell carrying the grand piano on his back." But the lady had chosen, and Dell, who had comforted her during her separation from Dreiser, moved on.

While he was still in the city, Dell's running quarrel with the publisher of the *Evening Post* came to a head, and he resigned in protest. After settling his affairs in Chicago, he joined the rebellion now fermenting in Greenwich Village.

With Dell now amicably out of Kirah's life, she, Jug, and Theodore settled into a kind of stable triangle. Kirah made the rounds of the theaters without much success and helped her lover with his work. By October, Harper's was sending an edited manuscript of *The Titan* to East Fifty-ninth rather than 3609 Broadway. The affair could no longer be said to be secret. After she had moved to a new place at 23 West Fifty-eighth Street, Dreiser notified Willard Huntington Wright that "Miss Kirah Markham . . . maintains an interesting drawing room Sunday evenings."

In February, a figure out of the past, Ben Dodge, arrived in town and offered him a post with a new publishing company for which Dodge had found a "doughbags." Dodge swore that he was "strictly sober and on the wagon." He proposed that the firm be renamed Dreiser & Company in his friend's honor. Dreiser would have a veto over all manuscripts, the reading of which he could delegate to Anna Tatum, now working as an editorial assistant at Harper's. Why was Dodge doing all this? Naturally he wanted Dreiser's name for its prestige value, but also, he said, he felt guilty about the thousand-dollar investment his friend had dropped in B. W. Dodge and had always felt "that I could come across with some kind of stunt that would give you a comeback for that money."

All this sounded too good to be true, and Dreiser asked Mencken and Dell for their advice. Mencken warned about Dodge's weakness: "If he takes to the jug again there will be hell." Other than that, why not? Probably Dreiser had the same qualms as Mencken, and he bowed out. By December Dodge was at a rural retreat in Vermont taking "a physical exercise cure" and thanking Dreiser for the "green goods" he had loaned him.

Although Dodge's scheme was probably doomed from the start, Dreiser's interest in a "liberal" publisher was sincere. He was unhappy with Harper's for business and literary reasons. The sales of *The Financier*, which had raced to a promising start in the latter part of 1912, tailed off in 1913 to only 1569 copies in the first six months and 1727 for the entire year. *Jennie* had sold 5000 copies in its second year, but now it had slowed to a trickle; the same held true for *Sister Carrie*. If *The Titan* didn't sell, he would slide deeper into debt, with only *The Genius* available to rescue him. But that manuscript bristled with potential moral problems.

His resentment against the censors was growing. When he received a rather innocuous letter from John O'Hara Cosgrave, a former colleague at Butterick, now an editor with the New York *World,* asking him to join the Authors League and support its struggle to reform the copyright law, he shot off an angry reply. Cosgrave had mentioned that the novelist Winston Churchill and Theodore Roosevelt would become president and vice president, respectively, of the organization. Dreiser reminded Cosgrave that Roosevelt had condemned Tolstoy for immorality and advocated the banning of works by Rabelais, Rousseau, and others. An authors' society that would fight "bureaucratic & reactionary interpretations of morals and individualistic thought in books, plays, sketches & the like" might interest him, but he could not see the worth of one dominated by "the pseudos, reactionaries and pink tea and chocolate bon bon brotherhood of literary effort" who were concerned primarily with "second serial and moving picture rights."

By fall he was asking Mencken to help him find another publisher. The latter advised him to talk to George H. Doran, who was reputed to be liberal-minded. Dreiser followed up the lead promptly and wrote Mencken that Doran "will give me full liberty this side [sic] criminal libel & will arrange for debts." Doran looked inviting because Dreiser had just passed through a terrible row with the Century Company over the *Traveler* manuscript.

CHAPTER 7

The Woman Stuff

> After I am dead please take up my mss of The Financier,
> Titan & Travel book & restore some of the woman
> stuff. . . .
>
> —Dreiser to Mencken (1913)

The arrival of batches of the *Traveler* at the Century offices at Union Square must have resembled a series of earth tremors. One can imagine the editors reading the latest chapters with mounting alarm. Dreiser's encounters with those gay Parisiennes, Marcelle and Mme de Villiers, are described, if not in full. Two chapters are devoted to a Berlin prostitute named Hanscha Jower. A charming dalliance in Venice (not mentioned in his travel diary) is given its due, complete with a moral: "I think true passion is silent and lust is deadly." Needless to say, as Dreiser wrote Mencken, the editors "objected . . . like hell" to these vignettes.

On top of that, Richards was still sniping away. When Doty forwarded proofs of an article on London carved out of the script for the British edition of the *Century,* Richards dispatched a telegram warning that the description of the Carlton Grill was libelous. But really, there is nothing in the manuscript stronger than what he himself called "invidious comparisons" with "the garish splendour, the ornate vulgarities of the American hotels [Dreiser] had most admired. . . ." To say that the Carlton did not measure up to the opulent, though arguably vulgar, decor of the Waldorf surely did not constitute libel, even under the draconian British laws. Perhaps Richards was really worried that publishing those remarks would cost him his favorite table at the Carlton Grill.

The Century Company's objections were more serious, and the raciness of parts of Dreiser's manuscript seems to have precipitated an internal battle between the new breed, represented by Ellsworth, Doty, and others, and members of the *ancien régime*, led by Robert Underwood Johnson, who wrote Hamlin Garland that Dreiser had included descriptions of "illicit relations with five different women, with disgusting details." What is more, he had "made defense of his conduct from the moral point of view—the most unblushing and immoral thing I have ever read." Already incensed by the efforts to rejuvenate the aging *Century*, Johnson regarded Dreiser's articles as profaning the temple.

He took his revenge. Garland, responding to criticisms that the National Institute for Letters had too many Easterners in its ranks, had proposed Dreiser for membership, and Johnson's letter was written to inform him that he would certainly blackball Dreiser.

On the face of it Dreiser appears to have lurched into another controversy he should have avoided. Some of his copy he could hardly have expected to be published. Probably he thought that all the furor about the "social evil" made prostitution respectable. The topic was very much in the air after a New York grand jury headed by John D. Rockefeller Jr. began probing the so-called white slave traffic in 1910, and the Chicago Vice Commission published its report on prostitution the following year. Magazines had been full of lurid articles about young women who were drugged by swarthy foreigners and spirited off to bagnios in Hong Kong or Rio de Janeiro. If Dreiser had not written about the subject with sociological objectivity, it was because he was a novelist, not a social scientist.

Nor had Dreiser been overly indelicate in his handling of the theme. Describing his affair with Marcelle in Nice, he mentions that they kiss, then adds, "The rest need not be related. . . ." In his chapters on Hanscha Jower, Dreiser does say that he availed himself of the woman's services, but he would have felt hypocritical if he had not done so.

His travel diary shows that he regarded their encounter as more than a casual sexual transaction: "Back to Alexander Platz where I get off & encounter Hanscha Jower. A most remarkable experience. All my life I have been seeking to encounter a woman of the streets who was safe, pleasant, innocent in a way. . . . Here she is, Hanscha Jower. Born in Tilsit, East Prussia. Lived in Stettin (pronounced Steteen). Large, soft, innocent, mild eye—like one of Ruben's [sic] women—like Jennie Gerhardt."

How many novelists are granted by life the opportunity to make love to a character in one of their books?

She took him to her little room and related the story of her life—how she had learned weaving but fell in love and became pregnant. The father of the child left her to join the army, and she worked for a time in the mills of Stettin, but the job made her ill. She tried clerking in a department store, but had no head for figures. "Occasionally I went with a man. I had to." Dreiser gives his answer to Johnson: "It is so easy for those born in satisfactory circumstances to moralize." The sketch ends with a question: "Why might not life have been kind to Hanscha Jower?"

There are other scenes of the underside of Europe that Baedeker does not talk about—sleazy cafés where prostitutes hang out, working-class slums, drab bars where poor people drink themselves into numbness. All of this was cut of course—and the encounters with Marcelle, Hanscha, Signorina X of Venice, Mme Culp as well. For serialization in the *Century*, Doty found material for two articles rather than the three originally planned. As for the book, he assured Johnson, "I'm cutting the Dreiser copy from 500,000 down to 100,000 and then [there] won't be anything left that is unprintable."

In London, Richards continued to slash away with abandon at anything unflattering to himself or his friends. Worried that nothing would be left, Doty suggested Dreiser disguise his friends' identities wherever possible. At one point he tells him rather than kill the Paris and Riviera sections entirely, "it would be better to resort to fiction,—to eliminate your personality entirely and project a new character as a traveling companion."

By now Dreiser was apparently aware of what Richards was up to and protested. Doty told the Englishman that, trying to satisfy them both, he felt he was "between the devil and the deep blue sea."

Meanwhile, the rift within the Century Company widened. In July Ellsworth wrote Richards that the articles selected for the magazine were "much liked by the liberals, and rather frowned on by the elder statesmen— of whom, by the way, we have now very few left." Johnson had resigned the previous month after management rejected his proposal that the company start a new, popular magazine like *Ainslee's*, while continuing to publish the *Century* in the old way.

With the domestic opposition vanquished, Doty and Ellsworth turned their fire on Richards. Ellsworth gently laid down the law:

> Mr. Dreiser thinks, and we all think, that you are asking him to take a great deal out of "A Traveler at Forty" which could be there just as well as not and hurt no one. I read the galley proofs of the book last Sunday, and it seems to me wonderful,—one of the most remarkable travel books ever issued, and I believe it is going to become a classic. Why should you not be embodied, like a fly in amber, in this classic?

He reminded Richards that he was the one who had brought Dreiser to Union Square; surely he had been aware that Dreiser "meant to tell the story of everything that happened to him."

When the book was safely in galleys, Doty told Richards that he had restored some of the cuts, mainly descriptions of friends whose identities had by then been sufficiently disguised. Richards himself had been given the elegant pseudonym "Barfleur." As for the alleged libels against the Carlton Hotel, Doty would promise only to *try* to remove the references; however, the plates were already made and he was not sure that he could (they were not removed).

And so *A Traveler at Forty* went to press, Doty sighing with relief: "The damn book has surely worn me out!" Many cuts had been made, and some padding added, it appears. Mencken, after reading the advance galleys, sensed that something was missing. While the section on Italy was "dragging in tempo," in the Paris chapters he noticed "an effect of reticence. You start up affairs which come to nothing." Dreiser replied, without elaboration, that he wished he had cut "the last half of the book more or left in a lot of woman stuff. . . ." He begged Mencken, "For heaven [sic] sake don't over emphasize the dullness of the Italian scene or you will have every critic in the U.S. yelping your remarks like a pack of curs." For he now believed that Mencken's reviews set the tone of his books' critical reception.

The published version of *A Traveler at Forty* had the same relation to the original manuscript as the Venus de Milo in the Louvre to the original statue. Though it is only a torso, there is enough of Dreiser left to make it identifiably his. In some places he exhibits a vivacity of style and humor, but his fatalistic philosophy runs through the book like a ground bass, reminding Mencken of Conrad: "He is an agnostic in exactly the same sense that you are—that is to say, he gives it up." Dreiser expresses, more openly than in any previous work, his skepticism of all laws and conventions: "For myself, I accept now no creeds. I do not know what truth is, what beauty is, what love is, what hope is. I do not believe any one absolutely and I do not doubt any one absolutely. I think people are both evil and well-intentioned."

Describing his elation over embarking on the journey, he recalls that the news of a friend's suicide had just arrived. The thought gave him pause: "I acknowledge the Furies. I believe in them. I have heard the disastrous beating of their wings."

The book is subjective, impressionistic; reporting is obviously not Dreiser's purpose. He mentions the beefy capitalists and voracious British labor leaders he met in Manchester as symbols of opposing forces in an economic war, but offers no reports from the battlefield, not even mentioning the general strike taking place in England while he was there. He has nothing to say about the British suffragists who were chaining themselves to the gates of Parliament and being force-fed in prisons.

His social comment is largely confined to England and consists of brief but telling descriptions of the London slums. As his diary shows, the gap between rich and poor, and the hopelessness and passivity of the latter, made a deep impression on him and permanently etched his opinion of England as a class-ridden country with a ruling elite that was indifferent to the fate of the poor. By contrast America seemed a land of opportunity; at least young people of ambition and "genius" (like himself) had the hope of bettering themselves. A London shopgirl he talked to, unlike Carrie, could not conceive of marrying above her station.

Readers unaware of his ulterior purpose of following the amorous trail of Yerkes would conclude, even from the Bowdlerized account that was published, that he showed an inordinate interest in women of uncertain virtue. He was following his nature, of course, but in his diary prostitutes like Lilly Edwards become stand-ins for women of the underclass. The published account of his meeting with her shows little of the compassion expressed in the omitted Hanscha Jower chapters. Instead, Dreiser presents himself as a detached investigator eliciting the sordid facts of her life. He condemns commercial sex as dreary but is skeptical of moralists' efforts to eliminate it, human nature being what it is.

Had the Hanscha Jower chapters and similar material been retained, the book might have showed a more darkly evocative picture of the underside of Europe, providing an ironic contrast to the guidebook Europe that remains. As published, *Traveler* is an editorially battered child. Only in the final chapters, culminating in Dreiser's account of how passengers aboard the *Kroonland* reacted to the sinking of the *Titanic*, does the book develop a cumulative emotional power. The ship, built by Britain in an effort to claim victory in the running competition between its and Germany's transatlantic passenger fleets, epitomized the bellicose commercial and nationalistic rivalry between the two nations. Its demise provided Dreiser with an unwitting epitaph to the pre-war era.

Determined to recoup its sizable investment in Dreiser, after emasculating his book, the Century Company produced a handsome edition of *A Traveler at Forty,* with pencil sketches by William Glackens and a binding stamped in gold. The critical reception was respectful, for the most part, taking the book as a welcome detour from the heavy black line Dreiser was drawing on the literary map. Among the nay-sayers was, surprisingly—or perhaps not so surprisingly—Floyd Dell in *The Masses,* where he was now assistant editor.

His attack on Dreiser had more to do with the generation gap than with bitterness over the loss of Kirah Markham. Dell spoke for the young radicals of the Village. He was irritated by Dreiser's tragic pessimism about the possibility of political change and accused him of preaching the outworn Darwinism of the Victorian era. Darwin, Dell writes, "made people think of change as something outside human effort. With the chill of his doctrine he froze the blood of revolution for a generation."

Dreiser offers no solution for the poverty and injustice he briefly describes and is skeptical of all efforts at reform (particularly the moralistic kind). He can only vaguely predict that change will come: "In due time, after all the hogs are fed or otherwise disposed of, a sense of government of the people, for the people will probably appear. . . . There are some things the rank and file are entitled to . . . and these they will eventually get." He fatalistically places his faith in the blind forces of natural conflict and the Equation Inevitable.

Dell, speaking for the Bohemian rebels around *The Masses,* sounded the radical tocsin: "We can have any kind of bloody world we bloody want." Later, he continued this dispute with Dreiser in person, once shouting at him: "Look, this world is changing. . . . It's changing before your eyes—changing because of human effort."

Summing up, Dell complains that in *A Traveler at Forty* Dreiser takes "one last look at mid-nineteenth century Europe—a Europe of streetcorners and drawing-rooms, cafés and cathedrals, repartee and women, and over all a sense of lovely futility as of flowers and toys." But in hindsight, Dell's radical optimism is more dated than Dreiser's chronic pessimism. Bloody world indeed.

Dreiser may have seemed a political fossil to Dell and some of the Village radicals, but he was not entirely out of sympathy with them. He had acquaintances among the orthodox socialists (whom the *Masses* radicals thought stuffy), and the *New York Call,* a socialist organ, had reprinted the previous year his sketch about unemployment, "The Men in the Dark."

On cultural and social issues he was even more in step with the younger generation. Because of the troubles in his own marriage, he shared the ideas on the family, sexual morality, and contraception proclaimed by Emma Goldman, Margaret Sanger, and the Swedish feminist Ellen Key, who held that the marital union should not be enforced by law. *A Traveler at Forty* contains an attack on the Christian doctrine of the indissolubility of marital ties: "in marriage, as in no other trade, profession or contract, once a bargain is struck—a mistake made—society suggests that there is no solution save in death." (He had used the marriage vow—"forsaking all others," etc.—as an ironic epigraph for *The Genius.*) Dreiser also predicted that as new demands for greater "intellectual, social, spiritual freedom" bubbled up, the state "will guarantee the rights, privileges and immunities of the children to the entire satisfaction of the state, the parents and the children." Elsewhere, he expanded on that theme, saying that the state should raise children where the parents were unfit. That led him to extremes; in another interview, he renounces the ideals of *The Delineator*'s Child Rescue Campaign, proclaiming, "An orphan asylum can bring up a child better than the average mother." But he continued to advocate the pro-feminist views he had encouraged, albeit cautiously, in the magazine's pages, telling one interviewer: "I am an intense individualist, and it seems to me that the beauty and interest of life will be increased in proportion to the growing number of great individuals among women as well as among men. I believe that the feminist movement, taken as a whole, has a distinct tendency to strengthen and enrich the individuality of woman."

He failed to link feminism with any specific program of laws or reforms; presumably it must come naturally, as a product of the larger forces of change, led by great individuals—male and female.

Dreiser's convictions on artistic freedom would also have been acceptable to the Village radicals. There had been some developments on the censorship front, however, that suggested a counterrevolution was developing. In September Anthony Comstock, head of the New York Society for Suppression of Vice, led a raid on the offices of Mitchell Kennerley, the British-born publisher who specialized in radical writers like Vachel Lindsay, Joseph Hergesheimer, Max Eastman, and Walter Lippmann. What aroused Comstock's ire was a novel Kennerley had just published called *Hagar Revelly*. Written by one of those earnest social reformers Dreiser despised, the novel could have been subtitled "Why Girls Go Wrong." The author was concerned with the temptations and pitfalls facing New York's underpaid shopgirls; there were a couple of overwrought seduction scenes.

The threat that Comstock posed to publishers was dramatized by the raid—Kennerley was arrested and the plates and sheets of *Hagar Revelly* impounded. Previously, Comstock had concentrated his fire on fly-by-night pornography peddlers and publishers of sex manuals rather than mainstream publishers. Kennerley was personally erratic, his firm small and financially shaky, but he was a publisher of serious books.

Rather than withdraw the novel and pay his fine, Kennerley became the first publisher to fight the ban in court. He hired John Quinn, a literary lawyer and art collector, to defend him. Comstock, who was also an inspector for the U.S. Postal Department, had charged Kennerley with sending obscene material in the mail in violation of the 1873 statute Comstock had helped write.

The trial judge urged the jury to deliver a guilty verdict, but the independent-minded panel declared Kennerley not guilty. His acquittal was hailed as a vindication of freedom of the press, and B. W. Huebsch, another publisher of modernist literature, pointed out that *Hagar Revelly* "went no further than a hundred novels of the past decade" and that it "possessed both literary merit and social significance."

But as Mencken noted in a letter to Dreiser, Kennerley had not been permitted to offer testimony of experts as to the book's artistic and sociological integrity. Furthermore, the jury was not allowed to consider the book as a whole, only Comstock's list of isolated allegedly obscene passages and words. Indeed, the decision was something of a fluke, probably contrary to law, by a runaway jury.

Comstock scared a lot of publishers, including *Smart Set*'s John Adams Thayer, who was worried that he might be next as a result of the "advanced" material Willard Huntington Wright was injecting into the magazine. Complaints from readers and advertisers poured in. Mencken himself worried that Wright was going too far, too fast, and warned him, "Be careful with the sexual stuff, at least for the present."

Wright had turned the magazine into a lively journal, one that published undiscovered geniuses like D. H. Lawrence, as well as Max Beerbohm, Frank Harris, Louis Untermeyer, and Sara Teasdale. But the older readers, who were used to society novelettes, were baffled and angered by the new fare. And so when circulation took a dip in December, Thayer panicked, and Wright, who was tired of all the rows, left by mutual agreement to fill an opening as book editor of the New York *Mail*. The *Smart Set* settled back into its old ways.

The upheaval had been a stressful time for Mencken. On top of that, he wrote, "I am in rotten shape physically & mentally. A hell of a world." Shocked by this gloomy note from his chief morale builder, Dreiser anxiously inquired, "What is the trouble? Are you seriously ill? Is there anything I can undertake for you? or do? I'll even review books if necessary. Command me. It distresses me to hear you seriously complain."

As it happened, he was not so cheerful himself. He had asked Mencken, "Do you suppose I will ever reach the place where I will make a living wage out of my books or is this all a bluff & had I better quit. I am getting ready to look for a job. Yours—fronting the abyss." To generate some needed cash he had proposed to the Century Company that he write a travel book about India. But his motive for choosing the subcontinent was not entirely mercenary. Some months previously he had clipped an interesting item from a New York paper about Emilie Grigsby: "For several years, since the fiasco of her social aspirations in England at the time of King George's coronation, she has taken a great interest in the Yogi philosophers of Hindustan. Her trip to India will take her into the extreme interior, where ancient philosophy may bring ease to her mind and take the place of her waning beauty."

But Doty was not interested in another travel book, and had told Dreiser: "I believe it would be wiser to wait until [*A Traveler at Forty*] is out so that we can see what sort of reception it gets, before we decide on the nature of your next travel book."

The reception was not encouraging—only 2745 copies sold in the last two months of 1913, and the usual falloff after that. In December Century advanced Dreiser $500 and in January $300, but that was it, Doty told him.

There was no hope of any further money from Harper's, and he was casting about for another publisher who might take over all his books and sell them.

Mencken tried to buck him up, saying, "Certainly you'll reach the place where your novels will keep you. . . . 'The Titan,' with its melodrama, ought to make both a popular and an artistic success. And once you escape from Harpers, all of the books will pick up."

With *The Titan* now on press, after considerable last-minute sweat, Dreiser departed for Chicago—and Kirah. Aside from the usual complaints about eleventh-hour revisions, Hitchcock was apparently satisfied with the result. Since the book ended before Cowperwood moves on to London, the "inadvisable" material alluded to in his letter to Holly more than a year before that might rile J. P. Morgan was not an issue. In any event, the old man died in March 1913.

CHAPTER 8

*The Same Thing
Over and Over*

My Dear Mencken:
How is your health?—and fortune? Since writing you last
I have some slight news.

— Dreiser to Mencken (1914)

An eternal pox upon the Harpers.

— Mencken to Dreiser (1914)

Other than for a rest and an idyll with Kirah, Dreiser had no particular reason to go to Chicago. Probably he hoped to stir up publicity for the new novel. *The Financier* had sold well in the city and was for a time the number-one fiction title— Yerkes was well remembered. *The Titan* follows Yerkes' business career in Chicago closely, culminating in his grandiose plan to wrest a monopoly of the city transit system. Exiled by society despite his efforts to buy his way in with lavish soirées and civic gifts, he and his Mary Adelaide were left to take drives in solitary splendor. When he tired of his wife and sought comfort in the arms of others, Mary Adelaide turned to drink and raged up and down the empty echoing corridors of their vast mansion on Michigan Avenue.

All of this Dreiser put in. He was accused of exaggerating Yerkes' amorous career, though much later he told biographer Robert Elias that he had learned from his researches that Yerkes had mistresses all over the country. But there was no real-life counterpart to the woman in the novel he calls Stephanie Platow, the art-smitten young actress. Or rather none in Yerkes' day, for she is clearly based on Kirah Markham. It must have amused

Dreiser to play fictionally with an affair he was having in real life, even creating a character based on Dell, a "young, smug, handsome drama critic," as one of Cowperwood's rivals for Stephanie's favors. He added three other rivals, one based on Maurice Browne, another on Michael Carmichael Carr, and a third, a "tall, melancholy" journalist and would-be poet, on his own younger, Chicago self. In a bizarre denouement Dreiser has the journalist gaining Stephanie's favors, only to have Cowperwood interrupt their tryst and send him packing. Thus did an older, stronger Dreiser write off his weaker, youthful self, revealing how deeply he identified with his Titan.

Cowperwood at last finds the ideal woman he has been seeking for years. She is Berenice Fleming, a schoolgirl when he first meets her but possessed of such promise of beauty and refinement that he plays Pygmalion, sculpting her with his money into a cultured young lady. It is doubtful Yerkes followed that course with her prototype, Emilie Grigsby, but, like Berenice, she was many years younger than he, and her mother had also been the madam of a high-class brothel in Louisville, Kentucky.

While Berenice is blooming in a hothouse finishing school, Cowperwood is pyramiding his street railways into a monopoly. Only one final step remains: to create a holding company that controls the entire operation and to sell the watered stock at a huge profit. But to make the new company a success he needs a long-term franchise; otherwise he will be at the mercy of the "sandbaggers"—corrupt city council members who set up dummy companies ostensibly to compete with that of the franchise-seeker—and demanded that the latter buy them out before granting the privilege he sought. To obtain the fifty-year monopoly he seeks, Cowperwood first bribes the state legislature—and then approaches the governor. But the latter is incorruptible (the character is based on the reformer John P. Altgeld). Next, Cowperwood focuses on the city council—as ripe a collection of boodlers as ever looted a city. But a downstate paper exposes his subornation of the legislature, and the Chicago press takes up the cry like a pack of hounds on the scent.

A typical headline of the time read: NEW GRAB BY YERKES; YERKES IS INSATIABLE. Dreiser's notes express amazement that the press could have treated the man who had become his hero so ferociously. ("Fighting Yerkes must have created circulation," he decides.) Cowperwood's enemies in the business community supported the vendetta, and Dreiser scores their hypocrisy in one of his notes: "Imagine them sitting solemnly on the fate of Yerkes!"

The novel reaches a climax with the defeat of Cowperwood's fifty-year franchise proposal at a turbulent meeting of the city council, which has been cowed by a mob of infuriated citizens, who threaten to lynch them if they vote their pocketbooks. Again, Dreiser dramatized a page from Chicago's history. But then he departed from reality. Cowperwood retires to his mansion to brood; enter Berenice, who declares her love and encourages him to resume the fight on another playing field. Actually, Yerkes was barely scratched by his defeat. He immediately went to the Sunset Club, a meeting place for the city's power brokers, and coolly defended his attempt to bribe the city council: "We do not want the eternal sandbagger after us all the time. When they say there is bribery in the City Council why not give us the fifty year franchise we ask for and thus stop the bribery." And then he sold his streetcar lines for a reputed $20 million and moved on to London, where the unfinished Underground offered a new challenge. But the Sunset Club scene might have detracted from Dreiser's romantic climax.

In late February Dreiser suffered a setback of his own. Harper's informed him that it would not publish *The Titan*. The reason, Dreiser laconically informed Mencken, was that "the realism is too hard and uncompromising and their policy cannot stand it." (To Alfred A. Knopf he explained that Harper's found the book "hard, cold, immoral.") He was inevitably reminded of a similar incident in his career: "If this were Sister Carrie I would now be in the same position I was then." He said Doran was considering the book.

"The Harpers be damned," Mencken fumed. "Jump to Doran, by all means," despite reports that he "is running to religious bosh." Ironically, Mencken had also been approached by a representative of Doubleday (probably Knopf, who started his long publishing career there), who asked if Dreiser would be interested in coming back. Only if Doubleday were the last publisher on earth, Mencken had retorted.

There were other reminders of *Carrie*. In the summer of 1900, Dreiser was out of New York and had to rely on his friend Arthur Henry to conduct negotiations for him. This time he depended on Anna Tatum and William Lengel, who had recently moved to the city to work for *Real Estate* magazine. Both sounded out publishers besides Doran, while Dreiser wrote to Charles Scribner, who was friendly but uninterested. Mencken's suspicion about Doran turned out to have been close to the mark. As Tatum reported, "He is a 'gentleman' and a conventionalist," and considered the book unsalable because Yerkes was an "abnormal American" and "the Grigsby woman" an adventuress.

Anna would be a rock in the ensuing days, although she was "literally penniless" and her father was dying. Kirah had supplanted her in Dreiser's affections, but now Anna found in him a cause commensurate with her idealism. As she told Dreiser, calling him by a pet name, "Oh, Dodo, how I love you. And how I love even more, the artistic ideal." Lengel too was eager to be of service to his old chief, even though he was immersed in getting out his first issue of *Real Estate*. Fortunately, he approached J. Jefferson Jones, manager of the American branch of the John Lane Company, whom Anna sized up as "a far more generous, idealistic type than

Doran." Not only was he liberal-minded, he was willing to take a chance on new and unconventional American writers. He also had the large British firm's financial resources behind him. For a second opinion Jones passed on the galleys to Frederick Chapman, a literary adviser for Lane who was in New York City.

Other publishers were approached, and Alfred A. Knopf, who had recently left Doubleday and was now working for Kennerley, was interested. Knopf became known to Mencken and Dreiser as a champion of Joseph Conrad. Dreiser, however, did not think much of Kennerley, who had a reputation of not paying his authors. Not long after Dreiser left Butterick he had sent Kennerley the manuscript of *Idylls of the Poor* at the publisher's request. But Kennerley never returned it, later explaining he had been in a nervous state and unable to tend to business affairs.

Dreiser informed Knopf that he doubted Kennerley saw him as a "commercial possibility" but allowed him to read the manuscript and render "a frank honest opinion." But "the reading must be speedy as well as the decision," he added as an afterthought, which Knopf took as authorization to pass it on to his boss. Kennerley was outraged by the depiction of Grigsby, with whom he had been in love, and predicted she would sue. (She was now living in England and moved in the highest circles.) At a dinner he repeated the warning to Frederick Chapman, who had by then written a highly favorable report on *The Titan,* calling Dreiser "the leading American novelist." Chapman had told him that John Lane might well publish the book, which irritated Kennerley.

Lengel and Tatum also tried the Century Company but received no encouragement from that quarter. After its experience with *A Traveler at Forty,* the firm was reluctant to go once more into the breach. According to Dreiser, Doty et al. thought that *The Titan* was "abnormal & impossible."

While *The Titan* hung in limbo, Dreiser gave interviews to publicize it. One was with Ben Hecht, a young reporter on the Chicago *Journal,* who found Dreiser's knowledge of the city's political and business history staggering. To a reporter from the *Evening Post* Dreiser held forth on censorship. He had identified so deeply with his hero that he seemed to conflate his troubles with censors and Yerkes' with civic reformers. Both of the latter were seeking to tear down the strong, the builders and creators. "A big city is not a teacup to be seasoned by old maids," he said. "It is a big city where men must fight and think for themselves, where the weak must go down and the strong remain." Let the fittest survive, so that "the future of Chicago will then be known by the genius of the great men it bred." He attacked Major Funkhouser, the city censor, who had banned the painting "September Morn," calling him "Bunkhouser." Censorship, he warned, was "a terrible thing that is overtaking this whole country, appointing someone . . . to tell you and me what is right for us to think—mind you, think!"

. . .

Upon his return from an excursion downstate with Masters, Dreiser was visited by another trial—a painful attack of carbuncles. The condition required surgery, and he was given nitrous oxide. After the operation, and still under the effects of anesthesia, he began hysterically giggling, and Kirah, who was at his bedside, heard him exclaim, "I've got it . . . the secret of the universe, the same thing over and over. . . ." Was that revelation inspired by the resemblance of his present troubles with Harper's to the *Sister Carrie* case—or was it a vision of the Spencerian universe, with its sempiternal rhythmic undulations, equilibrium after equilibrium until the final synthesis? Shortly after the operation he wrote Mencken that he was planning an article—"a new philosophic interpretation of earthly life."

Five days later, on March 21, he reported that his carbuncles had been vanquished. And there was even better news: Jones had sent him a telegram saying he would be "proud" to publish *The Titan*.

The mystery of the entire affair is why Harper's acted so precipitously. It had 4000 advance orders for the book and had printed sheets for 10,000 copies. Apparently the abrupt cancellation order came from high up in the company, probably from George Harvey himself. The financial stewardship of the jaunty, enigmatic president of the House of Harper was under increasing criticism from his overseer, Thomas Lamont, of the Morgan bank, and changes had been demanded. Knopf told Lengel that Harper's feared a novel about financial chicanery might antagonize its leading creditor. "*Too much truth told* about the *high financier*. Do you *get it?*" Anna wrote Dreiser, presumably referring to Morgan. And then there was the problem of Volume III—dealing with Yerkes' battle in London against Morgan's agents. George Harvey's position had become too shaky to risk offending his bankers. That portrait of Pierpont Morgan in his office glowered at him daily, and the old man's son was now in charge of the bank.

Even before the *Titan* affair, gossip had it that Harvey refused to be introduced to Dreiser, regarding him as an "immigrant vulgarian" and a "sex maniac." That may have been his personal feeling, but Dreiser was invited to the lavish seventy-fifth birthday dinner Harvey gave for William Dean Howells. True, Harper's had been nervous about Dreiser's "immorality," but it seemed prepared to back him for the long haul. Its objections, moreover, were to *The Titan*, with its muckraking content, rather than to Dreiser himself. The firm insisted on keeping *Carrie* and *Jennie* on its list; and as Dreiser wrote Mencken on March 31, "If you will believe it Harpers have asked me to permit them to publish . . . *The Genius*. This sounds wild but it is true and they backed it by an offer of aid. They feel they have made a mistake . . . the same people who think me unfit for publication. Am I mad or is this good red earth we are standing on."

A footnote to the Kennerley-Grigsby matter: Jones told Dreiser that Kennerley had written to John Lane, for whom he once worked, urging him not to publish *The Titan* in England because of libel. Jones asked Dreiser to indemnify the John Lane Company against any legal damages if Grigsby did sue and to provide documentation for his fictional portrait. Seeking legal advice, Dreiser had written to Masters, who replied that truth was a defense in libel actions and when Yerkes' liaison with La Grigsby was reported by the press after his death, she hadn't sued.

Whatever the reasons for Harper's actions, fear of a Comstock raid did not seem to be among them. As Mencken assured Dreiser, "There is not a word in the book that will give Comstock his chance. He must go into court with some specific phrase—something that will seem smutty to an average jury of numskulls. The fundamental and essential unmorality of the book is beyond his reach."

Publicly, Dreiser took the Harper's affair with his characteristic fatalism, although inwardly he probably had some bad moments. He told Mencken that he was full of plans and projects, but he was still peering into the financial abyss. He now owed various publishers $3800, counting the money Century loaned him. He had complained to Knopf that no one wanted to back his career; publishers were interested only in immediate gains: "The book of the season is the thing and the opinion of small fry critics. My contempt for the situation is so great that I heartily desire to drop out at times."

He had Mencken's private prediction that *The Titan* would sell, as well as his enthusiastic endorsement of the novel as the best picture of an immoralist in all modern literature. Anna Tatum had rushed the typescript to the critic so he could write a *Smart Set* review before leaving for Europe April 11. Unfortunately, Mencken was too pressed with last-minute arrangements to do so and this time was not in the critical van. Confirming Dreiser's belief in his crucial influence, the reception for *The Titan* was on the whole tepid, notably in Chicago, where Dreiser had counted on a brisk sale. A bellwether was Lucian Cary, who was sympathetic to Dreiser. While praising the accuracy of the Chicago backdrop, he thought the book too reportorial. "The story is always dangerously close to actual event," he wrote, "dangerously close because Mr. Dreiser has depended on this actuality to convey reality . . . outward facts are significant only when they are the sign of inward meaning. And Mr. Dreiser simply does not know the inward meaning. He has never for a moment stood in Frank Cowperwood's shoes and looked out upon the Chicago of twenty-five years ago with Frank Cowperwood's eyes." The schoolmarms, male and female, were out in force. Some complained that Dreiser was wrong to acclaim this rather commonplace financial freebooter as a superman. He was "a satyr not a titan" and "no more a Superman than the barber around the corner." "The book tells a story, a sordid, disagreeable one," wrote the Chicago *Tribune*, "with many blemishes of split infinitives, unnecessarily coarse speech and rough colloquialisms." Adding to the growing collection of Dreiser's overworked words was "rich" (as in "rich" thrills or a person who takes "rich" strides); and such solecisms as "Quite like a character in a Japanese print might be" and "She was probably something like her own mother would have been."

Defenders praised Cowperwood as an accurate portrayal. To say, as some reviewers did, that presenting "abnormal" types like Cowperwood without any mitigating goodness was not realism was to confront Dreiser on his strongest suit—truth. The world of Chicago politics and finance in the latter part of the nineteenth century was not populated by exemplary characters, and Dreiser created a powerful portrait of a type of financier whose greed and amoral methods were representative of an age.

Where he faltered was in his too close identification with his character. Just as other men are Cowperwood's tool, so is the financier himself, Dreiser claimed, a "useful tool" of the universe, creating, building, providing better public transportation. At this point Dreiser's model belies his invention, for Yerkes created nothing but watered stock and rickety trolley cars. Dreiser was of course free to depart from the historical record, but he never really makes a case for Cowperwood's beneficent effects. As a quondam municipal socialist himself, he was conflicted about the utility of nineteenth-century municipal plunderers like Cowperwood. In a larger sense, he believed at that historical stage of industrialism, great greedy barons had been needed to build up the country—the Rockefellers and Carnegies, and Armours. But he also believed they had acquired too much power and robbed the masses.

He resolved this ambivalence through his philosophy of opposing forces and Equation Inevitable. The trilogy was conceived as a saga of Spencerian dissolution. The meteoric Cowperwood must ultimately fall to earth. As Dreiser writes in the coda of *The Titan*, the masses have their role to play in the Spencerian dialectic. The people of Chicago rise up and assert their claim against the individual who has gone too far: "a balance must be struck. The strong must not be too strong; the weak not too weak. . . ."

But Cowperwood is also motivated by an ideal higher than money and power, which becomes the means to this end: beauty in both its feminine and artistic incarnations. When he meets Berenice, he realizes he has finally found the meaning of his existence.

Dreiser's European Diary attests to how deeply personal was this conviction. He was obsessed by the passage of time, the need for feminine warmth and beauty (an unconditional, maternal love). In Rome he had noted the need of even the most powerful and successful person for love—not any love, or ordinary love or bland steady uxorial love—but *new love*, love fired by romance, a restorative of lost youth, love like Venus-Aphrodite rising pink and new from the waves.

And what was art but a redirection (sublimation, if you will) of the erotic impulse? Love was madness; art was divine madness. Artistic beauty was a realization of the feminine ideal, only a picture's beauty never faded as a woman's did. Indeed, that was the reason for the eternal quest for Aphrodite—to find a fresh feminine beauty to replace the fading charms of the present love-object. And ultimately, only feminine solace—Eros the eternal foe of Thanatos—could assuage the pain of encroaching mortality. He had written in his diary that even death he would not fear, if he could slip into it obliviously in the arms of a beautiful woman.

And so in this saga of Spencerian dissolution, Cowperwood seeks to stave off death—temporarily—by acquiring beauty through power and wealth. In *The Financier* Cowperwood recalls having read about a man who lived a shabby lonely life in a little room for twelve years and finally committed suicide. He should have done it long before, Frank thinks, for he had long been dead. Most of us sink back into the undifferentiated herd, never having *lived*. Radical individualism—freedom—is man's boldest defiance of his inevitable fate. For his death-haunted creator, Cowperwood was the incarnation of the life force.

Part Three

THE VILLAGE
1915–1918

CHAPTER 9

Scènes de la Vie de Bohème

Only youth and enthusiasm and love of freedom and color
and variety together with all but unbelievable illusion and
an incurable detestation of the humdrum and commonplace could have achieved it.

—Dreiser, "Greenwich Village"

Back in New York, Dreiser rented a post office box and slipped away to the home of his sister Mame on Staten Island. Since Mame took his side in the battle with Jug, she provided a perfect hideaway. When William Lengel and his new bride, Nelle, called at 3609 Broadway, they found Jug alone. She said vaguely that Dreiser was "away," but she probably wistfully hoped that he might return; she always thought he needed her and would sooner or later realize it. She was resigned to his philandering, but she simply could not imagine the truth—that he was drunk on Cowperwood and needed others, not her.

Kirah Markham had joined a touring company, which opened in Philadelphia. He joined her there and they had trysts in his rented room when she could sneak away. "Don't give this address to anyone," he wrote Mencken on April 5, 1914, from 4142 Parkside Avenue, adding that he was considering a permanent move to Philadelphia.

He wrote Mencken that he was about to tackle revisions of *The Genius*, which would "surely" be published next spring. At Mame's he had begun working on an autobiography, writing under her nose about things in her and the family's past she wanted forgotten. He called it *Dawn*, and finished thirteen chapters by April 24. In an interview with the New York *Sun* more than a year before, he had announced that he would like to write "an absolutely accurate autobiography . . . a literal transcript of life as it is," to be called "The Sealed Book." Only Rousseau in the *Confessions* had made an honest self-revelation. Any halfway truthful account would demonstrate that "all lives are failures."

In the press he continued to defend his capitalist superman against the moralists, reformers, and levelers. He complained to a reporter from the Philadelphia *Public Ledger* that Americans tend "to discard the opinions of those at the highest point of the intellectual scale for the prejudices and stupidity of the multitude. Everything is for the vast, ruling majority. . . . The idea that all men are created equal is one of the fundamental errors of our system of government. For to the distinguishing mind it is quite apparent that the degree of mental endowment with which individuals come into this world varies enormously. But to level down is the cry of mediocrity everywhere." No wonder that Mencken admired *The Titan* as "a great Nietzschean document." But no wonder too that Reedy, a Nietzsche hater, had written in his review that the towering figure of Cowperwood had obscured for Dreiser "the people in the mass whose blood and sweat made the glory for which Cowperwood fought." They were present only as supernumeraries in the crowd scenes. He had, for example, said nothing about the Chicago trolley strike, which he had witnessed as a boy, for that would have meant considering the justice of the workers' demands. There was inconsistency as well as elitism in his stance.

In May he was at Mame's, working and absorbing the reviews of *The Titan*. The novel's performance was turning out to be a disappointment: some 6000 copies in the first two months, but only 2000 or so more during the rest of the year. Not only was this a falloff from the not large total for *The Financier;* it meant that Dreiser would collect no royalties from either Harper's or Lane. All the more reason to revive *The Genius*. Possibly because of the controversy over Volume II of the Cowperwood trilogy, Dreiser decided to shelve Volume III (which would be called *The Stoic*). There was much more research to do on it, and continuing fears of libel (Berenice-Emilie was a central character).

Jones was eager to publish *The Genius;* he wanted to recoup his advance on *The Titan*. But Dreiser was restless; he carried on some mild flirtations with other publishers and at times even thought of giving up the writing game. He told Knopf, "Bouncing around from publisher to publisher does not appeal to me at all. I would rather, if I might, become a high-priced editor." He was exaggerating, but his low opinion of the financial returns of the authorial trade showed in a letter to a fellow scrivener, Charles Fort, a couple of weeks later. "All authors are gamblers and worse," he wrote. "They are pinchbeck speculators in human emotions—myself included."

In July Masters wrote Dreiser that he was still writing "the Spoon River stuff into which I am pouring divers philosophies—taking the emptied tomato cans of the rural dead to fill with the waters of the macrocosm." These poems would become the *Spoon River Anthology*. After reading the first ones in Reedy's *Mirror*, Dreiser urged Lane to publish them, but the firm was dubious of their sales potential and suggested that the author try Kennerley. Masters, aware of Dreiser's bad experiences, declined. Reedy, acting for his pseudonymous author, received an offer from Macmillan and Masters accepted.

Another Chicago poet sought Dreiser's help. Ben Hecht forwarded a batch of poems by a fellow reporter named Tom Kennedy, and Dreiser replied with a detailed critique. Save for a few, he found that Kennedy's work lacked that "blinding poignancy of expression or preciosity of words, framing an inspiration of thought or mood" that he regarded as the hallmark of great verse. But he offered to submit the manuscript to Lane or the *Century* if the author wished. He also called Mencken's attention to the work of Vachel Lindsay; to that of Dell's friend Arthur Davison Ficke, like Masters a lawyer; and to *Spoon River Anthology* in the *Mirror*. The poetic gusts from Lake Michigan may have caused Dreiser to revive his own bardic ambitions, for within a year he was writing *vers libre*.

In June he reported to Mencken that he was at last going to "try to edit" *The Genius*, after having it retyped, adding with a broad hint, "I am such a poor editor." Mencken, of course, stood ready to oblige; he had designs on the novel. The letter to H.L.M. revealed Dreiser to be in good spirits: "I have many schemes or plans but only one pen hand—and meanwhile my allotted space ticks swiftly by. Greetings—and let's pray we keep good stomaches and avoid religion."

One of Dreiser's schemes, which might have surprised Mencken, involved the infant motion picture industry. Lengel's employer, Hoggson Bros., was planning to set up a movie company, Mirror Films, and Lengel suggested his old boss for the post of editor-in-chief, or some such title, responsible for choosing original scenarios or books and plays that could be converted into scripts, as well as writing some. When or how Dreiser formed such a precocious interest in the cinema—indeed, whether he had even seen a movie at this time—is not known.

He was also testing the Broadway waters. The agent Gabrielle Welch was dickering on his behalf with a Boston producer who was interested in dramatizing *The Financier*. But that effort fell through when the producer refused to come up with an advance. Financial need was surely the main goad for his extra-literary forays, but that did not mean he was steering his own writing into more commercial channels. Far from it. He was working on some philosophical one-act plays.

A major preoccupation at the moment, though, was finding a permanent abode, since he could not stay with Mame indefinitely. Inevitably, his thoughts turned to Greenwich Village, where a spacious floor-through flat could be had for $25 to $30 a month. And he needed a large place because Kirah—under parental orders to come home if she could not find an acting job—was to join him, at least for a time.

The Village was now entering its Golden Age. Recalled the poet Orrick Johns, "The winter of 1913–1914 was the fine flowering of the village, a period of sincere, hard-working and productive social freedom." This was the Village of John Reed, Max Eastman, Harry Kemp, Floyd Dell, Art Young, John Sloan, George Bellows, Louis Untermeyer, and *The Masses;* of Polly Holladay's restaurant, the Liberal Club, and the Boni Brothers' bookshop next door.

In July Dreiser took a flat at 165 West Tenth Street, a nondescript brick tenement. His place consisted of two large rooms with broad splintery floorboards that had cracks between them so wide a pencil would fall through. The back chamber he used as a bedroom, and the larger front room served as his living room and study. A small kitchen and a bathroom completed the amenities. He had to boil water on the stove when he wanted a bath. The only other source of heat was a small coal-burning grate. At times the place was so cold that he would go to Polly's to write. Gradually he added chairs, rockers, tables, and other things, and the loving inventory of his accumulated possessions he made after he moved out included

> one upright piano, victrola . . . one antique mahogany couch . . . imitation mahogany encyclopedia stand . . . antique brass candle stick . . . imitation mahogany sewing table, white with bench and with back . . . fancy hearth brush . . . wicker tea tray, red porcelain tea set . . . framed picture of Kirah Markham, framed picture of Christ . . . small silver mazuza [sic] attached to right jamb of front inside door . . . one pair brass candlesticks, one pair mahogany candle sticks, one seven-branched brass candlestick . . . lamp on brass chain. . . .

The most prominent piece of furniture was a large rosewood desk fashioned from a piano that had belonged to his songwriting brother, Paul Dresser. This would be his worktable for the rest of his life; it was large enough to hold piles of books and the various manuscripts he was always engaged on simultaneously. On the walls were two large paintings, fully 7 feet by 9 feet each—one of a black odalisque. These had been stored with him by Anne Rice, the artist he had met in Paris. Scattered strategically about the floor were six throw rugs, the windows were adorned with pink draperies, and usually there were bowls of flowers or fruit about, for Dreiser loved color. At night the available electric lighting was weak and so Dreiser developed a taste for candlelight.

By fall Kirah had joined him. Their happiness was not spoiled by the proximity of Jug, who had moved in with her sister Ida on nearby Waverly Place. Kirah remembered seeing Jug, who did not recognize her, in the neighborhood shops. She felt no remorse, for Dreiser had told her what a narrow conventionalist his wife was, how he had married her when he had been too green to know better, and how she refused to give him a divorce. Still, the younger woman must have perceived the wife as a kind of hostile presence, for she later claimed that Jug would stand for hours beneath the streetlight, watching the apartment. (Oddly, Dreiser has Kirah doing the same thing in a story about her.)

But there were more congenial neighbors, he would discover, and a stream of visitors, who were told not to call until after five, when Dreiser's working day was over. He remained aloof from the Village scene. Louis Untermeyer recalled that when Dreiser occasionally showed up at *Masses* editorial meetings he cast a pall over the proceedings because he was considered—or thought to consider himself—a "Great Person." Yet he could be sociable when he chose. Orrick Johns recalled a long evening at Polly Holladay's with Dreiser grieving for the British poor and railing at the callous aristocrats and intellectuals who allowed such conditions to exist. He belonged to the Liberal Club and the Pay-As-You-Enter Club, dined at Polly's and the Dutch Oven and Mouquin's and the Brevoort, and roamed the streets, a familiar tall, well-dressed figure with a rolling gait.

For a time he and Kirah held regular "at homes" on Sunday evenings, though he eventually gave them up, he said, because the guests always became noisy and argumentative, giving him a severe headache.

But Dreiser blocked off a part of life for work, a compartment in which he remained solitary. He never had any illusions about the quality of the art the Village rebels were producing: "Genius? I doubt if there was ever much more than a trace of it in the entire Village." But he enjoyed the spectacle. The Villagers seemed to him a gaudy group of strolling players, performing a commedia dell'arte in a grim slum.

The month of May in New York was a rainy one, and toward the end of it Dreiser wrote Mencken that he had a window box of morning glories that didn't need watering. The rumbles on the Continent in the wake of the June 28 assassination of Archduke Francis Ferdinand were far from his mind.

Aside from the robust state of his morning glories, Dreiser reported that he knew a place where they could get broiled lobsters for fifty cents each.

But then he let slip a hint that work was driving him: "Underneath my table is a bottle of Gordon Gin & a syphon of seltzer. Life is difficult & I must keep up."

While waiting for *The Genius* to be typed, he had composed three one-act plays, with the idea of Lane's advancing him money for a collection to be called *Plays of the Natural and the Supernatural*. The new efforts fell into the latter category. In one, *The Blue Sphere*, a monster child is lured to its death by a benevolent spirit holding an azure globe. In the second, *In the Dark*, a poor Italian immigrant who murdered his brother is hunted down by police while spirits hover about crying murder most foul. That play may have had its origin in a nightmare; Dreiser had recurrent ones of being pursued by some menacing foe. The origin of the third play, *Laughing Gas*, was another kind of dream—his hallucinations under nitrous oxide while his carbuncles were being removed. A brilliant scientist—a useful tool in the evolutionary scheme, like Cowperwood—lies on the operating table, while his unconscious self speeds through uncharted dimensions of time and space and discovers the meaning of the universe: humans are "mere machines being used by others." We have lived before and "Society has done the things it has done over and over." The scientist must by an effort of will create himself, or else he will die.

These dramas were "reading plays," not intended to be staged, Dreiser explained to Mencken with a hint of salesmanship, adding defensively, "I am not turning esoteric, metaphysical or spiritualistic. These are merely an effort at drama outside the ordinary limits of dramatic interpretation." They show a revival of Dreiser's preoccupation with the spirit world, where the dead are alive. The pieces meld expressionism and realism; there are spirits as well as human characters, and fluid scene changes that dissolve the frame of the realistic stage (making them practically unstageable) and the psychic wall between past and present, the visible and the invisible worlds.

This esoteric subject matter left Mencken undaunted. By all means send them, he said; he had a "particular reason" for wanting to see them. This soon emerged: he and George Jean Nathan had taken over the editorship of the *Smart Set* and wanted to "blaze out with some Dreiser stuff." The magazine had gone into receivership and was now under new management. Mencken was optimistic about its future, claiming it could rapidly become self-sustaining once overhead was reduced. He promised "cash on the block" but begged Dreiser to have a heart in setting a price.

Dreiser was glad to give Mencken the plays, and, in an entirely un-related gesture, offered him the manuscript of any of his books. Accusing Dreiser of having taken to "heroin, Pilsner, formaldehyde," Mencken said he would esteem the manuscript of *Sister Carrie* "more than the gift of a young virgin."

On August 17 he told Dreiser, "We simply *must* have something from you." He and Nathan had agreed that a light satirical tone would be best for the magazine, but he needed Dreiser and other serious writers to give it artistic ballast.

He saluted the German invasion of France with a "God's benison upon the Kaiser." His loyalties lay with the land of his ancestors, and he blazed out with pro-German sentiments in his "Free Lance" column in the Baltimore *Sun*. He closed each column with "In Paris by Thanksgiving!" which inevitably gave way to "In Paris by Christmas!" In October he wrote Ellery Sedgwick that he was being "bombarded daily" by letters from angry readers and that "public sentiment seems to be rapidly turning in favor of England."

Dreiser emitted some modest cheers for the Kaiser in his letters to Mencken, but devoted his writing time to the completion of his autobiography. In early August he reported that he expected to be done by September. And then—on to *The Bulwark*! Although he didn't come close to meeting that schedule, he accomplished an amazing amount, writing at a furious rate as the memories of the hard times in Indiana rushed back. One day he unleashed a torrential eight thousand words—and spent the next day in bed, recovering.

Then, as would happen so many times, his momentum ran out, and he turned to shorter projects in the hope of raising some quick cash. He concocted an exotic *Arabian Nights*–style tale, "The Princess and the Thief," which he hoped to sell to Pathé Frères, a movie company, but sent a copy to Mencken for possible use in the new *Smart Set*, along with "The Lost Phoebe," which his new agent, Gabrielle Welch, was now trying to sell. According to her tally, it had been rejected by sixteen magazines. Mencken thought "Phoebe" was "fine stuff—a story in your best style," and wondered if they might come to terms on it. But after the plays what they really needed was something representative of the Dreiser with whom the public was most familiar, the Dreiser of *Jennie Gerhardt* and *The Titan*. *The Genius* promised to be that Dreiser, so perhaps they should run an excerpt from it next.

Dreiser, however, still hoped to serialize *The Genius* in a better-paying magazine. He had told Mencken that he needed at least $1500 to carry him through the writing of *The Bulwark*. And he mentioned casually that he had shown the three plays to the *Century* and *Metropolitan* and "from one or two tentative opinions I have secured . . . I could get about $1,000 for them." But he would be happy to have them in the *Smart Set* if they ran consecutively and were published with appropriate fanfare.

Mencken guaranteed payment for each play as soon as it was set in type—in case the magazine should suddenly go under. He suggested that they publish a short excerpt from *The Genius* different from the material selected for serialization, and gave the first of the three plays "the place of honor on the front cover" of the December issue. But then, on October 13, he confessed with chagrin that "Nathan is so full of the notion that this 'Lost Phoebe' lies far off the Dreiser that we want to play up that I begin to agree with him." What they really wanted was something from *The Genius*.

Dreiser darkly interpreted this turnabout as a slap from Nathan, for whom he had formed a vague mistrust. He complained that in order to help them out he had recalled "The Lost Phoebe" from *Red Book*, which had offered $125 for it. That was not quite the truth. Ray Long, the editor, had expressed lukewarm interest, but said the price was too high, and Dreiser refused to lower it. As for the plays, he again mentioned the alleged interest of the *Century* and the *Metropolitan*. In fact, both magazines had turned them down.

Unaware of all this, Mencken assumed the entire blame for the confusion about the story and insisted that Nathan had actually liked the plays. Dreiser forgave them but requested the return of "The Lost Phoebe," for which he probably still hoped he could get a higher price elsewhere. He said the editors could postpone the plays and run an episode from the novel. Visibly relieved, Mencken replied, "We are in your hands, and damned glad to be." In early November Dreiser forwarded the first half of *The Genius* manuscript, apologizing that it was an unedited version.

Despite their differences over money, Dreiser and Mencken were finding a new bond between them: the war. Many other German-Americans felt as they did. The issue of dual loyalties in World War I proved traumatic to this ethnic group, which had hitherto enjoyed a benign stereotype— hardworking, prosperous, and patriotic. After the lurid propaganda about atrocities in Belgium, however, popular opinion turned against Germany and then German-Americans. America's linguistic, historical, cultural, and legal ties to Britain were too strong; and the German propaganda efforts were clumsy and exuded arrogance.

Anglophobia played as much a part in Dreiser's pro-German views as ethnic loyalty. That prejudice derived from his trip to the Continent and his quarrel with Grant Richards. He considered Richards to be a representative of all British intellectuals, and lumped him with the fox-hunting nobs who oppressed the poor. And so Dreiser and Mencken's attitude toward the war set them apart from other American intellectuals, who opposed the war out of pacifism or because they thought the munitions profiteers were pushing America into it or because of the disastrous effects of war fever on constitutional liberties.

"I may talk pessimism," Dreiser once wrote, "but I never cease to fight forward." But his current literary efforts seemed as bogged down as the Germans at the Marne. Even Mencken's sturdy faith in him was wavering. He had plowed through *The Genius* with mounting distress. Some preliminary cavils issued from 1524 Hollins Street, Baltimore, in December. He grumbled that Eugene Witla's early career had been "under-described" and informed Dreiser that there was no such word as "alright." Dreiser eagerly assented to both criticisms, but he surely recalled that the reaction from Baltimore for his previous books had not been so long in coming. Something was up.

Mencken delivered his verdict in person while visiting New York in January 1915. There was a "friendly row," which became so noisy that Kirah Markham fled the house. Mencken's chief complaints were verbosity and repetitiousness. He also was bothered by the novel's sexual frankness, not because of personal objections but for fear of Comstock. In later years, he recalled suggesting that a scene in which the hero touches a female character's knee be eliminated. Dreiser refused, saying, "But that's what happened." The most autobiographical of his novels, *The Genius* was closest to his heart. He was adamantly opposed to cutting the script. The immediate result of their meeting was that no excerpt appeared in the *Smart Set*. As it turned out, no other magazine was interested, and the serialization income Dreiser was counting on did not materialize.

And so *The Genius* was the first of his novels since *Carrie* to go to press untouched by his favorite critic's hand. Dreiser had, however, heeded the objection of Eleanora O'Neill, a Boston book critic and old friend, that Eugene's interest in Christian Science seemed mere New York intellectuals' faddishness, not worthy of a truly pagan novelist. He altered the chapters about Eugene's visits to a practitioner so that they do not represent a conversion but rather a form of emotional therapy. And realizing that the description of his hero in the title was open to challenge, he added quotation marks around "Genius," explaining to Mencken that he wanted to inject a note of doubt; also, another book with the same title had recently appeared.

The most important change was his own idea. He jettisoned his original ending, in which Eugene and Suzanne are wed, and substituted a new one that was truer to life. In his revised version they see each other only once, at a distance, and Eugene snubs her. In the end he has returned to painting and lives alone with the child Angela conceived to hold him, only to die of complications of a Caesarean section.

Jones, at least, found the manuscript publishable, and he turned it over to Chapman for editing. Chapman cut 50,000 words, but in the proof stage Dell was hired, at Dreiser's suggestion, to slash even more. Dell succeeded in lightening the novel by another 20,000 words, but Dreiser restored much of what he had taken out. The following August, when the book was in page proofs and Dreiser was out of town, Jones asked Markham and Dell to excise an additional eight pages. According to Dell, they simply lopped off the paragraphs of philosophizing with which Dreiser habitually began or ended his chapters.

Much of what was cut was fat, but some problematic allusions to the sex drive were purged, as well as animadversions on Angela Blue's possessiveness and conventional mind. The specter of Comstock probably explained the former cuts; as for the latter, Dreiser had reasons at this time not to offend Jug, on whom Angela is based in more ways than the play on her maiden name (White). Yet, for all her jealous rages, Angela Blue is one of the most sympathetic characters in the novel. Dreiser later explained that he never regarded Angela as a repellent person; she was merely a limited one who was unfitted to be Eugene's wife, "the kind of woman who regards a man as property."

By "property" Dreiser meant that Jug clung to him for financial support. When he could no longer afford his hundred-dollar-per-month payments, she hired a lawyer, and Dreiser was forced to sign a separation contract under which she agreed to an eighteen-month reprieve of his obligations. In consideration for this concession, he gave her all his property. The "consideration" part may have been legalese, since she had their furniture and he had conveyed to her the lots in New York and Washington states two years previously.

Kirah was understanding. She wrote him bravely from Chicago, where she had been spending time with her family and rehearsing a play, not to worry about "the madame." She said it didn't matter to her whether they got married or not.

There was probably as much prudence as emancipated thought in her attitude. She must have realized by now that any marriage to Dreiser would be an unconventional one. His varietism was already showing, for she remarks in another letter that he seems to be seeing a lot of people she hasn't met, including Mrs. Roberts (undoubtedly Mary Fanton Roberts, an old friend; his interest in her was almost certainly professional—unlike the other women, including Lillian Rosenthal, whom he met clandestinely). Kirah charged that when she was away he found others to console him, and when they were together he treated her like a jailer. Such a primitive emotion as jealousy was passé for a New Woman, and she begged him either to tell her that she was first in his affections or to drop her.

For all his strayings while they were apart, Dreiser would always regard Kirah as one of his great loves. She was undoubtedly drawn to him as an older, stronger man, a father figure. Explaining his attraction for her, she told biographer W. A. Swanberg that Dreiser was an "emotional steamroller" possessed of "animal magnetism" rather than charm. He also had a strong will and an "utter sense of loneliness" that brought out her maternal instincts. What she remembered most was their walks through the mean streets of the Lower East Side. "Few realize how the man suffered over Life," she said. "Many nights we walked the streets, Theo holding my hand in the pocket of his overcoat while the tears poured down his face."

· · ·

Meanwhile, his closest masculine friendship, that with Mencken, had, during the spring of 1915, undergone another shakeup, an aftershock of the quarrel over *The "Genius."* When Mencken casually asked him to "dash off a few lines" about the *Smart Set,* saying "that it has shown progress during the past six months and is now a magazine that the civilized reader may peruse without damage to his stomach," Dreiser let fly: "Under you and Nathan the thing seems to have tamed down to a light non-disturbing period of persiflage and badinage, which now and then is amusing but which not even the preachers of Keokuk will resent seriously. . . ."

Mencken admitted that the April number was weak, but explained that the magazine "represents a compromise between what we'd like to do and what the difficulties we face allow us to do." He pointed to the two stories by the young Irish writer James Joyce in the issue that Dreiser criticized. But, he went on, "the light touch is what we want." Consider the magazine's name—hardly that of a vehicle for "revolutionary fustian." Actually, Mencken said, he had invited Benjamin De Casseres, a Greenwich Village poet and essayist; Floyd Dell; and "the rest of the red-ink boys" to contribute, but found their stuff was "inexpressively empty . . . hollow-headed and childish."

Dreiser replied that he too had no use for parlor socialists. "I sometimes think that because I have moved into 10th Street and am living a life not suitable to the home streets of Baltimore that you think I have gone over to the red ink family. . . ."

Mencken was predictably irritated by the crack about "the home streets of Baltimore" and warned: "For far less insults I have had gentlemen killed by my private murderer, a blackamoor but a deft hand at the garotte."

There followed a four-month hiatus in their correspondence. In the meantime Dreiser had found another critical champion, who, it happened, lived in the Village—John Cowper Powys, who was about the same age as Dreiser. A displaced Englishman, Powys made his living lecturing on literature to American audiences in the hinterlands. He had been drawn to Dreiser since the day he had picked up a newspaper on the train and read an interview in which Dreiser said, "I have no hope, yet I do not despair, life drifts." Astounded to hear such stoical sentiments from the lips of an American writer, he eagerly hunted down *Carrie* and *Jennie* and became a convert. In Philadelphia, in December 1914, he paid tribute to the living American novelist he admired most, before a full house of 1500 avid matrons at the Broad Street Theater, including an admirer of Dreiser's who sent a detailed report of Powys' "epileptic enthusiasms"—a reference to the Englishman's flamboyant platform style.

The acquaintanceship with Jack Powys began in gratitude and progressed to respect for a fellow artist and philosopher. They were both strong individualists and mystics. Powys' religiosity ran to animism; he was also something of a latter-day druid and prayed to his Welsh ancestors. But he was open to all phases of the supernatural and thus in sympathy with the occult side of Dreiser's temperament.

J. Jefferson Jones was beginning to worry about Dreiser's next book, which was nowhere in sight. The autobiography, *Dawn*, was on the shelf, *The Bulwark* still mulching in his unconscious. He told Mencken he was planning a short novel or story about a man condemned to die in the electric chair. This was apparently his first try at the novel about a murderer he had mentioned to friends wanting to write as long ago as 1907.

He had, through Elias Rosenthal, obtained the record of the murder trial of Roland Molineux, who had fatally poisoned a rival for the hand of a wealthy woman, using a slow-acting substance that mimicked the symptoms of diphtheria. After marrying the woman he craved, Molineux quarreled with the manager of the Knickerbocker Club and tried to dispatch him with a bottle of Bromo-Seltzer laced with cyanide. Another person took the poisoned potion instead, however, and died. Police traced the doctored bottle to Molineux, who had not realized that cyanide interacting with bromide creates a more potent toxin. As Dreiser wrote in his notes, "Important: Molineux intended to provide only a lingering death. The hydrocyanic acid accidentally precipitated the murder inquiry!"

This malign intervention of chance was one of the elements of the case that fascinated Dreiser. Actually, Molineux was not executed. Acquitted by reason of insanity, he died of a brain disease in 1914. His death touched off a flurry of stories about the earlier trial, sparking Dreiser's interest in the case. Although he never responded to Mencken's queries about his progress, he did make a start on the novel, which he called *The Rake*.

About all that can be said for the dreary, aborted narrative that survives is that the hero, Ausley Bellinger, resembles young Theodore Dreiser more than he does the calculating socialite Roland Molineux—or any type of that class. Bellinger has an artistic temperament, love of beauty, and a "keen passion for sex." Through his father's connections he obtains a job in a factory, where he ogles the female workers, who exemplify natural sexuality. Dreiser had done the same thing at the Chicago laundry where he worked as a boy. Ausley meets a wealthy young woman, and another man enters the scene. Perhaps Dreiser intended the two men to compete for the heiress's hand, leading to Ausley's murder of his rival. But he lost confidence in the story well before the key incident. One of his major difficulties was bringing to life the Long Island society milieu, a setting he knew from weekend visits during the *Delineator* days.

According to his later reckoning, this effort was his first step on the road leading to *An American Tragedy*.

CHAPTER 10   *Desire as Hero*

> Don't despair. The philistines will never run us out as long
> as life do last. Given health & strength we can shake the
> American Jericho to its fourth sub-story.
>
> —Dreiser to Mencken (1914)

I n early August Masters came to town. At the age of forty-six, he
could be said to have awakened to find himself famous. The
publication of *Spoon River Anthology* in April had caused a sensation, and the book had become that rarity, a best-selling work of
poetry.

Dreiser and Kirah invited a congenial group to honor him at one of
their regular Sunday evenings. A reporter was on hand to describe the
festivities for uptown readers. The guests included "parlor socialists, artists,
bobbed-haired models, temperamental pianists, girls in smocks and sandals
and a corporation lawyer in a soft boiled shirt." People seated themselves
on the floor, and Miss Kirah Markham, "Mr. Dreiser's secretary," presided
over the punch bowl. Among the guests were Franklin Booth, the artist;
Bobbie Edwards, a poet who wrote songs about Village life; Floyd Dell;
Charles Fort; Berkeley Tobey, of *The Masses;* Ben Huebsch; Virginia For-
rest, an actress; and Willy Pogany, a Hungarian artist.

Dreiser was a rollicking host. As Masters described him, "His teeth
stuck out, his face was red from health and excitement. His eye turned up
with added bubbling of spirits, as he folded his handkerchief and poured

forth thunder-lizard words. Altogether he was the most waggish, quizzical serio-comical, grotesque, whimsical character I had ever seen." The highlight of the party was a reading from the *Anthology* by Masters.

For Dreiser the party was one of those turning points of fortune he sometimes attributed to his guiding genius or "control." In the course of the revelry, Franklin Booth casually asked, "How would you like to go out to Indiana in my car?" Booth, in his early forties, was a prosperous illustrator and maintained a studio in his hometown of Carmel, Indiana, in addition to his New York atelier. Since beginning *Dawn,* Dreiser had thought about returning to his home state, visiting the towns where he had lived as a boy—Terre Haute, Vincennes, Sullivan, Warsaw, Bloomington. And so he proposed that he write a book about the trip and Booth illustrate it. The latter agreed, and all that remained was for Dreiser to raise his expense money. On August 6 he called on Jones, who agreed to advance him $200 for *Plays of the Natural and the Supernatural.*

Dreiser visited the Automobile Association of America, where he obtained a map showing the various passable routes to the West, and secured from Mame a list of addresses of the houses where they had lived in Terre Haute. He managed also to bid Lill goodbye—not a very pleasant occasion, apparently, since in his diary Dreiser mentions that they rode around on the bus quarreling. There was also a luncheon at Mouquin's with Masters and Dell and his latest mistress, at which they discussed "Sophocles and Plato and Oscar Wilde and Homo-sexuality," according to Dreiser's notes. Masters, whose new style in *Spoon River* derived from ancient Greek epitaphs, sonorously quoted a line from Sophocles that greatly impressed Dreiser: "O ye deathward-going tribes of men, what do your lives mean except that they go to nothingness?"

On August 11 they set out in Booth's large open touring car, a gleaming sixty-horsepower Pathfinder, driven by "Speed." As they tooled through New Jersey, Dreiser noted in his diary, "40 miles an hour!" Motoring was a new experience for Dreiser, and venturing into the interior on unpaved roads was akin to an African safari.

Nevertheless, they turned the trip into an extended picnic. They stopped frequently by the road for al fresco lunches or to inspect some notable sight, which Booth would sketch, or to engage in philosophical arguments. They ate in small-town cafés, bought postcards of the local sights, and spent the night at whatever inn or resort caught their fancy. This peripatetic life suited Dreiser, a varietist in all things.

The sensation of speed and movement, the "Tr-r-r-r" of the engine, and the "chip, chip" of the tires induced a mild state of euphoria, sustained by endless, unfolding novelty—"the blue hills of Pennsylvania, piles of coal and slag, red brick houses, plumes of steam."

Rushing west, he went back in time as well—to places holding boyhood memories that had not all been pleasant.

. . .

When they arrived in Warsaw, Indiana, the first stop on their itinerary, he was overcome by nostalgia, a keen pang of change and loss. The sites he had known were altered or gone—the house belonging to the richest family in town was now a Knights of Pythias home, the slough where red-winged blackbirds used to flock in the spring to eat wild rice had been drained and planted in corn. Wraiths of girls he had once yearned for with budding desire materialized in the corner of his eye.

He walked to Center Lake on the edge of town, where the houses of the wealthiest families stood. But the lake had receded and the houses no longer bordered the water. He searched in vain for "houses which I had made sure I would be able to recall should they chance to be here"—where lived the gay, well-dressed youths of Warsaw society, whom he envied. The houses were still there, but the remembered glamour of them had faded.

As he walked in the yard around the old brick house where he had once lived, mentally restoring vanished things, he felt that "somewhere down in myself, far below my surface emotions and my frothy reasoning faculties, something was hurting. It was not I, exactly. It was like something else that had once been me and was still in me, somewhere, another person or soul that was grieving, but was now overlayed or shut away like a ghost in a sealed room." Inside the house, which had been subdivided into four apartments, he peeked into his old room. The sight of another boy sleeping there touched him deeply. As he later wrote: "It brought back the lapse of time with a crash. . . . To my host and hostess I said, 'beautiful,' and then that whimpering thing in the sealed room began to cry and I hurried down the stairs."

Or so he wrote in the finished book. In the notes he made at the time, there is no mention of the workingman or the sleeping boy in his room. Yet the scene he created contained an emotional truth. As he recorded, "Life is not a matter of fact but of fancy, as I well know."

Terre Haute was the next stop. They drove about aimlessly, looking for the house where he had been born but, lacking the correct address, could not find it. He did locate the large house where the family had lived the longest, on a grimy, treeless street. And then the last stop: a dreary slum. The houses all looked alike to him: any of them would serve to mark the nadir of the Dreiser family fortunes when there was nothing to eat but fried mush and the children picked up coal along the railroad tracks.

Next they drove to Sullivan, traveling past fields of rich black soil baking under "a blazing hot Egyptian noon." The house where Sarah Dreiser and the three youngest children—Theodore, Ed, and Claire—had lived was still there, considerably run down. A new chauffeur, named Bert, drove them to Evansville, where more than thirty years ago Paul Dresser had magically transported them to a clean new house. Dreiser visited the

German Catholic school he had unwillingly attended years ago, where he was terrorized by the nuns in their batlike robes and flaring headdresses and the priests who whipped wrongdoers.

On August 26, the eve of his forty-fourth birthday, they arrived in Bloomington. It had grown considerably from the dusty little country town he had seen in 1888 when he came to attend Indiana University as a special student. "New life. New age. A rich town, instead of a poor one," he records. Though they went on to Indianapolis and Carmel, he had reached the end of his pilgrimage into the country of memory. He had returned as a somewhat famous native son, an author in a state that had produced an unusual number of them. But no one had heard of him; when folks thought of a writer they thought of Gene Stratton Porter, author of *A Girl of the Limberlost* and other sentimental best sellers.

His journey carried him to his Midland roots. He deplored the conventional rural minds in the small towns along the way, the narrow provincialism, the illusions about religion and morality, but he was half-charmed by their friendliness, the easy democratic ways, in contrast to "smug and sophisticated" New York. "America is so great, the people so brisk. Everywhere they are fiddling with machinery & production & having a good time of it."

This was the rural America he evoked in *Newspaper Days,* the countryside that produced a Lincoln, a Jackson, a Bryan; Elwood Haynes, making the first automobile in Kokomo; General Lew Wallace, writing *Ben-Hur* under a beech tree in Crawfordsville. An idyllic land, where the judge lent a copy of Shakespeare to the poor boy, who dreamed of the big world beyond. A dream of equality and opportunity that was only a dream, now that the trusts and monopolies had gained control. But a good dream.

But he also remembered the places where he grew up, a lonely outsider. He had gone home to where he never had a home.

The rush of memories stirred him, and back in New York he immediately set to work on a book about the trip, which he called *A Hoosier Holiday*, tapping a reservoir of memories, observations, contrasts with the past. As was becoming his practice, he had *The Bulwark* on the go—started sometime in 1915. Because of the money Dreiser owed on *The "Genius,"* Jones was in no mood to advance him any more for *A Hoosier Holiday.* The same held for *The Bulwark,* in its embryonic state. *The "Genius"* was now out, however, and Jones—and Dreiser—had reason to hope that it would be a strong seller. In October the reviews began pouring in, and they were the most vehemently pro and con of any of his books. Literary opinion in the United States was sharply split, and the battle line divided along a growing fissure in American culture.

On the liberal side were, first, the familiar Dreiser partisans, Reedy,

J. C. Powys, and Edgar Lee Masters, all of whom held forth at considerable length and eloquence on the virtues of the novel. Floyd Dell temporarily defected to the anti-Dreiser camp, with whose values he had little in common; however, his review was full of compensatory praise. Mencken had sworn to Dreiser that he would reread the novel with an open mind, but he was not converted. His notice was a grand clash of negative and positive judgments, all cymbals and kettledrums, like the final movement of Beethoven's Seventh Symphony, and really a tribute of a kind. But Dreiser was wounded by the lash of Mencken's incomparable invective, in passages such as this one: " 'The "Genius" ' is as shapeless as a Philadelphia pie-woman. It billows and rolls and bulges out like a cloud of smoke, and its internal organization is as vague. . . . The thing rambles, staggers, fumbles, trips, wobbles, straggles, strays, heaves, pitches, reels, staggers, wavers."

Rallying behind him, though, was a new set of boosters, the younger generation of poets and novelists who saw him as a leader in their rebellion against literary conservatism. A critic for Margaret Anderson's *Little Review* who called himself "Scavenger" hailed Dreiser as "the greatest novelist in the country . . . the only real, uncontaminated genius of these States."

John Cowper Powys, not chronologically young but European in sensibility, articulated the new generation's case for Dreiser, calling *The "Genius"* the "American prose-epic . . . concerned with the mass and weight of the stupendous life-tide as it flows forward, through vast panoramic stretches of cosmic scenery." In Dreiser the "great life stream" is the hero, and he writes with the spaciousness and drab accents of America's "large flat, featureless scenery," evoking the "curious sadness" of the land.

A review by Randolph Bourne, the spokesman for the literary radicals, titled "Desire as Hero," singled out the same inchoate force of vitalism, the "subterranean current of life . . . that desire within us that pounds in manifold guise against the iron walls of experience," against "the organized machinery of existence." Dreiser writes about the erotic "with an almost religious solemnity." Eugene Witla is lashed and tossed by passions he does not understand. "One feels," Bourne writes, "that this chaos is not only in the Genius's soul, but also in the author's soul, and in America's soul."

Both Powys and Bourne echoed the new ideas in the air—Freud's libido and Henri Bergson's *élan vital*. Freud's explorations of the terra incognita of the mind, where dwelt the chained Promethean id, inspired fresh interpretations of everything from politics (Walter Lippmann's *A Preface to Politics*) to small-town lives (Anderson's *Winesburg, Ohio*). Freud seemed to have exhumed buried wishes and provided the solution to the mystery of human behavior; he also gave the intellectuals a theory of human nature that challenged the reigning morality.

Bourne pointed out that Dreiser's conception of desire stemmed from Herbert Spencer's philosophy: "What Mr. Dreiser has discovered is that 'libido' which was nothing more than the scientific capturing of this nineteenth-century desire." The post-Victorian novelists, of whom Dreiser was the pioneering voice, glimpsed the Freudian tragedy of civilization and its discontents, the beating of the wings of desire against the cage of convention. Yet Bourne and the other voices of the American Renaissance with youthful optimism believed that an upwelling of repressed forces of desire or vitalism would shatter the crust of outworn morality, law, and convention, creating a freer, more just society. As Dreiser said, they were out to shake the American Jericho to its foundations.

All this ferment among the literary radicals sparked a counterreaction from the conservatives, who invoked a kind of clubman's code to blackball Dreiser. According to the code, there were only two types of characters suitable for fiction—gentlemen and bounders (or three, if one counted the generic virtuous heroines that they favored). As a corollary to this, a gentleman did not write sympathetically about a bounder. But in *The "Genius"* Dreiser had taken a bounder for his hero, and the conservatives rose to the challenge. The Kansas City *Star* scored the novel as "a procession of sordid philandering." The Minneapolis *Journal* called Dreiser a "literary Caliban" who wallowed in depravity. *The New York Times* charged that Dreiser had chosen "an abnormal character and written an abnormally long novel about him." Eugene Witla was denounced as a "contemptible cur," a "drummer in a frock coat, a Don Juan of the streets"—certainly no gentleman, asserted H. W. Boynton in *The Nation*.

And, driven by the wave of anti-German sentiment that swept America after the sinking of the *Lusitania* in May, a new note of prejudice appeared in several of the reviews. This ranged from a subtle hint ("the book is German in its quality of thoroughness"), through heavyhanded humor ("We hope that 'The Genius' will immediately appear in a German translation. That's how kindly we feel toward the Germans!" said N. P. Dawson), to the flag-waving of Elia W. Peattie in the Chicago *Tribune*: "I have not yet lost my patriotism, and I will never admit such a thing until I am ready to see the American flag trailing in the dust dark with stains of my sons, and the Germans completing their world rule by placing their governor general in the White House in Washington."

Mrs. Peattie angrily denied that *The "Genius"* was the "American prose-epic." It had a "human tom-cat" for a hero, a cad who wished his wife dead and ravished poor men's daughters. She cites the case histories of several men she has known who followed Witla's degenerate path: one died in a madhouse, another committed suicide, a third is "a shame and a by-word."

Ironically, Dreiser himself had described the disasters that Eugene's wayward desires had brought down upon him. He had not written a tract for sexual freedom. Witla agrees that "the licentious were worn threadbare

and disgraced by their ridiculous and psychological diseased propensities."
But Dreiser did not judge him by Christian morality; his values were closer
to those of the success code, which called for hard work and sublimation.

Dreiser did not really believe in sublimation, at least now; his impulse
was for expression, in art and in life—expression of sexuality. His ideal was
Cowperwood, not Witla. Yet the latter was a part of him too, the compulsive
guilt-ridden side of Dreiser's sexuality, which had its origins in the Victorian
sexology of his boyhood. His earliest sexual gropings had been haunted by
stern admonitions against masturbation and promiscuity, by the shibboleth
that libidinal excesses cause physical enervation, and by his fears of conceiving a child and being trapped in an unwanted marriage.

But he had been courageous enough to lay before the world his troubled
sexual history as honestly as he thought the times permitted. To Dreiser, as
Bourne says, sex is a solemn business. Witla is an idealist, a searcher for
meaning and beauty, not carnal freedom. Dreiser's heroism lay in his attempting to say, more assertively than any other novelist of his day, that
society must recognize subterranean urges as part of human nature, and that
his "pathological" hero was more normal than official morality admitted.
So-called decent people, in the privacy of their hearts, would confirm the
existence of similar urges in themselves.

The battle over *The "Genius"* represented a wider war in American culture,
one that was related to strong political passions unleashed by the real war
in Europe. The forces of the Old Order reacted to the alien threat and
sought to restore the primacy of Victorian or "Anglo-Saxon" culture and
purge the nation of "foreign" values clustered around naturalism, Freudianism, and socialism. It was an intellectual war, but a sociological one as well.
Behind the genteel critics stood the cruder forces of the old nativism, on one
hand, and of the state on the other.

Dreiser had become a larger symbol of all that those groups deplored.
Most of the reviewers of the patriotic school lacked the intellectual equipment to challenge the hypotheses of modernism, and so they retreated into
moral criticism or patriotism. In the December 2 issue of *The Nation*, however, Professor Stuart P. Sherman, of the English faculty at the University
of Illinois, unlimbered the big intellectual guns. Sherman had been a student
of Irving Babbitt's at Harvard in the early 1900s, and had imbibed from his
mentor the precepts of the aesthetic ideology called humanism. Humanism
was a form of classicism that anathematized romanticism and science—the
former because it substituted pity and feeling for reason and moral standards, and the latter because it replaced God with Nature. Dreiser stood out
as the leading exponent of the fallacies of romantic pity and the naturalistic
or scientific view of humankind.

Sherman's polemic, meaningfully titled "The Barbaric Naturalism of

Theodore Dreiser," was in parts the most effective statement yet uttered of the conservative case against Dreiser's method. But it was fatally marred by a descent into a kind of polite nativism. Asserting that "In the case of the realist, biographical details are always relevant," Sherman notes that Dreiser was born of German-American parents. Turning to Dreiser's five novels, he continues, "I am greatly impressed by them as serious representatives of a new note in American literature, coming from the 'ethnic' element of our mixed population which, so we are assured by competent authorities, is to redeem us from Puritanism and insure our artistic salvation"—a reference to Bourne's call for a "trans-Atlantic" literature. (He makes no mention of such American-stock rebels as Sherwood Anderson, Edgar Lee Masters, Floyd Dell, Max Eastman, Ezra Pound, and Bourne himself.)

Like Darwin, he says, the naturalists have a theory; it is a philosophy "such as we find in the mouths of exponents of the new *Real-Politik*" (read, the German militarists). This view holds that society is a jungle, that civilization is window-dressing to conceal brute instincts, which are the real determinants of human behavior. "By thus eliminating distinctively human motives and making animal instincts the supreme factors in human life," Sherman continues, Dreiser "reduces the problems of the novelist to the lowest possible terms . . . he has confined himself to a representation of animal behavior."

Sherman's attack made Mencken itch for battle. It was "a masterly exposure of what is going on within the Puritan mind," indicative "of its maniacal fear of the German." Dreiser agreed. Next to Sherman's definition of the realistic novel, he wrote "rot" and to the description of his theory of "animal behavior," he scribbled, "Animal behavior being evil of course." He did not pen a reply, but found a willing surrogate in Harold Hersey, a poet who was working in the copyright office of the Library of Congress. Hersey had already dispatched a letter to the New York *Evening Globe* criticizing N. P. Dawson's screed. In a letter to Hersey, Dreiser revealed how deeply Sherman's, Dawson's and others' personal attacks had affected him: "These moonbeam chasers are trying to make a devil of me. . . . I am now being tied up with all the evils which the Germans are supposed to represent. I am anti-christ."

Morality aside, *The "Genius"* had serious technical flaws—the inept language, the silly lovers' dialogue, the lack of clear point of view. Dreiser had been unable to detach himself from his central character. He later wrote that Eugene Witla was not autobiographical, and he does make him softer, more easygoing than himself. But he had too deep an emotional investment in his characters to discuss them with detachment. When he shows Eugene being charming at a tea party—using his own favorite expression, "nix"—he cannot see that he is not charming at all. When he describes the affair with

Suzanne, he must shovel pages and pages of moonlight-and-roses romance; he cannot see how foolish Eugene's supposed grand passion looks—as silly as Dreiser's for Thelma. Yet he solemnly tells her: "You have . . . made me over into an artist again."

But Dreiser admired Eugene's commercial success (his career follows closely the author's own at Butterick) so greatly that he had not dramatized the dilemmas of the artist in a business society. Dreiser still believed, as he told an interviewer: "Each of us is an expression of the will-to-power, but in America business is still the swiftest, surest method of obtaining great power. . . . It never occurred to anybody that greatness could be achieved as a writer, a musician, an artist. Therefore all potentially great men poured into business."

Admiring ambition, the will to power, as he does, Dreiser cannot critically probe Witla's career with the United Magazines Corporation. The question of betraying his talent never arises, though surely the frustration of Eugene's artistic gifts was an aspect of his condition worthy of discussion. But Dreiser sees the fruits of material success as so dazzling that there is never any conflicting pull to the world of art. Eugene hardly misses painting. He is happy becoming a Somebody. He is a poor boy's fantasy of the artist as businessman, a person of worth and standing accorded by money. Only sexually is he unhappy. In researching his novel, Dreiser had spoken to artists like John Sloan, but he seems to have missed Sloan's dissatisfaction with the commercial work he did to support his painting, his political radicalism. Perhaps if he had made Eugene a writer, dramatizing the conflict between journalism and creative writing, he could have explored more deeply the tensions between art and commerce. Those quotation marks around "Genius" inject a note of doubt that Eugene really had it in him to be other than a commercial artist. But Dreiser tries to have it both ways at the end, implying that Eugene has returned to his true vocation, and is dreaming "great art dreams."

And yet *The "Genius"* succeeds as a portrait of the artist's life in America. Without irony or artifice it relates the journey of an ambitious young man, driven by dreams of wealth, fame, and beauty, from his rural backwater to the city. That is the archetypal Dreiser story: the young man from the provinces, illusioned and naive, who escapes a dull Middle Western village and dreams, miraculously, of Beauty (often in the form of a young woman, the most immediate form beauty takes in a small town). This young Eugene is appealing, as he shoots up like a green plant from the common soil. There are moving descriptions of gropings for expression—such as the scene at the Chicago art school when he begins painting.

Although the early chapters are the best, the later ones contain individual scenes that rank among the finest that Dreiser had written, meaning among the finest written in any American novel up to that time: the deadly office politics at the United Magazines Corporation and Angela's death after giving birth to a child by Cesarean section, for example. Depicting the ferocious battle between Eugene and Angela over Suzanne, Dreiser does achieve detachment, presenting Angela's side of the argument fully. He makes Eugene a breathing, suffering man rather than an unwitting fool; both partners are caught in a marital trap after desire has died and only hatred and pity are left.

He continued to work on *A Hoosier Holiday,* making good progress, but with no advance on it, he was supported by Kirah. His other writing in 1915 consisted mainly of poetry. They were short poems, conceived "out of mystic despair," he once said, conveying some image that had kindled a mood. He submitted a batch of them to the *Smart Set* at Mencken's urging.

Mencken liked four of them, and such was Dreiser's extremity that he haggled over the fee. To which Mencken replied: "The market price for first-class verse, dear heart, is 50 cents a line. At this rate we are offered endless consignments of sound goods by the best firms in the business." Too proud to beg, Dreiser threw up his hands. All right, he would make them a present of the "horrible things." To which Mencken eventually replied, after consultation with Nathan, that he would accept the gift of three poems, but that "Wood Note" was so good he insisted on paying $25 for it, which came out to $3.62 and ½ cents a line. "Ye Ages, Ye Tribes" was correctly categorized by Mencken as a statement of Dreiser's philosophy:

> Lo, the earth resounds with the bells of creed, and
>   all men pray.
> They bow down in wonder and know not.
> They gaze upon one another, and find no answer.

The dominant mood was one of questioning. As a realist, he could contemplate and report on the spectacle of life, in all its horror and beauty, but, with nation-tribes slaughtering their young men in Europe, it was becoming urgent for him to ask *Why* all the suffering and meaningless death. Could that conceivably be part of the great evolutionary scheme? Was God a sadist? He contemplated those questions in *A Hoosier Holiday.*

In January 1916 Dreiser decided to seek a milder climate in which to finish *A Hoosier Holiday* and work on *The Bulwark.* He suffered from bronchitis in New York's cold winters and this lowered his spirits, and he was also enduring a siege of prostate trouble.

On January 26 he boarded a steamer bound for Savannah, Georgia. Once at sea, Dreiser breathed a deep exhilaration as onshore entanglements fell away. Watching the gulls, he wondered, "What brooding spirit of life generated them? What thing is it, in nature, which wants to be a gull, haunting the grey sea. Or is it a curse—but I do not see any form of life as a curse. I never did, not in my darkest, most unhappy hours. Change in life, not less life or no life was what I craved." He groped for that greater reality, that Something on the other side of the veil—which expressed itself, perhaps, by being a gull.

Once he disembarked in Savannah the rosy clouds dissipated. Conserving his funds, he rented a room in a private home for $2.50 a week, then walked around the city. Southerners, he decided, were a "thin, anemic prejudiced people." Puritanism was to blame for their character. The "respectable" whites suppressed their natural instincts and became envious, gossipy, hypocritical. Feminine purity was idealized; the women were "like saints craving subconsciously what they sniff at openly—sex." In its present culturally arid, repressive incarnation, the South had no future.

He was "Very lonely." The main cause was that he missed Kirah and had not heard from her. He managed to complete chapter 48 of *A Hoosier Holiday,* then sent her a telegram asking why she hadn't written. It was raining; he couldn't work. Bypassing Western Union, he transmitted a telepathic appeal. A little later a wire arrived: SWEETHEART HAVE WRITTEN EVERY DAY SINCE FRIDAY LOVE. KIRAH.

With that boost he was able to work on his book, despite the unseasonably cold weather, his painful prostate, and bad food. He continued to grouse about being lonely: "I despise life without a woman." "See how I live, day after day, with scarcely a word with anyone. The curse of life is loneliness." "It is a bad thing being an intellectual. One is too distant & people do not draw to one."

After finding a more pleasant room, he pounded steadily toward the finish of *A Hoosier Holiday,* completing the final chapter on February 13. It was another long manuscript, more than 250,000 words about a journey that had taken a bit over two weeks. But the lengthy travelogue would also be one of his most genial, relaxed books, a rich pudding studded with humor, autobiography, philosophy, and mellow perceptions of roadside America.

"In a fine philosophic mood all day," he announced after completing the manuscript. The next morning he took out the draft of *The Bulwark* and began revising chapter 1, having good success and breaking off at three to go to town to buy 500 sheets of paper and check the post. On the way he spied a broken horseshoe, then a whole one. He interpreted these conflicting omens as meaning, "My spiritual guardian & enemies are fighting."

He was now receiving an ample flow of mail, including a letter from Mencken inquiring about John Lane's integrity as a publisher. Dreiser had already asked Mencken to check with the Baltimore booksellers on sales of *The "Genius,"* suspecting that his publisher was withholding royalties from him. In another bulletin Mencken reported that he had attended a Billy Sunday revival meeting—a "convention of masturbators."

Kirah arrived for a short, inconclusive visit, and Dreiser left Savannah alone at the end of March, returning by rail via Washington.

CHAPTER 11

Battle of
The "Genius"

The exact specifications are these.
Lewd:
Pages 20-21-43-44-46-51-52-55-56-7—70-71-79-124-125-126-
127-128-129-130   131-150-151-154-155-156-159-160-161-163-164-167-
168-171-179-180   183-245-246-340   341-342-343-344-345-348-350-
351-445-446-531-533-539-540-541-542-551-552-553-554.   555-556-
557-558-567-569-585-588-595-596-597-599.
Profane:
192-335-356-379-389-408 409-410-421-431-469-566-618-678-
713-718-722
Greeting.
Visit me in my cell.

—Dreiser to Mencken (1916)

ack in New York, correspondence between Dreiser and Mencken in May was consumed by inquiries from Mencken regarding Dreiser's books; he was composing a critical study and wanted to get the facts right. Mencken planned to combine it with three other essays—on Huneker, Conrad, and "Puritanism as a Literary Force"—in a book that John Lane would publish.

The most explosive essay in his bag was "Puritanism as a Literary Force," an all-out attack on the literary moralists. The prevailing view of literature in this country, he wrote, is "still a moral one, and no other human concern gets half the attention that is endlessly lavished upon the problem of conduct, particularly of the other fellow." Pointing to the torment of writers who had dared to defy Puritan morality, such as Poe, Whitman, Mark Twain, he concluded: "The Puritan's utter lack of aesthetic sense, his distrust of all romantic emotion, his unmatchable intolerance of opposition, his unbreakable belief in his own bleak and narrow views, his savage cruelty of attack, his lust for relentless and barbarous persecution . . . have put an almost intolerable burden upon the exchange of ideas in the United States."

Sherman and Comstock surely headed the list of contemporary Puritans. Others ranged from Bible-thumpers like Billy Sunday, moralizing lady journalists, anti-German academics, and the antivice societies, which had stepped up their attacks on alien ideas. The patriotic chauvinism of the time, bolstered by President Woodrow Wilson's censure of "hyphenated Americans," gave them a hunting license. Comstock had pronounced foreign literary classics to be more harmful than the crudest pornography, and tried to ban the *Decameron,* Rousseau's *Confessions,* and *Arabian Nights.* More recently, the New York Society for the Suppression of Vice had begun to compile, in its *Annual Report,* a table showing the national origins of every person arrested on obscenity complaints—to strengthen the immigration authorities "in their efforts to keep undesirable classes from our shores."

"Alien" ideas were the true enemies of these censors, dangerous new viruses rampant in the social body. Censorship was about *control* of the strange and thus threatening, from foreign agitators to extramarital sexual drives. And the controllers represented the class that held power, largely Anglo-Saxon in origin and determined to keep labor cheap and docile. Middle-class people of "American stock" felt menaced by the 14 million immigrants who had arrived on America's shores in the last decade.

Anthony Comstock had died in 1915, but his successor, John Sumner, was emerging as an effective smut-smiter. He was more public-relations conscious than his predecessor, and more legalistic. Comstock was a brute, a hard-eyed cop with gamboge whiskers who boasted about the number of filth merchants who had committed suicide as a result of his persecutions (fifteen) and who loved to invade the dens of evildoers, gun drawn (in addition to pornographers, he went after abortionists and lottery-ticket sellers).

Because of his dolorous trade, Sumner was not a popular figure, and the society, while enjoying the financial support of Andrew Carnegie and John D. Rockefeller, had only about three hundred members. But it purported to act on behalf of ordinary citizens, and it received full cooperation from the legal establishment. The New York Society had been chartered by the State Legislature with the power to arrest violators of state and Federal obscenity laws. As secretary of the society, Comstock acted either on the complaint of a citizen (who could remain anonymous) or else on his own initiative. He would threaten prosecution unless the book was withdrawn and swear out a warrant before a local magistrate if it was not. Once the complaint had been served, he had the legal right to confiscate all copies of the questionable book. If the state court found it obscene, the society was empowered to destroy all copies, unbound sheets, and plates. He rarely lost, since he picked jurisdictions where the judges were sympathetic to him, and few magistrates wanted to be seen on the side of the pornographers. And few publishers were willing to risk the accusation of selling pornography, a serious threat to their business and social reputations in this gentlemanly profession. Public opinion passively supported Comstock, who was avowedly protecting their children, so legislators were loath to modify the laws he had helped draft.

Comstock was also a special agent of the Postal Department. Under the law, the ultimate power to bar material from the mails resided with the solicitor of the Postal Department, but this official had traditionally backed Comstock when he fingered a malefactor. And Comstock could also bring a complaint under the state obscenity law against any dealer who sold the book locally.

When Sumner took over as executive secretary of the antivice society, he apparently realized that he must broaden his attack. Old Anthony had been so effective against the clandestine pornography peddlers that there were few of them left, so Sumner redirected his fire at the above-ground publishers. Whereas Comstock's main challenge had been to purveyors of well-known classics, Sumner plunged into the briar patch of contemporary literature. His pristinely literal mind saw a radical younger generation demanding free expression and access to the franker literature produced on the Continent and concluded that the chief menace to the innocence of the young women was the Village radicals who preached and practiced the doctrine of free love. One of his first raids was on *The Masses* bookshop, where he seized a sober sex manual.

Early in 1916, surely not unaware of Mencken's columns guying the Baltimore antivice league, Sumner had turned on the *Smart Set*—or rather *Parisienne*, a subsidiary publication. The *Parisienne* foray could have been part of a clever strategy by Sumner to put Mencken and Nathan out of business, since it was their most profitable venture. If so, he miscalculated. The editors had cynically chosen the title to capitalize on pro-French sentiment generated by the war (privately they called it "the parasite"). And although the name also connoted naughtiness—at least to the average cigar-store patron—they expunged the slightest hint of it from the stories, many of which had first been published in *Smart Set* and transplanted to a French setting. Sure enough, Sumner's complaint was dismissed by the judge.

The "Genius" continued to draw the conservatives' fire. In a discussion of recent books in the May *Atlantic,* the anonymous author defending literary romances against the realistic school chose *The "Genius"* to exemplify the faults of the latter, and added a sly reference to Dreiser's "quite Teutonic" thoroughness. Mencken pounced on that tactic as "typically and beautifully Anglo-Saxon" and said he wanted to mention the review in his book. For he was constructing a defense of Dreiser, neutralizing the nativist attacks by demonstrating that "He shows even less of German influence than of English influence"—which happened to be true.

As Mencken was polishing his argument, Dreiser asked him to edit the manuscript of *A Hoosier Holiday.* Not only that; could he dash off 150 words of jacket copy? And not to stint on requests, he also wondered if Mencken might find an editorial job for Anna Tatum, "one of the best and sanest brains I know anything about." As usual, Mencken was amenable, asking for the typescript as soon as it was ready and meeting with Tatum. He had no openings on the *Smart Set* staff, but he did promise Dreiser that he would give her some literary work to do.

The first portion of the *Hoosier Holiday* typescript was dispatched on June 23, and with manuscripts on his mind, Dreiser wrote Mencken that he had deposited the uncompleted holograph of *Dawn* in the safe at Jones's office. In the event of his sudden demise, he asked Mencken to take charge of the script, since "If it ever fell into the hands of Mrs. Dreiser or some of my relations I am satisfied they would destroy it at once." The manuscript describes rather bluntly the sexual escapades of his sisters Mame, Emma, and Theresa (which, disguised, he used in *Carrie* and *Jennie*), and he knew they would complain, since all of them were now respectable married ladies.

Dreiser had not drawn on this autobiographical material in the account of his childhood in *A Hoosier Holiday*, concentrating mainly on his mother and father. Indeed, in a cursory account of the Dreisers' social failures in Terre Haute he changed a mention of his sisters and brothers to "relatives and friends."

Mencken was probably relieved to find that he liked his friend's latest effort. "The book is full of splendid stuff—some of the very best you have ever done," he wrote Dreiser. He was, however, "outraged . . . by banalities," and his hands itched to clean them up. Also, the book was too long— 200,000 words, he reckoned. No, only about 125,000, Dreiser countered. Fine, Mencken retorted, he would suggest cuts to bring it down to a more seemly 100,000. Subsequently, he did slash repetitions, mostly philosophical passages, and some of the descriptions of Dreiser's clumsy attempts at seduction at Indiana University, which Mencken thought "very unwise." Dreiser chuckled at the thought of Mencken's removing all "lewd, obscene and lascivious references."

Three weeks later a more drastic censor struck. One of the jewels in Anthony Comstock's empire—almost the peer of Boston's almighty Watch and Ward Society—was the Western Society for the Suppression of Vice, based in Cincinnati. Its secretary, F. L. Rowe, was a tireless soldier of the Lord. But it was one of his vigilant supporters who started it all. The Reverend John Herger, a Baptist divine, received a telephone call from an anonymous informant complaining about The "*Genius,*" which he had purchased in a local bookshop. Reverend Herger passed on the tip to Rowe, who acquired a copy and found it riddled with "obscenity and blasphemy." He promptly demanded that stores remove it from their shelves and filed a complaint with the U.S. Postal Department to have it banned from the mails. The department dismissed the complaint as improperly drawn.

Rowe reported his actions to New York, but Sumner already had been alerted. He had received in the mail pages torn from the novel, containing allegedly obscene matter. Rather than swear out a warrant for the publisher's arrest, however, he went directly to the offices of John Lane and requested that Jones either consent to delete the obscene passages or withdraw the book and stop advertising it. This move was in keeping with Sumner's new, low-profile strategy. As the New York *Tribune* explained: "The essential feature of the new method is to get rid of objectionable publications without giving authors and publishers the benefit of free advertising, such as followed Comstock's attack on the picture 'September Morn' and the novel Hagar Revelly."

On July 27 Dreiser sent a laconic bulletin to Mencken: "In passing—the censor has descended on The 'Genius' and ordered Jones to withdraw it from the market. . . . Jones is apparently anxious to compromise and I do not intend that he should unless I have to but I have promised silence until the specific objections are laid down." In fact, Jones had capitulated, halting shipments and requesting stores to return their copies of The "*Genius.*" Sumner also notified the local postal authorities, and two inspectors duly collected copies of the novel to determine if it should be barred from the mails.

On July 28 the Cincinnati and New York societies jointly issued a list of the pages containing lewd, profane, and blasphemous matter—nearly ninety in all—followed by the phrase: "Information filed. Book ordered withdrawn." No explanation of why the material on those pages was obscene was given or needed; the societies' word was sufficient.

Thanks to this scholarly industry, depraved persons could easily locate the ripe stuff, starting with page 20, where they were confronted with the following "lewd" passage (Eugene is skating with a girlfriend): "She stood before him and he fell to his knees, undoing the twisted strap. When he had the skate off and ready for her foot he looked up, and she looked down on him, smiling. He dropped the skate and flung his arms around her hips. 'You're a bad boy,' she said." On the next page, Eugene plants "a long, sensuous kiss" on her lips.

With such a lecherous hero, the book becomes steamier. By page 44 Eugene is involved in a physical relationship (not described) with another feminine acquaintance, and Dreiser notes, "his sex appetite became powerful" (no further details). On page 51 he is seduced by Bouguereau's nudes—"great, full-blown women whose voluptuous contour of neck and arms and torso and hip and thigh was enough to set the blood of youth at fever heat." After that his downhill slide is rapid; on page 55 he is painting a "naked model."

. . .

After receiving Dreiser's letter of July 27, Mencken went on full alert, sending advice and encouragement. However, the upshot of his thinking was that a compromise might be best. It could be that only a few sentences would have to be removed; better that than the suppression of the book. To resist would be folly, advised Mencken the realist. "After all, we are living in a country governed by Puritans and it is useless to attempt to beat them by a frontal attack—at least, at present." Besides, Sumner was a boob; he could be gulled into restoring most of the questioned matter.

Dreiser, however, wanted action. He briefly considered mailing a copy to see if the Federal authorities would arrest him. He would gladly go to jail, he told Mencken; it would save him living expenses. Worried by his friend's seeming lust for martyrdom, Mencken tried unsuccessfully to telephone him when he was next in New York, then wrote him to do nothing until Mencken had perused the society's complaint.

Meanwhile, Dreiser urged Jones to resist, but Jones dithered, saying that he had to consult with the directors of John Lane in London before deciding what to do next. "A fight is the only thing & I want Lane to fight," Dreiser told Mencken. "I hope & pray they send me to jail."

After reading the scores of words, sentences, pages cited in Sumner's complaint, Mencken agreed that resistance was the best course. The allegations were so infantile that they would not hold up in court, as had happened in the *Parisienne* case. But, he warned, any trial would be tainted by the current German spy mania: "A man accused of being a German has no chance whatever in a New York court at this time."

In his next letter Mencken asserts that Sumner had overplayed his hand by enumerating so many allegedly obscene passages. He was all bluff, and if Jones stood up to him, he would "compromise on a few unimportant changes." Of course, if Sumner demanded the excision of "essential things," Dreiser should fight—but he must give up the idea of going to jail. There was "very heavy work" before the war was over, and he would be needed.

According to Dreiser's information, Sumner was in no mood to compromise, so why not fight him? If the list of alleged obscenities was as ridiculous as Mencken said, Dreiser was sure to win. As it turned out, on further examination Mencken found three passages that he considered so unacceptable that Dreiser would probably lose in a trial; and advised him to settle out of court.

Mencken was a shrewd, worldly man, but he leaned toward the side of caution in matters of sexual material. That was understandable at the *Smart Set*, which was too wobbly to risk a run-in with the comstocks. But a novel by the man he called America's greatest writer was surely a different matter. Mencken's distaste for the novel may have swayed his judgment: he thought the thing so grossly overweight that "a few thousand words might be easily cut out without damaging the whole in the slightest." Hence it was not worth fighting over the three obscene passages.

Mencken should have known better than anyone how much the novel meant to Dreiser, personally, and how fiercely protective of every word of it he was. But Mencken had been badly bloodied for his pro-German opinions in "The Free Lance" and though he would never back down, he decided it was time to lie low. The real battle against the Puritans could wait until after the war, he told Dreiser.

By now word of the antivice committee's action was percolating through the literary community. Some of Dreiser's friends in New York were talking about organizing a defense committee. "Money will be provided from upper aides," he cryptically assured Mencken on August 8. On the propaganda front, he was circulating copies of two Mencken columns about him, soon exhausting the back-issue files of the *Sun*. Hearing that Wright had complained that Jones hadn't paid him $500 owed for a book, he asked for further details, promising "I may break with Lane yet—and soon." What Jones intended to do about Sumner at this juncture is anybody's guess, but Dreiser's instinct that he wanted to avoid a fight was probably correct. He had turned the matter over to his lawyer, who, coincidentally, had also found three "danger spots." Dreiser urged Mencken to send Jones an encouraging letter to stiffen his spine. He seemed naively to think that three counts of obscenity would be easier to refute in court than the original laundry list.

Despite the Sumner shock, he continued to work on *The Bulwark*, and Jones was preparing a dummy volume, containing the first chapter, for his salesmen to circulate among the bookstores. But a minor complication had arisen: Anna Tatum was "down" on Dreiser, raising the possibility that she might bring some sort of "spite" suit.

The quarrel with Anna may have been an indirect result of his break with Kirah Markham, who was in self-styled exile in Chicago. He may have turned to Anna out of loneliness, and she had demanded a commitment that he would not make. At any rate, she returned to her home in Pennsylvania. As for Kirah, Dreiser still insisted on his freedom to cultivate friendships with other women, while she held out against all outside emotional entanglements. She didn't want to spend the rest of her life in his "intellectual harem." Some women thought so little of themselves that they could give a "big man" their "dog-like devotion," but not she.

In May he rejected her demand that he devote himself only to her: "If I could for any living woman I would for you, but I can't. You are a ranging vigorous intelligence, each day growing more individual. Our fates are slowly, but surely, diverging. . . . On the long roads that we go alone my thoughts—loving thoughts will always be with you. Goodbye and good luck. If I can serve you in any way let me know."

Possibly he didn't send that letter, since it is the only one to her that survives. She wrote him a few more times that month. In the last one extant, dated May 31, she says she is coming to New York and expresses her hope that they won't have to separate. But it was over between them. She could not live with those unknown rivals, whose letters she occasionally discovered, and he could not give them up. But even more, as she once told him, "You want me to compete with a wraith, an illusion, a phantom. Well it can't be done and I don't propose to try." She meant that ideal woman, who would forever be younger, prettier, richer, more loving, more brilliant, more sacrificing than the woman he was with. She was not the first to be defeated by this rival—nor the last.

By the fall he had taken up with thirty-year-old Estelle Bloom Kubitz, small and pretty, with bobbed hair and dark eyes, a bright, cynical, yet vulnerable flapper. Mencken had met her sister Marion in Washington in 1914 and grown fond of her. He encouraged Marion's literary ambitions by publishing her epigrams in the *Smart Set.*

Estelle, whom Mencken had nicknamed "Gloom" because of her liking for dark Slavic novels and her moodiness, had read Dreiser's books and greatly admired them. While Kirah was away he took her for rides and deep conversation on the top deck of the Fifth Avenue bus. Eventually he enlisted her to do some typing for him in connection with the *"Genius"* case, and they entered into an informal arrangement under which she did his secretarial work. She refused to accept a regular salary, for she liked the job and wanted their relationship to be on a personal, rather than employee-employer basis. In any case he couldn't pay her regularly. She continued to live apart from him, at his behest, and at times shared Marion's rooms.

Mencken was apparently uncomfortable with the idea of his girl's sister going out with Dreiser. Knowing all about Dreiser's philandering, he worried that Estelle was letting herself in for trouble. Also, the affair thrust him into a backstairs intimacy with Dreiser. He became Estelle's father confessor and this put him in the awkward position of knowing more about Dreiser's private life than Dreiser knew he knew and, what's more, disapproving of what he heard.

Meanwhile he had charged into the thick of the *"Genius"* affair, writing friends to solicit their support and counseling Jones on strategy. His shrewdest idea was to circulate a petition supporting Dreiser among leading writers. On August 9 he had written to Dreiser's young admirer Harold Hersey, who was now assistant to Eric Schuler, the executive secretary of the Authors League, suggesting that the organization back Dreiser. "A public protest signed by twenty-five or thirty leading American authors would have a tremendous effect," he pointed out. Although still hoping for a compromise, he realized there was safety and power in numbers. And an attack on Dreiser was an attack on all writers: "If the moralists score a victory against a man of his range and attainments, they will undoubtedly run amuck." Indeed, Sumner had let it be known that after suppressing *The "Genius"* he intended to slap bans on Dreiser's other novels.

Possibly as a result of Mencken's overture, Dreiser was invited to plead his case before the league's executive council on August 24. He delivered a grim warning: "A band of wasp-like censors has appeared and is attempting to put the quietus on our literature which is at last showing signs of breaking the bonds of Puritanism under which it has long struggled in vain." He concluded, "A literary reign of terror is being attempted. Where will it end?"

Impressed, the council members passed a resolution affirming that *The "Genius"* was not "lewd, licentious or obscene" and warning that the present "too narrow and unfair" test for obscenity might choke off the circulation of literary classics. They sent a statement to the Post Office opposing a ban from the mails, and Hersey was instructed to circulate a protest petition among the members. That document, which was based on Mencken's draft, tried to anticipate objections from conservatives who disapproved of Dreiser: "Some of us may differ from Mr. Dreiser in our aims and methods, and some of us may be out of sympathy with his point of view." But, it went on, the vice society's "attempt to ferret out blasphemy and indecency where they are not, and to condemn a serious artist under a law aimed at common rogues," was unjust and absurd, and writers and publishers should be "free from interference by persons who, by their own statement, judge all books by narrow and impossible standards." The protest closed with a vague call for the amendment of existing obscenity laws.

Jones continued to mark time, but he told Dreiser that if the authorities did not act within two months, he would test the *de facto* ban by selling a copy of *The "Genius."* Dreiser remained steadfast in his determination "to stand pat and fight." He, Jones, and others apparently hoped that the popular protest would pressure the postal authorities and Sumner to drop the threat of prosecution.

At least it gave Dreiser and his supporters a feeling that something was being done. In addition to those Hersey sent out, statements were circulated by Mencken, Francis Hackett, Willard Huntington Wright, and John Cowper Powys, who contacted British authors. Powys struck gold when Arnold Bennett, H. G. Wells, W. J. Locke, Hugh Walpole, and others cabled their support. The press was also sympathetic, and editorials critical of the ban appeared in the New York *Tribune* and *Sun,* and the Des Moines *Register,* among others. Even the conservative *Saturday Evening Post* criticized the comstocks.

Mencken was determined that the protest signers be impeccable members of the literary establishment, meaning no red-ink boys, who, Mencken believed, wanted to hijack Dreiser's cause for their own revolutionary ends. He appealed to conservatives like William Dean Howells, William Lyon Phelps, Brander Matthews, Hamlin Garland, George Ade, Bliss Carman, Rex Beach, Owen Johnson, Robert W. Chambers, and William Allen White. Dreiser did not disagree with that strategy; he had actually mentioned those names to Mencken as worth going after. Nevertheless, Dreiser saw no reason to exclude radicals like Max Eastman, editor of *The Masses,* and Hutchins Hapgood, an independently wealthy anarchist and writer.

The red-ink-boys issue surfaced like a spouting whale when Dreiser relayed a request from the Liberal Club for Mencken to speak on censorship at a symposium. His Baltimore adjutant fulminated against "tinpot revolutionaries and sophomoric advanced thinkers." (Two of the proposed speakers were Eastman and Professor Franklin H. Giddings, of Columbia University, a pioneering sociologist.) Mencken grumbled to Ernest Boyd that Dreiser was unable to extricate himself from the clutches of the "Washington Square mountebanks" and that he was "a fearful ass and . . . it is a very difficult thing to do anything for him."

The letter to Boyd was an expression of his growing disillusionment with Dreiser personally. In part, ideological differences were to blame: mention the Liberal Club and Mencken saw Reds. When Dreiser mailed a flier to 200 secondhand book dealers, asking them to display *The "Genius,"* and included a preliminary list of signatories to the Authors League protest, Mencken went off like a Roman candle: "Despite our talk of last week," he wrote, "you have inserted the names of four or five tenth-rate Greenwich [sic] geniuses, including two wholly unknown women and left out such men as [Winston] Churchill and [George] Ade."

Dreiser reacted angrily. He resented Mencken's "dictatorial tone" and his constant cavils about ties to the Village radicals, whom he insisted that he had little to do with socially, and even if he did, it was none of Mencken's business. He added: "I still seem to sense something in this letter which is not on the surface by any means and which I resent . . . if you have any real downright grievance come across."

Mencken wrote back that he had no secret grievance. He just thought it bad politics to cite "professional revolutionists" like Eastman and "nobodies" like the two women on the list. Such people dragged Dreiser's banner into the muck of free love, birth control, and other dubious causes, giving "the moralists the very chance they are looking for." And involving them undercut Hersey, who already faced opposition from the conservative members.

A few of the Old Guard in the Authors League did growl about the executive council's support for Dreiser. One of the most vociferous dissidents was Hamlin Garland, who thought the petition "a shrewd advertising move" on Dreiser's part. On October 2 he warned Executive Secretary Schuler that it would promote discord.

Garland aside, it turned out that Mencken and Hersey had exaggerated the threat from the league's Tories. The only holdouts were Garland and the playwright Augustus Thomas, whom Mencken dismissed as a has-been. Dreiser had the league's support, though it was largely symbolic. It did not include, for example, legal or financial help. Indeed, Frank Harris, then editor of *Pearson's,* resigned in disgust because he felt the writers' group was being too timid. As he wrote Hersey, "I think any decent Authors League would have got up a defense fund to stand the cost of the whole case for Mr. Dreiser."

In November Mencken launched "a general offensive against the lice who have refused to sign the protest." With the help of a stenographer he churned out letters at the rate of twenty-five a day. To the reluctant ones, he wrote personal notes, sometimes three or four of them, patiently answering the objections they had raised. Each letter was "carefully designed to fit the mental capacity of the recipient"—a polite way of saying that he was buttering up writers he considered hacks.

The tactic worked on some, but others recused themselves, pleading that they were unfamiliar with Dreiser's writings; still others, however, knew them only too well. William Dean Howells, who had disapproved of *Sister Carrie* in 1900, wrote, "I have no doubt that half literature, prose and poetry, could as reasonably be suppressed as Mr. Dreiser's book." Nevertheless, he supported censorship to protect immature minds.

Unsurprisingly, the younger writers better grasped the issue of freedom of expression at stake than the Old Guard. The poet William Rose Benét regarded Dreiser as "the most overrated writer in America" but signed because "the freedom of American letters" was at stake. Robert Frost was not familiar with Dreiser's novels ("beyond that they are honest"), but he joined "with all my heart" because of the principle involved. The doyenne of imagism, Amy Lowell, wrote, "Nothing would be more pernicious to the future of literature in America than to have it in the hands of bigoted and fanatical people, who judge it for reasons quite other than its artistic merit." And Ezra Pound indited an editorial in *The Egoist* condemning "the suppression of serious letters" in the United States and particularly the ban on "poor old Dreiser, who is, perhaps, the most serious and most solemn of contemporary American prosists."

Despite the variegated opinions of this highly individualistic group, the basic language of the protest held, and Mencken's yeoman work significantly lengthened the list of signers to 458 in all. Such a collective statement was unprecedented in American letters, and it temporarily united a broad swath of the literary community, radicals and conservatives, younger and older generations, behind the principle of opposition to *unreasonable* censorship.

Sumner, however, was unfazed. In September he had written Alexander Harvey, editor of a small literary weekly called *Bang* and a Dreiser partisan, "Authors taken as a whole may be very good judges of the artistic attributes and the literary merits of any particular writing, but as judges of the tendency of that writing on the manners and morals of the people at large they are no more qualified than are an equal number of mechanics of ordinary education."

But in a communication with George T. Keating, a liberal editor, Sumner got to the heart of his complaint about *The "Genius"*:

> through the story there are very vivid descriptions of the activities of certain female delinquents who do not, apparently, suffer any ill consequences from their misconduct but, in the language of the day, "get away with it." It is wholly conceivable that the reading of the book by a young woman could be very harmful, and that is the standpoint from which this society views the matters which become the subjects of its activities to wit: the effect on the young and impressionable mind.

There it was in a nutshell: any book that might corrupt a young girl must not be published. For forty years American literature had labored under that sweeping, vague standard, applied informally by editors and legally by Comstock and his epigones. Now the informal editorial consensus was slowly being eroded by the new literature and the growing public demand for that literature, but the laws that formed the superstructure of the Victorian sensibility still stood.

The only way to undermine that superstructure was in the legislature and the courts. There was little hope that the former would happen, but *The "Genius"* case conceivably provided an opportunity for a sapping operation via the latter, depending on how vigorously Dreiser's lawyers pressed his cause. And he now had lawyers. The firm of John B. Stanchfield and Louis Levy had agreed to take the case for no fee. Stanchfield was a conservative, but he was a bitter foe of Sumner's; according to Mencken, he intended to fight the case through to a complete victory and then sue Sumner for libel.

The Dreiser cause was looking up on other fronts. In Washington, a newspaperman named James Hay Jr. was in touch with Judge Lamar, the solicitor of the Post Office Department. Lamar assured Hay that *The "Genius"* would have to be "a mighty tough book" before he would bar it from the mails. If the solicitor came through with a clearance, Sumner would be completely thwarted as far as a postal ban was concerned. But Lamar dawdled and was not heard from until late December, when he announced that the novel was not bannable.

Lamar's procrastination was paralleled by the Manhattan district attorney's backing and filling. A lawyer at Stanchfield and Levy who worked for the DA sounded him out privately and reported that he thought Sumner an ass and would not carry the water for him in a court action. Later, however, after meeting with Sumner, the official reversed himself—or so Dreiser heard via the legal grapevine.

Until the *de facto* ban was legally tested it remained in force. Dreiser proposed a deal: if Jones would risk prosecution, Stanchfield and Levy would defend him at no cost. Jones made the ritual reply: he would have to consult his principals in London. Smelling another stall, Dreiser gave him twenty-four hours to write a letter promising to test the ban. Jones's response was ambiguous. He addressed himself to Dreiser's "proposition" that Stanchfield and Levy be retained to defend any John Lane employees prosecuted by the U.S. Post Office or the Society for the Suppression of Vice "at your expense or no charge to us." He said nothing about selling *The "Genius."* And then Jones told Dreiser "to let [his] attorney, Mr. Stanchfield, loosen the dogs of war on Sumner and his crowd at once." In other words, let Dreiser's attorneys bring some kind of suit. In a letter to Mencken in October, Jones said he was leaving all legal decisions to Stanchfield. In fact, he had no intention of offering himself up as a test case.

Nor, apparently, did Dreiser. In early December he wrote Mencken with excessive optimism that the lawyers would bring suit "by Monday" and that he might be "arrested here to accommodate" Stanchfield and Levy. But the lawyers brought no action until the following year.

All this delay was not helping the Dreiser exchequer. *The "Genius"* had been out of the stores for nearly six months now, a considerable financial loss for him. Although sales had dropped in early 1916, the novel seemed destined for a continuing life, had not Sumner quashed it. According to his most recent royalty statement, Dreiser owed his publisher $1600.

Jones did handsomely by *A Hoosier Holiday,* which was published in November in a pale-green, gold-stamped binding that Kirah Markham had designed and which contained Booth's charming pencil sketches in the best smudgy *Masses* style. The book had hardly come off the press when a controversy arose. A telegram from John Lane himself arrived objecting strenuously to two anti-British passages. These were mild by Dreiser-Mencken standards but certainly would hurt sales in England. Dreiser had written, for example, "One German was worth about fifty Italians in force and capacity,—and as for England, if left to contest with Germany alone, she would have been beaten to her knees in three months or less." Dreiser refused to permit any changes, but Lane went ahead and made them.

Jones had not read the manuscript himself, possibly reserving one of Kennerley's defenses in the *Hagar Revelly* case in the event that *Holiday* provoked Sumner in some way. He had hoped, he told Dreiser, that Mr. Mencken and the Lane editor would have caught the anti-British allusions. One wonders where he had been when Mencken was castigating perfidious Albion in "The Free Lance."

John Lane's reaction aside, *A Hoosier Holiday* elicited glad cries from American reviewers, who regarded the relaxed, ruminative style as a refreshing departure for Dreiser. One writer welcomed the absence of Dreiser's usual preoccupation with sex; this view was quickly challenged by several conservatives who found sex lurking in every chapter. Mencken wrote a long, perceptive review in the *Smart Set*, calling *Holiday* "the high tide of Dreiser's writing—that is as sheer writing. His old faults are in it, and plentifully. . . . But for all that, there is an undeniable glow."

Objection! cried an old nemesis, the Chicago *Tribune*. The book was done in "worse than slipshod English" and contained "a mass of radical cant. . . ." But from another part of town, the *News* announced that "Never—a word used after deliberation—has there been a more incisive and yet just criticism of America and Americans written in this country." Dreiser was like a child: "To him to tell the truth is natural, and to dream is natural." *The Nation* agreed he was like a child—"an ill-bred, undisciplined" brat who was "outside all the conventions and decent loyalties of the society which he professes to represent."

A majority of the reviews were favorable, though coverage was sparser than for previous books. Sales were sparse too; only about 1600 copies in the first six months. Perhaps the price was too steep, the book too thick, and, above all, it was not a novel. Or had Dreiser's name been irreparably linked with Germany and immorality?

A Hoosier Holiday is perhaps Dreiser's most accessible book, philosophical in parts and pessimistic in outlook, yet steeped in the sights, sounds, and talk of the Middle West and leavened by his rather ponderous humor. At the outset he compares his memories of his Indiana boyhood to a "rose window" in his life, like that at Chartres: "In symphonies of leaded glass, blue, violet, gold and rose are the sweet harmonies of memory with all the ills of youth discarded." He tests these illusions by going back, and in the end they remain, though now tinted by the darker hues of maturity. The memories themselves were not illusions—they were *of* illusions, the illusions of youth, the dreams that briefly gild the world before disillusionment sets in.

He sees Americans living by a similar set of illusions, the old dreams of the founding fathers, of equality, liberty, and justice for all. He doubts that Americans were really free. Yet why not dream the old dreams? Some day historians would say, here was a country where "men were free, because they imagined they were free—"

CHAPTER 12

Neurotic America

We are to have no pictures which the Puritan and the
narrow, animated by an obsolete dogma, cannot approve
of. We are to have no theatres, no motion pictures, no
books, no public exhibitions of any kind, no speech even,
which will in any way contravene his limited view of life.
    —Dreiser, "Life, Art and America" (1916)

You fill me with ire. I damn you in every European language. You have a positive genius for doing foolish things.
    —Mencken to Dreiser (1916)

J ones had announced *The Bulwark* for spring 1917, extravagantly
predicting that it would be "the greatest novel that has ever been
written." The Lane Company also published a promotional brochure, "Theodore Dreiser: America's Foremost Novelist," containing a garland of poetic tributes by Masters and Arthur
Davison Ficke and a reminiscence by Harris Merton Lyon, originally published in *Reedy's Magazine*. It was the late Harry Lyon now; Dreiser's old
protégé at *Broadway Magazine* had died in the summer of 1916 and Dreiser
was helping his widow find a publisher for a collection of short stories.

Jones's commercially inspired festschrift was his last hurrah for Dreiser.
He had advanced him $1800 and was pressuring Dreiser to sign a contract,
rightly fearing that he might take *The Bulwark* elsewhere. Dreiser complained to Mencken that the publisher had made him a "distinctly wrong"
financial proposition. What was more, the Lane manager was a "bag of
mush" and had "no real publishing acumen." In late November Dreiser had
Schuler of the Authors League vet the proposed contract but put off signing
it. By then Jones's failure to test the ban on *The "Genius"* had created further
ill feeling. Under the circumstances, Dreiser did not really want Lane to

have the novel and asked Mencken to help him find another house. Actually, his reluctance to give Jones *The Bulwark* may have been the main cause, at this time, of the slow progress he was making. A tug-of-war had developed between them, Dreiser trying to pull *The "Genius"* out of his publisher's warehouse and Jones trying to extract *The Bulwark* from him. Dreiser may have psychologically resisted working on a novel, seeking to punish Jones for his timidity.

Dreiser's difficulties with the novel were not due to any fear of Sumner. That is shown by a play he wrote in November called *The Hand of the Potter* (an allusion to *The Rubáiyát of Omar Khayyám:* "What! did the Hand then of the Potter shake?"). The subject was sexual perversion, and the central figure was Isadore Berchansky, a child molester. Was Dreiser deliberately defying Sumner, hoping to goad him into the legal test that Jones's refusal to risk arrest had denied him? Had he himself been goaded into a kind of self-destructive act of defiance? Or was he, as his enemies charged, seeking to profit by sensation? Even a Dreiser sympathizer like George Jean Nathan would later impute this motive: "That Dreiser wrote *The Hand of the Potter* with a Rolls-Royce in view seems to me as certain as that he writes novels with nothing in view but the novels."

Actually, Dreiser had been talking about writing a dramatic tragedy for two or three years, and a play about a pervert was hardly the route to a Rolls-Royce. What inspired this particular subject matter is unknown. Nathan may have been right when he speculated that the Leo Frank case in the South was one source. Although Dreiser had been repelled by the lynching, he may have shared the common belief that Frank was guilty of raping the girl. But the papers were full of child-molestation cases (in Dreiser's days as a reporter in St. Louis he had reported one such story and the editor spiked it). Ben Hecht, not the most reliable of witnesses, recalled that Dreiser had based the play on a Chicago incident he read about. Certainly the sensationalistic press treatment of these crimes—and what it revealed about American prurience—was a motif in the *Potter.*

Another was sexuality itself; Dreiser's own drives, his womanizing, had earned him the censure of Jug and of Mai Dreiser and his sister Claire. There was some feeling in the family that he was abnormal, even talk that he should be sterilized. He had attempted to write about his strong sexual drive in *The "Genius,"* an effort that drew the same moral condemnation from literary conservatives that his philandering had brought from his relatives. Eugene, whose sexuality hardly seems abnormal today, was dubbed "pathological" by critics. He ends in disgrace, an outcast; Dreiser surely felt much the same about himself. And gossip about his private life was fanned by his literary reputation as a writer of a banned book. Exaggerated accounts of his amours were circulating in New York literary circles.

Dreiser still bore the childhood scars of social censure in Terre Haute and Warsaw, when his sisters' affairs had brought obloquy on the family. His projected autobiography was a kind of apologia for their own lives. He intended to show with scientific detachment how an individual could not control his or her chemical makeup; it was shaped by the hand of the Potter, by Nature, and thus individuals could not be held to the illusory standards of traditional ethics: "Life and the individual should be judged on their chemical and physical merits and not on some preconceived metaphysical, religious notion or dogma," he had written.

He sought to tie together American sexual attitudes and censorship in an essay called "Neurotic America and the Sex Impulse." In it he accuses Americans of being both puritanical and "sex struck," citing the example of a Southern city he had recently visited—obviously Savannah—where books and movies are vetted by censors and the old-fashioned morality is dominant. And yet the young people flock to roof gardens, where they cling together in "suggestive dances," after which they go off to lovers' lanes in Model T Fords to consummate their aroused desires. Their behavior, however, is normal, he insists; what is neurotic is the official denial of the instinct driving them and the artificial conventions set up to regulate it.

The essay alludes to Freud and Krafft-Ebing, and he quotes a passage from a book by an American disciple of Freud, the psychiatrist H. W. Frink, the gist of which is that "the sexual factor [is] dominant in every neurosis." But his description of the sexual drive as "a fire, a chemical explosion" is pure Dreiser. Sex is "an all but dominant force of life," superior to man-made laws. It underlies both love and lust; it is protean, surfacing in many guises, often displaced or sublimated, but always the mainspring of human effort. The conflict between the "amazing super-impulses of sex" and the rules of those who fear it has continued throughout history, generating all that is poetic and tragic in life.

The Hand of the Potter is an attempt to show how irrelevant are society's laws and conventions to the primal force of sexuality. The protagonist is a young man who cannot control his desires. Like Cowperwood or Witla (or Dreiser), he is bewitched by female sexual magnetism, but he lacks their consciousness of beauty. Witla and Cowperwood were higher-class individuals. Witla suffered for his sexuality, but emerged a stronger person; Cowperwood defied the conventions at the cost of an entrée into Society. With the character of Isadore, Dreiser made an abrupt descent from super-man to *untermensch*. Isodore is the crude embodiment of Dreiser's own sexuality in its primitive, destructive form: he is a projection of Dreiser's guilt feelings—a scapegoat, as it were, a pariah. Significantly—perhaps—he had made him a mental defective, a Jew, *and* the son of an immigrant.

Isadore comes from a poor immigrant family like Dreiser's own, but

Russian-Jewish in origin. The Berchanskys reside on New York's First Avenue, in the Thirties, and their children are following the familiar second-generation road to a more prosperous, materialistic life. One daughter has married a successful businessman who represents the respectability and material well-being to which the others aspire. When the family begins to suspect that Isadore has gotten in trouble, the son-in-law urges them to deny any knowledge of what happened. Another daughter, Rae, is the most sensible. She has long been telling the family that Isadore should be put away, but they feared disgrace.

Isadore has only recently completed a two-year prison term for an attack on a little girl. He has tried to get a job, but his criminal record bars him; the old urges gnaw. By the end of the first act, he has strangled an eleven-year-old girl who lives in his tenement. Hunted by the police and hiding out in a shabby little room, starving and without money, hearing newsboys shouting scare headlines about himself, he resorts to the gas pipe to save society the trouble of executing him.

Dreiser does not blame society for making Isadore what he was; rather, he holds society guilty of averting its eyes to the slip of Nature that made him a murderer and then hypocritically condemning him for a flaw in his makeup that he could not help. Dreiser took that idea to its logical conclusion in a rambling article on eugenics published in 1918 by the *Call*. In it he contends that society has a duty to put to death children born with congenital defects that, according to Dreiser's glandular theory of human nature, point them inevitably to idleness or criminality. (How such children are to be identified he doesn't say.) Such people were destined to become a burden on society, and the religious people who object to eliminating them are the ones who will do nothing to help them when they grow up. Rather than cruelly executing them or letting them rot in deplorable institutions, why not eliminate them at birth, or at least sterilize them so that their progeny won't continue the cycle of failure? Sooner or later: "only the fit, or those favored by accident or chance, regardless of moral or inherent worth, can or do survive. . . ." In the play, he also makes a tacit plea for birth control, when old Berchansky says that having so many children made it impossible for him to supervise their upbringing.

Those notions derived from Dreiser's growing advocacy of a "scientific" morality as an alternative to religious or traditional codes, which are based on religious ideals—"theories, dreams" that ignore glands and Darwinian law.

Dreiser finished the first draft of *The Hand of the Potter* in early December, working uncharacteristically at night, six, eight hours at a stretch, stimulating himself with cups of strong black coffee à la Balzac. He was aware of the touchiness of the theme and did discuss it with Edgar Lee Masters and Hutchins Hapgood before writing the play. They approved, but with such a topic, execution was all. Deeply immersed in the drama as he was, he thought he had handled it with discretion, and so when he sent it to Mencken for an advance reading he mentioned that "the one thing I am concerned about" was the accuracy with which he had rendered a character's German dialect, and asked Mencken to "look after" it.

He must have been taken aback by the vehemence of Mencken's reaction—the most outraged critique in all their friendship. The first letter was comparatively mild. The play was hopeless, he said, "not only because the subject is impossible on the stage, but also and more especially because the treatment is lacking in every sort of dramatic effectiveness. . . . Nor does it seem to me that you illuminate the central matter in the slightest. . . . The whole thing is loose, elephantine and devoid of sting." The very mention of certain subjects, Mencken insisted, "is banned by that convention on which the whole of civilized order depends. In no country of the world is such a thing as sexual perversion dealt with in the theatre." What was even more appalling was the timing. Dreiser's worst enemy could not have conceived of a more tactically stupid move. The comstocks would fall on this play with knives drawn.

Dreiser lashed back. He had told the story of a family that had concealed a "weak pervert" in its bosom "for social reasons." The man commits a crime—not shown—bringing disaster on the entire house. If the play was a total botch, the critics would duly condemn it. But when Mencken told him what could and could not be shown on the stage he was revealing his own prudishness. As for Dreiser's alleged mishandling of the social problem he had dramatized—"I wonder really what you assume *the central matter* of this play to be. You write as if you thought I were entering on a defense of perversion . . . if you would look at the title page you would see it is labeled *a tragedy*. What has a tragedy ever illuminated—unless it is the inscrutability of life and its forces and its actions."

Dreiser urged Mencken not to reveal his opinions to anyone or publish a review in advance of the other critics, lest he doom the play before it had a chance. (Mencken seems to have heeded the first part of that request, but, he told Dreiser: "As for the review, my chaplain advises me to promise nothing. For such a disease as you show the most violent remedies are indicated.") With the dismissal of *The "Genius"* and now the bitter attack on *The Hand of the Potter,* Dreiser was beginning to feel that his champion was turning his back on him. Then too, he resented the way that Mencken was taking the upper hand in their relationship, signified by the hectoring tone he sometimes used.

On his side, Mencken felt that Dreiser was writing "cheap pornography," as he later told B. W. Huebsch. Mencken had staked his reputation on Dreiser's books, so he felt a proprietary interest in his career. But he was beginning to fear that he had become too closely identified with him, especially after his efforts to rally support in *The "Genius."*

Taken aback by Mencken's hostility, Dreiser kept asking, why so angry, why so violent? He had now tried the script on Powys, Stanchfield, and Levy, who thought it "great"; ditto Rella Abell Armstrong and Estelle Kubitz. But Mencken had admonished: "Take the advice of men with hair on their chests—not of women." That dig, out of the blue, let slip Mencken's private view of Dreiser as a sultan surrounded by an adoring harem that fanned his brow and cheered his every venture into pornography. Such gibes in turn fed Dreiser's suspicion that Mencken's distaste for his recent writings reflected a bourgeois judgment on his lifestyle rather than a criticism of the works themselves.

In this theory he was not entirely wrong. Mencken could not stomach the promiscuous way his friend conducted his romances. He once said, "In all matters of manners I am, and have always been, a strict conformist. My dissents are from ideas, not from decorums." Decorum was foreign to Dreiser's temperament and upbringing. Significantly, Mencken's animadversions on Dreiser's sex life in letters to friends began after Dreiser took up with Estelle Kubitz and, to Mencken's mind, treated her rottenly. On top of this came his consternation at Dreiser's penchant for martyrdom, for playing the fool, for associating with Bohemians, and all the rest of the litany recited in previous quarrels.

As they had in the past, both men eventually backed down. Mencken fired a final blast, then emphasized his respect: "You are the one man in America who can write novels fit for a civilized man to read and here you waste yourself upon enterprises not worth ten minutes of your time."

On Christmas Day, Dreiser returned to the salutation "Fairest Mencken," which he used when he had a favor to ask or gratitude or affection to convey, and invoked their common ethnic ties: "In the face of so much pro-British subterfuge how can you turn on a fellow Menschener [man] in this cruel fashion." He closed with an uncharacteristic "Merry, Merry Christmas."

In February 1917 the *"Genius"* case at last began its snail-like journey through the legal system. Stanchfield persuaded the parties to agree to a plan whereby Dreiser would launch a friendly suit against the John Lane Company for breach of contract. To start the wheels turning, Dreiser wrote his publisher a letter asserting that the novel was not obscene and therefore its withdrawal from the market constituted a violation of their agreement. Jones replied that he would allow the courts to decide whether or not it was obscene. To whet the judges' interest Dreiser claimed to have suffered

$50,000 in damages, though he admitted that the exact amount was difficult to ascertain. In March the controversy was submitted to the Appellate Division of the New York Supreme Court.

Dreiser did what he could to keep the censorship issue before the public in an article for *Seven Arts*, a new literary magazine nominally edited by James Oppenheim, though it was his brilliant young associate editor, Waldo Frank, who provided the literary taste, publishing such key radicals as Randolph Bourne, Carl Van Vechten, Witter Bynner, Paul Rosenfeld, Hendrik Van Loon, and others. Some of Sherwood Anderson's stories that became *Winesburg, Ohio* first appeared in *Seven Arts;* also an early play by Eugene O'Neill, and another by Robert Frost, the poet's only dramatic effort. Considering Dreiser one of the major American writers and the *"Genius"* case a crucial cultural issue, Frank published "Life, Art and America" in the magazine's February 1917 issue (after a dispute with Dreiser over the fee), and followed it with Mencken's essay "The Dreiser Bugaboo."

"Life, Art and America" is one of Dreiser's most durable, certainly most impassioned essays. It is an extended critique of American culture, which Dreiser considers to be dominated by capitalism and the Anglo-Saxon–Puritan ethic, with little space for independent thought or artistic beauty. By virtue of his talent for selling paint or coal or stoves, the business-man "has strayed into a position of counsellor, or even dictator, not in regard to the things about which he might readily be supposed to know, but about the many things about which he would be much more likely not to know: art, science, philosophy, morals, public policy in general." As a result, the nation has produced few poets, painters, and writers comparable to those of Europe.

Dreiser ends with a passionate plea for freedom of thought. The censors' pernicious meddling with serious letters and science is "the worst and most corrupting form of espionage which is conceivable to the human mind. It plumbs the depths of ignorance and intolerance; if not checked it can and will dam initiative and inspiration at the source." New ideas and works of art arise out of free inquiry into the workings of Nature, not stale dogmas and creeds. He concludes: "Life is to be learned as much from books and art as from life itself—almost more so." Now books were at risk. "Art is the stored honey of the human soul, gathered on wings of misery and travail. Shall the dull and the self-seeking and the self-advertising close this store on the groping human mind?"

As *Seven Arts* presaged the intellectual revolt of the 1920s, so Dreiser's essay previews some of the themes of that revolt—the artistic poverty of a business civilization, the provincialism of the average American, the unchecked power of Big Business, the overriding materialism. The generation of Frank, Bourne, Van Wyck Brooks, and the others to come would push further in the coming years, and abandon or take for granted the battles fought by Dreiser's generation. But in 1917, in *Seven Arts,* young and old rafted together the rapids of change.

As an artist, Dreiser had claimed the genius's privilege of remaining aloof and superior. Now he saw that he was not above the battle.

CHAPTER 13   *Surrounded by*
Women

I feel a stormy sex period brewing there.
—Dreiser, Diary (1917)

Dreiser is going on with women like a crazy college boy;
his place is full of them all day and all night. Result: he has
stopped the Bulwark and is doing nothing.
—Mencken to Ernest Boyd (1918)

To launch an anticensorship campaign, Dreiser, Frank Harris, Harold Hersey, and Theodore Schroeder, head of the Free Speech League and an expert on obscenity and the law, convened at Harris's home at 3 Washington Square for the purpose of founding an "authors' aid society," which would extend financial assistance to talented writers (chosen by a panel of critics) whose work was too advanced for conventional publishers. Legal assistance to authors under attack by the censors would also be provided.

Harris, short, organ-voiced, with a Guardsman's mustache, called for a campaign of ridicule against the big-business supporters of the antivice societies; *Pearson's* had already published articles questioning Sumner's integrity. Schroeder wanted to expose the New York Society for misuse of its trust fund, and Dreiser proposed periodic bursts of anticensorship propaganda to keep the heat on the comstocks.

Although the critical-society idea would sporadically occupy Dreiser for the next two years, it never got beyond the stage of a proposed dinner to which wealthy patrons of the arts would be invited, along with artists, intellectuals, writers, and editors like Max Eastman, Finley Peter Dunne,

William Marion Reedy, Masters, John Dewey, and Arthur Brisbane. The difficulties of assembling such a heterogeneous group proved insurmountable, however, and the dinner was never held.

Meanwhile, the comstocks, encouraged by their success in suppressing *The "Genius,"* were in full cry. Sumner had raided *Pearson's* offices, ostensibly complaining about a racy article on New York's night courts in the May issue but actually retaliating for the pieces about him. He also impounded a novel by *Masses* contributor Albert Kreymborg, called *Edna: The Girl of the Street.* The little-magazine impresario Guido Bruno asked Dreiser to contribute to a symposium on censorship in his latest new weekly. Chastened by the row with Mencken over *The Hand of the Potter,* Dreiser declined, this time implicitly agreeing with his Baltimore conscience that some anticensorship fights were best steered clear of.

On April 6, 1917, Congress declared war on the Central Powers, and Sumner exchanged his vice crusader's mufti for the khaki of a YMCA officer. He was posted to France. While Sumner was trying to shield American manhood from the temptations of Paris, the Vice Society struggled on, but its work was eclipsed by the government agencies set up to mobilize public opinion behind President Wilson's crusade to make the world safe for democracy.

Once war was declared, Mencken saw his worst caricatures of democracy as mob rule come true. Local governments and vigilantes mobilized to purge the country of Teutonic influences. German-language sermons in Lutheran churches were barred, a minister who preached against hatred of Germany was horsewhipped. German-Americans were interned; school districts across the country banned the teaching of German; textbooks that were not sufficiently critical of Germany or too emphatic in their descriptions of past conflicts between the United States and Great Britain were banned. College professors engaged in an anti-German orgy, and one of the loudest voices was that of Stuart P. Sherman, who warned against "Prussianism streaming into Anglo-Saxon communities through the forty volumes of [Thomas] Carlyle." Aliens of all stripes became targets of the amateur spy hunters, and ordinary Americans took pride in denouncing neighbors as agents of the Kaiser. The slogan "one hundred percent Americanism" came into vogue, and woe to the "hyphenates" who preached such foreign doctrines as socialism or the eight-hour day.

The most serious blow to constitutional rights was delivered in June when Congress passed the Espionage Act, followed later by an amendment known as the Sedition Act. Together these laws forbade speaking out against the war, or expressing contempt for the flag, the military, and the Constitution, or hindering military recruitment, or inciting mutiny in the armed services—even writing a "disloyal letter" or an antiwar article. The law empowered the postmaster general to ban from the mails any printed matter he found seditious (a measure that bore some resemblance to the

Comstock Act and showed the close affinity between moral and political censorship), enabling the government to revoke the second-class mailing privileges of radical publications.

Nearly two thousand people were arrested for violations of the Espionage Act. Rose Pastor Stokes, controversial radical and signer of Dreiser's *"Genius"* petition, received ten years for saying, in a letter to the editor, "I am for the people and the government is for the profiteers." Socialists and members of the IWW were favored targets. The most prominent publication put out of business was *The Masses,* whose editors and several contributors went on trial twice, both cases resulting in hung juries. Another, indirect casualty was *Seven Arts,* which had been publishing the vigorously pacifist essays of Randolph Bourne. The magazine was not banned, but its financial backer demanded that the editors cease publishing antiwar articles, and Frank and Oppenheim refused. The last issue appeared in November 1917, one year after it had begun. Its demise and that of *The Masses* were the last gasps of the Renaissance, which would go underground until the 1920s.

To avoid the slightest note of controversy, Nathan and Mencken kept the war out of the *Smart Set* (unaware that the government had appointed publisher Eltinge Warner to keep an eye on them lest they preach sedition or run a spy ring from the office). In his letters to Dreiser, Mencken confined himself to mock pledges to serve his country. Upon hearing that suffragists were enlisting, he proposed that he and Dreiser volunteer as midwives. But in a more serious vein he worried about being drafted, despite his age and severe attacks of hay fever. Also, his *Prefaces* book was turned down by John Lane because of its anti-British sentiments.

Dreiser's letters contained similar mock-patriotic exhortations. In one, he resurrected a Kiplingesque poem Mencken had composed more than ten years before called "The Orf'cer Boy" and extolled "the touching lines to a worthy English soldier." But mainly he remained wrapped up in his personal concerns.

In May Stanchfield and Levy filed their brief in the *"Genius"* case. A member of the firm, Joseph S. Auerbach, had prepared it, and his basic strategy was to prove that the novel was actually a moral work demonstrating how Witla's libidinous excesses led "to artistic futility and business disaster"—a not inaccurate description, as we have seen. Since the novel did not "exult in debauchery" or glorify vice, it could not tend to "deprave or corrupt those whose minds are open to such immoral influences." The brief also argued that The *"Genius"* was no worse than other works challenged by the Society that the courts had refused to ban, e.g., *Arabian Nights, Tom Jones,* and *Madame Bovary.*

It would be a year before the case was argued, however, and Dreiser again found himself financially pressed, subsisting at times on ten dollars a week. With Estelle Kubitz putting in long hours at sweatshop wages (when she was paid at all), he set up a literary assembly line, switching over the next several months from *The Bulwark* to short stories (when he needed quick money) to philosophical essays. He sold the publishing rights to *Sister Carrie* to Frank Shay, who had purchased the Washington Square Book-store from the Boni brothers and who planned an edition of 1000 copies. Previously, Dreiser had been selling by mail the copies he had on hand. He mailed out a flyer saying that his books "have been continuously attacked by Puritans solely because America is not used to a vigorous portrayal of itself." The recipient could obtain *Sister Carrie* by writing to "George C. Baker," who happened to live at 165 West Tenth Street.

The cutoff of royalties from *The "Genius"* bothered him, especially when the book, which was listed at three dollars, was being sold under the counter for five or ten dollars. Later he and Mencken tried to obtain fifty copies of the novel to sell at the black-market rate, but Jones's board of directors, fearing that the comstocks would get wind of the scheme, refused to approve it. His books with Harper's had at last earned back their advances—*Jennie* and *The Titan* had sold some 24,000 copies, *Carrie* only 4000—but sales were down to a trickle now.

His debt to Lane was mounting. Jones doled out an occasional advance ($200 in February), and would have given him more. Dreiser later told Mencken that aside from the *"Genius"* matter, his relations with the Lane manager now were "of the friendliest." But when he offered his publisher *The Hand of the Potter*, Jones demurred, saying its publication would do Dreiser's career "immeasurable harm."

Short stories and articles temporarily alleviated his financial pinch. In February he sold an article on New York to *Hearst's* for $500; in March, a story, "Married," to *Cosmopolitan*, for $600; in August, "The Second Choice" to the same publication; and in December, "Free" to *The Saturday Evening Post* for $750. He also received a $1000 option payment from Arthur Hopkins, a theatrical producer who was brave or foolhardy enough to want to stage *The Hand of the Potter*.

His relationship with Estelle was now complicated by sexual posses-siveness. The first entry in a diary he began keeping in May 1917 reads: "Little Bill cold to me. We have argument in bed as to how many women I have watched suffer under my indifference." "Little Bill" was one of his nicknames for her, along with "Bo" and "Bert" ("Gloom" was really Mencken's appellation). Their quarrel was the usual one over his desire for "freedom" and fear of a woman dominating him. The eternal issue was, as he wrote in his diary, "Tension of opposition—who is to control?"

So it went, quarrels and reconciliations accompanied by bouts of stren-uous lovemaking. Sometimes she was "a gay, laughing girl," at others sulky, tearful, and depressed, consumed by jealousy after discovering the remnants of the tea he had served a recent visitor. Her favorite song was "Poor

Butterfly." She was the prototypical flapper, at once cynical and idealistic, one of a train of literary-minded young women drawn to Dreiser by a need to give meaning to their lives by serving a great artist. As she told Marion, she knew she was a doormat, but life was an "empty dance card" anyway and the only solution was "to live in somebody else."

. She obsessively recorded his flaws and betrayals and inconsistencies while complaining of being left to do work while he went out and played with others. She called him "Old Moloch" because of his stinginess. Mencken urged her to leave him and offered to lend her the money to go to Washington and find a job. "Why in hell a woman of your talents should be a slave of a man is beyond my comprehension," he admonished her.

Dreiser marched with Estelle in a suffragist parade, buying her flowers beforehand (and guiltily noting that it was the first time he had ever done so), but he compulsively lived by the double standard. He seemed to fancy—and sometimes seriously advocate—polygamy. Once he was talking to an attractive woman who had come to his studio. When she said that the independence of women led to unhappiness, he agreed. He describes in his diary what happened next: "I advocate Mormonism and prove that she already accepts it in fact while denying it in theory. As we talk I pull her over to me and feel her breasts. She kisses me, and in a few minutes I persuade her to undress. . . ." So much for theoretical discussions.

He was fonder of Estelle than she seemed to think, but his feelings were, at best, tenderness and pity, never love, which requires a loyalty and reciprocation he could—or would—not give. At least in the early months of the affair, though, she put him through some hoops, and he paid her the backhanded compliment of continuous jealousy. Indeed, at times *her* alleged infidelities (she had men friends but apparently not lovers) caused him to think of breaking with her. He told himself, "I am fond of Bert really. It will hurt me very much to leave her but she couldn't behave herself any more than I can. And should I ask her to? I think not—and yet I do!" When she was gone he wanted her back, couldn't sleep, felt wretched, and fretted, "what is to become of me in my old age."

But when she returned, he continued to see other women. Once she refused to help him choose slipcovers for his couch because her rivals would be seduced on them. "I would like one room," she told him, "in which I would not always be finding traces of other women."

One of the women he was still romancing was Lillian Rosenthal, now a singer in vaudeville, who would visit him at odd times for passionate liaisons. And that same turbulent spring, he formed still another feminine friendship. She was Louise Campbell, young, pretty, spirited, cynical—a "hoyden" he called her—from Philadelphia. She had sent him a fan letter after reading *A Hoosier Holiday,* describing her vague ambition to be a writer and adding, coquettishly, "I seem to have more success in being decorative than intellectual. My friends all seem to think I make a much better fashion model than a writer." A month later, when she was in the city, she called him and he invited her to drop by. She was impressed by the Bohemian ambience of his studio, though frightened by the pet mouse he kept on his desk in a wire cage. He had caught it in a trap and couldn't bear to kill it. (Some might find the caged mouse a symbolic expression of his possessive attitude toward women.) He asked her to read a short story he was working on and, after listening patiently to her criticisms of his style, took her to lunch at the Brevoort. Like many women, she was impressed by his sympathetic attention, his way of listening closely and asking questions that got to the heart of the matter.

In May he arranged a tryst with her at a hotel in Trenton. Telling Estelle he had an appointment, he spent a rainy afternoon with Louise at a "fierce" (shabby) hotel, returning that night to pick up a cross Bert at her apartment. He comforts her, and "we fall to screwing. Work at this almost an hour. During afternoon I come four times, Louise seven or eight. We finally come down to studio and go to bed . . . and after an hour of tossing about get excited and have one more long fierce round. Then am able to sleep."

Such accounts of his sexual adventures are sprinkled throughout Dreiser's diary. They were confirmations of his potency, which he had, irrationally, worried about since adolescence. He felt the same documentary urge to record that a day ended with lovemaking that he did to describe the weather, or the name of a caller, or the price of a purchase at the store. Once he noted, "No sex." Sexuality had become as much a part of his relationship with a woman as a meal or a conversation. When he has tea with a Barnard English professor, a brilliant, attractive, but no longer young spinster, he decides she was "thirsting for passion," and though he was not attracted by her, contemplated "sex charity."

With a beauteous female libertine like the writer Nina Wilcox Putnam, who had an open marriage with her publisher-husband, he met his equal. He suspected she was toying with him as a possible addition to her list of male conquests, and they engaged in a couch wrestling match that was less foreplay than a contest to determine who would control. Finding her too aggressive, he spoke roughly, seeking to regain the upper hand. She pushed him away: "You talk like a thug."

At times it would have taken a Mack Sennett to direct the complicated exits and entrances at his studio. There were Lill and Louise, of course, more or less regulars, both wanting to marry him but, since one frequently traveled and the other lived in Philadelphia, not too demanding. Then there were friendships, not all of them involving sex, with women like Rella Armstrong, who told Dreiser it was his mind that interested her (he scoffed, writing in his diary that it was "her driving lust"); Edith De Long Jarmuth, who had an arrangement with her wealthy husband in the West whereby he subsidized her artistic, or rather Bohemian, career; and red-haired Mary

Pyne, the Bohemian poet Harry Kemp's mistress, whom he saw as the embodiment of the modern Village woman—a "bad-good" girl—that is, one who exercises her sexual freedom yet is decent, intelligent, and moral; and a Louisville housewife who had written him a fan letter and who had been drawn to him as the creator of the masterful Cowperwood.

At times, his promiscuity resembled addiction. He worried about his health, writing, "I must give up so much screwing or I will break down." He did not drink to excess, except on occasion, or take drugs. Women were the most delightful drug of all.

Despite these affairs, he never got over the old loves. Or they him. Thelma Cudlipp, now a successful magazine artist for *Vanity Fair* and other magazines, saw him in a restaurant accompanied by a drab-looking woman and thought he looked "oh, so down-at-heels." Kirah Markham turned up in New York, after spending a year in California working with a little theater group and trying to get into the movies. On the rebound from Dreiser, she had married Frank Lloyd Wright Jr., son of the architect. Lengel told Dreiser that when he saw her last she had burst into tears at the mention of his name. When she came to Dreiser's apartment he cleared out the mementos of their life together; another time he imagined she was willing to make love, but he made no move; he did not want another affair to start. She separated from Wright but returned to him, speaking for many New Women when she told Dreiser, "What's the good of a freedom I don't want and can't use?"

Nor was the oldest love of all, Jug, ever completely out of his mind—or his life. Walking by their old place on 123rd Street would trigger a rush of memories of those "sad, beautiful days." Lengel's untalented wife's trying to sing reminded him of Jug's irritating desire to "be someone"; and when Lengel described his own sexual restlessness, Dreiser was reminded of the frustrations in his marriage.

In November 1917 Jug wrote him that she'd lost her job at *The Delineator* and demanded that he provide financial help. Still under an obligation to her, he had been thinking seriously of a divorce. He had sent her little if any money, pleading poverty because of the ban on *The "Genius."*

"It is so hard for me to completely rid myself of old loves," he wrote after seeing Kirah. But he could also write: "I believe it would almost kill me—be absolutely impossible for me to be faithful to one woman." Yet he had not forgotten the times as a young man when he thought himself homely, unattractive to women, and unable to interest any. As he wrote in the diary: "I have so many girls now compared with my one-time luck." He adds in the next sentence, "Will I ever have money, I wonder, to contrast with my poverty?"

To answer such questions he resorted to Jessie Spafford, a Village fortune-teller. When she asked his three wishes, he told her, "Money, success in work, beautiful women," and she predicted that he would have money by November 15 and also a "great triumph with some book." He had faith in her, for she had once accurately forecast a new love affair. Sure enough, before the prophesied date he received a $200 payment from the Washington Square Players for the stage rights to *The Girl in the Coffin* and a $100 royalty payment for *Sister Carrie*.

Hutchins Hapgood, who regularly dropped by for a chat, concluded that, despite his amorous reputation, Dreiser placed work first. He saw no one until the end of the day. His talk was almost always about literature or the moral restraints on it.

Even his visitors were pressed into service as readers, typists, or copy editors. When Louise came, he would give her a manuscript to critique "between rounds." And he used events in their lives as raw material. Campbell's account of her marriage provided him with the theme for a short story called "Love" (later called "Chains"). The sight of places associated with Jug generated two stories, "The Victim" (which he apparently never finished) and "The Old Neighborhood," which he conceived while walking through the Bronx neighborhood where they once lived. When he bought Estelle some new lingerie and watched her trying it on, he thought of a play called *The Nobody,* "the story of a poor drab of a woman who never gets anything." He never wrote the play, but the incident tells volumes about his relationship with her.

For all the competition, Bert remained at the center of his life, and they spent many hours of quiet domesticity, reading together in bed, going to restaurants or the theater. He stayed with her not only because she had a "perfect body" and was (when not in one of her moods) bright, companionable, gay, and loyal but also because she helped him make his way through the tangle of projects in which he was embroiled. He needed her to type and edit the manuscripts he wrote with such prolific haste, cutting excess words and improving grammar as she typed.

The two of them spent a working vacation in June and July at her brother-in-law's farm. Dreiser alternated *The Bulwark* with a new project, the second volume of *A History of Myself,* which he called *Newspaper Days.* He wrote his old Warsaw schoolteacher, May Calvert Baker, that he had finished twenty-eight chapters of the Quaker novel.

The correspondence with the woman he called an "angel" had begun earlier that year after she wrote him that she had read *A Hoosier Holiday* and was gratified that he had made good, but she worried about him. "It does not appear that you have won happiness with fame." He replied, "I suppose I am not happy yet as I might be—who is—but I am much more philosophic." From Maryland he wrote that he had not forgotten her—"if I've thought of you once I've thought of you a hundred times." He informed her he was now 6' 1/2" tall and weighed 190 pounds. She had not seen him for more than thirty years and had married and raised children in the interim.

At the farm he also finished a forty-three-page essay on the war, which he called "American Idealism and German Frightfulness." The burden of the piece was his theory that England had started the war to deny Germany colonies in Asia and Africa. American boys were being sent to die for British commercial interests. The United States was no paragon of democracy itself. Big business ground down the workers, and the Puritans suppressed free thought.

He sent the 10,000-word manuscript to Waldo Frank at *Seven Arts,* asking for a higher than usual fee. He also suggested that Frank approach wealthy German-Americans to finance a wider distribution of the essay, "not so much because it is pro-German—it is not—but because it is anti-British and pro-American." Fortunately for him, Frank declined (the magazine was about to go out of business), as did several other editors. Its publication would have landed him in an internment camp, as Mencken, who read it, warned him.

When Mencken drove up to the farm, he found himself in the middle of a spat between Dreiser and Estelle. She accused him of planning an assignation with Louise Campbell, which was very likely the case. When Dreiser asked Mencken to drive him, he refused and watched with growing displeasure as Estelle meekly withdrew her objections. Later, he attacked her for giving in to Dreiser: "If you fall for that bunk again I'll have you arrested. When you went back last time, I wrote to Marion that you were ripe to be read out of the human race."

While at her brother-in-law's, Bert did some writing too—a play with two characters: Old SOB and Miss Damn Phool. Lying in a hammock with Miss DP sitting at his feet, Old SOB announces that he must go to New York on business. She tells him that if he leaves she will walk out for good: "I've worked and played with you for a year now and done ten times as much of your work as you have, and yet this business I'm to know nothing about. . . . I'm just raw enough to want some return for what I do for you and am for you."

It really wasn't a very funny skit. The author was too close to her subject matter.

CHAPTER **14**   *Over Here*

As for Dreiser, he is full of some obscure complaint against me, which I can't understand, and so I don't see him. In brief, I suddenly find myself very lonely in New York.
—Mencken to Boyd (1918)

Dreiser and Estelle patched up their differences, but Marion refused to speak to him, in protest of his treatment of Estelle. As a result, he declined an invitation to dine with her and Mencken but relented after she sent him a conciliatory letter. They capped the evening with a session at the Ouija board at Dreiser's studio—to Mencken's disgust. Mencken took his revenge by pushing the Ouija. Dreiser sought cosmic, rather than mundane, answers from the spirits: at a previous session an anonymous shade informed him that there was no evil, no God, and perforce no reason to lead a moral life.

Ten days later, August 13, Mencken again intervened in Dreiser's destiny. Merton S. Yewdale, the Lane editor, told him that Mencken, in his *Book of Prefaces*, which Alfred A. Knopf was about to publish, had dismissed *The "Genius"* as "a mass of piffle" and said that Dreiser's early work was his best while the recent stuff represented a deterioration. This news hit Dreiser hard, and Estelle did not help his self-esteem when she remarked that Mencken's evaluation would influence posterity's opinion on Dreiser's entire oeuvre. Later, when Lill called and asked how he felt, he told her he was "horribly blue and sad, feeling eventual failure staring me in the face."

The article was far from an attack—quite the opposite. It was the fullest, most sympathetic account of Dreiser's artistic struggles and achievements yet written, save perhaps for Randolph Bourne's essay in the June *Dial*. But after reading it Dreiser felt that his Baltimore scourge was taking an unholy glee in enumerating his faults. One passage in particular drew blood. Mencken says that one half of Dreiser's mind is usually intelligent and thoughtful,

> but there come moments when a dead hand falls upon him, and he is once more the Indiana peasant, snuffling absurdly over imbecile sentimentalities, giving a grave ear to quackeries, snorting and eye-rolling with the best of them. . . . The truth about Dreiser is that he is still in the transition stage between Christian Endeavour and civilization, between Warsaw, Indiana, and the Socratic grove.

Dreiser later said he objected to Mencken's "slapstick familiarity and condescension in regard to myself personally, which at times becomes a little too familiar to be agreeable." He decided Mencken had fallen behind the times, preferring earlier works like *Sister Carrie* and *Jennie Gerhardt*, which "represent really old-line conventional sentiment."

As a result, their friendship went into a deep freeze. When they met by chance in a New York restaurant, and Dreiser came over to shake hands, Mencken would have none of it.

More troubles with the patriots. In October, when Mencken's *Book of Prefaces* appeared, Stuart P. Sherman was lying in wait. In a review of the book published in *The Nation* in November, the innuendos he had strewn about in his anti-Dreiser essay were replaced by heavy-handed sarcasm: "Mr. Mencken is not a German. He was born in Baltimore September 12, 1880. That fact should silence the silly people who have suggested that he and Dreiser are the secret agents of the Wilhelmstrasse. . . . He is a member of the Germania Maennerchor, and he manages to work the names of most of the German musicians into his first three discourses. His favorite philosopher happens to be Nietzsche. . . ."

After Sherman had downed him, the critical pack tore Mencken to pieces. He was pilloried up and down the land as a seditious mouthpiece of alien and licentious ideas. His contributions were not encouraged at the *Sun*, and he suspected the paper would be relieved if he took his opinions to another forum. The *Smart Set* was shaky. He and Nathan wrote much of the magazine under pseudonyms, and their prolific Chicago contributor, Ben Hecht, had eight stories in one issue, under such Mencken-inspired Anglo-Saxon *noms de plume* as John Henslowe Saltonstall, the Rev. Dr. Peter Cabot-Cabot, and Ethan Allen Lowell. Editorial salaries were in arrears, and his other sources of income had dried up. When his friend Philip Goodman, an advertising man who would briefly become his publisher, suggested some hackwork, Mencken replied: "Why ask me if I am willing to do a little whoring? Tell me what it is and I'll do it. If necessary, I'll do a piece proving that [Secretary of the Treasury] William G. McAdoo is the Son of God." He signed a contract with the *Mail* for a series of nonpolitical articles, which turned out to be some of the best he ever did, including the bathtub hoax and "The Sahara of the Bozart," a caustic look at cultural aridity below the Mason-Dixon line.

In addition, he assembled two books for Goodman, *Damn! A Book of Calumny* and *In Defense of Women,* both of which provoked even greater outrage among the critics and sold few copies. Then he began his great work, *The American Language,* a scholarly declaration of linguistic independence from Anglo-English and a cerebral celebration of the native lingo. But all in all it was a bleak winter.

Dreiser was meanwhile no more beset than usual: his literary troubles lay in a heap, like a pile of lingering, dirty snow on the city streets. Contrary to Mencken's gossip, he was writing as much as ever, though a lot of that was short stories intended to raise quick cash. But it was not hack stuff; he continued to write truthfully and to avoid formula romances.

Initially, at least, he had some success. "Am rather cheerful these days because my money problems are not pressing," he concluded in October. He and Bert were in temporarily calm waters. He was sufficiently well heeled to escort Estelle to Arnold Constable, a swank department store, and buy her a new suit and a pair of silk stockings. They dined at the Koster Glocke, a favorite German restaurant, and attended the theater and a vaudeville performance starring Eva Tanguay and featuring Sarah Padden, a tragedian for whom Arthur Henry suggested he write a play. His old comrade of the *Sister Carrie* days, whom he had not seen in nearly ten years, was back in New York, married to Clare Kummer, a Broadway playwright and songwriter, whose verses Dreiser had published in *The Delineator.*

Although Dreiser made scant progress on *The Bulwark* during the winter of 1917–1918, he became engrossed in Volume II of his autobiography, *Newspaper Days,* completing nearly forty chapters. He also rescued the manuscript of the first volume of *A History of Myself* from J. Jefferson Jones's safe and sent it to Louise Campbell, who had volunteered to type and edit it. And he accumulated enough short stories for a book. He was also reworking some of his early stories and sketches, hoping a publisher would issue a collection. In most cases his revisionary pen deepened and improved them. He made "The Lost Phoebe," for example, more psychologically plausible than in its first incarnation, showing the effect of his greater interest in the science of the mind.

Following in the Financier's footsteps.
Dreiser, left, on the Riviera in 1912, with
Grant Richards, center, and Sir Hugh Lane.

(UP)

Helen Richardson in 1920: "Full
of delightful and innocent dreams
of beauty and peace under simple
circumstances."

(UP)

Estelle Bloom Kubitz (aka "Gloom,"
"Bert," "Bo "), Dreiser's secretary
during the Village years.

(UP)

Dreiser in 1920. The inscription—"For the returned Helen"—was prophetic. She always came back.

(UP)

H. L. Mencken, Dreiser's early critical champion: "He was my captain in a war that will never end, and we had a swell time together."

(Alfred A. Knopf)

Helen in the black lace afternoon dress she wore in *The
Four Horsemen of the Apocalypse.*

(UP)

Helen and Dreiser at one of
the houses where they lived
in Hollywood in 1921.

(UP)

The 1916 bust of Dreiser
by Onorio Ruotolo
displayed in the reception
room at Boni & Liveright.
(Smithsonian Institution)

Dreiser in the 1920s.
(Courtesy of Vera Dreiser)

An American Tragedy

An American Tragedy

Chapter 1

"Dusk — of a summer night".

And the tall walls of the commercial heart
of an American city of perhaps 400,000 —
such walls as in time may linger as a mere
fable.

First page of the holographic
manuscript of *An American Tragedy:*
"Dusk—of a summer night."

(UP)

Dreiser correcting a typescript
in the 1920s.

(UP)

Top left: The Glenmore
Hotel as it appears today.
Here Chester Gillette
rented the rowboat.

Top right: The waters
of Big Moose Lake where
Grace Brown died.

Chester on the witness stand, as
depicted in the New York *World*, 1906.

Courthouse, Herkimer, New York,
where the trial took place.

Dreiser in Russia. Left to right: L'Étienne,
a Latvian agronomist; Dr. Sophia Davidovskaya,
physician and scourge; Dreiser; Ruth Kennell,
his American-born interpreter; and a guide.

(UP)

He took another look at *The Hand of the Potter*. Dissatisfied with the authenticity of his Jewish characters, early in 1918 he asked David Karsner, an editor at the socialist *Call*, to suggest someone who could introduce him to a typical family on the Lower East Side. Karsner chose a young member of the *Call* staff named Irwin Granich—who in the 1920s would take the nom de plume of Mike Gold and write a classic Lower East Side memoir, *Jews Without Money*, which appeared in the 1930s.

Honored to help Dreiser, who was a hero to him, Granich invited him to Friday night sabbath dinner at his mother's East Side tenement. The visit enabled Dreiser to add some touches of Jewish life to the play, but apparently it was all for naught. Hopkins demanded more substantial changes that Dreiser was unwilling to make, and in April the producer bowed out, saying, "It is the best American play that has been submitted to me, and I would eagerly have produced it had not Dreiser imposed on me so many bulls, caveats, and salvos." Dreiser later accused Mencken and Nathan of talking Hopkins out of doing the play, although Nathan actually favored its being staged.

Not long after the falling out with Hopkins, he found a publisher, if not a producer. His name was Horace Liveright.

Their meeting came about in the summer of '17 when Dreiser discovered that *Sister Carrie* had been issued by the house of Boni & Liveright, which had purchased the rights from Shay, who was about to be drafted. The firm had been formed the previous year by Liveright and Albert Boni, who had hatched the idea for the Modern Library of contemporary classics—cheap editions bound in limp lamb's-leather covers and retailing for sixty cents each.

Liveright had done a stint as a bond salesman on Wall Street and then married the daughter of a wealthy paper manufacturer. With his father-in-law's backing, he decided to go into business for himself. His first venture was manufacturing an extra-fleecy toilet paper. The name of the product— Pick-Quick Paper—suggests that even then Liveright had a literary flair of sorts, and indeed, at age seventeen he had written a drama that almost made it to Broadway.

After the toilet tissue flopped (it was too costly to have a market but the paper was later used as the top liner in candy boxes), Liveright found temporary refuge at an advertising agency, where he met Boni. His father-in-law had promised to back him in one more venture, and when Boni outlined his idea for the Modern Library, Liveright offered to put up the money.

Liveright was the dynamo of the firm, a salesman with flair. Dreiser, he decided, would be the figurehead on the prow of the Boni & Liveright ship. He was interested in publishing new American writers, preferably undiscovered Village geniuses, and Dreiser's name on his list would give the house prestige and attract the young talent.

Liveright called on Dreiser and wove his spell, promising to put twice as many copies of *Sister Carrie* in the stores as Shay would have, and, what is more, to advertise them. As for the future, he proposed that B & L acquire the rights to all of Dreiser's books, including *The "Genius,"* and publish them in a uniform set—something Dreiser had been longing for. And of course they would bring out all his new works and would support him with generous advances. Liveright coveted that much-rumored novel, *The Bulwark*, which he had heard was a devastatingly ironic swipe at religion. Liveright was already years ahead of the Genteel Age.

Dreiser had recently been talking to Harper's. The older house seemed a safer home than a new outfit like Boni & Liveright. The fact that both partners were Jewish may also have given pause, but it was probably not a major issue. He had well-off Jewish friends like Elias Rosenthal and his daughter Lill, and when he later met Abraham Cahan, novelist and editor of *The Daily Forward*, he deeply admired him, telling Nathan, "I don't believe in saints, but there's one man on this earth who strikes me as being one, and he's Abraham Cahan." He could weep over the poor Jews of the Lower East Side, but he resented the newly visible class of nouveau riche Jews (whom Cahan himself would satirize in his 1917 novel *The Rise of David Levinsky*) like motion-picture-theater owner Samuel J. (Roxy) Rothapfel, with whom he spent an evening. As he described it in his diary: "That apartment! And his wife! Former kikes* all, raised to ridiculous heights by wealth. . . . The men start a gambling game, $1 ante, out of which I stay. A typical American parlor evening—puritanism, until all are thawed out and sure of their ground. . . . What a trashy land!"

A Jewish-run publishing house was a novelty in New York in 1917. There were two others besides Boni & Liveright—Alfred A. Knopf and B. W. Huebsch. Almost by default, the Jewish publishers became the innovators on the scene, the ones who were most open to foreign writers and new, "daring" American ones. Partly this was a matter of sophisticated tastes and partly it was because they could not compete with the establishment houses for the best-seller writers or literary gentlemen and had to go elsewhere—the same situation in which renegades like Mitchell Kennerley and newcomers like Jones found themselves. And so it was Huebsch who published not only James Joyce's *A Portrait of the Artist as a Young Man* but Sherwood Anderson's *Winesburg, Ohio*. Knopf had Mencken, of course, and a growing list of distinguished foreign authors.

Liveright lacked the others' impeccable literary taste, but he had an instinctive sense of what the public would like (with an emphasis on erotic material), and was attuned to the avant garde. He was a most persuasive

*He was using "kike" in its original meaning of a recently arrived Eastern European Jew.

character, a man of sinuous charm and abundant ego, slim and handsome in an almost Mephistophelean way (he liked to remind women he was trying to seduce of the resemblance between his profile and John Barrymore's). With his chronic suspicion, Dreiser saw through Liveright's charm to a different, enigmatic, vulnerable soul underneath.

Liveright, the ex-stockbroker, analyzed Dreiser's portfolio—his books—and found it underperforming. In September he reported to Dreiser that the total sales of his eight titles in print for the year ending June 30, 1917, came to only about 2000 copies, bringing in $700 in royalties. That was "ridiculously small"; B & L could easily double it. He wondered if there were any additional titles that could be included in the package. Might he obtain *The Bulwark* without having to pay anything to Lane?

Dreiser pointed out that there was the matter of the advances Jones claimed he owed the company; perhaps Liveright could be induced to make good on those as part of the price for his transferring to B & L. But money wasn't the only thing. Did Liveright sympathize with what he was trying to do artistically? Could Dreiser depend on him not to succumb to a faint-heart attack like Jones and Harper's?

Liveright outlined what he would guarantee: he would publish every-thing Dreiser submitted, promote the books to the hilt, fight any legal challenges raised by the comstocks, and pay advances of $500 to $1000 on each title, more for a novel. Those were astonishing concessions. But Dreiser still wasn't sure and so responded with a test. He offered Liveright *The Hand of the Potter* and also a collection of his short stories. When Liveright balked at the play, Dreiser told him the deal was off. The publisher came down to his studio and tearfully agreed to do the play.

The Hand of the Potter was scheduled to go to press in February 1918, but Dreiser began making extensive revisions to reflect his recent researches. When he felt doubts about something he was working on, he would gather more background material (hence the visit with Granich) and seek scientific confirmation on problems of character.

Liveright warned that the changes would be "a mighty expensive mat-ter for you." More than 100 pages had to be reset, almost the entire book. Dreiser was undeterred. Then a proofreader at the printing house pointed out that because of Dreiser's earlier alterations certain references in the last act no longer applied, so more fixes had to be made. Because of the delays in the book, Liveright, who had sent out advance publicity, complained it would have to be "sold all over again."

Before he could start, there was another delay. A wealthy couple dab-bling in the theater wanted to produce *Potter* and paid Dreiser $1000 for the option. Liveright postponed publication until after the play was staged, to take advantage of the publicity. But after scoring a Broadway success with another, more conventional drama, the backers had second thoughts and backed out. The book was not issued until 1919.

The short story collection, *Free and Other Stories,* also ran into delays because of Dreiser's insistence on revising it "on the stone." In June, shortly after the *Potter* debacle, Liveright was complaining that "you have practically rewritten the whole book." It too would have to be postponed. But when Dreiser accused his publisher of caring only about the costs (rather than his desire to improve the book), Liveright swallowed his anger and apologized. It was becoming a habit.

Meanwhile Dreiser plugged on with *Newspaper Days.* He was in truth blocked on *The Bulwark,* later explaining to Mencken that he did not think a novel about a Quaker was appropriate in the prevailing martial atmosphere. He may well have been right, but the story of a Quaker family set in the late nineteenth century could only by a stretch of the imagination be considered pacifistic. Still, at a time when the top sellers were stirring accounts of life at the front, it would have had a poor sale, and the antireligious passages in a book by him would bring out the comstocks in force. Also he needed money to carry him through the writing of the novel, and he was having trouble selling short stories.

Although on Christmas Day 1917 he received a timely $750 check from *The Saturday Evening Post* for his story "Free," the New Year ushered in hard times. W. A. Swanberg added up Dreiser's rejections in 1918 and came up with the figure seventy-six. As Swanberg suggests, some of the pieces were rejected because they were poor work—melodramatic tales like "Khat," "Phantom Gold," and "The Hand," or pessimistic, radical philosophical essays like "Hey, Rub-a-Dub-Dub!" "Equation Inevitable," "The American Financier," and "Neurotic America and the Sex Impulse."

Only the last might have been spurned because of the subject matter, but the reason bluntly given by Douglas Doty, now at *Cosmopolitan,* was probably more to the point: "Once again you have written over the heads of our audience." The others in this philosophical vein, which expounded some of Dreiser's theories about man and the cosmos, were equally ill-suited to mass magazines; even his old friend and supporter Mary Fanton Roberts called one of them "too complicated and weird."

The short stories were another matter. Some, like "Free," "Love," and "The Old Neighborhood," were among Dreiser's best work in the form, and the lesser stuff was at least an honest attempt at psychological horror aimed at the popular audience. Most of the stories were eventually published in magazines—but not in 1918. His score for that year was four stories and articles sold, bringing in a total of $1650. A fine story like "The Old Neighborhood" fetched only $300 from the *Metropolitan.*

Dreiser was out of step with the national mood and the requirements of commercial magazines. "Butcher Rogaum's Door" was rejected by *Red Book* because the characters were Germans. Doty warned that "American

Idealism and German Frightfulness," which Lengel had sent him in an excess of loyalty, "comes clearly under the head of those proscribed writings that 'give aid and comfort to the enemy.' " Reactions to "Chains" fell into a pattern: "one of the best things you've done" but "extremely dissatisfying to the average reader" (Doty); "Perhaps . . . the finest piece of short fiction . . . you have accomplished. . . . We are the ones who have to face the Philistines" (T. R. Smith, *Century*); "We like [stories] with some meat in them, but not too much" (Arthur T. Vance, *Pictorial Review*).

At *The Saturday Evening Post,* the editors' enthusiasm for Dreiser's work quickly dissipated after "Free" drew a tide of angry letters objecting to its implicit endorsement of divorce. As a result of the protests, the *Post* shelved another story by Dreiser that it had purchased in the interim, "St. Columba and the River," a tale about a sandhog who is trapped in a tunnel cave-in.

The message was not lost on Dreiser. In the summer of 1918 he attempted a patriotic article. Called "Rural America in Wartime," it describes home-front activities in and around a farming community in Maryland. The general tenor was, Now that America is at war and her sons are dying, any reservations about the war on grounds of pacifism, ethnic loyalty, or socialistic antipathy toward "trusts, plutocrats, the growth of class distinctions" were out the window. And he continues, as though it were the country people speaking, "America is now important—America first, as it were, regardless of anything else that ever was or again may be." One could read the entire piece as concealed irony; yet he thought of himself as American first, German second (as did Mencken).

Dreiser's actual contributions to the home-front effort were few. He nominally belonged to the Vigilantes, a propaganda organization founded shortly after the U.S. declaration of war by a group of writers, editors, and artists led by the maker of the famous Uncle Sam "I Want You!" recruiting poster. In July 1917 Dreiser received a request from E. L. Harvey, publicity director of the superpatriotic National Security League, calling him to the colors "as a member of the Vigilantes" to write an editorial of 200 words on "What the Victory and Defeat of Germany Means to Every American." Seven months later, Harvey asked where his statement was. In 1919 Harvey was back to tell him that the war having been won, the League was concentrating on "the menace of Bolshevism to America."

Again no response. Dreiser's attitude toward Russian communism was, in fact, favorable. In November 1917, when Lenin's forces overthrew the parliamentary government of Alexander Kerensky, he wrote "Good" in his diary. And when Senator Hiram Johnson later made a speech criticizing U.S. participation in the Allied intervention against the Bolsheviks, Dreiser requested a copy of the speech from the senator's office.

In a March interview with David Karsner, associate editor of the social-ist *New York Call*, he unburdened himself of some near seditious thoughts: "The United States is intolerant because she is grossly ignorant, and knows nothing, cares for nothing and boasts of it, but money, money, money. We worship the man on top of the human pile and kick the man underneath who holds up the man on top."

He went on to criticize the jailing of Wobbly leader "Big Bill" Hay-wood and a number of IWW members in a recent Federal crackdown aimed at smashing the union. He praised Emma Goldman, soon to be deported because of her opinions, as "one of the noblest women who ever lived." Karsner noted that Dreiser still preached Darwinian individualism, but he told the *Call* editor that if he were president, he would put the "big brains" to work running the country and require "absolute obedience" to their dictums—socialism from above, as it were. In an article for the paper in 1919, he inveighed against the "autocracy" of big business which suppressed free speech, adding, "In what other lands less free are whole elements held in a caste condition—the Negro, the foreign born, the Indian?"

Karsner had published a tribute to Dreiser in the *Call* and com-miserated with him about the unfairness of Mencken's critique in *A Book of Prefaces*. Karsner's essay and the one by the radical Randolph Bourne in *Seven Arts* conveyed the message that Dreiser's only friends were on the left. The war had radicalized him, but he was a radical without a program, still a believer that social change was the product of natural forces.

An essay called "The American Financier" contains the fullest declara-tion of Dreiser's socioeconomic views at this time. He continues to hail the great individual—artist, inventor, capitalist, scientist—as the source of inno-vation and progress. But then he points to the recent advent of ideologies seeking to curb the individual and protect the masses. Foremost among the latter is socialism: "Marx, the humanitarian, appeared preaching solidarity for the mass and mass control, and his work will probably result in greater material battles between the individual and the mass than any yet wit-nessed." Dreiser still preferred the "big brains."

In the wartime Village everyone was talking about the Bolshevik revolution, Dreiser included, but he never went beyond talk. When the socialists held a parade in New York City in October 1917 to protest wartime censorship, he was not a marcher but a spectator who happened by. His comment on the demonstrators' demand for freedom of speech and the press was a sarcastic "They are likely to get it—here! Yes."

The omnipresent smog of wartime patriotism nauseated him. In his diary he grouses, "The present political and war situation makes me sick. The canting fol de rol of American politicians!" While dining at Lüchow's he was disgusted by the spectacle of "Germans singing *America!*" But he no longer cheered on the German army. Hearing news of a recent German victory, he comments, "I hope they get a draw out of the war anyhow. It would never do to let England win."

The mindless slaughter in Europe had cooled his enthusiasm for the German cause. What good could come out of this war? Ludwig Lewisohn, back in the city after nearly losing his job at a Middlewestern university because of anti-German sentiment, remembered an evening with Dreiser after a meeting with some other writers: "We walked toward his house in a flurry of early snow. He lifted his cane toward the sky with an unusual passion and denounced the blood and hypocrisy and tyranny of the war. . . . His grim and reasoned denunciation heartened me. . . . I left Dreiser . . . more than ever convinced that he was not only a great writer, but a good man and a lover of his land."

Mencken's estrangement from Dreiser deepened at a time when both men felt acutely isolated. He told Boyd that Dreiser was "full of some obscure complaint against me, which I can't understand so I don't see him." Mencken knew that what he had written in his essay was the cause of Dreiser's displeasure, but he would never, never apologize, dismissing Dreiser's grievances as "idiotic petulance."

In the spring of 1918 Mencken's letters were peppered with jabs at Dreiser's amorous proclivities. "He is doing little writing but devotes himself largely to the stud." "He still keeps his manly powers and is first cock in Greenwich Village."

When Dreiser began circulating broadsides on various topics, such as one against the American press, Mencken suspected that he was becoming a pamphleteer, rather than an artist, as a result of the moralists' attacks. As Mencken said of Ezra Pound: "He has gone the Dreiser route, Puritan pressure has converted him into a mere bellower."

The coolness between them had become common knowledge in literary circles, and when in March Ben Huebsch wrote them offering to mediate, Mencken replied that Dreiser had the mistaken idea that he was engaged in a critical vendetta. Far from it: "All I propose to do is to let him alone. . . . He has his own work to do, and I may be wrong. But my experience with the Dreiser Protest showed me exactly how susceptible he is to the flattery of self-seeking frauds, particularly those with cavities between their legs." To Estelle he wrote: "It goes without saying I would do anything in the world to help Dreiser as an artist, but I have a feeling I have written my last word about him." To Boyd he expressed relief that he had Dreiser off his chest; he was tired of apologizing for him.

In his reply to Huebsch, Dreiser sounded a wistful note: "I am overly fond of Mencken, literally. He is and always will be to me a warm, human, boyish soul, generous, honest and superior—so far above the average run that I cannot even think of him in connection with it." But he thought nothing could be done to repair the breach.

Although the exchanges with Huebsch had no immediate result, they served to draw off some of the venom. In May Dreiser apologetically sent Mencken a play, *Phantasmagoria,* and the essay "Hey, Rub-a-Dub-Dub!" which outlined his skepticism of all ethical credos. Mencken replied politely but foisted on Nathan the job of rejecting the play. He declined the essay on the ground that the *Smart Set* was in precarious financial health and "a serious article would appear in it like a flash of common decency in a Methodist." But to Boyd he described the play as "awful stuff" and the essay as "ghastly," adding, "The latest news is that he is at work on a 'philosophical book.' You may well guess that fornication will be defended in it." A truce was in effect, he said: "I still avoid the old boy, though we do not quarrel."

But he continued to upbraid Estelle for staying with Dreiser, and when she decided to remain with him, Mencken called her a "door-mat." She had had a chance to escape to a good-paying job, but "one roll of the evil eye was enough to make you throw it up." If she was willing to be a slave, it was no wonder Dreiser exploited her. He refers to Dreiser as "old Warsaw" and "the Warsaw lothario" and "that ancient guinea pig."

Unaware of this hostile undercurrent, Dreiser sent out peace feelers through the fall, until Mencken relented, handsomely requesting a copy of *The "Genius"* to lend to some friends who hadn't been able to buy it. When he received *Free and Other Stories,* he broke his tentative vow of silence and told Boyd that, while the book was "awful stuff," he had reviewed it and "tried to be as gentle as possible." Dreiser said nothing about the review and continued to correspond sporadically.

In November Mencken revived the humorous note that had been missing from their letters. He reported that while in New York recently he had "succumbed to alcohol" with a friend and while in their cups they discussed Dreiser's sterling virtues and decided to pay him a call. Finding no one home, they deposited their "cards"—joke presents like religious tracts, Black Hand threats, menus of Armenian restaurants, frankfurters tied with red, white, and blue ribbons, inscribed photographs of the Czar and the like, with which Mencken and Nathan had in the past filled his mailbox.

At Christmastime, Dreiser sent Mencken an inscribed copy of a novel by Bertha M. Clay, a writer of sentimental romances, conveying "all my best wishes for your dearest happiness throughout the coming year May heaven protect and prosper you, Henry dear." To "Bertha Clay," Mencken wrote gratefully on Christmas Day: "What angel whispered to you to send me your lovely book? Last night, anticipating a heavy strain upon the liver and lights today, I took a dose of castor oil. Unluckily, my mind was upon other things, and so I swallowed a whole seidel of the damned stuff. Today I have been a prisoner within white-tiled walls, but my long vigil has been made happy by your incomparable tale of true love."

And so their anger cooled.

. . .

Mencken later said that in one way the war had been a boon to him. It had freed him from daily journalism, giving him the leisure to write five books, recharging him with new ideas and new material. Dreiser, however, drifted into a backwater. True, he wrote a handful of good short stories (the reviews of *Free and Other Stories* were mostly unsympathetic, however), but much of his work was dedicated to keeping himself afloat.

Money dribbled in, little of it in book royalties. The most recent check from Harper's was a bit over $47; the one from Lane, a trifle less than $35—the total returns on six books. Liveright was his main support in these threadbare times, advancing him sums of $500 to $1000 on three collections in 1918 and 1919—two of short stories, one of philosophical essays, which Dreiser had tentatively titled *The King Is Naked*, after the fairy tale about the little boy who recognizes that the emperor has no clothes.

The $200 advance he received from the Washington Square Players for *The Girl in the Coffin*, per Mme Spafford's prediction, was a welcome windfall. The Village group, which later moved to Broadway as the Theatre Guild, gave the piece a creditable production. On opening night, December 2, the audience summoned the actors to eighteen curtain calls, and cries of "Author!" rang out, but Dreiser was too shy to attend. He had taken an active interest in rehearsals, criticizing the diminutiveness of the coffin and bringing one actress to tears with a lecture on how her role should be played. The play earned him a total of $300 for its six-week run. When he walked by the Comedy Theater at Fifth Avenue and Forty-first, he felt no great thrill at seeing his name on the marquee, but his youthful appetite for the stage was revived and he set to work on an American counterpart of Hauptmann's *The Weavers*, which would show the effects of mechanization on workers. The drama went nowhere, however, and he abandoned it after twenty pages.

He made several false starts on short stories as well. He tried to sell some character sketches, several of them written years previously, which Liveright agreed to publish under the title *Twelve Men*, but editors were resistant, finding the pieces plotless and too grim. But he continued to write them. He had quarreled with Liveright over the advance, demanding $1000. Liveright thought that $500 was plenty, but he relented and met Dreiser's terms. Despite the meager returns on the three books, his faith in Dreiser never wavered.

Dreiser's most successful short stories dealt with love and marriage, but those themes also invited editorial censorship. In April 1919 he sold three stories, including "Love," to Burton Kline at the New York *Tribune* magazine section for only $150 each. Kline had rejected a fourth, "Sanctuary," about a prostitute, telling Dreiser that "it might get me scalped if I put it in this polite family journal." He proved a poor judge of his employers' threshold of tolerance. "Love," an account of a faithless wife and an older husband who cannot break with her, cost him his job.

In July the Appellate Court at last handed down its decision in the *"Genius"* case. In essence the justices ducked the issue; they held that since no prosecution had been brought, the question of obscenity was not before them. It was a narrow, legalistic ruling, and the upshot was that Sumner had banned Dreiser's novel without a court's determining that it was obscene. *The "Genius"* was now adrift in a legal limbo.

Jones wrote Dreiser that while he found the decision regrettable, "any delays [in the publication of *The 'Genius'*] are the responsibility of you and your counsel, since we left all matters pertaining to the trial in your and their hands." He also reminded Dreiser that he owed Lane $2175.11, which included "the advance royalty we paid you on your next complete novel."

Dreiser had no intention of giving Jones financial satisfaction, even if he could have afforded to. Liveright was willing to publish *The "Genius"* if Jones would sell him the copyright, plates, and stock for a reasonable price. He also had his lawyer, Arthur Garfield Hays, determine what contractual claims Jones had on *The Bulwark*. Jones, however, demanded $5000 for *The "Genius,"* although the book was earning nothing for him; and insisted that Dreiser must either give Lane his next completed novel or pay back the unearned advances. The price, said Liveright, was "out of the question." Both sides dug in for a long war.

As for *The Bulwark*, Dreiser hadn't signed a contract for it, so it was presumably available. The snag was that Dreiser's contract on *The "Genius"* gave Lane an option on his next novel, and Jones had advanced him $1800 and had made up salesmen's dummies. Dreiser contended that the sums advanced him had come from a general drawing account and were not for a specific title. He could point to letters from Jones suggesting that the publisher thought so too.

He also argued that Jones's failure to issue *The "Genius"* in effect voided the present contract. Jones countered that Sumner's complaint was sufficient cause for his refusal to publish. Dreiser's contract contained a standard clause warranting that the book "contains nothing of a scandalous, immoral or libelous nature." Since the high court had refused to say the book was not obscene, Sumner's informal finding of immorality held.

Dreiser's only legal hope of freeing *The "Genius"* was to bring another suit to invalidate the contract. Liveright's lawyer leaned toward the theory that *The Bulwark* was not covered by that contract, but warned that even if it wasn't, Lane could sue Dreiser for the advances.

.   .   .

Early in 1919 Mencken wrote Dreiser, "Why in hell don't you move out of New York, settle down in some small town, and finish *The Bulwark*? In brief, get away from visible America." Dreiser suspected he was playing mother hen: "I have the feeling that you are under the impression that I am idling in the extended arms of a harem dreaming sweet dreams and killing time. It is your Dreiser complex I fear." He defended his recent production: he had completed Volumes I and II of his autobiography, known as *A History of Myself*, which was not quite true. A part of Volume I, *Dawn*, had been retyped by Louise, but he had abandoned it, fearing family censorship; Volume II, *Newspaper Days*, was still not done, but he had it well in hand. He had also written thirty-one essays, assembled sketches about turn-of-the-century New York, many of them written years ago for the collection called *Idylls of the Poor*, and composed some 200 poems. And he planned to write another play: "I like tragedy and am looking for a great picture to be done briefly."

Dreiser was optimistic and hoped that the play and short stories would provide money to see him through *The Bulwark*, but he closed: "Personally, at this age, I have concluded that literature is a beggars game."

CHAPTER 15

The Tragedy of Desire

> [Freud] reminded me of a conqueror who has taken a city, entered its age old hoary prisons and [proceeded] to release from their gloomy and rusted cells the prisoners of formulae, faiths and illusions which have racked and worn men for hundreds and thousands of years.
>
> —Dreiser (1931)

> Cries and moans all night. Claims she has no friends now and cannot leave me. I try to cheer her up, but no use. She lies beside me all curled up and weeping. Of such is the tragedy of desire.
>
> —Dreiser, Diary (1917)

Following the *"Genius"* decision, Dreiser tried again to form a group that would help authors muzzled by the comstocks. In early 1919 he engaged in two projects toward this end: (1) an organization with the clumsy name of the Society for Certification and Endorsement, an attempt at setting up a mechanism to subsidize the publication or exhibition of worthy but uncommercial manuscripts or art works; and (2) a radical literary magazine similar to *Seven Arts*.

An organizational meeting of the critical society was held in January, and twenty people showed up at Dreiser's studio, a mix of artists, writers, and publishers, including George Luks, Douglas Doty, George Jean Nathan, Alfred A. Knopf, John Cowper Powys, and Ludwig Lewisohn. Once his guests were seated on the floor, as was customary in Dreiser's chairless abode, the host rose to speak haltingly of the sorrows of neglected geniuses in America—an obsession of his that was not shared by his raucous guests. Nathan objected that no unsung talent escaped *his* eye at *Smart Set*, and Knopf said the same held at his publishing house. Luks, who had liberally sampled the contents of a hip flask, challenged Dreiser to name just one neglected genius. Dreiser was unable to, and Luks declared the meeting adjourned.

Despite this hostile reception, Dreiser plunged ahead. A small sum of money was raised and Harold Hersey hired at a minuscule salary to invite prominent figures in the arts to join. He sent out 275 letters in all and received only 50 favorable responses. In March he reported to Dreiser that artists were an antisocial lot; he had spent $200 to raise $140. The critical society quietly died of inanition.

As for the magazine, Liveright had volunteered to back it, and Merton Yewdale agreed to serve as unpaid managing editor, supervised by Dreiser, who would personally select the material. The journal would be a quarterly, sold in bookstores. Mencken, who had been thinking about starting a magazine of his own, suggested the name: *The American Quarterly*. Fliers were printed announcing its imminent advent, and an impressive editorial board recruited, including Mencken, Reedy, Lewisohn, Robert Frost, Masters, Hapgood, and Henry B. Fuller.

Among potential contributors Dreiser listed the names of several radicals, including Eugene Debs, Emma Goldman, John Reed, and "Big Bill" Haywood. Yewdale protested, pointing out that Reds in the magazine's pages would bring the postal authorities down on their neck. Wartime sedition statutes were still in effect. Indeed, Mencken offered Dreiser the satirical "Declaration of Independence in American," then withdrew it for fear of trouble with the law.

The response from other writers Dreiser hoped to bring in was tepid. Masters contributed a poem (no sacrifice, since he had a large inventory) and Randolph Bourne, who had died in the influenza pandemic of 1918, was represented by a posthumous essay. Then Yewdale resigned to take an editorial post with Harper's. Dreiser had no time or energy to devote to starting up and running a magazine, and so when he could not find a dogsbody willing to do the detail work, he abandoned the project. He was undoubtedly sincere in his efforts to advance the twin causes of serious literature and free expression in the United States. Reedy, who said he thought Dreiser might make a go of *The American Quarterly*, nevertheless was gently skeptical, pointing to the high rate of failure of such ventures, which "have more freedom than they have art and the number of people who can really appreciate either freedom or art is very thinly dissipated through the mass of the population."

Dreiser's relations with his old critical champion had been rather distant during the war, for Reedy was strongly anti-German and privately thought Mencken's Teutonic ideas were a bad influence on Dreiser. However, after Harris Merton Lyon, the young genius both men had encouraged at different times, died in 1916, Dreiser had in an obscure rite of homage devoted considerable time to assembling all of Lyon's stories for publication. He asked Reedy to write a foreword to the book (which was never published), but the latter procrastinated and finally admitted he no longer cared for Lyon's work. To Dreiser, Lyon represented a thwarted American genius, reduced to commercial hackwork and in the end killed by America's indifference to her talented. And so he grew cool toward Reedy and avoided him when he was in New York. On his part, Reedy was disturbed by Dreiser's portrayal of Lyon's mother in a sketch called "De Maupassant, Jr." He had shown it to Mrs. Lyon, who complained of its inaccuracy, blaming her jealous daughter-in-law for feeding Dreiser malicious gossip.

That sketch had appeared in Dreiser's new book, *Twelve Men,* published in April 1919. It was not the big novel his publisher was hoping for, but it was vintage Dreiser, and Mencken hailed it as "a capital piece of work." Dreiser accepted the kudos in silence; the book was, after all, a return to his earlier style and to turn-of-the-century America—as though he had at last heeded Mencken's criticisms of his avant garde stuff. And perhaps he had.

Some of the sketches in *Twelve Men* had been written as long ago as 1902 and 1903. But Dreiser reworked them considerably. The changes were more in substance than in style, however. He told Dorothy Dudley, a Bryn Mawr graduate whom he enlisted to condense the manuscript, that fine writing was a lost cause in the United States. Here, one wrote for businessmen, who didn't care about style.

The most significant changes were in his conception of the characters. For example, in a 1904 essay, "The Toil of the Laborer," he had portrayed Mike Burke, the foreman he met while working on the New York Central, as an authoritarian brute. In the later version, a story called "The Mighty Rourke," Burke becomes a stern but kindly father-figure who sacrifices his life for his men. Similarly, the brawny wrestler William Muldoon, who ran the sanitarium where Dreiser recuperated from his nervous breakdown and whom he had depicted in 1903 as a sadist, is now a more likable character, whose gruff, bullying ways mask the benevolent heart of a healer. Time had mellowed Dreiser's memories of those years, and he altered his own persona in the stories from a superior intellectual to a timid, introspective soul who learns from these rugged men that life is to be lived.

They exemplify, too, Dreiser's idea that goodness comes in unconventional guises. Most of the twelve men are the opposite of churchgoing do-gooders; their virtue is natural, uncontaminated by society. The portraits of his father-in-law, Arch White, and Charley Potter, a storefront evangelist, remnants of the Christian-Socialist phase of Dreiser's life, show them practicing the simple faith of the Sermon on the Mount and Christ's admonition to visit the afflicted and comfort the widows and orphans—the religion of deeds, not creeds.

This theory of unconventional goodness was embodied most fully in the portrait of Paul Dresser, the Broadway rounder and womanizer, who is tenderhearted and "generous to the point of self-destruction." There are contradictory aspects of Paul's character he doesn't touch on in order to highlight the sweet, naive side of the man. But the essence of that corpulent figure was packed into the sketch's thirty-four pages.

Reviews of *Twelve Men* were generally good, and a few conversions were announced—the anonymous critic of the New York *Morning Telegraph,* for example, admitted that prior to reading this book he/she had agreed whole-heartedly with Stuart Sherman's assessment of Dreiser's "barbaric natural-ism." From the liberal end of the spectrum, Burton Rascoe, in the Chicago *Tribune,* wondered aloud at what Sherman would think of this book, which roundly refuted the professor's charge that Dreiser was sex-obsessed. But a member of the younger generation observed smugly that Dreiser was "con-stantly at war with his puritanical instincts . . . in an age when others have fought free."

Critically, *Twelve Men* was a holding action until the long-awaited important novel appeared. It did not win him a wider audience. Sales through June 30 totaled 1600 copies, and only 125 more were disposed of in the rest of the year. Still, it would be one of Dreiser's most enduring books. His vision of life is expressed movingly in the last sketch, the tribute to the artist W. L. Sonntag, who died young: "We toil so much, we dream so richly, we hasten so fast and lo! the green door is opened. We are through it, and its grassy surface has sealed us forever from all which we apparently so much crave—even as, breathlessly, we are still running."

Dreiser told Mencken that "for years" he had been planning a counter-part to *Twelve Men* called *A Gallery of Women.* "God what a work! if I could do it truly—The ghosts of Puritans would rise and gibber in the streets." Actually, an editor had suggested he do a series of articles on emancipated women in December 1917. But that would require new material and more research; besides, some of the subjects he had in mind were still in his life. During the past decade he had followed the program he conceived in the early 1900s—*Jennie,* the Cowperwood trilogy, and *The "Genius."* He had virtually abandoned the third volume of the Cowperwood saga, leaving only *The Bulwark* and that elusive novel about a murderer. After the aborted effort with Molineux, he persisted. He continued to research murder trials, seeking the "right" one. In July 1916, for example, he had read the morgue clippings on the William Orpet case, which involved a young man who had murdered his former sweetheart after taking up with a new girlfriend. He clipped some stories on the 1906 trial of Chester Gillette for the murder of his pregnant sweetheart, Grace Brown. And he very probably discussed these and other cases with Edward Smith, who was planning a book on criminology that would elucidate a glandular theory of criminal behavior.

Vying, so to speak, for Dreiser's attention was *The Bulwark*. As he now envisioned it, that novel would be ironic in tone and expose the illusory nature of religion and idealism. As he wrote in the *Call:* "All truth is inherently un-Christian, for Christianity—its theory—is a delusion." But the novel was a product of his Cowperwood period; indeed, the hero, Solon Barnes, is a pallid, pious counterpart of the financier: "Solon was an idealist and as such it was his disposition to turn away from the hard cruel facts of life."

Solon's banking career coincides with late-nineteenth-century industrialization, the age of the Robber Barons. Among Dreiser's extensive notes is a chronology of milestones in the business history of that period. But Solon's austere faith condemns the conspicuous consumption of the new rich. Like his father before him, he is bound by the precepts of the Quaker Book of Discipline, which teaches prudence and frugality in business. One can feel Dreiser invidiously contrasting their stinginess with Cowperwood's lavishness and panache. He does not appear to like Solon very much; the man is a stick—almost a caricature. In later chapters he toys with making Solon a bluenose reformer. Reflecting Dreiser's own troubles with the censors, the novel seems to have evolved into an attack on the moralists. But that change warred with Dreiser's original conception of Solon as a tragic figure. It also took the story far afield.

Dreiser's great strength as a writer was his ability to present sympathetically a wide range of characters, including those with whom he disagreed—to become them and think as they did. If the vital energy of sympathy did not flow, the character lay dead on the page, and that is what happened to Solon Barnes.

His intellectual drift in these years had been away from a character like Solon who represented the problem of goodness (in the conventional, religious sense). Now he was more interested in the problem of evil in the social sense—that is, crime, murder—rather than the theological sense. In Savannah he had read Dostoevsky's *Crime and Punishment,* with its portrait of the murderer as a sinner outside the human community. Raskolnikov's crime is a pure expression of the will to power—why should the pawnbroker live when she has the money that the brilliant young student needs? But Raskolnikov had no ambitions; he was contemptuous of society's rewards. Dreiser's heroes and heroines struggled in the social web (save Cowperwood, a spider who preyed on the flies).

Not incidentally, he had around this time met Aleister Crowley, the self-proclaimed witch and devil-worshiper, who fascinated him. Dreiser later told Burton Roscoe that Crowley represented the principle of misrule, of anarchy and disorganization. For all his unconventional ways, Dreiser viewed society, at least in the abstract, as requiring organization and stability. This need for order, deriving from his rootless childhood, represented one side of his temperament; the other being his hatred of convention and his need for spontaneity and creative and erotic freedom.

Crowley, then, was the incarnation of evil, of supreme selfishness, like Dreiser's black-sheep brother, Rome, "that strange Poe-like figure in our family," he wrote in *Dawn.* "Self, self, self—he never saw anybody but himself!" Sinister and frightening when on a drunk, Rome was a perverse force in the family who strove against his mother's effort to achieve respectability and a stable home.

Eugene Witla, reflecting on his amorous drives, believes he is possessed by the devil. Freud was opening the door to another closed room of Dreiser's life—sexuality. In 1918 Edith De Long Jarmuth had introduced him to Freud's basic essay "Three Contributions to the Theory of Sex." She or Edward Smith had also introduced him to A. A. Brill, the American translator of Freud. Brill, a sociable man, enjoyed convivial evenings of beer-drinking and philosophical disputation. A prison psychiatrist, he was always willing to explain the criminal mind and had advised Smith on his book.

Dreiser later described the effect of his first reading of Freud: "At that time and even now quite every paragraph came as a revelation to me—a strong, revealing light thrown on some of the darkest problems that haunted and troubled me and my work." He likened psychiatry to a key that unlocked the mental prisons where guilty secrets were entombed.

Dreiser's studies of psychiatry were not systematic, and he resisted the idea of being analyzed. But reading Freud provided insights into his own compulsions. Indeed, at one point, he experienced the "medical student syndrome"—imagining one has all the symptoms one is reading about. He recounted his reactions to Brill, who assured him that his depressions were normal, and later informally counseled him.

Dreiser had personally experienced the tangled motives of sex, jealousy, and violence in his relationship with Estelle Kubitz. In November 1917, while they were dining at the Café New York (the pre-war Kaiserhof), they quarreled over her possessiveness and his philandering, and he delivered an ultimatum: henceforth he would come and go as he chose, sleep with her or not as he liked. She burst into tears and fled to the ladies' room. When she returned, she announced that she was going to walk out on him. Dreiser told her, "If you do I'll run a knife through you. . . . If you go and leave me here before all these people I'll kill you. They've all seen you crying." "Yes," she sobbed, "every restaurant in New York has seen that, thanks to you." Afterward they went to a movie, then returned home. Dreiser resolved that he must break with her, but they made up.

. . .

Following his introduction to Freud, Dreiser sought to describe the role of the unconscious in an unpublished article he wrote some time in 1918, titled "It." *It*, inspired by Freud's id, is a primal animating force "compelling the body to act, and act vigorously, often violently." *It* is a dynamo humming silently in the basement of the mind, "ever at work, apparently, wishing, dreaming, ceaselessly planning. And of a sudden, growing weary of wishing or Its method of procedure finally thought out, It presents you, the general organization (the body), with Its idea. You are to do thus and so. And thus you do and so you must, or suffer the tortures of inhibited desires. . . . The ego which lifts the poison to Its own lips (the machinery by which It eats), that whips from Its pocket the knife or the revolver, that defies laws, scoffs at governments, taboos, philosophies—what does It know or sense that we do not?"

He was too wedded to the physical and chemical explanation of human conduct to embrace Freud completely. In particular he was troubled by the lack of laboratory verification of the Viennese doctor's theories. As he wrote Brill in December 1918, "Just below Freudianism lie the outer clouds of pure mysticism." And so in April 1919 he asked Mencken for a letter of introduction to Jacques Loeb, the physiologist. Dreiser had read some of Loeb's books, including *The Mechanistic Conception of Life*, but now he wrote him directly at the Rockefeller Institute, reiterating his doubts about the Freudian method.

Loeb was pleased to receive the inquiry. Few literary people had any sympathy with his work "on account of the frankly materialistic or chemical conception of life expressed in my writing." As to Freud's theories, Loeb was skeptical. Freudianism was a vogue, like hypnotism, he said. Although it had some basis in fact, "the methods are so amateurish and crude that nothing permanent has or can come of it."

But Freudianism provided an "X" factor that was missing from the behaviorist equation—that locked room of psychosexual compulsions that Dreiser recognized in himself. Estelle exemplified "the tragedy of desire," of love that is not returned. The criminal case histories he discussed with Brill had "the appeal of great tragedy." He had told Mencken, "I like tragedy and am looking for a great picture to be done briefly." Murder—desire—tragedy—the elements were revolving in his mind.

On May 11, as Dreiser was crossing the street at Columbus Circle, he was struck by a car and suffered lacerations on his right hand and scalp. After receiving first aid, he was released, in considerable pain. Estelle insisted on nursing him, and he stayed with her for a time. Among his visitors were Kirah and her new friend, a husky blond engineer named Howard Scott, known in Village coffee shops as an eccentric advocate of a new economic doctrine called Technocracy. Scott had picked up some medical knowledge and performed chiropractic manipulations that relieved Dreiser's pain.

Mencken, a medical buff, dispensed sympathy and expert advice: "Let me hear what the x-ray shows. Don't let them flash it on your seeds. Ten seconds exposure will shrivel them." He prescribed bed rest, telling "Gloom," "I think all his pains are due to movements of the bruised muscles . . . if he goes west, the railroad journey will get him into the hospital. . . ."

The railroad journey Mencken referred to was a trip to Indiana. Dreiser had planned to visit May Calvert Baker and his old copy editor, John M. Maxwell. The accident delayed his departure, and then, on June 5, Edith Jarmuth, who had married Edward Smith, died suddenly of influenza. Dreiser, who had been best man at the wedding, sat with the distraught husband at the hospital and comforted him. Afterward, Smith wrote him, "I truly don't know how we might have weathered this shock without the aid of a few friends, conspicuously you and one or two others."

He could provide a unique mixture of strength and tenderness in times of illness. He was not squeamish about hospitals and illness; in 1917, when John Cowper Powys underwent a gastroenterostomy, Dreiser insisted on observing the operation and later told Powys that he had held in his hand "some important portion" of Powys's guts. The novelist John Dos Passos once spoke of an accident too terrible to look at. Dreiser couldn't understand this. He claimed he could look at anything.

On June 15, his pain nearly gone but his writing hand *hors de combat*, Dreiser boarded a Pullman for Indiana. His first stop was Huntington, where his old "mother-teacher," now nearly sixty, lived with her sister. To a reporter from the Huntington *Press,* Dreiser announced that he supported the League of Nations *if* Germany were admitted. He also called for government ownership of public utilities. Sounding more socialist than ever, he blasted the Horatio Alger myth. An ambitious lad, he said, had no more chance of becoming another Rockefeller here than he did anywhere else in the world. And he scored the Red Scare sweeping the country, charging that anyone who criticized the "monied class" was clapped into jail as a Bolshevik.

May and Dreiser next drove to Warsaw, where they picnicked with some of Theodore's classmates and May Baker's old pupils, and on the way passed Pike Lake. Something about the sight of the lake and the clusters of water lilies struck a chord of memory, for Dreiser noted them in his diary, adding, "An old ache." That night he and May sat up late under the stars, talking about his books and the old days. "Life passes so achingly," he thought as memories rushed back.

The following day they drove to Culver Military Academy, and he took May for a rowboat ride on adjacent Lake Maxinkuckee. That night he fell into bed exhausted, only to have "dreadful dreams." Was there something disturbing about those Indiana lakes that brought back old terrors and provoked nightmares? Did he remember rowing on Center Lake in Warsaw with his scapegrace brother Rome, who had rocked the boat, frightening him? He must have also recalled Warsaw's upper-crust boys and girls in white flannels and bright dresses plying the blue waters in sailboats.

While in Indiana he was thinking about a crime story he was writing, called "Her Boy." It was not based on an actual case, though Dreiser may have been recalling his brother Paul's boyhood friend in Sullivan, "Red" Bulger, who was executed at Sing Sing for a robbery-murder. The protagonist in the story had a brutal father, like Bulger's, but he grew up not in Sullivan but in the Philadelphia slums. He was no ordinary hoodlum; he had "an errant mind, subject to dreams, vanities, illusions, which had nothing to do with practical affairs"—a description that would have served for Clyde Griffiths.

The rest of the summer passed uneventfully—too much so, perhaps; he seems to have done little work. Mencken was bubbling with projects and book ideas. Dreiser could show no similar activity. His latest royalty statement listed total sales of 2700 for *Free and Other Stories*, 1086 copies of *Sister Carrie*, and 2600 of *Twelve Men*—the net effect of which was to reduce his debt to Boni & Liveright to $367.16. Mencken informed Ernest Boyd in August: "Dreiser, I hear, is in a hell of a fix financially. His 'Twelve Men' has not sold enough to keep him, and he has no other means." Mencken thought Dreiser a fool for giving up his old job and trying to live by his books. (He had forgotten that seven years ago he had assured Dreiser that he could make a good living out of the literary game.)

But he did provide concrete help, buying Dreiser's story about a prostitute, "Sanctuary," which the general magazines had found too grim or immoral. Dreiser was glad to have the sale, but complained that he was "practically giving it away."

In August Dreiser wrote Jones demanding that he "state definitely whether you will resume publication" of The "*Genius.*" Jones replied like a broken record that until Dreiser's lawyers assured him that Lane could issue the book "without making ourselves liable to prosecution" he could do nothing. As though to show him up, *The Hand of the Potter* landed in the stores in September and provoked not a peep from the antivice society. The reviews were violently for or against, with the negative side reviling the play as gloomy, clinical, repulsive, and unconvincing. Several critics were offended by Liveright's advertising copy calling the play "Stark naked and unashamed." One Dreiser-hater thought the theme of the play a fit subject for a medical treatise. As if on cue, the *New York Medical Review* praised it as a "pathological drama" of more literary than scientific worth, faulting the psychological interpretation of Berchansky but still recommending the book to "every physician or student of psychology who is interested in psychopathological conditions. . . ."

As a *cause célèbre, The Hand of the Potter* fizzled. Liveright must have been disappointed. He would turn to publishing, more profitably, straightforward erotica in "private editions" sold to a select list of subscribers, thus avoiding interference from Sumner.

In the watershed year 1919, an anti-labor, anti-radical, anti-foreigner, anti-Semitic, anti-Negro, anti-anything-not-100-percent-American mood hung over the country like mustard gas. The country was shaken by a wave of strikes and race riots. Gangs of returned doughboys performed their patriotic duty by stamping out the menace of Bolshevism in the United States. On May Day a mob of them beat up staff members of the *New York Call*, and on Armistice Day bravos from the newly formed American Legion castrated and hanged an IWW member in Centralia, Washington, after the Wobblies had fired on paraders bent on destroying their union hall.

As ever tacking against the wind, Dreiser told Berenice Sidelsky, of the Brooklyn *Eagle*, that the war had "blown religion and hard-and-fast ethics to bits." Workers should demand "complete reorganization of the economic system. . . . They can get it. They have the ballot; and if they haven't they have the bricks." Dreiser had come a long way from the executive who argued that the Butterick company's workers had no right to strike. Now he endorsed the coal miners' call for industrial democracy (though he thought the AF of L too conservative and pro-business). Authors should organize too, Dreiser said—or publish their own books.

So repressive was the national mood that even Mencken found himself reading *The Liberator* (Max Eastman's successor to *The Masses*), and he told Louis Untermeyer that he might vote for the socialist Eugene Debs in the next election. The Hollins Street freeholder hadn't converted to socialism; rather, he regarded the radicals as the enemies of his enemies. He told Untermeyer that he was giving up belles lettres because "We live, not in a literary age, but in a fiercely political age."

For Dreiser 1919 was a time of uncertainty and ambiguity in both love and work. He had long wanted a liberal publisher and now had him in Liveright. But his frustrations with *The "Genius"* and *The Bulwark* remained. He needed money; his landlord was raising his rent. Also, he was tiring of the place, now so full of Estelle's presence.

They were sinking into a kind of Bohemian domesticity. They went to restaurants and plays together, dinners at Marion's, weekends at the shore, and he found this routine dangerously close to monogamy. But when she announced a new plan "to stay away nights," he immediately suspected that she had a lover, noting, "She has so little interest in sex now." Jealousy was followed by reconciliation. "Feel very sad to think affection is always jealous and painful, in myself and everyone," he writes after a quarrel. Like the couple in "Chains," they were locked together by bonds of need and sexual desire. He had written of such a love in a poem: "And love that need is, and would love its need—"

At times she rebelled against her state and railed against the immorality of their relationship, crying out that they were both "in the gutter." That description made Dreiser furious, and another stormy scene erupted. He concludes, "Jealousy is at the base of it, a desire to impregnate me with the idea that I should stick to her." (Surely Freud would have noted the use of the word "impregnate" to describe a woman's hold over him.)

More than a year previously, after a particularly stormy period, she had threatened to leave him. The threat and subsequent reconciliation had a purgative effect on them both, and Dreiser describes his loving mood: "Amazing feeling I have for her. Almost the wildest kind of romantic love. Can't explain it. Intensely happy in her company."

Such moods were as fickle as the March weather. A month later he told Estelle that he was through. They made love, but that "phase of her is no longer of any great importance to me." Again she threatened to walk out, but he called her bluff and she backed down. He sums up his attitude toward her: "I feel sorry for her, truly, but what can you do in this world, which is so unbalanced, all running after the few successful, all ignoring the hopelessly poor or unsuccessful or defective. Life is made for the strong. There is no mercy in it for the weak—none."

In August 1919, "worried about my work & income," he summoned his "psychic control"—the genius or oversoul he believed watched over him—and asked it to send him a sign. That night he had a dream: "I was possessed of a key by the aid of which I was able to fly—much to my delight." He flew over cities and vast territories, to the admiration of all. Then he landed on a high rock, and was unable to go farther because his magical key's powers had run out. Interpreting the dream, he wondered if it meant that his "mental & literary soaring days were over."

If he had consulted Freud's book on dreams, he would have read: "The close connection of flying with the idea of birds explains how it is that in men flying dreams usually have a grossly sensual meaning, and we shall not be surprised when we hear that some dreamer or other is very proud of his powers of flight."

The dream obviously derived from his fears that he was losing his potency, and concomitantly the literary power that enabled him to soar above admiring crowds in cities. In the dream appeared "one with a key like mine who imitated me"—a generic younger rival, sexual and literary.

A month later he wrote in his diary: "This day I met Helen."

Part Four

HOLLYWOOD

1919–1922

CHAPTER 16

The Golden Girl

> We whisper & dream of New Orleans & Los Angeles &
> what the west will bring us. Such dreams. Helen wants a
> bungalow & a car & flowers and a pet lion & what not. It
> is a fairy tale come true.
>
> —Dreiser (Diary)

On Saturday, September 13, Dreiser was writing at his desk when the doorbell rang. He slipped on the Chinese robe he wore about the house—in his haste putting it on inside out, an omen of impending change. Standing shyly on the stoop was a young woman he judged to be nineteen or twenty. She told him she was a distant cousin from the western branch of the family—her grandmother, Esther Schänäb Parks, was Dreiser's aunt, whom he had never met. She asked for Ed Dreiser's address, and he gave it to her, then requested hers. His left eye—the good one—was, he felt, sending him a message, meaning he was extraordinarily attracted to her. He gave her a copy of *The Hand of the Potter*, autographed "To my little Oregon cousin."

That was the first meeting of Dreiser and Helen Patges Richardson. She was not nineteen but twenty-five, beautiful with a kind of "lympathic sensuality" that acted on him, he said, like an aphrodisiac. Her golden-brown hair hung down to her shoulders, her figure was full and shapely, and her eyes glowed with a mischievous gaiety. Not the least of her desirable qualities was her disdain for "strident, aggressive and vain youth" and preference for "age, weight, grey hairs and intelligence and force when combined in a man." Also, she liked "only good books, plays and poems," the out-of-doors, riding, driving, singing, and dancing. The sound of her voice suggested "youth, summer and happiness."

He tossed most of the night thinking about her, and the next morning called her and asked her to meet him at the Pennsylvania Roof. She agreed to come in the afternoon, and over a late breakfast they talked for hours. She showed her sympathy to his work by praising *The Hand of the Potter* and promised to read all his novels. He asked her to have dinner with him on Tuesday, but she said she couldn't. He was desolate: maybe she didn't like him after all. They walked to the subway station, where he parted from her plunged in gloom. She promised to come again on Wednesday, but he didn't believe her. He was sure he had lost her forever.

All day Wednesday he waited for her call. He was trying to revise his book of philosophy, but could not concentrate. A letter from Lill arrived, boasting of her triumph in a new show, but that merely bored him. He visited Estelle, "but my interest in her is so dead that I merely wonder how I can get away—once & for all." He was amazedly in love and recording as evidence his lack of attraction for others.

At 6:30 Helen appeared at his door. He took her in his arms and kissed her; she responded passionately, but she refused to stay with him that night. He told her that there must be a physical relationship between them; he could not be just friends. Finally she agreed to come Friday.

After their first night together, he wrote in his diary: "a new chapter in my life is opening which [may] lead anywhere. . . . My life seems torn up by the roots. Feel that I am in for a long period with her, maybe years."

The dreams and omens were right. Change had come. In the space of less than a month, he and Helen decided to go to Los Angeles, where she would try to break into the movies; he accepted an offer from Jesse Lasky, head of the Famous Players–Lasky studio and a friend of Liveright's, to write screenplays; he signed a contract with Liveright for *The Bulwark* under which he would receive an advance of $4000, to be paid in twelve monthly installments of $333.33; and he sublet his apartment to his old friend Eleanora O'Neill, now married to William McQuaid.

Lasky had bought out Mirror Films, for which Dreiser had written a few scripts. Lasky apparently hoped a writer of his stature would produce some usable scenarios, while Dreiser hoped to reap bushels of Hollywood dollars by tossing off screenplays and selling his novels to Famous Players or some other studio. A Hollywood agency had offered to represent him.

Possibly Dreiser's arrangement with Lasky precipitated the signing of *The Bulwark* contract in August. Liveright wanted the novel badly, and his lawyer had advised him that although Lane could be expected to sue, he had no contractual claim on the book that would stand up in court. For a gambler like Liveright it was worth a flutter.

And so with a stroke Dreiser cut through his publishing entanglements, and Helen, through her powerful sexual magnetism, provided the solution to his romantic ones. He couldn't have gone off with any woman, but she seemed to be All-Woman.

Born in Oregon, she was the daughter of the former Ida Parks and George Patges, a Danish immigrant who one day walked out for good, leaving his wife with two daughters to raise. When Ida's mother, Esther, sold her farm and bought a hotel in Portland, Ida and her children tagged after her; Helen was around five at the time. The hotel was frequented by vaudevillians who performed at the theater next door. There was also a local repertory theater nearby. The little girl was fascinated by the actors and longed to accompany them on their travels. She had the run of the theater, sometimes taking children's parts in the rep company's productions. By age fourteen she was performing in amateur theatricals. She had also worked in an art-supply store since she was ten. A beautiful child, she caught the eye of older men and learned to exploit them for money and presents. One old man gave her a dollar if she would let him fondle her. By the time she was a teenager, she was prematurely wise to the ways of sex and strung along a wealthy old man, who gave her presents.

When she was sixteen, she met nineteen-year-old Frank Richardson, a slender, handsome visitor from Charleston, South Carolina, who was as stagestruck as she was. They fell in love, were married, and Frank formed an act with three other young men, singing in saloons around town. With that experience he worked up a ballroom-dance routine for himself and Helen. They had a modest success, making up to ninety dollars a week playing cities in the Northwest. After bouncing around the circuit for three or four years, they decided to try San Francisco. But there the act reached the end of its run. Richardson decided to return to his family in Charleston, while Helen tried to go it alone.

After a year of struggling, Helen became discouraged and joined him. Fed up with the theater, Frank had embarked on a business career. But the marriage was on its last legs; she found southern ways too confining for her Bohemian spirit and hankered for New York. In 1918 William E. Woodward, a friend of the Richardson family and vice president in charge of public relations at the Industrial Finance Corporation, owner of the Morris Plan loan societies, visited Charleston, and Helen told him of her ambition to go to New York someday. He was attracted to her and offered to help her if she ever made the move. In 1918 she did, leaving Frank for good.

Woodward hired her as his secretary after she took a refresher course in typing and shorthand, and they had an affair.

Woodward confided in her that he was bored with business and planned to quit his job when he was fifty and write a novel. He admired Dreiser and gave Helen a copy of *Twelve Men* to read. When she told him Dreiser was her second cousin, he urged her to call on him. She naively extolled her new lover's prowess to her boss, who was not at all pleased to hear about it, and she realized it was time for her to leave.

She had saved some money toward her goal of becoming a film actress. When she revealed her dreams to Dreiser, he immediately fell in with them because of his own movie ambitions. Both of them were drawn by the golden dream of an abundant life and an Edenic climate that was luring thousands of Americans from the Middle West.

On October 8 Dreiser and Helen boarded the liner *Momus* (God of Ridicule and Censure, he noted in his diary) bound for New Orleans. Sequestered in their cabin, they told each other fairy tales of a land of perpetual sunshine, rose-trellised bungalows, fruit trees, and shiny automobiles. "We were like two children, hand in hand, united in a common bond—the love of beauty," Helen later wrote.

In New Orleans they holed up in a romantic old hotel on a picturesque square. It was there that she gained her first insight into him. There was a picture in the room showing a farm scene, and he remarked it was like one his mother had. Watching him gaze fondly at the picture, Helen realized how strong was the cord of memory that bound him to Sarah Dreiser; later she would learn how much the loss of her had instilled in him "a fear of losing anything he loved very much."

The four-day train trip to Los Angeles was an erotic fantasy come to life. "Her beauty just knocks me. It is unbelievable. . . . She looks like an angel or a classic figure & yet is sensuality to the core." The allure of her naked body was "simply maddening," her white skin was blue-veined like marble. He couldn't believe "she is as insane over me as she seems. It seems as though some one must have hypnotized her & told her that she was in love with me." He was in the perilous role of adorer and worried about it: "The constant distrust of Helens beauty & how it may make me suffer tortures me."

After continuing their idyll in Los Angeles, they rented the lower floor of a two-story house in the small town of Highland Park, set amid rolling golden hills. The area was swarming with cults. Their landlord would greet them each morning with a stentorian "PRAISE THE LORD!" Dreiser sent a jaundiced report to Mencken: "The place is full of healers, chiropractors, chiropodists, Christian Scientists, New Thoughters, Methodists, Baptists,

Ana-Baptists and movie actors. . . . This climate is 90 percent over advertised. There's not one decent restaurant & the drinking water has alkali in it. I have lost 10 pounds in weight."

His disenchantment may have been caused in part by the obstacles he was encountering. The first time he dropped in at the Lasky studio in Hollywood, he was turned away at the gate. The same day he received a telegram from Liveright saying that Jones was threatening to sue over *The Bulwark.* Liveright tactfully inquired about his progress on the novel, which had been promised for delivery on August 1.

He had put in a day or so on the manuscript, then set it aside for two months to work on photoplays. One of his first efforts was called "Lady Bountiful, Jr.," a plotty tale of a young singer who is cheated out of her inheritance by her stepfather and in the end is rescued by her real father, an opera star, who reunites her with her lover. Dreiser described it as "pure hoakum [sic]—& sweet morale [sic] optimism prepared for movie sale." He eventually tried to sell it to Mary Pickford, who expressed polite interest but no more. Another effort, "The Long, Long Trail," was one of the first of several crime scenarios he wrote, all revolving around the theme of the hunters and the hunted. In this one, the main character, who was named Giffen, is accused of a crime he didn't commit and spends years as a fugitive.

He at last gained admission into Lasky's sanctum on December 30, only to learn that all his screenplays had been rejected. It was a depressing finale for the year 1919, and his spirits were not helped by the news from New York City of the death of an acquaintance who was only four years older than he was. "Life seems so futile—a mere nothing," he sighed to his diary.

Dreiser then tried to generate some subsidiary-rights income. A New York admirer of *The Hand of the Potter* was translating it into Yiddish, with Dreiser's blessing. He dickered with Literary Productions, which was trying to interest a Broadway investor in *The Financier.* Dreiser demanded $10,000 for the rights and the guarantee of "an adequate artistic production."

To Estelle Kubitz, from whom he had parted amicably, probably not even telling her about Helen, he confided his despondency over his failure to sell anything to Lasky, and she passed the word to Mencken, who scoffed, "It would be quite easy for him to get money if he went about it shrewdly. But he is an impracticable fellow." But he sympathized with Dreiser's inability to get on with *The Bulwark;* he was an artist, not a merchant slicing cheese. Suspecting Dreiser was hard up, he invited him to contribute to the *Smart Set.*

Dreiser didn't take up the offer. He and Helen explored the hills near their rented home and made excursions to Catalina Island and San Diego. After a month of this, Dreiser wrote in his diary, "More idling with H—— which worries me—however delightful." The weather was bad, prices were too high, and the honeymoon was fading. They were discovering irritating qualities in each other. Helen had petulant streaks; she was like a child who becomes angry when real life doesn't live up to her dreams. She would throw tantrums in shops when they didn't have what she wanted.

He was liable to fits of jealous fury when he imagined she was flirting with some man or when she received letters from former male friends. She thought he was pompous and overly critical of her. Once, when she forgot to take his silk shirts to the laundry, he blew up and called her "the most infernally lazy creature I ever knew." Such outbursts would make her freeze with anger, then burst into tears, and Dreiser would console her and feel guilty afterward.

For all the minor frictions, he was crazy about her. She had an intuitive love of beauty, combined with a crass materialism; she admired a sunset and a dress in the store window with equal rapture. He liked her earthy humor and recorded her mannerisms in his diary under the heading "Babes Cute Ways." He liked her wisecracks, the way she said "Next" when coming out of the bathroom; her baby talk. She was vain, bawdy, and refined. She wore high heels wherever they went, applied makeup before going to bed, favored beribboned shortie nightgowns called teddy bears. She was the most wanton and sensual woman he had ever known; in her transports, she recited "the most coaxing and grossly enervating words. . . ." But her seductive presence distracted him from his work: "From 10 to twelve I work on mss. Two to 4:30 play with Helen. We copulate 3 times. At 5 return to work & at 7 get dinner. 9 P.M. to bed."

After several months of this, Dreiser began to experience heart pains. ("We stage an orgie [sic]—so delightful that it knocks me out. Copulation is beginning to affect my heart.") He took sulfur baths, and the treatment relieved the pains, but a doctor at the facility told him he had heart trouble. But in May another doctor, who examined him for a life insurance policy that Liveright asked him to take out, assured him that his heart and lungs were sound.

Those first months together contained moments of the keenest happiness they would ever know. Once, while walking in the hills, they came upon a group of Japanese farmers working and singing in the fields below. As they watched the figures lit by the slanting golden light of the setting sun, swaying to the immemorial rhythms of the harvest, they experienced an epiphany of joy. As Helen describes it in her autobiography, "Teddie caught by the mood of the scene, running to me and taking my hand in his, saying with a sob in his voice: 'I shall never leave you, Helen! Never!' "

Nearly twenty years later, during a bad time between them, she remembered that scene and wrote a sonnet about it, which concluded:

> "I'll never leave you," rode a far-flung sigh,
> As then your soul did wing the azure sky;
> And as I turned and saw your face alight,

And felt your hand in mine so warm and tight—
A tear—your tear—fell to eternity,
As a rare pearl is dropped into the sea,
But in my heart that tear will always be
For it was never seen by ought but me.

They were living in a private garden, seeing no one in Los Angeles; he was a fugitive, so it was no wonder he wrote screenplays about them. To all his correspondents he gave only a post office box number—"the address of a pickpocket," grumbled Mencken.

Two reasons for his furtiveness were Jug and Anna Tatum. The former was trying to collect something under their separation agreement, which had fallen into abeyance because of Dreiser's pleas of poverty. Hearing that Dreiser was under contract for *The Bulwark,* she assumed his fortunes had improved and demanded confirmation from Liveright. The publisher assured Dreiser that he hadn't discussed their "financial relations." As for Anna, Dreiser continued to fear that she would sue if he published *The Bulwark,* or else was trying to cut herself in for a share of the royalties.

Dreiser's concealment of his whereabouts was also motivated by fear of a scandal. He and Helen earnestly discussed "Society & what people would think" about their relationship, and he was heartened when she told him she was for him "once & for all—whatever happens." He was after all a married man, and Helen had not obtained a divorce from Frank Richardson, who had lately written, begging her to come back to him. He had landed in Chicago, and she heard he had made a lot of money in mysterious ways, possibly related to the Volstead Act. Apparently at Dreiser's urging, she asked him to send her some of it, but Frank pleaded poverty.

As their stay in California lengthened into months, Dreiser began observing the curious folkways of Hollywood. The movie industry was rapidly taking over the conservative little agricultural town. Land formerly planted in orchards was overrun by actors and camera crews; sets were erected under the skies and covered by canvas when an indoor lighting effect was desired. The whole town was a set, and its citizens watched as cars full of Keystone Kops careered along the streets. By 1920, large, walled studio complexes were rising up, with massive gates before which hordes of hopefuls gathered each morning for casting calls. Ever more grandiose sets were being erected, sparked by the success of D. W. Griffith's *Intolerance*.

Dreiser's first impression was that he had landed in a unique colony of anti-Puritans. In a letter to Margaret Johnson, an actress he had known in New York, he writes approvingly of Hollywood's amorality: "When I watch these men & beauties in the seething movie world where success and pleasure hold their proper place as goals, I see what a brilliant interesting thing a pagan world is. Moralistic cant & religious theory kill life."

Once, he and Helen strolled by the Beverly Hills Hotel and Douglas Fairbanks and Mary Pickford's mansion. As Helen spoke fervently of her movie career and her bungalow dreams, Dreiser cursed his financial state: *"She is too beautiful not to have a car & I resent our poverty."* A few days later, in a kind of symbolic protest, she pawned her ring and went on a shopping binge, buying two hats, a dress, a pair of shoes, and some stockings. It was, Dreiser thought, an act of "wild desperation over not having all the money she wants." As she tried on the clothes she described them in excited tones, her eyes glowing feverishly. The debauch was a psychic release from the frustration of watching the starlets in their expensive wardrobes, sailing regally around the city in large touring cars, while she and Dreiser lived in boardinghouses and ate at Boos Brothers and the Pig-'n'-Whistle Cafeteria. They were extras in a crowd scene—standees in long lines at eating places and the movie theaters.

At times he felt he was slipping into the anonymous Los Angeles mass, a mere hanger-on at the fringe of Hollywood. Boarding a trolley car, he dropped his coin, and when the conductor commanded him to step off and pick it up, he automatically did so, feeling "confused and ashamed at so easily being made to obey." This scourge of officious bureaucrats and rude waiters now found himself behaving like a timid clerk.

He grew more depressed about the paucity of money coming in and the impending cutoff of the Liveright subsidy for *The Bulwark*. Helen, who had been devoting her time to typing his screenplays, decided to launch her long-planned assault on the studios. They moved to 588 North Larchmont Street, within walking distance of Hollywood and Vine.

In early May she landed her first job as an extra. When she came home, she tactfully presented him her first paycheck—for $7.50—then regaled him with stories of how the director and the producer had flirted with her. Although she swore she rejected their overtures, it was for Dreiser an unsettling introduction to the pressure on pretty young women to be friendly with their male bosses if they wanted a job.

As Helen's absences during the day became more frequent, he sank into despondency. "Greatly wrought up in my nerves because of fruitless results of my efforts to write & impending separation from Helen owing to no money. . . . I wish so that we could stay & live here. Money helps so much." He was thinking seriously of returning to New York, where he could work. She did not want to leave, and broke into tears when he suggested it; he decided they should go in June, then changed his mind.

One day, "horribly" lonely, he conceived a story called "Bleeding Hearts," about a drab clerk who grows jealous of his beautiful wife's success in the cinema and murders her.

At other times he felt himself a has-been, and this crept into another story, called "Fulfillment." To the extent that the story is autobiographical, it shows Dreiser purging his sense of failure, symbolized by having the hero's paintings command higher prices after his death than they did in life.

Helen's next job (ironically, at Famous Players–Lasky) required her to work nights. "Helen gets in at 7 A.M.—delivered by auto. She has made a big impression," he records. She gossiped about the intrigues on the set and fending off passes and the resentment of the rival actresses and about the star, Bebe Daniels. Helen was filmed undressing behind a screen and in a Teddy bear nightgown; in another scene she danced on a table. "This sex struck country," Dreiser sniffs in his diary. The houri of his private fantasies would display her beauty on the screen before millions of strangers.

She scaled the Hollywood ladder rapidly—a week's work at $10 a day, directors asking for her by name, an increase to $12.50. In contrast, he was alone all day, futilely trying to write serious stories and screen "hoakum." His confidence ebbing, he was losing his way. He felt depressed because he could not offer her a life as exciting as she was leading on the set. He seriously wondered if she might leave him for her more exciting friends in the movie world—even as she was accusing him of growing bored with her! They were a symbiotic pair, need feeding on need.

But he grew fascinated with her career, vicariously participating in it by helping her choose a new wardrobe, suggesting the materials for three new gowns, supervising the taking of a set of glamour photographs. He admired her "youth & beauty & force & ambition" and hoarded her gossip about the movie business, amassing enough material for several articles. She held herself superior to the actresses who submitted to the directors' demands. It was all right, she told him, for a "low" type of woman to rise via the casting couch, but not a "refined" woman.

Then some money came in from the sale of two short stories to *Live Stories* for $400, and an optimistic letter from Lengel about a possible sale of the abridged version of *The "Genius"* to the same magazine for $3000. His gloom lifted temporarily.

At the center of his literary troubles was *The Bulwark.* He returned to it at the end of February, but after a few days' desultory work, he and Helen made a trip to Santa Barbara. When they came back, he was in no better frame of mind about the novel. On April 4 he writes in his diary, "I am depressed about Bulwark," and five days later he announces that he has finished reworking chapter 13, but it was "terrible hard work. No gayety of soul here." On April 22 he wrote Liveright that he was drudging on the book "with little joy and with small expectations." The small expectations part was a dig at his publisher for the poor sales of *Twelve Men,* although those had reached a fairly respectable 4000 by this time and were continuing. Liveright reminded him that it was unfair to compare a collection of short stories with a novel—speaking of which, where was *The Bulwark*?

Dreiser had promised to let Liveright see the first fifteen chapters, but he was dissatisfied with them (he refers to the finished chapter 14 as being part of the *"new version"* of the book). Yet he still hoped Lengel might be able to sell advance serial rights. Perhaps, too, he was worried about Anna Tatum's threatened suit.

He finally finished the fifteen chapters and returned to *Newspaper Days*, on which he worked with much greater confidence, as though in excavating memories of his youth he was recovering his own identity. By April 22 he had completed sixty-five chapters; by August he had done the final revisions. In May he confessed to Liveright that *The Bulwark* was delayed and offered him *Newspaper Days* instead. Liveright said he would be glad to read it, "but frankly, what I want is *The Bulwark.*"

But Dreiser was fatally blocked. In July he mentioned to Lengel that he might start another novel. A month later he wrote Mencken that *"The Bulwark* lags but should be along by Christmas or if not that—then a novel of equal force." He said nothing further about this mysterious other novel, but the evidence suggests that he began writing it in August. The first allusion to it in his diary does not occur until September 6: "In the morning Helen & I walk over the hills above Echo Park Ave. into Alessandro Street. The woman on the hill who looked like Mrs. Dreiser. . . . I work on 'An American Tragedy' till 4 P.M."

Helen wrote in *My Life with Dreiser* that the fundamentalist religious atmosphere in Highland Park "supplied the necessary climate" for starting *An American Tragedy*, which at this point he sometimes called "Mirage." The generative climate was also the Hollywood air, electric with sex, success, and money, charging Dreiser's and Helen's yearnings. Murder was, surprisingly, also in the air for one whose mind was attuned to suggestions of it. At a restaurant Dreiser frequented, The Welcome Inn, the owner was an Englishman who quarreled viciously with his wife. After seeing one of those rows, Dreiser wrote in his diary in July, "I suspect he plans to kill her." Many of the plots of his screenplays revolved around criminals who are falsely accused or who find some kind of redemption—like the heroine of "The Door of the Trap," a young woman branded a thief, who finds love with a good man after overcoming her past.

In a letter to Edward Smith, who was writing an article about him for *The Bookman*, Dreiser implicitly describes the hero of his novel: the "sensitive and seeking individual in his pitiful struggle with nature. . . . We would, all of us, like to live and be somebody in this great, indifferent cruel swirl. And only see what in the main happens to us."

A sensational murder that dominated the front pages when he arrived may have revived his interest in the novel about a murderer. Harry New, the illegitimate son of former Senator New, now postmaster general of the United States, had killed his lover. Harry had been unaware of his real father until he was a grown man. Senator New had offered to help his son, but just as this unexpected bounty came to him, Harry's sweetheart, a lower-class girl whom he did not love, told him she was pregnant and demanded that he marry her. Apparently fearing a scandal, Harry murdered her in July 1919 and immediately confessed. The elder New had previously got him out of a scrape in Denver, but this time he could do little. His son pleaded guilty to second-degree murder and served eleven years until he was released on parole.

Also influencing Dreiser's choice of a protagonist was the book he had just completed, *Newspaper Days,* in which he recalls standing on Euclid Avenue in Cleveland, gazing at the mansions and "envying the rich and wishing that I was famous or a member of a wealthy family, and that I might meet with some one of the beautiful girls I imagined I saw there and have her fall in love with me." He fantasized a beautiful, socially elect woman who would solve all his troubles. Instead, he becomes engaged to Jug.

Money was so crucial for a rootless, untrained boy without prospects; lack of it could even drive him to murder. In an editorial in *The Delineator* he wrote: "The average person, swept by unknown forces into an unknown, hardly understandable world such as this, finds himself confronted in early youth by a widening field of desire and little or no opportunity to gratify any of its various phases. . . . Only money seems to answer for most of the things which are actually worthwhile. . . ."

For such youths money was the Aladdin's lamp that procured the objects of desire. Success was the end of striving—the world Carrie conjured up as she rode past the mansions on Lake Shore Drive, catching glimpses of their gaslit interiors and imagining "that across these richly carved entrance ways where the globed and crystalled lamps shone upon paneled doors, set with stained and designed panes of glass, was neither care nor unsatisfied desire. She was perfectly certain that here was happiness."

The reacquaintanceship, as it were, with the struggles of his youth predisposed Dreiser to choose a protagonist with a similar background, making the crime a tragedy of youthful ambition and desire. He had abandoned the novel about Molineux because he could not work up empathy with a character from an upper-class background. He had tried, in "Her Boy," to tell of a slum-born criminal, but Eddie Meagher's criminal career is a product of environment—the slums—which Dreiser did not know.

He had followed so many false scents. The most recent was the Richesen case. In 1914 the Reverend Clarence Richesen had killed Avis Linnell, his pregnant lower-class sweetheart, after being called to the pastorship of a fashionable church in Boston, where he met a beautiful young woman from a good family who fell in love with him. Dreiser later said, "I planned to write this as *the* American tragedy, and I did write six chapters of it before I decided to change to Clyde Griffiths." The character of a minister was too alien to him, and his failure to bring to life the pious Solon Barnes of *The Bulwark* was fresh in his mind.

Richesen's story offered the kind of love triangle that was a motif in the cases he had collected. It always involved, he later wrote, "the young ambitious lover of some poorer girl." The fatal design was formed when "a more attractive girl with money or position appeared and he quickly discovered that he could no longer care for his first love. What produced this particular type of crime . . . was the fact that it was not always possible to drop the first girl. What usually stood in the way was pregnancy, plus the genuine affection of the girl herself for her lover, plus also her determination to hold him."

An ambitious young man kills "Miss Poor" because she stands in the way of his marrying "Miss Rich." In the tragedy of ambition, then, pregnancy becomes a snare for the romantic, inexperienced youth. He had already raised this theme in *The "Genius"* and put Angela Blue through horrible suffering, as though wreaking symbolic vengeance on her for becoming pregnant. But her death was an accident of fate; now he contemplated his hero murdering the entangling girlfriend.

After eliminating the Richesen murder—he had collected more than a dozen such cases in all—Dreiser turned to the one that he had been looking for all along: the Gillette-Brown murder. On August 13 he wrote to W. Earl Ward, district attorney of Herkimer County, New York, who had prosecuted Gillette, requesting the record of Gillette's appeal, which would include transcripts of the court proceedings. Ward was unable to furnish it, but suggested he try Gillette's lawyer, Charles D. Thomas. Dreiser did not get hold of the transcripts, since they comprised three huge volumes. The only other source would be newspaper accounts, but, as we shall see, he relied on the New York *World*'s coverage of the trial in writing his novel.

In Chester Gillette Dreiser must have seen a poor, ordinary, seeking young man with whom he instinctively identified. Another link was the fact that Gillette's parents had been Salvation Army officers. He had once told Mencken that he intended to write a story about a "street preacher," and it was no great step to imagine his protagonist's parents running a small mission. Perhaps the precipitating factor was a cinematic image that became the opening scene of the first draft and remained in the book when it was published more than five years later:

> Dusk—of a summer night.
> And the tall walls of the commercial heart of an American city of
> perhaps 400,000 inhabitants—such walls as in time may linger as a mere

fable. And up the broad street now comparatively hushed, a little band of six,—a man of about fifty, short, stout, with bushy hair protruding from under a round black felt hat, a most unimportant-looking person, who carried a small portable organ such as is customarily used by street preachers and singers. . . .

And then the description of a twelve-year-old boy named Clyde Griffiths, unwillingly trudging behind this family of street evangelists, as though ashamed of them and of the work they did and their willful poverty and inane faith that "God will provide," when He obviously hadn't, feeling the first stirrings of a desire to escape the drab piety of their lives.

Now this Clyde Griffiths bore little relation to Chester Gillette other than having the same initials. Gillette testified at his trial that he had run away from home at age fourteen and shipped out to the Hawaiian Islands. After his return, with the aid of a wealthy relative, he attended Oberlin preparatory school but dropped out and worked as a brakeman on the railroad (as had Dreiser's brother Rome). After a year or so of *wanderjahre,* in Chicago he met his uncle, N. H. Gillette, who offered him a job in the skirt factory he owned in Cortland, New York, where he met Grace (Billy) Brown. Chester said little about his parents, perhaps to shield them from notoriety, but after reporters tracked them down in Denver, they were revealed to be very religious, former Salvation Army missionaries and now too poor to help Chester.

This was the sketchy background Dreiser had to work with. Had he looked further into the story, he would have discovered that Gillette's parents were different from the ones he imagined for his novel. The father, Frank Gillette, had practical training in engineering in Spokane, where the family, particularly one of the brothers, had done well in the restaurant business. Frank had impulsively converted to evangelicism after hearing the singing at a Salvation Army mission. His wife, Louisa, followed him into the fold, and for nearly ten years the family lived the itinerant life of Salvation Army officers.

During Chester's childhood, the family moved from one town to another—as did all Salvation Army workers (the Army transferred its soldiers every six months). It was a life they had chosen. Eventually they were assigned to Hawaii. Chester apparently never went to the islands, but worked in San Francisco as a printer. Eventually Frank became ill and lost his vocation. The family returned to the States and joined the Dowie colony, a healing cult presided over by a bearded patriarch who grew progressively more grandiose. Ultimately the colony went bankrupt.

To Dreiser the precise details weren't important. What struck him was Chester's strict religious background, his seemingly ineffectual father and stronger mother, his poverty, his early wanderings, his chance meeting with the rich uncle—like a scene from a Horatio Alger novel—his ambiguous social position as a poor relation in Cortland, his affair with Billy Brown, and his involvement with a girl from a wealthy family, which drove him to murder his pregnant factory-girl sweetheart.

But there was no "Miss Rich" in the Gillette case. A young woman named Harriet Benedict, daughter of a wealthy lawyer, was called to the stand because letters to her were found in Gillette's effects. But she testified that she had had only one date with Chester, and that he went out with several girls from well-off Cortland families whom he met at various parties and church socials, while carrying on with Billy. The yellow press, taking its cue from the prosecution, blew up Harriet's role in Chester's life to that of the "other woman." From that fiction, Dreiser took his plot; if Harriet Benedict hadn't existed, it would have been necessary to invent her.

Another element in the case that intrigued Dreiser was the manner in which Gillette murdered Brown. According to the prosecution, and the jury concurred, he took her out in a boat on Big Moose Lake in the Adirondacks, struck her with a tennis racket, and pushed her overboard. This more dramatic crime had a private resonance for Dreiser—his subconscious fear of drowning that traced back to his childhood experience in a boat on the Wabash River with his black-sheep brother, Rome. His visit to Warsaw and Lake Maxinkuckee two years before with May Calvert had stirred up those old fears, as well as his sense of rejection by the town's "better" families—as a result of his sister Sylvia's illegitimate child. The water lilies he mentions in his diary were an associational link to Billy Brown, who had been picking the flowers just before she died.

In a midden of memory he discovered the shards of *An American Tragedy*. Now he must begin piecing them together.

CHAPTER 17

The Tangled Web

> I am and have been conducting an individual struggle to
> live and write and I will continue so to do as my best wits
> help me.
>
> —Dreiser to Mencken (1920)

While Dreiser worked on the *Tragedy,* Helen's career gained momentum. In September she won a small role in Metro's production of *The Four Horsemen of the Apocalypse,* starring Rudolph Valentino. She scored "a great hit" on the set. Her modest rise, fueled by extravagant hopes, made success seem almost in hand. Now she was torn between Dreiser and her career—and feeling guilty about neglecting him.

Her dependence on him emerged when he traveled to San Francisco to attend a reception in his honor given by Paul Elder, a bookseller of the city. One of the sponsors of the fete was George Douglas, literary editor of the *Chronicle,* who had planned to deliver a speech on Dreiser and attack puritanism in America. But the guest of honor wrote Douglas that he could not bear to listen to a tribute, and he told the poet George Sterling, to whom Mencken had introduced him in New York, that he preferred not to meet any of his admirers in the city, though he would be glad to talk to Sterling and perhaps a few of his friends. He even discouraged Sterling from providing him with feminine companionship, perhaps because he planned a secret rendezvous with Lillian Rosenthal, who was touring in *Hello, Alexander.*

Helen suspected he would see another woman. Only a month before, while in a restaurant with her, he had been guiltily thinking about the various women in his life and regretting "the injustice and folly of leaving one for another." Suddenly she began crying and accused him of wanting to leave her. "The rank materialist would say coincidence," he thought. "I say attuned chemisms—one highly responsive to the other." Helen recalled their mutual possessiveness, their intense desire "to become as one . . . to merge one's identity in the other. . . ."

When Dreiser found no letter awaiting him upon his arrival, he immediately assumed she was cheating on him. He berated her by telegram. In a state of hysteria she replied: YOUR TELEGRAM FINAL BLOW GOOD GOD IF YOU KNEW AGONY OF THIS LONELINESS FEAR BREAKDOWN. She followed that message with a letter, explaining she had been distraught. But he could never know how much she had suffered and she begged him to come back as soon as the reception was over. "It is so easy for you to make me suffer and would soon [sic] kill me." After receiving that missive he spent a vinous evening with Sterling and his lady friend. "Get drunk & a little wild," he reports. "We empty a hamper of rose leaves on the floor & put our heads in it. At 1:30 carried home in a taxi. [Lill] waiting. She is very cheerful. After a round—we sleep."

The bacchanal continued. "Nightly I was led to my room full to the ears," he wrote Mencken, who had sampled Sterling's bibulous hospitality that summer when he covered the Republican Party's national convention. Dreiser was enchanted by the town that Sterling called "my cool grey city of love."

Upon his return, Helen was aggressively seductive, improvising amorous fantasies of watching him "in transports with other girls" and "to get me girls & watch me manhandle them." Was Helen projecting her own masochistic or revenge fantasies? She was, he decided, "the most dangerously jealous beauty I have ever had."

He was making some progress on *An American Tragedy*. One day he took time off to visit a storefront mission, for background on Clyde's parents. He worked a bit on another project at this time, an article on Edgar Allan Poe. Even this was not completely alien to the novel. He was drawn to Poe's excursions into the terrain of horror and the irrational, his anticipation of Freud. Poe's phantasmagorical stories reflected the nightmarish aspect of modern life, a dimension, Dreiser believed, that traditional realism neglected.

In a 1921 interview he said that much contemporary realistic fiction lacked "the power of imagination." Alluding to the current celebration of the seven-hundredth anniversary of Dante's death, he said that if the Italian master were alive today, "he would have gone beyond mere realistic description and shown us the half-monstrous proportions of our city like a giant sphinx with wings. The power of such imagination would lift a modern book into glorious fantasy. . . . [Contemporary novelists] are content to examine the inside of a boarding house or chronicle the mere number of windows in the colossal stone and steel shells of our buildings. They stick close to the curbstone. They rarely climb any such heights as Dante climbed to look out over the tremendous wastes of lives."

A related influence, surely, was the cinema. He had seen *The Cabinet of Dr. Caligari* and was much taken by its expressionistic style, which suggested, in surreal backdrops and cinematography, the subconscious, or soul, as the Germans would have it, and which evoked the subjective world of madness. The film graphically dramatized the power of delusions; dream and reality intermingle and nothing is what it seems. (And in the movie there was a somnambulistic murderer—a killer without volition.)

But there was also an element of identification with Poe. Probably drawing on Mencken's essay on Puritanism, Dreiser had concluded that Poe was a martyr to the Puritans, who had "a horror of reality" and who drove him to drink and despair. Dreiser sometimes felt that he too had been hounded by the Puritans into obscurity. One of the several biographies of Poe he read while in California was Dr. John W. Robertson's *Poe: A Psychopathic Study.* He wrote John J. Newbegin, a San Francisco book dealer who had sent him a copy, that

> I accept wholly, [Robertson's] theory of morbid heredity in the case of Poe with its corollary that, "he was not always to be held responsible either for his words or acts." . . . I have always accepted with intense sympathy, Poe's own explanation:—"I have absolutely no pleasure in the stimulants in which I, sometimes, so madly indulge. It has not been in the pursuit of pleasure that I have periled life and reputation and reason. It has been a desperate attempt to escape from torturing memories."

Poe's temperament, being artistic, was too sensitive and vulnerable, Dreiser believed. He had known people "so open, emotionally, to every breath of mood and the whips and goads of life as to necessitate a refuge of some sort." Few respectable people had any conception of the mental torments these "physically denuded spirits" suffered. Drink provided Poe an escape into illusion; religion served that function for others. As he wrote to Edward Smith, who accused him of embracing Christian Science in *The "Genius,"* "Religion is a bandage for sore brains. Morality ditto. It is the same as a shell to a snail. The blistering glare of indefinable forces would destroy most, were it not for the protecting umbrella of illusion." And he added, "My next novel, which will soon be ready, will clear the air once and for all." At this point he could have meant either *The Bulwark* or *An American Tragedy*, also known as "Mirage."

. . .

The psychological motifs of those letters would find their way into the first draft of *An American Tragedy*. He writes that Clyde Griffiths was teased by other children and as a result developed "a concealed somberness or morbidity which grew directly out of the wounds inflicted upon a sensitive and decidedly responsive psyche." And a fight with another youth causes a "deep psychic wound . . . which was destined to fester and ramify in strange ways later on." Dreiser concludes with a pseudo-Freudian interpretation. The wound "by some psychic process of inversion . . . gave him a greater awe of wealth and comfort—or at least a keener perception of the protective qualities of a high social position in life."

Clyde is also troubled by sexual desires, and wonders if his sister has them too. Working for a firm of wholesale grocers (a variation on the wholesale hardware company Dreiser worked for in Chicago), he dreams of success, even if it comes "via love or favoritism or some other freak of fortune. . . ." When the family packs up to move to Denver, Clyde imagines a "Western Paradise" and "mines of silver and gold."

And Dreiser derives Clyde's family background from his own family history. The father in the novel, Asa Griffiths, resembles John Paul Dreiser Sr. as much as he does the Civil War pensioner Asa Conklin, who Dreiser says in *Dawn* was the model for the character. Like many fathers in Dreiser's novels, he is a failure; he is cut out of a family business because of his incompetence and later squanders in a foolish investment money he has inherited. Dreiser is obviously harking back to his own father's failure in the woolen business, which plunged the family into poverty.

Inevitably the narrative became bogged down in Dreiser's own history; the characters had no independent lives and no link to the murder that lay at the heart of the novel. This tragedy must show the inexorable workings of fate on character, but what Dreiser had written—as was the case with his previous stabs at the novel about a murderer—was entirely background. The plot, after some twenty chapters, had not moved Clyde out of adolescence. Dreiser seemed to have had no conception of where he was going. He needed more information on the crime and the trial, and the execution too, so that he could extricate the narrative from the bog of his own life and move it to a fictional plane. Dreiser needed reality on which to ground his fiction.

The last time he mentions working on the novel is in January 1921, although in June there is a single reference to "revising" it. Thus the twenty-one chapters Dreiser wrote were probably completed sometime between January, when the diary breaks off, and April, when it resumes. Later he sent the revised chapters to Estelle Kubitz to type.

. . .

In June, having received nothing from his author beyond fifteen chapters of *The Bulwark,* Liveright took the offensive: "Everyone is waiting for a Dreiser novel. When I tell some of the most important people in the trade that I have already received the first third of the book, they laugh and say, 'Oh, that was written several years ago; we thought Dreiser was West finishing the book.' Other people whisper in my ear that they hear through some subterranean channels that you haven't been doing anything on *The Bulwark.*"

In July Liveright revealed that Lengel and "another source" told him that "*The Bulwark* was far in the future." The publisher begged Dreiser to be frank with him; after all, $4000 was a substantial advance.

And he twisted the knife a little by mentioning that Francis Hackett, in his unfavorable review of *Hey, Rub-a-Dub-Dub!,* a collection of his philosophical essays, which had been published in January, called Dreiser "our leading novelist," implying that Dreiser should stick to his last.

If Liveright meant to shame his author, which he surely did, he was going about it the wrong way. *Hey, Rub-a-Dub-Dub!* was close to Dreiser's heart, and the reviews of it had been by no means all bad. Dreiser's philosophical effusions, while subjective, unconventional, even eccentric, expressed the temperament (in all its contradictions) behind the books. Dreiser's ideas—articulations of his bleak, mechanistic vision of the universe—were integral to his novels. Taken out of context, they seemed murky to some, bluntly offensive to the moralistic, banal to sophisticates. Mencken roasted the book in *Smart Set,* as he had warned Dreiser he would do. He explained to Dreiser, "I could have done that book much better myself, whereas I couldn't have done a single chapter of *Twelve Men* or *Sister Carrie.*"

Liveright continued his hectoring. "You are keeping your public waiting entirely too long," he said. "Everyone is clamoring for a novel from you and what they get instead is short stories, essays, plays or whatnot." Dreiser countered by accusing Liveright of not promoting his books, and he informed Mencken, "Quietly and under cover I am negotiating a return to Harper and Brothers."

Unaware of Dreiser's maneuvers, Liveright appealed to Dreiser's vanity: "We simply must not let Sinclair Lewis, Floyd Dell, Sherwood Anderson, etc. do all the writing of the 'great American novel.' "

This tactic succeeded in drawing from Dreiser a confession that he was unable to finish *The Bulwark* and had begun another novel, about which he would have nothing further to say until it was completed. As for those writers who were threatening his preeminence: "The truth is, as you ought to know by now, that my love is for the work itself and after that I would like to see it sold so that I might get a little something out of it. Beyond that little interests me, not even the arrival of a thousand geniuses. They do not help me to write my books and they do not stop me. As I say I do the very best I can."

Dreiser was aware of the recent success of Sinclair Lewis's *Main Street*, nearly 300,000 copies sold in 1921, praised and damned throughout the land. He apparently had not read the book, but he rarely had a good word to say for it (calling it a "catch novel"). This was not merely envy of Lewis's success; he was jealous of the other's succeeding so well with the realistic novel he felt he had fought and bled for, with little financial balm for his wounds.

When Liveright heard that Dreiser was dickering with other publishers over *Newspaper Days*—or rather *A Novel About Myself*, as Dreiser was now calling the book—his patience ran out, and he dispatched a telegram: PLEASE ASK LENGEL OR MENCKEN TO SEND ME IMMEDIATELY MANU-SCRIPT NOVEL ABOUT MYSELF FOR SPRING PUBLICATION. WIRE AN-SWER.

He followed that with an angry missive, one of the few he wrote Dreiser, reproaching him for remarks about his friend T. R. Smith, managing editor of the *Century* magazine, who would soon join B & L.

Dreiser drafted a tortuous reply to Liveright's telegram. Because of Liveright's harping on *The Bulwark*, Dreiser said, he had assumed he was not interested in *Newspaper Days*. He criticized his publisher's "insane" idea that he had been shirking on *The Bulwark*. He had written the nonfiction book as "a pledge" to Liveright, to enable him to recoup the money he had advanced on the novel. He said that Harper's had offered him $2000 for *Newspaper Days*, but he had no objection to Liveright as a publisher: "Where you are really interested you seem to do a great deal. The only thing for an author to do though is to get your real interest or move. For more reasons than one I always feel that I am entitled to considerable interest and aid, because . . . my public connection with a house is of great value to it."

As ever, Liveright backed down. He wired Dreiser an offer of $1000 for *Newspaper Days*. It might not be as good as Harper's tender, he explained, but "after all you know that an advance is really more or less in the nature of an evidence of good faith." The ideal plan would be to publish *Newspaper Days* in the spring and the new novel in the fall. Naturally he would not regard the latter as a substitute for *The Bulwark*, but would advance an amount commensurate with what it was worth.

The bid of $2000 that Dreiser mentioned was a fantasy. Yewdale had simply asked to see the manuscript. On January 4, 1921, William H. Briggs, editor-in-chief of the firm, wrote Dreiser that he thought *Newspaper Days* a "splendid work"; however, Dreiser's proposal that Harper's issue all four volumes of his projected autobiography was out of the question. "The present is not the time to announce and to begin the publication of a three or four volume autobiographical work. It is the time for a fine big piece of creative imaginative fiction by Theodore Dreiser." Now, if he would only send them a novel, one that was not contracted to another house and preferably "one with some commercial possibilities," then Harper's would be willing to talk about publishing the four volumes of the autobiography.

Mencken blamed Dreiser's publishing tangles on his willingness to accept advances. He contended that "advance royalties benefit the publisher vastly more than they benefit the author. . . ." Once Dreiser took an advance, the publisher gained a hold over him, and "you are bound to quarrel with such a fellow soon or late, and when the quarrel comes his advances give him a chance to knock you in the head." Witness, Jones.

Advances weren't the cause of Dreiser's problems; it was his inability to finish the books contracted for. He was not defrauding publishers; *The Bulwark* had been seriously conceived and he had done considerable research and writing on it before running into a psychological block. And the dispute over *The "Genius"* had put him deeper into the hole. What he needed was a publisher whom he could trust, who would fight the censors, and who was willing to wait five years for a Dreiser novel. Actually, in Liveright, he had such a paragon, though neither of them knew it.

He could be pardoned for being disheartened by the poor commercial prospects of a serious writer in America. He told Edward Smith, preparing his profile for *The Bookman*, "I can safely [say] *all* who have attempted liberal and artistic writing in the best sense in America have failed, not of artistic achievement in the main but of public recognition and support." To write a book that criticized the American businessman, or father or mother or family, ensured unpopularity: "the writer of a serious interpretation of America is more or less a scoundrel, a low fellow. I hope I have the honor to be one."

Liveright continued to plead: "My confidence in you doesn't waver. Why does yours in me?" But the *Tragedy* was stalled. On March 31 Dreiser had wired his publisher: DEVOTING ENTIRE TIME TO NOVEL NOT THE BUL-WARK WHICH SHOULD BE DONE ABOUT AUGUST 1. Perhaps he still had hopes for *An American Tragedy,* but there was no sign that he was working on it. Indeed, a month and a half after his letter, he announces in his diary that he has begun a novel called *Mea Culpa.* Judging from the surviving manuscript, and making allowances for a first draft, it was an unbelievably bad effort. Dreiser's chief problem seems to have been in his hero, whom he wants to show as both a rich idler and a parvenu.

He spoke confidently to Briggs and Liveright of the first volume of his autobiography—*Dawn*—being almost ready. But it lay untouched in his files. In February he had asked Louise Campbell to dig out the manuscript to see if the family references could be toned down to eliminate objections from that quarter. Then he urged his agents in New York to devote all their efforts to selling serial rights to *A Novel About Myself*. He claimed to Mencken that Lengel had, contrary to his orders, sent the entire manuscript to Harcourt and to the *Metropolitan,* and both were so offended by certain passages he hadn't intended them to see that they refused to consider excerpts. (Actually, Lengel had told him he was doing this and Dreiser didn't object.) Eventually Lengel took the manuscript, carved out five chapters, and sold them to the *Bookman* at $500 each.

Liveright heard about none of this and was patiently waiting for Dreiser's go-ahead on *A Novel About Myself.* In October Liveright observed that there seemed to be a "mix-up" regarding that book. "As I understand my position with you . . ." he wrote confusedly. He wasn't sure if Dreiser had accepted his offer months ago of $1000 for *A Novel About Myself.* At one point he wailed, "It's almost humiliating to be forced to wire you time and again regarding whether there's to be one of your books on the fall list."

Thus, after nearly a year's correspondence, Liveright and Dreiser were no further along than when they started; nor had Dreiser found another publisher. Nor had he progressed on his novel. Nor had his screenwriting career advanced a fraction of an inch. Lasky and others had rejected all the scenarios he wrote, causing him to mutter darkly to Estelle Kubitz of a "plot" against him at the studio.

He took his revenge on Hollywood by writing a gossipy, three-part series called "Hollywood: Its Morals and Manners," which ran in late 1921 in a film magazine called *Shadowland.* Apparently movie executives were shocked by the series, which appeared not long after the Fatty Arbuckle scandal hit the front pages. Dreiser had excised from the piece some gossip about the case, in which the rotund comedian had been charged with raping and fatally injuring a starlet during an orgy in a San Francisco hotel. Three juries failed to indict Arbuckle, but he was barred from the movies for life, and Will Hays, a Republican politician, was brought in as "czar" to clean up the movies. The effect on Dreiser of all this was to make novels like *Sister Carrie,* with its heroine who goes unpunished for her sins, and *The Financier,* with its immoralist hero, unfilmable.

A more direct repercussion from the *Shadowland* article was that *Photo-dramatist,* which had solicited a similar piece from him, backed out. The editor, Ted Le Berthon, apologized, explaining that the studios would put him out of business if he ran an article by Dreiser. The majority of the movie magnates, Dreiser replied, "are muddle-brained braggarts or fat lechers, or both, and all they know is the commercial,—not the artistic or creative side" of filmmaking. As for Le Berthon's praise of Dreiser's courage and honesty, "my personal sincerity . . . is deliberate and merits neither compliment nor sympathy. It has cost me much more than the average person would imagine . . . yet I have had the satisfaction of facing the facts of life as they show themselves to me and for this I would not accept all the cash lost though it were accompanied by compliments and genuflections."

Up to that point Dreiser had envied the movies their sexual frankness, and a producer had even been interested in filming *The Hand of the Potter*, though that project fell through. But in November came the news that the avant garde Provincetown Players wanted to stage the tragedy. George Cram Cook, the director, dickered with Dreiser over the guarantee, with the latter demanding $500 and Cook pointing out that in the small theater the maximum weekly gross was only $1400. They compromised on a lower figure, and the play quickly went into rehearsal.

Opening night was December 5. In their notices the next day the critics from the major dailies were divided on which was worse—the production or the play. The headline over the *Herald*'s review read PROVINCETOWN PLAYERS IN REPULSIVE PLAY. The *World*'s tag was "A Misuse of the Theatre" and its critic's verdict was that the play was "conspicuously offensive." Most of the major papers did not send their top reviewers, and the notices that appeared were brief and dismissive.

According to Edward Smith, one of the platoon of scouts Dreiser had mobilized for the occasion, the opening night performance had gone very badly. The actors were amateurish. The curtain stuck in the third act, and when it was wrenched free it upset a spotlight and some pieces of furniture. As a final touch the house cat began wailing, then leaped onstage and made her exit to resounding laughter. In a subsequent letter Smith said that perhaps he had been a little harsh; still, the play was better than the performance it received.

Edna Kenton toted up the plus and minus reviews: the dailies were all scathing, but the Brooklyn *Eagle* was generally favorable. Lewisohn, in *The Nation*, Karsner, in the *Call*, and Abraham Cahan, in the *Forward*, were predictably positive, as was the *Jewish Tribune*. Kenton bravely concluded, "with only three brief weeks to its credit in a theater that seats say 200 and with no advertising the play is really the talk of intelligent New York,— even of those who did not hear of it in time to see it."

And so *The Hand of the Potter* faded into theatrical history, one of the most controversial plays to appear in the decade. Clumsy as it was, Dreiser's tragedy had stretched the moral boundaries of the theater in a healthy way. It deserves a place on the honor roll of plays that are historic events, if not monuments of dramatic art.

In January Dreiser wrote in his diary: "Am wishing for money & success in my work." He sat in a dark room and meditated, "trying *to repeat Experiment of 1909.*" He meant 1919, when he had asked his control—the genius or guiding spirit that he speaks of only in his diaries—to send him a sign, and dreamed of flying. This time the message was, "Help will come." But it didn't.

He missed the energy and intellectual stimulus of New York. "There is no art in Los Angeles and Hollywood," he complained to an interviewer. "And never will be."

Even the financial insecurity that chronically plagued him was absent, despite his unproductiveness. Helen's movie earnings enabled them to achieve their original dream of buying a little bungalow. Both had tired of the gypsy life they were leading—they had lived in six different places since they had arrived. Driving through Glendale one evening, they spotted a white cottage with green shutters on a small plot of land with a vacant lot next door. They decided to buy it. The price was $4500, and they paid $1000 down and $50 a month on a mortgage, which was cheaper than their rent at their previous residence, a tiny brown stucco house in Hollywood.

Dreiser settled in comfortably. He wrote in the mornings and early afternoons in the tiny breakfast nook, stacks of manuscripts overflowing the table. After he had finished, he watered the zinnias he had planted, fed the chickens they were keeping in the backyard (which he could not bear to kill), and watched a resident horned toad he had befriended. He bestowed such loving care on his flowers that the neighbors would come over to admire them and ask for horticultural advice. The picture of him gardening late in the day when she came home from the studio would be etched in Helen's memory. It seemed to her that "his mother's temperament was expressing itself through him, for so much of the time he was like a big warm grandmother. . . ."

For a while Helen's sister Myrtle and her boyfriend, Grell, were their constant companions. Grell conveyed the four of them around in his automobile on weekends. The young couple livened up Dreiser's cloistered existence, and he unconsciously absorbed their slangy banter, their fascination with cars and clothes, and their tastes in popular songs. No longer did he play gloomy Slavic symphonies on the Victrola; now it was "Whispering," "Avalon," and "Cherie" (which Lill had written).

Myrtle was materialistic, something of a tease. She had dreams of Hollywood affluence like Helen's, but lacked her beauty. Grell went into debt to buy her the fashionable raiment she craved. After smashing up his car, he bought a new Hudson to impress her, giving a note for the down payment. This stretched him beyond the limit, his creditors began to close in on him, and he fled without saying goodbye. To support herself Myrtle took a job as an elevator starter in a downtown department store and moved in with them, an arrangement Dreiser tolerated, for Helen needed her sister's company.

Their only socializing took place on visits to San Francisco, where they had a small circle of literary and artistic friends whom Dreiser could visit while retaining his privacy in Glendale. There was Sterling; George Douglas and his wife, Mollie; Henry von Sabern, the German-born sculptor and his wife, a dancer; Newbegin, the bookseller; and others. On one occasion the Powys brothers—John Cowper and Llewelyn, who had recently immigrated after living in Africa for a time—were in the city. Llewelyn later raved to Dreiser about Helen: "how divine, how lovely. God! what a rascal you are to have discovered anybody so wonderful. Think of it living there in retirement in Los Angeles with so exquisite a companion."

Helen came down with severe stomach pains while in San Francisco, and on the strength of testimonials by Sterling and Llewelyn (who had tuberculosis), she and Dreiser consulted Dr. Albert Abrams, a well-known quack. The piercing-eyed, bearded physician was brisk and authoritative; after analyzing their blood he informed Helen that she had a sarcoma and Dreiser that he harbored tuberculosis. Helen says she didn't believe the diagnosis, though she continued to experience what Dreiser calls "cancer pains" in his diary. Her pains were probably chronic gastritis related to stress.

Helen's indisposition deeply worried him, but rather than urging her to go to a doctor, he encouraged her to take the Abrams treatment from a Los Angeles disciple, apparently hoping for a miracle cure. When the pains persisted, he ordered the man to administer longer doses of electricity from Dr. Abrams' patented "oscilloclast" and wrote in his diary: "Get a little frightened of what I would do in case she died." At this point in his life he would have found it difficult to function without his "Golden Girl," as he called her. Whenever she was away he felt at a loss and wrote her long letters.

With her it was the same. On the eve of her birthday, when they were lying in bed together, she cried, "Hold me, Teddie. We have such a little time on earth and we will never have each other any more in any other world forever."

Meanwhile, back East, further complications reared up that made Dreiser regret his isolation from the publishing center. Edward H. Dodd, head of Dodd, Mead, which had recently purchased John Lane's American branch, told Dreiser's lawyer, Arthur Carter Hume, a friend, that he was interested in clearing up Dreiser's debts and becoming his next publisher. In March Hume and Mencken conferred with Dodd, and Mencken dispatched a favorable report of the session. Dodd, he said, wanted *The Bulwark* if Dreiser could get Liveright to release it, and stood ready to publish *The "Genius"* with a few cuts to make it acceptable to Sumner.

Dreiser recalled Ben Dodge's characterization of Dodd, Mead as "pious Presbys" and told Mencken, "The Dodd people . . . approach me about as a Baptist snouts a pervert. . . . They do not want *The 'Genius'* unless it is properly pruned around the vitals."

Mencken assured him that the Puritans were on the run; why, even Doubleday would print *Sister Carrie* today, and Briggs had recently declared that Harper's would be glad to have *The Titan* back on its list. If Dreiser weren't so obsessed with preserving every precious word of *The "Genius,"* Mencken could get it past Sumner with a few, hardly noticeable deletions. He volunteered to negotiate with the antivice crusader—on the condition that Dreiser approved and would not back out later. Dreiser told him to go ahead, but insisted he make only the minimum number of cuts necessary to placate Sumner. Mencken promised that if Sumner's demands were too extreme, he would instantly adjourn the meeting.

But Dreiser continued to have doubts and proposed that Hume test Dodd's liberalism by showing him one of the "more daring and honest" of the sketches on women he was writing. Since he also wanted the firm to undertake the three volumes of *A History of Myself,* which contained frank material, the reaction to the sketch would tell Dreiser whether Dodd would want to publish the autobiographies. He chose one called "Olive Brand," a fictionalized version of the life of Edith Jarmuth.

In May Dodd wrote Hume that although he found nothing objectionable about the story "on the sex side" and would be willing to publish a collection of the woman sketches, he doubted that such a book would be profitable. In a subsequent letter Dodd let it be known that he was really interested in *The Bulwark* or another novel of equal stature. Dreiser asked Dodd if publishing *The "Genius"* would be tied to his turning in *The Bulwark.* Lane, he said, "succeeded in putting me very much out of the mood for [*The Bulwark*] and I have never been able to complete it," though he would in time. Dodd wanted *The Bulwark,* but if Dreiser had anything else as good he would take it.

Liveright reluctantly agreed to cancel *The Bulwark* contract and take *A Novel About Myself* as a replacement. But he too had designs on *The "Genius,"* and had independently spoken to Sumner and secured from him a list of the cuts demanded, which Dreiser forwarded to Mencken, asking him if the number could be reduced. Mencken thought it could and made an appointment with the antivice lord for May 31, telling Estelle he was not looking forward to the session: "It will be a hard sweat and in the end the Hollywood Fornicator will accuse me of swindling him."

Mencken persuaded Sumner to abandon perhaps four-fifths of his original demands and to acquiesce in "reasonable" cuts, a list of which he appended. Dreiser was willing to accept many of the trims, but some he found impossible to stomach—with reason. For example, Sumner had insisted that all of page 534 be lopped off—actually a few paragraphs ending a chapter. The compromise Mencken wrested from him called for cutting the part implying that Suzanne experienced physical desire. The language is elliptical to say the least: "Were there ever thoughts and feelings like these in so young a body? . . . She was like the budding woods in spring, like little white and blueflowers growing." The other compromises were along those lines: where Sumner had wanted to excise an entire page, Mencken succeeded in limiting the damage to a specific passage.

Dreiser also objected to expurgating Angela's debate with herself over whether or not she should have a child to tie Eugene to her. That meditation, Dreiser pointed out, was essential to the plot, since her decision to bear a child leads to her death. If Mencken could save that particular passage, Dreiser said, he would allow Dodd to reissue the expurgated version with blank spaces where the cuts had been made. Subsequently, Mencken reported that Sumner had agreed to restore the section about Angela's decision to have a child.

Dreiser swallowed his qualms, thanked Mencken profusely, and admitted that any chance *The "Genius"* had of selling "was done for long ago." And so there the matter rested. In August Mencken sailed for Europe, but after Dreiser's June 24 letter correspondence between them temporarily ceased—a possible sign that Dreiser was unhappy. Furthermore, Dreiser did not give Dodd his approval of the expurgated version; indeed, the publisher heard not a word from him.

Meanwhile, Liveright had at last received the manuscript of the elusive *A Novel About Myself*—a title, he informed Dreiser, no one at the house liked. Dreiser really preferred *Newspaper Days*, but Liveright and his editors decided on *A Book About Myself*, which was the worst of the lot.

With the tensions over *The Bulwark* dissipated, Dreiser and Liveright worked smoothly on this book. The publisher edited it himself and was "tickled to death" that Dreiser approved of his surgery (with some exceptions). There were no expensive changes in the page proofs, and the book appeared in December on schedule.

Dreiser's original handwritten manuscript, which he and Estelle Kubitz cut down, was full of scenes and language that would have brought Sumner and his minions swarming to the doors of Boni & Liveright; for example, a description of one of his landlady's "passionate transports" and "brief blazing orgasms."

What remained was a compelling narrative. The critic H. W. Boynton, one of the Greenwich Village literary radicals, was correct in saying that the book, like Hamlin Garland's *Son of the Middle Border*, "ought to be read as a novel. . . ." The little-magazine editor Edwin Seaver heard echoes of the 1890s and "that mad scramble for success, to get somewhere in the world, which made America spread from coast to coast in so short a span of years." Whereas Garland in his confession recounted the disillusionments that dogged his family's pursuit of the pioneers' dream, Dreiser created the figure of an untrained young man drunk on the exhortations of Horatio Alger and Samuel Smiles, going east to make his fortune as a journalist. In city rooms along the way he learns that life is a stinking, cutthroat game. He sees the jarring contrasts of wealth and poverty of a country in the "furnace stage" of industrialization where the "big brains" exploit the workers. The book ends with Theodore in New York, without a job after quitting the New York *World,* worrying about his future.

"Before we realized it the summer of 1922 had almost passed," Helen recalls in her autobiography. "Teddy was becoming noticeably restless. . . ." Actually he had been growing restless long ago, and his various chaotic negotiations had emphasized to him the extent to which he had become a literary exile. Mencken urged him at every opportunity to come home, writing, for example: "How long are you going to stay out there among those swamis, actors, tourists, and whores? Why not move back to Christendom, and give connoisseurs a chance to look at you? . . . you are so damned securely buried that thousands of boobs are growing up who have never heard of you."

Dreiser replied: "So you would like to see me back in New York . . . I wish I were, to tell you the honest, God's truth. And I expect to be, one of these hours." For more than a year he had been dropping hints to friends that he might return. Estelle Kubitz had earlier written Dreiser a scathing letter telling him he was wasting his talent—that he should come east forthwith and finish *The Bulwark* and *An American Tragedy.*

But he was reluctant to leave California's balmy climate, and Helen had her career. Also, his apartment building in New York had been sold, and he would have to find a new place to live. There was a serious housing shortage in the city, and he was worried about high rents. Money would be a problem without Helen's income. She had recently invested some of her savings in real estate, and they had bought a lot in Montrose with the idea of building a house on it.

With his writing career in the doldrums, seemingly stalled on *An American Tragedy,* unable to finish other projects, he spent much of the year in search of a quick financial return. He even considered going back to article writing, and forwarded some ideas to Lengel at *Hearst's International.* Fearing he had acquired a reputation of being too gloomy for general magazines, he told Lengel: "In the matter of novels and plays I am a natural born tragedian of the silk hat and husky voice variety. When it comes to articles I lug in no tragedy. I have written tons of them. . . . I could take any given condition, anywhere, investigate it and write an intelligent account of what was going on and why."

Nothing came of that rather sad effort to revive his career as a magazinist (which he had abandoned twenty years earlier, save for occasional reviews and "think pieces"). He spent several months adapting *The "Genius"* for the actor Leo Ditrichstein. It was an onerous task, but he managed to finish a draft in May, at which time Ditrichstein came to the Coast. They were supposed to rework his draft, but they quarreled over financial terms and the project was abandoned.

Then in September a letter arrived from Ray Long at Hearst, rejecting four "Gallery of Women" sketches. It was a painful blow, since Long had contracted for six of them for *Cosmopolitan.* The entry in Dreiser's diary that day reads: "Bad news from Cosmo agent anent sketches. . . . Personally feel very depressed and soon go to bed. At the moment see no very clear way out of money troubles or that I am making any real artistic headway with work. The relentless push against the individual on and away into dissolution hangs heavy on me."

"The days go by like a dream," he had written in his diary. Now it was time to return to New York and reality. He could not work in California; life was too easy. Around this time he told a Los Angeles reporter, "I want to be back where there is struggle. . . . I like to wander around the quarters of New York where the toilers are. . . . I don't care about idlers or tourists, or the humdrum, or artistic pretenders that flock out here, or the rich who tell you—and that is all they have to tell—how they did it. They would have interested me when they were struggling."

More practically, he knew he must do further research on the Gillette-Brown murder—pore over detailed reports of the trial and visit the scenes of the crime and the trial. But he would need an advance to live on, and so it was time to huddle with Liveright and possibly show him the twenty-one chapters he had completed, and talk about other books, including *The "Genius"* and the woman sketches (which he had described as a book that would "rub Sumner the wrong way"), and untangle his publishing affairs.

Helen was reluctant to go, but realized that the move was inevitable. Dreiser later said she gave up a promising movie career, but it is doubtful that she would have gone much further than bit parts. Then too, she feared that Teddie would find someone else in the East. On his part, he had given her three years of fidelity—a long time. Although he still regarded her as the most beautiful woman he had ever known, he missed the romantic tensions of his former life in New York.

Helen may have feared as much, but she says she did not hesitate about choosing to go with Dreiser: "I longed to develop spiritually, mentally and artistically. Where, I thought, could I do this better than at the side of so great a man as Dreiser?"

Part Five

TRAGEDY

AND TRIUMPH

1923–1926

CHAPTER **18**   *Scenes of the Crime*

> And what did you do after coming back to South Bay?
>
> We went up toward the east end of the bay again to get some lilies. We rowed around for a short time and we talked . . . about what we were going to do. We talked about how we were going to meet the condition which confronted us. . . . We were talking this way when she sprang up suddenly on the side of the boat and it tipped over. . . . As she went into the water I grabbed for her, but I was not quick enough.
>
> —Chester Gillette on the witness stand (1906)

Helen and Theodore arrived in New York in late October. After two weeks' search they found an apartment in Greenwich Village at 16 St. Luke's Place.

After living so long in California, New York struck Dreiser as "immense, congested, smoky . . . smeared over by millions of insignificant people. I never saw such a change in a city." The frantic commercial pace, the building boom that was throwing up new skyscrapers that fragmented the skyline, the febrile flush of prosperity on Wall Street—all seemed a change for the worse. The "old vivid searching idealism has gone," he told Margaret Johnson. He blamed the decline on "Too many unidealistic Jews." He confided to Mencken, who had just returned from a trip abroad, that he might head for Chicago.

Mencken's spies in New York had reported that an unexpurgated issue of *The "Genius"* was in the works, and he politely asked Dreiser, Was it true? If so, he must notify Sumner, who "acted very decently and I don't want him to think that I was stringing him."

It was true. Liveright was more eager than ever to challenge Sumner and publish *The "Genius"* without the cuts Mencken had so laboriously negotiated. The main obstacle was Dodd, Mead, which claimed the sanitized version by right of succession to John Lane's American branch. Dreiser confessed that an uncensored edition was indeed a distinct possibility, but said if that fell through he would let Dodd, Mead issue the pruned version.

But Edward Dodd wanted none of second best. He wrote Arthur Carter Hume, who had been acting as intermediary in the negotiations, "He must not get the idea that . . . he is free to go on with *The 'Genius'* with another publisher." He had offered Dreiser a contract for it and *The Bulwark* or another novel, but Dreiser had not replied while in California, probably waiting to see what kind of deal he could make with Liveright, who for all his faults was a liberal publisher.

Once in New York, Dreiser sent Dodd an intemperate letter on Boni & Liveright stationery demanding that he publish an unexpurgated edition or nothing; he had forty-eight hours to answer. The ultimatum angered Dodd, who decided to rid himself of the vacillating Dreiser in return for suitable compensation.

The bargaining with Liveright went smoothly, probably because the publisher gave Dreiser just about everything he wanted: a drawing account of $4000 a year, paid in monthly installments, through 1927; Liveright to secure the copyrights and plates of all his books formerly owned by Lane and those now owned by Harper; in January 1927, B & L to publish a collected set of all of Dreiser's titles in a limited edition of 1000 copies, guaranteeing the author a minimum of $10,000 in royalties; the house to take a five-year lease on Dreiser's books and pay him a 20 percent royalty on all save *The "Genius,"* on which he would receive 50 cents a copy.

Thus Liveright had *The "Genius"* and Dreiser's backlist as security for money he would advance on future books. There was, of course, no guarantee that the old books would sell, but Liveright was willing to take a chance.

In return, Dreiser promised to deliver two new books a year, through the spring of 1926. Those included titles already finished or nearly so: *A Gallery of Women*, Volumes I and III of *The History of Myself* (Volume II, *A Book About Myself*, aka *Newspaper Days*, having already been published), *The Color of a Great City*, a volume of poems called *Moods*, and a collection of short stories. But he also pledged two new novels: the prizes, Liveright really thought; he had small commercial hopes for the other books. No specific deadlines were set for the novels, but if Dreiser did not deliver, the advances would be deducted from royalties on the other books and the guarantee for the complete set. *The "Genius"* would be published first, in spring 1923, assuming all was quiet on the censorship front.

For Liveright the arrangement entailed a sizable capital outlay. To acquire the rights to Dreiser's books at Dodd, Mead and Harper he gave cash notes for nearly $5000. But B & L was on its way to becoming the hottest publishing house of the 1920s. Liveright and the gifted staff he had assembled, led by T. R. Smith, had a knack for discovering bestselling authors in the unlikeliest places.

Liveright's biggest bet was on Dreiser. The contract was signed on February 7, and Dreiser's fortunes were changing. In January Lengel sold the serialized version of *The "Genius"* to *Metropolitan Magazine*. That, of course, was not the Mencken-expurgated version; it was a condensation, of about 100,000 words, to run in three installments. Dreiser netted $2700 from this transaction, and suddenly he was relatively prosperous. Later he sold two of the woman sketches—"Reina," a portrait of Helen's sister Myrtle (who would also appear in *An American Tragedy* as the mercenary Hortense), and "Ida Hauchowout" to the *Century*, and resold, as it were, "St. Columba and the River," the story on which *The Saturday Evening Post* had reneged, to *Pictorial Review* for $800. And Helen had sold two Montrose lots at a $1000 profit.

By then they were quarreling. They had hardly settled in when Helen began overhearing telephone conversations between Dreiser and people she did not know who belonged to a world of which she was not a part. Like Kirah and Estelle, she resented being segregated from his friends. The engagements were mostly with male acquaintances, but there was a Mrs. Howey with whom he said he was discussing the Russian theater. The painful exclusion drove home to Helen the precariousness of her position. Insecure and fiercely jealous, she realized that she was losing the hold over him she had in California when they were cut off from his world back east.

At last she rebelled, announcing that she would find a place of her own. This thrust hit Dreiser in his weak point, his fear of abandonment. The "mother-boy" inside him cried out. "Helen packing. We discuss this move. I do not want her to go. The pathos of it." The next day: "Helen begins to pack & then I realize that actually she is leaving. The sinking sensation in the pit of my stomach. The sense of loss. I can hardly believe that she is going. . . ." He went out for a luncheon engagement, but could think only of her. "What will the future be like now. So they slip away from me, one by one, & periods close . . . forever."

But she could not stay away for long; his pleas and promises brought her back. After an intensely passionate reunion, Helen returned to 16 St. Luke's, at least part time, and took singing lessons as a substitute for her abandoned career. They attended the theater and made excursions to Newark and Asbury Park on the Jersey Shore, where Dreiser was seized by nostalgia for his earlier great loves—Jug, Kirah, Estelle. Each affair had ended, closing an epoch of his life, never to be reopened, reminding him of the inexorable passage of time. He simply could not write finis to Helen, whom he still loved, but neither could he break with all those other women, past present and future.

While passing through this turmoil with Helen, Dreiser found more public distractions. Early in the spring of 1923, the antivice crusaders were astir. Sumner had formed an alliance with New York Supreme Court Justice John Ford to lobby for passage of the Clean Books Bill in the State Legislature. The measure was designed to negate every defense or legal argument raised by defendants in obscenity cases in the past decade.

Some had successfully argued that the legal definition of obscenity was unconstitutionally vague, so the Clean Books Bill defined obscenity by saying the word should be taken in its "generally accepted meaning." Others had called critics and scholars to attest to the artistic integrity of the work (as in the prosecution of James Branch Cabell's *Jurgen*). And so the bill prohibited expert testimony, particularly that of artists or writers, at trials. A judge in an important New York case had ruled that the prosecution must prove that the work excited lustful and lecherous desires. The bill said that such proof was not required. And defense counsel had argued in many cases that the work as a whole must be considered, not isolated words or passages. Ford and Sumner's legislation pre-empted that defense by stating that a ban could be based "exclusively upon a part or parts, of any publication." In other words, a jury's finding that a single word or passage was obscene might be sufficient to proscribe the entire work.

Dreiser jumped into the fray. In an interview published in the New York *Evening Telegram* he called censorship "bunk and hokum," and proceeded to deplore the arid state of American culture, which put Philistinism in the saddle. Businessmen, he said, talked like nine-year-olds, while university graduates could converse only about Babe Ruth. "America," he summed up, "is a hopeless country for intellectuals and thinking people. . . . The majority of its people have the mentality of a European or Asian peasant."

When hearings were called by the Senate Judiciary Committee, Liveright led to Albany a hastily assembled anticensorship cavalcade consisting of Gertrude Atherton, author of the current B & L best seller, *Black Oxen;* two Hearst executives; a psychology instructor; and a lawyer. At the hearings Judge Ford repeatedly tangled with the sixty-six-year-old Atherton, a doughty battler for greater frankness in sexual matters. Sumner solemnly presented the committee with a sealed package containing allegedly pornographic passages from recently published novels.

Liveright set up headquarters in an Albany hotel suite and for the next two weeks presided over nightly poker games at which the liquor freely flowed. Either a bad poker player or engaging in a subtle, time-honored form of bribery, Liveright regularly dropped such large sums to the senators who sat in that a messenger from B & L made regular cash runs to New

York. He and Senator James J. Walker, one of the bill's few opponents, applied other forms of persuasion as well, and sentiment swung against it. Walker drove the final nail in the coffin with a widely quoted speech on the floor of the Senate, full of Irish sentiment and blarney, evoking "dad's sweetheart who afterward became dad's wife." This paragon lived in the days when there were as many salacious books as today, yet "went down to her last resting place just as clean and pure in mind and heart as the day she was born." Thus, "No woman was ever ruined by a book." Evoking the hypocrisy of Prohibition, he observed that many of this bill's supporters "vote one way and drink another." Similarly, "Some of the best tellers of shabby stories in this Senate have been worrying their hearts out . . . about somebody reading something which may not have been good for him or her." A former songwriter ("Will You Love Me in December as You Did in May?") and a protégé of Paul Dresser's in the old days, Beau James managed to defend Home and Mother while attacking hypocrisy, thus appealing to urban sentimentalists and sophisticates alike.

While all this was transpiring, Dreiser made one of his periodic, unintentionally comical efforts to rally the literati. He called a meeting at his studio, inviting Mencken, Carl Van Vechten, Ernest Boyd (who had moved to New York), Burton Rascoe, Sherwood Anderson, Llewelyn Powys (now living at Patchin Place), and others. The primary purpose of the affair was to launch the new edition of *The "Genius,"* a prime candidate for censorship should the Clean Books Bill go through, though few guests remembered this pretext. Their memories of the evening focused on the lack of hard liquor. Possibly Dreiser did not know a good bootlegger as yet; at any rate he provided only beer and wine.

That soirée did little to advance the fight against the Clean Books Bill. As the author of a banned book, Dreiser could not go to Albany to testify, but he did get into a public row with the Authors League, which had been slow to take a stand against the bill and, when the chips were down, confined itself to a telegram and a letter of opposition.

What triggered Dreiser's outburst was a form letter from Rex Beach, the adventure novelist, inviting him to attend a conference "to advance the artistic and cultural standards of motion pictures. . . ." Dreiser wrote Beach that the league should be mobilizing against the depredations of the comstocks instead of conferring with movie magnates. His letter received wide publicity, and league vice president Gelett Burgess, complaining that Dreiser hadn't attended the hearings, boasted of the league's effective behind-the-scenes lobbying, concluding that if Dreiser devoted "as much time furthering the cause of literature as he does to seeking personal publicity, he wouldn't need to ask an association he doesn't belong to help protect his dubious sex fiction."

Dreiser pounced. Drawing on inside information provided by Liveright, he demolished Burgess's claim that the league had helped defeat the bill. As for his debt to the league for its help in the *"Genius"* case, beyond a statement of support he had "received no further aid of any kind from the Authors' League, and I fought the *'Genius'* issue single handed for five years. And I am still fighting—single handed." And then he retaliated against Burgess's "personal attack" on him with one of his own. It seemed that Burgess had sent him a note two months before asking him to read a story by his wife that was published in *McClure's* and "give her your most brutal criticism." Not mentioning any names, Dreiser asked how a fellow writer and executive of the Authors League could ask a purveyor of sex fiction to give his wife an honest critical opinion of her work.

Mencken sullied Dreiser's triumph slightly by reminding him that "a critic in Baltimore" had "laid out $300 in cash" to round up authors to sign a petition. Said Baltimore critic had another, unrelated gripe: a Boni & Liveright advertisement had quoted him as saying, "In 'The Bulwark' especially the big power of Dreiser's massive impetus is evident." Mencken had, of course, written no such moonshine (unless while in his cups), and he hadn't even read the manuscript of *The Bulwark*.

The culprit was Liveright, whose vaunted promotional skills had been unleashed. The offending passage was part of a series of advertisements treating Dreiser "as an institution," as Liveright put it. The version that had aroused Mencken was apparently an early one, for in August, to coincide with the publication of *The "Genius,"* Liveright poured $2000 into a revised, more dignified campaign, conducted primarily in the pages of *The New York Times Book Review* and announcing "with pleasure and pardonable pride" that B & L had acquired the rights to Dreiser's books.

Liveright's claim that he was the best promoter of Dreiser's work was no idle boast, but Dreiser was impatient for results, and even the prominent bust of him in the ornate "Italian Renaissance"–style reception room at B & L's new offices did not pacify him. When Liveright informed him that *A Book About Myself* had sold only "a lousy 3,000 copies," he did not hang his head in shame. He all but accused his publisher of cheating him—and of not advertising enough.

Liveright usually replied to such complaints with soothing words: "In spite of your letter, which it is possible I have misinterpreted, my admiration and affection for you remains the same"; he was for Dreiser's work "heart and soul." In another communication he outlines his advertising plan, offers to go over it with Dreiser, and promises "real results" with *The "Genius"* even though "it's only a *republication.*" The next time Dreiser came to the office, Liveright promised, he would "gently lead you down by the hand" to Arthur Pell, the treasurer, and open the ledgers for his inspection. "I am going to make you believe more and more," he said, "that Liveright's word is as good as his bond. . . . But when, as and if, you demand your pound of flesh—you old fundamentalist—it's going to be accompanied with a sworn statement of printings from the printers, and you, yourself will be able to see the books on hand here and at the warehouse." Dreiser subsided for the time being. He was too suspicious and had an inflated ego; still, he might have wondered why it was that every book he had submitted to Liveright since 1917, save *Twelve Men,* had routinely sold from 2000 to 3000 copies. He thought, probably rightly, that Liveright was interested only in a novel and cared little for his other work. In the back of his mind formed a suspicion that Liveright was keeping him in economic thralldom until he produced the big book.

One of those lesser books, *The Color of a Great City,* appeared in 1923, in a handsome edition with drawings by C. B. Falls. It was a miscellany, a time capsule of New York at the turn of the century—short, impressionistic sketches of city scenes saturated with Dreiserian cosmic moodiness about time, loss, and fate. There is an undercurrent of mourning for the lost city Dreiser had known as a young man, "more varied and arresting and, after its fashion, poetic and even idealistic than it is now." *Color* was a minor work but not an uninteresting book by any means.

As though to prove Dreiser's point, Liveright instead shone the publicity spotlight on the new edition of *The "Genius."* Although delayed until the serialized version in *Metropolitan* had run its course, the novel was relentlessly promoted and took off, selling more than 12,000 copies by the end of the year; sales would reach 50,000 copies before the decade was out. Of course, the past controversy surrounding the novel stimulated interest, but not all the buyers were sensation seekers—else why the steady sales? Dreiser had been at least partly right in insisting that there was a public for that book. It was the young of all ages who had a soft spot for Eugene Witla's idealistic art-dreams.

Now Dreiser was ready to resume the novel on which Liveright would gamble some $25,000, the book he described to Helen as "our dream." He spoke confidently of finishing by fall 1924.

But first he shored up the foundation of reality on which he must erect his book; he carefully amassed facts not for their own sake but as a kind of backdrop, a real world bolstering the imagined one in which his characters moved and lived. He needed a form of scientific confirmation of his vision of the workings of that world, so he met with Dr. Brill, his informal technical adviser on matters criminological. The primary purpose was to gain further insight into the mind of a murderer. One suspects that the case histories the psychiatrist narrated over cocktails interested him far more as tales and as examples of the bizarre workings of the mind than for their Freudian insights. (Dreiser would inscribe in Brill's copy of *An American Tragedy* a reference to their "Thousand and One Nights.") Hearing these psychiatric mystery stories stimulated his imagination and gave him insights into the mind of a murderer.

They probably also discussed the *Arabian Nights,* which Dreiser had read as a boy and reread in 1918 with Estelle Kubitz. Brill's *Psychoanalysis,* which Dreiser perused in 1919, interprets fairy tales as expressions of forbidden wishes. It contains a passage about children who took fairy tales literally and became "phantastic dreamers entirely unfit to cope with the stern realities of modern life." When these individuals grew up, Brill asserted, they subconsciously clung to the childish desire for omnipotence. They were "constantly wishing for the unattainable that could only be gotten through some of the charms of fairy land, such as magic books, invisible caps, Aladdin's Lamp. . . ."

The Aladdin tale would become a central motif in the *Tragedy.* It tells of a poor young man who acquires magic powers and wins the Sultan's beautiful daughter. It appealed to Dreiser as a metaphor for every poor youth's desires for power and wealth (he had in *Sister Carrie* used Aladdin's cave as a simile for opulence and luxury) and the hand of the princess. But the dreams were unattainable; they lured and tricked like mirages.

In an unscientific (but artistically necessary) way he linked these ideas with the seemingly contradictory findings of the early behaviorist Jacques Loeb, particularly his theory of tropisms. In January Dreiser called on Loeb at the Rockefeller Institute. He found the scientist "quite old," and deeply pessimistic about the future of the human race, perhaps a lingering aftershock of the Great War. Loeb's books had helped cure Dreiser of the Victorian faith in Progress, which also peeped out of Spencer's writings. In his notes on the meeting Dreiser writes that the old man was "very positive that all is accidental—no thought, no plan—no intelligence and great danger of dark ages returning. Thinks intelligentsia ought to hold together in a kind of brotherhood." The words "all is accidental" confirmed Dreiser's predisposition to tell the story of a crime not as an act of free will, but as the product of a chain of circumstances, "physico-chemical" (shortened by Dreiser to "chemic") compulsions, and the workings of the subconscious. The sexual chemism hypothesized by Freud was the link between psychiatry and behaviorism.

The next step was research on the ground. He and Helen left on July 1 for upstate New York to inspect the places associated with the Gillette-Brown murder. They were in a holiday mood, and on the way to the Hoboken ferry stopped at Mame's place to pick up three bottles of gin. She and her husband, Austin, were now managing the Rhinelander apartments, a row of ornately balconied buildings on West Eleventh Street.

Their first destination was Cortland, where Grace Brown and Chester Gillette had met while working in his uncle's skirt factory. They arrived at 7:00 P.M., and the next morning walked around the town, which now had a population of about 25,000, compared with about 9000 in Chester Gillette's day. They inspected the factory, now in a different building and occupied by the Newton Shirt Company. Helen says Dreiser made a point of exploring the "best" part of town and then the poorer neighborhoods, something he had often done during his reporter days, when he first began brooding about the contrasts between wealth and poverty in America. But that was the extent of his research in Cortland, the Lycurgus of the novel.

Their next stop was Little York Lake, where Chester had taken Harriet Benedict for an outing on July 4, a week before the murder. From there they went on to the village of South Ostelic, where Frank Brown, Grace's father, had sold the milk and cheese produced on his dairy farm. They jounced along a narrow dirt road to the farm itself, where the girl had lived from the age of three until, at nineteen, she left to find a job—and, she hoped, a husband—in Cortland. The place looked run-down and forlorn to Helen, although in Grace's day it had been a 200-acre spread, with barns, meadows, orchards, and fields. Helen pitied the girl who grew up in such an out-of-the-way place, although, judging from her letters, Grace had fond memories of her childhood on the farm and had gone frequently to South Ostelic for shopping and band concerts. Frank Brown had died in 1918, but Dreiser met a farmer who had known him.

After driving through the nearby town of De Ruyter—Fonda in the novel—where Grace joined Chester at the Tabor House at the beginning of her journey to Big Moose Lake, they spent the night in Cazenovia. The next morning they proceeded to Big Moose Lake, via Utica and Eagle Bay (Three Mile Bay in the novel), to which Chester hiked on a forest road after the murder, caught a boat for Inlet and later joined two Cortland girls, whom he had met by chance on the train coming up.

At Big Moose Lake, surrounded by vast forests, in the heart of the rugged Adirondack country, they took a room at the Glenmore Hotel, where Chester and Grace had registered on the morning of July 11, 1906, the young man using a false name. According to Dreiser's diary, he and Helen went for a row on the lake, then had dinner and afterward listened to the music and watched the dancers at the hotel. In her autobiography Helen describes the lake as "an isolated spot, very beautiful. One felt the weight of the surrounding woods stretching for miles in every direction." Dreiser matter-of-factly records the price of the rooms and the fact that it rained from 3:00 A.M. until dawn, suggesting he spent a restless night.

By Helen's account, the next morning they hired a rowboat at the hotel dock. Dreiser merely notes that the attendant remembered seeing Grace and Chester on the fatal day, and he repeated the gist of his testimony at the trial that Chester had taken his suitcase with a tennis racquet strapped to its side in the boat. The prosecution later theorized that the racquet was the murder weapon, and the presence of the suitcase showed that Chester intended to flee after killing Grace.

In Helen's account they rowed to the inlet called South Bay, where

Chester and "Billy" Brown had drifted around during the blazing hot afternoon and she had picked the pond lilies that grew in profusion near the shore.

On July 11, 1906, South Bay had been almost deserted. It is concealed from the lake's western shore, where the Glenmore and a few other hotels stand, by a long spit of land, forming a sizable bay. There were few houses or "camps" along the shore in those days, but a man living in one of them, on the point at the head of the bay, recalled seeing the couple drifting by. A boater passed them on his way out of the bay. After that they were alone.

Even today, South Bay can seem—at least to one mindful of the tragedy that took place there—a forsaken place. The water is almost black, except near shore, where Grace's body was found and the weedy bottom can be faintly discerned. Along most of the shoreline a tangle of pine and hardwood trees crowds close to a narrow beach, and the cottages are barely visible. The horizon is dominated by the green-furred humps of the Adirondacks. A smaller inlet, known as Punkey's Bay, where searchers dredged up Grace's body with a boathook, her bloodshot eyes open and staring, was probably uninhabited when Dreiser was there. Beyond the shore is a marsh matted with tangled grass and weeds. Elsewhere, the trees press claustrophobically against the water's edge, some growing grotesquely atop huge glacial rocks, their roots clutching them like tentacles. One can imagine—as Dreiser must have—Grace and Chester drifting purposelessly about on a blazing July afternoon, not in a lovers' intimate seclusion but rather lost in a profound solitude, remote from human eyes, mutual desperation and recrimination seething below the surface. The fat, round, yellow-and-white blooms of the pond lilies protrude on thick stems above the surface like pods of some primitive plant—or, to a fanciful eye, clenched fists stabbing up from the dark depths.

Certainly, Helen's imagination worked overtime. As they both sat transfixed by the "quiet, deathlike stillness" of the spot, she thought:

> "Maybe Teddie will become completely hypnotized by this idea and even repeat it, here and now."
> The air was motionless, as though we had been raised to a different level of existence or had become a minute part of the ether itself. It was a little as one feels when, looking over the side of a very tall building, one is tempted to jump. I wished something would break the awful spell of the moment. . . .

While Helen reflexively identified with the victim, Dreiser slipped into the skin of the boy, contemplating murder. There was no likelihood of his committing some violent act, of course. Envisioning the scene for his novel, he understood why he (Clyde) would not, could not, do such a thing. Beyond moral compunctions, enough of him was in Clyde that the fictional projection would have shared Dreiser's inclination, when trapped in a dilemma, to procrastinate; his tendency (as when he let Grant Richards take charge of his life) to drift, to let fate decide. Drifting in a boat on the opaque glassy surface was the dominant image of that July day in 1906, as he would imagine it. No, he (Clyde) could not do it.

The thoughts that actually ran through Dreiser's mind he didn't record in his diary; but surely his photographic memory registered the atmosphere of this forsaken place, where Nature seemed hostile, a sinister landscape out of Poe, under a pitiless sun.

By Dreiser's account they departed after talking with the boatman who had seen Grace and Chester and drove back on the road on which Chester hiked to Eagle Bay, clutching that incriminating suitcase. He buried the tennis racquet in the woods along the way.

The winding dirt road was muddy, and their car frequently got stuck; then a tire blew out. After changing the tube, they headed toward Herkimer, the county-seat town where Gillette had been tried for the murder of Grace Brown. Midway in the seventy-mile journey they stopped by a woods, slung a hammock between two trees, and took a nap. The route to Herkimer led them through picturesque small towns and bucolic country with rolling green hills and clear streams. A "beautiful, simple, life," Dreiser observed, as though relieved at seeing Nature restored to a benign, pastoral state.

He found Herkimer, the county seat, a large, bustling small city, more urban than the city where a jury of backwoods farmers had stared with stony disapproval as the district attorney elicited the details of Chester's seduction and abandonment of Grace Brown. They found the courthouse at the foot of Main Street; directly across from it was the county jail, a solid gray-stone structure where Chester had stayed for months in relative comfort awaiting trial. The courthouse is constructed of red brick with a tall wooden cupola atop a steeple, containing an open belfry. (In the book Dreiser would place the courthouse in the square and give it a clock tower; he was describing the courthouse in Warsaw he had known as a boy.) The courtroom, which could hold 1000 spectators and was packed during the trial, is on the second floor of the building, with rows of high windows and stern dark woodwork. This ample chamber, comparable to a Broadway theater in dimensions, would be transferred intact to his novel.

Their inspection completed, they journeyed homeward.

And so Dreiser's research consisted of speaking to at most two or three people with direct knowledge of some aspect of the murder of Grace Brown. A historian later discovered that he did at some point visit Mrs. Ward, widow of the Herkimer County district attorney, who showed him her husband's scrapbook of clippings on the case. He may have taken some notes on the contents, but he depended mainly on morgue clippings from the

New York *World,* which he could as easily have obtained in New York City. He evidently did not visit the shirt factory in Cortland that had replaced the Gillette Skirt Company, where Chester worked. But in the novel he puts Clyde in a collar factory, and he subsequently did tour such a factory.

There were still many people in Herkimer with knowledge of the trial, including the defense lawyer, the presiding judge, and the undersheriff who arrested Chester and saw him daily in jail. But Dreiser had no particular desire to interrogate them. None of them could have provided the key to his story, the essence of the case—why Chester Gillette murdered Grace Brown (if he did) and what went through his mind that day on Big Moose Lake. Even if they could have, Dreiser might not have been interested. He would formulate his own theory of what happened to Clyde and Roberta Alden on the lake.

Later that month, seeking privacy and relief from the city heat, they rented a secluded cabin they had noticed on the way to Cortland, near Monticello in the Catskills.

News from New York invaded his rural hideaway; first an "oily" letter from Liveright responding to Dreiser's gripes about the poor sales of *A Book About Myself.* In it the publisher praised the *Moods* poems, but Dreiser decided that Liveright was flattering him. Then a more momentous communication from Mencken: "Confidentially I am at work on plans for a new review—something far above anything hitherto seen in the Republic." That "review" would become *The American Mercury.* He and Nathan had wearied of editing the *Smart Set,* and they persuaded their publisher, Alfred A. Knopf, to back a new journal. Mencken wanted a magazine that was more serious than the dandyish *Smart Set,* with iconoclastic articles on history, science, and politics, and fiction of uncompromising realism. To Dreiser he proclaimed a New Freedom: "You may attack the Methodists by name, and call the Baptists the Sewer Rats of God if you please."

As Mencken planned the magazine that would make him the most influential social critic of the 1920s, Dreiser was making a painful beginning on the book that would win him his greatest fame. That summer he worked at an improvised desk under a tree, fair game for ambient mosquitoes, worms, and spiders. He was racked by doubts. He mentions his trepidations in letters to Sally Kusell, a pretty young blonde woman from Illinois with literary ambitions whom he had hired as a literary assistant. She had previously worked for her brother, a theatrical producer, and gained some experience at "play construction," as he put it, leading Dreiser to think she had the editorial skills that Helen lacked.

Kusell's first task was to edit and type the "studies," as Dreiser called them, for *A Gallery of Women.* By the time he left for the country, he was calling her "my little Yankee Zulu" and "my bobbed-haired pirate." In early August he wrote that they had much to do together and he wished she were there; however, he realized that working with her would be fatal: "The trouble with you is that you have a gripping sex appeal for me. I doubt—apart from *that*—if much would be done because I'd fag myself daily and then lie about. . . ." A week later he wrote that he has been working every other day, "and that in the face of the damndest qualms and struggles in connection with the book. The trouble with me when I set out to write a novel is that I worry so over the sure even progress of it. I start & change & change. . . . What I really ought to have is someone who could decide for me—once & for all when I have gotten the right start—when I am really going ahead—or one who would take all the phrases I pen down & piece them together into the true story as I see it. That is what I eventually do for myself—but oh the struggles & the flounderings." Despite his qualms, he had finished six or seven chapters, which he would give her when he returned to the city to see Liveright.

While Helen was packing she noticed a bundle of Sally's letters on top of his bag. "Ordinarily I would not have touched them," she writes ingenuously, "but at that moment I could not overcome the feeling that they concerned me in some way and I should read them. After reading two or three, I replaced the rest, for I had seen enough to know that this was a more serious triangle than I had supposed." Confronting Dreiser with the evidence, she told him she was through. They drove back to New York in a sulfurous silence, and she let him off at St. Luke's Place with the advice that he need never try to see her again. Nevertheless, she was back at the studio the next morning, and he looked tired and distraught. "I walked the streets all night long," he told her. "Where were you?"

She softened but could not take him back. They decided they would live apart but continue to see each other. He would move into the Rhinelander apartments, where Mame would look after him. Two large ground-floor rooms with a fireplace and separate entrance at 118 West Eleventh Street were available, and he settled in with his desk and a few pieces of furniture. As it happened, Kusell lived nearby on West Ninth Street. He would meet her regularly for breakfast and give her manuscript to type and edit. One evening he took her to Mouquin's and then to the Ziegfeld Follies, featuring in this year's edition "Six naked women . . . behind very transparent screens."

Helen suspected that he was still seeing Sally, but there was little she could do, other than reproach him when he stayed away for days at a time. After one such flare-up at Christmastime, he took her to Atlantic City. She cried most of the way, but eventually he soothed her and they had a relaxed holiday. They returned home on December 27, and the next day Dreiser writes that he was "glad to be back & working." By then he had finished thirty-two chapters of the *Tragedy*.

.   .   .

A hint of his thinking about the novel—and The Novel—emerged in an interview published in *The New York Times Book Review*'s Christmas issue. "Realism is not literature; it is life," he told Rose Feld. He attacked the brittle novels of cynicism and disillusionment that were in vogue. The younger generation of writers "choose one dark dank, ugly corner of life . . . forgetting that life consists of many corners, many open spaces. . . . The realistic novel of America is not the torpid, sick neurasthenic novel. Life in America is not like that." Here there was opportunity, said the immigrant's son. He quoted a "foreign writer" who had told him, "There is always a push upward . . . the life, or the soul if you will, of an individual needn't stay poor."

Contemporary novelists, he complained, were overly preoccupied with form and technique—"Gertrude Stein stuff"—at the expense of substance. As for the inevitable topic of sex, Dreiser took a moralistic swipe at the current wave of flaming-youth novels, saying he was "sick of the exaggeration of sex in our novels today. But the person who ignores sex is as much a fool as the person who over-emphasizes it. You can't write a novel of realism and let sex out of the picture, even as you can't write a novel full of sex and call it realism."

The allusive realism of Stein's lost generation could not have produced a *Madame Bovary* or *Crime and Punishment*. The Russians and the Victorians needed "breadth and length. They took the trouble to make their picture complete. The little canvases of today will never displace the larger ones of yesterday." Writers had abandoned the social novel and were retreating into subjectivity, he declared. As he would observe of another novelist, now forgotten, he "is thinking more of himself than he is of life."

Dreiser apprenticed on the expansive novels of the Victorian era. He could not fully appreciate how much the 1920s writers' rebellion against the Victorian masters was a rebellion in *form*. Substance was part of it in a negative sense: the young rebels had no desire to expose or describe social evils. And so they turned to language and technique, as well as greater psychological depth, reflecting private disillusionment and hurt.

Caught between the Victorian and modern age, Dreiser in his *Tragedy* was writing a large-canvas novel documenting American society and its false values. Though he was sensitive to the changes in those values, Dreiser, unlike the writers who emerged in the 1920s, could not believe that the old idols were shattered. His entire career had been one of struggle against the reticence of the genteel tradition and official censors and popular taste; he had defined himself by opposition. As he wrote David Karsner in December 1923, "Like a kite I have risen against the wind—not with it." He needed the wind to keep aloft.

And so he found himself something of a troglodyte, and this revealed itself in his lack of sympathy with methods of the new writers, though it was not a simple hostility, for he admired some of them, such as Evelyn

Scott, an English novelist published by Liveright, whose truthfulness he liked, but "not her bitterness," he told Mencken.

When he observed modern youth, in the larger sense, he could not see a generation of rebels, but rather one of complacent materialists. Responding two years previously to a journalist's query asking if he believed that the younger generation was throwing off the shackles of convention, he had said that the vast majority of young people

> are interested in but one or two things, and chiefly one . . . getting into business where he will be able to make money quick . . . and, having made a little, lording it over the people in his vicinity. He yearns to build a stuffy home wherein, soon, he can intellectually lie down and take the count, spending his days thereafter in riding around in a Ford, at the worst, and joining, if they will have him, the Rotarians, the Shriners, the Elks or the Odd-Fellows. . . .

There was truth in that description; flaming youth was overrated.

The young people in Dreiser's work in progress faced a dilemma that urban sophisticates would regard as quaintly antique, something more typical of 1906 than 1923. (In his first draft he set the novel in Chester Gillette's day—remarking on the rarity of automobiles, for example. But in subsequent versions, the story is vaguely located in the late teens and early twenties, as evidenced by scattered references to clothes, songs, and movies of the time.)

Although the situation of a pregnant girl who fears disgrace and ostracism might seem anachronistic in Manhattan, it would not in Cortland or Herkimer, New York. As the sociologists Robert S. and Helen M. Lynd would write in *Middletown*, their 1925 study of Muncie, Indiana, "A heavy taboo, supported by law and by both religious and popular sanctions, rests upon sexual relationships between persons who are not married." Moreover (as the Lynds discreetly point out), it was the young people of the upper-middle class who were sexually sophisticated, who knew about contraceptives and doctors who, for a price, got girls out of trouble. Dreiser was well aware of this class barrier of ignorance, so to speak; it was one link in the chain of circumstances pushing Clyde Griffiths to his doom.

CHAPTER 19

An *"Unholy Task"*

> But by this time a change had come over the affections of Chester Gillette. He had discovered that the name of Gillette was a social one in Cortland. He had found out that it would open the doors of Cortland's exclusive circles. He had found out that the name would bring him in contact with girls of a different class, girls of education, and whose families had position; girls who moved far from the sphere of the class of factory and farmer girls to which Grace Brown belonged.
>
> —District Attorney Ward's opening statement (1906)

Toward the end of March Helen decided to go west. They were still living apart, but the strain of typing his manuscripts all day and going out with him at night was too much for her, she explains. But jealousy was at the heart of it—not only Dreiser's affair with Sally but the fact that she was playing a more important role in the writing of the book than Helen was. And so, in what would become a pattern, she fled to her mother's in Portland.

He assumed the separation would be short-lived. He would finish the novel by August 1 at the latest, he told her. When he was free they would take a trip and then "settle in a little dream place with a garden," preferably in San Francisco. The day after she left, he received "troublesome" telepathic waves from her and thought he heard her crying (she cried all the way to Chicago). He continued to believe that they were in mental communication (as did she). Sometimes he received hostile, sometimes loving thought-waves. He repeatedly reassured her that he was interested in no one in particular. "I know you think I have a girl hanging on my arm every night," he wrote in April. Not so. He told her about a couple of his engagements, one an invitation to a soirée at the actress Clair Burke's, which he had accepted only because Mencken would be there. He promised, "If this seeing people without you is going to torture you I am content never to see anyone save with you." He had, he reminded her, done that for three years in California.

He was attuned to her moods, "so like my own," and sent her copies of poems. The first one would bring him an unwanted fame. It was called "The Beautiful," and he had not written it at all. He had borrowed the words from Sherwood Anderson's story "Tandy," added a few sentences, and rearranged the lines on the page. It is a tribute to a long-suffering woman, who says, "They think that it is easy to be a woman—/to love and be loved,/ But I know better." But Dreiser adds some lines describing the kind of love he needs: "Complete and ceaseless/And insatiable and yet generous." Such was his demand of Helen.

Helen remained in Portland for several weeks, trying to put the pieces of her life back together. By April, she felt better and went to Hollywood, where she had once been happy, and rented a room in a private home belonging to a family with three daughters. For a time she occupied herself with buying and selling real estate and discovered that the properties she still owned could yield profits of greater than 100 percent. After making a fair sum and speculating in other tracts they owned, using additional money Dreiser sent her, she decided to resume her voice lessons. But she missed Dreiser, and he began begging her to come back, swearing that he loved her more than anything in the world, promising to do better. But she had set a more drastic condition: marriage.

He forwarded periodic reports of his progress on the *Tragedy*. At first he is full of doubts, and he tells her that he had finished a chapter, but "I boast not. I only hope for the best and that I may not destroy [the manuscript] in a crazy dark mood." He was lucky, he said, if he did a chapter in two days—but he spent five days on one, knowing what he wanted to say but so nervous and wrought up he couldn't get it down. He was working hard, rising at 7:30 or 8:00, lighting a fire, having breakfast and "a drink"—a morning pick-me-up, taking a walk around Washington Square Park and then writing from 10:30 until 6:00; sometimes he returned to his desk at 8:00 P.M. and continued until 11:00. He ate in restaurants, often wolfing down two hot dogs and a cup of coffee. He went out only two or three times a week, and spent much of the time by himself in his room, tending to his "regular job," eight hours at a stretch.

His room, he said, had become a kind of prison where he was "fixed & struggling all the time." The novel was an "unholy task." "I might as well be chipping it out of solid rock," he told her. "But I am chipping." At times he feared the task was beyond his strength. His attitude toward the story was at times almost religious. "When the book is finally done maybe I'll get credit for the contest & maybe I won't," he told Helen. "But just the same & failure or no failure I feel it an honor to be permitted to even attempt to tell such a tale & on that basis I am working on."

By April he felt more confident, telling Helen that he was "surer now than I have been in a long time that I will bring it to a successful conclusion." He had pushed the story "to the point where . . . I know now that it will come through & I am not suffering mentally like I was before." When he has finished Part 2, which ends with the death of Roberta on the lake, he will know that "the top of the range is crossed & I'm descending the other side. . . . For the approach of this story is longer than the conclusion." That is, he must establish the causes of the murder and then the rest—the trial and execution of Clyde Griffiths—would inexorably follow, though not as easily as he encouraged himself by believing.

He was unable to write this novel as rapidly as previous ones: "It is too intricate in its thought & somehow my method if not my style has changed. I work with more care and hence difficulty. My style is not as fluid. Whether its worse I can't say—yet." This was in part because of the more painstaking care he was taking with the progression of the story, the placement of scenes, the sequence of events.

For example, after Clyde has seduced Roberta Alden, his co-worker in the collar factory, he meets the dazzling Sondra Finchley: "I'm to where the factory girl & the rich girl in Clyde's life are entangling & by degrees destroying her. Hard! . . . It seems simple. I know the story. The right procession & selection of incident should be as nothing but it just chances to be everything and so I write and rewrite."

He was not an agile, inventive plotter; the sequence of scenes must deepen the central reality. He couldn't, for example, decide when to show Roberta's awareness of the developing triangle. In the first draft he has her reproaching Clyde for breaking a date with her to attend a dance, in early December. But in later versions the dance takes place at Christmastime. Dreiser felt that it would be more revealing to show Roberta waiting for Clyde, alone in her room, with the simple presents she has bought.

In June he complained to Helen that he felt wretched and "spiritually alone." The July heat wilted him: "My body appears to be made of heavy, wet leather & my nerves & joints of rusty wires & iron." He had so much to do and didn't have the right person to help him.

She asked who was typing for him (read: Was Sally Kusell still around?). He replied no one at the moment and that he had a backlog of six chapters and an article. Liveright had offered one of his secretaries to help out, but he had refused. He did not want his publisher to read the book now: "He might begin with annoying suggestions & I'd have to pull out." He was working under conditions of virtual secrecy.

Liveright reveals the state of his ignorance in a letter written on April 2: "The new book, as I understand it, is to be called An American Comedy. . . ." Apprised of the true title, he suggested it be changed to "Griffith, An American Tragedy." The *s* in Clyde's surname, he explained, was difficult to pronounce. And a week or so later, fresh from a booksellers' convention in Chicago, Liveright *implored* Dreiser to call the book "Ewing" or "Warner," presumably more pronounceable names. He also thought the word *tragedy* was too depressing.

Dreiser did not dismiss the idea of a new title out of hand, writing Helen that he was considering something like "Orion" or "Icarus" or "Xion"—all mythical Greek heroes "who were misled by & suffered through love." He even hunted in the library for a picture of Icarus (who had not suffered from love but from flying too high) falling into the sea, for possible use on the jacket. Another possibility was "The Love Cast," which was cryptic indeed. He soon abandoned the search for a better title, and stuck to the one he had used from the beginning. It expressed precisely and boldly his conception of the story: "I call it *An American Tragedy* because it could not happen in any other country in the world."

Liveright was now "yelling for the book," Dreiser reported to Louise Campbell, whom he had recently enlisted as an editor-typist. Probably his quarrels with Kusell had become too distracting; he needed an efficient, impersonal secretary who would steadily turn out the endless revisions he was making.

Louise's recollection was that he was about one-third finished when she began. She had arrived in the city in early April to audition for the chorus of the Ziegfeld Follies. But she took part of the manuscript with her to the theater, began reading it while waiting her turn onstage, and decided then and there that she would rather work for him. Louise was a faster typist than Sally, and he gradually came to value her editorial suggestions. She lived in Philadelphia, removing any sexual complications; and in any case their affair was probably over.

He was working hard, but not spending as much time cloistered in his room as he led Helen to believe. While continuing the relationship with Sally, he had casual affairs with Mrs. Howey, who was also a friend of Edgar Lee Masters; Maude Guitteau, a twice-married former showgirl whose quick seduction made him think, "Without the fame of my books I personally could not achieve this relationship at all"; and Magdalen Davis, who aspired to be a writer but at present worked for the Standard Oil Company and had some connection with the Greenwich Village Theatre.

These transient amours provided companionship and sexual release: "Magdalene [sic] & I meet here at 10:30 P.M. for pleasure." "When I invite [Mrs. Howey] in & close the door she immediately begins to undress—which makes me laugh. I hadn't assumed that copulation naturally followed. However—always willing to oblige."

Sally provided companionship. They went to the theater frequently. He roared at W. C. Fields in *Poppy,* and at Jimmy Savo and Fred Allen in *Vogues.* He took Magdalen to hear Sumner debate on censorship at the Civic Club. He attended a soirée at the drama critic Alexander Woollcott's rooms. He went to a writers' dinner and had four drinks, he wrote Helen, but no feminine companionship. He spent a weekend in April at the actress Laurette Taylor's place, accompanied by T. R. Smith, the Liveright editor. In May he stayed at the rented Larchmont mansion of W. C. Fields, and was bored by the smart Broadway chatter.

In August, again accompanied by T. R. Smith, he traveled to the Hedgerow Theater near Philadelphia to see the play *Art,* in which Kirah Markham was featured. Their affair was definitely over, he confided to Wharton Esherick, the sculptor and cabinetmaker at whose rural home they spent the night. If Kirah were in a play in Africa, he would hop on a boat and go see her, but there would be nothing romantic in it. He had a rule, he once told Dorothy Dudley, "not to moon around over anyone." Speaking of the painter Anne Rice, he said, "She was one of those women where I lost out. She didn't want me, that is, not until years later, and then I wouldn't have her." By then she had known too many men.

So the summer passed. His eldest sister kept a worried eye on him. The book, that "unholy thing," was taking a toll on his nerves. To soothe them he started smoking cigarettes, something he had rarely done in the past because of his bronchitis, and he was increasingly resorting to gin as a creative stimulus. Once, in a fit of drunken despair, he told Mame that he would never finish the book and began weeping.

In July he confessed to Liveright that he was stuck and could not possibly meet the deadline for fall publication. The publisher pressed him to finish *A Gallery of Women* as a substitute. But that would take him too long to complete, he complained to Helen, and further delay the *Tragedy.* Still, he did write more "studies," including one about Helen that he never finished, and he accepted a magazine assignment to interview Ty Cobb. He was so lonely for Helen that he was contemplating going west and took the Cobb assignment to pay for the trip.

By September his morale hit bottom. Sometimes he was troubled by nightmares in which Helen figured. The dreams reflected guilt feelings about his treatment of her, and he asked for forgiveness, or rather under-standing: "I may have seemed cruel and to you have been cruel but I have tortured myself more in so doing because within me you have always been—safe and centered in my very heart—and when I have hurt you I have felt so sad afterwards—ah—so very sad."

Like a child petitioning his mother, he pleads, "If I promise to be very, very good from now on . . . do you suppose you could be happy with just me." Perhaps he was worried about the "handsome" movie star friend she was now dating. It is difficult to believe that a woman of Helen's strongly sensual nature was celibate.

Absence always made him fonder—and loneliness and need of mother-ing. He assured her that compared with the other women in his life she was "on a pedestal and quite alone." Once her beauty had struck fears of inade-quacy in him; now, from a distance, he was idealizing her. She played hard to get, peremptorily dismissing his offer to divorce Jug or hiding behind her refinement, coyly suggesting, "Perhaps you like a coarser type." Recalling their private orgies in California, he responded, "since when have you become delicatessen in that field?" He did indeed need a "coarser type," in the sense of an illicit relationship. The mistress became the wife, who inevitably became the controlling mother, making him *mind.* And then the Golden Girl was gone.

Yet such was his need that he forgot his determination never to be vulnerable in an affair. Now he was in the uncomfortable position of peti-tioner, like Clyde with Sondra, like Roberta with Clyde. Helen felt her power over him, and used it to negotiate a renewal of their relationship on her terms. He stepped to her tune, making every possible promise to lure her back, every plaintive appeal to her sympathy.

The transcontinental debate continued through November. He wrote her that he had had a dream that they were seated at a table in their own place, and all sorts of people were with them, including "young Krog." On the walls were drawings by a woman he had known, but somehow Helen wasn't jealous. As they were going out, they came to a pile of discarded women's clothes. He feared that Helen would see them and throw a jealous fit, but she merely kicked them into the corner.

The pictures were, of course, Thelma's. And the pile of clothes symbol-ized all the old loves whom Helen briskly kicks out of his life.

He was waiting for her when her train arrived at Pennsylvania Station in mid-December. "Well," he kept saying foolishly, "it's Babu, all right." She thought he had "a hollow look about him, a seeming lack of vitality" which worried her.

Her presence had a rejuvenating effect on him, and they spent a few days in Washington while he researched in the Library of Congress. But when they returned, as they were getting out of a taxicab, a woman rushed up and said something "sharp and accusing" to him. Calmly, he told Helen to go inside and while she waited she could hear them talking, his voice low and firm, the woman's shrill and insistent. To Helen it must have seemed a new variation on an old triangle. But she had come this far and there was no going back.

CHAPTER **20**   *Death by Water*

Overwhelmed by the distractions of Manhattan, Dreiser suggested that Helen find a place in Brooklyn. In March, at the suggestion of his friend J. G. Robin, the fallen financier of "Vanity, Vanity" in *Twelve Men*, who was now a lawyer and author of a tragedy called *Caius Gracchus* that Dreiser admired, he took an office in the Guardian Life Building at 50 Union Square. Robin was associated with Arthur Carter Hume, who had an office in the building, and the two of them advised Dreiser on legal points in the story.

Brooklyn and Union Square would be the poles of his life for nearly nine months, as he completed Book 3 of the *Tragedy*. He worked at both places but used the office also as a staging area for nocturnal forays, and, presumably, for assignations.

Helen later offered the theory that he needed a romantic triangle to stimulate his creativity. "He tried to place himself between opposing forces in order to gather reactions of a stimulating quality and character, and at the same time to safeguard himself against being weakened or destroyed by the indispensability of any one person."

Although the second part of that proposition was probably true, the first seems a rationalization or defense mechanism for preserving her self-esteem. Implicit in her theory was the idea that he was not especially fond of the women, that he was merely using them as grist for his mill. That, as we shall see, was not always true. At this point in his life, though, he needed Helen and the home in Brooklyn as an emotional anchor, a gravitational center in the emotional chaos of his life. But to escape the confining domesticity he had so resented with Jug, he needed affairs with others. It was not only sexual fulfillment he sought from them, although that was becoming increasingly important as Helen assumed more of a surrogate wife's role and less of the mistress's. She understood his resentment of too much control and tried to give him a long tether—pretending not to know about the other woman, for example. Still, she was there and their relationship had moved to a plateau of semi-permanency and this dampened his desire for her.

But he also needed the other woman for mental stimulus and for editorial reactions to what he wrote, since he did not value Helen's opinion. But there was a limit to his acceptance of editorial suggestions, as Louise Campbell perhaps knew as well as anyone—an invisible line which if crossed would provoke an argument or worse.

Finally, further complicating this sexual quadrille, Dreiser craved the ego boost and stimulation, sexual or mental, of still other women. That is, one triangle necessarily bred another, so that he could feel that no single woman dominated him.

Not long after they moved, Helen was called on to render the kind of service he needed from her—nursing him through a bout of near pneumonia. That illness laid him up for three weeks, causing wailing and rending of garments at Boni & Liveright, which was now pressuring him for the book in time for fall 1925. His recovery was slow, but he was well enough by the end of March to propose to Mencken a night of beer-drinking. To launch the evening properly, he offered cocktails at his office in the Guardian Life Building. The revels did not take place until April 8, but they must have been strenuous, for soon after, Dreiser complained to his Baltimore correspondent, "Sex and beer parties do not agree."

Dreiser and Helen also entertained in Brooklyn, "about 30 minutes from Times Square," he assured Mencken, who made the subway journey, as did Claude Bowers, an editorial writer for the *World*, who had lived in Terre Haute as a young man and heard stories about the Dreiser family before he ever met its most famous member. Bowers admired Dreiser and thought him a typical Hoosier—not only his accent but his naturalness and lack of airs. At their first meeting Dreiser suddenly asked him, "Do you ever get terribly depressed?" Bowers said he was generally in good spirits. "I wish I could say that," said Dreiser wistfully. "There is the old saw, to know all is to forgive all," he declared another time, "though in some cases in my experience it seems hard to believe." But Bowers felt in him the deep compassion that saturated his novels.

The pages of manuscript proliferated. Louise Campbell said that at times he seemed knee-deep in paper, for there were always several versions of each chapter in circulation. Esherick called on him and found the living-room floor and every other available surface covered with pages.

A kind of editorial assembly line had been set up. A note he wrote on the final typescript shows how many hands it had passed through: "Finally revised and cut copy—with cuts by myself, Sally Kussell, Louise Campbell and T. R. Smith." Sally and Louise took the manuscript in turn, editing and typing successive drafts. They both cut and condensed chapters with Dreiser's approval. (Book 1, for example, was slimmed down from the original thirty-two chapters to nineteen in the published volume. Later reports that his original manuscript contained more than one million words seem exaggerated, however.)

Having refused to have any dealings with Liveright on editorial matters, he worked with T. R. Smith, an erudite, cherubic man who wore a pince-nez. Smith often invited Dreiser to the legendary parties Liveright gave at the four-story brownstone at 61 West Forty-eighth Street that had become the firm's offices in 1923.

By day Liveright's office was a place of business, but after hours it became his club and pied-à-terre. Liveright gave two kinds of parties: "A" and "B." The A parties were intended to publicize a new title, and a cast of famous authors and celebrities in other fields was assembled for them. The B affairs were—or became—private orgies, and the guest list for them drew on a more raffish circle of Liveright's social acquaintances. His Broadway connections ensured that plenty of pretty showgirls were on hand, and he often had one in tow himself. The best bonded liquor flowed. By the end of the evening the hard-core drinkers ended up in Horace's office, which also served as an aid station for those who had passed out earlier.

Dreiser avoided most of Liveright's affairs. He did, however, attend a party at the Van Vechtens' that June, hearing James Weldon Johnson, the black writer and educator, recite "Go Down Death," and Paul Robeson sing spirituals. It was the height of the Harlem Renaissance, the flowering of black culture, which Van Vechten brought downtown with his book *Nigger Heaven.* An aficionado of black music, George Gershwin, was there, and he played show tunes at the piano while Dreiser sat "heavy and brooding, the direct antithesis, almost a contradiction of all that Gershwin means."

Yet these contradictory spirits somehow blended in the potent cultural cocktail that was Manhattan in 1925. Gershwin's tunes bathed the boozy amours of liberated couples in the warm glow of elegant romance, and his jazzy rhythms caught the frenetic energy of the city streets. Dreiser retained a provincial's awe of the congealed power and seductive glamour of the tall buildings, which sometimes seemed to him a mirage. Walking the streets one night, he composed a poem called "Tall Towers":

> *Tall towers.*
>> *Clustered pinnacles.*
> *Varied and fretted flowers of stone and steel.*
> *That island the upper air—*
> *That top the fogs and storms.*

And he later wrote another, "My City," which evoked the polyglot human swarm in the canyoned streets.

The alcoholic excesses and hedonism of the time foamed over into novels, from Fitzgerald's *Gatsby* to Van Vechten's *Firecrackers,* in which a writer intones a Dreiserian credo: "that life is largely without excuse, that if there is a God he conducts the show aimlessly, if not, indeed, maliciously, that men and women run around automatically seeking escapes from their troubles and outlets for their lusts." There was a callousness, a success-at-any-price materialism, a cynical egoism, an indifference to communal ties, which Fitzgerald caught in *Gatsby;* everyone came to Gatsby's parties but no one went to his funeral.

Everyone came to Liveright's parties that year. . . .

Dreiser was not impervious to his times, and the novel he was writing in the 1920s would be different in its setting and the relationships among the characters from those he wrote before the 1920s. He had absorbed, almost unconsciously, the social and intellectual influences that went into the making of the decade's literature. But his cynicism was more weathered, his hedonism more tired, his alienation more profound than that of most of the younger writers. His despair was philosophical, almost detached, sometimes almost cheerful; life had on the whole used him fairly well, he liked to say on his better days. He had the weary air of one who has peered into the black deeps of space and found nothingness.

In writing he paid back the universe for its implacable indifference, siding with humanity against it, pityingly tracing the careers of characters in his novel, plotting their fates as he believed the Unknowable often cruelly plotted his and all men's. There was Roberta, experiencing "the first flashing, blinding, bleeding stab of love" for Clyde, and then, just after discovering she is pregnant, sitting alone in her room because he has fallen in love with Sondra. Love, to Dreiser, was pain. Clyde feels the "stinging sense of what it was to want and not to have." When Clyde's attempts to arrange an abortion for Roberta come to naught (for these scenes Dreiser drew inspiration from Mame's search for a doctor reputed to perform the operations in Indiana when he was a boy in Sullivan), the trap closes and the mirage of love vanishes, leaving barren hostility.

Dreiser had reached the point where Clyde formulates his plot to kill Roberta. Here he summons up a figure in the *Arabian Nights*—the mysterious efrit, who whispers to the boy the answer to his problem. The efrit is a kind of perverse genii—genius, control. The efrit is *It* (which is perhaps why Dreiser chose the archaic word for genii):

> . . . the very substance of some leering and diabolic wish or wisdom concealed in his own nature and that now abhorrent and yet compelling, leering and yet intriguing, friendly and yet cruel, offered him a choice between an evil which threatened to destroy him (and against his deepest opposition) and a second evil which, however, it might disgust or sear or terrify, still provided for freedom and success and love.

This was no textbook or theological representation of evil, but a force Dreiser had read into Freud and sensed in himself. Helen recalled, "His was a dual nature, and there were times when I felt the opposing force struggling for control within him so powerfully that I felt he might be torn apart by it." Marguerite Tjader Harris, who was Dreiser's literary companion in later years, speaks of "those veiled mysterious forces of darkness that he had believed in almost more than forces of Light . . . the weird, the inexplicable, the evil, even the super-evil. . . . For did he not *see* faces at the foot of his bed, sometimes, evil faces such as he had described in [his short story] 'The Hand'; and also later, described to me?"

The efrit, or genii, personifies Clyde's "darker self," Dreiser often said, leaving it at that. It could be called a projection of a forbidden wish which the conscious mind cannot countenance and so imagines in the form of an external spirit. Once Clyde opens the subterranean prison where the efrit dwells, he is in its power. Like the fisherman in the *Arabian Nights*, he cannot put it back in the bottle.

The efrit speaks in calm, reasonable tones, overwhelming the objections of Clyde's conscience, his fears of punishment, his repugnance toward such a deed. The efrit makes murder seem a sensible course—the rational way out of his dilemma.

But in the end, on South Bay of Big Bittern Lake, Clyde loses his nerve and "confides his dilemma to circumstances." Dreiser sets the boat adrift in a moral void—"in endless space where was no end of anything—no plots—no plans—no practical problems to be solved—nothing." The lake is like "a huge, black pearl cast by some mighty hand." As they drift on the opaque cobalt water, Roberta sings a banal little song, "I'll Be There Sunday If You Will," evoking her long wait for him to come for her. The relentless sun in the blank sky is focused, as if through a magnet, on the boat, so it becomes a single burning nodal point. Clyde nerves himself to act, the conflict within him is reflected in his face, "distorted and fulgurous." He is torn between a "chemic revulsion against death" (deeper than conscience) and a subconscious desire to kill (personified by the voice of the efrit); behaviorism and psychiatry, Loeb and Freud, clash at the "cataclysmic moment"—and nullify each other. All volition is gone; he suffers a "palsy of the will." It is as though a giant invisible hand is now writing the script. In his prose Dreiser shifts to the passive voice to describe somnambulant beings—mechanisms controlled by a higher Author:

> And yet fearing to act in any way—being unwilling to—being willing only to say that never, never would he marry her. . . . But angry and confused and floundering. And then, as she drew near him, seeking to take his hand in hers and the camera from him in order to put it in the boat, he flinging out at her, but not even then with any intention to do other than free himself of her—her touch—her pleading—consoling sympathy—her presence forever—God!
>
> Yet (the camera still unconsciously held tight) pushing at her with so much vehemence as not only to strike her lips and nose and chin with it, but to throw her back sidewise toward the left wale which caused the boat to careen to the very water's edge. And then he, stirred by her sharp scream . . . rising and reaching half to assist or recapture her and half to apologize for the unintended blow—yet in so doing completely capsizing the boat—himself and Roberta being as instantly thrown into the water. And the left wale of the boat as it turned, striking Roberta on the head as she sank and then rose for the first time, her frantic, contorted face turned to Clyde, who by now had righted himself. For she was stunned, horror-struck, unintelligible with pain and fear—her lifelong fear of water and drowning and the blow he had so accidentally and all but unconsciously administered.

In the end Clyde's lethal act is a reflex triggered by a subconscious rejection of Roberta's entwining, mothering arms. Then, out of the depths of the lake rises the efrit to persuasively whisper the forbidden wish: how convenient simply to let her drown. Clyde swims to shore, thinking of "that last frantic, white, appealing look in her eyes. . . ."

His bottled-up rage had lashed out against the pregnant wife, the Mother, who is his only love but who betrayed him; the Mother who kept him in her thrall, denying him forever (God!) sexual happiness. He is free to go to the all-giving Mistress-Mother, Sondra the Golden Girl.

Dreiser lived deeply in his characters. In the tragedy on Big Bittern Lake, he had expressed his own tangled forbidden wish, not Clyde's.

·   ·   ·

Dreiser's description of what happened in the boat does not derive from any evidence offered at the Gillette trial. District Attorney Ward introduced this scenario: "He expected to throw her into the water and drown her, but he found it more difficult than he bargained for, and he was compelled and obliged to render her unconscious, to still her in the first place by striking her blows upon the head. . . . Then, having accomplished his purpose, he threw her body into the water."

Gillette testified that he had never promised to marry Grace and had taken her on the trip with no clear plan as to what he would do next. They had originally headed for Tupper Lake but didn't like it there and Grace had suggested they go on to Big Moose for the day. They decided to take a ride on an excursion steamboat but changed their minds after the desk clerk at the Glenmore Hotel advised them that the trip would take so long that they might miss dinner and recommended they hire a flat-bottomed rowboat instead (the clerk confirmed this on the stand). Out on the lake they rowed and drifted for several hours, then pulled in to shore to eat the picnic lunch Chester claimed he had packed in his suitcase (thus explaining why he brought the latter along). After lunch they drifted about some more and discussed what they should do about Grace's condition. Chester said he suggested they tell Grace's parents the truth. At that, she began to cry, stood up, and said, "Well, I will end it here." She then "stepped up onto the boat, kind of throwed herself in." When he tried to pull her out, the boat tipped over, and when he surfaced he could not see her. He swam around for a few minutes looking for her and then gave up.

District Attorney Ward in a brutal cross-examination tore this tale to shreds. And, given Gillette's previous lies—his use of phony names at the hotels, in an attempt, Ward said, to create a "straw man," a third person with whom Grace was having an affair; his suspicious failure to summon help; the incriminating suitcase he carried when he made his getaway; and the tennis racquet he buried in the woods—the circumstantial evidence weighed heavily against him. This, along with his seemingly callous demeanor in court and his admissions of sexual misconduct with Grace, caused the jury to convict him. (One juror believed him to be not guilty, but, under pressure from the others, capitulated.)

Unlike Clyde, Gillette had not visited beforehand the lake where the murder took place; nor was there any evidence that he was inspired by a news story, though there were plenty of drownings in Adirondacks lakes in the summertime. And he had originally intended to take Grace on the steamboat, from which it would have been difficult to stage an accident. The choice of Big Moose as the scene of the crime, and the skiff in which they went out as the vehicle, seemed to have been happenstance rather than part of a murder plot. The use of false names on hotel registers could have been the self-protective action of a man traveling with a woman not his wife.

It is possible that Gillette did not plan the murder but acted on impulse, or that the drowning was a tragic accident, or even that Grace did jump from the boat (she had talked of suicide). Chester does not seem to have been capable of conceiving and executing what the DA called a "well made and cunningly and shrewdly devised" plan. Nor did he appear "bloodthirsty and brutal," with "more stability of purpose, more determination, more cunning than a wolf has got." A small-town roué, he seduced the inexperienced Grace and thereafter made love to her two nights a week in the parlor of her boardinghouse while her landlady was asleep. He soon lost whatever romantic feelings he had for her and never took her out or gave her presents; he always invited the socially superior women he knew to parties and dances. When fellow workers at the factory criticized his shabby treatment of Grace, he told them to keep out of his affairs. He even ignored a warning by N. H. Gillette's son Harold that the affair "wasn't good for business." (In the novel, Harold becomes Gilbert Griffiths, greatly altered from life into Clyde's physical "double"; his opposition to Clyde originates in snobbery, and he knows nothing about the liaison with Roberta.)

Although Chester insisted that he loved Billy Brown, on the stand he never referred to her by name, calling her "she" or "her" or "the girl," transforming her into a nonperson as he had in life—provoking an outraged comment by the district attorney. He had drifted through life, seemingly untouched by any serious thoughts or deep emotions. Women, his mother told reporters, were his weakness.

He steadfastly denied that he had murdered Grace Brown until the very eve of his execution, and there are enough ambiguities in the case to leave a residue of doubt as to his guilt. The circumstantial evidence against him was compelling, but the crucial autopsy, which supposedly proved Grace had died from a blow to the head *before* she entered the water, had been so botched that it should have been ruled inadmissible.

But Dreiser was not interested in flaws in the prosecution's brief against Gillette. He selected from the facts of the case and transmuted them into a metaphorical murder full of sociological, psychological, and moral ambiguities. He examined the ultimate antisocial act from every perspective of guilt—except his own.

On January 9, 1925, Dreiser wrote a cheerful letter to Louise Campbell, announcing he had finished Book 2. Then, in an aside, he opened a window into his mind: "This book will be a terrible thing."

When I was leaving mother,
Standing at last in solemn pause,
We looked at one another;
And I—I saw in mother's eyes,
The love she cannot tell me . . .

—Chester Gillette's last poem (1906)

Book 2 passed through further revisions before it reached T. R. Smith's desk. On June 3 the editor told Dreiser that he had read "the last five or six chapters . . . with real agony. The slow, fatal working-up to the death of Roberta is one of the grimmest and most gripping tragedies that I have read in years. The whole idea was so powerful that I had difficulty in re-editing it for you." But with barely concealed anxiety he asked, Where was Book 3? They had received no copy whatsoever.

In July Smith sent Books 1 and 2 to the printer. Planning on October publication, he urged Dreiser to finish the final section as speedily as possible. Liveright was aiming for the novel to be out in time for the Christmas season and had already begun beating the drums, stimulating advance interest among booksellers and reviewers.

Since the novel would be a long one, he planned a two-volume edition to be sold for four dollars a set. That was a stiff price, so Liveright offered booksellers a larger than usual discount to induce them to take it. He budgeted $10,000 for advertising. Nevertheless, he told Dreiser (through

Smith) that he would increase the author's royalty from fifty to sixty cents a copy.

The year 1925 was the firm's most brilliant yet. The authors it published or had under contract included Ernest Hemingway (*In Our Time,* his first book to appear in America), William Faulkner (*Soldier's Pay,* his first novel), François Mauriac, Hart Crane, Robinson Jeffers, Djuna Barnes, Dorothy Parker, Conrad Aiken, Heywood Broun, and Frank Sullivan. He had a surprise best seller in Anita Loos's *Gentlemen Prefer Blondes* (on which he actually managed to lose money), and excellent sales for Sherwood Anderson's *Dark Laughter,* Eugene O'Neill's *Desire Under the Elms,* Frances Newman's *The Hard-Boiled Virgin,* and Maxwell Bodenheim's torrid *Replenishing Jessica,* which Sumner banned.

Yet on more than $1 million in sales, the company made only $8600 in profits, as a result of some expensive flops in the theater, high advertising budgets, and Liveright's personal losses on the stock market. To solve his perennial cash-flow problems, Liveright sold the cash cow of his operation, the Modern Library, to Bennett Cerf, then an editor with the firm, for $250,000, thus losing a profitable backlist.

On August 17 Smith begged Dreiser to forward all of the manuscript that had been typed. But Dreiser would not be rushed, and he continued to revise. He was still wading through the proofs of Books 1 and 2, working night and day to keep up, and Louise came up from Philadelphia to read and cut on the spot.

In September Mencken wrote Dreiser that the *Mercury* was in "easier waters" with 60,000 subscribers and that he had more money to spread around among "worthy literati." He was still not collecting a salary, had almost gone crazy from overwork during the first year, and feuded with Nathan over content, with the result that their friendship was shattered and Nathan resigned as co-editor. Otherwise Mencken was cautiously optimistic.

Dreiser promptly offered him a story called "The Power of Convention," which, he said, ran to 6500 words. Oh yes, he wouldn't consider cutting it. Mencken accepted it, and Dreiser could not resist noting that a certain critic had once proclaimed that he could not write short stories.

"Convention" tells of an adulterous love affair between a St. Louis newspaperman and a beautiful widow, and it came straight out of memories of Dreiser's newspaper days in St. Louis. The story was not so far afield from the *Tragedy,* after all. Both were about what Dreiser calls "the old eternal triangle—the woman who was not interesting, the woman who was interesting, and the man interested by the more interesting woman." What is more, murder is involved, although it is the younger woman who is accused of sending poison chocolates to the wife (for this *modus operandi* Dreiser drew on the case of a St. Louis intern who employed that technique to do in his former sweetheart). And in recounting the press coverage of the affair—

especially the factitious psychologizing of the "sob sisters"—he had the similar coverage of the Gillette case in mind.

In the end, the newspaperman meekly returns to the purgatory of domesticity—the fate Clyde would kill to avoid.

Despite his immersion in the novel, he might have been sardonically amused to hear of an episode that summer at the Fire Island cottage of Gene Fowler, the flamboyant journalist from Denver. On a weekend in August, while Dreiser was sweating over proofs, Fowler entertained Jug. Among her male friends was an editor of *The New York Times,* and that connection probably explains her acquaintanceship with the raffish Fowler. The latter was struck by her obsession with Dreiser more than a decade after their marriage had ended. After reciting a litany of the sacrifices she had made for his career, she said, "Theo hasn't written anything worth while since our separation—and he never will."

None of his novels after *Jennie Gerhardt,* with their tomcat heroes, interested her, and she had watched his career with growing dismay, thinking: if only she had been there acting as his balance wheel. She clipped and saved all her life a 1914 review of *The Titan,* underlining a passage that characterized *Sister Carrie* and *Jennie Gerhardt* as "the height of reticence" compared with Dreiser's latest novel—which she probably took as a tribute to her vigilance.

A contemporary photograph shows a stylish, smiling Jug. But one can see in the lines of bitterness etched in her face hints of the spurned wife in "Convention"—"so pinched, so homely, so faded—veritably a rail of a woman, everything and anything that a woman, whether wife, daughter, mother or sweetheart, as I saw it then, should not be."

Jug was in the *Tragedy* too, as to a lesser extent were all the women who had tried to bind Dreiser with the chains of marriage or guilt. (Clyde's nickname for Roberta is "Bert"—the same as Dreiser's for Estelle Kubitz.) Significantly, Dreiser made Roberta two years older than Clyde, the same discrepancy as between his and Jug's ages (Grace Brown was twenty when she died and Chester nearly twenty-three), strengthening the subconscious triangle of wife-mother vs. giving mistress.

Having completed the first two parts of the *Tragedy,* Dreiser had crossed the mountain range. For Clyde's trial he drew on the *World's* account, quoting snatches of testimony and counsels' remarks, but significantly rearranging the order of events. His most notable borrowing was several passages from Grace Brown's love letters, the reading of which had stunned the spectators at the Gillette trial. The headline from the *World* the following morning conveys some of the impact:

COURT IN TEARS
AS LOVE LETTERS
BARE GIRL'S SOUL.
MISSIVES EPIC IN THEIR
WOMANLY SWEETNESS.

Dreiser was later accused by Morris Ernst, the civil liberties lawyer, of plagiarizing those letters; and the additional charge was made that the letters had themselves been concocted by some of the New York journalists who covered the trial. The latter idea was preposterous; the letters had been found among Gillette's possessions. Indeed, he had accommodatingly told the DA where they were located, almost pronouncing his own death sentence, for no upstate New York jury in 1906 would have let him off after hearing the plaintive voice of Grace Brown reincarnated in court. In the last one she wrote, just before she left to join Chester on the wedding journey that ended in Big Moose Lake, she said farewell to the places on the farm where she was born:

> First, I said goodbye to the spring house with its great masses of green moss; then to the apple tree where we had our playhouse, the beehive, a cute little house in the orchard, and, of course, to all of the neighbors that have mended my dresses from a little tot up to save me from thrashings I really deserved.
> Oh dear, you don't realize what all of this is to me. I know I shall never see any of them again. . . .

Even the reporters dabbed their eyes.

Dreiser's use of this material was not plagiarism, and the girl's letters to Clyde earlier in the novel were made up out of whole cloth. It is only to show their effect at the trial that he does quote passages from Grace's, compressing them and changing the wording slightly—muddying their simple pathos in the process.

He altered the facts in the 1906 trial in more important ways. To emphasize the political ambitions of the district attorney, who is a candidate for county judge, he sets the trial before the election. In real life there was partisan rivalry between the prosecution and defense counsel Mills, a former state senator, but Ward had been elected before the trial. The fictional DA, Mason, is also given a more extensive background in local politics than Ward had.

The most significant departure was Dreiser's staging of the courtroom drama. In the first place, he altered the sequence of the trial. For obvious dramatic reasons he has the DA read Roberta's letters last. Ward introduced them before the crucial testimony of the five doctors who signed the autopsy report. (In Dreiser's first draft he follows the sequence of the trial more slavishly.) Clyde's attorneys do not make an issue of the bungled autopsy, as did Chester's—with good reason to do so.

He also transformed the tactics of the lawyers, particularly Ward's. Mason in the novel is a much more aggressive and adroit cross-examiner than was the real-life DA. The latter jumped around in time and place in an attempt to confuse Gillette, which succeeded. But to follow that course would have confused the reader of the novel as well. Rather than tediously exposing each of the inconsistencies of Clyde's alibis, Dreiser stages a dramatic confrontation: Mason hauls in the very boat in which Roberta and Clyde rowed on the lake and has Clyde reenact what happened. Ward had Chester describe the overturning of the boat while Chester was seated in the witness chair. (Showing how much influence press reports had on Dreiser's imagination, there was a false story that Gillette would reenact the crime in the boat on a nearby river.)

And while Ward contemptuously dismissed Chester's story that after looking around for Grace and seeing nothing, he swam ashore, Mason dwells far more on the fact that Clyde let the girl drown, since that is an element of his moral guilt. Ward, of course, was espousing the blow-on-the-head theory, so Clyde's omission was not as important to his case, although he stressed that Chester was a good swimmer and boatman.

In contrast to Gillette's defense team, Clyde's attorneys press the theory that Clyde was bewitched by love. "A case of the Arabian Nights," observes the philosophical lawyer Jephson, "of the ensorcelled and the ensorcellor." "I don't know what you mean," Clyde says. Jephson replies: "A case of being bewitched, my poor boy—by beauty, love, wealth, by things that we sometimes think we want very, very much and cannot ever have. . . ."

Far from slavishly cribbing from the transcript, Dreiser staged the trial in masterly fashion and wrote dialogue that stated afresh the themes of his novel.

After the verdict and the sentence, Dreiser follows closely real-life events—Clyde's transfer to the death house at Auburn prison, his appeal, the clemency hearing before the governor (though the cast in the novel is different), the execution. Little was known about how Gillette endured his last months. As his appeals dragged to their fruitless conclusion and his hopes that he would ultimately be freed were dashed, he saw virtually no one but his mother, his sister, and the Reverend Henry MacIlravy, an evangelist who had met Chester's mother during her unsuccessful lecture campaign to raise a defense fund for her son. With Louisa Gillette's approval, MacIlravy set out to convert Chester and succeeded. The minister is the inspiration for one of Dreiser's strongest characterizations, the Reverend Duncan McMillan.

The nature of the spiritual transactions between Gillette and MacIlravy is unknown, but in a state of intense isolation and after all hope of a reversal on appeal had vanished, Chester confessed his sins and accepted Jesus Christ as his Redeemer. The scenes when the minister is exhorting Clyde parallel Ward's cross-examination in court; each inquisitor cracks the young man's defenses, but he retains intact a core of belief in his innocence of murder and of unbelief in a Hereafter. Just as Clyde was also preserving a false innocence in court—his lawyer's concocted version of how Roberta met her death—so he at first withholds the true story from McMillan because he does not want to undermine his legal appeal. But when the appeal fails, and then the governor turns down his pleas for clemency, he confesses to McMillan, revealing the ambiguity in his own mind about whether he was guilty, legally or morally, of murder.

Society's judgment is rejected by Clyde after many sleepless nights. He admits the wrongfulness of his treatment of Roberta and his moral coward-ice in not attempting to rescue her; but how could a jury of farmers and shopkeepers judge him—men who never understood the compelling power of his dream? Or the compulsion of his desires? Or experienced the priva-tions and shame of his boyhood? And God—did He really consign sinners to Hell? And would He, in exchange for an act of contrition or penitence, reward Clyde with Eternal Life? What was the Hereafter to him, who wanted to live, who had spent only twenty-one years on the earth—who never had a life? The Heaven McMillan conjured up was the last mirage.

Weary, alone, and afraid, Clyde composes a statement, with McMillan's help, addressed to the young men of America, calling on them to accept Christ and live clean lives. Here Dreiser quotes verbatim the statement that Gillette issued on the eve of his execution. He confessed to MacIlravy and the prison chaplain that he had killed Grace; the details of the confession were never made public. Just before the execution, Governor Charles Evans Hughes, who had conducted exhaustive inquiries into some alleged new evidence, finding it neither credible nor relevant, called the prison and was told of the confession. The news eased his conscience, Hughes wrote in his memoirs, and he slept soundly for the first time in many weeks.

In Dreiser's version, only the minister and Elvira Griffiths plead with the governor. And it is the man of God who betrays him. Asked point-blank by the governor if he knows any reason why Clyde should not be executed, McMillan retreats into theology: Clyde sinned in his heart. The one man who might have saved Clyde forsakes him—does not even mention his sincere contrition, or the extenuating circumstances, which seemed so com-pelling when related to him by Clyde and which, Dreiser implies, might have moved the governor to grant clemency. Instead he adheres to the letter but not the spirit of the Word.

·   ·   ·

As Clyde is awaiting word on his appeal, a letter arrives—typed, unsigned, mailed from a large city, but unmistakably from Sondra. She can never understand his deed, but she "is not without sorrow and sympathy" and wishes him "freedom and happiness." No words of love to confirm that the dream for which he had risked all had not been a mirage: "His last hope—the last trace of his dream vanished. Forever! It was at that moment, as when night at last falls upon the faintest remaining gleam of dusk in the west. A dim, weakening tinge of pink—and then the dark."

Once upon a time Dreiser and Helen had shared a dream of the West. She was the Golden Girl, so beautiful that he feared she might suddenly vanish. California for a time held a promise of a life of sensuous ease and fulfillment, of money and luxury and beauty. But the mirage had dissipated, and he reluctantly returned to the reality of New York. Because of this dream of Helen, he could better dream with Clyde of Sondra. Of course Sondra was not literally modeled on Helen, but what she represented was. She did, however, share Helen's penchant for baby talk. With touches like this, and the initials C.G. for Gillette/Griffiths, the nickname Bert, the disparity between Clyde's and Roberta's ages, Dreiser dropped clues to his plagiarism from life—and his own subconscious.

Dreiser once called death the green door; in the novel it is iron-gray. In the first chapter of the *Tragedy*, Clyde and his family disappear through the portal of their mission—"The Door of Hope." When Clyde finds himself on death row, he is in a "gloomy and torturesome inferno," "a kind of inferno of mental ills" with the words *Abandon hope—ye who enter here* figuratively above the gate. Two doors: one offering the hope of an afterlife, the mirage of religion, the other offering extinction, nothingness.

Clyde's desires had taken him through successive doors of hope, each seemingly leading to a new opportunity, but instead leading him deeper into a high-walled labyrinth. First the walls of the factory, which he enters in hope of rising in the world, and then the door to Roberta's room, which he forces her to open, admitting him to the ecstasies of sexual love. But the invisible barriers of class block his ambitions for a finer life; then the walls of convention force him to choose between two doors: marriage to Roberta and "the way of the lake"—murder which promises freedom. He chooses the latter, loses his nerve, tries to flee—and finds that the last door has slammed shut. He is incarcerated in the gray walls of the legal system, convicted in an unfair trial by a district attorney who wants retribution not justice and a jury that has prejudged him. He has no help, save from his ineffectual family, no money to purchase rich man's justice.

On death row, Clyde is given two books to read: The *Arabian Nights* and *Robinson Crusoe*. The first, tales of fantasy and magic, of sorcerers and the ensorcelled; the second, an early work of realism describing how a man cut off from civilization survives by practical efforts. Dreiser was evoking his recurring themes: illusion and reality. Clyde's vacillation in the rowboat was "a reflection of the conflict between illusion and reality that was visited upon him by his early training and environment," Dreiser explained in an interview. At the last moment Clyde cannot face the reality of killing the beauty of soul that is Roberta for the bright, blinding illusion of Sondra.

And so the day finally comes when Clyde is to pass through that other door that he has feared for so long, and he says goodbye to his mother, speaking the illusion that will comfort her: "God has heard my prayers. He has given me strength and peace." But he adds under his breath: "Had he?" His weeping mother—so like Sarah Dreiser in her unconventional ways, her maternal strength. Dreiser must have recognized a kindred spirit in Louisa Gillette when he read how, unable to raise the money to come east for her son's trial, she had taken a job as special correspondent for a Denver paper. She had arrived in Herkimer just in time to hear the death sentence passed on her son. When Gillette received the guilty verdict, he telegraphed his father; Dreiser used the same wording for Clyde's telegram but has him send it to his mother. And in the end, Clyde is returned to the arms of his mother. The oedipal triangle is resolved, the mistress-mother lost, the wife-mother dead; the real mother reasserts her claim: "My son—my baby," she cries in their last *Pietà* embrace with the overwhelming, unconditional love of grief.

And then Clyde is hustled through the gray door. He walks toward it as if reliving a dream he has had a thousand times, though no dream because he has seen the other men on death row go the way of this door: "Now it was here; now it was being opened. There it was—at last—the chair he had so often seen in his dreams. . . . He was being pushed toward that—into that—on—on—through the door which was now open—to receive him— but which was as quickly closed again on all the earthly life he had ever known."*

Reverend McMillan accompanies him on the last walk, and after it is over he is sick, thinking only of Clyde's eyes. Those eyes are his most prominent feature throughout the novel. Marguerite Tjader Harris wrote that "eye magnetism fascinated Dreiser. His right eye impaired from birth and virtually useless to him, he believed he himself had become mystically endowed with eye magnetism at the moment of his mother's death." To

---

*To show how determinedly Dreiser worked over his manuscript, this is the first draft of that passage: "Here was the first door—here the second—the fatal door. Now it was being opened. There it was—the chair—and he was passing through into it. 'Goodbye, Clyde!' They had called that to him. Yes it was goodbye. . . .

"And then at last the final march. But to those who have read all that has gone before no word as to that will now be necessary—the final deathly chill—the few last confused and decidedly meaningless and unimportant thoughts."

Dreiser, the eyes were potent, flashing power and ambition, and instruments of artistic voyeurism, gatherers of "material," registering coldly and clinically. McMillan recalls Clyde in the chair: "his eyes fixed nervously and . . . appealingly and dazedly upon him. . . ."

The manuscript ends with an Envoy, called "Souvenir," which loops back to the beginning—the scene of the little band of missionaries amid the tall walls of the city that "in time may linger as a mere fable." Clyde's sister Esta's illegitimate son asks his grandmother for a dime for ice cream. She gives it to him, thinking she must not deny him pleasures, as she had her boy Clyde, for she now understands how denial in Clyde's early life magnified his hungers. Here Dreiser echoes a description he wrote nearly twenty-five years previously in a sketch about slum children in New York, their faces pressed against shop windows at Christmastime, gazing yearningly at the baubles with "an earnest, child-heart longing which may never again be gratified if not now." But the corollary was: if those dreams were so pervasive, so compelling, why should a few attain them, and the many stand outside the window, looking in? And if there was no answer to that question, why not kill to attain that which was denied?

Before that scene Dreiser had originally placed a section containing various "documents"—a newspaper account of Clyde's confession, written by McMillan; denials of guilt by Clyde's attorneys; a statement by Mason reaffirming his culpability, and finally a news story of McMillan's suicide, eighteen months after the execution, reporting that the minister had changed his mind and decided that Clyde was innocent. But this material was cut from the final book. Let the reader imagine McMillan's leftover life—and debate Clyde's guilt or innocence.

As he approached the end of Book 3, Dreiser became uneasy about the death-house scenes. On November 14, more than two weeks after the chapter had been set in type, he asked Mencken to intervene with friends at the *World* and wangle him a pass to the death row at Sing Sing prison—though "not the Execution room," he added. He had no desire to witness what went on behind that metal door. Mencken wrote James M. Cain, then an editorial writer on the paper. Cain replied that the visit could be arranged.

But when a judge granted the necessary order, Dreiser was surprised to learn that it authorized him to interview a convicted murderer named Anthony Pantano and that, moreover, the *World* expected him to write a story about it. The day after the visit Mencken received a telegram from the newspaper saying that Dreiser had demanded $500. Mencken wired his displeasure to Dreiser: "THIS PUTS ME IN A NICE HOLE INDEED." Furious, Dreiser hit back: "THE WORLD LIES YOUR TELEGRAM IS AN IN-

SULT." Caught in the middle, Mencken called down a pox on both sides. Dreiser wrote him a spluttering letter belaboring the *World* and the American press in general, and insisting that he had never been told that he was supposed to write about Pantano for nothing.

The paper had probably induced the judge to approve the visit by saying that Dreiser was on assignment to check out a rumor that Pantano was about to make a confession. But after granting the request, the judge heard about Dreiser's novel and suspected that the assignment was not bona fide. The *World*, fearing that he would deny them access to convicts in the future, pressed Dreiser to write the article to prove the commission was legitimate. Dreiser, oblivious to these maneuvers, busy packing and closing up the Brooklyn apartment, and assuming that the visit was arranged through Mencken's connections, demanded a fee. The *World*, which had expected him to do it out of gratitude, refused. The affair was settled amicably: Dreiser related his impressions to reporter Dudley Nichols, and it was published on page one under the banner: "Dreiser Interviews Pantano in Death House: Doomed Man Avows Faith in a Hereafter."

In the interview Dreiser described the layout of death row, the "heavy silence" that hung in the cellblock, the guards in their black uniforms and felt-soled shoes, who reminded him of an apparition in *The Cabinet of Dr. Caligari*, "a strangely stretched-out being, with thin, twining arms that twist above his head. . . ." An odd association, but evidently to Dreiser the place had a surreal quality like the movie. The inmates lay silently on their bunks. "One opened an unwinking eye and regarded me stilly, as if he were in another medium beyond communication, like a fish in an aquarium."

Dreiser told Mencken that the visit added little to his description of death row in the novel: "my imagination was better—(more true to the fact)—than what I saw." He did add a few details on the galleys—describing how the men played checkers with numbered boards, changing "No newspapers" to "No privacy," because the prisoners were allowed newspapers, changing a "solid Irish trusty" to a "tall cadaverous guard," like the one he had seen. Otherwise, the layout of his death house and the one at Sing Sing were completely different, and he may have made up his out of whole cloth. Clearly he wrote his description before he visited Sing Sing, and that description, save for a few touches, remains. The visit served to confirm his point that the death house was a psychological torture chamber.

The contretemps with Mencken soured their relations after five years of relative harmony. Mencken chose to ignore Dreiser's squawk, but privately he was exasperated, as was Dreiser with him for initially taking the *World*'s side in the dispute. On December 5 he sent Dreiser a copy of Isaac Goldberg's recently published biography, *The Man Mencken*, inscribed, "For Theodore Dreiser, Enemy for 18 years!" A joke of course.

．　．　．

Dreiser completed the novel on November 25, Helen writes. He made some small changes on the proofs, mostly the corrections in the death-house scenes. He had done more extensive rewriting on earlier galleys, particularly in Book 2 (Book 1 was little changed). Many of these changes consisted of adding scenes, rearranging events, clarifying motivation, or altering or expanding Clyde's perceptions. For example, Dreiser inserts some language to intensify Mason's hatred of the rich, emphasizing the force of class behind his early determination to "get" Clyde, who he assumes is a wealthy young idler. There are some minor changes in the trial, including interpolations of legal maneuvers by another hand—probably J. G. Robin's—to make the lawyers' tactics more authentic.

Now the book was too late for the Christmas season. What is more, the manuscript was already long—some 400,000 words—and it would be necessary to charge five dollars for each two-volume set. Smith, and Manuel Komroff, production manager at B & L, had already sought to lighten it by some 50,000 words. When they told Dreiser the news, he supposedly said, "What the hell is 50,000 words between friends?"—and then restored more than half of them.

But he had at last delivered the book begun six years before, and meditated even longer. Liveright set December 10 as the publication date, although finished books weren't available until the fourteenth. The publisher also planned to issue a luxury edition at $12.50 a set, signed by the author. He had advance orders for 10,000 copies of the trade edition, and excitement was building. By that time Dreiser was too exhausted to care, and desperate to get out of town, partly for a rest and partly to escape the reviews, which he expected to be hostile.

Helen was worried about him. He had been "battered" by the book (and by the love triangle in which he had been embroiled). From the novel, however much he tried, he could never escape; the writing machine kept pumping relentlessly, never giving him surcease for long, until the job was finished. At times depression radiated from him like a malign aura. Louise Campbell recalled: "You'd almost feel the air was black around him as he sat there for long stretches and said nothing." Sally Kusell thought him megalomaniacal, totally self-absorbed.

Helen was spiritually battered too. She later summed up that last year: " 'The dark days of Brooklyn,' he once wrote. And so they were. Dark days for all of us."

Walking with Clyde that last mile had taken him to a private philosophical dead end: for if the individual could be swept into dissolution without help or fellow-feeling, meaning, or hope of hereafter, life was a bleak business. Dreiser had faced the implications of his mechanistic philosophy before, but never so emotionally as in writing about the death of Clyde, alone and afraid, without hope of eternal life or any consolation of religion or philosophy, without even understanding why he must die. The door of hope clanged shut.

CHAPTER 22

"The Great American Novel"

Your writer, your scientist, your chief official, all have lost the power to revive the early illusion concerning fame and high place. Their beauty and delight is like the mirage in the heavens only plain to the eye outside. Within is nothing. . . .

I have seen youths, bright eyed and fair, groping after bubbles in rapture and conceiving them diamonds and the glitter of fine jewels . . . until their hand closed over a something that was not to be felt nor longer seen—mere colored air. I have long known . . . that an illusion it was which made them run. . . .

—Dreiser, "The Bubble of Success" (ca. 1898)

fter vacating the Brooklyn apartment, Helen and Dreiser moved to temporary quarters. He was considering a walking trip, his favorite therapy for bad nerves, but the weather was too cold, and they decided to drive to Florida. Helen had to rush about obtaining a new license plate. Dreiser let few people know of his plans. Just the previous Saturday he had told Sally Kusell what he had earlier written Mencken—that he was going hiking in the mountains of Virginia—alone.

That was propaganda. Sally had retreated to Larchmont and thus did not work on the final ten chapters of the *Tragedy*. But she and Dreiser managed to sneak a "glorious Saturday together." Dreiser did not tell her that Helen was driving him to Florida.

They got away on December 8. Dreiser climbed into the Maxwell beside Helen and they were off. Helen had a terrible cold and he had caught it. When they reached Philadelphia, both were miserable.

After consulting with Louise about editing *The Financier* for a new, trimmer edition, he joined Helen at the Eshericks', near Philadelphia. Then they drove to Baltimore, and Dreiser called on Mencken unannounced, leaving Helen in the car. After almost an hour, Mencken suddenly realized that Helen must be with him and rushed outside to invite her in. He had just that day taken his gravely ill mother to the hospital for an operation, and was too distraught to talk about much but his fears that she would not survive an operation. Dreiser, however, appeared to be more interested in obtaining a bottle of Scotch from Mencken's private cellar. After some desultory conversation, Dreiser left without saying anything about Anna Mencken. Helen uttered some platitudes at the door, but it was too late. Mencken was deeply offended by Dreiser's apparent insensitivity.

That night, when they reached Washington, he quarreled with Helen over Sally. Both of them were feeling exhausted and sickly. The prospect of listening to her recriminations for the rest of the trip annoyed him, and he threatened to return to New York if she didn't lay off.

In Florida the great land boom was just then passing its zenith. The speculative fever was exacerbated by the stock-market boom, which created a mirage of ever-rising prosperity. Dreiser was initially impressed by the new developments sprouting in recently drained mangrove swamps. "Here wealth builds," he exulted in his diary; compared to this, California was "a world of moderate means." But after seeing one Venice-by-the-Sea after another, he soured on the ubiquitous boomers, writing Mencken: "The state is all ready completely sub-divided in lots 50 × 80—and being sold off at from 150.00 to 50,000 per lot. . . . All the awnings, water piles & lanterns—domes and lattices of Venice, Sorrento, Capri—and Spain & Italy are being copied in plaster & papier-maché, and sold to crackers as romance, gaiety." Despite his cynicism about the real-estate boom, Dreiser caught the fever and paid a $200 binder on a lot, which was later washed away during a hurricane. Although the bubble had burst by then, the hurricane administered the coup de grâce. Within a year the real-estate offices were closed, and the landscape was littered with abandoned developments.

In his letter Dreiser promised Mencken a copy of the special edition of the *Tragedy,* "personally inscribed." (The inscription read: "Dear Heinrich: As my oldest living enemy I venture to offer you this little pamphlet. Don't mind if it emits a destructive gas. Us Germans—you know. D.")

Mencken's reply, written six days later, carried a subtle reproach: "My poor mother died the day after you were in Baltimore. I suppose that you noticed I was rather disturbed when we met." Unfortunately, he didn't know Dreiser's address and so sent the letter c/o Liveright, so Dreiser didn't receive it until his return to New York, in early February. Only then did he pen some consolatory words: "These things are in the chemistry and the physics of this immense thing and *'wisdom'* avails not at all. Yet fortitude is exacted of us all whether we will or not. I offer—understanding."

. . .

Dreiser and Helen continued to squabble. The mere sight of a letter from another woman was enough to touch off a fresh outburst from her.

Physically, he was run down, he wrote T. R. Smith, and had been "all but sick in bed." He was experiencing symptoms of that postpartum depression that hit him after he finished the first draft of The "*Genius.*" But as the weather warmed up, his spirits revived. Settling in a reasonably priced hotel in Fort Lauderdale, he and Helen took early-morning dips in the ocean, drove to Lake Okeechobee, and hiked along the Indian River.

Donald McCord, Peter's brother, was one of the first to congratulate him on the *Tragedy.* Dreiser replied, "Letters such as yours—(not the general run of criticism by any means) have satisfied me that the work is sound. I hear the usual drivel concerning style." He was putting up a bold front, for he had received no word about the reviews. On publication day, Liveright wired that he had ordered paper for another large printing, but the critics were still to be heard from.

At first the news was not very encouraging—a letter from T. R. Smith saying that Sinclair Lewis had declined to compose a prepublication blurb after reading the galleys. A more flattering letter arrived from the poet Arthur Ficke. Dreiser displayed his usual phlegmatism, saying he had fled New York "to avoid a deluge of knocks." But whatever the critics said, the book was done: "And that's that. I hope it soothes some. It entertained me for many a day."

Then came a telegram from Sally Kusell reporting that Stuart P. Sherman had written a favorable review in the *New York Herald Tribune Books* on January 3. Sherman's prominent notice was only the beginning. On January 9, Smith wired: THE REVIEWS ARE AMAZING ENTHUSIASTIC AND DIGNIFIED YOUR POSITION IS RECOGNIZED THE SALES ARE EXCELLENT.

This was followed by another telegram from Kusell on January 12 informing him that 17,000 copies had been sold. According to Liveright's figures, 13,378 copies were sold in December alone, netting Dreiser $11,872.02 in royalties. In one month he made more money from the *Tragedy* than he had from any of his previous books. Dreiser wrote Lengel: "It seems to have gone over the top. And none more surprised than myself."

It was ironic that the bellwether review had been written by his old foe. Sherman even alluded to his earlier crusade against Dreiser, but he explained that, in the years since The "*Genius,*" Dreiser had grown to understand American society, a polite way of saying he had become assimilated. As a result, his books had gained a greater artistic "detachment," "objectivity," and "impartiality." Dreiser's analysis of the psychological forces that drove Clyde to his doom, he said, was "complete and convincing"; more significant, his understanding of the predicament of poor Roberta showed that Dreiser had become a "good moralist." One need only compare Dreiser's "romantic glozing" of Jennie Gerhardt with his "exhaustive and astoundingly intelligent study of the shame and misery and torment of Roberta Alden in being pregnant, penniless, without a husband" to grasp how much he had matured since he published "that earlier sentimental tale."

The real comparison was between the Jennie who "got away with it" and the factory girl who pays for her transgression; the portrait of Roberta is true, Sherman says, because it illustrated the wages of sin. With unintentional humor, Sherman quotes a young woman to whom he has recommended the novel because "it would deter her from folly." Eyeing the two hefty volumes, she replied, "Yes, but by that time it would be too late."

Sherman's praise included the "usual drivel about style" and the much-quoted dictum: " 'An American Tragedy' is the worst written great novel in the world." He was, however, an accurate barometer of middlebrow taste. Only a decade earlier, reviewers could praise Dreiser's realism but warn of his immorality. Now Sherman grafted his own moral on Dreiser's novel— and certified it morally pure and aesthetically wholesome.

Late in January, Dreiser told Helen, "Well, it looks as if I've hit the mark this time. I think I'll go back home and collect some of the spoils." On January 25, 1926, they sailed from Miami on the *Kroonland,* the ship on which Dreiser had returned from Europe in 1913.

A pile of reviews—the finest of his career—awaited him in New York. The writers heaped on the superlatives:

> . . . the biggest, most important American of our times. (Sherwood Anderson, *Saturday Review of Literature*)
>
> The appearance of "An American Tragedy" is an event of first-class importance in the history of American letters. . . . (Abraham Cahan, *Jewish Daily Forward*)
>
> "An American Tragedy" is, in fine, the greatest of its author's works, and that can hardly mean less than that it is the greatest American novel of our generation. (Joseph Wood Krutch, *The Nation*)
>
> . . . the Mount Everest of American fiction, and . . . one of the high hills in all the fiction of the world. (Heywood Broun, New York *World*)
>
> . . . the best novel yet written by the greatest of American novelists. (Gretchen Mount, Detroit *Free Press*)
>
> [*An*] *American Tragedy* is . . . one of the very greatest novels of this century. (H. G. Wells)

Phrases like "The Work of Ten Years" and "After ten years silence" appeared in the headlines and leads of reviews. Dreiser was nominated "the outstanding literary figure of America" and even the "dean" of American letters, thus inheriting the mantle of the late William Dean Howells, who had died in 1920, "a dead cult" he himself admitted, widely scorned by the younger generation and forgotten by the reading public.

The *Tragedy* was praised for the soundness of its construction ("as solid as a bank building"); its exhaustive documentation ("He has fortified his charges with informing detail of every sort, biological, erotic, anatomical, contraceptual" [sic]); the tragic power of the narrative, especially the final scenes ("Oh, it is a painful story, a harrowing story, relentless and awful in its inevitability"); the catholicity of understanding shown the characters ("the author, with large sympathy and admirable impartiality brings out all that is strong and touching in the narrow and deluded religionist [Elvira Griffiths]"; the probing critique of American culture ("a tacit record of a parching absence of beauty in the common life").

Being Dreiser, he could not escape "the usual drivel concerning style." One critic insisted that the style was the man. Dreiser could not write as he does, "mixing slang with poetic archaisms, reveling in the cheap, trite and florid, if he were not, in himself, something correspondingly muddled, banal and tawdry." But in a letter to the editor of *The New Republic,* a poor young novelist named Henry Miller took issue with this attack, contending, "He uses language, consciously or not, in the manner which modern writers, notably Joyce, use deliberately: that is, he identifies his language with the consciousness of his characters."

Literary conservatives, such as William Lyon (Billy) Phelps, led the opposition. Phelps compared the novel to "a colossal derelict on the ocean of literature" that would "float around awhile" but "eventually sink." Moralistic reviewers read the *Tragedy* as an exposé of Errant Youth. It was true that as an inveterate observer of the conflict between generations, Dreiser had unintentionally probed in a profounder way than the flaming-youth novels the youth culture that flowered in the twenties, when young people of the white middle class were drawn away from the parental authority by mass cultural forces—magazines, movies, styles, music, dances—and had become independently mobile in their own Fords as well as socially mobile in their separate peer worlds centered in high school and college, a subculture with its own mores, initiation rites, secret societies, dress codes, slang, and manners and morals.

In the 1920s, mass culture (which Dreiser had amply observed in Hollywood films) set the styles. Clyde's initial break from his family is via a working-class peer group—his fellow bellhops, who teach him to drink, patronize prostitutes, and speed to roadhouse dances. He acquires the hedonistic values that clash with his parents' religious ones. Later, in Lycurgus, when he infiltrates Sondra's set, he is exposed to broader vistas of youthful pleasure—summers at the lake, tennis, dinner dances.

It is in Lycurgus that the barriers of class rear up in Clyde's path.

Dreiser's inspiration is to delineate the tenuousness of his position as a poor relation of one of the town's wealthiest families. To his fellow employees at the shirt factory, to the clerks in the stores he patronizes, and above all to Roberta, Clyde is a Griffiths, part of the Lycurgus elite of power and money, and he begins playing this role to the hilt. But to the Griffithses he is a poor relation and a potential embarrassment (unlike Gillette, who was accepted by his uncle's set). Once he has been taken up by Sondra, who befriends him just to spite Gilbert, Clyde assumes the airs of a young socialite. He tells Sondra's friends that his parents run a hotel in Denver. (This is necessary, Dreiser points out, because, "despite his looks and charm and family connections here, the thought that he was a mere nobody, seeking . . . to attach himself to his cousin's family, was disquieting . . . if he had a little money and some local station elsewhere, the situation was entirely different.") Even the place where he works is congruent with his social climbing. The pompous Gilbert tells a friend that the family business has a "social importance" because it produces cheap collars, "giving polish and manner to people who wouldn't otherwise have them. . . ." Collars are more than articles of clothing: they give status to parvenus like Clyde.

Dreiser shows the class relations between the characters by the logical formulation "X is to Y as Y is to Z." Roberta is to Clyde as Clyde is to Sondra. Roberta increasingly regards him not as her lover but as a socially superior being. She sees rich and poor in Lycurgus "divided by a high wall." And as he is admitted to Sondra's set, he begins to treat Roberta as an upper-class youth would—a factory girl with whom one takes his pleasure and then drops in favor of a more socially desirable woman. But unlike his lawyer, Belknap, who was involved in a similar scrape in his youth, Clyde hasn't the money and social connections to buy his way out—arrange an abortion. (He and Roberta are also ignorant of contraceptives.) Resenting Roberta's demands, Clyde snobbishly compares her condition to his sister Esta's, seduced by a wayward actor: *she* had not compelled anyone to marry her. How were the Aldens any better than his family?

The comparatives multiply: Sondra is a finer Hortense Gable, the novel's gold-digging shopgirl in Kansas City, while Clyde is a poorer Gilbert, his cousin and double. At Clyde's first meeting with Sondra she mistakes him for Gilbert. To Sondra, Clyde is the better-looking and more charming of the two, but she is too superficial a person to see Clyde's shortcomings other than his lack of money. His entrée into the social dance of Lycurgus derives from her patronage.

The physical resemblance between the two cousins is Dreiser's reminder that if Clyde had had similar advantages and family, he too could have been upper class. "After all you didn't make yourself," the lawyer Jephson says rhetorically at the trial.

Gilbert is also contrasted with his father to make another observation about American society: the change from a manufacturing to a consumer economy. The honorable, commanding Samuel Griffiths exemplifies the old producer class, living by an inner-directed credo, the Protestant ethic of hard work and postponement of gratification. Gilbert embraces this ethic as an ideology of control over the employees; but he expects material and social rewards as a matter of right, not as the result of hard work. Clyde, the arriviste, is drawn to the conspicuous-consumption lifestyle of the "fast set" and tries to slip into their ranks by imitating their dress and manners and by love, just as Carrie Meeber rose by attracting men of higher social position and then by practicing her allure on audiences in the theater.

Just as Dreiser made Carrie's career upend the values of the shopgirl novels of the 1890s, so he uses the Alger myth (hoary but still honored by the business society of the twenties) to ironic effect in the *Tragedy*. Dreiser subverts the Alger story not because he thought it pernicious (the idea of a poor, worthy lad rising in the world had inspired him as a boy) but because he believes that American culture has betrayed it by making the end, success, more important than the means and by condoning a money-oriented, inegalitarian society. Even Samuel Griffiths belies the myth, for he started his business with $15,000 he had inherited (the luckless Asa Griffiths was cut out of the will).

With the scalpel of irony Dreiser probes the dreams—and nightmares—of American culture, its ordinary terrors and tawdry illusions. Therein lies his lasting claim as one of America's most acute social novelists—not of mere manners (like Sinclair Lewis) but of the psychological, economic, and social structures that undergird class and manners. Not that Dreiser wrote a Marxist analysis or a sociological study. He molded his massive indictment of American society out of the pain of exclusion and hunger for material success. The prosaic dream of wealth and romance is heightened into a craving for beauty—and so it would be seen by one who has known the dirt and humiliation of being poor. Yet it is all a mirage.

At the core of the novel is not the American dream but the American nightmare, a vertiginous fear of falling, of social extinction, of being a nobody. Icarus plummeting into the sea. This dread is carried to the ultimate nightmare—of being a criminal hounded by society for a horrible crime one both did not and did commit. After the terror of flight from the Furies, Clyde is tried and found guilty. He is taken to death row, dressed in drab prison garb, and placed in the company of pariahs, like himself. He has been stripped of all the symbols of his former status. And then the great machine of the state impersonally, indifferently exterminates him.

Dreiser's power not only emanates from his patient accretion of fact; it also comes from the psychological resonances behind the facts. He drags the reader beneath the social surface into black depths of terror and desire, death and dreams.

Dreiser sensed that he must avoid the philosophizing that marred his earlier books; perhaps he had learned something from the younger novelists about understatement and from the visual power of film. He later told an interviewer, "I never once intruded upon this book my own point of view or interpretation or philosophy, nor even indulged myself in the relief of painting a word picture here and there. . . ." When he was finished, "the result seemed so foreign to me that I simply couldn't adjust myself to it at all. . . . It struck me as being . . . a monumental failure."

> Now we waited about the large bare table, while the lady
> set the cake before her and sat down. "A chocolate cake!"
> Dreiser licked his lips. The lady cut a slice. Dreiser grew
> nervous. The lady cut a slice. Dreiser's eyes bulged, his
> hands thrummed. She cut a slice. Dreiser tipped his chair,
> sprawled forward. . . . Swiftly, as if working against a
> possible crisis, the good lady put a piece of cake on a plate
> and handed it to Dreiser. He fell to, happy, rolling his eyes.
> —Waldo Frank (1926)

No one, least of all Dreiser, would have predicted that his novel would strike the lucrative vein it did. The first intimation of wealth came not long after his return when Liveright suggested dramatizing *An American Tragedy*. He needed a Broadway hit, and it looked promising—an acclaimed novel that his showman's instinct told him could have a sensational impact in the theater. To do the adaptation, Liveright chose an unknown, Patrick Kearney, a young actor with one produced play to his credit called *A Man's Man*, which had caused a minor stir in a little theater production.

On March 8 Kearney went to Liveright's home in New Rochelle, and the publisher reported to Dreiser that they had labored until 1:30 in the morning, blocking out a scenario that called for four acts and twelve scenes. "I'm honestly bubbling over with enthusiasm about it," he said.

Horace wanted to move quickly because now was the time to exploit the novel's success; also he was eager to sign two young stars, Glenn Hunter and June Walker, for the roles of Clyde and Roberta while they were at liberty. Kearney was happy to work on a novel he admired and readily agreed to take 45 percent of the author's royalties and 35 percent of the motion picture rights, leaving a bigger share for Dreiser. A contract was drawn up that gave Dreiser a generous share of the gross receipts at the box office, on a sliding scale of 5 percent on up to 7½ percent of anything in excess of $7000. The only sticking point between them was Liveright's share of the motion picture rights. In his initial letter the publisher had noted, *en passant*, "You know of course that the producer of the play always gets 50% of the motion picture rights." But Dreiser objected strenuously to this provision, and rather than haggle, Liveright suggested that Dreiser should receive one-third of the money if the play ran for ten weeks in New York with an average weekly gross of $12,500. However, if Dreiser sold the motion picture rights for a sum of $30,000 or more before the play opened, Liveright would receive nothing. Thus Liveright was in effect betting Dreiser $30,000 that he couldn't sell the movie rights before the play was produced.

At any rate, the publisher told Dreiser in his March 8 letter, the question of movie rights was academic. Given the present moralistic climate in Hollywood, "it's extremely doubtful that *An American Tragedy* can even be done on the screen. Tremendous pressure would have to be brought on Hays to let him pass it, and then the theme is such that it's rather unlikely that any company who would make a good picture out of it would care to go on it."

Liveright was repeating what Jesse L. Lasky (whose readers had rejected the *Tragedy* in galleys) told him. But after the studio head saw Quinn Martin's movie column in the New York *World* on March 7, he changed his mind. Martin wrote that *An American Tragedy* "if courageously treated would make the greatest film yet produced." He doubted that Dreiser would entertain the thought of such a film·"out of sheer pride of authorship," because Will Hays "would annihilate it." No producer would risk his money on such a chancy property, and no director was capable of filming it with integrity. Nevertheless, Martin's column stirred up much interest at the Famous Players–Lasky office in New York. Director George Cukor urged Lasky to buy the property. Producer Jed Harris dropped by and became so enthusiastic about the idea that he outlined a presumably Hays-proof scenario on the spot.

The upshot was that the movie mogul vowed he must have the book, and what Jesse wanted Jesse bought; price was no object. Also, he was on good terms with Will Hays, whom he had helped install as president of the Motion Picture Producers and Distributors of America after the Fatty Arbuckle scandal, and may have thought that given the novel's reputation as a serious work of art, the arbiter of movie morals could be persuaded to approve it.

On March 17 Dreiser wrote Louise Campbell that he had decided to stay in New York for a while rather than take Helen on a long-promised junket to Paris, because "they're making a play of the *Tragedy* & there's something else in the wind." Two days later, when he appeared at Liveright's office to sign the play contract, the publisher announced that he was having lunch with Lasky and his special assistant, Walter Wanger, to discuss terms for a movie sale. This surprising intelligence planted in Dreiser's suspicious brain the idea that Liveright had been lying to him about Lasky's lack of interest and had some kind of sub rosa arrangement with him. Hadn't Liveright told him ten days ago that it was doubtful a movie could be made of the book, and that Lasky would pay $35,000 at most and only if the play were produced? The publisher's friendship with Lasky (Liveright later said he gave "absolute loyalty" to the movie company) exuded the smell of collusion.

Dreiser didn't know that Lasky had suddenly blown hot and had been trying to reach him for several days. Once he had decided to buy the novel immediately, he didn't need Liveright's play—or Liveright. In his autobiography Lasky says that the publisher had engaged in "delaying tactics" by concealing Dreiser's whereabouts.

Thus began a chain reaction of misunderstandings. Presumably, all Liveright knew was that the movie sale hinged on the play. For taking the risk of producing the dramatic version of *An American Tragedy* he felt he was entitled to a portion of the Hollywood gold. Horace was suffering from chronic cash-flow shortage. He planned two new productions (*The Best of Us* and *Black Boy,* a play about a Negro prizefighter, starring Paul Robeson), and producing the *Tragedy* would be costly.

Liveright asked Dreiser what he wanted for the film rights. When he said $100,000, the highest amount ever paid for a novel, Liveright opined that $60,000 was more realistic, but told Dreiser to stick to his guns and invited him to come to lunch with the film people and state his demand in person. Then he asked if Dreiser would "take care" of him: anything above $60,000 should be his. To that Dreiser merely smiled sardonically—amused, he later said, at how Liveright had so quickly changed his tune. The publisher, however, took the smile as a sign of assent. The two of them had a few drinks and strolled to the Ritz. En route, Liveright again asked Dreiser if he would take care of him and Dreiser said he would.

And so they joined the two movie men in the soigné dining room. Over coffee Liveright, in one last try at steering the negotiations, announced that he and Dreiser had agreed on a price: $100,000, of which he would receive $30,000 and Dreiser $70,000. The two men's recollections of what happened next diverge. Liveright said Dreiser seemed to assent to that formulation. Dreiser insisted that he had promptly told Lasky and Wanger that such a split was news to him. Liveright then excused himself from the table to say hello to June Walker and Glenn Hunter, who were lunching with his theatrical partner.

In the ensuing discussion Dreiser bluntly asked Lasky why he was buying the film. The other replied: "The way it is, the movies are under criticism today and we want to do something; as a matter of fact, we want to make a gesture and we can do it through this book." Dreiser then asked Lasky if he would make "a great feature picture" out of the book. The other promised he would. Then, Dreiser said, price shouldn't stop you. He also claimed he requested an additional fifteen or twenty thousand for Liveright as part of the deal.

When Liveright returned to the table, he inquired about his 30-percent share. Dreiser protested that he was obligated to give him only 10 percent. (This was true. Quite apart from their agreement on *An American Tragedy*, an earlier contract awarded Liveright 10 percent of any movie sale he made.) The publisher protested that they had agreed on the higher figure. Dreiser retorted, "That's a damn lie." The publisher's smiling mask vanished. "You're a liar!" he shouted. The other diners looked on in shocked silence as a furious and red-faced author rose to his full 6 feet ½ inch, shouted an oath, and told his publisher to stand up and fight. When the 130-pound Liveright prudently remained seated, Dreiser picked up a cup of warm coffee and dashed the contents in his face. A waiter mopped up the drenched victim as Dreiser stalked out.

The following week Lasky and Dreiser agreed on a total price of $90,000, of which Liveright would receive $10,000. Liveright was hurt by what he saw as Dreiser's ingratitude and stunned by the sudden turn his fortunes had taken at that lunch. In private he remained embittered, telling friends that his efforts alone had made the sale possible. As for Dreiser, he firmly believed that Liveright had tried to pull a fast one by concealing Lasky's interest. Yet the entire quarrel had come about because Lasky, after telling Liveright about the difficulties of filming the novel, had changed his mind upon reading Martin's column and talking to his associates. Liveright acted on the basis of what Lasky told him before the column. Moreover, Dreiser might well ask, how could Liveright claim a 30-percent slice before the play was produced, contrary to their agreement? In the light of what Lasky told him at lunch, about trying to reach him, Liveright's conduct seemed suspicious indeed. He already mistrusted the man; this was the proof.

Still seething, Dreiser dispatched a harsh letter to Liveright demanding a written apology. As usual, the publisher turned the other cheek. He really could not afford to lose his now-profitable author. In his first reply, he swore that the Ritz meeting was not a "set-up" to bilk Dreiser. His main desire all along was to see that Dreiser "got everything possible out of this book." Six days later, Donald Friede, who had lunched with Dreiser in the interim, reported to him that Dreiser had been hurt by the charge that he had lied. Liveright formally apologized and tried to put the fracas behind them. He dangled the promise of a new promotional campaign for the *Tragedy* which he would personally supervise and which would exploit the movie sale.

That campaign was duly launched with a statement by Lasky to the press that the movie of *An American Tragedy* "will be the most ambitious effort made by our company." Every studio in Hollywood had wanted the book, he said, and Famous Players won the contest only "after the payment of a record sum, and also after we had given a guaranty to Mr. Dreiser that the book would be filmed exactly as it is written." Dreiser would later have reason to question those words.

Another imbroglio marred Dreiser's return to New York. H. L. Mencken's review did not appear until *The American Mercury* hit the stalls in late February, but he had written it in January. On January 28 he had warned Dreiser, almost apologetically, "I have taken a dreadful hack at the book in the Merkur for March, but there is also some very sweet stuff in the notice. I am sending a proof to Schmidt [Smith]."

It was devastating. Mencken calls *An American Tragedy* a "shapeless and forbidding monster—a heaping cartload of raw materials for a novel, with rubbish of all sorts intermixed—a vast, sloppy, chaotic thing of 385,000 words—at least 250,000 of them unnecessary!" Whole chapters could be spared; it is full of "banal moralizing and trite, meaningless words." "Is Freudism stale, even in Greenwich Village? Ahoy, then, let us heave in a couple of bargeloads of complexes. . . ." And, quoting an awkward sentence: "What is one to say of such dreadful bilge? What is one to say of a novelist who, after a quarter of a century at his trade, still writes it?"

He relents a little in his summing-up, writing, " 'An American Tragedy,' as a work of art, is a colossal botch, but as a human document it is searching and full of solemn dignity, and at times it rises to the level of genuine tragedy. . . . Hire your pastor to read the first volume for you. But don't miss the second!" But the damage had been done.

Mencken had come of age as a critic when the chief literary battles were against the censors. Now Dreiser not only was acceptable in the better literary circles; he was popular with Puritans like Stuart P. Sherman. The broadside in the *Mercury* had little effect on the sales of the *Tragedy* or the canonization of Dreiser, but it would destroy a friendship. A few years later, writing in his diary, Mencken blamed the *World* quarrel for the rupture, along with Dreiser's insensitivity about his mother's death. He writes that Dreiser did not offer any condolences, forgetting that he had written a sympathetic letter upon his return from Florida. Mencken says nothing about his hostile review of the *Tragedy,* and he had often urged Dreiser not to take critical opinions personally. But Dreiser did; to him the review was a betrayal.

In a letter to Mencken written February 8, Dreiser starts out normally enough, reporting that he and Helen are staying at the Empire Hotel and inviting Mencken to dine with them sometime. But then his anger boils up in a postscript: "As for your critical predilictions [sic], animosities, inhibitions,—et cet. Tush. who reads you? Bums and loafers. No goods. We were friends before ever you were a critic of mine, if I recall. And,—if an humble leman may speak up—may remain so—despite various—well—choose your insults."

Mencken disdained to reply; the feud was on. Encountering Mencken's assistant, Charles Angoff, a few months later, Dreiser remonstrated, "That boss of yours ought to stay in Baltimore on the *Sun* and keep out of writing about books. [Eugene] O'Neill is luckier than the rest of us. He has George Nathan to write about him. Now, Nathan knows playwriting. I can feel it inside me. But Mencken—oh well. What does it matter, anyway?"

As time went on, Dreiser's festering rancor became gangrenous. As he had blamed Mrs. Doubleday for the suppression of *Sister Carrie,* so he concocted a plot by Mencken to destroy the *Tragedy.* As the latter described it to Irita Van Doren, book editor of the *Herald Tribune,* "Poor old Dreiser has been going about New York saying that I rushed my review of 'An American Tragedy' into The American Mercury in order to get ahead of Sherman, and so poison the wells. It is, of course, nonsense. Dreiser, I fear, is a bit ratty." Dreiser was probably inflating the idea that Mencken had reviewed the unrevised page proofs into evidence that he had rushed out the notice—forgetting that the review had appeared long after Sherman's.

Mencken acted throughout as though he couldn't understand why Dreiser was angry, and professed indifference to the sudden chill in their relations. He seems to have been genuinely surprised that Dreiser would take his *An American Tragedy* review so hard. After all, the book was selling well. But, as Dreiser suggested to Angoff, he had expected Mencken to hail it and instead he had hurled the same kind of wounding invective that he'd used in his review of *The "Genius."*

Around the time Dreiser lashed out at Mencken he shed another friend, Sally Kusell. The provocation seems trivial. Apparently she had asked him to give her a personally autographed copy of the *Tragedy* recognizing her contribution to it, and he resented the request, having begun to feel she was crowding him too close, calling him "Master," and all that. It may have been ingratitude on his part or else she demanded more credit for the success of the book than he was willing to give her. Like Dreiser's other lovers, she made the mistake of finding her identity in his greatness. She admitted she was jealous of Helen, but assured him that she didn't aim to intrude on his life with her, as she had done when they were in Florida. To put a stop to that, Dreiser had refused to give her his New York address. A week later he hit her with a formal indictment, as it were:

> The trouble between us springs . . . from the firm conviction that
> your interest in me is somehow based more on a desire for mental and
> artistic recognition through me than it is on any innate personal and

ineffective as well as effective qualities which may characterize me. . . . The matter of inscribing the book was one of those chance flashes which reveal so much. There must be some form of written recognition consoling to an ego that sees—or did see in me as a writer—not as a man,—some form of personal achievement & stimulation for you.

Sally sent him a stream of beseeching letters. Finally, in March, she departed for California. Helen, whose resentment against Sally had erupted in Florida, could claim a victory. Indeed, she had the satisfaction of personally receiving her rival's surrender. Just before Sally left for California, she called Dreiser to tell him that her train was scheduled to depart Penn Station at such and such a time. Helen, who had answered the telephone, politely agreed to relay the message. Then Sally told her, "You are the only one I was ever afraid of. . . . You have him *always,* he comes *home* to you." Helen agreed that he did, though that had not made life any easier for her. Sally commiserated with her sufferings, then confessed she knew she had lost after Helen's return from California, when she noticed "a definite change in him, a psychic strength I felt I could not beat." Sally conceded first place to Helen. "I felt as though I wanted to put my arms around her," Helen writes.

"I just sold the moving picture rights for $100,000 [sic]" Dreiser wrote Lengel. "I'm likely to be rich." He began to invest in stocks after boning up on the subject just as he had immersed himself in the technicalities of nineteenth-century finance before writing about Cowperwood. But he did not speculate. Most of his investments were in blue chip stocks and supposedly gilt-edge bonds from which he could draw a steady income.

Scarred by many disappointments over a twenty-year career as a full-time novelist, Dreiser found himself at the age of fifty-four in the promised land of wealth and ease that Clyde Griffiths had died trying to attain. Innately frugal and suspicious of wealth (he had seen it destroy his brother Paul), his instinct was to hoard what he got. Financial security and freedom to write what he pleased were his primary aims; money would give him more independence in his dealings with publishers.

But he was not an ascetic. As his bank account was enriched, his wardrobe blossomed. Waldo Frank, in a *New Yorker* "Profile," offers this snapshot: "If you see him nowadays, his ruddy face shining above the dapper clothes and his spatted boots pounding along beside the pumps of a flapper, you have a grotesque sense of an old college boy on a vacation. . . ."

Around this time Dreiser strode into John Cowper Powys's shabby Patchin Place flat and announced, "I am opulent, opulent! What can I give you?" Powys asked for a particular rare edition he had long coveted, and Dreiser bought it for him. Powys, a novelist never fully appreciated in his lifetime, once wrote that success "is an invariable sign, not of superiority, but of vitality . . . more brute force than imagination, and more *luck* than anything else!" Dreiser, however, was a "special case . . . one of those formidable Men of Destiny. . . . For once in human history the exploiters of genius have met their match in Dreiser. He can give as good as he takes, and a little more."

Dreiser found himself beset by a swarm of distractions—pretty women, letters from total strangers begging for financial assistance, decisions involving large sums of money and future publishing arrangements. He had known a modicum of fame, but nothing like this *celebrity* (a word he had used in *Sister Carrie,* long before it was in currency, to describe the patrons of Hurstwood's "gorgeous" saloon).

For all their reputation for frivolity, the 1920s were a time when books had a wider impact on popular culture than any era before or since. Movies, though popular, were still too lightweight to receive much more than fan-magazine treatment. Authors of best-selling—even artistic—books were not as well known as some movie stars, but they were celebrities, and their words and days were chronicled by literate New York columnists.

Dreiser's reputation, fanned by Liveright's publicity mills, grew apace. His public correspondence became so voluminous that he was forced to hire a secretary to handle it. The letters fell into four general categories: fan notes, appeals for money, pleas for advice from young writers, and requests for autographs, public statements, lectures. In the first category were heart-felt thanks for writing *An American Tragedy,* which was "comparable to no story I know of in its sympathy for the ignorance and weakness of young men. . . ." People wanted advice or understanding. An actress hoped that he was not in the "mist [sic] of a story, for my heart wants to pour out its life story all the secrets and heart aches the world must never know are mine."

To the requests for his time he gave a standard reply: he had "inviolable rules" against public speaking, joining clubs or societies, serving on committees and boards, and autographing books or pictures.

For young writers, however, he was a soft touch, dispensing sincere advice or kindly criticism (it would become his practice to have various literary assistants read any manuscripts that came in and report on them to him). He advised one hopeful that writing could not be taught. He recommended working on a newspaper, "if you do not stay at it too long," as the best school. He urged a poet not to be deterred by the criticisms of his college professors. "Your faith in your own ideas & dreams must not waver. All writers are, and must expect to be, criticized." If he really had it in him to be a writer, he would keep on writing and eventually find something to say.

To the begging letters he had a standard response: he had so many needy relatives that he was precluded from extending help to strangers.

He helped George Sterling get his tragedy *Lillith* published, writing a foreword to the book, but later had reason to feel he should have done more: in November came the news of the poet's suicide after a bender.

One of Dreiser's correspondents was a voice from the past. On March 31 Jug sent him congratulations on his "wonderful good fortune," meaning the movie sale. She followed that with a second letter in which she asked if he might provide for her so that she could go back to Missouri and adopt her late sister Rose's daughter, Rosemary (now an orphan), thus fulfilling at last the dream of motherhood that Dreiser had thwarted. Dreiser replied, Wasn't it wonderful that, after all these years, without a comment from her about any of the twelve books he had published, she should suddenly take an interest in his literary career? Did the fact that he had come into a considerable sum of money have something to do with it?

Unfair, Jug protested. Her admiration for his writing had been just as great before *Carrie* was even published. As for the other books, well, she had leafed through a few of them but had no time for reading. She reminded him that she had supported herself and had not bothered him about money over the years (though that was not for want of trying) because he had told her his income was erratic. Now, she assumed, he could afford to help her. At the age of fifty-seven and in frail health, she was in danger of losing her job in a dress store. In May, having heard nothing from Dreiser, she advised him to get in touch with her attorney.

Dreiser's old bitterness resurfaced. He told his lawyer, Dudley Field Malone, that when they were living together Jug had never been sympathetic with his work "and did everything to discourage me from proceeding with it." Her idea of success "was along very different lines." He had done his best writing while living apart from her. As for the alleged shower of wealth, he estimated that he would earn $20,000 from sales of *An American Tragedy* that year (too low by half, it turned out) and had "tentatively" sold the movie rights to the novel, receiving $35,000 as a "binder" (no mention of the additional $45,000 he had coming). He intended to invest as much of those funds as he could, "in order that the income . . . may keep me independent of publishers—permit me to work in my own way—guarantee me against a rainy day in the future, and possibly permit me to do at least a few of the things I have always wanted to do."

Having vented his old grudge, he agreed to pay her $200 a month for the rest of her life. In return she absolved him of liability for any debts she might incur and relinquished any claims on his estate after his death. There seems to have been some promise that she would agree to a divorce—or so

Helen always insisted. But it is not at all clear that Jug would permit one. And Dreiser may not have pushed her for fear that a divorce settlement would have cost him even more. Also, there were advantages in preserving the status quo: the tie to Jug gave him a convenient out when other women started importuning him about marriage, as they usually did.

He was contemplating a separation of another sort. His contract with Liveright ran out in January 1927, and he entertained feelers from Harper's and Doubleday. The spat with Liveright had inflamed his distrust of the man, though they were still speaking on business matters. He took up Liveright's offer to inspect the sales ledgers, though Bennett Cerf, who disliked Dreiser, considered the procedure something of a joke.

Dreiser's suspicions were not mollified, and he began checking with booksellers. In April he sent a letter to a wholesaler to inquire about sales of *The "Genius"* and the *Tragedy*, coyly explaining that he needed the information "because of a special type of novel I am writing." These inquiries probably yielded no hard evidence that Liveright was cheating him, but he remained convinced that he was being shortchanged—that the company kept two sets of books and skimmed off some of his returns.

But Dreiser did have some cause for mistrust of Liveright's freewheeling ways, and as a further check, he cultivated Arthur Pell, the firm's hard-nosed treasurer, who could presumably give him the straight story on finances since he was the only real businessman in the place. It was Pell who complained about the unlimited expense accounts top editors enjoyed, Pell who made certain the books were always short of the actual cash on hand that day, to prevent Horace from advancing the money to Greenwich Village geniuses, Pell who had opposed the Modern Library sale and then demanded that Cerf and Donald Klopfer come up with an additional $25,000 immediately. Perhaps flattered by the attentions of the famous author, the treasurer began handling his investments, but moved on to other services, including, presumably, keeping tabs on sales. Dreiser later wrote, ". . . except for you I wouldn't be with the house at all—only I know you know that."

Harper's was the more serious suitor, and Dreiser retained a nostalgia for the prolific years of his association with the firm when he wrote *Jennie*, *The Financier*, and *The Titan*. In May the company offered to publish a uniform edition of his books. Such a proposition was not as risky as it had been a few years earlier; thanks to the success of the *Tragedy* and Liveright's institutional advertising campaign, sales of Dreiser's other novels had picked up. *Carrie* sold 3412 copies in 1926 (twice as many as the previous year); *Jennie* nearly 1400; and *The "Genius"* more than 8000. Harper's thus stood ready to harvest the fruits of Liveright's investment. In return, the house promised to throw the full weight of its publicity apparatus behind the collected edition and spend $10,000 annually for an advertising campaign hailing

Dreiser as "America's greatest author." Half of the money for this "fund" would be siphoned from Dreiser's royalties, however.

Liveright rose to the challenge and performed his usual financial leger-demain, weaving a spell of future wealth that lured Dreiser despite his misgivings. He counseled Dreiser to stay with B & L, whom he knew, whom he could trust [sic]—especially if it was a matter of a ten-year con-tract, which was one of Dreiser's demands, along with "a sense of absolute security" and greater participation in the business affairs of the company. His offer, which after further discussion was embodied in a memorandum of agreement running for five years, amended the 1923 contract in the follow-ing particulars: 20-percent royalties on all of Dreiser's books; a $500-a-month drawing account; in the fall of 1927 B & L to launch the "great Dreiser set"—the long-promised collected works of Theodore Dreiser in a limited edition; in the spring of 1929, the publisher to print a "popular library edition" from the limited edition plates; $10,000 to be expended on advertis-ing the *Tragedy* during the remainder of the year; commensurate sums to be laid out on future books; and a weekly advertisement of Dreiser as institution or of one of his books to run in *The New York Times Book Supplement* throughout 1927.

To deal with Dreiser's desire to participate in the affairs of the house, Liveright offered to make him a member of the board of directors. Dreiser's initial reaction to that suggestion was huffily to reject it, saying it would be "a fine thing for Boni & Liveright, but not such a fine thing for Theodore Dreiser." Liveright then proposed that Dreiser meet once a month with the editorial and sales staff and go over plans for promoting his books and his name, with Dreiser given the right to veto any scheme he disliked. Dreiser apparently didn't know what he wanted, but in the final agreement he was given a seat and one share of stock, subject to an amendment of the corporate bylaws. This was necessary because Liveright and Donald Friede each owned half the total shares, and giving Dreiser a vote on the board would upset the balance between them (hence Liveright's caginess). Dreiser appar-ently feared that if B & L went on the rocks, he would be held financially liable; thus the new memorandum exempted his share of stock "from assess-ments or any obligations of any kind." But Liveright, whose ego matched Dreiser's pound for pound, staunchly resisted giving him any managerial responsibilities. Still, Dreiser could hardly refuse such an attractive package, which came as close as any agreement could to fulfilling his dream of artistic independence and absolute financial security.

But what had he really won? He had bound himself tighter to the fortunes of a man whom he distrusted, who embodied the spirit of ballyhoo he found undignified yet approved when it was his books that were being touted, and whose profligate spending and plunges into the stock market and the theater should have sounded alarm bells. In return he was put on a dole of lavish advances that must be earned back by royalties from future books. He was betting on two long shots: his ability to produce more best sellers and Liveright's continued solvency. Swollen by the success of the *Tragedy,* he seems to have forgotten that he was an artist and could not crank out books to order. Of course he had the uncompleted manuscript of *The Bulwark* and an outline of *The Stoic,* the third volume of the Cowperwood trilogy, in his trunk; they should do well, based on his current fame—*if* he could finish them in reasonable time, which was by no means certain. As he himself had said, his books never came in an orderly progression.

He once told Nathan, "What I am still looking for in the midst of all this success that seems to have come to me is some little, greasy one-horse publisher who . . . has a high and very real love for literature and who, though he may be poor in money, will have time to talk sincerely with me about my work. . . . I am sick of these business-men publishers with their offices that look like the *Ile de France* and with their minds that look on books as if they were so many boxes of merchandise."

Now, seeking "absolute security"—a need dictated by his chronic insecurity—he had bound himself in golden chains to a publisher with offices like the *Ile de France.*

His business affairs presumably in order, and his desk cleared of literary projects (which that year consisted chiefly of an article on the Florida boom and the preparation for press of a limited edition of his poems, *Moods Cadenced and Declaimed*), Dreiser decided it was time to enjoy the fruits of his success. Helen would at last have her trip to Europe.

They sailed on June 22 and spent four months abroad, meeting prospective publishers in Scandinavia, cruising Norwegian fjords and trekking through still pine forests, visiting the graves of Ibsen and Björnson. Then on to Germany, where Helen "felt a strange harmony come over Teddie," as he communed with his ancestry. Yet he did not call on relatives in his father's birthplace, Mayen, and, echoing his father, criticized the Prussians as "too drastic. . . . They think too much about abstruse and esoteric problems—life, death, the destiny of man—too little of their immediate surroundings." He saw this heredity in himself, but was helpless to change.

In Vienna he missed Freud, to whom he had a letter of introduction, and in Prague stayed with Tomas Masaryk, the nation's first president and an admirer of his books. In Paris he met his translator, Victor Llona, who took him to visit Balzac's home. Deeply moved, he gazed on Balzac's memorabilia. Dreiser stayed a long while, saying little, perhaps thinking of his own amazing and unsettling prosperity and envying this monastic cell where Balzac hid out from creditors and completed his Human Comedy.

After ten days in London, where he researched Yerkes' career for the third volume of his long-postponed trilogy, bantered with George Bernard Shaw, and formed a fast friendship with Otto Kyllmann of his British publisher, Constable, they boarded the *Columbus* on October 15, and docked in New York on the twenty-second.

In September, Franklin P. Adams had reprinted side by side in his column an excerpt from Sherwood Anderson's story "Tandy" and a poem of Dreiser's called "The Beautiful," which had appeared in *Vanity Fair.* That poem was the one Dreiser had written—or rather "adapted"—in 1923 and sent to Helen as a plea for forgiveness. Anderson defended Dreiser when reporters called him and later wrote a friend: "My own private notion is that the man—perhaps as an exercise—tried to put some of my prose into verse form. He might have left it lying about, forgetting in the end the source. . . . It does not matter except that it must make him feel very foolish and uncomfortable when it comes to his notice. . . . I admire him greatly."

Dreiser maintained a public silence on the controversy, but it was an object lesson in the pitfalls of celebrity. A poem he had sent to Helen three years before and forgotten had branded him a plagiarist. Critics had already retailed the erroneous idea that he had copied his novel from the court records of the Gillette trial.

He now had a "position" to maintain and must be more careful. Helen begged him to let her look for more appropriate quarters. Liveright was also urging him to establish himself in a suitable place where he could play host to Manhattan's literary world as befitted a great American novelist. More practically, the publisher needed to know how to find him. Only Arthur Pell was entrusted with his address, and this arrangement had become inconvenient since a new collection of his short stories, *Chains,* was in the works, and Dreiser was needed to read proofs.

Dreiser gave Helen an equivocal go-ahead, but she had already seen just the place—a large duplex in the Rodin Studios at 200 West Fifty-seventh Street, across from Carnegie Hall. The lower floor had an enormous living room with large windows admitting the north light, a wall of glass-fronted bookcases, adjoining dining room and a kitchen. A stair led to the upper level, which was divided into two bedrooms.

Dreiser, however, bridled at the rent—$3500 per year. At the time he was negotiating some lucrative deal that Helen does not identify. But how could she keep them straight? He was deluged by offers—$5000 from Hearst for a newspaper serialization of the *Tragedy,* $1000 from Abraham Cahan for a story to appear in the thirtieth anniversary issue of the *Jewish Daily Forward.* The magazines were crying for his stories, and he sold "Fine Furniture," a slick tale that had been rejected nine times in 1923, to *Household* magazine and "Typhoon" (based on one of the murders he had considered for the *Tragedy*) to *Cosmopolitan* for hefty fees.

In addition, the dramatized version of *An American Tragedy* was a palpable hit, grossing $30,000 a week, of which Dreiser's share was more than $2000. And the novel continued to sell steadily. Donald Friede wrote Dreiser in Europe in July that it was receiving almost daily mention in the press: "if it's not the book it's the play; if it's not the play it's the movie." By year's end, more than 50,000 sets had been disposed of, earning Dreiser some $47,000 in royalties. His total income that year was $91,225.65, according to his tax return.

At last Helen got her way, after persuading the landlord to lower the rent by $500, and by mid-December they were able to move into what she calls "my dream home."

In October Friede took Dreiser to see the Broadway version of the *Tragedy*. Dreiser was totally caught up in the spectacle of the characters he had lived with so long in his mind materializing onstage. He would not even leave for intermission, and when Clyde was led away through the steel door and the curtain fell, Dreiser had tears in his eyes. "The poor boy!" he said to Friede. "The poor bastard! What a shame!" In a way, he was weeping for himself, and the unsated desires of youth.

Part Six

RUSSIA

1927–1929

CHAPTER 24

Thursdays at Home

> I was beginning to realize that genius was like the sun. One could be warmed, nourished, sustained and strengthened by it or horribly burned. . . .
> —Helen Dreiser, *My Life With Dreiser* (1951)

A fter Dreiser and Helen had settled in their new apartment, they began entertaining at regular Thursday-night "at-homes," an attempt to create a kind of salon for a mix of personalities from publishing, Broadway, Wall Street, and the Village.

The venue for these affairs was the large drawing room, which rose the full two stories. Dreiser was often to be found seated in a high-backed ducal chair, listening, absorbing.

Claude Bowers attended the Thursday-night levees from the start and observed Dreiser's attire evolve from a soiled blue artist's smock to a dinner jacket, sartorially recapitulating, presumably, his rise from a cold-water flat in the Village to an uptown duplex. Initially, Dreiser was pink-cheeked and as enthusiastic as a boy at his own birthday party. But he began to worry that the affairs were dominated by the speakeasy crowd who were more interested in sampling his excellent whiskey than in conversing about art. He confided his anxiety to Bowers.

The following week, Bowers noted, the cultural level of the guests had edged a few notches higher: first-nighters in evening dress, fresh from the premiere of *The King's Henchman,* an opera by Deems Taylor with a libretto by Edna St. Vincent Millay. Max Reinhardt, the director, was there, looking like a stockbroker, and the short, seigneurial financier Otto Kahn.

Although the conversation did not markedly improve and Dreiser continued to fret about the lack of culture, the affairs became a popular stop on the Manhattan circuit. As many as a hundred people would show up. The mix included literati like the novelist Ford Madox Ford; the beautiful Elinor Wylie, who posed "like a peacock spreading its tail" to invite admiration; the inevitable "Carlo" Van Vechten; big, rumpled Sherwood Anderson; Fannie Hurst; tiny Anita Loos; dapper George Jean Nathan; erudite Ernest Boyd; the Van Doren brothers; Joseph Wood Krutch; Broadway luminaries like actress Lillian Gish and torch singer Libby Holman; artists like George Luks, Jerome Blum, and Willy Pogany; business and professional people like Liveright, Dr. Brill, the Reverend Percy Stickney Grant (who had defended The "Genius" from his pulpit), Liveright's lawyer Arthur Garfield Hays; and numerous others.

This was Helen's element; not only sharing Dreiser's glory as his publicly acknowledged mistress, but complementing his moodiness with her hospitableness and warmth. She had "an almost reverential regard for literary talent," Louise Campbell remembered.

Louise had been brought to New York to help on one or another of Dreiser's literary projects. Upon her arrival he took her to meet Helen, and stood back and pretended he was "a helpless male facing two female rivals." Helen, however, flashed Louise a tolerant smile and took her away to show her the apartment. The two became friends, and Louise listened to Helen's sad stories about Dreiser's absences in pursuit of this or that woman. Once Louise chided Dreiser for his treatment of his companion and he told her, "Helen will be there to close my eyes at the end."

But now they slept in separate bedrooms, and his inattentiveness to her must have been a damaging blow to Helen's fragile sense of self-worth. She lashed back and their quarrels became more public. Louise charitably attributed his volatile temper to long hours at the writing desk, and he seemed always to be writing, though nothing of much consequence. He might be chatting with Helen and Louise over a drink and then casually drift back to his desk and go to work.

Bowers wondered if Dreiser's elevated lifestyle would cut him off from the common people, who were his subject matter. He once asked him point-blank if luxury would soften his writing. "No," Dreiser said, missing the point. "I see no one during the day, and it's quiet up here."

He was working hard, but his energies were dissipated among various projects, including hasty, superficial feature stories for the lucrative syndication market that his new agent, George Bye, diligently cultivated. For the Metropolitan Newspaper Service, he undertook a series of three articles, at $400 each, on American manners and morals. One, on the theme of "American Restlessness," was an expression of his own itch for change, variety—

"Moving from place to place, and more because of a desire for change than for economic betterment," he wrote, "appears to be an innate part of the American spirit." Another, "Fools for Love," subliminally advertised his success-guilt. He extols a woman (Louise?) "endowed with ample equipment for success in novel or play writing," who chose to take care of her mother and help other relatives. Some would say her life was a failure: "What nonsense! What rot! To me she is really a great and appealing success." He concludes that he prefers to cast his lot with "those who feel and respond emotionally, and poetically, in simple and inconspicuous ways—not with those who thunder and battle and, at the last, find their hands and hearts empty and their strong boxes stuffed with gilt-edged and meaningless 'securities.' "

He, of course, had a strongbox at the Central Hanover Bank and Trust Company stuffed with bonds. The market was heating up and Pell sent him tips: Financial and Industrial was now up to 82. . . . Too bad he hadn't purchased Manufacturers Trust at 600; it was now 785. . . . He should keep some cash on hand so he could act quickly when a hot tip came along.

Exaggerated reports of his wealth appeared in the newspapers. A story in the Dayton *Herald* reported "American Tragedy Brings Fortune to Theodore Dreiser." According to the reporter, Dreiser's total receipts from the book, movie, and play had passed $1 million. Another paper, however, noted that Dreiser still rode the subway.

The phrase "an American tragedy" had entered the language. His face would become so well known that it was used as a clue in the daily crossword puzzle ("American author pictured here"). Newspapers solicited his opinions on questions of the moment. Boni & Liveright ran a national contest with a prize of $500 for the best answer to the question, "Was Clyde Griffiths guilty of murder in the first degree?"

Dreiser would tell an interviewer that he had derived little happiness from the money he garnered from the *Tragedy*. "It was too late. Who wants money after the fires of youth have died. . . ." Anita Loos told Carl Van Vechten that one evening she discovered him in the butler's pantry, "dissolved in tears, shed no doubt for the sorrows of the world."

Wealth had not made his life with Helen any more idyllic. He had taken an office in the Manufacturers Trust Building on Columbus Circle, which he used for romance as well as work. As a result, his companion was experiencing the pangs of neglect. Out of need, and in retaliation, she developed a passion for a handsome young Hungarian-born pianist-composer named Ervin Nyiregyhazi. He lived in a little room on Fifty-eighth Street. He had no piano to practice on, he told them, so Dreiser, always ready to assist thwarted genius, offered the use of his Steinway grand on afternoons when he wasn't writing. The first time the young artist came,

Helen tiptoed out to the balcony to watch, and was so moved that she wrote a poem, called "Heavenly Infant":

> *Your hands run over the keyboard,*
> *And with your touch,*
> *the heavens open,*
> *And*
> *Showers of filtered stardust*
> *Rain upon the keys*

"I felt myself physically drawn to him," she confesses in her autobiography. Dreiser left her alone night after night until the early-morning hours "in that tomb of a studio," she once told Ralph Fabri, the Hungarian artist who became the confidant of both of them; yet with "his terrible ego he thought I was not human and could go on and on and on with *no one.*" In her autobiography Helen writes that she held back, but to Fabri she spoke of a "short (so terribly short) intimacy."

Late in March, overcome by restlessness and nerves, Dreiser departed on a walking trip through Pennsylvania. He may have been having love problems of his own; he was involved with three or four women at this time. Helen decided to join him and caught up with him at a hotel where he was spending the night. There she asked if it would be all right if she formed "a constructive emotional attachment to help me live through the time you leave me so much alone." He exploded: "Do as you please. But when you do, I'm out!" He demanded the name of her lover. Much distressed, she told him. Helen mulled over her problem and finally concluded that if she must choose between the Hungarian and Dreiser, she would choose the latter.

Helen telephoned Nyiregyhazi that the affair was off. Later the Hungarian wrote Dreiser a letter describing the affair with Helen in the "most evil & shocking way." Dreiser was so furious that he sat down at the typewriter and copied it. When Helen happened by and asked what he was doing (he rarely used the typewriter), he showed her the letter and shouted, "This finishes you, I can tell you that!" The pianist was a "cad" for writing such a letter, and Dreiser never wanted to see him again.

Dreiser wasn't letting Helen off easily, however. After the incident of the incriminating letter, her life became more lonely. "An impregnable door was closed against me," as she puts it. Dreiser still came home to her—most nights—but that was no consolation. She would lie awake for hours waiting for the sound of his key, crying herself to sleep.

Desperate for peace of mind, she began reading books on yoga and talking with the swamis from the Vedanta Society. She took up breathing exercises and achieved "the distinct sensation of an expanding consciousness, as though my mind was opening to a deeper understanding and wider perception of life."

The arrival of Helen's mother for a visit bolstered her morale, and since Dreiser liked Mrs. Patges, an earthy woman who did not hesitate to tell him that his neglect was to blame for Helen's affair, peace of a kind returned.

In 1927—the gaudy year of Lindbergh's lonely flight, Babe Ruth's sixty home runs, the stampede of the bulls on Wall Street, the Dempsey-Tunney long count—Dreiser produced little writing, beyond the Sunday-supplement pieces. His turbulent private life and the demands of celebrity had, as Bowers predicted, distracted him, but he had no fresh inspiration. The revised version of *The Financier* was as close as he came to working on a novel. Otherwise, he tidied up some short stories for a collection called *Chains* and began reworking some of the "studies" for *A Gallery of Women*, but he seemed dissatisfied with the latter.

Liveright was hungry for anything with Dreiser's name on it and was aggressively exploiting Dreiser's fame. In 1927 he published not only *Chains* and the new version of *The Financier*, in which Dreiser and Louise had made numerous cuts, but he also reissued *The Hand of the Potter* and brought out *The Songs of Paul Dresser*, a collection of lyrics, to which Dreiser had written a foreword. The last title had a small sale, but it was close to Dreiser's heart and Liveright indulged him. Finally, the *Tragedy* was still selling, though tapering off. The play was also tapering off; reports in April showed the gross was down to $9000 per week.

Partly to breathe new life into the novel, Liveright decided to protest the ban of *An American Tragedy* in Boston. Actually, it was not officially banned, but it was rumored that the police might act. Liveright's motive was not entirely publicity-seeking. Censorship was heating up in Boston, and nine books had been suppressed in 1927, two of them published by B & L. And on April 12, Sinclair Lewis's *Elmer Gantry* was barred, and the police had said that the *Tragedy* was one of several books under scrutiny.

So Liveright made a pre-emptive strike, taking as his model H. L. Mencken's fight against a ban on the *Mercury* in 1926. The Watch and Ward Society had confiscated copies of the magazine on the ground that an article in the April issue about a small-town prostitute, "Hatrack," was obscene. Mencken journeyed to Boston to get himself arrested (a stratagem he had advised Dreiser against in 1916). With an audience of Harvard students cheering him on, he sold a copy on the Common to J. Frank Chase, secretary of the society. He was bound over for trial, but by chance his case was assigned to one of the city's few liberal judges, who read the story and dismissed the charges. The next day, at Chase's behest, the U.S. Post Office banned the April issue. Mencken's lawyer, Arthur Garfield Hays, appealed but eventually lost on a technicality.

The "Hatrack" case was a national *cause célèbre*, but history did not repeat. Donald Friede sold a copy of the novel, was arrested and tried by one of the pro-censorship judges, who found him guilty and fined him $100. Hays appealed, but it would be two years before the courts would get to it and meanwhile the *Tragedy* was unavailable in Boston.

Dreiser attended Friede's trial, and on the train to Boston met Clarence Darrow, who had delivered a highly favorable verdict on *An American Tragedy* in a review for the New York *Evening Post*. The two men were inveterate determinists and shared the belief that murderers were driven to their acts by uncontrollable forces. Indeed, the novel echoed in spirit Darrow's summation in the Leopold-Loeb trial, which saved the two thrill-killers from the electric chair. Dreiser had followed the Leopold-Loeb trial closely in 1924 while he was writing the *Tragedy,* though he was more interested in the psychology of the murderers than in Darrow's tactics. He wrote Helen that the case "interests me enormously. . . . Just a desire to kill doesn't seem to explain it. There must be something more it seems to me. A great novel there somewhere."

In May he made a substantial investment that would bring him much joy and pain. This was the purchase of thirty-seven scenic acres overlooking one of the lakes in the Croton reservoir system in Westchester County, about four miles from the town of Mount Kisco.

When Dreiser bought the land, the only structure on it was a hunting lodge constructed of white birch logs. To reach it from the main road, one had to drive along a narrow, winding dirt track through high grass. The lodge was perched on a rocky hill, with a view of the surrounding meadows, woods, and the rolling green Berkshires. Below the house was a small spring-fed pond which Dreiser would deepen for a swimming pool. He also enlarged the house and the porch and commissioned Wharton Esherick to design two gates painted Prussian blue and emblazoned with the word "Iroki," a Japanese word meaning "the spirit of beauty."

For all his restlessness, he had long hankered after a country seat where he could write undisturbed and sink down some roots. He found a modicum of tranquillity gazing from his veranda at the rolling hills. "The peace of that place," he wrote in his diary that fall. "The silence of the stars."

In early October came another distraction—an invitation from the Soviet government to attend the November 3–10 celebration of the tenth anniversary of the Bolshevik revolution. Dreiser was intrigued but wary. He grilled the man who conveyed the summons, F. G. Biedenkapp, executive secretary of International Workers Relief, a Communist Party auxiliary: how could he learn much about the country in a week? He did not want merely to ornament the Moscow celebration. He could stay as long as he wished, Biedenkapp told him, a month, six weeks. "Go where you will, accompanied or unaccompanied by Russian officials, and judge for yourself what has been done and what is happening." Finally Dreiser agreed to go, provided he receive official letters confirming that he would be reimbursed for all his expenses, including travel and his "time," and guaranteeing freedom of movement. He told Biedenkapp that he wanted to visit "the real, unofficial Russia—the famine district on the Volga, say—some of the small towns and farms in Siberia and the Ukraine, some of the mines and fisheries." The Russian said the letters would be produced but that he must be prepared to leave within nine days if he was to arrive in time for the celebration.

Dreiser's interest in the Soviet experiment went back to the Village years, but he had no deep commitment to radical programs or doctrines. He did not, for example, join the intellectuals who protested the verdict in the Sacco-Vanzetti case, which radicalized many American writers in the 1920s.

Nearly a year previously, Dreiser had written the Soviet critic Sergei Dinamov, who had asked his opinions of social conditions, that he had no "theories about life or the solution of economic and political problems." There was no plan or ideology, including Christianity or communism, that could deal with man's "primitive and animal reactions to life." Because greed, selfishness, vanity, hate, passion, and love were ineradicable, there could be no Utopia. The law of the survival of the fittest still held, among individuals and among nations, "whether in the monarchies of England, the democracies of America or the Soviets of Russia." He did express interest in making "an exhaustive study" of the Soviet system at some time, but confessed that now he knew so little about it that he could not predict whether it would succeed or fail. However, "I do hope something fine and big and enduring does come of it."

And that is roughly where he stood when Biedenkapp appeared in his living room. He was sympathetic to communism as an experiment in making life better for the masses, but he still believed that the strongest individuals would dominate the weak, the big brains would—and should—rule, though he opposed the excessive power of big business. Yet he was inwardly restless, an individualist wondering if there weren't something more than self. Could a system dedicated to eliminating greed and inequality work?

After Biedenkapp departed he discussed the Russian's proposal with Helen. She begged him to take her with him, but he told her that he would want to travel under rough conditions, and she would not like that. She teased him about becoming involved with Russian women. "Who me," he replied. "Russian girls? Those wild Bolsheviks? Aren't these American girls bad enough?"

> This enormous giant is at last rousing itself from the sleep
> of centuries—equipping itself—entering . . . upon a strange
> new day and mission.
> —Dreiser's Russian Diary (1927)

Dreiser was booked on the *Mauretania*, sailing October 19 for
Cherbourg, whence he would proceed via Paris and Berlin to
Moscow. He was but one of 1500 Americans invited to the
decennial festivities, but the only one to rate a private tour with
all expenses paid. The official notification he had requested soon
arrived in the form of cables from Maxim Litvinov, assistant foreign minister, and Mme Olga Kameneva, Leon Trotsky's sister and director of VOKS
(Society for Cultural Relations From Abroad), the government agency that
was in charge of his tour. From Joe Freeman, a young American communist
who had worked in Moscow, he received letters of introduction to various
artists and officials.

There were many goodbyes to be said, most of them, it seemed, to
female friends. His current favorite was a woman identified in his diary only
as "B———," who was married to a prominent Broadway producer. She
was upset by the impending separation, and comforting her required several
romantic interludes at his Columbus Square office. On October 15 he records
a busy afternoon: from 1:00 to 2:00, "play with B——— in office"; from 2:00
to 3:00 "go over finances with Pell," setting aside $8000 for Helen (who was

"all agog because of responsibilities descending on her") for household expenses, and at 3:00 meeting J. G. Robin at 200 West Fifty-seventh to discuss the lawyer's dramatization of The "*Genius.*" B———— was "more passionate than ever" because of his leaving, he records on October 18; after which, "return to work on Gallery of Women."

Elsewhere, he notes that he has received letters from Louise Campbell, Esther McCoy (a recent college graduate who was doing research for him), and Maud Karola ("am conscience-stricken about Maud").* Yet he can still write, after one of his consolatory sessions with B————, "In spite of all my varietism I realise that I really care for Helen. It is spiritual, not material. I feel sad at leaving her."

Still, on his last day he managed to see B———— at 1:00 for a final goodbye before he and Helen went to the ship to settle him into his cabin. The *Mauretania* did not sail until 11:00, and Dreiser attended a going-away party followed by an impromptu shipboard press conference. He told reporters that if anyone asked him to trot along on a government-conducted tour, he would "take the next train out of the country."

Aboard the *Mauretania* were several congenial passengers, including publisher Ben Huebsch, the lawyer Morris Ernst and his wife, and Diego Rivera, the Mexican muralist, a communist, with whom Dreiser got on famously, even though the artist spoke little English and the writer had no Spanish.

After a placid crossing, Dreiser lingered briefly in Paris and sat for an interview by a reporter from the Paris edition of the New York *Herald.* He had time for some sightseeing at Sainte-Chapelle, which moved him to indite a passionate homage to the "god of Beauty" in his journal. ("I will kneel & strike my breast & touch the dust with my forehead I will! I will! Only do not forsake me, oh God of beauty.") Then he met Huebsch at a sidewalk café. Joining them were Dreiser's translator, Victor Llona, and a husky young man named Ernest Hemingway, whom Dreiser identifies as the author of *The Sun Also Rises* but says nothing further about. There was much "talk, talk, talk," about the falling franc, the state of art, and James Joyce. That night he recorded an inspiration for a "psychopathic novel," featuring a character unhinged by "sexual weakness; strong sexual desire (mental)" and modeled on the homosexual King Ludwig II of Bavaria or the scandalous Harry Thaw, who shot Stanford White.

After Paris the way of the pilgrim led through Berlin. Dreiser traveled with Huebsch, and en route they had a long talk about communism. Dreiser resolved to look hard at "its theory & actual practice" and "its consonance or conflict with human nature as we find it."

Arriving in the German capital, he checked into the luxurious Adlon

---

*Let it be stated for the record that not all the women who were friendly with or worked for Dreiser were amorously involved with him.

Hotel, where he was met by some Soviet officials. In a letter to his old friends Franklin and Beatrice Booth, he vowed that "once out of the hands of these government agents I will prove more simple—even to the extent of riding third class" with the mujiks and "sleeping on a mat." He complained about the strain of travel, and two days later his bronchitis was "worse than ever." Nevertheless, he met various delegations and a representative of the Hearst papers, who offered him $3600 for two articles on Russia. He wrote Louise Campbell that he was ill, "but I'll be better tomorrow I hope. The doctor just left."

The doctor had prescribed some medicines and a Turkish bath to decongest him. The steam relieved his symptoms temporarily, and he sat up that evening with Huebsch and Sinclair Lewis, who had pursued the foreign correspondent Dorothy Thompson to Berlin in the course of a whirlwind European courtship. Dreiser's distaste for Lewis had not abated, although the latter seemed eager to be friends. He explained at length why he had not reviewed *An American Tragedy*, "as though the matter was of the greatest importance," Dreiser sniffed, not even bothering to record Lewis's reasons.

The next day he felt worse, and consulted two other doctors, who advised him to have an X ray. This disclosed that his health was "very bad," the doctors said. There was an enlargement of the aorta, which was pressing against his left lung, producing bronchitis. The physicians advised him to cancel the trip to Russia and enter a German sanitarium immediately. "I am not going into any sanitarium," Dreiser told them. "I am going into Russia. My condition may be bad but I do not happen to be afraid of death."

He talked over his situation with Lewis, who was worried. Then, alone in his room, he was overwhelmed by depression and cabled Helen, explaining later in a letter to her that he had experienced "a case of real homesickness, almost to the point of vomiting. . . ." In his diary he wrote that he felt "like a cast away in a small boat. Here I am—nearly 4000 miles from N.Y. . . . Supposing I were seriously ill—to die. And Helen so far away. And I have been so bad to her."

On November 2, with a group of American delegates, Dreiser boarded the Moscow train. After crossing the border into Russia, the people all reminded him of characters in Tolstoy, Gogol, and Dostoevsky—"the heavy and yet shrewd peasants; the self-concerned and even now, under communism, rather authoritarian petty officials." On the afternoon of November 4, he arrived in Moscow. At the station there were a lot of boring welcoming speeches and a band that played the "Internationale"—a "most uninspired" anthem.

His hotel, the Grand, was "rococo and shabby grand." Later, Sergei Dinamov, from the American section of Gosizdat, the state publishing house, arrived to welcome him, accompanied by a tall, attractive American-born woman named Ruth Kennell. Dreiser gave Dinamov a list of people he wanted to see and dashed off a report to Esther McCoy: Russia was "an armed dictatorship. Workers and peasants are drilled like soldiers to fight and can be called to fight at any time." And to Helen: "The only difference between the Russian government & ours that I can see is that it is poorer—as yet. And that no one is allowed to pile up large fortunes—or not to work at something." The people voted just like in America, and he predicted that in ten years Russia would be "as gay & wonderful & happy a place as any on earth. I hope so. There is no lack of liberty. . . . I think really there is much less liberty in America than there is here. For one thing there is no Negro or Catholic question:—the church is down here. A child cannot receive religious instruction & education is the watchword everywhere." So much for first impressions.

Still receiving VIP treatment, Dreiser was moved to a large room overlooking Red Square, from which he could observe the anniversary parade on November 7. With Dinamov he went to the Hotel Lux, where foreigners who worked for the government lived, among them Ruth Kennell, who was writing a preface to the Russian edition of *Chains* for Gosizdat. The three of them then paid a call on "Big Bill" Haywood, who had fled to Russia in 1920 and was now living at the hotel. The old Wobbly had gone "flaccid and buttery," and was staying in a shabby room with a wife who was "a kind of Slav Slave," surrounded by "dubious radicals." "Life has beaten him as it beats us all," Dreiser concluded. The following year Big Bill was buried in the Kremlin wall.

After leaving Haywood, the trio strolled around Red Square and viewed Lenin's temporary tomb. Eventually Dinamov left, and Dreiser thought he seemed peeved at the way the two Americans were hitting it off. He writes in his diary that when he told Ruth how lonely he was, she agreed to come up to his room.

He was now in open rebellion against his officious hosts from VOKS. When a guide from the agency arrived the next day, he sent him packing. The American radical Scott Nearing called and found Dreiser sulking in his room, morosely drinking vodka and complaining that VOKS was trying to push him into a package tour, with a "Russian lackey as a guide."

He felt trapped, harried by manipulative strangers. He needed someone whom he could trust to translate and to take notes during interviews, and to handle the logistics of travel in this huge, baffling country.

Nearing suggested Ruth Kennell; she was American, spoke Russian, and knew the country. Dreiser liked the idea, "since we are already so close." He interviewed her, learning that her political sympathies had drawn her and her husband to Russia in 1922 as technical workers. Her husband eventually returned to the States, but she had insisted on staying. Now Dreiser offered her a job as his secretary, and she accepted.

On November 7, anniversary of the Bolsheviks' seizure of power,

Dreiser was awakened by the sound of bands and the tramp of soldiers' boots in Red Square. Later he went to a grandstand to watch union and nationality delegations stream past bearing red banners with slogans such as "Workers of the World Unite" and effigies of obese capitalists and swinish kulaks and speculators. From 11:00 until 7:00 that night the human river flowed past the reviewing stand atop Lenin's mausoleum. The marchers waved to the Party leaders smiling down at them. Deeply moved, Dreiser wrote in his diary, "I think—if only human nature can rise to the opourtunity—here is one for the genuine betterment of man. But mayhap the program is too beautiful to succeed;—an idea of existence to which frail & selfish humanity can never rise. Yet I earnestly hope that this is not true—that this is truly the beginning of a better or brighter day for all."

That evening he and Ruth were joined for dinner by Dorothy Thompson, who was writing a series of articles on Russia. Dreiser and the Juno-esque Dorothy discussed the relative advantages of communism and capitalism. She thought the Russian system a "drab affair—more a matter of mental or idealistic enthusiasm on the part of its members than of actual material improvement." Later, with Nearing, they went out to a dance recital. On the way home Dreiser received an impression that Thompson was "making overtures" to him. At the hotel, Dreiser notes, "D T——— & I continue our flirtation. After a supper with the American delegation she comes to my room with me to discuss communism & we find we agree on many of its present lacks as well as its hopeful possibilities. I ask her to stay but she will not—tonight."

He was surely exaggerating the lady's attraction to him. She was radiantly in love with Lewis, and later wrote him that she was bored "with being facetiously nudged by old Dreiser, who has turned quite a gay dog in Moscow, constantly making rather lumbering jokes." Yet she found him "sympathetic because he has a sort of healing common sense about life. And, curiously enough, he has a genuine—if rather elephantine—sense of humor. Last night . . . both he and I were almost in hysterics with the accumulated laughter of the day, and irritated our earnest friends highly thereby." Evidently her conspiratorial laughter encouraged Dreiser (who usually needed little encouragement) to think she was available.

Since a ten-day holiday had been declared and he could do no traveling until it was over, he spent the next few days sightseeing with Ruth, tramping through churches, day nurseries, museums, and schools. In a large cemetery they located Chekhov's grave, an obscure marker crowded in among the others. He deplored the state of literary men's graves and wished in his diary that their remains be either cremated and scattered to the winds or placed in a suitable resting place where one might come and meditate on that author's books.

Perhaps he was thinking of his own mortality; he notes that he is feeling lethargic, a sign of growing old. That night he had a reassuring dream, in which he was "delightfully vigorous & gay—not changed in years or strength." In the dream he danced nude down a garden path, swinging an Indian club. As he was cavorting with abandon, he noticed "an elderly man in dark clothes—one of the conservative and learned types" approaching him. He feared that the mysterious pedagogue meant to harm him, but then thought: "How can he?" Did the sinister figure represent Death? The Freudian censor? Stuart P. Sherman (who had drowned in 1926—ironically in a boating accident)?

Whatever else it meant, the dream was a portent of returning health; in the dry, cold climate his bronchitis subsided. Full of energy, he engaged in a heated argument with the assistant director of the State Academy of Artistic Science over whether creativity could be studied scientifically, with Dreiser taking the negative. Ruth, who had now begun typing up the interviews for his diary, noted: "You behaved like a steam roller in a china store."

One evening he and Ruth were invited to Dinamov's apartment, and Dreiser got his first view of crowded living conditions in the capital. He questioned the thin, dedicated editor-critic, who, with his thick glasses and ascetic face, looked like a student in a Dostoevsky novel, about living conditions. His host had foresightedly invited three workers who lived in his building to join them, and Dreiser interrogated each of them in turn. He was most attentive to the textile worker, who said he had no ambitions for his daughter to become a respectable married woman. She could live with a man and divorce him for another if she liked. "The important thing is that she should be an independent person, able to support herself." Thinking of his own marital state, Dreiser whispered to Ruth, "Get this all down."

That night, when one of the guests asked him about the United States, he launched into a paean of praise for American prosperity and industrial might, climaxing in a tribute to the Robber Barons like Rockefeller and Carnegie who had made it all possible. Dinamov, whose mother was an Old Bolshevik and who himself had fought in the civil war and was a dedicated Party member, almost choked upon hearing these blasphemous names mentioned in his own house, and though he had told Dreiser he considered him "the greatest writer in the world," he would in future consign him to the outer circle of "bourgeois radicals."

They walked about the neighborhood, and Dinamov showed him a new workers' housing development. Dreiser was appalled to learn that as many as fourteen people lived in a three-room apartment. The rooms were furnished in wretched taste, he thought, reminding him of a "Pennsylvania mining village under the rankest tyranny of capitalism."

The ten days nearly up, he met with a secretary at VOKS named Kerenetz, who assured him that all was in order for his tour. A most genial and accommodating man was Kerenetz. To whatever demand Dreiser made he would reply, "Why of course, of course." A meeting with Stalin? "Done." Reimbursement of all expenses thus far? Send us the bill.

Arrangements for the tour apparently settled, he and Ruth visited an elementary school and then the Mother of God chapel near Red Square, once considered "the holiest spot in Russia." A line of people was waiting to be blessed by a priest. On the wall of a building opposite the church was a huge sign reading: "Religion Is the Opiate of the People," prompting Dreiser to observe, "And possibly such an opiate is worth something, although for me the soviet idea is better."

The same day he called on the filmmaker Sergei Eisenstein, *auteur* of the revolutionary classic *Potemkin*, who plumped for realistic dramas illustrating historic principles and explained his theory of movies without a plot or professional actors, in which daily life was the drama. Eisenstein admitted the cinema was under strict government controls, but argued that in America the churches exercised similar censorship. Dreiser accused him of being an "uplifter," a propagandist, and defended the drama of the individual, saying that "only through the individual could the mass and its dreams be sensed and interpreted." Eisenstein was not persuaded, but he greatly esteemed Dreiser's work. He was somewhat disillusioned, however, to find the author rather slow of speech and, by the Russian's lights, provincial in outlook.

During an audience with Constantin Stanislavsky, cofounder of the Moscow Art Theater, Dreiser was lectured about the political role of theater, though when he asked if communism had generated any great plays, Stanislavsky said no, dutifully adding that such plays as had been written were "good as chronicles of the revolution."

Dreiser would become personally acquainted with the mysterious ways of the censor when he submitted the dramatic version of *An American Tragedy* to Stanislavsky, who seemed enthusiastic about doing it. Several weeks passed, and then the director told him that regrettably the play had been disapproved. When Dreiser asked why, Stanislavsky explained that the censors had objected to the religious scenes in the death house between Clyde and the Reverend McMillan and also "the relationship between employer and worker"—presumably not sufficiently evocative of the class struggle. The incident gave a double edge to Stanislavksy's statement that "The line of art is eternal and passing conditions do not change it."

Yet this was the time of the flowering of "NEP culture," after Lenin's New Economic Policy, which permitted a measure of economic and political freedom, and Dreiser witnessed experimental productions of American plays at the Jewish theater and attended opera and ballet at the Bolshoi Opera House. A spectacular dance drama based on Victor Hugo's *The Hunchback of Notre Dame* caused Dreiser to note approvingly that the novel's anticlerical message was highlighted. At least there was no religious censorship in this country. Over a late supper at a gypsy restaurant, William Reswick, correspondent for the Associated Press, urged Dreiser to speak to Otto Kahn about bringing the Russian Ballet to America.

At the Bolshoi he caught a brief glimpse of Stalin, seated in a dimly lit box reserved for high officials. That would be his only sighting of the Russian leader. Despite the VOKS man's assurances, Dreiser's requests for interviews with Stalin and Trotsky produced no results. When he arrived in Russia he hadn't realized that Trotsky was out of favor and would soon be expelled from the Party and later banished from Moscow, along with Zinoviev and other "left socialists."

He learned more about the Party schism over collectivization and extension of the NEP when he received a surprise visitor at his hotel—Karl Radek, a veteran communist who would be purged along with Trotsky. Dreiser had tried several times to telephone him at the Kremlin but was always told he was out. Now Radek proceeded to elucidate Kremlin politics: he was being watched because the anti-Trotskyists feared that he and other members of the left opposition were plotting against them. He gave his version of the doctrinal dispute between Trotsky and Stalin and reminisced about Lenin.

Radek was the only high official Dreiser had seen thus far, and he was beginning to feel like a capitalist orphan adrift in a communist sea. Finally, at a glittering banquet of the Presidium of the Moscow Soviet, he had a tantrum. Spotting an American who worked in the New York office of VOKS, he berated her until she trembled. "I have been treated vilely," he thundered. "Madame Kameneva and the Soviet government can go to hell." He demanded reimbursement for all his expenditures, including his steamship fare and Kennell's pay, and then he would go home. Mumbling that she was sorry, the woman scurried off, and soon Kameneva herself appeared, an interpreter in tow. There had been a mistake; tomorrow her secretary would help arrange a trip—anywhere he wanted to go; any interview he wanted would be arranged. Dreiser looked at her "meaningfully" and said he would let it pass—for now.

After this outburst several officials granted him interviews. His social life picked up as well. He was invited to a cocktail party, where he met the English-born Madame Litvinova, wife of the assistant foreign minister. She extolled the "restfulness" of life in Russia compared to her homeland. There was no competition for wealth, no social climbing. The onus of economic failure was not placed on the individual; everyone was guaranteed a minimal living, housing, health care, old-age assistance, and fifteen rubles a month if he or she couldn't find work.

Although this side of the Soviet system drew his warm approval, he would obsessively return to the theme of individualism—free enterprise, in economic terms—versus socialism and collectivism. He told Commissar of Trade Anastas I. Mikoyan that Russian consumers would soon crave more luxuries. Mikoyan replied sternly, "Russia will never be a luxury-consuming country. Luxury can only lead to the destruction of communism." Dreiser was silent but later said, "I wonder." To another official who preached austerity, he defended American advertising "and other stimulants to buy." Wouldn't their absence "take away the spirit and color of life"? The average American, he told still another functionary, "gets good wages, has an auto, wonderful roads, every farmer has a telephone and radio, every farm girl has silk stockings." At home he chastised Americans for their bovine material- ism, but he was not being inconsistent, for he had always praised the material comforts of his homeland while deploring his countrymen's obsession with them to the exclusion of art and thought.

The big brain vs. little brain controversy came to a head in an interview with Nikolai Bukharin, leader of the "right socialists," heir apparent to Lenin and the Party's top theoretician. Now co-ruler with Stalin in an uneasy duumvi- rate, he was a tough, doctrinaire communist, but unlike the suspicious, conspiratorial Stalin, he was charming and popular. After Lenin's death in 1924, Bukharin had become the architect of the New Economic Policy and advocated a more humane and open form of socialism than Stalin, who supported rapid and massive industrialization from the top down.

Dreiser was not being greatly misled by those like Dinamov who told him that the lot of the average Russian had improved under communism. The work day was down from ten hours in prewar Russia to seven and a half; there was a comprehensive social welfare scheme and free medical care. True, urban unemployment had shot up because of a massive migration to the cities. And the sinister face of Stalin's repression would be briefly un- veiled in January when he unleashed a crackdown on "Kulak speculators," with armed militias forcibly confiscating hoarded grain.

The meeting with Bukharin was Dreiser's only penetration into the Kremlin. He was so excited that he forgot to wear a tie, but the VOKS guide, Trevis, told him not to worry; Soviet leaders were too busy to care about sartorial conventions. Bukharin, a handsome, boyish-looking man, greeted the American delegate heartily and sat back for what he probably thought would be an exchange of polite generalities. But Dreiser had come to debate.

He declared that communism led to "intellectual despotism." He ac- cused the Russian state of being as doctrinaire and authoritarian as the Catholic Church or the czarist government or "any form of tyranny or propaganda of which you can think. You take the ignorant and make them believe your way because you are sure your way is best. But is it? Do you know yet?"

Bukharin said communism was "the fairest form of human government yet devised. Our dream is to make all happy." To which Dreiser observed,

"Personally I think good often needs as much tyranny to establish and maintain it as evil. A benevolent tyranny—at least until all men have brains sufficient to appreciate good. Why not adopt that as a defense?"

Bukharin said he did not believe it. "Left alone humanity moves in the general direction of its best ideals."

Dreiser pressed on to the heart of the matter: "Should the big mind rule the little one?" Bukharin contended that the proletariat could produce great minds and that under capitalism workers were denied equal education. Gesturing toward the window, Dreiser asked if the man sweeping the street was Bukharin's class equal. Bukharin said he was, that all Russians had the same opportunities and rights. Dreiser countered, "I think big minds will always sit in high places and have comfortable rooms [like Bukharin's office] and lead the little minds in the street."

Bukharin riposted that under communism personal ambition would disappear, replaced by a universal ambition to serve the general good. Given proper education, the socialist ethic would ultimately become ingrained.

"So you're going to have a perfect world, against human nature," Dreiser said. "And you think God will accept it? That's the bunk. Contrasts will remain forever that's what makes life interesting. That's the way the universe is run, in spite of your Marxian theories."

"My God, take him away!" Bukharin muttered to Trevis. "I can't stand any more." Outside the Kremlin walls Dreiser watched a ragged street sweeper cross himself before the Chapel of the Siberian Virgin. "I suppose next year he'll have Bukharin's place," he said, having the last word.

Turning to literary business, Dreiser met with representatives of Gosizdat to discuss a contract for the Russian rights to his past and future works. He complained about pirated editions and the state publishing house's recent abridged versions of *Color of a Great City* and *Twelve Men*. Ossip Beskin, head of the Department of Foreign Literature, offered Dreiser 750 rubles ($375) for the rights to those two titles. Dreiser acted insulted and said Gosizdat could have them as a gift. At length, he settled for $1000. After further haggling, it was agreed that he would receive advances of between $600 and $1000 for each new title and semiannual royalty statements. They shook hands, and the staff was summoned to welcome the new author on the Gosizdat list. Afterward he attended a banquet for foreign writers given by the state publishing house, where the poet Mayakovsky perceptively toasted him as the first visiting American to admit he had formed no definite impressions or conclusions.

On November 21, the seventeenth anniversary of Tolstoy's death, Dreiser and Kennell made a pilgrimage to Yasnaya Polyana. They had to catch a 1:00 A.M. train, which was packed. Although they arranged with the ubiquitous OGPU man at the station for accommodations in the crew compartment, the train began pulling out and they had to jump into a fourth-class car—popularly known as "Maxim Gorky" cars—the lower depths. Dreiser later described the scene:

> I choke as I enter, for not only is the car full of vile smoke but of indescribable odors—odors . . . odors of unwashed feet, with ancient wool socks over them, or none, and the same protruding from the ends of a line of wooden bunks or shelves . . . on all of which are piled heavy, and even loggy-looking humanity, as in a jail or inferno.

That would be the last time Dreiser rode with the mujiks. At the first stop, they ran up to the front car, where they could lie down on wooden benches and sleep intermittently the rest of the way.

They arrived early the next morning at a silent village, surrounded by snow-laden pines. Hiring a sleigh, they bumped over icy roads to the estate, a two-story frame structure that reminded Ruth of her grandfather's house in Kansas. Only a sleepy caretaker was on hand to show them through the unheated rooms. They returned to the village and visited the local soviet, located in a log hut. The officials immediately notified Tolstoy's daughter Olga, who lived in another part of the house; she invited them back for another tour. Then they traveled by sleigh to the novelist's grave and watched as schoolchildren piled pine branches and flowers on the unmarked mound and sang a dirge, *Vechnaya Pamyat,* which means "Eternal Remembrance," but which Dreiser, in a letter to the Booths, hopefully translated as "There is no Death."

Meanwhile, there seemed to have been no progress on arrangements for his trip to the hinterland. Now he had a financial incentive to see "what these Russians are up to," as he liked to say: a contract with North American News Alliance (NANA) for five 1200-word articles on his trip, at a total fee of $6000. Irritated by the foot-dragging, Dreiser decided to go to Leningrad. He was put up at the Hotel Europe, a truly *luxe* establishment, and surrounded by obsequious VOKS employees wherever he went. "It would be easy for a fool to get a false impression of his importance," he wrote in his diary. He was homesick for West Fifty-seventh Street and Mt. Kisco.

Leningrad was one of the most beautiful cities he had ever seen. They toured the various palaces, still with their original furnishings; he was disgusted by this show of idle wealth. The fortress where political prisoners had languished in subterranean dungeons imprinted in his mind a vision of ancient tyranny.

On the political *carte du jour* was an interview with the vice chairman of the district soviet, a former metalworker, whom Dreiser hectored about workers' crowded living conditions. "When the workers made a revolution they didn't do it for bath tubs," the official replied. "They did it for political power."

Back in Moscow, the American Gulliver raged at the Lilliputian functionaries who bound him in red tape. Sinclair Lewis, who had pursued Thompson to Red Square, found him in a dyspeptic state—"impatient at the still universal inefficiency of a nation which has had to make something out of nothing."

Dreiser also grumbled about the general uncleanliness of the people and feared that out in the hinterlands there would be bedbugs and cockroaches in the borscht. It was odd, he wrote in his diary, "that a nation of 150 million beside modern Europe could not have developed a disguise for uncleanliness." Marxism without deodorants was hard to take.

The crowded conditions in which the people lived stimulated Dreiser to posit a native "herd instinct." And the ubiquitous "Lenin corners" in public housing—lounges devoted to study and propagandizing—affronted him. He concluded there was "something strange, almost mystic in the fever of these people to consolidate their gains—make themselves sure that what they have shall not be later taken away from them."

At last Dreiser was summoned to Madame Kameneva's office, but when he arrived she was just leaving. She told him airily that there were only 2000 rubles left in the budget for his expenses. He said he would take that and go back to New York. She said nothing had been said about paying his expenses to and from Russia. He reminded her of the promises made to him by Kerenetz. She said the man had no authority. They parted frigidly.

It turned out that VOKS was unwilling to pay Kennell's salary, since she wasn't an employee or even a Party member. But the real hitch, Dreiser thought, was a complication that had cropped up during the trip to Leningrad. The guide had made advances to Ruth, which she repelled. Out of spite, he had complained about her to his superiors and now she was considered unreliable.

On December 7 Dreiser marched to the VOKS office for what he called the "final battle." A "stormy session" ensued during which he once again told VOKS to go to hell. At this point the head of the Foreign Affairs Department interjected some soothing words. Meester Drayzer should understand that they were merely concerned about his health. That was the reason for the delay. The tour would go ahead as planned, but VOKS would assign him a new guide, Dr. Sophia Davidovskaya, the house physician at the Lux, whom Ruth knew and liked. Dreiser could retain Kennell as his secretary, but at his own expense. VOKS would pick up his tab in Russia, and Workers Aid would reimburse him for his steamer ticket.

On December 12, with $1000 in expense money Bye had cabled him, Dreiser and party boarded the night train for Kiev. It departed three hours late, setting the pattern of rail journeys to come. In Stalino, bundled up in furs against the brisk, sleety wind, they were driven in an open car to a large state farm—10,000 acres in all. Then on to a coal mine, followed by a good dinner of beer and schnitzel at a cooperative restaurant. A violinist rendered "Yankee Doodle" in honor of the American delegate. The sight of two heavily rouged prostitutes at a nearby table set Dreiser off, however. He challenged Dr. Davidovskaya (whom he had nicknamed "Davi") to explain the presence of these ladies of the evening. The government claimed that these social parasites had been eliminated. She in turn accused him of seeing only the bad things. He retorted that he was having his doubts "about this Soviet thing." Had the communists really built that much new industry? Many of the factories he'd seen had been erected under the Czar, and even now weren't up to their pre-war production. The argument raged on until, fortunately for the little group's cohesion, the violinist began playing "On the Banks of the Wabash Far Away." The wistful strains pacified the irascible visitor, and he began singing along the words he had long ago helped his brother Paul compose.

For all his lambasting of the Russian system, a part of him was absorbing the socialist message, and he wrote in his diary: "In America our task is to catch and harness for the good of all that escaped, world-making, world-running thing industrial & financial enterprise & bring it back to the service of the general good." Whether communism was achieving this was an open question. Still, "One sees really a country with no abandoned—if as yet wretched poor; no foolish and meaningless rich."

Yet he still played capitalist's advocate during interviews with local officials, and he and Ruth had almost daily arguments. The cold, damp climate had revived his bronchitis, and he was coughing alarmingly into his handkerchief. As they reached the last leg of their journey, Dreiser and Ruth continued to rag and wrangle. For all their disputation, however, they had formed a close camaraderie. When they weren't arguing, their talk was full of shared jokes; both had a fine sense of the ridiculous, which could dissipate any lingering rancor from their doctrinal disputes. She treated him as a kind of lovable if eccentric rich uncle, and he regarded her as his companion "Ruthie"—and the only person in all of Russia he could trust.

Dr. Davidovskaya, however, never wavered in her opinion of him: he was rude, arrogant, impossible. As she later told Ruth, "He is a terrible man! All the time it's swine this and lice that, and yet you lick his boots!"

So the merry little group made its way along the Caspian Sea to Tiflis, where they spent a quiet New Year's Eve. The following night they caught a train to Batum, and there boarded a ship that would take them to Odessa. At this point Dreiser's spirits were at their lowest ebb. As they waited for the vessel, he huddled next to a stove, coughing phlegm into his last clean handkerchief. Ruth looked at him pityingly: "His smart light-gray topcoat was grimy, his scarf bedraggled, his suit untidy, his bow tie missing, and he himself was unwashed. There was something touching in the spectacle of America's foremost novelist at the age of 56 braving the Russian winter to examine the workings of a new social system which was at variance with his own theories."

They arrived at their final destination, Odessa, at 8:00 A.M. on January 8, a dank, cold day. He had long ago arranged to meet Helen in Constantinople, but now discovered that the next steamer did not leave until January 18. That was too long to wait, so he wired her to meet him in Paris instead.

But she was already aboard the Orient Express. She had sailed on the *Mauretania* on December 30, expecting some word from him upon her arrival in Paris, but there was nothing. After waiting a few days, she elected to press on to Constantinople. As it turned out, he had sent a telegram to the wrong hotel; eventually it reached her and she returned to Paris.

Meanwhile Dreiser was snarled in red tape. He would not be allowed to take his notes and manuscripts out of the country without a special permit. And, oh yes, he could not take out more than 300 rubles. These official intrusions into personal papers and personal funds represented to him the final blows of Soviet petty tyranny. And so, when a reporter from the *Odessa News* came to interview him, he gave the country a piece of his mind: "I made him a long speech about what I thought of conditions, that it was an interesting experiment, but—they had a long way to go before they could try to put the system in other countries. I had no objection to their trying it out here, but they should not try to change other countries until they had proved the system here."

The next day permission to take out his papers and money came through, as Ruth had predicted it would. Back at the hotel he dictated another statement, summing up his impressions. He confessed a bias: "Personally, I am an individualist and shall die one. In all this communistic welter, I have seen nothing that dissuades me in the least from my earliest perceptions of the necessities of man. One of these is the individual dream of self-advancement, and I cannot feel that even here communism has altered that in the least."

Ruth was seated on the foot of the bed, taking it all down on her portable typewriter, just as she had those past weeks recorded most of his diary entries. He doubted that "the right of the superior brain to the superior directing and ruling positions has been done away with," and asserted that in Russia as elsewhere "you will find the sly and the self-interested as well as the kind and the wise slipping into positions of authority, executing for the rank and file the necessary program which guarantees their comfort. And as time goes on, if not now, with a much larger return for their services."

He praised communism's achievements, in particular the elimination of dogmatic religion, which gave "the collective mentality of Russia freedom to expand. . . ." Although this expansion "is a little too much colored by the new dogmas of communism," he could not object. He was impressed by the housing programs, the new factories, schools, hospitals, but the "indifference to proper sanitation" was a national disgrace. Even the poor in other European countries didn't live that way. Here Ruth interjected, "But TD, they haven't developed the means and equipment of those Western European countries yet." He continued dictating without missing a beat: "It will not do, as some insist, to say that this is a matter of prosperity and equipment. It is not, I insist it is not."

So it went, Ruth's objections always swept away by the flow of Dreiserian logic. He said that "more individualism and less communism would be of great advantage to this mighty country." And: "There is too much effort to make the laborer socially comfortable, and too little to make him thoroughly efficient. Really, there should be no talk of the seven-hour day until the workers are earning enough to pay for the latest type of machinery which would make such a day possible."

His statement was never published in Russia, but he sent a copy to an American correspondent, Junius Wood, and it appeared in the United States. In one of the two papers Wood represented, the Oakland *Tribune*, the headline read: SOVIET PLAN TO FAIL, DREISER SAYS ON RETURN. The Chicago *Daily News* was more accurate: THEODORE DREISER FINDS BOTH HOPE AND FAILURE IN RUSSIAN SOVIET DRAMA.

On January 13, visas in hand, Dreiser and Ruth prepared to board a train that would take them to the Polish border. There the train would be divided, and she would return on one section to Moscow while he would go on to Warsaw and Paris. When it was time to part, he accompanied her to her compartment and bade a hasty goodbye.

Later, she completed typing his diary notes, adding a farewell message. When the trains separated, "it seemed as if it were a physical separation of just us two, as if you were cut away from me, or worse, that only a part of me had been cut away from you and the rest had gone on with you in the darkness in that other coach. . . ."

CHAPTER 26

A Contrarian at Home

Russia has a dream. Human nature is malleable. Government can exert pressure on the individual and make him a collectivist. I don't care about that. Ideals are what I want.
— Dreiser in an interview (1927)

I have been digging into biology & getting a strange new light on life.
— Dreiser to Ruth Kennell (1928)

The next Ruth heard from him was a letter from the Hôtel Grand Terminus in Paris. His relief at escaping from Russia was palpable, and he exhorted her to do the same: "Come out into the sunlight. Only Russians can solve that mess if they ever do." Paris was "warm and bright.... And not a smell anywhere since leaving."

Obviously, Dreiser was happy to be back in the land of sanitation, clean sheets, and palatable food, but he was, Helen says, haunted by memories of the poverty he had seen, talking about it as he luxuriated in the fleshpots of Paris and the Riviera. He had come to believe that, whatever its demerits, the communist system was seeking to help the wretched of Russia.

Ever the contrarian, he began defending Russia to the West just as he had stood up for the United States in Russia. In London he interviewed Winston Churchill for a syndicated article and was incensed by the Tory politician's prediction that the communist government would collapse within seven years. Dreiser praised the growing military and economic power of the New Russia and challenged Churchill to explain why England didn't improve the living conditions of its millworkers.

Yet, to a British writer, he prescribed not socialism but enlightened capitalism as the way to eliminate slums. "In America," he explained, "the rich men would be called upon, for the honour of their city, to come forward with the money necessary to clean them up."

He was, in short, of two minds—at least—about the Soviet experiment. Arriving in New York on the S.S. *Hamburg* on February 21, he faced a battery of shipping reporters eager to learn his views on the Soviet Union. "I wasn't a Communist when I went abroad and I don't return as one," he assured them. Still, although Russia was no utopia, there were programs there that the U.S. might emulate. He offered his own interpretation of the power struggle in the Kremlin: "Trotsky and some of his associates in the minority group were in a temper of revolt. . . . Stalin and his group were in the majority and there was nothing left but that they [Trotsky's group] be ejected. And, though he has a tremendous following he was ejected, for the Russians realize their strength lies in unity." Stalin, he reported, "is a big man, handsome, dark. He is astute and silent."

When one of the reporters asked him to comment on the breadlines on the Lower East Side, Dreiser said, according to the *Evening Post*, "Nowhere in Russia, whether the nation is prospering or not, will you find men without overcoats standing in breadlines." (The *New York Times* reporter gave it a less sensationalistic spin: "I cannot understand why there should be breadlines in a nation as rich as America. . . . Nowhere in Russia will you find men without overcoats standing in breadlines waiting for a handout.") The *Post* also quoted him as saying, "Contrasting the free and uncontrolled grafting we face here with the regulated accumulation centered in the Soviet government, I much prefer the Russian system." The article appeared with the headline NO RED BREAD LINE, SAYS DREISER.

His quotes made him seem to favor communism over the American way of life. No matter that he also criticized artistic censorship in Russia ("Unless artists turn their talents to propaganda for communism there is little hope of recognition") and quoted the conservative Winston Churchill as favoring more social spending in Britain to forestall a communist revolution. His remarks about breadlines and grafting in the United States drew the headlines.

Dreiser had been trying not to let the personal discomforts he experienced on the trip color his public statements. He later explained his shipboard remarks to Ruth Kennell:

I decided that, however little I might, I should not seriously try to injure an idealistic effort. Besides, learning that there were bread lines here—the first since 1910—I became furious because there is too much wealth wasted here to endure it. Hence, while I am going to stick to what I saw favorable and unfavorable, I am going to contrast it with the waste and extravagance and social indifference here. I may find myself in another storm. If so, well and good. . . .

His first interview did not result in a storm, but there were gale-force winds. An American Legion official, delivering a lecture the next day on "The Ideals of Washington as Opposed to the Ideals of Karl Marx," charged that Dreiser had been on a "cooked" tour. A week later, Simon Strunsky, writing in *The New York Times Book Review,* made the same point more elegantly. How could Dreiser say that there were no unemployment lines in Russia, when Stalin himself had declared that "unemployment is Russia's No. 1 problem"? It was a well-known fact that there were long queues at food stores and "conditions suggesting famine." Strunsky hinted that Dreiser had been misled, since "Joseph Stalin placed at his disposal two secretaries who traveled with Mr. Dreiser wherever he went."

In a letter to the editor of the *Times,* Dreiser pointed out that he had not said there was no unemployment in Russia. As he had told the New York *Herald Tribune,* "Russia will not let anyone starve. If people can't pay their rent, the Government pays it. The Government feeds the hungry." As for the secretaries, they were furnished not by Stalin but by VOKS. And "more than once, and by these same secretaries, I was threatened with not only exposure to the Russian Government but desertion and even ejection from Russia . . . [for] being nothing less than an . . . incorrigible American materialist. And worse, an anti-Communist come to spy on the honest Communist government." His claim that there was no famine in Russia, though, was generally correct. There were food shortages, the result of peasants withholding grain from the market because of low prices, and queues at the shops, but no famine.

In the ensuing weeks he wrestled with his conflicting impressions as he wrote the series of syndicated articles for NANA. The result was hasty but not unbalanced journalism.

He begins by describing the virtues of the communist system: "pursuit of this ideal of work for everybody, unearned idleness for none and the elimination of the individualist who wishes everything for himself and as little as possible for any other. . . ." He provides more specific examples of communist concern for the people's welfare: improved education ("which seeks to eliminate from the human brain or chemism all personal self-interest"—an echo of Bukharin's argument, which he pooh-poohed at the time), "the legal and political emancipation of women," the ease of divorce, and the absence of the "clatter . . . covering immoral plays, books, vice societies and their crusades, public censors, police raids, elopements, shooting, rape, sadistic murders, due to sex repressions and the like." That last mouthful (the articles were wretchedly written) was a prolix way of saying the Russians have a healthy attitude toward sex, regarding it as (what else?) "normal and natural."

But Dreiser's critical faculties were overrun by his prejudices and predilections. He continues, "There are sex murders in Russia to be sure, and rapes also," but then announces, a few sentences later, "If there is no rape and no murder there is no real crime." And after seemingly praising the absence of sexual censorship, he complains in a later article, "plays that glorify religion or dwell too heavily on love or sex are mostly taboo."

Those confusions aside, he could be bluntly critical, deploring "the endless outpour and downpour of propaganda," the omnipresence of spies and secret police, the censorship of the stage and cinema and overemphasis on didactically optimistic plays, the repression and intolerance of dissent by the ruling single-party state. He chides the press for its uncritical praise of the government and suppression of any news "which does not tend to glorify the principles of Marx and Lenin. . . ." He describes and quotes some of the various dissenters he encountered; tells of complaints by farmers that they could not afford to buy boots or coats. He also bemoans the lack of sanitation, the uncleanliness of the people, the overcrowded apartments, the shortage of bathing facilities (later implying that such conditions were the result of a communal philosophy imposed by the government). He is disturbed by the indoctrination of schoolchildren, the pervasive garrison psychology, the "spyhunting" mania with its "rumors of secret trials and executions."

He wonders if the workers' state caters too much to the industrial workers at the expense of the peasants, and if "the elimination of the old-time creative or constructive businessman" is engendering a society "from which the urge and tang of competition had been extracted." He questions Marx's dictum "From each according to his ability, to each according to his need." Who is to determine need and hence reward? "Is Edison to receive the same as a swineherd? Rockefeller no more than a steelpuddler?" And what of the lack of private incentives under communism: "can man be made to work as enthusiastically for others as for himself?" He decides that communism is a "semi-religious, semi-moral theory," no more scientific than Christianity or Islam, yet by the same token no less compelling.

Perhaps the communists are right, he sums up, and men and women's selfish instincts can be trained out of them. Stalin et al. would testify to the affirmative, but "Mr. Darwin, Mr. Haeckel, Mr. Spencer and Mr. Voltaire will tell you no—that these Russians are fools, dreamers and that some day that great people will wake up." In the end, he throws up his hands, writing that the final word has not been written on "that fascinating, stimulating, crazy topsy-turvy land."

Emotionally, however, he had committed himself to the socialist ideal. In a single aside, he gets to the personal heart of the matter:

[Under communism], this collective or paternalistic care of everybody for everybody else, it is possible to remove that dreadful sense of social misery in one direction and another which has so afflicted me in my life in America ever since I have been old enough to know what social misery is. . . .

For if [communism] has lessened the glitter and the show it has at any rate taken the heartache and the material tragedy from millions and millions of lives.

NANA was anxious to publish a paperback edition of the articles, but Liveright objected, asserting his contractual rights to Dreiser's writing. He proposed that B & L publish a hardcover book of Dreiser's reflections on Russia. Dreiser was not averse to the money or the chance to propound his views on a country that was badly misunderstood in America. The problem was that he would have to pad the articles to have enough material for a respectable-sized hardcover book.

He was juggling a number of projects at this time, including *A Gallery of Women,* for which Liveright had set a deadline of September 15; an exposé of the Catholic Church, which Esther McCoy was researching for him; a dramatization of *Sister Carrie,* which a young Broadway writer-producer named Hy Kraft had hired the playwright John Howard Lawson to do.

The study of Russia was the most pressing, and he enlisted Campbell to help him cobble together his material. He did send her a rough draft of a manuscript that built on the newspaper articles, which he had reworked or sliced up and sandwiched between new material. Working with his notebook and newspaper clippings, including a set of Dorothy Thompson's articles, which had run in February, Louise edited and expanded the manuscript and organized it into chapters. After she finished, she returned the script to Dreiser, who rewrote some more and revised her organization plan. For example, he decided that "the G.P.U. stuff will have to be set off by itself as a separate chapter. It concerns a kind of thing which the Russians love— terrorism & will have to have the psychology of that discanted on."

He might have been better advised to bring in Ruth Kennell as a collaborator. In May she had decided to return to the States. On her way to visit her grandparents in Oklahoma, she stopped in New York and Dreiser took her to lunch at an elegant restaurant. She felt ill at ease with the man with whom she had once been so close and shared so much. He gave her some letters of introduction to editors and publishers to whom she might pitch articles and books on Russia. But apparently he didn't mention the Russia book to her. He later explained that as she was going west and would not be around to help him, he didn't bother.

At least in hindsight, she had a better conception of the book than he did. She thought he should have written a more personal, chronological account, drawing upon the diary she had helped compile. The result might have been a more relaxed travel book in the rambling style of *A Traveler at Forty* and *A Hoosier Holiday*, but doing it that way would have meant writing a new book rather than building on the newspaper series. Instead he reorganized the material under subject headings such as "Russia's Post-Revolutionary Political and General Achievements," "The Russian Versus the American Temperament," "The Current Soviet Economic Plan," and "Communism—Theory and Practice." Only the last three chapters contained his personal impressions. Such an approach may have seemed the quickest way to get the book done, for it provided pigeonholes into which various blocks of material could be filed.

In July he and Helen drove their new Chrysler Imperial convertible to Woods Hole on Cape Cod, where they had rented a cottage and where he intended to finish his various writing projects. Construction was under way on the Iroki house, so it was impossible to work there. But also, through the Russian-born scientist Boris Sokoloff, he had been invited to spend a month at the Marine Biological Laboratory as a sort of writer in residence.

Watching the "direct, undogmatized gaze of these workers toward the unknown" was inspiring. He adjured Ruth Kennell to study biology: it "will remove your moralistic—or semi-dogmatic inhibitions & let you set up a decent social code for yourself." He was ushered into a new mental realm—"the fairy land which lies just below the microscope," he wrote Franklin and Beatrice Booth. "I am awed and so amazed by the processes visible to the eye that I grow decidedly reverent."

He interrogated the scientists in his deceptively naive way. A writer for the *Collecting Net*, the weekly newsletter published by the laboratory, described him in action: "He has that rare talent developed in his earlier experiences as a Chicago newspaper reporter, of asking questions which require hours of enthusiastic monologue to answer. Silent scientists have burst into profuse verbiage at his questions, to explain themselves. . . . Mr. Dreiser sits, profoundly interested, and listens."

But two nonscientific questions kept recurring: Is there a God? Is there life after death? He reported to the Booths that the scientists were "all mechanists & in so far as life is concerned hopeless. It is a good show—sometimes—but ends for man here." But the longer he peered into the microscope, the more he thought he saw clues to God's existence. For there must be some creative intelligence behind the intricately beautiful forms of even the lowliest creatures. In another letter to the Booths he reported that he had discovered scientists who were not mechanists. "Some are agnostics, some mystics, some of a reverent and even semi-religious turn."

He lived, John Cowper Powys said, in a universe of chaos, but, peering into the microcosm, he glimpsed form and design.

On the Cape he labored nine hours a day at putting the finishing touches on *Dreiser Looks at Russia* (the title was the one used by the New York *World* for his articles) and reading proofs of *A Gallery of Women*. He had written a new "study" for the latter, called "Ernita," which told Ruth Kennell's story. He sent her a copy, and she said she was "torn" about whether to allow him to use it. "Does Ernita get anywhere with her life?" she wondered. She feared that he liked the story because it supported his belief that puny man was always defeated. She left it to his judgment whether publication of the story "would injure anyone."

When it was time to leave, he sent a bread-and-butter letter to his hosts at the Marine Laboratory, which was published in the *Collecting Net*. It bespeaks a wistful admiration for the cloistered life devoted to the pursuit of pure truth. There was in Dreiser, among other conflicting traits, a Monk and a Sensualist, the former dwelling in silence in some remote cell in his mind, performing rites of penance for the Sensualist, calling him back to an austere life of work and contemplation.

The manuscript of *Russia* was rushed to the printer, and by mid-August he had received galleys. At this juncture he consulted Ruth, now in Palo Alto visiting her mother. He asked her to check the text for accuracy of names and facts and to make any other changes she thought necessary. He explained that "Some of the bits are material verified by others and offered me for use."

She found the book in its present state "a hodgepodge, a carelessly thrown together conglomeration of impressions, facts and evaluations," but she wrote him an encouraging letter, praising the "delightful and true pictures." There was not much she could do beyond rearranging the order of chapters so that the three personal ones came at the end, correcting errors and quarreling with some of his interpretations as well as his bad grammar. She objected to some anecdotes that reflected unfavorably on the Revolution, such as a description of pigs living in peasants' huts.

He accepted many of her factual emendations, but declined to cut the story about the pigs because Tolstoy's daughter Olga had told it to him. As for the mistakes in grammar and the superfluous words, he pleaded guilty on all counts. "I have been so offending all my life. All my books are full of them." She had criticized a passage that seemed pro-religious, and he lectured her on the difference "between religion and dogmatic religion." The former could be "a response to as well as an awe or reverence before the beauty of wisdom or creative energy"—an idea bolstered by his contemplations at Woods Hole.

Ruth seems to have felt a proprietary interest in the book, for she asked why he failed to mention her work as his secretary. (He had referred only to anonymous interpreters and guides.) He reminded her of "a possible situation here in America (a personal one I mean) which might . . . dictate silence in regard to any particular female secretary." He meant Helen, of course, though his sudden accession of reticence was odd.

A Gallery of Women moved toward publication. He had more material than he needed, and Lengel sold three of the surplus portraits to *Cosmopolitan* for a substantial fee—$10,000. Louise was put to work polishing these stories. She may have been overconscientious in making them suitable for *Cosmopolitan,* for he chided her about cutting a scene involving "a little youthful stuff in the wretched family parlor." He would put it all back in the galleys, he said, and teased her about growing stuffy in her mature years.

The serialization in *Cosmopolitan,* titled *This Madness,* required the postponement of the *Gallery.* With additional time Dreiser began to write other sketches, possibly as replacements for the weaker ones in the present manuscript. He was eager to do one on Emma Goldman, whom he had encountered in a state of near destitution in Paris in 1926. He later sent her money and tried to find a publisher for her autobiography. Now he told her that a study by him might whet public interest in the autobiography. And by presenting her sympathetically he might help rescind the deportation order that had propelled her into exile. Unfortunately for her confidence in him, he was under the monumental misapprehension that she had shot and killed Henry C. Frick of the Carnegie Steel Works. (Goldman's lover, Alexander Berkman, had done the deed; Frick recovered from his wounds.) She chided him for these mistakes and doubted his sketch would help her much. Nor did she want help: "As for trying to justify me to society, why should anyone want to do that."

There seems little doubt that Dreiser was more interested in aiding Goldman than in writing about her. He was taking up her cause as he had taken up that of Tom Mooney, the labor leader wrongly convicted by perjured testimony for bombing a Preparedness Day parade in San Francisco in 1916. On November 15 Dreiser wrote a letter to Governor C. C. Young of California asking him to pardon Mooney. Young eventually refused, and Mooney would not accept parole because that carried a presumption of guilt.

As he identified with radicals like Goldman and Mooney, he also distanced himself from the mainstream political parties, though that was nothing new. When, that September, Bruce J. Bliven, editor of *The New Republic,* solicited his views on the 1928 presidential candidates, he dismissed Herbert Hoover, the Republican, as "a hall boy for American corporate power" and rejected Governor Al Smith as a captive of Tammany Hall and the Catholic Church, "an earthly organization which seeks to dominate all governments and whose animating motive is by no means pure and undefiled spirituality but *power.*" He supported the efforts of the philosopher John Dewey to organize a third party.

.   .   .

As he was revising *This Madness* and expanding *A Gallery of Women*, another woman from his past surfaced in his life. He had already written about her in *The "Genius"*—his old love from the Butterick days, Thelma Cudlipp. After *An American Tragedy* appeared she had read *The "Genius"* and been touched by the account of his sufferings for her sake, although she also felt he had been unfair to her mother. She wrote Dreiser a social note and later invited him and Helen to dinner.

Thelma had married Edmund Grosvenor, a rich, socially prominent attorney, in 1918 and now at thirty-six, with two children, was living the life of a Park Avenue matron. For Dreiser the reunion was fraught with emotion. When they had a moment alone, she told him, "I have read your *'Genius.'* " "You have been a long time coming to it," he said. When she told him that her mother had committed suicide, he said, simply, "I am glad." He made a movement as though to embrace her, but let his hands drop, saying, "It is too late." Or so she describes the scene in her unpublished autobiographical novel, "October's Child." The dinner went well, but like many other women before and after her Thelma noticed that he ignored Helen the entire evening. Helen didn't seem to mind, Thelma thought. Later she and the children visited Iroki, and she and Dreiser maintained an occasional correspondence. After their reunion he wrote a cryptic poem, "The Muffled Oar":

> *You—*
> *I.*
> *But from whence?*
> *And to where?*
> *You?*
> *I?*

The seas of time had washed away their common past; whatever he had once felt for her was gone.

The demands of the present summoned him. In addition to his onerous writing schedule, he was bedeviled by the responsibilities of his country home. What he really wanted, he decided, was a country place someone else owned which he could visit. But by the end of September, he wrote Beatrice Booth that work on the house should be completed in three weeks. The spring-fed pool, a new road, a stone wall, and the Prussian-blue gates emblazoned with "Iroki" were in place. Wharton Esherick had designed a thatched-roof guest cottage, modeled after the huts in which Washington's army wintered at Valley Forge.

He could afford to indulge his architectural whims. His income for 1927 had been a substantial $97,000 (worth, at 1990 prices, nearly five times that amount), most of it insulated from the tax collector by his personal corporation, the Authors Holding Company, of which he, Helen, and Arthur Pell were salaried officers. He now espoused the antitax convictions of a Wall Street banker, the following year stating his approval of a newspaper campaign for lower taxes. Although sales of the *Tragedy* dwindled in 1928 to some 2600 copies, the revised *Financier* sold only 4000, and *Chains*, a respectable 12,000, he was earning sizable sums from foreign sales, syndication deals, and magazine fees, including several sketches from *A Gallery of Women* that he had sold to *Cosmopolitan* before *This Madness*. Also, a road-company production of *An American Tragedy* was harvesting royalties.

That fall he and Helen resumed the Thursday at-homes. Now, friends noticed, he could talk of nothing but his Russian journey. Claude Bowers and W. E. Woodward, Helen's one-time boss and now a debunking historian, both remembered his passionate defense of the Soviet government. He also praised Russian culture and spoke about bringing over the Russian Ballet. At one of his soirées he presented the Russian soprano Nine Koshetz, who been a favorite in Czarist days. When she finished her recital, he announced to Bowers, "The best is yet to come." And then a group of leaping, sweating, near-naked African dancers hurtled into the room, shouting and menacing the guests. Dreiser thought the dancers wonderfully primitive. That evening was considered the highpoint of his Thursday salons.

His life was as chaotic as the dancers in his living room. Part of him was the wealthy and famous impresario of the Rodin Studios, part of him yearned for the hall bedroom, the one-horse publisher, the tranquillity of science. Part of him believed that the Soviet experiment was idealism in action; another part said it was "a wholly lunatic theory in regard to altering the very nature of man," which practiced "the ruthless suppression of individualism . . . peace and prosperity under a gun." Like the Americans he wrote about for the Sunday supplements, he was restless—"to do what? attempt what?" He told Margaret Szekely, one of his set of Hungarian friends, "Life is so difficult, so complex that I have to knock my head against the wall to regain my equilibrium."

In search of the "detail secretary" who might shoulder some of his burdens, he hired Esther Van Dresser, a pretty, red-haired divorcée from St. Louis. She recalled to William A. Swanberg that Dreiser was a difficult boss. "He was highly critical, not tolerant of an error, though of course he made many errors." He would fly into rages over petty matters—"it was like working for a volcano." But Beatrice Cole, who performed part-time secretarial tasks around this time, thought him an easy boss. When there were letters to answer, he never dictated but told her to say this or that and left it to her to fill in the blanks. The handwritten manuscripts he gave her were sometimes difficult to read, and she would rewrite parts that were illegible.

He never complained. And although "he was a womanizer from the word go," he never bothered the petite and recently married Beatrice.

Esther was another matter; he was having an affair with her, which explained their stormy relationship. He was domineering and scoffed at her religious beliefs. "He planted in me a seed of disbelief that hurt me many years," she later said. He kept six or eight bottles of pills on his desk, and had a phobia about tuberculosis (she wasn't aware that he believed he had contracted TB as a boy in Chicago). He confessed that there were times when he would remain in bed for days and "just brood and grieve and ponder." He feared that he was losing his creative powers and that his wealth wouldn't last. (This latter idiosyncrasy Helen dubbed his "poverty complex." According to Mencken and others, however, she compensated for his parsimony with her frequent shopping sprees. Living well was Helen's best revenge for his infidelities.)

With Dreiser, the personal was metaphysical; inner chaos led to spiritual chaos: at the height of fame he had lost sight of himself, of his place in the great scheme. When *The Bookman* asked him and other writers for a statement of their views on the meaning of life, Dreiser could only reaffirm more strongly what he had said in 1912, what he had said in *Hey, Rub-a-Dub-Dub!*: "Life is to me too much a welter and play of inscrutable forces to permit . . . any significant comment. . . . I catch no meaning from all I have seen, and pass quite as I came, confused and dismayed."

The appearance of *Dreiser Looks at Russia* in November injected further turmoil into his life. On November 13, two days after publication, Franklin P. Adams once again found it his droll duty to point out in "The Conning Tower" some curious correspondences between a Dreiser book and one by another author. This time it was Dorothy Thompson, whose *The New Russia* had been published on September 7. The next day Percy Winner, in the *Evening Post*, which had run Thompson's articles, provided a detailed list of the "amazing similarities" between passages in both books. Beatrice Cole recalled his reaction when he first saw Winner's article: "I never read her Goddamn book." He immediately dispatched Esther Van Dresser to the nearest bookstore to buy a copy. But Winner accused Dreiser of undue borrowing from Thompson's articles (the basis for her book), citing examples of nearly identical paragraphs.

Dreiser denied that he had lifted words from Thompson and countercharged that he had given *her* material while they were in Moscow, which he later used in his book, thus explaining the similarities. Thompson hotly challenged this theory: "I wonder when he gave me that material. As I recall it, we met only two or three times and then had merely casual conversations," which was true. When *could* he have given her the material?

They had met early in Dreiser's Moscow stay when he fancied she was flirting with him, and they talked generally about communism and capitalism. He wrote Ruth Kennell, "She took three separate pieces of stuff I gathered . . . all of which I talked over with her & when I didn't know she was rushing off daily letters to New York or contemplating a book. . . ." But at that point Dreiser had seen very little, and would not have had much information to give her.

Then he offered another explanation: they had obtained material from the same source, the weekly bulletin of the Soviet Foreign Ministry. Thompson retorted that she had drawn on official handouts only to verify some transcriptions of speeches. Furthermore, the plagiary involved descriptions of Moscow scenes, not the kind of stuff that would be found in government releases.

She had a good case. For example, Dreiser wrote: "There are the N.E.P. men. . . . They sit moodily in the restaurant of the Grand Hotel, drink Russian wines, watch the dancing and think themselves lucky if a ballerina from the opera dances with them." Thompson's account reads: "The businessmen sit moodily in the restaurant of the Grand Hotel watching the dancing and thinking themselves lucky if they have a ballerina from the opera to dance with." There were several other parallels. Thompson later wrote a friend, "The old beast simply lifted paragraph after paragraph from my articles; I'm not speaking of material—we all got that where we could—but purely literary expressions. And, of course, ideas as well, because it never occurred to anyone else, for instance, to write about the social life of Moscow."

Thompson's attorney, Melville Caine, demanded that Dreiser's book be recalled, the plates destroyed, and any profits paid over to Thompson as recompense for the injuries she had suffered. In her formal complaint, forwarded by Caine to Arthur Garfield Hays on November 26, she asserts that eight of the eighteen chapters in Dreiser's book "have been distinctly and strongly influenced by my articles." (That was lawyer's overkill.) Dreiser hired Arthur Carter Hume to represent him, not trusting Hays, who was Liveright's attorney.

Vincent Sheean thought that Lewis was behind the suit. Sinclair and Dorothy had been married in May and had just moved into a duplex on West Tenth Street. Playing the outraged husband, he was more eager than his bride to punish Dreiser, and Caine was his lawyer, not hers.

But Dreiser proceeded to poison the air with wild countercharges. He began circulating the tale that he and Dorothy had been intimate in Moscow and, as she heard it, "that I may have gone into his room and purloined his *notes!*" As he explained to Ruth, he believed Dorothy was jealous of his competing book and she and Lewis were trying to stir up publicity for hers.

The irony of the entire affair was that he didn't need to borrow any material from Thompson. He had spent three months in the country, while she had spent a month in Moscow and then hurried off to join Lewis. Take the NEP men scene quoted above. In his diary Dreiser describes a similar group whom he saw in Leningrad's Hotel Europa. He could well have used that description but perhaps felt he must provide some Moscow color. Leningrad NEP men wouldn't do.

Rushed and needing filler material, he took a shortcut. The Thompson passages appear in the original manuscript. They are written in Dreiser's own hand. He had always regarded newspaper stories as grist for his novels, and it could be that he lumped Thompson's articles with their conversations in Moscow. This was the material he told Ruth Kennell had been "offered to me for my use."

A scandalous trial was brewing, with lawyers on both sides primed to impugn the character and integrity of the opposing parties. Dreiser seemed eager for battle, writing Kennell in December, "I have good lawyers & she & Lewis will know something more about plagiarism than they do now before it's all over." His attorneys planned to introduce a fourteen-page concordance between Thompson's book and *New York Times* columnist Anne O'Hare McCormick's previously published Russian memoir, *The Hammer and the Scythe.* In December Harry Hansen, in his literary column for the *World,* had written that "both ladies seem to have emerged from Russia with similar ideas, similar information, and sometimes even similar little characters to report." Having run Dreiser's original articles, it was not surprising that the *World* was on Dreiser's side.

Amid all the fuss, the reviews of *Dreiser Looks at Russia* were somewhat anticlimactic. Many critics alluded to the Dorothy Thompson imbroglio, but most were bemused rather than indignant. Lewis Gannett in the New York *Herald Tribune* put it best: ". . . the impression is abroad that Dreiser's book is like Dorothy Thompson's. Except in a few details it isn't. It is as different as Theodore Dreiser is from Dorothy Thompson. . . . Dreiser is not sure of anything about Russia. And who else has ever written a book about Russia without being abundantly sure?"

CHAPTER 27   *This Madness*

> But in the interim . . . there came a form of satiation most
> characteristic of my disposition—and perhaps of all nature
> in one form or another. . . . The changefulness of my
> moods! The cruelty of them!
>
> —Dreiser, *This Madness* (1929)

reiser Looks at Russia found no strong response among readers;
U.S. sales eventually totaled only 4000 copies. As usual Dreiser
blamed his publisher's inadequate advertising for the poor showing. In February Thompson withdrew her suit, which might
have publicized the book. Probably she had no heart for a bruis-
ing court battle at which she would be accused of stealing from Anne
O'Hare McCormick. Not that she had plagiarized, but like most reports by
journalists about Russia, the two books contained similar themes.

Dreiser's complaints about the book's sales were just another shot in his
running battle with Liveright. A larger grievance was the failure of Horace
Liveright Inc. (as the company was now known) to bring out the limited
edition of his complete works, which under the contract was to have been
launched in 1927. Once again Dreiser was entertaining suitors, including his
old but apparently constant love, Harper's, which had offered to take over
all his books for ten years and invest $75,000 in advertising; Dreiser would
receive a flat 10 percent of sales. Another bidder was Simon & Schuster, the
publishing house that the crossword-puzzle craze built. It would guarantee

him $16,000 a year for ten years, regardless of sales, and spend $50,000 on promotion over the first five years of the contract.

Liveright once again baked a savory financial pie to tempt him into staying. He had hopes for another Great American Novel—*The Stoic* or *The Bulwark*. In the meantime there was *A Gallery of Women*, for which a presumably large public was waiting. Dreiser on women—well, his reputation was getting around. At any rate, Liveright dangled a guarantee of $15,000 a year for ten years, plus 100 shares of stock in the company, currently selling at $275 a share.

Despite the competing bids, Liveright held the inside track, but Dreiser was not going to grant him victory without a fight. He demanded a greater role in the affairs of the reorganized company, of which Liveright was now sole head. With Horace's approval Dreiser hired an accountant to comb the ledgers, and then he sent Esther Van Dresser as his proxy to a meeting of the board of directors in early February 1929. According to her notes, Dreiser had a proposal for the board:

> That in consideration of the prestige and position [Dreiser] occupies and because of his foreign contacts and connections, as well as influence among various authors here, he believed that he could be of considerable service to the publishing firm of Horace Liveright, Inc. by securing various authors for them, and that by joining hands with the publishing house and coming in with them as a stockholder, the firm could be developed into one of the largest of its kind in the world.

Liveright responded that because of the professional jealousy among writers, it would be unwise for one of the company's authors to assume a directing role. He added that if Dreiser really wanted to strengthen the house, he could do so from outside, primarily by bringing in new writers. The board did not act on Dreiser's request, but it did raise his annual payments from $6000 to $15,000, retroactive to January 1, 1929, under a contract running six years. This pact had not as yet been signed by the author, who favored a ten-year agreement.

Dreiser was surely aware that Liveright Inc. was falling on hard times. The glory days of 1927 and 1928, when its titles regularly rode the best-seller list—six of them simultaneously, at one point—were behind it. The year 1929 would be the worst in the company's history; its only best seller was Francis Hackett's *Henry VIII*. And without the Modern Library or any other backlist, Liveright needed multiple best sellers just to stay afloat.

Horace Liveright had suffered heavy personal losses as well. A musical he produced, called *The Dagger and the Rose*, had flopped out of town, costing him $90,000. He dropped $100,000 on two stocks alone. Finally, the company had been riven by internal dissension, culminating in the departure of Donald Friede in 1928 to form his own house. Liveright had to borrow money from Pell and others to redeem Friede's shares, pledging his own as collateral.

When Dreiser read Liveright's remarks at the board meeting, he fired off an angry letter demanding an explanation of his "fine bit of imagining [as to] an author's duties to his publisher." He starchily informed Liveright: "You now have the privilege of writing me a letter in which you will state what did happen from first to last. . . . I am not willing to wait longer than Monday afternoon for your reply."

The day after the meeting, Dreiser wrote Otto Kyllmann, of Constable, suggesting that he team up with an American publisher, following which Dreiser would move "bag and baggage" to the new house. Kyllmann was all for it and suggested that he could work out some arrangement with Harcourt Brace. Dreiser replied that he did not much care for that house (which was Lewis's publisher) and would consider moving only if Kyllmann had a controlling voice, which was out of the question. On April 29, 1929, Dreiser signed the new contract with Liveright Inc., calling on him to deliver a new book every other year.

Dreiser's Russian trip embroiled him in another project at this time, one close to his Slavic soul—bringing the Russian Ballet to America. The idea had been suggested to him by William Reswick, the AP man in Moscow, who proposed that Otto Kahn be the chief angel. At least $250,000 would be needed. The logistical problems were formidable, and the impoverished company needed new sets and costumes.

Kahn, a latter-day Maecenas of the performing arts (now president of the Metropolitan Opera, he had sponsored Nijinsky's American tour with the Ballet Russe), was receptive. He pledged $25,000 seed money and promised to underwrite half of the $250,000. As business manager Dreiser engaged Hy Kraft, the producer whom he had authorized to mount *Sister Carrie* for the stage (the project was abandoned when Dreiser refused to approve John Howard Lawson's script and the writer left for Hollywood).

With the prestige of Otto Kahn behind the enterprise, a few society people pledged money. But then some snags reared up. According to Kraft, communication with the Moscow authorities, with whom he was dealing through Reswick, broke down. No one, it seemed, in the labyrinthine communist bureaucracy had the authority to approve the tour Kraft had mapped out. Later Kraft heard that Reswick had fallen in with some shady officials who sought to profit from the deal.

In early April Kraft set a deadline for a decision by Moscow, and when none came Dreiser decided to cancel the tour. On April 14 he wrote Kraft that the "deal is off. Sorry. Financial responsibilities will be quickly determined and I will see about meeting them. . . . I'm off for Boston."

. . .

"Boston" meant the long-awaited trial of Donald Friede for selling a copy of *An American Tragedy*. Liveright and his attorneys, Arthur Garfield Hays and Clarence Darrow, were optimistic about winning the case. Dreiser was ready to testify in behalf of his book, and there was support among Hub intellectuals. But the city's Puritans—Protestant and Catholic—were all-powerful.

Hays suffered his first setback when he tried to introduce the entire novel into evidence and was overruled. The statute clearly permitted a finding of obscenity on the basis of specific passages or words. He then tried to introduce artistic intention as a defense, but that argument also got nowhere. Finally, he asked if the author could be called to the stand to *tell* the entire story, providing at least some context for the offending passages. Again a negative response from the judge. With that, the trial recessed.

That night an anticensorship rally was held at Ford Hall. Dreiser, the two lawyers, and Friede attended. Margaret Sanger sat onstage with her mouth taped shut in a gesture of protest against the city's ban on birth-control information. Skits were performed satirizing the Watch and Ward Society, and Upton Sinclair, whose novel *Oil* had earlier been banned in Boston, sent a defiant telegram. The meeting drew extensive newspaper coverage, but the stories generally portrayed the participants as advocates of dirty books. Moreover, Sanger's presence served to link Dreiser's novel with birth control—anathema to the powerful Catholic hierarchy. The district attorney had charged: "A story like this is indecent. It's an invitation to young people to learn birth control."

It is doubtful, however, that Dreiser's cause would have prevailed even if the rally had not been held. In his presentation, the district attorney needed only to cite the twenty-four questionable pages in the novel. The level of argument was epitomized by his comment on the scene in which Clyde visits a prostitute: "Well, perhaps where the gentleman published this book, it is considered not obscene for a woman to start disrobing before a man, but it happens to be out in Roxbury where I come from." In his charge to the jury, the judge backed the district attorney, telling the panel they need only consider whether the passages were obscene and tending toward the corruption of the young. Artistic intention or quality was irrelevant.

Hays knew the game was up, and he telegraphed Liveright that the jury would "vote Catholic." It did on April 18, leaving Friede the choice of paying the $300 fine or appealing. After a discussion among the principals, Liveright agreed to finance an appeal to the Massachusetts Supreme Court (which, a year later, upheld the lower court's verdict).

At the trial, Dreiser audibly chuckled at the district attorney's concern for the moral sensibilities of the good folk of Roxbury, but the Boston banning was a fire bell in the night, activating his anticensorship juices. He laid the blame on the altar of the Church Temporal. When Claude Bowers sent him an editorial he had written for the *World* condemning the banning of the *Tragedy* and the confiscation by a Boston customs official of thirteen copies of Voltaire's *Candide,* Dreiser replied in fury: "I have stated over and over that the chief menace to the world today is the Catholic Church because it is a world wide organization and because chiefly it attacks intelligence . . . since for its own prosperity's sake it believes in mass stupidity."

He suspected that religious groups were also behind the delay in the filming of *An American Tragedy* in Hollywood. Three years had passed since the stormy luncheon at the Ritz, and not a line of the script had been written. Dreiser had received reports that Will Hays was holding the picture hostage on moral grounds. Paramount-Publix (as Famous Players–Lasky was now called) was probably complicit. When Lasky announced with great fanfare the purchase of the screen rights to the novel, the studio had received a deluge of protest mail, and the recent verdict in Boston was a sign that in some quarters at least, *An American Tragedy* was an immoral book.

At this time Hays was calling for the adoption of a stricter Production Code. After seven years of guiding movie morals with a loose set of rules known as the "Hays Formula" (which applied only to films made from books and plays), he smelled another storm brewing akin to the Fatty Arbuckle tornado. The antivice groups were active and bills for a Federal censorship law were perennially before Congress. Since the industry preferred self-regulation, Hays thought it politic to announce a tougher code, one with a religious provenance. And so that summer, when Martin Quigley, publisher of movie magazines, sent him the draft of a code that he had written with the Reverend Daniel A. Lord, a Jesuit priest, Hays had the answer to his prayers. The Martin Quigley standards were adopted in 1930.

Dreiser evidently had heard premonitory rumbles of all this, and he surely noted the Catholic involvement. In an article for *Theatre Guild Magazine* titled "The Meddlesome Decade," he did not specifically refer to the Church, but he echoed his earlier statement to Bowers, declaring that "today we are faced with one of the most fanatical and dangerous forms of censorship that ever existed because the effect of all such activity is to reduce all human intelligence to one level—and that level about that of a low-grade (not even a high-grade) moron!" He protested the outmoded 1915 Supreme Court decision affirming the right of state review boards to ban movies. (The Court held that motion pictures were a "spectacle" like a circus and therefore not protected by freedom of speech provisions in state and national constitutions.)

Having fired those blasts, he found himself encountering another kind of censorship. The serial *This Madness* that he had sold to *Cosmopolitan* was bowdlerized by the editors. The stories were semiautobiographical, describing the love affairs of a famous novelist who goes by the nicknames "Dodar" and "T" and whose books include *The Financier* and *The Titan*. The editors played up the autobiographical angle, and Dreiser gave the series his imprimatur: "You people may not realize it, but in 'This Madness' you are publishing the most intimate and important work so far achieved by me." To which the editors chorused, "We do realize it, Mr. Dreiser. We realize that no man, certainly no American, has written so honestly, so frankly, about the part love plays in the life of a great artist."

This Madness is subdivided into three episodes titled "Aglaia," "Elizabeth," and "Sidonie." Although some events are fictionalized, Dreiser painted his portraits of ladies from life. The title character of "Aglaia" is loosely based on Lillian Rosenthal, and the story covers their affair from the time he occupied a room in Elias Rosenthal's apartment on Riverside Drive while writing *Jennie Gerhardt*. "Elizabeth" is Anna Tatum, and Dreiser takes care not to say too much about her family, probably still fearing a lawsuit. Kirah Markham is "Sidonie" in the final memoir.

The theme of this "honest novel about love" is the male character's inability to remain faithful to one woman. Each affair necessarily ends in grief, the abandoned woman mourning her loss and the narrator racked by guilt for the pain he has inflicted. The contrasting emotions are mutually reinforcing: the man wants the woman to grieve as an affirmation of her devotion, then he can expiate his guilt by self-recrimination. The editors of *Cosmopolitan* were stretching things when they termed *This Madness* Dreiser's "finest work," but he dealt more honestly than they knew with the compulsions that had driven him in his affairs with women.

Whatever its confessional value, *This Madness* was second-drawer. The stories lack irony, tension, detachment; the language is at times turgid, weighing down the slight subject matter, at times lushly romantic.

After the first two episodes appeared, Ruth Kennell chastised him for writing "pseudobiography with the unreality and romanticism of a schoolboy, and the social snobbery of Robert W. Chambers." The stories encouraged the "false conception engendered by capitalism . . . that woman is a commodity for the use of men, which loses its value when youth or beauty decline." She was right. The women in *This Madness* are figments of desire.

Dreiser at least deserved credit for not completely succumbing to the formula of slick magazine fiction; there are no happy endings. But he did have to conform to the standards of woman's-magazine morality. The material was cut by almost a third, he told Grant C. Knight, a University of Kentucky English professor, in order to make it "suitable to the censorship in various states and possible prejudices of some of their readers. . . ." Dreiser's final typescript suggests that the trims were not as large as he said, but cuts there were. The phrase "I let my hand wander to her breasts outlined beneath the filmy material of her dress" was deemed unsuitable. The outcome of a romantic rendezvous between the author and a scantily clad Aglaia one moonlit night in the country was not left to the imagination in the manuscript. Nor would the editors permit Dreiser to allude to Aglaia becoming pregnant and visiting an abortionist. The "uncompromising realist" shown in the author's photograph had made some compromises.

Dreiser told Knight that he intended to publish the complete stories, along with four others, accompanied by "an introduction and a philosophic commentary at the close, which will throw some light on the book as a whole." He was not coy about their source: "In regard to the material—it is autobiographical." A lot of people already suspected that.

Now that he had money, he was able to subsidize a group of researchers, some of whom were mistresses. He was secretive about his affairs, so that, like the members of a communist cell, each woman rarely knew the identities of the others. One of his later women friends says he did this to avoid hurting anyone's feelings; avoiding jealous confrontations may have been another motive.

Yet he was sincere in his fashion, making each woman feel he loved her. Yvette Szekely, whom he had seduced as a teenager, said when asked if Dreiser used or exploited women, "Why were they being used? They were happy. They loved him. . . . He told everyone that she was the only one. He really did care about the person—not that he pretended to love and didn't. If he had five women, he really cared for them."

When a former mistress needed help he usually provided it. He sent $500 to Sally Kusell, who had fled to England and was discovered broke and ill in a London nursing home. Another of his woman friends caught pneumonia after they had broken up. Dreiser paid for her hospital room and sat by her bed, holding her hand.

One of those who did literary work for him at this time was Marguerite Tjader Harris. She recalled their first meeting, at one of his Thursday nights: "He turned to look down at me as if I were a glass and he wanted to see what sort of liquid was in it." She was living the life of a society matron, and he teased her about being a "parasite" and offered to put her to work. She was interested and began performing various research tasks, commuting from Connecticut during the week to a rented room in Manhattan. He visited her infrequently, never notifying her ahead of time, as though he were trying to conceal his movements. But the uncertainty also gave a romantic piquancy to his affairs, Harris thought; he preferred to respond to "the urgency of the moment" rather than adhere to a fixed routine. She was struck by his "utter simplicity" and his strongly emotional nature. "Dreiser simply *was* his own emotions, his own instincts, or intuitions, attempting to communicate them directly, often in terms contradictory to each other."

A tall, intelligent woman with a determined chin and wide brow, Harris came from a wealthy family. Dreiser liked to take her to fashionable restaurants, the opera, or the theater. He would don a tuxedo and she, evening finery. She provided a glamorous outlet for his secret craving for admission to society, Harris thought.

All this extracurricular life generated constant tensions with Helen, and Dreiser found a sympathetic ear in Margaret Szekely, Yvette's mother (this was before his affair with her daughter). Sometimes he would ring her in the middle of the night and ask if he could come to her place on West Ninety-first Street. "He would come and cry on my bosom because Helen didn't understand him," she later told Swanberg. "He needed a mother and I supplied the need."

By June his relationship with Helen was approaching a crisis. Ralph Fabri, the Hungarian painter, who met Dreiser through Margaret Szekely, began playing the same role with Helen as Margaret did with Dreiser. Dreiser had admired Fabri's portrait of Helen's singing teacher, Maria Samson (who complained to the artist that Dreiser made advances to her), and asked Fabri to do one of Helen. She posed with her wolfhound, Nick, at Fabri's studio on Washington Square, often walking all the way from Fifty-seventh Street. During the sittings she poured out her troubles with Dreiser. He recorded in his diary that she told him they hadn't had sexual relations for two years, but that there was a durable spiritual affection between them.

Helen was particularly wounded by his taste for younger women, and also feared he was endangering his health. He boasted that sex was the most important business of his life, and once told Helen he had slept with three women in the same day. His run of amorous luck made him more libidinous but also more lonely. As he had written in *This Madness*, he could never be sure a woman cared for him or his fame. And clearly some of them were drawn to him by a combination of hero-worship and literary ambition, which he always encouraged to the point of commending their work to his agent of the moment. And in most cases his praise was sincere.

But women only satisfied a need; they did not provide the answers he was seeking or soothe his restless spirit (indeed, on balance, they brought him more unrest). It was in a philosophically questing mood that he re-turned to the Woods Hole Marine Laboratory in August. Accompanied by Calvin Bridges, the Nobel Prize–winning geneticist from the California Institute of Technology, he spent a weekend on Nantucket with Marguerite Harris and her husband. He had developed a friendship with Bridges, a towheaded, boyish man with an easy grin, who was as dedicated an admirer of femininity as Dreiser. They picnicked on the beach and talked well into the night about the philosophical questions that obsessed him. Bridges ar-gued that philosophers had no hope of learning the "why" of existence, but he believed that eventually science would fill in all the "hows." His theory was that human lives are determined by higher laws of cause and effect, and the best we can do is to live to the fullest, enjoying the spectacle of the harmony of nature or the form of a beautiful woman. Dreiser liked this idea,

Harris noted, but thought Bridges's scientific approach excluded "those veiled mysterious forces of darkness that [Dreiser] had believed in almost more than forces of Light. . . ." He envisioned the universe in mechanistic terms as the setting of a Manichean drama in which light and darkness clashed in an eternal struggle.

The struggle with Helen continued after his return to New York in September. One day in October she announced, "I just had a fight with Teddy. We're breaking this time. He's going to a lawyer." Later she reported, "He must be fixing up a place for himself. He probably wants to leave me in the street." But the next day, when Fabri went to 200 West Fifty-seventh to return a book, he found Dreiser at home, worrying about the stock market crash. It was October 29—Black Tuesday.

The question of how much Dreiser lost in the plunge elicited various opinions from his friends. He himself said that before the fall he had a paper fortune of $400,000. Esther Van Dresser estimated his wealth at only $200,000, and said she had saved half of it by selling a block of stocks in August, on a tip from the broker Julian Bache. Dreiser himself boasted that by lucky intuition he had redeemed a number of shares before the bottom dropped out. With some of the money he purchased $50,000 worth of gold coins, which he stored in a safe deposit box.

A partial list of his holdings, compiled by Arthur Pell, shows that as of September 1929 he owned nearly $65,000 worth of industrial and foreign-government bonds. Adding the stocks he held, his total worth was well over $100,000, roughly half of the $200,000 Van Dresser said he had been worth before she persuaded him to sell in August.

On the whole, then, he seems to have weathered the storm relatively well, and he did not noticeably curtail his lifestyle. His income from bonds continued, and he had the regular monthly stipend of $1250 from Liveright plus a steady stream of article and permissions fees. He also had hopes for a good sale of *A Gallery of Women*, which appeared in late November in a two-volume $5 edition. He had argued for a $3 edition but Liveright talked him out of it, saying that his prestige would be hurt by the lower price. And why take a 40-percent cut in royalties?

The advertising campaign for *Gallery* was the prince of literary ballyhoo's last hurrah. It was inaugurated with a full-page Dreiser-as-institution advertisement in *The New York Times* describing him as "the rock on which the future of American letters must be raised." This was followed by daily ads in several papers for a solid month. Posters covered the sides of trucks and buses, depicting beautiful women who were purportedly the characters in the book. No matter that one of the studies was about an Irish scrubwoman, another about a drab farmwife, and a third about the eccentric fortune-teller Jessie Spafford. Liveright huffed and puffed but could dispose of only 12,000 copies—"a terrible flop," Donald Friede later described it. The $5 cover price and economic uncertainties surely diminished sales. And there was no titillation in the book to live up to Liveright's advertising.

If *Gallery* was a commercial disappointment, the critics weren't writing Dreiser's epitaph. A majority of them were favorable if unenthusiastic. Most of the stories were praised as honest, unadorned examples of realism, devoid of stylistic tricks and imitating life in all its inconclusiveness and ambiguity. There was criticism of Dreiser's "monotonous" preoccupation with sex, but his perception that most women are troubled by sexual problems happened to be one of his acutest insights. As Harry Hansen observed, most of the women in the book are undone by love: "Success does not attend them. Whether they restrain their passions, or become 'varietists' . . . happiness is not for them."

Hansen's observation was apt as far as it goes. Dreiser might have chosen a different group of women he had known who could have exemplified either professional success, such as the reporter Rheta Childe Dorr or the novelist Fannie Hurst (he did include the literary agent Ann Watkins—"Emanuela"), or heroic struggle for a cause, such as Emma Goldman and Margaret Sanger, both of whom he genuinely admired. But he did not know them well enough. In writing the sketches he drew on firsthand knowledge or gossip from friends. (Estelle Kubitz, for example, was his main source for "Regina C———" based on the nurse Miriam Taylor, who became a morphine addict. She also wrote a version of "Giff," about Spafford. And to complete the circle, Dreiser wrote a sketch about *her*, entitled "Gloom," never published.) Most of these females run afoul of convention; whether they defy it or bow to it they ultimately lose.

Observing liberated women (and several unliberated ones as well), he concluded they could not free themselves from men—to their detriment. The title character in "Lucia" oscillates between Bohemian-style free love and marriage to a conventional man, finding happiness in neither. She ends up neglecting her artistic talents and searching for a man with "a strong compelling force . . . before whose strength and temperament I could be humble—maybe." With others—Ernestine, Olive Brand—the denouement is death, but the same predestined failure haunts their lives, as Ruth Kennell had feared when he told her he was writing about *her* life. Dreiser might well have taken as his text the remark Kirah Markham once made to him: "What's the use of a freedom I don't want and can't use."

But he missed the sociological point. As Estelle could have told him, the rebellious post-Victorian women of the teens and twenties faced great odds. She had made a sensible marriage rather than continue to fight them. *A Gallery of Women* lacks the unifying music of pity and elegy that made *Twelve Men* so moving; it seems more grab bag than gallery. It is an uneven performance—though certainly not a "kiss and tell book"—and contains some haunting portraits.

A Gallery of Women stirred up some objections among those who knew the real-life models. "Ernestine," for example, was based on Florence Deshon, a beautiful young actress Dreiser had met in Hollywood, who had been the mistress of Max Eastman and Charlie Chaplin before she committed suicide. Eastman wrote, "His portrait corresponds only in two small remarks to my knowledge of her life and character: She was 'sensuously and disturbingly beautiful and magnetic' and she was 'almost abnormally ambitious.'" Eastman appears in the story as Varn Kinsey, a radical poet with a talent for fund-raising for political causes, keeping some of the money for himself as a salary. All this material was based on Dreiser's conversation with Florence Deshon in Hollywood.

Eastman apparently did not bear a grudge about Dreiser's portrayal, but Edward Smith had been disturbed by the sketch about his wife, Edith Jarmuth, in "Olive Brand." In February 1927 he made some sharp remarks to Dreiser for which he later apologized. The story had not been published at that time, but it had been making the rounds since earlier in the decade. When it did appear in *Cosmopolitan* the following year, it had necessarily acquired a new ending: Smith, disconsolate over Edith's death, had begun drinking heavily and died of pneumonia. Actually, "Olive Brand" is one of the finest portraits in the book; Olive is like a female Peter McCord of *Twelve Men*, an ardent, seeking temperament crushed by fate.

Ruth Kennell would be another aggrieved party. The sketch "Ernita" describes in some detail her personal troubles. After at first leaving to Dreiser the decision on whether to print the story, her domestic situation altered and she asked him not to do it. Her shock when she read it in the book was considerable. Dreiser had offered her $500 for the story, but she refused to take it. Sergei Dinamov, to whom she confided her troubles, agreed with her that Dreiser had not adequately disguised her identity but shrugged, "a writer is always a writer."

Dreiser asked Dinamov to act as peacemaker. The Russian wrote Ruth and forwarded her reply to Dreiser, who was moved again to send her a check for $500. In February 1930 she wrote Dinamov that upon further consideration she was inclined to take the money. Dreiser's motives were generous, she realized, and besides the harm could not be undone. In his letter to her, Dreiser apologized, then proceeded to lecture her about her New England conscience, calling her the "indestructable American school marm." He reminded her that people weren't always lovable or worthwhile, and where would the moralists be without the sinners to chastise? To Dinamov she remarked on "the weird logic" of Dreiser's letter. And so it was. It would be several years before they again communicated.

Hutchins Hapgood was another disgruntled victim. He is portrayed as J.J., the wealthy, cold-blooded lover of Esther Norn, who is based on Mary Pyne, as Dreiser recalls her from his Village days on West Tenth Street, when she would come to his studio from the unheated flat she shared with

Harry Kemp and warm herself before his fire like a cat. Kemp is shown as a mountebank, egoist, and self-promoter who treated Mary rottenly, having affairs while she was ill. Hapgood—or J.J.—happens on the scene and becomes her lover. Hapgood felt that Dreiser had taken an unpardonable liberty with his life by saying he and Mary were lovers; he insisted their relationship was platonic.

A likely cause of the unflattering portrait of Hapgood, with whom Dreiser had been friendly while in the Village, was jealousy. Estelle Kubitz had told him that Hapgood attempted to seduce her, and Dreiser concluded that Hapgood was operating behind his back. For aesthetic purposes the character J.J. serves as a foil for the Harry Kemp figure. The story is about an almost saintly "bad-good girl," as Dreiser once called Mary, who is exploited by her two lovers—the opportunistic Bohemian and the hypocritical Puritan.

"Esther Norn" was not the only portrait that settled a score. In "Rona Murtha," the tale of Anna Mallon and Arthur Henry, Dreiser pays back his friend of *Sister Carrie* days for the depiction of himself as a fussy neurotic in Henry's book *An Island Cabin* more than twenty-five years ago. But there is sympathy, too, for Henry's futile dreams and for the woman he casually tosses aside when she no longer serves him.

Dreiser was drawing his material from life as he had always done, but he did not warrant that every portrait was literal truth.

No one sued, but there were psychological repercussions. Hy Kraft received a call from him one Saturday and when he arrived at the Rodin, Dreiser announced, "Kraft, I'm going to die." He had no particular complaint or physical symptoms, just a premonition of doom. He had not gone out for two days because he was afraid he might collapse in the street. Kraft, who had recently undergone psychoanalysis, attributed Dreiser's depression to the publication of *Gallery*. He was ashamed of it, thought it "pretty cheap stuff, and [was] overwhelmed with a sense of guilt."

That explanation seems superficial. One guesses Dreiser felt more guilty about the slick and lucrative *This Madness* than the *Gallery*, on which he had worked for nearly ten years and which could not be considered cheap exploitation. He always experienced postpartum depressions after completing a book. What he felt this time may have been a free-floating anxiety, a fear of some nameless retribution for his exposés. All but three or four of the women were dead, but he had taken liberties with their lives, broken the sheer membrane between fact and fiction, and now regretted it.

Depression over the book was just one of the clouds hanging over him. There were his stormy relations with Helen, various woman troubles, the Crash, and the failure to bring over the Russian Ballet, which had embarrassed him socially. As it was for many people, 1929 had been a bad year for Dreiser. He had heard the beating wings of the Furies.

Part Seven

EQUITY

1930 – 1938

CHAPTER **28**   *Going Left*

> I say this country is facing Communism. Is it to be met like
> a political doctrine—soberly—in a civilized way—or tyran-
> nically?
>
> —Dreiser (1930)

D reiser's personal demons seemed distinctively those of a rich man, the anxieties of surfeit—juggling the financing of a country home and a luxury studio in Manhattan, conserving his capital against the gyrations of the stock market, extracting his rightful share from an increasingly shaky publisher, parceling himself among various mistresses. Many of his fellow Americans were not so fortunate in their neuroses. As the country slid into the worst depression in its history, their anxieties focused on starker problems. Speaking for the 1920s intellectuals, John Dos Passos pronounced the end of an era: "Anyway, the Jazz Age is dead." Gone was rebellious hedonism and private angst; in came politics, social conscience, the writer *engagé*.

Dreiser had begun speaking out; his involvement in the Mooney case had broken a kind of psychic barrier. But he was still groping toward an economic philosophy that would explain the weird malaise stalking America. Having been to Russia, communism in some form was his sovereign remedy, but he had doubts that it would work in the United States. In his last public utterance on the subject, he had affirmed to readers of *Jewish Day* that he was still an individualist and praised America as "the ideal country for the individualist who is capable of getting ahead" (Jews, who were "natural-born traders," being a prime example). He had the "greatest interest" in the communist experiment in Russia and predicted that even if it didn't bring heaven on earth in fifty years, it would "eventually alter the relationship of the people to their governments." But communism was the antithesis of individualism: "It's the cutting off of every kind of independence! You've got to obey every law and rule of the community; you've got to swear you'll do it."

Meanwhile early rumors emanating from the Swedish Academy in Stockholm indicated that Dreiser had an excellent chance of winning the Nobel Prize for Literature. He had an adoring German admirer who boosted him in Europe, and he also paid Esther Van Dresser's way to the Continent. Her dual mission was to talk him up for the prize and to collect past-due royalties from his foreign publishers. A man who met her on the ship later related a revealing incident to Robert Elias. She claimed she was really Dreiser's daughter and described "the horrible life she was leading under his mistreatment." In Prague Esther was successful in collecting money from Dreiser's Czechoslovakian publisher. In the course of her business dealings she fell in love with the son of the American consul, and they were later married.

To replace Esther, Dreiser hired Kathryn Sayre, a brilliant Columbia graduate student in philosophy. Then, in March, plagued by bronchitis; unable to work on his next book, *Dawn*, because of distractions, particularly a love affair he was trying to break off; and curious about the state of the country under the lengthening shadow of the Depression, he boarded a train for Tucson, stopping off at the Grand Canyon on the way. (His effusive descriptions of this phenomenon of nature prompted George Jean Nathan's mot that "One always finds Dreiser surprised and amazed at what has long been familiar to most persons.") He was alone for at least the first leg of his journey, apparently seeking solitude. Loading some blankets and camping equipment in the trunk of a rented car, he headed for New Mexico, pulling off the road at night and sleeping on the ground, an old rifle by his side.

He was a blundering driver. In cities he maneuvered a car as he used to drive his laundry wagon in Chicago, weaving in and out of traffic and ignoring stoplights. On country roads he was liable to fall into a reverie and veer into a ditch. After a week or so he realized he was a hazard to himself and others and summoned Kay Sayre to chauffeur him around and help him with *Dawn*, which he was trying to work on en route.

In transit he wrote his new Hollywood agent, I. M. Sackin, assigning him the task of selling his novels for the screen. His minimum price was $75,000 for each title, he told Sackin—more for *The "Genius"* and the *Tragedy*, which was still stalled at Paramount. He was also willing to write scripts if the price was right. He explained to his artist friend Willy Pogany, who had steered him to Sackin, that stiff demands were necessary to command respect from the studios.

The same day he issued Sackin's marching orders he wired George F. Hummel, an editor at Liveright, that an MGM film called *Wonder of Women* had certain parallels to *The "Genius."* He had heard that the film was adapted from *The Wife of Stephen Ironhold,* a novel by the German author Hermann Sudermann, and he instructed Hummel to obtain a copy of that work and ascertain the copyright date. If it was later than *The "Genius,"* he intended to try to enjoin the film. This is the first manifestation of Dreiser's persisting suspicion that Hollywood studios were plagiarizing his work. Sudermann's novel, a translation of which had been published in America in 1927, is about an artist who is averse to marriage, but there are only coincidental resemblances to *The "Genius."* Dreiser's theory was that the studio, unwilling to pay what he demanded for his novel but dying to make a picture based on it, adapted the German book (which was also a plagiary of his novel) instead.

Perhaps his itinerant life far from New York City had detached him somewhat from reality and he was seeking to assert himself. He shed his cloak of anonymity and began sounding off in interviews. In Albuquerque he inveighed against reformers and YMCA secretaries who censored books. He gave the horse laugh to the Hays Code and moral movies, and dismissed the Ten Commandments as "a bunch of bugaboos." Prohibition was "bunk," he told the press, and he couldn't wait to reach El Paso, where he could cross the border and get a decent drink. Capitalism also drew his ire: "Money is the hallmark of all that is best in America," he proclaimed. "Because he has money, Henry Ford is an authority."

The quixotic traveler surfaced again in El Paso, where he informed the man from the El Paso *Post* that religion was "just fool dogmatic bunk." The citizens of El Paso were advised to "boot out your . . . ministers along with all other religionists and your city and America will be much better off." Two days later, holding forth in Tucson, he continued the antireligious harangue. His point seemed to be that organized religion had no social utility. The only people helping "the defective, the insane, the criminal, the deficient" were "the up-to-the-minute, generous-minded warm-hearted sociologists and economists, trained in the exact truths of science, and not in the worn-out and threadbare dogmas of the churches." Close the churches, he proclaimed, and seek the meaning of life in scientific laboratories; only there could truth and beauty be discovered.

In Dallas, less than a week later, he told the *Morning News* that a communist revolution was possible in America and that democracy was a "farce." He loosed another blast at American materialism, offering himself as a leading sinner. For thirty years, he said, he had dreamed of owning a place in the country, but now that he had one, he had spent $150,000 fixing it up ($50,000 was probably a more accurate estimate, still a sizable dent in his *Tragedy* gains)—and he didn't like living there.

Dreiser's tone in these interviews, as conveyed in newsprint, sounds unvaryingly irascible. Gone was his wariness of the press. Perhaps the availability of tequila just south of the border had something to do with it, but talking politics always seemed to raise his decibel level. Politics brought angry emotions seething to the surface. His views were fired by passion rather than analysis. He was getting sore (as he might have said) about the way the country was being run. Also, as he once confessed, he liked to shock reporters with outrageous statements.

Driving along the peaceful New Mexico highways with Kay Sayre, he was more tranquil and philosophical. This is shown by some of the *aperçus* that she recorded in flight, as it were:

"Sadness [comes] from certainty of limitation of enjoyment."

"Art is not disciplined freedom—it is psychogenetic—[it] springs fully formed from the creative energy itself. God damn it, it leaps like a winged victory!"

In an advance comment for a debate at Carnegie Hall between his ancient enemy Irving Babbitt, the Humanist, and Carl Van Doren and others, he reaffirmed the faith of a realist. The New Humanism, as it was now known, was enjoying a revival on campus, and its spokesmen, led by Babbitt, were attacking Naturalism, Menckenism, Sinclair Lewis, and other heresies. From Dallas, Dreiser hurled a philippic: "I appear to be charged with being a realist. I accept the insult, but with reservations." He reiterated his old idea that "Art is life seen through a temperament." What *his* saw was "beauty and ugliness, mystery and some little clarity in minor things, tenderness and terrific brutality, ignorance, sodden and hopeless, and some admirable wisdom, malice and charity, honesty and dishonesty, aspiration and complete and discouraging insensitivity and indifference. Yet . . . in the main, [a] fascinating picture from which but a few of us, however great our ills and complaints, are prepared to step out."

After attending to Babbitt, Dreiser set forth to tangle with the Babbitts of Hollywood. Warner Brothers, it seemed, was vaguely interested in filming his books. Helen was now along. She joined him in Dallas with their nine-passenger Chrysler. Warner Brothers' interest turned out to be ephemeral, so they pushed on up the coast to San Francisco for a visit with one of Dreiser's causes, Tom Mooney, at San Quentin. They found America's most famous political prisoner desperately longing for freedom. Dreiser tried to comfort him by reminding him of the worldwide renown he had gained while in jail; once out he would be a nobody. But that was small consolation to Mooney, who was weary of martyrdom and began weeping. Dreiser, deeply moved, promised that he would do all he could to win his release and traveled to Sacramento to speak with Governor C. C. Young, who was weighing a pardon. Young told him he couldn't act until a decision was handed down on the appeal of Mooney's codefendant in the San Francisco bombing. Concluding that publicity was Mooney's best hope, Dreiser tried to interest publisher William Randolph Hearst in the case, and he and Helen had lunch at San Simeon. Hearst was sympathetic but noncommittal.

Stopping at Los Angeles en route to Portland, Dreiser conferred with a director from Universal Pictures, who intimated that his boss, Carl Laemmle, Jr., who had the previous year taken over the studio founded by his father, was interested in filming the *Tragedy*. Fine, Dreiser told him, but he was leaving in two days. No summons came, but a telegram from the studio asking him if he would return arrived in Oregon. All right, Dreiser said, but send $500 for expenses. This was done and Dreiser met with Laemmle, who was trying to move the studio away from its customary low-budget output to more ambitious films. But nothing further was heard from Universal.

So, empty-handed as far as Hollywood was concerned, Dreiser and Helen drove homeward, stopping at Rochester, Minnesota, where he was scheduled for a checkup at the Mayo Clinic. The examination revealed signs of youthful fibroid pulmonary tuberculosis. His left lung was "so densely scarred that multiple small cavities are present." This condition was equivalent to a chronic bronchitis, producing persistent coughing, repeated respiratory infections, and quantities of sputum, often foul-smelling and sometimes containing blood. Dreiser also had an enlarged prostate, which was of no medical concern. And so, as Dreiser had always believed, as a boy in Chicago he had contracted TB while working in the hardware warehouse (perhaps the scar was the "tumor" the doctor in Berlin saw on the X ray).

The next stop was Chicago, where they picked up his long-missing brother Rome. Dreiser had suspected that the money he had been sending to his brother's hotel was being diverted into other pockets. His suspicions turned out to be correct. They decided to take Rome, who was physically debilitated, to New York, where the recently widowed Mame would look after him.

When they arrived in New York in June, more reporters were demanding his views on the state of the nation. He held forth in the *World-Telegram* under the headline DREISER NOW REDISCOVERS AMERICA. The corporations were running the country, he charged, so why not draft prominent tycoons into the cabinet? Make John D. Rockefeller secretary of oil and gas, for example. He let fly at wealthy business leaders with their "gold swimming pools at their country houses. They can buy thousand-acre tracts to keep off neighbors and indulge in all that swill, but they can't arrange things so a man can have a job."

Perceiving like everyone else that the national economy was coughing along on one cylinder, and lacking essential facts and analysis, he lashed out at an old Populist demon—monopoly capitalists extorting money from the masses to pay for their gold-plated swimming pools. But the problem was much more complicated than swimming pools, whether gold-plated or spring-fed like his own at Iroki.

In June four publishing houses announced they were slashing prices on all new titles. Novels would be sold for $1 a copy and nonfiction titles reduced 40 percent across the board. The publishing trade had fallen into the doldrums, and the action was an attempt to revive sales. Horace Liveright, just back from a frantic search for best sellers in Europe, wrote a friend: "This doesn't hurt the concerns with big text-book departments or with cheap lists which they can reduce in price if they want to. But by and large we have a highbrow list of authors who are worth from $2.50 to $5.00 and we won't make a cut." Dreiser was for once of the same opinion as his publisher: he went on record as refusing to give his books to any publisher who cut prices. To hold the line Liveright pared down his fall list to eliminate inferior titles, but it was a dying gasp.

Liveright's own financial situation had deteriorated badly. He had no hope of paying back the loans from Pell, who now owned most of his 2150 shares. In July Pell called in his loan, forced Liveright out, and began slashing costs—selling the brownstone on West Forty-eighth, moving to cheaper quarters and cutting salaries. There were also back royalties to be paid—Eugene O'Neill was owed $19,000, requiring borrowed money, and Isadora Duncan's brother had not long before hit the firm with a court order for royalties on his late sister's autobiography. Liveright asked Pell: "Was this money for royalties put in escrow or is this another blow?" Pell responded: "Sorry—just another blow." The monthly $1250 to Dreiser had become a millstone, but the author refused to reduce it. T. R. Smith told Mencken that when he suggested to Dreiser that his demands were excessive, the other replied, "Whoever said I was fair?" Later that year he sued Liveright for the stock-company rights to *An American Tragedy,* which he contended had reverted to him under a clause in the contract requiring Liveright to produce the play at least seventy-five times on the road each year.

Although Liveright was in fact out, he told friends and the press that he would continue as a director and chairman of the executive committee. He was going to Hollywood to take a vaguely defined job with Paramount (which Otto Kahn had arranged for him), but he hoped to return to the business he loved.

Dreiser owed his publisher *Dawn* by the end of 1930, so he retired to Iroki and brought Campbell up from Philadelphia to assist him. In July he wrote Otto Kyllmann in London that he was now finally revising the manuscript for publication, but he would not complete the task until January. The original manuscript was graphic about Mame's and Sylvia's illegitimate babies and other sexual matters, including Dreiser's youthful masturbation. Although some of this was cut, he got in much of it in condensed form. And he had Kay Sayre go through the manuscript and camouflage his sisters' identities by giving them fictitious names and eliminating telltale descriptions such as a reference to Sylvia's belief in Christian Science. As a disciple of Rousseau, he was determined to include at least partial glimpses of his and his family's sexual history.

Politically, he continued his leftward march. When International Labor Defense, the Communist Party's legal arm, asked him to speak at a rally, he declined but authorized it to use his name, thus inaugurating a practice that would become habitual. He agreed to become chairman of the Emergency Committee for Southern Political Prisoners, an adjunct of ILD and the John Reed Club. The real power in this organization was Joe Pass, a young Communist Party member. The group had been formed to draw attention to the harassment (and worse) of communist labor organizers, who had become active in the South. Dreiser's only pronouncement in its behalf was indited at Pass's request—a condemnation of the arrest in Atlanta of several communists who had been distributing literature demanding jobs and higher wages. The charge, under a hoary statute, was inciting to insurrection, which carried the death penalty. The two blacks in the group, Herbert Newton and Henry Story, were to be tried first.

The issue, Dreiser asserted in his hastily written statement, was not communism, the desirability of which was not for him to say, but whether communists could get a fair trial in this country. The tactic of trying the Negroes first looked like "a frame-up to convict the whole lot," since in the South blacks were considered guilty as soon as they were arrested and some were simply lynched without even that formality. It was better to respect the communists' rights and permit them to advocate peaceful change. This was hardly a radical position, even though the John Reed Club, a CP auxiliary, was behind it. The club had in May persuaded 135 intellectuals to sign a statement protesting arrests of labor organizers and workers. Among the signatories was H. L. Mencken, a vehement anti-communist.

Dreiser was more lucid in an article on the Mooney case for the Scripps-Howard newspapers, which had decided to campaign editorially for the imprisoned man's release. In it he moved beyond Mooney's cause, calling it "a chestnut," and attacked the "indifference—the real Imperial Roman indifference" of Americans to cases like Mooney and Billings and Sacco and Vanzetti; the communists arrested in Georgia; the New York CP leaders, including William Z. Foster, who were given indeterminate sentences for leading a New York protest march against unemployment; a Minnesota prior-restraint case. Working people, he said, should stop being indifferent to the growing concentration of power in the hands of "a financial autocracy already too anxious to enslave them."

But he was still living in a capitalist society, and in his dealings with that exotic species of tycoon *Tyrannosaurus Hollywoodus* he was a combative businessman. Just before Liveright left for the Coast, he wrote Dreiser that Lasky needed to be sold on the idea that a talking film of *An American Tragedy* would be good box office; otherwise Paramount might vend the rights to another company.

Dreiser contended that the silent-film rights he sold to Famous Players–Lasky in 1926 had lapsed because of the company's failure to film it. He had, he claimed, done everything to overcome any possible objections, even granting permission to change the title. But Will Hays, who was in cahoots with Lasky, had declared the book immoral so that Paramount-Publix could wriggle out of the contract. He threatened the film company with a suit for breach of contract. If, however, it decided to make a talkie, it must negotiate a new contract with him; otherwise he could vend the rights elsewhere. He had been advised by the Dramatists Guild that Paramount held only the silent rights.

At his end, Liveright was trying to claim the 30 percent of the motion-picture rights to the Kearney play of *An American Tragedy* that he owned. At any rate, he asserted that Dreiser must pay him $5000 if he sold the talkie rights. He said that he had "stirred up great interest" in a movie version directed by Sergei Eisenstein, whom he and Lasky had met in Paris and signed to a six-month contract. Eisenstein admired Hollywood's technical achievements and was eager to observe them firsthand.

While Dreiser and Liveright were exchanging recriminations by mail, Eisenstein arrived in Hollywood in June with his assistant Grigori Alexandrov and his cameraman Eduard Tisse. The trio of Bolsheviks settled into a pleasant bungalow and cast a wondering eye on the movie capital, which seemed a fantasy world, far removed from the realities of Depression America. The wild-maned Russian excited much comment in the gossip mills.

Eisenstein looked for a film to make. He rejected the studio's suggestions, but his own ideas were considered too controversial or too costly. Then, perhaps at Liveright's suggestion, he was offered the *Tragedy*. He was aware of the troubled history of the project; several directors, including D. W. Griffith, had turned it down. But he was determined to go ahead because he admired the book.

Liveright was appointed supervisor of the project and tried to involve himself in the writing, but Eisenstein disliked him. In a diary he wrote at the end of his life, he says he can remember nothing about Liveright other than his reputation as a publisher of "daring" books. Actually, Liveright never had a chance to supervise because the project was aborted.

What happened? According to the scriptwriter, Ivor Montagu, the studio originally envisioned a simple love triangle–murder story, devoid of social significance. (A Paramount writer put it more succinctly, describing *An American Tragedy* as "the story about the guy who got hot nuts, screwed a girl and drowned her.") Eisenstein had his own perspective on the novel. The real tragedy of this book, he decided, was the "tragic course pursued by Clyde, whom the social structure drives to murder." Clyde lost his nerve at the crucial moment and thus was innocent of the crime. To underscore this point, Eisenstein alters Dreiser's story by having Clyde try to rescue Roberta after the boat overturns. "But the machinery of crime has been set in motion and continues to its end, even against Clyde's will. Roberta cries out weakly, tries to retreat from him in her horror, and, not being able to swim, drowns." That version eliminated the last semblance of Clyde's guilt in a legal or moral sense. Eisenstein was primarily interested in showing the implacable operations of fate. An innocent man is subjected to a sham trial that is actually a political contest between the district attorney and his opponents before a prejudiced jury.

To depict Clyde's change of heart in the climactic scene in the rowboat on Big Bittern Lake, Eisenstein invented a new technique, which he called the "interior monologue," the cinematic equivalent of James Joyce's stream of consciousness (he had discussed *Ulysses* with Joyce in Paris). Sound, words, and pictures are used to show the clash of conflicting desires in Clyde's mind; he hears voices alternately saying "Kill—Kill!" and "Don't—don't kill!" These voices are melded to visual images—waves, Sondra's face, Roberta's face. In the end, Roberta's image eclipses Sondra's—"Ending the conflict. Sondra is lost for ever. Never, never now will he have the courage to kill Roberta." Thus, contrary to the novel, Clyde has a change of heart before arriving at the lake.

Eisenstein made another major alteration in the book: he eliminated the character of the Reverend McMillan and has Clyde confess to his mother in the death house that he had originally planned to kill Roberta but changed his mind. At the pardon hearing it is she who seals Clyde's doom. Unable to free herself from her religious belief that "the thought of sin is equivalent to its execution," as Eisenstein puts it, she cannot affirm his innocence to the governor.

Thus, rather than recognize the moral claims of Christianity, in the powerful presence of McMillan, as Dreiser did, Eisenstein makes the mother's "purblind fanaticism" the villain. Outside the governor's chambers, she regrets her silence and cries out, "My son is innocent!" But it is too late. The scenario coldly contemplates her guilt: "The mother's fatal moment of silence cannot even be washed away by her tears." Perhaps

Eisenstein was expressing a subconscious hostility toward his own mother, who had temporarily deserted him when he was a child. Elvira Griffiths in the movie is no longer the *Pietà* figure of the book who pleads for mercy before the governor.

Eisenstein and Montagu began the script in September and finished it in early October. Paramount had called for a twelve-reel film, budgeted at $1 million. Eisenstein's scenario comprised fourteen reels, but he explained that he would cut it after hearing the comments of Paramount, Dreiser, and the Hays Office. The script was warily received by the film company. Eisenstein recalled that studio head B. P. Schulberg asked, "Is Clyde Griffiths guilty or not guilty—in your treatment?" When Eisenstein replied not guilty, Schulberg said, "But then your script is a monstrous challenge to American society." The screenplay followed the book in showing how Clyde's early life made his crime inevitable.

Also, as Eisenstein wrote his mother, when en route to New York for talks with Lasky and Dreiser, "there are many questions in connection with the 'propaganda' theme" in the light of Representative Hamilton Fish's investigation of communism in Hollywood.

Dreiser approved the script, and Lasky, though cautious throughout, was tentatively for it. After all, he had not only bought the novel but imported Eisenstein to film it. But at this time an internecine conflict was simmering at Paramount between the Hollywood studio, under Schulberg, and the New York office, headed by Lasky, who was production boss directly under Adolph Zukor.

Embedded in the novel was a seemingly insoluble problem: if Clyde is shown as innocent because of environmental forces, as Eisenstein saw it—as, indeed, Dreiser saw it, though less categorically—then he would be a sympathetic figure. The culprit would be American society. But if he were shown as guilty, with no mitigating circumstances, he would be an unsympathetic character, who well deserved the punishment ordained by the Hays Office. That was the dilemma that had frightened off directors like D. W. Griffith and Ernst Lubitsch.

Perhaps more troubling to the Schulberg faction was the cost of the picture at a time when the industry was reeling under the impact of the Depression. And Eisenstein was determined to use amateurs to play the leads, as had been his practice in Russia. He had already been scouting filling stations for a Clyde "type." If he had his way, this controversial film would not even have the box-office insurance of stars in the leading roles.

While Eisenstein and Montagu were in New York, talking to Dreiser and preparing to scout locations upstate, telegrams were presumably flying back and forth between the coasts. Then, on October 23, Lasky announced that the contract between Paramount and Eisenstein had been "terminated by mutual consent." What had swung him against the picture, he later said, was the pile of mail from patriotic Americans objecting to a film by the Red Dog Eisenstein. Lasky called Eisenstein and Montagu into his office, showed them the letters, and said, "Gentlemen, it is over. Our agreement is at an end." Eisenstein had probably expected this in his heart. He made no statements to the press, but soon after announced that he wished to buy the Soviet rights to Moss Hart and George S. Kaufman's hit play *Once in a Lifetime*. The play, a spoof of Hollywood, was, he said, "Grim realism. When you know your Hollywood, it is a sort of *Mourning Becomes Electra*." Fearing that he might sign with a rival company, Paramount offered to pay his way home, but Eisenstein hated to admit failure. He returned to Hollywood and persuaded Upton Sinclair to back him in filming a picture in Mexico—which turned out to be his second American tragedy.

In November Sinclair Lewis was awarded the Nobel Prize for Literature, the first American author to win it. Earlier, the Associated Press had reported that Dreiser was favored and that he had "several champions" in the Swedish Academy. Closer to the announcement day, however, a Swedish paper had reported on excellent authority that the choice was between Lewis and Dreiser. When the three-man committee from the Swedish Academy met, Dreiser had only one champion. The other two members reportedly preferred Lewis's satire to Dreiser's more ponderous, solemn style.

What Dreiser's immediate reaction was is not known. Fabri told Swanberg that for a time Dreiser was "almost suicidal." Losing to Lewis, to whom he felt he took precedence as an American realist, was particularly galling, and aside from the honor of the thing, the tax-free $46,350 would have been welcome in a time of economic uncertainty. But he stoically wrote a friend, "I cannot imagine the prize lessening or improving the mental standing of any serious writer—writing is, after all, his or her main business."

Dreiser would have been a more popular winner among American writers. Sherwood Anderson's reaction was perhaps typical. He found the choice "very depressing," he wrote a friend. "Dreiser has had real tenderness in him. Lewis never. It seems to me that Lewis must have got it out of European dislike of America rather than liking."

Some consolation for his loss came with the news that the sale of the talking rights to *An American Tragedy* had finally gone through. It had been a bumpy ride. In late October he accused Liveright of holding up the deal by his unjust demands for $5000. "Do you intend at whatever gate I apply, to seek to block the realization of this fine screen picture?" he asked. "If so, say so!" Sackin reported that Paramount contemplated a silent film but would do a talkie if Dreiser would accept $30,000. He refused and wrote the agent that Paramount could make a silent film if it wished but his price for a sound version was $55,000. Paramount probably had been bluffing about its intention to do a silent picture, for Adolph Zukor begged Josef von Sternberg, the director of *The Blue Angel*, who had brought its star, Marlene Dietrich, to Hollywood, to make a low-budget talkie and salvage the studio's already large investment in the property. Dreiser got his $55,000. The contract was signed on January 2, 1931, and Dreiser approved von Sternberg as director and Samuel Hoffenstein, whom he knew socially, as scriptwriter.

And so Liveright was left out in the cold. It was still another blow for the former publisher, who badly needed the money. An affair with an actress had broken up, and he was drinking heavily. In Hollywood, the splendor and flair of Horace Liveright died, leaving the ashes of a man.

CHAPTER 29

Droit Moral

I have a literary character to maintain and I contend that I have a mental equity in my product and in the character of my product. Even though [the movie companies] buy the right of reproduction they don't buy the right to change it into anything they please.

—Dreiser (1931)

By early 1931 Dreiser was more than ankle-deep in politics. He was now being asked for statements on this or that issue by leftist groups and publications. Anxious to say the right thing, he wrote somewhat self-importantly to Ann North, editor of *Solidarity*, "Although I know the Marxian theory thoroughly, and satisfied myself, by going there, of the experiment in Russia, I do not know the details of the larger issues which confront the Communists here in America." He proposed that she or Mr. Pass or the John Reed Club or *The New Masses* suggest pertinent topics and provide data "which could be either selected from or recast by me so that I would not be outside the facts most interesting to the Party and would be able to speak with the knowledge which is so necessary." He would consider any subjects they proposed and perhaps write an article, which publications like hers or *The New Masses* would be welcome to publish.

In May he took that offer a step further. When the *Daily Worker* required a contribution for the May Day issue on the press and political prisoners, he told them to write it themselves—"to assure you have just the statement you want"—and he would edit and sign it. "Make it strong," he told the editor.

In addition to saving himself time when responding to such pleas, he was trying to educate himself in political economics and amassing economic data for a book on the current crisis, with the help of his various researchers and from CP sources. In the fall of 1930, when Dorothy Van Doren of *The Nation* asked him for a piece on New York's unemployed, he gave her a compilation of figures and theories. She had hoped for a kind of Hurstwood updated, a subjective picture of conditions among the jobless, and rejected the article. In the spring of 1931, however, he did some firsthand research in Passaic, New Jersey. He found unemployment approaching one-third of the local work force; wages plummeting; the jobless running out of resources, private or public, and scrambling to survive; and health conditions deteriorating because of lead poisoning and other forms of industrial pollution.

Before he could proceed any further down the communist road, he became embroiled in another time-consuming dispute with the capitalists in Hollywood. Hoffenstein had in five weeks completed his screenplay of the *Tragedy*, a straightforward job of work that lobotomized the novel of all social meaning and found Clyde guilty as charged. Because von Sternberg's version was to be a more modestly budgeted eight-to-ten reeler, Hoffenstein had focused almost entirely on the murder and the trial. This was in keeping with von Sternberg's ideas about the picture. As the director explained, "I eliminated the sociological elements, which, in my opinion, were far from being responsible for the [murder] with which Dreiser had concerned himself."

Fearing some such jiggering, Dreiser had insisted on a clause in the contract stating that Paramount must send him the script and consider his "comments, advice, suggestions or criticisms." The company promised to "use its best endeavors" to accept them, but it was not legally bound to do so. There followed a series of errors and evasions and missed meetings, with Hoffenstein trying to fulfill, pro forma, Paramount's part of the contract by showing the script to Dreiser so the filming could begin and the latter rejecting the screenplay and carrying his objections to Lasky.

For all the words expended on this issue, Dreiser was claiming what the French call *droit moral*, the artist's right to preserve his or her work unaltered by subsequent purchasers—which was fine with a statue, but harder to do in a collaborative, commercial medium like the movies. After much back-and-forthing, Paramount flew Dreiser and Hy Kraft, who was working at the company's Long Island studio, to Hollywood, where they proposed a number of small, feasible changes that would suggest the hardships of Clyde's early life and reinject a tithe of Dreiser's social message. These were eventually added, but von Sternberg's movie, in the end, followed Hollywood morality. Where Eisenstein showed Clyde having a change of heart, von Sternberg shows him confessing his guilt to his mother in his cell; she gazes Heavenward and says, "I know that somehow, somewhere, you'll be given the right start."

Before the film was released Dreiser's lawyers sought an injunction to stop its showing. They warned their client that he had little chance of winning, and that if he did sue, Paramount might demand a sizable bond to indemnify it against loss. But Dreiser wanted to place his side of the dispute before the public. The case went to trial in July in White Plains, New York. Paramount's lawyer attacked the novel as a "cold-blooded plagiarism" of the trial record of the Gillette case and accused the author of being anti-Christian and a publicity-seeker. To that Dreiser shouted, "It's a lie!" and was cautioned by the judge. His counsel, Arthur Garfield Hays, was more effective: if the novel was mere plagiarism, he wondered, why hadn't Paramount based its script on the court records in the Gillette case? But Judge Graham Witschief ruled that Paramount had a perfect right to change the novel any way it liked, for it must answer to a higher court: "In the preparation of the picture the producer must give consideration to the fact that the great majority of people composing the audience before which the picture will be presented will be more interested that justice prevail over wrongdoing than that the inevitability of Clyde's end clearly appear."

Dreiser had to content himself with a moral victory. As he said when he left Hollywood, "I feel, in a way, that I am acting for the thousands of authors who haven't had a square deal, in having their works belittled for screen exploitation." And he had succeeded in forcing Paramount to make at least some of the changes he and Kraft devised.

Midway in the movie war, Dreiser returned to the political fray. Having received a telegram in Hollywood from Pass warning of stepped-up prosecutions of radicals, he agreed to invite a group of intellectuals to his apartment to discuss what should be done. Pass had in mind forming a successor to the Southern Emergency Committee, to be known as the National Committee for the Defense of Political Prisoners. This body was envisioned as a sort of intellectuals' auxiliary of International Labor Defense, and Dreiser was willing to lead it. His new secretary, Evelyn Light, a tall, efficient woman and former assistant editor of the leftist weekly *Plain Talk,* sent out fifty-three invitations—and later the same number of telegrams changing the date (for which Dreiser billed the committee). The subject of the meeting was declared to be "the matter of political persecution so rabid in the US today."

There was a good turnout at Dreiser's apartment on April 16. Malcolm Cowley, literary editor of *The New Republic,* thought only a writer of Dreiser's stature could have drawn such a crowd—editors, writers, reporters—"almost everyone in the literary world." Standing behind a table, white-maned, tall, and massive, Dreiser rapped for attention, mumbled something unintelligible and then, folding and unfolding his handkerchief, read a prepared statement. He described the abysmal state the country was in. Millions were unemployed—no one knew how many, for the government published no figures. Hoover and his cabinet had no idea of how bad things were. People were out of work, starving, hiding in holes. Striking miners in western Pennsylvania and Harlan County, Kentucky, were being shot by deputies and gun thugs hired by the mineowners. After this sorrowing litany, he looked up and said quietly, "The time is ripe for American intellectuals to render some service to the American worker." He proposed to his guests that they all join the NCDPP, which opposed politically motivated persecutions or deportations of union organizers, lynchings, and violence against workers. Mumbling a few more phrases, he then opened the floor for discussion.

For a while no one said anything. As Louis Adamic wrote, "Dreiser's own great honesty and bewilderment had engulfed everybody." Eventually, the old muckraker Lincoln Steffens rose to speak, recounting examples of how workers were crushed in labor struggles and how the press suppressed the truth. When the meeting ended, most of those who had come had no idea of what they were expected to do, but they wanted to do something. The answer arrived later, when they were contacted by Pass and enrolled in the NCDPP. An impressive steering committee was recruited for the letterhead, including Burton Rascoe, Edmund Wilson, John Dos Passos, William Rose Benét, Franz Boas, Clifton Fadiman, Granville Hicks, and Elmer Rice. Dreiser was made honorary chairman and Steffens treasurer, but Pass was "the real, practical head of the committee," according to Evelyn Light, and served as liaison with the Party.

The committee's first project was raising money for the defense of the Scottsboro Boys, nine black youths in Alabama who were accused of raping two white women in a freight car. The boys were probably not guilty. The NCDPP's role in the case consisted mainly of sending out fund-raising appeals and an open letter to the governor of Alabama. All contributions were channeled to International Labor Defense; the NCDPP was merely a conduit, a front if you will (which is not to depreciate the able defense the ILD conducted for its nine clients).

Dreiser kept a low profile, declining to address an NCDPP rally for the Scottsboro boys at New York's Town Hall later that month. Instead, he prepared or signed an 1100-word statement that traced the history of racism in the South. The death penalty for rape was "definitely aimed at the Negro male," he noted, rather than the white equivalent, "who miscegenates without serious opposition. But mixing the blood of a white man with that of a Negro woman is certainly the same as mixing the blood of a black man with that of a white woman." He closed by urging a "general broadening and humanizing of the universal treatment and condition of the Negroes, especially in the South."

The Party was a demanding mistress; issuing open letters and inviting intellectuals to his apartment wasn't enough. It was as though Dreiser were being put through a series of courtly tests to prove his love. In June the CP decided he was needed in Pittsburgh.

A brushfire of protests and strikes was racing through eastern Ohio and western Pennsylvania, touched off by the communist-led National Miners Union, which was seeking to supplant the enfeebled United Mine Workers. On May 26, 2000 miners were led out by NMU organizers. Soon 40,000 others were on strike, and Party leader William Z. Foster hurried to the scene to take charge. Incidents of violence proliferated, and Pennsylvania's Governor Gifford Pinchot brokered an agreement between the UMW and one of the largest operators, which preferred the AFL affiliate to the communist union. On June 22, strikers in Arnold City clashed with mine guards; a storekeeper was killed when deputies fired a volley into the miners' ranks after some boys threw rocks.

At this point, when tensions were at their zenith, Pass and Foster urged Dreiser to go to Pittsburgh. He agreed, though he specified, against Pass's urgings, that he would not go as a representative of the CP or the NMU. Either he was worried about being arrested or he felt that his neutrality as an observer would be compromised. His intention all along seems to have been to keep the NCDPP independent of the Party. The summons was perhaps the first example of the communist tactic of involving prominent literary people in their struggles. It was a smart strategy, for the local press tended to report strikes from the owners' viewpoint and would rarely quote the communist organizers who, at great risk to themselves, were fighting for the workers.

Dreiser arrived in Pittsburgh on June 24. He told reporters that he was gathering material for a book. At his hotel he questioned twenty-five miners and wives about living conditions. The following day he visited a mine at Horning, where an NMU organizer named Philips had been arrested. Confronting constable Deal Snyder, he demanded to know on what charge Philips had been incarcerated and was told "disorderly conduct." "Watch out or I'll take you in too," the officer warned.

Unintimidated, Dreiser visited mines and talked to strikers. He interviewed Sheriff Robert V. Cain, who denied that his deputies had interfered with the strike in any way. When Dreiser asked him about the case of a deputy shooting a miner which had been reported in the press, Cain replied that the reporters had lied. Later Dreiser witnessed state policemen driving pickets off the highway, even though they had a legal right to march there.

The next day he released a statement to the United Press describing the miners' tribulations:

> . . . from each person I interviewed I extracted a corroborated story of pay that insures a living only a little above the starvation line. . . . I learned the rent paid for company houses . . . ranges from seven to twelve dollars a month. . . . The houses were unbelievably bad, colorless, unrepaired, and sometimes enclosed and forbidden to strangers. The villages were slums.
>
> The workers were so poor they were unable to obtain decent clothing and decent food or enjoy entertainment of any kind, not even so much as a moving picture show, a radio or a phonograph.

Moved by what he heard, Dreiser abandoned his stance of impartiality by coming out in favor of the NMU as the miners' only hope. The statement blasted the AFL for collaborating with corporations and utilities "to put a quietus . . . on strike and labor troubles," and the United Mine Workers for abandoning its members. Roy Howard, president of Scripps-Howard newspapers, which used the statement at Dreiser's request, asked William Green, president of the AFL, if he wished to comment on the charges. Green did, at great length. The union leader, considered a sort of Warren G. Harding of labor, sought to refute Dreiser's charges that the federation collaborated with corporate officials to prevent strikes, that it did not help unskilled or Negro workers, and that the UMW had done little for the miners. He chastised him for defending the NMU—a communist union (the federation had a history of purging communists, workers' education groups like A. J. Muste's Brookwood Labor College, and "radicals" of whatever stripe).

After consulting with Party secretary Earl Browder and International Labor Defense, Dreiser issued his reply. It drew heavily on a point-by-point refutation of Green supplied by Browder, but in one instance at least he rejected the latter's counsel. Dreiser wanted to chastise the UMW for not seeking an injunction to enforce miners' constitutional right of assembly; Browder argued that the workers could expect no justice in the courts—"a class instrument of the capitalists." Thus Dreiser revealed the same stress on legal constitutional rights that he had shown in his statements for the Scottsboro boys. He might agree that the courts had an antilabor bias, given the series of decisions nullifying child labor and minimum wage laws, enforcing "yellow dog" contracts, and granting broad injunctions against union organizing. Nevertheless, he seemed to think that the rights that were guaranteed by the Constitution could be activated.

·   ·   ·

Embroiling himself in the political struggle provided an escape from the personal problems that were dogging him, particularly those involving women, what Helen described as "The latest phase of what Dreiser once frankly wrote about as *This Madness. . . .*" It had, she said, "brought about a new pattern of behavior that I found difficult to accept." As was her habit when the pressure became too much, she ran away, this time to Iroki. In effect, they agreed that she would live there and Dreiser would remain in the city, visiting her on weekends as he chose. Her mother and sister would join her from Portland, and Mame and Rome were now living in one of the guest cabins.

The swank studio on West Fifty-seventh Street would soon be no more. They had decided not to renew the lease, which ran out in the fall. In addition to their need to live apart, economizing was a consideration; expenses of remodeling Iroki were mounting. Not that he was hard up; that year he had a gross income of at least $40,000.

In August he wrote Louise Campbell, "I've had a hell of a summer. Hot. Work. Mental worries. Law suits. Just a day to day drive. Add to that moving." What with the Paramount suit, the Liveright suit over stock-company rights, as well as his political activities, his writing, and a hectic love life, Dreiser was pushing himself to the edge.

On top of all this, his sisters, particularly Mame, had been infuriated by *Dawn*. The next time Dreiser came to Iroki, Mame began berating him as soon as she spied him from the window. When a Terre Haute historian later asked her some questions about family history, she sniffed, "How *Dawn* could have been written is beyond human conception."

Perhaps Mame had seen Burton Rascoe's review in the New York *Sun*. After reading *Dawn*, Rascoe writes, he was less skeptical about the seduction scene in *Jennie Gerhardt*. Other reviewers marveled at the candor of the autobiography, and only a small minority were put off by its sexual revelations. The New York *Evening Post* called *Dawn* "one of the most ferociously frank and sensitively candid biographies I have ever read."

But for his struggling publishers, *Dawn* was another disappointment. The book would sell some 6000 copies. Yet, in tandem with *Newspaper Days*, it remains one of the greatest American autobiographies.

That summer when he came out to Mount Kisco for weekends, Dreiser seemed restless and tense, as though under a great strain, Helen thought. He took only fitful pleasure in the newly completed house, which she had filled with furniture from their apartment.

He may have been thinking about the cost of the place. The house and outbuildings represented four years of expensive labor. The main structure was a squat two-story stone and wood structure, with a steeply slanted roof covered with irregularly arranged log shingles, the bark left on, in imitation of a farmhouse he had seen in Norway. Louise Campbell thought it "looked as if a demented child had playfully tossed rough-hewn logs" on the roof. Dreiser's study occupied the lower level; it had a large picture window, a stone floor covered by a huge Oriental rug, a long trestle table carved by Esherick, its top a single huge slab of wood. Esherick also fashioned the andirons in the huge stone fireplace. The artist Robert Davis painted waves of colors on the walls and the floors of the dining and living rooms on the second floor; Henry Varnum Poor designed lighting fixtures for the studio which stood in each corner, like columns of light. Some of the windows were odd-shaped, reminding Esther McCoy of *Dr. Caligari;* she had scoured the city for panes of handmade amber glass to fill them. In one of the bathrooms there were erotic frescoes, à la Pompeii.

Ralph Fabri had supervised the building of the main house and the adjoining guest lodge, which were connected by a rustic-looking bridge. This house did not follow a blueprint; it grew organically in accordance with the whims of the owner, who later said, "There was no architect. Rather the house built itself."

Dreiser's Folly became a *cause célèbre* in Mount Kisco. Neighbors would drive by just to gape at the totem pole on the front lawn, near the four squat stone mushrooms from Russia. That summer he put up a large tent, decorated with colorful Indian designs. On hot nights, wearing a monk's habit and carrying an old-fashioned lantern, he would sleep in it. He thought of turning Iroki into a kind of monastic retreat for writers, and inquired of the Catholic diocese in New Mexico if he could purchase wooden beams from abandoned monasteries there.

To Helen the place was "her child"—literally a substitute for the infant she and Dreiser never had. To Dreiser it was a substitute for the novel he couldn't write; but it was also a nightmare of bills and quarrels. That August he turned sixty and was in a somewhat dyspeptic frame of mind when a reporter cornered him for the obligatory birthday wisdom. The talk turned to his wealth, and Dreiser insisted it had not made him happy. "When you get money you get encumbrances. . . . You find things to worry about that never entered your mind before."

Dreiser and George Douglas in Los Angeles, 1935:
two philosophers contemplating the riddle of life.

(Los Angeles *Examiner*)

Top: Bridge connecting the "little house" to the "big house." (UP)

Bottom: Helen and Dreiser on the veranda. (UP)

Top: The main house in winter.

(UP)

Bottom: Harriet Bissell, Dreiser's assistant; Edgar Lee Masters; and Dreiser.

(UP)

The 1933 Paramount
production of *Jennie
Gerhardt*, starring
Sylvia Sidney as Jennie
and Donald Cook as
Lester Kane.

(UP)

Dreiser addressing the international
peace conference in Paris in 1938.

(UP)

At Marguerite Tjader Harris's mansion
in Darien, Connecticut, in the late 1930s.

(UP)

Theodore and Vera Dreiser, who knew
him as a niece and as a psychologist.
(EU)

Dreiser and Paul Robeson.
(UP)

Helen and Dreiser in
the front yard of their house
on North Kings Road in
Hollywood in the 1940s.
(UP)

Clara Clark, who worked
with Dreiser on *The Stoic.*

(Courtesy of Clara Jaeger)

Sylvia Bradshaw, who reminded
him of the woman in Chekhov's
"The Darling."

(Courtesy of Sylvia Bradshaw)

Marguerite Tjader Harris, without
whose help *The Bulwark* might
never have been written.

(UP)

Last photograph of Dreiser, at the wedding
of Bernice Dorothy Tucker to Lieutenant
George B. Smith, December 21, 1945.

(UP)

CHAPTER 30　　"*Which Side Are You On?*"

> The minin' town I live in
> 　is a sad and a lonely place
> For pity and starvation
> 　is pictured on every face,
> 　　　　—"Aunt Molly Jackson's Ragged Hungry Blues"

In its September issue *The New Masses* published a special birthday salute to Dreiser. The editors said he had moved from critic and observer of America to a higher stage of social activism. The International Association of Revolutionary Authors cabled: "We are very glad to be able to call you comrade." In its editorial, "The Titan," *New Masses* admitted that although Dreiser was not a Marxist, he had the courage "to take sides openly with the world revolutionary movement of the working class."

Izvestia joined the happy-birthday chorus. The newspaper traced Dreiser's conversion to communism to his trip to Russia. To be sure, his book *Dreiser Looks at Russia* contained many "mistakes," but the trip changed Dreiser's thinking, and he began "attacking capitalism and America's pseudo-democracy." And so he had joined Romain Rolland and George Bernard Shaw on the literary barricades. Apparently *Izvestia* was too anxious to proclaim its latest convert to engage in haggling about the depth of his ideological commitment. There was a fear in Soviet political-literary circles that the bourgeois press would ignore Dreiser's baptism, so Moscow made sure it was broadcast to the world.

· · ·

In New York the object of these tributes busied himself with moving out of his luxurious studio on Fifty-seventh Street. He found new quarters in the Ansonia Hotel, a sixteen-story rococo edifice on upper Broadway that attracted a colorful clientele of musicians, playwrights, editors, prizefighters, baseball players, and showfolk. Dreiser's two-room suite had three French windows opening on a balcony with a spectacular view of the city and the Hudson River, and cost him $110 a month; he took a room on another floor as an office for Evelyn Light. The suite was sparsely furnished—the inevitable rocking chair, the rosewood-piano desk, some paintings, and a few other nondescript pieces—and he lived simply, eating his meals at the hotel restaurant or a nearby Horn & Hardart Automat.

With the help of Kay Sayre, Light, and various researchers, he was making good progress on a new nonfiction book about the economic crisis. In July T. R. Smith wrote to say he had liked the first two chapters but advised against the projected length of 125,000 words; 50,000 would be more like it. He probably knew that was a vain hope.

Dreiser had Earl Browder and William Z. Foster read an early draft of the book and asked for their advice on certain economic matters that were vexing him. The Party's researchers probably supplied considerable data for the book. Using this and other material he had collected, Kay Sayre worked up a first draft, which Dreiser later revised and expanded.

In October the Party summoned Dreiser for his most important mission yet—a trip to Harlan County, better known in the press as "Bloody Harlan." A brushfire war was raging there between the operators and the miners, most of whom were backwoods people who had been lured by the high wages during World War I. The demand for coal fell steadily throughout the 1920s and plummeted in the Depression, causing drastic retrenchments. Thousands of laid-off miners were stuck in squalid mining camps that dotted the rugged hills. They had grown too used to wage work and town life to move (assuming they could find jobs), and had long since lost the plots of land they once farmed. Mining had destroyed a way of life, as well as scarred the hills.

In the Harlan coal region, which comprised Harlan, Bell, Knox, Breathitt, and Hazard counties, the people were as badly off as anywhere in the nation, and the operators the toughest and most lawless. Wages had been falling and unemployment rising since the late 1920s, but the last straw was a 10-percent pay cut in February 1931. Miners who had jobs averaged sixty cents to a dollar a day. Most of their pay was siphoned off by the mine-owners in deductions—credit at the commissary, $5 to $10 a month for a rickety shack, $2 a month for a company doctor, a "burial fund" contribution of $1 a month, assessments for ministers and school funds, even check-offs for coal for their grate fires and kerosene for their lamps. Miners even had to pay for the carbide in their lanterns, explosives, and blacksmithing of their tools. What was left was issued in "scrip," good only at the company store. After all the "deducts," many miners had nothing; some actually ended up owing money. The checkoff system was a device for recycling miners' wages into the owners' pockets. Prices at the commissaries were 30 to 100 percent higher than in town stores; a miner who traded at the latter— some of which took heavily discounted scrip—risked losing his job.

As a result, most men worked in virtual peonage, and their families lived at the subsistence level. In one camp an average of seven children a week died of a form of dysentery called "bloody flux" during the summer of 1930. Most families lived on a diet of pinto beans, corn bread, bulldog gravy (flour, water, and lard), a little meat, and edible weeds. Milk for children was so rare it was regarded as medicine. Sanitation in the camps ranged from poor to nonexistent; streams, the only source of drinking water, were polluted, causing a high incidence of typhoid. The miners' houses were unpainted board shacks, the thin walls covered with newspapers or cardboard to block drafts.

So the companies' latest pay cut pushed the miners into open rebellion. As one said, "We starve while we work; we might as well strike while we starve." They turned to the National Miners Union for aid, and the operators responded by blacklisting those who attended union rallies and evicting them from their houses. As organizing efforts continued, Sheriff John Henry Blair's deputies, led by imported thugs like Jim Daniels (who boasted he had killed four men) and Marion ("Two Gun") Allen, launched a reign of terror.

A news blackout had descended on the county. Two reporters were shot, one while fleeing after he had been taken to the county line by Allen and other gun thugs and told he had five minutes to live. Two writers from *Scribner's* magazine were searched and intimidated; only the Knoxville, Tennessee, *News-Sentinel* provided objective coverage. Reporters from the Associated Press, which took care not to offend the powers that be, were tolerated, but much of the press service's information originated with its stringer, Herndon Evans, editor of the Pineville *Sun* in Bell County, who was in the owners' pocket.

That, more or less, was the gist of the ILD report that Dreiser read. The ILD wanted the NCDPP to conduct an investigation that would publicize the wholesale trampling on civil rights in Harlan. Dreiser was dubious, however, contending that a lay committee would face brutality or else no one would talk to it. He proposed instead forming a blue-ribbon panel of distinguished citizens. That idea was accepted, and Dreiser sent telegrams to a list that included Senators Robert La Follette and George Norris, newspaper publisher Roy Howard, William Allen White, and journalists, ministers, and educators from the region. (He had wanted to invite Arthur Garfield Hays, but Browder advised against this; Hays had helped the NAACP in the Scottsboro boys case and was considered a class enemy by the ILD.) All the invitees tendered their regrets, save for Bruce Crawford, the publisher of a weekly in Norton, Virginia, who had written stories critical of the owners and officials. His comments had aroused such anger that he was shot in the leg by a sniper while crossing a bridge near Pineville.

Abandoning that plan, Dreiser was forced to call for volunteers from the NCDPP membership. Lester Cohen and Samuel Ornitz, both novelists who had published with Liveright, immediately offered their services and met with Dreiser at the Ansonia. With a toothy smile, he told them he had hoped to have a committee of "representative Americans" but, having failed, "we are now reduced to writers."

Dreiser sent out some twenty invitations in all, but only six accepted on such short notice: John Dos Passos; Charles Rumford Walker and his wife, Adelaide; Melvin P. Levy; and Crawford.

Aware of the danger he and his committee faced, Dreiser dispatched telegrams to Governor Sampson and Sheriff Blair demanding full protection and holding them "personally responsible for the lives" of the group. He said the committee's findings would be turned over to Senator Norris, a farm-belt liberal who planned to hold hearings on the Harlan war. The governor responded that he would send a detachment of state militia to Harlan; he also appointed a committee of his own to look into the charges that miners were going hungry. Sheriff Blair apparently did not deign to answer. County Judge David Crockett Jones inveighed against the "snake doctors from New York."

Having turned a protective spotlight on themselves before they left, the members of Dreiser's committee departed on November 4 for Pineville. The others were surprised when a young and attractive woman boarded the train in Cincinnati and sat with their chairman for the remainder of the journey. Dos Passos thought her most elegant in her manners, and "her neatly tailored gray suit gave off that special Chicago chic I so appreciated." He thought it odd of Dreiser to bring a lady friend along, but later wrote it off as a flouting of convention, a "fetish" of Dreiser's generation. Esther McCoy, who knew Dreiser better, said he was just "doing what came naturally." Dreiser made no introductions, but his companion was later identified as Marie Pergain, probably a pseudonym.

In Pineville the committee checked in at the Continental Hotel, where Dreiser was interviewed by reporters from the wire services and the Louisville *Courier Journal* and chatted with the mayor, who promised to assist the committee without taking sides. Everyone was very polite until the imposing figure of Judge "Baby" Jones, six feet five, loomed up in the lobby. "Well they grow 'em big down here anyway," Dreiser quipped. The two verbally sparred for a while and were photographed. The colloquy ended when the wife of union organizer Jim Grace, who had been roughed up by deputies, demanded to know why her house had been raided, and Jones abruptly departed.

That evening some of the miners came to the hotel and began relating their stories. The committee moved to an empty room and Dreiser interrogated several witnesses, a stenographer taking down their testimony.

The next day, November 6, a fine fall morning, the committee traveled to the town of Harlan, commandeered a public room at the Lewallen Hotel, set up a long table on a platform, and began what resembled a congressional hearing. This staging was an on-the-spot improvisation, but it was effective. Word of the inquiry had got out and a stream of gaunt men and women in clean, patched-up clothes arrived to vent their grievances, ignored by townspeople who were more interested in the high school football game with Pineville. They had "faces out of American history," Dos Passos thought, their speech "the lilt of Elizabethan lyrics." Dreiser, wearing a blue suit and a bow tie, with his shock of white hair and probing blue-gray eyes, looked like a judge or a senator. Dos Passos thought "there was a sort of massive humaneness about him, a self-dedicated disregard of consequences, a sly sort of dignity that earned him the respect of friend and foe alike." Dreiser led the questioning of each witness, briskly pinning down the facts like an old newspaperman.

The burden of the testimony confirmed what they had already heard: miners blacklisted for joining the NMU, homes searched without warrants, men arrested for possessing copies of the *Daily Worker*, soup kitchens blown up by deputies, unionists jailed without formal charges and set free if they promised to leave the county. As a miner's wife put it: "The gun thugs are the law in this county now and not the judge and juries."

What made the national press, however, was an exchange between Dreiser and Herndon Evans. After undergoing some rather hostile questioning by the chairman on his income and a lecture on the need for "equity" in America, the Pineville editor asked if he might put some questions to his inquisitor. Certainly, said Dreiser. How much had he received in royalties from *An American Tragedy*, Evans wanted to know. "Two hundred thousand dollars approximately. Probably more," was the response. And how much did he make in a year? Why, he earned around $35,000 last year, Dreiser estimated. Did he contribute anything to charity? No, he did not. That is all, said Evans. Dreiser begged leave to expand his answer, saying he supported several relatives, paid four secretaries to gather data on economic conditions, and kept up the property he owned. Triumphantly, Evans pointed out that he gave more to charity than Dreiser did. What kind of equity was that? Dreiser launched into a garbled summary of his writing career, pointing out that for many years he had made probably $150 a month at most, but the damage was done.

The wire service reports on the Harlan hearing focused on that single exchange, and the thrust of their stories was, "Country Editor Turns Tables on Famous Novelist." Lost were Dreiser's long-held views that charity was inadequate to meet the problems of mass unemployment and that the government should assume the welfare responsibilities. Lester Cohen noticed that the miners in the audience listened to his admissions "with a sort of reverence and awe." Not because he had made all that money, but because they shared his attitude toward handouts. A mountaineer said, "I don't keer for charity myself. I only want what's coming to me." The audience also knew editor Evans as head of the local Red Cross, which denied aid to those who supported the union.

The next morning Dos Passos sensed "a war feeling in the air." Young men with cold eyes and bulges under their jackets were standing on every corner. The committee deposed prosecuting attorney William E. Brock, who explained that it was against the law to advocate communism in Kentucky, which was why people were being arrested for possessing copies of the *Daily Worker.* Of course peacable unionists had nothing to fear from his office. After the committee had thanked Brock for his cooperation, another lawyer, who had been listening with some agitation to the exchanges, asked Ornitz if any of his family came from Russia. Ornitz replied that he had some relatives there. "I thought you were connected with Russia," the attorney said triumphantly.

The delegation next drove to Straight Creek in Bell County, convoyed by two officers from the Kentucky National Guard—two-thirds of the "detachment" sent by Governor Sampson to protect them—and also by a carload of deputies, who hovered about looking mean but who did not interfere. The mining camp at Straight Creek was solidly NMU. The local could celebrate a small victory—an agreement with a few independent mines that raised pay to thirty-eight cents a ton and guaranteed check weighmen at the scales (it was later abrogated). They entered pathetically furnished shacks, the walls papered over and the wind coming in through cracks in the floorboards, yet bravely tidied up for "company." They heard "Aunt Molly" Jackson, the midwife, tell stories of children dying of the flux, doctors who wouldn't come, and burial societies that paid for no funerals.

The following day, Sunday, the committee split up. Dreiser's group went to Wallins Creek, where the novelist ate beans and bulldog gravy in an NMU soup kitchen and talked with miners and children at the school. They visited a dying man in a shack with rotting floorboards and a flimsy wall that collapsed when Dos Passos pushed against it to steady himself. That night, at a "free speech speakin' " at the Glendon Baptist church, they heard Mistress "Sudy" Gates praise the NMU for bringing the womenfolk into the fight. Aunt Molly Jackson sang her "Hungry Miners' Wife's Blues," and Jim Garland said the operators called the miners Red because their low wages had made them so thin and poor "that if you stood one of them up against the sun you'd see red right through him." George Maurer of the ILD told the audience that one day in America they would have courts like those in Russia, "where the workers are the judges . . . and where workers decide who is guilty and who is not guilty."

Watching Dreiser as he listened to the speeches, Cohen was struck by his deep attentiveness. He seemed somehow kindly and giving—qualities Cohen knew well enough were not usual with him; he had been profoundly moved.

On Monday, November 9, carrying a bulky transcript of the hearings, Dreiser boarded a train for New York. Marie Pergain was still with him; she had attended the hearings, saying nothing, and the other committee members still did not know what her role was. Before the day was out, however, they would have an answer of sorts.

The previous Friday night, two moral vigilantes, perhaps tipped off by clerks at the Continental Hotel in Pineville, learned that Pergain had entered Dreiser's room at a late hour. The "highly reputable citizens," as Judge Jones later described them, tiptoed to the room and placed some toothpicks against the door in such a way that they would fall if it was opened. The next morning the toothpicks were intact, proof that Dreiser had spent the night with a woman who was not his wife. On Monday, when the grand jury met, Judge Jones called on it to indict the culprits for adultery. And while they were at it, the veniremen should ponder an indictment of members of Dreiser's committee for criminal syndicalism. The purpose of the committee's visit, he maintained, was to "capitalize on the poor miners" and to "dupe them into joining some communistic organization."

The jury dutifully returned an indictment on the adultery charge, a misdemeanor carrying a maximum fifty-dollar fine and not an extraditable offense. Was the citizen-detectives' zeal prompted merely by small-town prurience or were the authorities out to get something on Dreiser in order to run him out of the county? After all, he was too prominent for the usual night-rider treatment—or to shoot in the back, as some hotheads were talking about doing. Better to trump up some legal pretext for expelling him and tarnishing his inquiry.

Learning of the charge while on the train, Dreiser was inspired to claim that he could not possibly have committed adultery because he was "impotent." Typical of Dreiser's literary career, the AP refused to publish the statement until the eight-letter word had been censored. Its story reported merely that he was *incapable* of adultery.

As Dreiser continued northward, bidding farewell to Pergain along the way, the farce continued. From Bristol, Virginia, he issued a longer statement: "The first thing before attempting to discuss any important economic or social matter in America is to assure, or rather convince everybody—church and state alike—of our complete and unabridged personal sexual morality. Otherwise we will not be able to get their minds off the matter...." Repeating that he was incapable of adultery, he charged Judge Jones with laying down a titillating smokescreen to hide "the really ... evil crimes that are being committed against the poorest and most underpaid and most long-suffering type of laborer, his wife and child, that I have ever seen." He asserted that the miners regarded the *Daily Worker* and the NMU as "their only friends."

He next surfaced in Norfolk, where he was tracked by reporters to the Atlantic Hotel. While they kept vigil in the lobby, he slipped out a back entrance to meet Helen, who had come by ship to Norfolk, bringing the car with her. And so he made a clean escape.

Safely in New York, he renewed the offensive against Harlan and Bell county officialdom. On November 12 he held a press conference at the Ansonia, with Dos Passos at his side. Speaking with a choking anger, at times almost incoherent, he said, "Something will have to be done about the state of things down there, and damned quickly, and put that in your papers if you dare." When the *Evening Post* interrupted him to ask what should be done, he snapped, "I'll tell you what they have to do, darling, they have to give them a living wage and damn quick." Dos Passos, who was terribly shy and hated speaking, exhibited miners' pay slips to illustrate how a man could end up earning nothing after the deducts.

Four days later the grand jury of the Bell County Circuit Court indicted the entire Dreiser committee. The bill charged that its members had banded together unlawfully "to commit criminal syndicalism and to promulgate a reign of terror" in the coalfields. The NCDPP's attorney asked New York Governor Franklin D. Roosevelt to meet with committee members before considering any extradition request the State of Kentucky might make.

Kentucky's syndicalism law, like those in many states, had been stampeded through during the post–World War I Red scare. Anyone found guilty of advocating crime, violence, arson, destruction of property, revolution, etc., could be imprisoned for up to twenty-one years. Legal scholars doubted the statute's constitutionality, but it remained to be tested.

The CP urged Dreiser and Dos Passos to go back to Kentucky and face trial. Dos Passos recalled Browder's "sneering tone" implying, Why don't you effete liberals make yourselves useful as martyrs? Neither man had any stomach for another sojourn in Harlan, particularly as guests in the overcrowded county jail. Dreiser called a press conference to announce that the NCDPP would fight extradition. He sent his own attorney, William D. Cameron (Hume's partner), to Kentucky to sound out the governor and other officials on whether extradition would be granted. The lawyer wired Dreiser that the charges would be dropped if, in effect, the committee shut up on the subject of Harlan. This Dreiser and the others refused to do. John

W. Davis, a Wall Street lawyer who agreed to defend them against extradition, also counseled silence, but Dreiser again bridled. He circulated a letter to wealthy friends asking for donations for the miners and gave a talk on radio about the mine war. Later he wrote a foreword to a book, *Harlan Miners Speak,* containing transcripts of his committee's hearings, which appeared in early 1932.

But he did not show up for an NCDPP rally in New York City on December 6, at which he was billed as the featured speaker. The 3000 people who attended were disappointed, but Sherwood Anderson substituted and praised Dreiser as "the first downright honest American prose writer" who had the courage to go down to Harlan and find out what was happening. "This is a speak-easy generation," Anderson said. "Dreiser spoke out loud in a speak-easy country—that's what criminal syndicalism is. What we need in this country is fewer speak-easy citizens and more criminal syndicalists."

In the end, the criminal syndicalism charges were quietly forgotten. Brock's talk of bringing back Dreiser and friends for trial was partly a publicity gesture intended to counter the negative image Pineville had acquired. On the publicity front, Dreiser, his committee, and, most important, the miners and their union were the clear winners. Dreiser's indiscretion in bringing a young woman along and taking her into his hotel room provoked some criticism, even on the left, but the press generally treated the adultery indictment as a joke or a red herring. Leftists tended toward the latter view—with the exception of Max Eastman, who was delighted by Dreiser's improbable claim of impotency: "It is both funny and sublime—an event in the cultural history of man." Dreiser replied, "You are the first of all those I know to get the real point I was trying to make." He said he had received many approving letters, some describing cures for impotency. He was interviewed for a newsreel on the toothpick incident, and theater audiences applauded him.

As for Marie Pergain, whom the papers described as a "vivacious blonde" or a "pretty, striking young blonde of French descent," she made a brief return to the limelight a few weeks later, when a tabloid reporter surprised her in the Ansonia. Before Dreiser came lumbering down the corridor to shoo him away, Pergain defended her honor: "The charges against me and Mr. Dreiser are untrue. I went with him to help the starving naked children of the miners. My life is my own to live as I see fit; I really don't care what people say."

To some, her words would have served as a silly summary of a naive, botched effort by some busybody liberals who had no business in Kentucky and caused more trouble. But the committee had accomplished what it set out to do—publicize the miners' plight. The new journal of Henry Luceian capitalism, *Fortune,* confirmed Dreiser's achievement when it wrote: "For the past year (as everyone knows since Theodore Dreiser and his committee went down to investigate and tell the world) Harlan County has been the scene of a bloody and bitter struggle between the soft-coal operators and their miners." If the public had learned just that, it was something.

Predictably, neither Congress nor the Hoover administration did anything to help the miners. Senator Norris met with Dreiser and reviewed the testimony the NCDPP had taken. He promised to introduce a resolution calling for an investigation, but doubted that Congress had jurisdiction.

Three more committees invaded Harlan the following year, one with Communist Party backing. But the reign of terror continued unabated, and the Pineville *Sun* editorialized that outsiders would be safe only "in a pine box six feet underground." The NMU, forbidden by an injunction to speak or demonstrate, called a last-ditch strike on New Year's Day, 1932. Perhaps 5000 miners went out, though "out" may be a misnomer, since most of them had been blacklisted or fired or had otherwise lost their jobs. Union headquarters was raided and organizers arrested; an NMU leader was murdered by a deputy.

Faced by overwhelming force, the CP again admitted defeat. The miners, whose hopes the NMU had raised so high, were left to fight alone. In 1933 the United Mine Workers returned to the state in force, armed with the National Industrial Recovery Act, which endorsed unionism and barred yellow-dog contracts. John L. Lewis negotiated a comprehensive bargaining agreement in which, as a writer for *The New Yorker* put it, "the defeated mine-owners agreed to all the things that deputy sheriffs usually shoot people for demanding." Meanwhile the Comintern heaped ignominy on the beaten NMU, criticizing its tactics and the "dual union" strategy. Thus was the courage of many CP "agitators" tossed in the ash can of history.

The Harlan trip was the high point of Dreiser's romance with communism. Sometime before he went to Kentucky, probably in the early fall, he had applied for Party membership, but, he told Lester Cohen, "they wouldn't take me." And he explained to Alva Johnson of the New York *Herald Tribune*, "I have been told over and over that I am much too much of an individualist and that I do not subscribe to the exact formulas [of] the Communist program, and therefore I would never be admissable."

Since the Party had so earnestly courted him and praised him and demanded his time, he naturally assumed that there would be no problem. And his vanity was such that he thought the Party would welcome the publicity coup and he suggested to Browder that his conversion be announced with maximum fanfare.

"There was no question about his sincerity," the former communist leader told W. A. Swanberg. "He sought publicity for his ideas as well as for himself. He did not seem quite adult, which was a part of his charm." When Browder turned him down, he was "surprised and hurt." Browder explained to Dreiser that he was more valuable to the communists outside the Party: "If he surrendered his right to be publicly wrong on very important issues he would no longer be Dreiser—but the Party could not afford to have a prominent member conspicuously wrong on anything in its then existing stage of development." This was a nice way of saying that Dreiser was a loose cannon. In Browder's estimation he was really an old-fashioned Populist. Then too, he was more useful speaking out as an independent, rather than as one under Party discipline, Browder may have thought. Not that Dreiser could ever be a dutiful soldier in the ranks, as Browder knew from personal experience; quite the opposite, he might use the party to publicize his own ideas.

Dreiser emotionally supported communism but was groping for an indigenous variety that would appeal to the average American. He felt that the Party was not making a sufficient effort to attract the middle class, the white-collar workers, and the professional people. In April, in an open letter to the CP, International Labor Defense, and other radical groups, Dreiser urged the formation of Societies of Karl Marx, to enlist middle-class Americans who were repelled or frightened by the obscurantist or revolutionary language in the Party's propaganda tracts. The societies would have no connection to the Party and would only discuss Marx's *ideas,* so no legal objections could be raised (he had in mind anticommunist legislation pending in Congress). They would also sponsor social events such as banquets, publish magazines, and hold conventions. This idea ("premature Popular Front-ism," it might have been dubbed) revealed Dreiser's tendency (in communist terms) to elevate the bourgeoisie to a coequal role with the proletariat and to downplay the worker revolution that the CP quixotically believed it was leading.

In a letter Dreiser wrote to a correspondent named David Agar Bailey, he emphasizes the need for a strong middle class to mediate between "the rank and file at the bottom [who] cannot think, or they would not be at the bottom so persistently" and the "strong and brilliant at the top [who] are not to be controlled by an indigent mass." Otherwise, he goes on, a revolution was a real possibility: "I have never seen a remedy this side of revolution that appears to work. When the atoms in any pot get too restless, the lid blows off." His "entire plan" was to reach the middle class and "to stir them to such action (and this is probably a vain dream) as will stop the lid from blowing off." Stopping the lid from blowing off was precisely what the Communist Party did not want. It wanted a radicalized proletariat.

Browder had heard enough of this firsthand to measure Dreiser's unreliability. Helen remarked that when the Party secretary visited Iroki, Dreiser bombarded him with advice on what course the CP should be taking. Helen (who said Dreiser had never mentioned to her applying for membership) recalled that he approved the communist program but felt "that the leaders of the Party in this country were without imagination. He could not tolerate their determination to hew sharply to the Party line."

After his rejection, his relationship with the communist *apparat* in America became more distant. The Party's behavior after his Harlan trip bruised his ego. Like Dos Passos, he had resented its martyrdom complex (that is, *you* be the martyr), and, though he wanted ideological direction, he did not like functionaries in New York making decisions for him with regard to "his" committee. He told Harriet Bissell, his secretary in 1937–1938, that he could never become a communist because of the way the CP had treated him in Harlan. It had set him up, he charged, either to be killed or to be disgraced. That was an exaggeration in retrospect, but the experience of other intellectuals in Harlan had borne out his suspicions.

Although he remained on civil terms with Browder, Dreiser preferred the company of William Z. Foster. Foster was an old-time radical, a former Wobbly who had led the great steel strike of 1919, and a convivial drinking companion. Browder was a rather mousy man (some compared him to Uriah Heep), an *apparatchik* who followed orders but who was also a shrewd political tactician and hungry for power. Foster was unpopular with the rank and file and had displeased the Comintern in the past.

Dreiser would remain a communist, but a highly unorthodox one. In the Marxist lodge he never moved beyond the degree of bourgeois liberal. He was motivated by a burning sense of injustice and unfairness and a deep sympathy, as Bissell described it, for "the poor dumbbells who really couldn't do anything but work themselves to death with illness and privation, with maybe a few years . . . in life of a little financial sunshine." His radicalism had its origins in boyhood poverty and early ambitions mingled with youthful envy of those who had undeservedly made it to the top due to family wealth and connections.

Guilt surely had something to do with his conversion—guilt over his wealth, his sins. The communist program offered an opportunity to expiate that guilt and to symbolically renounce his wealth by siding with the workers, the poor. Communism also promised cleansing action and sacrifice. When Dorothy Dudley interviewed him for a biography of him she was writing, he lamented that he found none of the idealism in New York City he had seen at the turn of the century—except "in the youngsters who want to change the whole face of the country and follow Russia." He told Dudley, "I would do anything if the moment came . . . an important moment, one that asked for sacrifice. . . . Communism has gone so far that there can be no change except a violent one from without." It also offered a quasi-religious ideal of a better society that was based on a "scientific" analysis found in the writings of Marx and Engels. And it had a plan for a strong government that promised to curb the rich and powerful and impose order on the American economic system, which seemed to have spun out of control. Such an order chimed with Dreiser's inner need to order the chaotic emotions, the urgent sensuality and anger, that drove his creativity when harnessed to a task but that harried as well as pleasured him in his private life; he could project on society a vision of coherence and order that he could not achieve in himself except through writing.

Not only did the communists provide a bolder program of social action for political change than anyone else; they offered camaraderie—the immersion of self in an idealistic community. "A revolutionary situation," Joe Freeman wrote, "fuses political and private life into one burning existence inspired by a common goal which is also your personal goal." Dreiser, who had long wandered in the wilderness of the artist's alienation, was deeply drawn to the young people who committed themselves to a cause.

Party literati like Mike Gold, now co-editor of *The New Masses,* unerringly probed writers' feelings of guilt and isolation, condemning the individualism, fashionable nihilism, aestheticism, and big-money corruption of the 1920s. When Gold read Dreiser's "What I Believe" statement in 1928, he told him that his bafflement lay in "a very profound and honest *social pity* & without . . . finding social reforms to express it—one must feel as bad as if one consistently repressed sex or other desires." He asked, "is the artist only a wonderful & special mirror of nature—& nothing more?"

At the time, Dreiser had reminded Gold that "the human race . . . is a predatory organism, fighting and killing to not only save but advance . . . at the expense of . . . every other type of organism." He saw no evidence that man could modify "the outstanding cruelties of the creative impulse," i.e., Nature. He had also argued that the true artist cannot be a reformer in his writing; the job of literature was to illuminate life, not issue manifestos.

Robert Elias later asked him how he could square social activism with his pessimistic, deterministic philosophy. He replied, first, that his sympathies had always been with the underdog, and, second, "When I take part in Communist activities . . . I am still a determinist and still a helpless victim of my own feelings and sympathies." There was no real paradox; he was driven by his nature to social action just as a capitalist was compelled by his chemistry to accumulate wealth.

But if Dreiser vented in pamphleteering and political action his sympathy for the lonely individual at the mercy of inscrutable forces which had motivated his best work, from *Carrie* to the *Tragedy,* would there be any energizing anger and pity left for a novel? He had not published one in five years. It was one of the ironies of Dreiser's career that, in his most radical period, the next book on his agenda was *The Stoic,* the third act in the life of Frank Cowperwood, arch–Robber Baron and individualist *par excellence,* whose motto was "I satisfy myself."

CHAPTER 31

The Stoic

> As for my Communism, it is a very liberal thing. I am not
> an exact Marxian by any means. . . . My quarrel is not so
> much with doctrines as conditions. Just now, conditions
> are extremely badly balanced, and I would like to see them
> more evenly levelled."
> —Dreiser to Evelyn Scott (1932)

As though to exorcise the old Cowperwood before taking up *The
Stoic,* Dreiser wrote an essay attacking individualism that appeared in several left publications and the foreword to *Harlan
Miners Speak.* Untrammeled individualism, he said, leads to a
state of nature in which every creature "is for itself, prowls to
sustain itself, and deals death to the weakest at every turn." But society "is
not and cannot be a jungle." Societies evolve like organisms; they progress
by creating "more and more rules to limit, yet not frustrate, the individual
in his relation with his fellows." The objective of organized society should
be to make it possible for "the individual to live with his fellow in reasonable
equity, in order that he may enjoy equity himself."

He saw no new Soviet Man on the horizon, only the same Old Adam.
Communism, he told the Russian novelist Boris Pilnyak, endured because
"Stalin uses the same ruthless procedures as dictators in other countries to
maintain his power. With the difference that Stalin is really exceptionally
gifted and a splendid character." Stalin was the apex of the Soviet state,
which represented the congealed force of the masses, enforcing equity and
curbing the excesses of individualism, according to the Marxian Golden

Rule: "From each according to his ability; to each according to his needs."

He could not have envisioned the democratic use of government under Roosevelt's New Deal to tame the free enterprise jungle—despite the unwittingly prophetic working title for his recently completed book, *A New Deal for America.* But Stuart Chase's *A New Deal* had appeared earlier that year (it probably was the inspiration for Franklin D. Roosevelt's use of the phrase when accepting the Democratic nomination for president), so the title was changed to *Tragic America* to capitalize on *An American Tragedy.*

Nervous about Dreiser's critique of industrialists and corporations by name, T. R. Smith had Arthur Garfield Hays vet the book, and in November Smith informed Dreiser that the lawyer had concluded that "much of the matter may be libelous." The company was in no financial position to defend itself against libel suits, and Smith demanded that Dreiser either cut the questionable matter or indemnify the publisher against any losses in court. Smith may have been trying to ease out of publishing *Tragic America;* what Hays said was that "we think you stand little or no chance of litigation." Dreiser's targets were John D. Rockefeller and other well-known corporate villains of the muckraking era. His sources were mainly magazines, newspapers, and government reports, so he was saying nothing new. His most important source was Gustavus Myers' *History of the Great Fortunes,* and shortly before the book went to press, Myers was hired to check the facts. His wife, Genevieve, recalled that he was offered fifty dollars and given twenty-four hours to complete the job. She thought the book read as if Dreiser had "stood on a soapbox and dictated at the top of his voice." Myers found thirty erroneous passages that had to be either eliminated or toned down. But in such a short time he could not catch every misstatement, and reviewers dredged others up by the handful. Stuart Chase claimed to have discovered eighteen miscues in one chapter. Some of the mistakes were typos or mental slips that when corrected seem less significant than the reviewer implied; for example, referring to Standard Oil rather than Standard Oil of New Jersey and saying that the Interstate Commerce Commission rather than the Railway Labor Board had reduced wages.

Kindlier critics thought Dreiser should have described the Depression in human terms—and even capitalists were people—rather than disgorging a lot of undigested statistics and leftist ideology. Reviewers in sympathy with Dreiser's analysis of capitalism, such as Edmund Wilson, said that, even though the book was full of inaccuracies and carelessly written, his sincerity and passion were such that attention should be paid. In *The New Masses* (which, oddly, did not publish its review until May) Bennet Stevens was respectful. However, he chided Dreiser for his failure to grasp Marxist principles—evidenced by his repetition of "the liberal fallacy that the use of the American government by the capitalist class is merely an abuse of the 'ideals of the Republic' "; his occasional subscription to "the Christian Socialist blather about the need to return to the teachings of Jesus," and his heterodox reference to leaders of the AFL as "cabbageheads" (he should have called them "deliberate misleaders").

Browder had read the manuscript in October and made some suggestions. But he wrote Dreiser, "It is entirely understood by us that you are taking only those opinions which can express your own profound convictions, and that our contribution is merely in the nature of assistance to help get the sharpest formulation of them." It appears that the Party was distancing itself from Dreiser as Dreiser was moving away from the Party.

From a literary standpoint, *Tragic America* was indisputably Dreiser's worst-written book. But it had an internal or psychological integrity. It was an eruption of rage; a venting of the molten core of felt injustice in *An American Tragedy,* a vision of America just as the *Tragedy* was a vision of America. His "characters" are trusts and monopolies and plutocrats, which, as Wilson notes, he presents "as blind and uncouth organisms with a kind of life of their own which expand and contract, galvanize and kill, and fight each other on international arenas."

As economic analysis or a statement of policy, as reportage or history, *Tragic America* is not worth much; but as a jeremiad, it was appropriate to the times and expounded a coherent vision of a real economic tragedy. It ends with Dreiser imagining a New Communist Utopia—an egalitarian society patterned after Russian communism (and Edward Bellamy's nineteenth-century utopian novel *Looking Backward*—a book Dreiser was advising his literary assistants to read), but tailored to the American character. In this last specification he is not entirely successful; he constantly falls back on Soviet examples to demonstrate that this or that provision would be workable here—dubious precedents. He seems to be enthusiastically endorsing the system headed by a benign, selfless Stalin, down to the last kulak deported to Siberia.

His central message is *"for the masses to build themselves new institutions."* This would entail scrapping the present Constitution and adopting one that would "guarantee official domination by the masses, rather than private interests. . . ." (He seems to have bowed to Browder's argument against legal remedies, for he cut from the galleys a passage reading, "I would recommend continuance of our American Constitutional system, which has at least some points of merit." He seemed to be saying that the Constitution should be changed so as no longer to protect private property.)

Private fortunes would be abolished; no one would be too rich or too poor. The economy would be run by government trusts in each of the basic sectors, just as private trusts run it now, "Only in this case, the immense profits of large scale production and distribution would, and should, enrich the government, and this should naturally tend to lower prices to every one as well as make for the physical as well as mental profit of the individual, *he being the first care of the state.* " The objective of Dreiser's collectivism was thus helping the individual.

Could it happen here? He thinks so. The system should be implemented "gradually," as in Russia (he apparently was referring to the Russia he saw in the 1920s, as if Stalin had not ousted Bukharin over the very issue of gradualism). The people would choose communism once they realized its obvious benefits. It would not go against the grain of American individualism. In the Soviet Union he "saw no lack of individualism . . . creative or otherwise. Arts and invention appeared to be flourishing there as here."

Although *Tragic America* was a "communistic" book, he had been edging away from the Party even before it was published. In the spring he had discussed with friends the formation of an American League for Equity. As he explained to Charles Yost, the small-town newspaper editor from Ohio, it was a matter of semantics: "Communism as technically stated by the Russians will not be accepted [by Americans]. Communism as practiced by the Russians, or at least most of it, can certainly be made palatable to the average American if it is properly explained to him and the title Communism is removed." He proposed that he and Yost, Bruce Crawford, Morris Ernst, and others get together to discuss his proposed league. He would take the leadership if enough followers could be attracted. The following year, when a reader suggested he organize Dreiser study clubs, along the lines of the John Reed Clubs, using *Tragic America* as their basic text, he was flattered enough to ask Esther McCoy, now living in Los Angeles, if she would be interested in starting such a club.

As a manifesto, however, *Tragic America* was a bust. It sold only 4600 copies the first year, but the author received scores of letters from strangers, troubled citizens looking for answers. Some reported incidents of censorship (one correspondent said that his Carnegie library had refused to put the book on its shelves because of its ideas; Los Angeles bookstores were telling people they couldn't obtain any more copies), and Dreiser began to suspect that the Catholic Church had blacklisted the book.

Despite his distaste for the way the Party was run, Dreiser did support his friend William Z. Foster, communist candidate for president. But it took some cajoling by Joe Pass, now director of the National Campaign Committee for Foster-Ford, before Dreiser would issue a 600-word statement on why he was voting communist. He said he was too busy to write it and asked Pass to draw one up. Then he decided that the draft written by Pass and Melvin Levy was "too colorless" and rewrote it.

He said that the communists prescribed a program under which all who worked would share "equally and generously" with their fellows. He favored such a program, and if that made him a communist "then most certainly I am a Communist" and would vote the CP ticket. Like many intellectuals in 1932, he voted for the CP as a protest against the major parties, which offered no programs to deal with the economic malaise.

The NCDPP entered the election with an organization called the League of Professional Groups for Foster and Ford, which published an open letter of support for the CP candidates, held a mass meeting in Manhattan, and issued a campaign brochure, "Culture and Crisis." Dreiser signed the manifesto but refused to make any further pro–Foster-Ford statements.

He was in fact trying to extricate himself from the committee, and in January 1933 resigned as chairman, explaining to Melvin P. Levy, its secretary, that he had no time since he was under contract to finish *The Stoic.* But the committee was a Tar Baby. By now the communist members dominated it, and in June he was asked to head the American delegation to the World Congress Against War, to convene in Amsterdam in August. Dreiser was too busy to go, and Evelyn Light, trying to protect him from misuse of his name, urged him to decline the invitation and resign from the NCDPP. Two letters to this effect were duly sent to Elliot Cohen, the NCDPP's latest secretary, but were ignored, and so Light appealed to a higher authority, William Weinstone, a Party official, to intervene. She had discovered who was really running the NCDPP. Unfortunately she hadn't heard that Weinstone was out of favor for opposing Browder.

With no satisfaction from that quarter, she instructed Rorty, secretary of the moment of the League of Professional Groups, to remove Dreiser's name from its letterhead. Dreiser was mystified as to how he had got on the list in the first place, and Light reminded him that he had signed the manifesto supporting the Foster-Ford ticket, and "now, of course, there is an organization, a league, a group, a committee, a collection, a mass, a whatnot. Anyhow, there is, and you are of it, in it (but not leading it, thank God) by virtue of being one of the original group who signed the statement. . . . If they keep on like this, all you'll have to do to become a second Stalin is to say hello to a Socialist." Relenting a bit, Dreiser had Light notify Pass that he would continue as a member of the league on the strength of the latter's assurance that it would dissolve after the election. As Light explained, Dreiser didn't want to find it was the nucleus of still another new group that would come into existence and draft him into its ranks. (The league did indeed live on after the election.)

In December Light wrote Eli Jacobsen, secretary of something or other, that Mr. Dreiser "has always felt that his independent and occasional support of any effort toward equity is more valuable than the constant use of his name in the diversified activities of the numerous organizations." Consequently, he had decided not to affiliate with any organization.

As Dreiser explained to Sergei Dinamov, "I've had to eliminate much detail in my revolutionary writing but still do whatever I can on important issues." When the Chicago chapter of the John Reed Club, which had been named after Dreiser, asked for an article for its magazine, Light searched his files: "I could find nothing in the Economic Article Completed file. Shall I dig something else out of *Tragic America*? On Why the Ballet, for instance." In a later instance of absentmindedness he apologized to a Soviet magazine for sending an article already published in Russia.

One of Dreiser's continuing causes was Tom Mooney, still languishing in prison but expecting a pardon at last. But when Levy asked him to write a letter advising Mooney to go on a speaking tour under the auspices of the CP after his release, Dreiser replied that he could not agree with Levy's draft; furthermore, if he were to rewrite it in his own words, it "would still align me directly and awarely with the motivating Communistic directorate in this country and that, as you know, is entirely false." Yet that same day a letter under his name went to Mooney, warning him off the socialists, who were competing for his blessing: "Among the Communists and even among . . . my own friends—artists, writers and scholars—the Socialist Party is now known as a Social Fascist organization." Dreiser suggested that Mooney let the NCDPP, which "is not a directly Communist organization," handle him. It is doubtful that Dreiser wrote this letter, for the denunciation of the socialists has the ring of Party rhetoric. And by now Dreiser knew that the NCDPP was communist dominated, for he had received statements from noncommunist members who had resigned in protest.

Unaware of the misuse of his name, he participated in a free-Mooney rally in San Francisco in early November. He met with Mooney in prison and the next day held a press conference. When a reporter asked, Even if Mooney was innocent, wasn't he a "dangerous anarchist"? Dreiser snapped, "If you meant that then you are an idiot and ought not to be at large." The rally at the Civic Auditorium attracted nearly 15,000 people, and Dreiser's speech drew noisy applause. He described his visit to Harlan and concluded that the Mooney case was "the same class warfare that has troubled Kentucky."

While in California, Dreiser made a quick change from radical advocate to capitalist writer, selling *Jennie Gerhardt* to B. P. Schulberg at Paramount. The terms were $25,000 to Dreiser for the rights plus 7 percent of Schulberg's one-third share of the profits as producer. Conspicuously absent from the contract was a clause giving Dreiser any say on the script. But Dreiser received oral assurances from director Marion Gering that the picture would be true to his book.

He had taken up *The Stoic* in earnest and acquired a new assistant to help him write it. Her name was Clara Clark; she was twenty-two, a dropout from Wheaton College and daughter of a distinguished Philadelphia Quaker family. Their collaboration started true to what was now a pattern: she wrote him an admiring letter after reading *An American Tragedy* and *Dawn*, and received an intimate reply: "Clara, Clara—Intense, aesthetic, poetic, your letter speaks to me . . . from Philadelphia, where, once, for a time I dwelt . . . would you come to see me here in New York, and we can talk?"

To Clara, bored, restless, unsure of what to do with her life, vaguely aspiring to be a novelist (she had written two unpublished manuscripts), his summons seemed "an open door, the only door on the horizon, a door leading to life." She decided to go to New York. He told her to stay at the Hotel Ansonia, and after she checked in he came to her room and they talked for a while. At first he was suspicious. Was she after publicity? So many were. She explained that she had recognized herself in *Dawn*, a misfit like him. He softened and told her to be thankful she was that way, rather than a dull conformist, and took her to his favorite French restaurant for dinner. When they returned to her room, he followed her in, shutting the door behind him. She realized that he had no intention of leaving.

He gave her a chapter of *The Stoic* to edit as a kind of test. She passed, and he offered her the job—six months' work at $25 a week. They settled into a routine. She would go to his suite in the morning, and he would sit in his rocking chair, an outline and research notes on Yerkes' career before him, and dictate the story to her. She decided that "for a famous novelist he was extremely humble about his writing. . . ."

He was trying hard to finish the book. As he wrote Louise, "If I can get it done I can do a lot with it because it completes a trilogy." He planned to "do some trading when the book is done." Not only would he have a new novel on the market, but after it had run its course his publisher could sell the trilogy as a set.

He was worried about money because in July, in an economy move (and also because *The Stoic* was overdue), the Liveright company had cut off his monthly stipend, "which means 7/8 of my annual income," he told Campbell. "That means Horn & Hardart, I guess. But with time I'll get down to bed rock—say $50 a week maybe. The good old days. . . . You don't need a janitor, do you?" He was thinking of moving to his old love, Harper's—soon, he hoped.

His other sources of income had dwindled. The mass magazines weren't paying as well as in the 1920s, and they weren't interested in the polemics he was writing. His name sold two controversial articles to *Liberty* for $1000 apiece, however. One, "The Seventh Commandment," was an attack on the laws against adultery and white slavery, and the editors added a disclaimer saying they disagreed with some of Dreiser's facts. (An excerpt from the article was clipped by an unidentified informant and sent to the Bureau of Investigation, U.S. Department of Justice. It is the earliest item in the security file the FBI kept on Dreiser until his death. The extract referred to the Federal authorities' reluctance to prosecute Mann Act violations except in actual prostitution cases.)

Other than those two pieces, Dreiser's magazine work was sparse, consisting of one short story, "Tabloid Tragedy," and some statements for left-wing publications. His returns from foreign sales of his books had dried up; his overseas publishers were hard hit by the Depression and had stopped paying royalties. His income from stocks and bonds had also dipped. In the 1920s his securities had yielded an income of around $6000 a year; now it was only $200. His living expenses were high, and he was still paying various researchers, supporting his three sisters and Rome, and sending Jug $200 a month.

To atone to Helen, he instructed Arthur Carter Hume to draw up a new will, leaving her two-thirds of all his property, including control of the Authors Holding Company, the copyrights to his books, Iroki, and the property they still owned in California. The will confirmed her status as the permanent woman in his life, however he might stray. He told Louise Campbell that in these chaotic times he admired Helen as much as anyone. "She keeps up a strong front & looks toward a simple form of existence under a new government. She likes flowers & dogs & the country & so I think she may come out OK. As for me!!?"

He must economize; no more sables for Helen. It was the simple life now. He let go some servants and reduced the payments to his sisters, who sent up a loud outcry. He decided to go to the Southwest for a month or so, where he could work undistracted and live more cheaply than in New York. He needed also to escape the myriad demands on him by this or that cause or organization. As he wrote Campbell, "I am sick of running a bureau & of being a clearing house for nothing. . . . Me for a simple hut in the west where I can write & save expenses. Everything seems to be going under."

And so in May 1932, Dreiser headed south, via ship to Galveston, taking Clara Clark along to do the driving and to help him work on *The Stoic*. From San Antonio, he wrote Helen that he was relieved to be out of New York. Now he wanted to get on with "writing or just living—and if it were not for my present women troubles I think it would be just living—certainly for a time anyhow—or vegetating." He wished he could talk to her without the usual "trouble waves of emotion & resentment . . . that lies between us. . . . I wish so much that we might be together in freedom & peace. But whether that can be I wonder. We are so individual and both of us were born free."

By June Dreiser had finished thirty-two chapters of *The Stoic*. In a letter to Esther McCoy from San Antonio he said he was working hard every day and believed that he could finish the book "in a month or so." But the fires of inspiration of 1912–1914 no longer burned as hot.

And there was also the matter of his new political commitment. Dorothy Dudley had asked him about his "turn away from interest in the financier to interest in the laborer." In a delayed reply he told her that "conditions as they are now are certain to be addled and to make ridiculous literary achievements. . . ." Nevertheless, he would complete the last volume of the Cowperwood trilogy, "which, I am sure, most of my critics will pounce on as decidedly unsocial and even ridiculous as coming from a man who wants social equity. Nevertheless, I am writing it just that way."

This *défi* to the Marxist critics was not entirely candid. For he did infuse his new views into *The Stoic,* though not in any obvious or didactic way. His main method was to soften Cowperwood so that he becomes less blatantly antisocial. The financier's motto is still "I satisfy myself," but Dreiser added a rationalizing gloss to those words in the early 1930s: "Intelligently or unintelligently [Cowperwood tells his mistress, Berenice Fleming], I try to follow the line of self-interest, because, as I see it, there is no other guide. Maybe I am wrong, but I think most of us do that. It may be that there are other interests that come before those of the individual, but in favoring himself, he appears, as a rule, to favor others."

In the novel, contrary to history, the London operation is proposed to Cowperwood by Berenice as something to keep him occupied and clear his name. (Yerkes said at the time that he expected London's transit system to be a bonanza—"the best chance I ever took.") Frank is already a multimillionaire and hardly needs the money. He will now create convenient, cheap transportation for Londoners, erase the stigma of his Chicago disgrace, and win acclaim as a social benefactor. He vows not to employ in Britain the "trickery he had been compelled to practice" in America or to engage in excessive profit-taking. But later, as though Dreiser sensed that his hero was becoming too saintly, he added, "In his heart, of course, he was by no means prepared to give over entirely his old tricks. . . ." He must still pyramid holding companies and sell the watered stock to a gullible public.

Dreiser and Cowperwood were at the same stage in their respective life cycles; fiction and reality rubbed uncomfortably close. Cowperwood's greatest triumphs were behind him; he was engaged in one final grand project, which he would not live to complete. Dreiser's greatest novel was behind him. Although he would tell an interviewer that his best work was still to come, he sometimes feared he was through. Recently, gazing at a portrait of himself by Wayman Adams, which Kirah Markham said he liked because it made him look like a successful financier, he had remarked despondently to a friend, "I am not that man any more." His sense of his own physical decline is refracted through Cowperwood. In one passage, later cut, he emphasizes the importance of Berenice's youth in reviving Cowperwood's vigor and confidence in himself—a function Dreiser's young women friends performed for him.

By the end of July he reported to Louise that he was on chapter 54. He had "sklaved" over the book, working from 9:00 to 5:00, sometimes 9:00 to 7:00. He sounded optimistic, pleased with what he had done. The first draft was of course too long, but when he had finished he would condense it and then "it will have a lot of go and color—and drama." In another letter to Campbell he reports that he has been cutting the script through chapter 45. He wonders why he has heard nothing from her, and thinks her silence "ominous." He began casting about for opinions and sent the manuscript to his old sounding board, Will Lengel, who liked it but wondered what sort of ending Dreiser had in mind. As the novel now stood, there was no foreshadowing of Cowperwood's ultimate fate: "Things come about almost too easily for him." It was a fair comment; the narrative lacked conflict and passion. Cowperwood is too bland; he sails smoothly through one squall after another, encountering few real storms save those of a domestic nature with his wife, Aileen. He meets some opposition to his plan for monopolizing the London transport system but easily overcomes it by wooing away its most powerful figures and upsetting the remaining rival. So it goes, punctuated by happy interludes with Berenice.

After completing a draft of chapter 54 (which corresponds to chapter 48 in the published book), Dreiser broke off. He would work on the novel sporadically in the coming months but to no avail. Possibly he had lost interest in the story, The last phase of Yerkes' career lacked the raw, dramatic conflicts that Dreiser had exploited so effectively in *The Financier* and *The Titan*, the revelations of the corrupt relationship between business and government that had stirred the cynical reporter years before. And he hadn't the visceral familiarity with London that he had with Philadelphia and Chicago, where the previous volumes had been set. Then, too, his English publisher, Otto Kyllmann, had warned of libel suits; some of Yerkes' rivals were still living. Cowperwood's financial maneuverings in Britain were just as audacious as his earlier schemes, but they didn't engage Dreiser, for the writing is flat. That left Frank's halfhearted social ambitions as a possible spark for irony, but Dreiser was not a novelist of manners.

Also inhibiting him were his problematic relations with the Liveright company. The publishers were breathing down his neck, and he always reacted hostilely to pressure. Canceling his monthly advance may have goaded him to retaliate by holding back the novel. Moreover, he did not believe his publisher could sell the novel. He later told Claude Bowers that the book business was so poor he had decided to keep *The Stoic* out of the market until better times.

A more immediate pretext to postpone the book was a new and interesting project that had come up in August. That was a literary magazine; Clara Clark had heard him discussing it with George Jean Nathan in a speakeasy the previous spring. Now Nathan had found a publisher and had invited Dreiser, Eugene O'Neill, James Branch Cabell, and Sinclair Lewis to serve on the editorial board. Ernest Boyd would be managing editor.

The magazine, to be called *The American Spectator,* intrigued Dreiser, and after various conditions were met—most important was that he would have a say in the editorial decisions—he signed on with an eagerness that suggests he was glad to get back into editorial harness. From Iroki and the Ansonia, and later from the *Spectator*'s offices, where Evelyn Light was given a desk, he loosed a swarm of letters to potential contributors.

The first issue was scheduled to appear in November, and frequent editorial meetings were held at Mike's, a speakeasy near the magazine's office on East Forty-first Street. These sessions were evidently heated as well as liquid, for after one Dreiser wrote Nathan, "You will always find me aggressive and insistent, probably irritatingly so, but the target and the goal is that evanescent thing, perfection."

As press time for the first issue drew close, he resorted to last-minute pleas reminiscent of his entreaties to Mencken for copy for the *Bohemian.* John Cowper Powys received this urgent summons: "Can you by some mystery swindle of your own let me have 12 or 15 hundred words for the Spectator by Friday." And to Nathan, two days later, a panicky telegram: WE MUST BE KIDDING OURSELVES. H.S. KRAFT JUST READ PROOFS. CALLS IT FLAT. INSISTS FATAL TO OPEN WITH THIS. . . PICKING UP CHAOS ARTICLE TONIGHT.

The "Chaos article" was not an account of an editorial meeting at Mike's, but the transcription of a conversation with Dr. Abraham A. Brill that never ran. By some mystery swindle of its own, the November issue of *The American Spectator* made it to the newsstands in more or less timely fashion. The format resembled a newspaper rather than a magazine, in keeping with the original title, "A Literary Newspaper," and the price was ten cents, which was not cheap since there were only four pages. The editors explained austerely that more pages would be added "only when and if the merit of sound copy on hand warrants it." They were permitted the luxury of integrity because there was no advertising. Its absence also assured them freedom from commercial pressures, and there were no taboos. The statement of editorial policy pledged that *The American Spectator* would prescribe no panaceas and had no axes to grind.

Swept along by his initial burst of enthusiasm, Dreiser continued in the ensuing months to solicit the kinds of stories that would ensure that the magazine reflected his concerns.

In January 1933, however, signs of editorial disharmony began to appear at the *Spectator.* In a letter to Nathan, Dreiser complains that the others aren't pulling their weight. "I do not think it is fair that . . . I should do all the pushing." And for the first time a piece he commissioned had been vetoed by his confreres. He told the contributor, a University of Wisconsin professor, "I cannot get the other editors to agree to any mention of Christ in connection with the economic and social dilemma in which we now find ourselves." More ominous was his complaint to Boyd and Nathan about an article by Thomas Beer that they had accepted and that Dreiser thought lightweight. His objections were overruled and the piece ran.

Meanwhile he had become involved in a film project, a movie called *Revolt*. It was based on a historical event, the rebellion of impoverished tobacco farmers in 1907 against the Duke tobacco trust. Hy Kraft was collaborating with him, and Dreiser sent him a three-page treatment: "It could be enormous—a sensational thing. I have not suggested here even a tithe of the powerful scenes, the sociologically and economically illuminating conversation that can and will be introduced." The picture would illustrate "the enormous profits that go to the top and the insignificant grains of reward that sift down to the man on the bottom. I think that now such things as that will not only be enormously illuminating but grimly and truthfully irritating, as well as sad."

This was to be Dreiser's contribution to the genre of revolutionary art. He even planned to direct the work, although he knew nothing about the technical aspects of filmmaking. He envisioned a powerful, even epic story à la Eisenstein, seething with social conflict and rebellious workers and heroes and villains. No love interest, though, he says in the brief treatment: "High drama in this instance will not require it. Tensity [sic] of economic emotion will replace love." The strike would result in a temporary victory for the farmers, but the great octopus of the trust will reach out to new sources of supply all over the world. "In the end . . . for all his struggles and pains, the worker will be where he was in the beginning—not much better and not much worse." No Hollywood *or* Marxist happy ending for Dreiser.

In February Kraft lined up a New York distributor and theater owner named Emanual J. Rosenthal to back the film, along with some others, including General Motors executive Joseph Fischler, who was serving as Dreiser's business adviser. In late January the principals decided to inspect locations for the film on the site of the actual tobacco wars in North Carolina and Kentucky, where the Night Riders, a group of tobacco growers, had burned out planters who would not join them in their fight against the Duke tobacco trust. In Hopkinsville, Kentucky, a firefight had erupted between armed growers led by an idealistic doctor named David A. Amass and a local militia defending the Duke interests. Amass became the model for Dreiser's hero.

The party, comprising Rosenberg, Kraft, Rothman (the director), and Dreiser, set off on January 29 in Rothman's car. By February 2 they were deep into tobacco country, in Durham, North Carolina. They inspected warehouses where auctioneers chanted their incantations and where ragged farmers, accompanied by their hollow-eyed children, brought their small crops to be sold for amounts that could provide only a bare subsistence.

By early March they were back at Iroki, and Dreiser, Kraft, and Rothman brainstormed a script while Clara Clark took notes. As she recalled, "I was set up in a corner of the studio to take dictation, which went on for several days, with a colossal amount of discussion and argument. We didn't get very far because suddenly they all disappeared."

Dreiser took over and, after some three weeks' work, completed a rough draft, which he then turned over to Anna Tatum for editing. She had reappeared in his life the previous fall, in need of a job, telling him she no longer objected to his writing *The Bulwark* and thinking it could be "an incredibly rich, complicated and tragic story." Anna, the model for Etta, Solon Barnes's rebellious daughter, reported that she had been cut out of her mother's will.

Dreiser tried to help her, but their collaboration almost foundered on the *Revolt* script, which Anna found too socialistic. Dreiser had strong feelings about the message he wished to convey—the importance of collective action—and accused Anna of being too individualistic and argumentative. Next he gave her some articles for the *Spectator* to rewrite, but that didn't work out either. In another letter (he seems to have met with her as little as possible), he confessed he was baffled about what to give her to do, since she told him she could work only on things that did not violate her convictions, which were "almost uniformly opposed to mine." Finally he assigned her to editing *The Stoic,* a task she found more congenial since she had helped him with *The Titan* in 1914.

Dreiser forwarded the revised script to Kraft in May. At this point the collaborators began to veer apart. In May he received a letter from Kraft, who reported, "I am still in the throes of preparing and adapting 'Revolt.' I am quite sure that this will be done before the end of the week. You know that I have worked diligently so that our joint efforts in this connection will meet with much hoped for success." Dreiser immediately suspected that Kraft was attempting to steal his script and wired him: YOU ARE NOT 'PREPARING' OR 'ADAPTING' 'REVOLT' FOR ME. YOU SHOULD BE ARRANGING A TECHNICAL SCREEN SHOOTING SCRIPT OF <u>MY</u> ORIGINAL MANUSCRIPT OF SAME AND NO MORE.

Dreiser soon linked Kraft with Rosenthal in a plot to steal his film and turn it into a Hollywood moneymaker, complete with love interest. All of his partners happened to be Jewish, including Kraft and Fischler, which did not smooth their business relationship. All but Fischler had some connections with the movie business, and at this time Dreiser was feuding with B. P. Schulberg over whether he, Dreiser, approved of the movie adaptation of *Jennie Gerhardt.* Schulberg had riled his touchy author in March by issuing a statement to the press in which he seemed to boast that Dreiser did not have a veto over the script. Dreiser countered that he had an oral commitment from Gering and the actress Sylvia Sidney, who played Jennie, "that this picture was to be made so that it would not only please but delight me." The quarrel raged in telegrams back and forth between Hollywood and New York and eventually petered out. When Dreiser saw the picture in June he wired Schulberg and Gering that he wholeheartedly approved of it. Schulberg replied that the movie had "previewed beautifully" and that "audience interest held throughout and steady tears from Vesta's death to end." Gering had made a four-handkerchief picture, which touched a sentimental nerve in Dreiser. Indeed, the coldness with which von Sternberg depicted Clyde may have been the critical factor in his dislike of the *Tragedy*.

The fracas with Schulberg may have soured Dreiser's relations with the producers of *Revolt*. He accused them of misleading him about the financing of the picture. The denouement came after Dreiser began referring to the financial arrangements as "kikey." Kraft was personally offended, and in Dreiser's suite at the Ansonia they had a violent argument and nearly came to blows. (In his autobiography Kraft improbably compares Dreiser to the Nazi Hermann Goering.)

It was a sad breakup for both men. Dreiser had relished the company of Kraft, who had an irreverent New York wit and acted as a kind of court jester and confidant—a younger Mencken, perhaps. For five years they had been very close. Dreiser would come to Kraft's room and talk to him for hours. Kraft would entertain him and sometimes tease him. For the younger man, who shared Dreiser's leftist politics, the breakup meant the toppling of an idol, a novelist whose sympathy for the oppressed he deeply admired.

In the aftermath, Dreiser and Kraft copyrighted their respective scripts so that if one tried to make the movie the other could sue. In Dreiser's more literary version, *Revolt* is a documentary about the tobacco industry, full of his brooding pessimism. In the end the doctor is fatally wounded in the skirmish following the torching of the tobacco warehouses; just before he dies, he learns that President Teddy Roosevelt has ordered the government to bring an antitrust suit against Duke's American Tobacco Company. The final scene is an unmistakably Dreiserian touch: a shot of a neglected grave in a rural cemetery. The tombstone reads: "Amos Haines—A Country Doctor."

Dreiser continued to try to interest a producer and changed the title to *Tobacco*, perhaps to make the picture seem less militant. When Fischler showed the script to an independent film company, the president suggested that the two leads—the doctor and the son of Duke—be rivals for a woman. Dreiser commented: "Just as I feared, what is on his mind is a picture narrowed down to the usual love story with some tobacco smoking in the background."

May 1933 was not a merry one for Dreiser. The break with Kraft was followed closely by the bankruptcy of Horace Liveright Inc. The latter news could not have come as a surprise, since the company had been in an increasingly feeble state. An estimated $115,000 was out in unearned advances to authors, including some $17,000 to Dreiser, who had not produced since *Tragic America.*

Dreiser was probably not completely aware of the disaster facing him, for the contract he had renewed in January 1932 carried a provision that in case of bankruptcy the agreement was nullified. Eugene O'Neill had negotiated a similar provision and transferred from Liveright to Random House with no problems. But Liveright still owed him back royalties, while Dreiser was in arrears. At this point in the company's fortunes, the unearned advances were considered assets—debts that could be collected. Of course many writers could never pay them, but the largest debtor was Dreiser, who was reputed to be quite solvent. If Dreiser had handed over a completed *Stoic* there would have been no further trouble. Arthur Pell, still head of the company, told Dreiser that his debt could be liquidated in four or five years through the sale of new and backlist titles. Pell wanted, or needed, a going concern, and obviously authors like Dreiser and O'Neill, plus certain other writers, would have formed the nucleus of a new, slimmer, but profitable company.

But Dreiser had no intention of staying. Even if he retained any liking for Pell, which seems doubtful, he had no confidence in him as a publisher. Now he wanted to use the unfinished novel as a bargaining counter in negotiations with his next publisher.

In July the assets of the Liveright company were sold for $18,000. Pell, who had held on to his majority share of stock, remained as publisher. Lost in the upheaval were two new books on Liveright's spring list: *Death in the Woods,* a collection of Sherwood Anderson's recent stories (some of his best), and a brilliant, mordant novel, *Miss Lonelyhearts* by Nathanael West.

Dreiser's next step was to exercise his rights under the bankruptcy clause in his contract. According to this provision, he was entitled to purchase plates, sheets, and bound volumes on hand at the manufacturing cost. If the parties couldn't agree on the price, the dispute would go to arbitration. Pell demanded a large sum, and Dreiser offered a fraction of it. Pell eventually reduced his price and counterclaimed for some $14,577 in unearned advances (mainly the total of the monthly $1250 paid to Dreiser between April 1929 and July 1932), and $2400 for copies of the luxury edition of a poem, *Epitaph,* he claimed had been sold to Dreiser. After further to-and-froing between the lawyers, Dreiser's side refused to go to arbitration, and the various claims and counterclaims were tossed in the lap of a judge. He ruled that the value of the plates and books must be submitted to arbitration per the contract but that the question of unearned advances must be settled in court.

All this came as a shock to Dreiser, who still thought that the new company had no right to print or sell his backlist titles because of the bankruptcy clause in his contract. Furthermore, he told Hume, Pell had assured him in the past that his name had been worth $15,000 to the firm, and if the company went out of business, he would write off that sum against Dreiser's debts. Now, however, Pell was suing him as a common debtor. Dreiser's backlist books were like contraband; some had creditors' liens on them, others were concealed in a warehouse somewhere. He feared, with some reason, that Pell was surreptitiously dumping them on the market. And the plates were in danger of being sold at a creditors' auction.

Dreiser wrote Hume that he was "dreadfully worried" about the entire business; further delay would do him "great harm," hampering him in finding another publisher and preventing the sale of his old books, notably *Jennie,* for which the movie might have created a demand.

In a sad footnote to these unpleasant proceedings, Horace Liveright died on September 4, alone, in a shabby hotel room in New York City, of pneumonia. He was only forty-six. At the time of his death he was supposed to have been readying a play called *Hotel Alimony* for Broadway production and writing his autobiography, *The Turbulent Years,* but those projects were only the last of Horace's ballyhoo. Dreiser attended the funeral along with a handful of others. If all the authors and editors whom Liveright had given a starting push had shown up, it would have been the literary event of 1933, if not the decade—O'Neill, Hemingway, Faulkner, Anderson, Katherine Anne Porter, E. A. Robinson, S. J. Perelman, among others.

That summer Dreiser and Helen visited John Cowper Powys and his companion, Phyllis Playter, and Arthur Ficke and his wife, Gladys, at their homes near Hillsdale, New York. Dreiser showed Ficke some of the new poems he had written with Clara Clark for an expanded edition of *Moods.* After one of those sojourns, he thanked the Fickes for "Heaving sunlit fields warm with sunheat. An old house permeated with genuine sweetness . . . mint juleps and the depths of life and space staggeringly suggested by diatoms. And naked bathing in rain and sunlight; and dreams and their sure evanescence." He added a P.S.: "Catch Jack alone in the fields. Throw a bag over him, truss him up and deliver him to me."

When the Fickes stayed at Iroki, Dreiser told Arthur about his deep sense of self-loathing. Ficke responded that "a man must learn to forgive himself." Dreiser repeated the phrase, "A man must learn to forgive himself," like a mantra. His angry outbursts were like the action in physics; his depressions, the inevitable reaction.

CHAPTER **32**   *Minority of One*

> What I cannot understand is why there are so many groups
> and why they waste so much time critically belaboring each
> other and ridiculing each other for their interpretation of
> Marx, when the world situation and particularly the Amer-
> ican situation requires a united front against a very obvious
> problem.
>
> —Dreiser to Max Eastman (1933)

Another incident in May 1933 had delayed-action consequences for Dreiser. This was the notorious "Editorial Conference (With Wine)," which appeared in *The American Spectator.* In May, Nathan, Boyd, Dreiser, Cabell, and O'Neill met for a sometimes facetious discussion of Jews, with a stenographer taking it down. The backdrop, if not the occasion, was the rising incidence of attacks on Jews in Germany and Hitler's accession as chancellor.

For Dreiser, the symposium, published in the *Spectator*'s September issue, had lasting reverberations. He uttered some foolish statements that took him almost the rest of his life to live down; for example, Jews were "altogether too successful in the professions, as well as in science, philosophy, education, trade, finance, religious theory, musicianmanship . . . painting, poetry, and the other arts." His "real quarrel with the Jew" was "that he is really too clever and too dynamic in his personal and racial attacks on all other types of persons and races." In certain professions "where shrewdness rather than creative labor is the issue" Jews unfairly excelled. They should be made to accept a handicap: "Thus 100,000 Jewish lawyers might be reduced to ten and the remainder made to do farming."

For weeks afterward, Dreiser was full of his great plan to solve the "Jewish problem." Eleanor Anderson, Sherwood's wife, made the following entry in her diary following a luncheon with Dreiser not long after the symposium appeared: "Teddy is really an evangelist raving about how you can get anything over. . . . He's now all hipped on a big exposure of Catholicism."

Dreiser's ideas were a loose amalgam of Zionism and anti-Semitism, the former picked up from Ludwig Lewisohn, an early American Zionist, and the latter a ragbag of notions and subrational resentments, common to his times and indigenous to his provincial, Catholic boyhood. He had written in *Dawn* of his resentment against the Jewish brothers for whom he worked in Chicago. In the original manuscript the description of them was harsh, but he later toned it down to say that all Jews were not like this. There are hints of bias in letters in the early 1900s, but from his experiences in New York and walks on the Lower East Side he gained a sympathy for poor, immigrant Jews. In the 1920s he associated with a few wealthy "our crowd" German-descended Jews of New York who looked down on the new immigrants and with the occasional one like Nathan, who obliterated their ethnic heritage. Then, there was his constant bickering over money with Liveright and Pell, and his fights with Jewish producers in Hollywood, which reactivated his dormant prejudices. Once again "clever Jews" had outsmarted him. And he was, in the case of Pell, scapegoating a Jew for the consequences of the Crash, which had forced Liveright Inc. into bankruptcy. It was in the early 1930s that friends began to notice his anti-Semitic remarks, though when challenged he would deny that he in any way hated Jews. And in a sense he did not: he was drawing on the deadly arsenal of anti-Semitism to express his grievances—at least partly imagined—against *certain* Jews.

He sincerely believed that Jews should have a national homeland; unfortunately he expressed this half-digested idea in sweeping language that blundered into the rhetoric of the brutal anti-Semites in Europe. At other times he seemed to advocate assimilation as an alternative to emigration— Jews should drop their insistence on a Jewish identity, Jewish customs and, more outrageously, Jewish "sharp practices," and become "Americans," as all the other immigrant groups had done. Here there were distant echoes of the trauma of the German-Americans deracinated in World War I and his own identity as a second-generation son in rebellion against his rigid, old-world father, and embracing American ways.

An interested reader of the "Editorial Conference" was Hutchins Hapgood, unwitting model for the character J.J. in "Esther Norn." Hapgood conducted a lengthy correspondence with Dreiser, he playing the righteous prosecutor as the latter further incriminated himself with wild statements like "If you listen to Jews discuss Jews, you will find that they are money-minded, very pagan, very sharp in practice. . . ." Hapgood was of old WASP stock, but he had written a book, *The Spirit of the Ghetto*, in the early 1900s that portrayed immigrant life sympathetically, and he had a more sophisticated, liberal attitude toward discrimination than Dreiser (though he, too, favored assimilation). He compared Dreiser's views to those of the Ku Klux Klan or the Nazis.

In a subsequent letter Dreiser backed down and for the first time took note of the sinister train of events in Germany:

> I am supposedly barbarous and anti-Semitic because in the face of all the attacks upon the Jews, their crucifixion in Germany and elsewhere, I rise to assert that these very gifted and highly integrated and self-protective people are, whatever their distinguished equipment, mistaken in attempting to establish themselves as Jews, with their religion, race characteristics, race solidarity and all, in the bosom, not of any one country or people, but rather in the lands and nations of almost every country the world over. . . . It is time for them . . . to realize that they are, after all, a dispersed and, in many ways, annoyed race or put upon nation, and that, as such—and anti-Semitism being what it is today, culture and liberality to the contrary notwithstanding—they should now take steps to assemble and consider their state and their future.

He was still convinced that a Jewish state was the best solution for anti-Semitism, and that "the Zionist movement being what it is," Jews would choose that option. But if no homeland was available, then there should be "a program of race or nation blending here in America. . . ."

Although Dreiser had begun to retreat from his extreme proposals, he still regarded Jews as an indigestible remnant, and blamed them for provoking anti-Semitism. He ignored the historical, medieval Christian roots of anti-Semitism. And he assumed Jews were a monolithic "race," which they weren't—certainly not in America.

Meanwhile, more trouble had befallen him in September. The three arbitrators had at last rendered their decision in his dispute with Pell, and it was an expensive one for the author. The panel set a price of $6500 for the plates—more than three times what Dreiser had offered and $2500 more than the receiver had paid for them at the bankruptcy auction.

At least he had by then found a new publisher. On September 28 he signed a contract with Simon & Schuster. He received an advance of $5000 for three books—The Stoic, a collection of short stories, and Volume III of his autobiography—and an additional $2000 toward purchasing the plates of published books from Liveright. Simon & Schuster would acquire the stock of his old books from his former publisher; this outlay was also considered an advance against royalties, making a total of $10,000.

The publisher announced the banns in a portentous advertisement:

"The Works of Theodore Dreiser, past, present and future will henceforth be published by Simon & Schuster. . . . The fame of Theodore Dreiser is an unshakable bulwark. He symbolizes the heroic mind and comprehending heart." And there was a lavish wedding feast—a cocktail party at Iroki attended by some 300 luminaries of the publishing and Broadway worlds, their spouses, husbands, and friends.

Messrs. Simon and Schuster had a prickly genius on their hands, but they were determined to humor him. The first test came when Dreiser submitted a manuscript. It was not, as they had hoped and expected, *The Stoic*, but a revised and expanded edition of *Moods*. M. Lincoln Schuster rose to the challenge. He read the manuscript over the weekend and sent an enthusiastic report to the author: "It is an outpouring of selfhood—in your own words, 'The demon of a secret poet.' What a sweep of phantasms, exaltations, dirges, and defiances." Dreiser replied that he was, at long last, happy to have "a publisher who speaks my own language." Schuster, however, had neglected to say whether he actually *liked* the poems.

After joining Simon & Schuster, Dreiser filed for a divorce from *The American Spectator* in January 1934, citing irreconcilable differences. He had the previous fall threatened to resign and Nathan made placatory gestures. But the problems he complained of were not remedied. In his bill of particulars Dreiser charged that the manuscript mail was being censored—articles of merit were rejected by Boyd and Nathan without consulting him. The two had blackballed a piece he commissioned, calling it "junk," and so, "I now find certain definite mental processes of mine being commented on as junk." He also contended that the magazine had a double standard regarding religion. Criticism of the Catholic Church was forbidden, while Protestants were fair game. This situation had grown worse after Catherine McNelis, a Catholic, succeeded Richard R. Smith as publisher. He objected to management's decision to solicit advertising to alleviate the periodical's deficit, on the ground that it would compromise editorial independence. Also, although he did not say it, Dreiser favored publishing more political material in the magazine. Not "direct social arguments," or ideology, he explained to John Dos Passos, but "presentations of specific instances of extreme social injustice as it relates to the individual."

Nathan and his ally Boyd would not relinquish editorial control of the magazine, so there was little Dreiser could do but resign. Asked if the editors had bickered, he told the *World Telegram*, "Of course there were quarrels. . . . That's why it was so good. There were enough fights to wreck a building."

Not long after the rift with Nathan, Dreiser reconciled with his oldest living enemy—H. L. Mencken. The reunion came about when Dreiser corrected an erroneous statement made by Burton Rascoe in a history of the

Smart Set. Breaking the nine-year silence, he wrote to Mencken, explaining what he had done. His old comrade thanked him and added, "I am seriously thinking of doing my literary and pathological reminiscences, probably in ten volumes folio. This is my solemn promise to depict you as a swell dresser, a tender father, and one of the heroes of the Argonne."

Dreiser's answer began with a one-word paragraph that seemed a sigh of relief: "Thanks." He proposed they meet on neutral ground in New York, "white flags in hand," and invited Mencken and his wife, the former Sara Haardt, a young writer whom he had married in 1930, to visit him at Iroki. "Helen and I still hold together," Dreiser said, speaking one couple to another. Mencken responded that he would be delighted to have a session with Dreiser, and forwarded a "recent portrait so that you might recognize me"—a fat, balding old man with a walrus mustache.

When Dreiser's Harlan investigation made headlines, Mencken was unimpressed, telling a friend that the communists were "making a dreadful fool of him, and taking him off his work. . . . I have no animosity to him, but he has become too tragic to be borne. Seeing him would be like visiting an old friend who has gone insane, or had both legs cut off."

Their first rendezvous took place on December 4 at the Ansonia. Mencken found Dreiser a bit grayer, a bit thinner, and possessed of two legs. Both men were at first uneasy, and Dreiser had taken care to have a third party present, Arnold Gingrich, editor of *Esquire,* who was awed by the two giants. But after downing two bottles of vodka, they were disputing as raucously as ever. They steered away from politics, though, and their fiercest argument was over which German restaurant they should dine at.

Hardly had they reconvened but Dreiser was asking Mencken's advice on whether to accept an invitation from Henry Seidel Canby to join the National Institute for Arts and Letters. Mencken replied as if it were still 1915: "Canby's letter offers you a great honor, and if you were a man properly appreciative you'd burst into tears." He pointed out that membership would elevate Dreiser to the august company of artists like Struthers Bart, Owen Davis, Hermann Hagedorn, and Edna Ferber—not to mention the venerable Hamlin Garland, who had refused to sign the *"Genius"* petition. Dreiser turned Canby down.

In a phrase Dreiser often used, it had been a long time between drinks.

Generally, he remained aloof from communist causes and especially the bitter sectarian disputes that shook the CPUSA. But there were times when he was forced to take sides. The first such occasion was a request from Eastman in 1933 that he sign a petition protesting the imprisonment of Trotsky's followers in Russia. After seeking advice from the head of the New York office of Amtorg, the Soviet trading company, Dreiser told Eastman, "Whatever the nature of the present dictatorship in Russia—

unjust or what you will—the victory of Russia is all-important. I hold with Lincoln: Never swap horses while crossing a stream." At that time, he regarded Russia as threatened by the Japanese invasion of Manchuria, the opening thrust in a general offensive by the capitalist nations to overthrow the Soviet state. Best to wait until the threat has eased before criticizing.

Later, he and Eastman (who was considered a renegade by the American CP) agreed that what the left needed was a united front, composed of all the various noncommunist splinter groups. Dreiser's main contribution was a plan whereby the followers of Alfred Bingham's independent radical weekly, *Common Sense*, would merge with A. J. Muste's American Workers Party. It got nowhere.

Dreiser was discouraged, writing Bruce Crawford early in 1935, "Personally I despair of communistic efforts in this country. There are too many groups, too much quarreling, and the main sentiment of America seems to be more anti-[communist] than pro." He then became enamored of Technocracy, which had recently enjoyed an enormous vogue as a panacea for the nation's economic ills. He had known Howard Scott when they were living in the Village, and Scott was espousing a total overhaul of the economic system, with engineers in charge.

Dreiser's relations with the CP reached a nadir in 1935. Hapgood published his correspondence with Dreiser, who had given his permission, in *The Nation*. The Party, which had a large Jewish membership in New York City and which was also anti-Zionist, felt it had to come down on its most prominent literary icon. It dispatched a delegation to Iroki to pray with the sinner, but the meeting produced only a partial recantation. In a statement published in *The New Masses*, Dreiser insisted that he made a distinction "between the Jewish worker and the Jewish exploiter. Everybody knows that I am an anti-capitalist. . . . I have no hatred for the Jew and nothing to do with Hitler or fascism. . . ." He admitted for the first time that perhaps his contentious business dealings with Jews had influenced him, but he resented the Party delegation's dictating to him what to think and reacted with predictable truculence, especially after some members insultingly hinted that perhaps he was getting old—in other words a little soft in the head. He told them, "I am an individual, I have a right to say what I please."

The Nation exchange (headed "Is Dreiser Anti-Semitic?") sullied his reputation, if not among the general public, then certainly among leftist intellectuals. Friends like Ruth Kennell stood by him, but she told him she was constantly having to defend him and asked him to explain himself; he evaded her. The incident seems not to have cost him any of his Jewish friends, but he made an effort to reassure them. To A. A. Brill he wrote, "all reports to the contrary I do not hate Jews as you must know." Brill apparently replied in a friendly vein, for Dreiser thanks him in his next letter. And he told Joseph Fischler, "In spite of my alleged anti-Semitism, I still pick and choose, as you know, and I would not trade one of my selections, for some ten thousand of the other kind." In the next sentence he mentions snubbing Hy Kraft in Hollywood; presumably Kraft was one of the "other kind." Dreiser continued to believe that Hapgood had exaggerated their "mild" exchange and predicted to Charles E. Yost that the storm would soon blow over.

Gradually, though, he backed off his extreme ideas. To a later correspondent, he pointed out that his books contained not a scintilla of anti-Semitism, citing *The Hand of the Potter*. He also cited the banning of his books in Germany as proof that he was *not* anti-Semitic. Dreiser believed that his blacklisting was the result of a mistaken idea that he was Jewish. Actually, the Nazis banned him because they considered him a communist.

The ban had hurt him financially; thanks to the efforts of his Hungarian-German publisher, Paul Zsolnay, he enjoyed a growing popularity before Hitler came to power. And so, rather than make a ringing protest against Nazi book-burning in general, he asked friends like Mencken to suggest someone in the German government to whom he could point out the mistake. Mencken told him that he knew no one in the Nazi regime, that Hitler seemed to be a lunatic, and that his German friends were all in the opposition.

As the Hitler regime's outrages against German Jews became more brazen, Dreiser reconsidered his view that the mistreatment was the victims' fault. In 1934 he had called for Jews to defy the world and "take whatever steps necessary to overcome" the persecution to which they had been subjected for centuries. Their power was sufficient to have an impact, he said. If they did not act, they might face increasingly cruel measures. At last he had recognized the abyss to which anti-Semitism led.

Out of favor with the CP *apparat* because of his earlier statements on the Jewish question, Dreiser decided henceforth to deal only with Moscow, turning out pro-Soviet statements on request. His relations with the Soviet cultural bureaucracy became strained, however, when Gosizdat was dilatory about paying royalties on his books. His response was to go on strike. To L. Cherniavsky, chief of the science and arts section of VOKS, he complained that he had performed "every known service from writing to speaking to entering dangerous areas in order to bring about favorable results for mistreated and injured American workers, and always at my expense. . . . Accordingly now I feel that if further material of mine is to be used it should be paid for in order that I might recapture at least a fraction of the money that I have expended on Russia's behalf here and in Russia." (His Russian tour had, of course, been paid for by the Soviet government. He probably bore the expenses of the Harlan trip—certainly he paid for the stenographer who recorded the miners' testimony, because he later billed the NCDPP for the amount.) The following year he received partial payment for a new Russian edition of *An American Tragedy* and asked Dinamov to find out what had happened to the rest of the money.

It was his nature to get what was coming to him from a publisher—capitalist or statist—and his love for the Soviet Union did not extend to donating free books to the Russian people. In fact, when a Soviet library asked him for a complete set of his works he refused on the grounds that he "did enough."

The sensational 1936–1938 Moscow trials of alleged traitors to the state puzzled Dreiser, as it did many communist sympathizers. He had even met some of the accused—the charming Bukharin, the disenchanted Radek, fellow novelist Pilnyak, who had earlier denounced one of his own books as heretical. In March 1937, participating in a symposium on the tribunal in *The Modern Monthly,* Dreiser confessed that he found the affair "very confusing." The parade of abject confessions, for example, he saw as "a real triumph of the spirit of self-abnegation. . . ." The psychology was puzzling, but, unless they had been tortured, these men seemed to be sacrificing their lives to preserve the system. It was all a Dostoevsky novel, full of murder and revenge, sin and repentance. The Russians stood revealed as "more capable than any other nationality of proceeding by devious, subtle, fanatical methods, incomprehensible and unjustified for the western mind."

In his psychological interpretation Dreiser was not echoing the Party; his views more closely reflected Walter Duranty's reports in *The New York Times* and *The New Republic*. He regarded Duranty as the best-informed, most objective American correspondent in Moscow. The *Times* man was an agnostic about the guilt or innocence of the defendants, but found reasons to believe that Trotsky and his supporters were plotting to overthrow Stalin.

Dreiser had always steered clear of U.S. Trotskyist groups. He was wary about associating himself with any faction, however impeccable its leftist credentials, that opposed the Stalin regime. When John Dewey and a committee of anti-Stalinist liberals undertook an investigation to ascertain the facts about the accusations against the Moscow trial defendants, Dreiser signed a petition condemning the probe because it would "lend support to fascist forces." The following year, however, his name did not appear among the 150 intellectuals who signed a statement that the trials had "by the sheer weight of evidence established a clear presumption of the guilt of the defendants." The two statements, taken together, might sum up his position: he didn't know if the defendants were guilty or not, but the Soviet Union should be left to its own devices in determining its internal enemies.

Stalin's wholesale purges began to hit home. In the summer of 1937, Calvin Bridges came to Iroki with a list of Soviet physicists whom Stalin had purged. Bridges had been sympathetic to the Russian experiment but denounced this rape of intellectual freedom. Shocked, Dreiser strongly agreed.

And in 1938 Sergei Dinamov, his staunch Russian admirer, was arrested. Dreiser could not understand what had happened, since Dinamov was a loyal communist, and attempted to learn his whereabouts, but to no avail. He wrote Ruth Kennell, "What has become of Sergei? Not a word in 7 months! . . . Are they going to try him? And he's so truly sweet and good." (It was not until 1943 that Kennell learned his fate: imprisoned for embezzlement and later killed in the war.)

Dreiser's doubts about the Soviet experiment emerged in a shaggy colloquy with John Dos Passos, which was published in Marguerite Tjader Harris's little magazine, *Direction*, in January 1938. He admits, "Well I was strong for Russia and for Stalin and the whole program, but in the last year, I have begun to think that maybe it won't be any better than anything else." When Dos Passos confessed that he didn't understand what was going on in Russia, Dreiser said damned if he did either. Dreiser thought that although the communists' economic and social program had succeeded, severe ideological constraints remained in force. Those perhaps represented "a temporary condition . . . an attempt to achieve cohesion and unity." He predicted that eventually "Russia will be liberalized" as a result of the people demanding religious freedom and "less standardization in life."

As ever, he was opposed to harnessing literature to the service of a political cause. To the novelist Evelyn Scott, a bitter anticommunist, he wrote that propaganda "is a very minor criterion in art" and that the U.S. communists were carrying it to absurd lengths. Why, only the other day, "some young writer was telling me that a man would write a better book if he had read and understood the Marxian dialectic! Imagine!" It was, he goes on, "better to praise books, no matter what the artist's point of view is, which have a broad, sympathetic, human view and which show the roots of all reforms and changes" rather than "call down the curses of heaven or communism on the real man who does not think in party terms at all . . . I don't think lack of social content is enough reason to call a book bad."

What he wanted for America, he later said, was "What Russia has plus mental freedom." Yet he gave the Soviet state the benefit of the doubt. As he had said to Bukharin in Moscow, a "benevolent tyranny" was needed "until all men have brains sufficient to appreciate good." But Dreiser's communism was a dream of justice and equity rather than an ideological creed. And he savored the joke about the communist speaker in Union Square who promises, "Comes the Revolution you'll all eat strawberries and cream." A heckler cries, "But I don't like strawberries and cream." The speaker replies, "Comes the Revolution you'll *have* to like strawberries and cream." Dreiser realized the jest was on him: he wanted strawberries and cream for all—but he didn't want anyone telling him to eat them.

CHAPTER 33

The Formula Called Man

> The mystery of life—its inexplicability, beauty, cruelty,
> tenderness, folly, etc., etc.—has occupied the greater part
> of my waking thoughts; and in reverence or rage or irony,
> as the moment or situation might dictate, I have pondered
> and even demanded of cosmic energy to know *Why.*
>
> —Dreiser, "What I Believe" (1929)

Disillusioned with politics, though not the cause of equity, Dreiser was also stymied artistically. "I've written novels," he once said to Marguerite Tjader Harris, "now I want to do something else."

Messrs. Simon and Schuster would not have appreciated that news. They were expecting *The Stoic,* the big book they believed would revive Dreiser's reputation and sales of his backlist titles. It was due by the end of 1935. But all they got was *Moods,* the volume of poetry, regarding which Richard Simon said, frankly, it would help sales if the book were shorter; it now ran to 570 pages. Dreiser complained that Simon's suggestions left him "very dubious as to the attitude of the house in regard to the book and to me." This book was different from an earlier edition that Liveright published. Dreiser had added many new poems and revised others in line with his scientific speculations. The new *Moods* was not a volume of lyrical poetry; it was an attempt "to express an individual philosophy lyrically, that is, cadenced and declaimed. . . ."

Moods appeared in 1935, trailing the unwieldy subtitle *Philosophical and Emotional (Cadenced and Declaimed)*—Dreiser's best effort to come up with a new name. Neither author nor publisher was happy with the result. It was sparsely reviewed, the critics apparently assuming that it was not a new work. It yielded the author about $400 in royalties.

Simon and Schuster continued to press for a delivery date on *The Stoic*. On January 21, 1936, Dreiser wrote Simon that he could not give them the novel, and he added, "Will it make much difference if I give you a really important book and follow it later with *The Stoic*?" Schuster replied that the firm was "deeply disappointed"; could they talk with him? Dreiser remained evasive, and the publishers did not track him down until the summer.

Another event had complicated relations between author and publisher. In June 1936 *The Nation* ran an article by the labor writer Ben Stolberg called "The Jew and the World." In a lengthy letter, agreeing with most of Stolberg's points, Dreiser's tone was sadder and wiser. He admitted that his attitude toward Jews was emotional, even prejudiced, resulting from unpleasant experiences with them in business matters. He confesses, "No doubt, today I look for what I dislike in Jews, and dislike what I would normally pass over in another. *Mea culpa!*" Such an attitude "in a time like this of social unrest, nationalism, jingoism, etc. . . . might in some groups lead to a pogrom. Yet this is decidedly what I do not want. Rather I have been always seeking a solution, for in a day of violence the obvious causes might not be the real ones. We in America might have as false justifications as there have been in Germany. We would have, of course, economic jealousy as a base. But still, there is always the much more powerful factor of the intangible fanaticism against the scapegoat through which we must always rationalize our unfulfilled desires and disappointments. *Mea culpa!*"

After the letter to *The Nation* was published, Dreiser worried about the effect on his publishers, and he wrote them that he had heard they were "surprised" about his views on the Jewish question. He assured them, "My personal friendship for you has nothing to do with the problems that Stolberg discusses." Simon and Schuster seemed not to have taken offense, but Dreiser got the idea they had, and this belief would have delayed consequences.

The "really important book" he offered them instead was the work of scientific philosophy that would obsess him for the next five years. In 1934 he had begun writing essays for it. As he explained to Sherwood Anderson: "What I am really doing is seeking to interpret this business of life to myself. My thought is, if I ever get it reasonably straight for myself I will feel more comfortable." He was at bottom seeking scientific confirmation of God, or a creator, just as he had consulted scientists for confirmation of his fictional characters. Marguerite Tjader Harris, who was probably more sympathetic to his quest than anyone, recalled, "He was searching for *facts*—in chemistry, in biology, in astronomy, in psychology . . . which, he hoped, would eventually make up answers, or some of the answers, to the questions he had endlessly asked. How? Why?"

An insight into his inner turmoil was a series of rambling conversations he had with Dr. Abraham A. Brill two years before, intended for publication in the *Spectator* under the title "Chaos." At one of these sessions, which were held at the psychiatrist's apartment on West Seventieth Street, Dreiser asked Brill: "Does life have any objective which means anything? Or is there nothing to hope for, nothing to live for, nothing to be honorable for, nothing to be honest for?" Brill responded, "Blessed are those who expect nothing, for they shall not be disappointed." Dreiser said: "I ask about rewards because I'm trying to establish from you that the whole process is practically chaos. Why don't you say so?" Brill countered: "You have never detached yourself from your early Christian training—you expect rewards." Dreiser yearned for a just God in Heaven; otherwise all was meaningless.

Once he told a woman whom he accused of being unfaithful, "God, how is one to live without faith? Hell is that lack of faith that breeds lack of hope." Hell, Dostoevsky said, is the inability to love. Love presumes a capacity for trust; in a universe of chaos there can be no trust.

Somewhere in the shadows of Dreiser's early boyhood, in the poverty and secret sorrows, his ability to trust had been severely crippled. This impediment left an aching void of loneliness inside him. Only his mother had given him the unconditional love he needed, and she had abandoned him. "I am the loneliest man in the world," he often said. Kirah Markham had long ago noted his "utter sense of loneliness." Hy Kraft had seen it in the 1920s: "He was . . . suffering a loneliness that must have been beyond his own powers of description." Kraft told Marguerite Harris, "He was very suspicious of everybody—always afraid someone was going to gyp him." And Yvette Szekely Eastman recalled, "There was a sad loneliness about him. He was always saying how lonely he was."

Clara Clark once took him to visit her Quaker relatives at the family summer home in the Poconos. He was enthralled by her brother, Warner, a sturdy, gentle, clear-eyed young man who worked for the American Friends Service Committee. Clara noted in her diary: "He always seems to be searching for people who will not let him down."

Out of his profound loneliness came his sympathy with the outsiders looking in, those who didn't belong, who desired the light and warmth inside the walled city. Out of it too came his surgical detachment which enabled a part of his mind to coldly observe life and to recount—with pity—the pitiless workings of fate. Buried in his abortive attempt to join the Communist Party was a need to find a symbolic communion with others in a cause. It had led to his conversion from extreme individualism to the ideal of a socialistic society in which extreme individualism was curbed. In a similar way he yearned to "join" the universe, to merge the isolated, outcast, mortal ego into a larger, immortal I. But always belonging must be on his terms.

A friend observed that Dreiser had "an orphan feeling," a sense of "neglect on the part of the world." A corollary to that was a need for erotic love and also universal love, in the form of success, fame, and applause. He sought a loving creator to whom all creatures great and small, human, animal, vegetable, and mineral, were of equal worth, as a mother's love bathes equally all her children.

But this mother had abandoned him. In a joking moment he once told Esther McCoy, "Life is a stepmother. You try to get her attention. You cry and hold on to her skirt and she pushes you aside. Then you give up and she calls, 'Johnny, do you want a pickle?'" Stepmother Nature was a more benign version of the creator he often envisioned, who might be devilish or demonic, at times malevolently inimical to him. He broached the problem of evil in the title essay of *Hey, Rub-a-Dub-Dub!* On the one hand Dreiser imagined "some great elemental spirit holding for order of sorts. . . ." And on the other, the Prince of Misrule—chaos—"vast schemes of chicane grinding the faces of the poor, and wars brutally involving the death of millions whose lives are precious to them because of the love of power on the part of someone or many. . . . Brute strength sits empurpled and laughs a throaty laugh." Life fed on life. There were blinding flashes of beauty in creation, moments of pleasure and tenderness, but how reconcile them with the principle of blind cruelty that seemed the driving engine of a mechanistic cosmos?

In February 1935 Dreiser was laid low by bronchitis, accompanied by an unusually severe and bizarre attack of depression. This psychic storm undoubtedly had physical causes, but its resemblance to a spiritual crisis, according to the criteria of William James, has been noted by Robert Elias. Dreiser wrote of this experience to George Douglas, the one friend in whom he perceived a similar mystical bent and with whom he felt a "psychic osmosis." He had already discussed with Douglas their collaborating on the work of philosophy that he had titled "The Formula Called Man." He had sent the journalist two essays to critique. Douglas's response, Dreiser told him, was the only one that was *completely* understanding."

At the heart of Dreiser's thinking was the idea of man as a tool or mechanism of the creator, an idea he had entertained since at least 1914 (and injected into *The "Genius"*), after his vision, under nitrous oxide, of the universe as "the same thing over and over." In the play *Laughing Gas*, about that vision, the central character discovers that human beings are "mere machines being used by others." In a recent essay, "You the Phantom," Dreiser said much the same thing. Man is "a mechanism for the mind and the intention of some exterior and larger mental process which has constructed [him] . . . for some purpose of its own." Elsewhere he describes all natural phenomena as "expressions" of the higher power, mere interchangeable tools turned out by a die press. He had shifted to a completely determinist position: even the faculty of human beings to ask *why* originates with the higher mind. *All* of man's thoughts and speculations emanate from the higher power. Hence we are phantoms. The idea that we can think, speculate, create, act out of free will is an illusion—"the myth of individuality."

Another of his earlier ideas he planned to develop in the book is relativity (with a bow to Einstein). Life is made up of contrasts: nothing can exist without its opposite—no cold without heat; no knowledge without ignorance; no justice without injustice; no truth without error; no poverty without wealth; no life without death; and so on. Evil seems evil only to the limited perspective of the human mind; in the larger scheme (unknowable to us) a balance between it and good is temporarily struck. Contrasts are one of the ways the creative principle expresses itself.

He told Douglas that he was prepared to devote "a considerable period of time" to writing the book. He did not want to hurry his thinking, and he worked very slowly, doing "an enormous amount of revising. But that is the only way I can work—thinking out illustrations from my experience, jotting them down, enlarging upon them, finding the proper subject head under which they belong and eventually combining them in some form as essays on the different topics I have in mind." He also took illustrations from magazine articles and scientific journals and pasted extracts or clippings on sheets of paper, then covered the page with his preliminary thoughts. These were filed under the several headings and later expanded into a short essay or quoted in a longer one.

He assigned researchers to write précis of scientific and philosophical works. He questioned eminent scientists, seeking information that would confirm some preconceived notion. For example, he asked Simon Flexner of the Rockefeller Institute if a paper the latter had written did not establish that the line "between matter and energy is lost or not to be determined. This seems to unite the two worlds, and on the plane of immensely creative intelligence."

He wanted confirmation that energy and matter were one, or rather, "two phases of the same thing," as he already believed. The two are united "on the plane of creative intelligence"; in other words, all is Mind. He had long believed in a nonmaterial or spiritual dimension of life, as stated in the Hindu Upanishads and in the doctrines of Christian Science, and now he sought scientific "proof" that the mind-matter dualism was false.

In January 1935 Dreiser proposed that Douglas come east and help him with the book. A gentle, erudite man who could quote poetry by the stanza,

Douglas was deeply unhappy turning out editorials for Hearst's Los Angeles *Examiner*. But he had a daughter in college and was reluctant to throw up his job. So Dreiser decided to go to California. Douglas insisted that he stay with him; his family would be away. Dreiser left at the end of April. The next five months were for both men one of the happiest times of their lives and a period of emotional and intellectual communion. During the day, while Douglas was at his job, Dreiser would read scientific books or write at a table littered with notes and the abstracts of articles and books he and his researchers had compiled. When inspiration flagged, he would wander into the garden and lounge by the pond, watching the goldfish and the birds.

In the evening the two of them would sit under the stars "saying over and over and over that life is what it is," as Dreiser later recalled, and then going inside and "opening Swinburne or Shakespeare or Shelley or [George] Sterling." A cook/housekeeper looked after them, and a French-woman named Brenetta Yerg, whom Helen and Dreiser had befriended, did secretarial work. Later, Helen came out, living in a rented room so as not to distract the men. She did some typing, handled correspondence, and occasionally joined the two men for dinner. Dreiser visited Calvin Bridges at the California Institute of Technology to talk over problems.

With Douglas, Bridges, and others providing stimulus and support, Dreiser felt he was making good progress on the *Formula*. He and Helen enjoyed life in California so much that they extended their stay into October, living in a house they owned in the Montrose section of Glendale. When it came time for them to go back, Douglas was miserable. He had been starved for intellectual companionship, and Dreiser's visit had been a revivifying experience. Now it was over. The night before they parted, he said, "There is a taste of death in every parting."

Back at Iroki, Dreiser tried to work on the philosophy, but several literary matters clamored for his attention. One of these was the production of a new dramatic version of *An American Tragedy*, written and staged by Erwin Piscator, the German director, from a scenario by Dreiser's friend Lina Goldschmidt. Piscator, a communist, highlighted the class divisions in the novel. Thus the stage was on two levels, denoting the upper and lower classes. There was also a "Speaker" or narrator who commented on the action didactically, as in Brechtian "epic theater." Retitled *The Case of Clyde Griffiths* and translated by Dreiser's erstwhile amanuensis, Louise Campbell (now working as a stockbroker), it eventually went to Broadway as a production of Harold Clurman's Group Theatre under the direction of Lee Strasberg. The didactic tone did not sit well with the critics; one called it "Drama with a pointer." Clurman himself disliked the play: "It was schematic in a cold way that to my mind definitely went against the American grain." After three weeks the producer, Milton Shubert, killed it.

In a letter to Douglas at the end of the year, Dreiser was sanguine, if vague, about his progress on the *Formula*. "I am slowly but surely lining up the answers to a series of propositions," he said. "The result should be presently visible." He had found a secretary to type and file his effusions, organize his research, and of course look after his correspondence. She was Harriet Bissell, a young woman recently graduated from Smith College. Dreiser's intuition told him that she was brilliant, a genius. When Harriet learned this much later, she was appalled. She thought herself unqualified for such a role, having had one course in philosophy and two in physics at Smith. She had assumed that her duties would be strictly secretarial and had taken a two-week cram course in Gregg shorthand before going to work.

Her first impression of Dreiser was of "a great old man," but otherwise she knew little about him, hadn't even read his books. There were 500 other applicants in that Depression year, so she was glad to have the job, which paid $25 a week, less $15 for board and room while she stayed at Iroki. Dreiser had closed his apartment at the Ansonia and moved to the country to save money and concentrate on the *Formula*. During the cold months he and Helen lived in the guest house, which was cheaper to heat.

For Dreiser and Harriet the day started at nine. She worked at her typewriter, set up on a card table, while he wrote at the large table Wharton Esherick had made for him. She noticed that, after two or three hours of work, his concentration would flag and he would break off and talk to her. He was a wonderful storyteller, with a sense of humor. Sometimes they would trade puns. "Perhaps we spent too much time doing this when we were supposed to be working," she later recalled.

He seemed incapable of putting in eight or ten hours of sustained writing anymore. And he took less interest than formerly in the details of his business affairs—the twenty or so contracts with foreign publishers, the royalty statements, tax matters, and bills. He could hardly balance a checkbook, Harriet said. The upshot was that business matters devolved upon the slender shoulders of a twenty-one-year-old woman just out of Smith.

That February his book received a serious setback when George Douglas died of a heart attack. Dreiser immediately wired Donald McCord in Pasadena: GEORGE'S DEATH HURTS BEYOND BELIEF. WILL YOU PERSONALLY SELECT FOUR DOZEN ROSES. SEND WITH CARD SAYING FROM DREISER TO GEORGE. Later, Henry von Sabern, the sculptor, wrote Dreiser, "You will never know what you meant to him and how he pulled himself together before you came. When you left for the East he wrote, I feel just awful. I don't know what I shall do now. And I felt like crying out, 'For God's sake, George, *don't* drink.'" Mollie Douglas wrote that after Dreiser left, George had written some articles, but when one was rejected, "he lost heart. He missed you dreadfully, but I am so glad that he had such a happy three months with you."

Dreiser had lost a friend he loved and a sympathetic ear to his specula-

tions. It was a devastating blow at a time when he was beginning to compre-
hend the magnitude of the task he had set for himself. The notes and
paragraphs continued to pile up, but what he had was to a finished philosophy as the pieces of jigsaw puzzle are to the picture on the front of the box.

All cosmic laws, he had decided, are "manifestations of some gigantic
mind." But what was the nature of that Mind? What was it thinking, feeling?
And why? Was it intelligent? Loving? Cruel? And if all individuals were
ultimately reducible to matter—energy, atoms and electrons, as science
showed they assuredly were—and were mere extensions of the greater
being, as science assuredly did not show, wasn't life itself a nullity? It was
as though he had at last stepped behind the screen and discovered the
ultimate mechanism in its laboratory, stamping out endless life forms, and
within the machine—Mind. Such a perception yielded neither faith nor
serenity.

In the spring Helen and Dreiser had a cataclysmic row over another romance of his. In mid-May she decided to flee to Portland and stay with her
mother and then go to Los Angeles. Dreiser accompanied her. He had a
lecture engagement at Purdue University and also wanted to discuss the
Formula with George Crile, author of *The Phenomena of Life,* a book that
deeply influenced Dreiser, in Cleveland. Esther McCoy, who was moving
to California after a futile job-hunting stint in New York, also hitched a ride.
Dreiser and Helen were amicable on the trip, but she seemed nervous and
tired. They dropped Dreiser off at West Lafayette, Indiana, and Helen and
Esther continued westward. They stopped in a small city for the night and
Helen immediately went shopping, as though, Esther thought, she was
feeling a sense of heady freedom and expressed it by buying shoes, although
she could have had a far better selection in New York. After leaving Esther
in her hometown in Kansas for a visit with her parents, Helen pushed on
to Oregon.

After a few weeks in Portland, she settled in Los Angeles for several
months' stay. Her plan was to talk to agents and producers about an idea
she had for a musical based on Paul Dresser's life. She had vague hopes of
getting a singing job, perhaps on radio.

Esther had dispatched Dreiser an anxious bulletin on Helen's health.
He replied, "I care for her truly although often enough we don't get
along. . . . So often I wish I wish I could make her wholly happy and when
she leaves me I am sorrowful and grieve for her and myself. . . . I will always
look after her to the best of my ability, as she knows. . . . I want her to get
well. I want to pull myself together and then maybe we can make a go of
it out there."

They had decided to put Iroki up for sale. The house was in Helen's name, but she used it as a hold over him, a way of financing their move to California, where, she thought, he would be healthier and happier—not to mention 3000 miles from his women friends in New York. He agreed to the move in principle. The upkeep of Iroki was becoming too heavy a burden. He owned the property free and clear, but his income had dwindled and taxes were high, forcing him to dip into capital. In February he wrote Yost ruefully, "If you want a fine collection of wolves at your front door, hang my picture outside. They never fail to respond."

That summer he rented the main house to a Manhattan doctor and moved into the cabins on the lower end of the property. Harriet did his secretarial work and sometimes prepared meals or kept him company when he went out to dinner.

Harris visited him, and one night while they were cooking supper in the cabin over a huge fire, Dreiser told her of seeing a large snake near the house—a puff adder. He shot it, only later to learn it wasn't dangerous. A few days later he saw another one and decided it must be the first snake's mate. He spoke to it, telling it he thought it was beautiful and was sorry that he had killed its mate.

"It stopped," he went on, "and I took a few steps toward it, telling it not to be afraid; that I was not going to harm it. Then slowly it turned and came toward me, passing right across the toe of my shoe—and disappeared into the grass on the other side." Was there more to Nature than the survival of the fittest?

In August Helen wrote from Los Angeles that she wanted to return. He told her to come home. "I feel unhappy about this whole business because if there were any chance or hope of my living with you affectionately and peacefully I'd like to do that." He said they must adopt a much simpler lifestyle. His first priority was to sell Iroki. Then he would cash in all his stocks and bonds, hide the money somewhere, "and tell Mrs. D. to go to ——"

His resentment at those monthly $200 payments to Jug had been been mounting for some time. After her plea of poverty from the hospital, her fortunes seem to have taken an upturn, for in 1934 she sailed around the world, playing Methodist hymns for the passengers on talent night and writing gossipy letters to her relatives in Missouri.

Dreiser wondered how she could afford a grand tour, but should have guessed the answer: she was very frugal, and had probably socked away the money he sent her. She shared a small third-floor walkup apartment on Waverly Place in the Village with sister Ida. The rent would have been low in such a neighborhood, and with a job in a dress shop and various economies, she probably was able to amass a sizable nest egg. (She was generous with her nieces and nephews, financing visits to New York for some.)

What particularly annoyed Dreiser was her continuing use of his name. Now he received letters from total strangers saying they had met his delightful wife.

Helen returned from California in November. That winter was so severe that they moved into the Park Plaza Hotel, adjacent to the Museum of Natural History. The Liveright suit over his unearned royalties came to trial in February, and it was an expensive defeat. The judge ruled that the author had plainly failed to deliver *The Stoic* and thus was liable for 75 percent of the money advanced him by the publisher between 1929 and 1932. The total came to $12,789, plus $3000 for copies of *Epitaph* and other books that Dreiser had ordered.

He was bitterly disappointed. Now the sale of Iroki became more urgent than ever. He had to make the Liveright payment, owed back taxes to the State of New York, and the Internal Revenue Service had questioned some stock sales on his 1931 return. He began seeking to cut expenses on petty items—buying copy paper at the 5 and 10 and complaining about the price, looking for cheaper brands of bourbon, his favorite tipple. Yet he did not stint on dining out or excursions to the theater.

He quarreled with the woman who had come between him and Helen, and she left New York. Helen thought she had won again and urged him to move to California. But Dreiser could not leave his work—or break with the woman, to whom he wrote letters full of sexual longing. In the spring of 1937 the affair resumed, and Helen again fled to Portland. She later said the winter in New York had been "a terrible one for me . . . terrible or useless." But she felt she had to be there, to make one more attempt to reclaim him. He treated her absence as a trial separation that might become permanent.

Iroki was rented, so he stayed at the Park Plaza for much of the summer, retreating into his work. In late August Calvin Bridges invited him to spend a month at the biological research laboratory at Cold Spring Harbor on Long Island. While there Dreiser had another epiphany. After an afternoon of peering at minuscule creatures under the microscope, he was walking along a path and noticed some small yellow flowers. He stooped down to study them and was struck by the beauty of the *design* of nature. There must be an aesthetic mind behind all creation, manifesting itself in the sublime correspondences among the microcosmos under the microscope, a flower, the star-seeded deeps of space.

That fall he moved to the Rhinelander apartments on Eleventh Street—where Mame had lived and he had written part of *An American Tragedy* in 1923. His quarters were comfortable, with French doors opening on a New Orleans–style wrought-iron balcony; a small bedroom, a large living room, and a kitchen with a stove, refrigerator, and counter, which he used mostly as a bar.

Dreiser had been told to cut down on his drinking after tests showed signs of diabetes. Knowing he wouldn't, his physician suggested he switch from bourbon to sweet vermouth. So he filled a medicine bottle with Martini and Rossi and took occasional swigs from it during the day, with no visible effects. He was subject to morning depressions, when his energy level was low. In addition, he gulped vitamins and other pills and kept an array of medicine bottles on his desk.

Robert Elias, a graduate student in English at Columbia who had written his master's thesis on Dreiser because he thought him a forgotten pioneer, called on him. They gossiped about Ernest Hemingway's fight with Max Eastman in Maxwell Perkins' office (Dreiser took Eastman's side) and discussed philosophy, free will, and man as a mechanism. If it were true that people were bundles of electrons powered by a central dynamo-mind, Elias wondered, why ask, Why? Dreiser didn't really answer the question.

Elias's final impression of that first meeting was, "When you see him close up, hot, in his shirt, standing above you pouring whisky, you realize he's not young. In a sense, I felt sorry for him. There seemed to be something so lonely."

During the winter of 1937–1938, Dreiser began writing quickie articles on topics like "Lessons I Learned from an Old Man" and "Is College Worthwhile? No!" According to Harris, he spent little time on them, and when she or Harriet complained about their sloppiness he would growl, "That's good enough for them." Dreiser wrote only two more short stories in the 1930s. The last one he published, "The Tithe of the Lord," was a disguised debate on the existence of God. A businessman named Benziger, whose wife has committed suicide and who has failed, promises God that he will donate 10 percent of his earnings to the needy if God will help him recover. He does prosper but breaks the covenant and again sinks into decline. Two friends analyze the implications of his life and decide that his conscience has punished him, and "conscience is God, or the only thing we know of as God, our guide."

With that story Dreiser abandoned fiction for philosophy. Alarmed by his dereliction, Sherwood Anderson begged him to return to storytelling. He said that the "notion of the writer being also thinker, philosopher etc." was wrong. He and Dreiser should "always be trying to tell the simple story of lives." Science wasn't the answer. "There is this terrible loneliness of the people in America. . . . This goddam science and mechanical development you talk of doesn't help all this while the other part of your work . . . the telling of the story always does."

Dreiser countered that science was not "dull, lifeless, nor even mechanical in a narrow way. I think the reason people reject it is because they haven't got the capacity to see how enormously rich, mysterious, varied, and in fact, entirely satisfactory in an emotional way, science as such can be. . . ."

There was really nothing Anderson could say that would persuade Dreiser to return to storytelling. Dreiser confessed to Mencken that he read "very few novels—mostly science and current sociology & economics." He thought the novel was dying "not only because of multiplicity but because of the movies, the radio and what is sure to be, television." After reading Pietro di Donato's violent *Christ in Concrete* in 1939, he wrote, "Literature cannot grow much more realistic, of that I am sure. I have a feeling that the tide is likely to turn (give way out of sheer weariness and news of horrors) to something less dramatic. Maybe." He admired John Steinbeck, considering *The Grapes of Wrath* one of the best novels of the decade, and Clifford Odets and praised a book by William Saroyan. In a letter to Saroyan he teased the younger man about being a "first rate pessimist" who thought that "life is a lousy mess, sex being the only thing that offers any letup and even that isn't what it is cracked up to be." He wondered why Saroyan didn't commit suicide but decided it was because he took out his pessimism in writing or else found "something in the lusty, and fierce, enjoyment and acceptance which a man can feel who can work in a slaughter house, eat a good dinner, and screw his girl. . . ."

He still regarded the movies as a potentially great art form, but his only dealings with Hollywood in the late thirties were entirely mercenary. In 1934 he had offered the Paul Dresser story to one of his pro-tem Hollywood agents as a vehicle for Mae West, who would play the "Sal" of Paul's song. Throughout the decade he tried to sell *Sister Carrie* and other novels and stories to a film company, employing a train of agents, empowered by the usual three- or six-month options, who sometimes found themselves treading on each other's heels in studio executive suites.

Lengel, who had left the magazine business to work as a story editor for Columbia Pictures and then became an agent, spearheaded a 1937 campaign to sell *Sister Carrie*. Warner Brothers gave the project a definite maybe, but Jack Warner was worried about the moral acceptability of the book and asked Joseph Breen at the Hays Office for an advisory opinion. Breen replied that the story's "kept woman" theme violated the production code. "At no time throughout the story," he wrote, "does she pay the penalty for her sins, and at the end is shown to be a highly successful actress." It was the same thing, over and over. For the story to win approval, Breen said, there must be "no suggestion of illicit sex anywhere." Also, Hurstwood's suicide violated a specific prohibition in the Production Code. "With this in mind could you find some other way to dispose of Hurstwood?" Warner backed out because of the censorship difficulties and economic conditions.

Lengel also conceived a radio series, which Dreiser, who was interested in the medium, would host. But the program never came off. He tried playwriting, attempting to create a vehicle for the British star Gertrude Lawrence, whom he met by chance at a restaurant. He proposed expanding his one-act labor play, *The Girl in the Coffin,* and the producer John Golden was eager to mount it. But they could not agree on the script. Golden found Dreiser's attempt "full of labor talk and plot." He didn't like the plot line about the planned murder of the millowner. He suggested that the millowner be portrayed as a "good fellow" who pays his employees well, "a sort of Henry Ford fighting the government on his own." He was probably unaware of Dreiser's opinion of Henry Ford fighting the government on his own.

Dreiser gave up and offered a dramatization of *The "Genius"* instead. But Golden didn't like that script either and proposed that Eugene be made less a Don Juan or else that the play be given a period setting. Dreiser replied: "The plan of the play as you suggested would probably be successful but it is not anything to which I would sign my name."

In December 1937 he wrote Helen, "I am in the midst of so many financial ills that I scarcely see how I can go on." As a result of not writing any books, Dreiser had fallen in debt to two publishers for some $22,000. He paid Liveright, but the advances from Simon & Schuster were becoming a millstone around his neck, and he resented their pressuring him, however politely, for a new book.

He tried to interest a new publisher in advancing him all or part of the money he owed Simon & Schuster, in return for rights to his entire oeuvre, past and future. In January 1938 he offered such a package to Charles Scribner, telling him, "I have the new book under way and I do not plan to be hurried into finishing it, or to have any kind of publishing pressure put on me about it." Scribner declined, as did others. The Liveright suit had probably hurt him in their eyes; unaware of all the facts, they regarded him as an author who welshed on a contract and then countersued his publisher for $52,000 in unpaid advances.

Although Messrs. Simon and Schuster didn't know it yet, Dreiser was again without a publisher.

CHAPTER 34   *Oh Change!*

I went on down to Spain (Barcelona) to see if I couldn't
be killed I guess.

—Dreiser to Donald McCord (1938)

The spring of '38 passed quietly, save for the Great Fire at Iroki. The Mount Kisco fire department saved the house, but there was considerable water damage inside, and Dreiser asked Ralph Fabri to submit a bill for the decorating work he had done, leaving the amount blank "to be filled in by me."

Now the headaches of Iroki far outweighed the pleasures. There was always something going wrong that had to be fixed—leaks, drainage problems, trouble with electrical lines. And the winters there had become too hard for him. He tried to mortgage the property, but no bank would give him a loan. He was too old to be a good risk, and they already had too many defaulted properties on their hands to take on this exotic domicile.

He had rented the property for the summer, and so in June he moved to Pratt's Island near Noroton, Connecticut, and set up housekeeping in a beach cottage rented by Marguerite Harris, who was otherwise engaged with her magazine, *Direction*. On weekends guests arrived, and there were picnics on the beach. Edgar Lee Masters came with his friend Alice Davis a couple of times, planting himself in a porch rocker like a courthouse loafer.

In early July arrived a telegram from the League of American Writers, asking Dreiser to attend, all expenses paid, the International Convention for International Peace to be held in Paris, July 23–24. Dreiser agreed; it was his first mission for a CP auxiliary since Harlan. But in a letter to Yvette Szekely, he was quite casual about it: "Last Sunday wires from the League of American Writers and the American League for Peace & Democracy began to arrive asking me to attend—all costs paid. . . . All I had to do was to go and say I represented them and that I believe in peace. That seemed easy, so, since I needed a lot of peace just then, I decided to do it."

Franklin Folsom, then executive secretary of the League of American Writers, recalled journeying to Pratt's Island to try to persuade a reluctant Dreiser to attend. It took much cajoling, and Dreiser was apparently unwilling to become associated with the League because of its CP ties. He insisted that the money for his expenses not come "from Russia" and said he didn't want it to look as if he were "bought and paid for" by the Soviet Union. Folsom assured him the writers group was paying his way.

Then, on the eve of his departure, Dreiser consternated his sponsors by refusing to join the League; he apparently wanted to go as an independent citizen, representing no group. Also, he was expected to speak out on the Spanish Civil War. He had sided with the Loyalists from the start, writing Ruth Kennell that he was working hard for the cause and "I think we'll pay for our indifference if Spain goes fascist." But that spring John Dos Passos, who had just returned from Spain much disillusioned because of the way the Soviet Union was acting, had visited Iroki. No doubt Dos told Dreiser about the purges and assassinations of anarchists and socialists being carried out by Soviet agents and sympathizers. So Dreiser was cautious and wanted no involvement with any group.

Aboard the elegant *Normandie* ("a floating candy box," he wrote Szekely), he fretted because he had forgotten his dress suit and lots of people were wearing black tie in the dining salon. Then he turned around and inveighed against the status-seeking chatter of the first-class passengers. The only person he liked was "a small, intense Jew driven out of Germany who is a natural thinker and of course shrewd."

His name was Samuel Groskopf, and he was a Parisian merchant. Dreiser's superstition about always meeting a "little Jew" at turning points in his fortune for once seemed accurate, though he doesn't mention it and the turning point was intellectual rather than pecuniary. What Groskopf did was to lend him an English-language abridgment of the Talmud. He wrote Harriet Bissell of his reaction:

And now I see if it were fully condensed & expressed it would . . . make clear that Christ must be a myth since all that he said is quite clearly there and thousands of years before. No wonder they [Jews] could never be converted. Even [Christ's] "love one another" is put in a more practical & possible way. Their strange dietary laws are now clear to me. And much of their shrewdness seems to [be] ordered by this book. Thus & so must they do—or fail & be unworthy of their Lord! Well, I stand illuminated as to that at last!

This basic text gave him a new understanding of Judaism, at a time when his philosophical studies had made him more open to religion.

He admired the French people's strong sense of family ties, in contrast to America, where "families blow up like seed pods of so many weeds and flowers and the members float away in the wind." He was thinking of his own kin—and now, perhaps, a void in his life. He complained to Bissell that he was sick of the "parlor radicals" he met like Louis Aragon, editor of *Ce Soir.* "I could write an article on radicals, they make me laugh."

And then he plunged into the conference, a wearying round of sessions and gaseous speeches in a variety of languages that no one listened to. He lunched with the co-chairs of the international peace conference, Lord Cecil and Georges Bonnet, the French foreign minister, and others, and got into an argument with them over the embargo on arms shipments to the Loyalists. As he later recalled it, "I talked to Bonnet, Pierre Cot and Lord Cecil. . . . Lice! Fakers! All wanted the combination of the privileged classes in all countries—but disguised as Democracy."

He was scheduled to speak at a session on "The Bombing of Open Cities." Despite the recent pulverizing of Guernica and Madrid by Italian and German planes, mention of the war was forbidden. Dreiser learned that his remarks, originally scheduled for the beginning of the session, had been put off until the end, following some boring committee reports. This maneuver made him more determined to be heard, and so when his time came he called to the delegates who were beginning to walk out. "Don't go! Don't go! I have something of importance to say!" He told them that public sentiment against war and the bombing of civilians was "very strong in America" and he called for an international conference "such as this one would like to be" to bring about a plan "to avoid the old cutthroat competition" among nations. It was his familiar call for equity extended to the international arena. Wars, he believed, were started by nations controlled by corporate and aristocratic interests seeking economic gain. Equitable societies (e.g., Russia), it followed, did not start wars. His address was enthusiastically received, and the Paris *Herald Tribune* gave it a prominent play.

Despite the minor triumph of his speech, he was feeling dreadfully lonely, slept poorly, and experienced "stupendous" morning depressions— "My blue devils," he wrote Bissell. "I am wholly too miserable to think of anything except dying or finding some soothing drug. All this business of living begins to pall on me. . . . Richard the III it was who screamed a horse! A horse! My kingdom for a horse. I would make it a drug. If I could only find one that would pull me through." He added that he expected soon to be in Spain.

He left toward the end of the month with an escort and car provided by the Spanish Loyalist delegation in Paris. (He had tried to contact Claude Bowers, now U.S. ambassador to Spain stationed in the south of France, but they missed connections.) He later wrote: "I felt war immediately as we crossed the border. . . . A sense of impending catastrophe difficult to define at first."

In besieged Barcelona the effects of war were more visible. The Ritz Hotel, where he stayed, had been damaged by bombs. The waiters tried to keep up standards in the dining room despite an acute food shortage. In the morning they served breakfast on silver platters—a single bun and a kind of "black juice" that was supposed to be coffee. There was no meat for dinner, only a fried mush composed of vegetables and drowned in sauce.

It was a "dangerous atmosphere," he wrote Harriet. "They are expecting a big push from Franco & more intense bombings every hour. Strange—sitting in a hotel room & being ready any moment to hear sirens all over the city & to have to grab your bag & make for an underground shelter."

He had come to Barcelona at the invitation of Republican Foreign Minister Alvarez del Vayo and Premier Juan Negrin, who had a mission for him: to persuade President Roosevelt to authorize the U.S. government to send humanitarian aid—food, medicines—to both sides. Dreiser agreed to try.

After five days in Barcelona, he departed for London via Paris (not telling the American writers delegation, which scoured the city for him). In London he called on certain wealthy people the Loyalists hoped would sponsor aid, with little success. He wrote Bissell: "I never worked harder. . . . You'd think I was an institution with a front office & 10 assistants and I'm just me & tired." Not that he had any great hopes of generosity from the moneyed class: "England is an aristocracy. The masses are underpaid; stupid, silent. The gang at the top wants not only to rule England but the world. They want beggars & stupid slogan-fed workers and they have them—while they loaf and entertain and shoot deer in great preserves! Oh Hell. . . ." He was frightened by the specter of a European war: "France, Spain, Czecho-Slovakia, and all the little states are enduring fear—pitiable unrest. I feel as though I would like to find a hole in a mountain and stay hidden & alone for good. It is truly dreadful."

After a brief, restful visit with John Cowper Powys at his ancestral village of Corwen in Wales, Dreiser sailed home on the *Lucania*. Folsom met him aboard ship, and when Dreiser saw him he said, "Folsom, we've got to do something about getting milk for the Spanish children."

The journey had imbued him with a deep sympathy for the Spanish people. As he wrote Bissell: "Their courage. They have so little to go on—their desire for their own type of Govt. . . . The pride. They won't beg! And their looks—how handsome the men & women even in poor clothes." His political batteries recharged, he gave interviews, wrote articles, and

made speeches to raise relief funds. He wrote President Roosevelt to request
a meeting at which he could relay the Loyalist leaders' message. On September 7 he spent the afternoon with FDR on his yacht on the Hudson. Roosevelt listened attentively but said the U.S. government must remain neutral.
Since the Neutrality Law permitted private donations of food and medicine,
he advised Dreiser to organize a committee for Spanish relief with a board
of distinguished professional, business, and religious leaders.

Dreiser immediately set about this task, pleading with people of whom
he disapproved, such as Father John A. Ryan, president of the Catholic
University; Nelson A. Rockefeller; and others. He talked to Joseph Medill
Patterson, the newspaper magnate (who, although he styled himself a socialist, was not enthusiastic), and Rufus Jones, chairman of the American
Friends Service Committee, which had been engaged in relief operations in
Spain for a year. Jones was the only one who was supportive, and Dreiser
was impressed by the big, homely Quaker philosopher, with whom he had
a two-hour talk at Haverford College. Shortly thereafter he formed the idea
of using Jones as a model for Solon Barnes, the father in *The Bulwark*. He
wrote the philosopher in December to request a copy of one of his volumes
of autobiography, explaining, "As you know I am very much interested in
the Quaker ideal. Like yourself I rather feel that it is the direct road to—not
so much a world religion as a world appreciation of the force that provides
us all with this amazing experience called life." That same month he wrote
Ruth Kennell and others that he intended to work on a novel.

Meanwhile his efforts on behalf of the Spanish people were a failure.
The dignitaries he approached declined to lend their names for fear they
would be accused of endorsing either the communist or fascist sides. Possibly they did not regard Dreiser, a well-known radical, as the man to organize
a neutral committee. President Roosevelt later arranged for shipments of
flour to Spain through the Red Cross. Dreiser thanked him, saying his action
showed "the enormous value of a great executive in the Presidential chair
at all times but most particularly in periods of stress and change."

That fall, Iroki being let to a doctor who was interested in buying it, Dreiser
moved his cache of notes and books into a room at the George Washington
Hotel in Manhattan and worked on the introduction to *The Living Thoughts
of Thoreau*. This book was part of a series of selections from great writers
published by Longmans, Green, which had offered him $500 for the job.
While he was away, Harriet Bissell had plowed through fourteen volumes
of Thoreau's journals at the rate of one a day in the summer heat, culling
key passages. Dreiser had read *Walden* and other Thoreau works as a young
man, and they had influenced one of his first published stories, "McEwen
of the Shining Slave Makers," almost a half century ago.

Writing the essay clarified his thinking on his own philosophy. In it he asserts that scientists are too cautious to admit what their data clearly shows—the existence of "supreme regulating and hence legal or directing force." Thoreau, he says, knew that life is directed "in the mechanical sense. Immutable law binds us all." Whatever Thoreau's views on the various philosophical problems, however, he is "tapping some marvelous, musical, lyrical source, which was life, which is a dream. . . ." He extolled the "optimism, the grandeur" of Thoreau's vision of "an unconquerably limitless universe, rushing and sounding furiously and noiselessly at once." The Concord sage had pierced the veil of appearances to "praise the whole."

Dreiser did not find his Walden at the George Washington Hotel. There were cocktail hours with old friends, including Richard Duffy, the sympathetic editor who published him in the dark days at the turn of the century. But there were also quarrels with a woman friend, whom we shall call the Dark Lady, not because she was evil or sinister—quite the contrary—but because their love had a dark-of-the-moon side, causing much torment for them both.

He had promised to join Helen in California but now felt a stronger pull to the younger woman. He told Helen bluntly that he was bored; although she had "a certain untutored and uncontaminated emotional response to beauty which is very moving," she was not interested in the scientific problems that were engaging him. And so he had "gone abroad for intellectual and emotional reactions which I felt necessary for me at the time." He was "in the midst of so many financial ills that I scarcely see how I can go on." In another letter he evoked the past: "it was lovely—unforgettable. . . . But today—the way things are—I don't seem to care whether life keeps or not. So I don't cry much. I think generally I am too sad."

As for Helen, she was happier in California, but she wanted him there, away from temptresses. She was lonely, and also, she told Fabri, "he should be using his personality in a way so as to be able to make a little money for himself so that he won't have to sit day and night writing articles. He is much too old for that slavery and I know that he would not have to do it" if he came to Hollywood. She was confident that she could make some movie sales that would enable them to live comfortably.

Helen suspected her rival was exercising some kind of voodoo on him and clung to her faith "that he really cares for me down deep, and very deep." This made her "fight on and come back and fight on some more."

In the diary she kept in California, Helen reveals a continuing search for inner peace. Testing the spiritual remedies of Mary Baker Eddy, she writes over and over, like a schoolgirl, "Am I demonstrating the healing power of Divine Love?" She wishes for "relief from nervous worry." She records the titles and numbers of the poems she has written and sends copies of them to Fabri. One is called "The World and I":

I stand before you, world, as one apart,
With wonder in my eyes, and open heart,
Seeking liberty and understanding too . . .

Earnestly she devotes herself to remedying the shortcomings Dreiser had lectured her about. She reads Dante's *Divine Comedy* ("It is a diary of redemption through love"), Thoreau, Matthew Arnold on Greek poetry, the poems of Emily Dickinson and E. A. Robinson. She reads *Looking Backward* and formidable works of science, including *The Evolution of Physics,* taking notes on colors and prisms and Newton's law of inertia, so that she could help Teddie on the *Formula.* She goes on a diet, reporting that she weighed 156 pounds at the start.

Dominating the entries, however, is one person—"T." While T. was in Europe, she records his itinerary day by day. And she finds consolation in a quote from Voltaire: "The friendship of a great man is a gift of the gods." But she was growing impatient and considers returning to New York to talk to him. She was in a kind of limbo, she wrote Fabri in July—"I have hung on and hung on and stayed away because I thought it best. But soon I have to make a move. Can you tell me anything."

In November Dreiser announced to Mencken, "I am moving out to the Coast for an extended period." Mencken wondered, How long would he be gone? Would he be back before the end of winter? "I am not planning an early return, maybe no return," Dreiser replied. He had decided, at last, to make the move.

He explained to Mencken that in 1935 he had found he could work well in California. "George Douglas and I ran a great household together—a fascinating group assembled about three times a week." This time, he said, he might tie up with Bridges or McCord. As for Helen, he was vague. "Helen will be with me a part of the time anyhow. She spends a good deal of her time with her mother in Portland." The doctor had made a good offer for Iroki.

The decision to sell Iroki carried the bittersweet taste of the end of an era. For all the headaches of country squirehood, Dreiser had grown fond of the place, a kind of eccentric museum to his tastes and to artists he admired. There had been good times during the 1930s, like the dinner for Diego Rivera at which the rotund Mexican muralist plucked ants from the flowers on the table and popped them into his mouth, pronouncing them "piquant."

When he was immersed in work, he was antisocial. He once telephoned the humor writer O. O. McIntyre, whom he had invited to dinner that evening, "Odd, don't come tonight. I'm in no mood for you." People sometimes drove through the open gates without an invitation, and if

Dreiser didn't want to see them he would lie on the floor of his study so they would think no one was at home.

Perhaps he was thinking of Iroki when he contributed a short statement for the first issue of Marguerite Tjader Harris's *Direction:* "As the antique order of an old house becomes the disorderly decay of a newer age, so with changing ideas. The refreshing tides of the seasons, years, generations, succeed each other not without sadness and despair and suffering for what was, but mainly with welcome and gladness for the vitality and promise of what will be."

From Germany that November came news of the anti-Semitic atrocities of *Kristallnacht.* The following month Dreiser issued a statement to a symposium published by the League of American Writers. He reiterated that he did not believe in the "social torture" of any race or sect "for reasons of difference in appearance or custom." Prejudice, though, had ancient roots, and its victims were many:

> You do not eat as I do; pronounce my native tongue as I do; dress, walk, talk or respond as fast or in the same way to this or that, as I do. Hence you are accursed. You should not live in the same world—or at least the same land or city with me. Out! I cannot induce you and I cannot wait for you to change. . . . Just now it is the Jews in Germany; the Negroes in America, the democratic-minded loyalists in Spain, the backward in China, the swart fellaheen in Egypt, the Moor in Africa, the Czechs in Czechoslovakia, who are being seized upon and exploited, restrained, oppressed or murdered—each according to some theory as to their unfitness in the past of some other nation or group—as often as not—really more often than not—for economic purposes; the desire and hope of profit on the part of the exploiters.

Dreiser had conducted a long and damaging education in public, admitting his prejudices with a candor few would dare, save the native anti-Semites and fascists (with whom he never had any truck). He had come a long way toward understanding that the "Jewish problem" lay within himself.

Just before Thanksgiving Anderson and Eleanor, Masters and Alice, Harriet and Dreiser gathered for a farewell dinner at Lüchow's. Bissell recalled that he mentioned Helen's need for an operation and his desire to be with her as the primary reason for his departure.

He left New York in a blizzard, and joined Helen in Portland. In her diary for November 30 there appears this entry: "8 A.M. T.D." They had been separated for more than fifteen months. As for the future . . .

Part Eight

EQUATION

INEVITABLE

1939 – 1945

CHAPTER 35 *Exiles*

Mentally, I am as alone as a tramp.

—Dreiser (1938)

All who come here come to lie down & take the count—die
& go to heaven (this being heaven).

—Dreiser to Masters (1939)

Dreiser returned to Helen dispirited and in shaky health. Helen believed he didn't eat well or rest when she was away; he may also have been feeling the effects of his stormy love affair. He wrote the Dark Lady, "Living with you is a kind of fever coupled with strain. It plays on my vitality." As for returning to Helen, it was a trial reunion—she was on trial and "I am the judge." They would "come to some working agreement that will give [Helen] plenty to do and leave me wholly free. . . ." But Dreiser was not sure where he stood with the Dark Lady. He had left her because of the conflicts between them but hoped they would "come to a clarifying and reforming sense of what is needed to make the relationship permanent."

Money was now a pressing problem. He had cashed in all his securities and his hope was to sell *Carrie* or another novel to the movies before the nest egg ran out. Some of his California friends thought he was on his uppers. Part of the impression was conveyed by the place he and Helen took in Glendale in early December: a small "court" apartment.

Edgar Lee Masters was worse off. He wrote, in January 1939, "I am hanging by tired fingers to the edge of the cliff." Dreiser tried to help. He talked up a movie based on *Spoon River Anthology* and suggested to Longmans, Green that it sign up Masters to do an edition of *The Living Thoughts of Emerson.* That commission was extended and worked out well, for the scholarly Masters knew his Emerson.

Helen and Dreiser had some old friends in the area—Lillian Rosenthal, now married to Mark Goodman; Donald McCord; the artist Willy Pogany, whom Dreiser had known since he lived in the Village; Clare Kummer, Arthur Henry's widow, who went back to the *Delineator* days, as did Upton Sinclair and his wife, who lived in Pasadena. The actor Edward G. Robinson, one of the many Hollywood "progressives" at that time, invited them to dinner; John Howard Lawson, who had adapted *Sister Carrie* for the stage and was now a rising screenwriter and active in CP affairs, dropped by for literary and political talks. He later remembered the social world of Glendale as an intellectual atmosphere in which "wild ideas and concepts were always floating around."

But an old friend Dreiser had counted on to provide intellectual stimulus, Calvin Bridges, was dying of heart trouble. At the hospital Dreiser sat with him, held his hand, and told how much he loved him. Bridges' suffering eyes briefly lit up and he whispered, "Well, if three or four people care for me so much it can't be that I mean just nothing." He sank into a coma and died shortly after. Dreiser attended the funeral but was put off by the "stiff priestly crowd—the new and pretentious royalty of science." Bridges was of another era—the hard-drinking atheistic scientist like Jacques Loeb, whom Sinclair Lewis immortalized as Max Gottlieb in *Arrowsmith.*

Dreiser was living with a woman he didn't love and had nothing to say to, while the one he did (sometimes) love (but could not live with) was 3000 miles away. And then he received a letter from her informing him that she was getting married. It had come about suddenly, she later explained—"on the rebound," a chance meeting. She still felt a great affection for him, but she was adamant. She wanted no more triangles; it ran against her conscience and pride to come running after him, only to play second fiddle to Helen. She had recognized, like others before her, Helen's tenacious hold on him, which he described variously as pity, a sense of obligation, guilt, or memories. The bond between them was like a cable composed of all these strands, individually weak but together severable only by death.

Now he experienced the pain of unreturned love. "Lord, lord but this life is cruel," he wrote her. "Life is hateful to me. I seem often a fly entangled in a net by an invisible spider. Ills. Ills. Ills." The next day he sent her a telegram: "ALL THAT IS LEFT IS WORK. THE ONLY REFUGE." She held the high hand—the strength and freedom of youth.

On New Year's Day 1939 Helen wrote her resolutions in her diary:

> *Let no destructive thoughts in*
> *Hold to course*
> *Steadfast*

"He won't let anyone go really," she fretted to Fabri, who was acting as her eyes and ears in New York. In February he reported that the marriage had taken place. Helen was exultant.

Not only romantically but professionally Dreiser was caught between two stools. He should be working on *The Bulwark* but felt the pull of the *Formula*, which he regarded as practically finished, a matter of assembling his examples under the appropriate headings. That was wildly overoptimistic. He had a jumble of notes and typescript packed in cardboard boxes; some of his files were still stored at Iroki. Privately, Harriet Bissell had become convinced that he would never finish it. He was no philosopher, had no talent for metaphysics or logic; nor was he a scientist.

His inability to reach a final conclusion about the nature of God and the universe lay at the heart of his inability to write *The Bulwark*. All along his skepticism had inhibited him from sympathizing with his central character. Now he had Rufus Jones as a model, and that was leading him to a reconsideration of Quakerism. To Harriet he had given Jones's autobiographical volumes a lukewarm review: "He strikes me as sincere, if nothing more." But that was not entirely candid: he had heavily annotated his copies. Beside a passage describing the influence on Jones of John Woolman's *Journal,* he wrote "Solon." The writings of the eighteenth-century antislavery Quaker mystic had also touched Dreiser. In January he ordered from a Friends bookstore in Philadelphia copies of George Fox's *Journals* and of the 1871 edition of Woolman's *Journal* that Jones had read.

He traveled to Whittier College to look up Quaker sources in the library, and while there he spoke with some professors. They were charmed by the transparent sincerity of his interest in Quaker thought. He spoke informally to the students, making a strong testimonial in favor of Quakerism. Later, a woman who heard him wrote to praise something he said about God. Cautioning her that he meant "nature or God," Dreiser replied that "the entire talk was intended to convey the idea that the enormous revelations of Science in regard to nature indicate a necessary balancing of forces that at one point of man's limited grasp appear evil and at another point good, but which same, in order to achieve the seeming reality called life, are both necessary. Also, that under those conditions no intentional evil or cruelty can be attributed to the *creative force* or *God,* but only a life structure which on the whole appears more good than evil, and so desirable."

For most of his life he had lived in a Manichean cosmos; and in the microcosm of his soul the psychological equivalents of darkness and light warred. As he told the students at Whittier, "Up until I was forty years of age I believed fully that the world belonged to the Devil." In a letter to the Dark Lady, written in December, while in a state of depression, he conjured up a chilling vision of the Supreme Being:

> I look at all I see now—all life really—as the product of either a blasé or disordered super-genius that can find no comfortable, workable illusion into which to enter and rest. And death & despair for all save the chemically fresh and immature—those brief and so futile extensions of his own restless, irritable, irrational cravings for an escape that is, after all, no real escape—but only a savage, chattering, creaking and screeching process called life that will not come through to any real smoothness of functioning & so peace for the creative energy that produces it. It seems to me to have been seeking to make a protoplasmic bed—in or on which to lie and dream. And yet only to have achieved a hairy or wiry board on which is no rest but veritable phantasms of aches and stings. . . . I write all this because I am so truly sad—disappointed with myself & all else.

Fear of death, the steely chill of a mechanistic universe, had penetrated the marrow of his being. He knew that his vision perhaps originated in his own sense of despair over the way his life was going, and the dwindling of the life-renewing energy of youth. As he wrote Masters, "Edgar, all that is needed to beat this sustenance and pleasure problem in this world is *youth—* ignorant, energetic desirous youth. . . . Age is an old man on your back and much too much to carry."

But in July he wrote Harriet a letter in a decidedly different tone: "I hang over the markings & colorings and formation of a flower or an insect—or a worm or snail and at such times, and only so, seem to *see* and *know* something of the instincts, and intents as well as powers of the sublime creative force that permits and maintains us all. Then the only other question is *why?*" But, even if one could not answer that, in the sheer contemplation of design one found "a kind of peace and rest. For—be life what it will—this aesthetic skill . . . seems so not only respectable but awesome. I *admire* until I border on affection—maybe love." Now he understood how Thoreau had "sensed and was comforted by the presence of not an *invisible* but a visible personality. One so wholly and so magnificently mental. And so wholly beyond all good or evil as man senses those things."

The lash of financial necessity turned his energies away from the *Formula* to selling *Sister Carrie.* He engaged a new agent—A. Dorian Otvos. He had received an offer of $35,000 from Harry Cohn, the Neanderthalic head of Columbia Pictures, but it was conditional on approval of the outline by Joseph Breen.

To raise some quick cash, he took to the speakers' circuit. His lecture agent, Briggs, had set up a strenuous course for a sixty-eight-year-old man: seven speeches over two weeks in three states. But at the end of the trail was a pot containing $1000. A sign of his desperation was that he accepted fees of $200, well below the $500 he once demanded. His topic was "What I Think About Life." He scored the Catholic Church as anti–free thought and praised George Fox as "the greatest prophet since Jesus Christ." He castigated Britain's undemocratic class system, causing a near riot in Portland.

In Utah, where he had four speaking dates, he warned that Americans must stop dreaming and prepare for war. "They think it can't happen here. The hell it can't." He predicted, "If we don't give the unfortunate a break we're going to go fascist. There is no reason why capital should kick labor around."

Along the way, Otvos wired him that an Associated Press reporter wished to interview him about the motion picture industry and urged Dreiser not to bite the hand that might feed him. He did his duty, admitting that "the motion picture is first of all a business and then an art medium. Certain story revisions in the interest of moral codes and state censorship are quite all right. . . ."

Returning home exhausted, he went to bed and stayed there for several days.

Rumors of the imminent sale of *Sister Carrie* rose and fell with the fickle Hollywood tides. Columbia had withdrawn its offer, but Harry Edington, the head of Famous Pictures, a production unit attached to Universal, promised Dreiser that he would assign two writers to prepare a script that would meet with both the author's and Breen's approval. The scriptwriters' solution to the censorship problem was to expand the character of Ames, the wholesome Midwestern inventor whom Carrie admires. In the end, he and Carrie would wed and live happily ever after in a small town. Hurstwood would expire of natural causes in a breadline. Dreiser seemed resigned. He had to "face the music," he told Harriet.

But Edington backed out, and in September Lengel began negotiating with RKO. The agent assured the studio that Dreiser had "agreed to permit changes" that would take care of Breen's objections. Later that fall Breen approved an outline, but, as Dreiser tried to explain to Masters, in Hollywood "even selling does not mean production because political and financial and religious whispers and interpretations stalk like ghosts all over the place." And, even more darkly, he confided to another friend, the writer Dayton Stoddart, "This is a selfish, self-concentrated, mean, loafing town. The business and political world is hard boiled & cruel. The movies are solidly Jewish. They've dug in, employ only Jews with American names and buy only what they cannot abstract and disguise. And the dollar sign is the guide—mentally & physically. That America should be led—the mass—by their direction is beyond all believing. In addition they are arrogant, insolent and contemptuous."

The virus of anti-Semitism had not been entirely cleansed from his system; it had only been in remission. He concealed it from all but Stoddart, who was once called "the American Céline." His animus contained a seed of paranoia; more, he may have fantasied Jewish revenge for his past anti-Semitic statements. A tired, lonely old man desperate for money, he was scapegoating those remote, powerful executives who held his survival in their hands and who seemed as arbitrary and capricious as the inimical Creator he sometimes believed in.

He now owed Jug $4000 to $5000 in support payments, and wrote her lawyer, Leo Rossett, who was threatening to sue, that he was in a low period financially and in poor health. To whom was his obligation—a woman who had been out of his life for thirty years and in it for only ten? "I have had the help of another woman for twenty years through my creative life and that woman has asked nothing. She makes no demands. But she helps. To whom is my moral duty, I ask you." He would pay when he sold something; as for now, "you can't get blood from a turnip."

The object of his moral duty was watching *her* rival's moves. Receiving a report from Fabri that the marriage was breaking up and the Dark Lady might come to California, Helen said, Let her come, she will find that she has wasted two or three years of her life "and at the end of that time I will be where I have always been, right at T''s side." She and Teddie had reached a "complete harmony and understanding." She was in a stronger position now, and she had a hold on Dreiser that was deeper than youth or sexual attraction: "There is a blood tie between T. and me, and that stays." She meant their distant cousinhood, but something more. Not only was "he . . . in a *position*, which I have helped him achieve more than anyone else in the world, but . . . he is the same as a Father to me. . . . Our relationship is exactly the same as father and daughter with a little added." Dreiser was the parent who abandoned her long ago.

She hoped to "give him some comfort in himself," spiritually. His health also gave her cause for worry—a painful blockage of the urinary tract and related bladder and kidney complications. His symptoms had their origin in his chronic prostate troubles. One doctor advised removal of the enlarged gland—devastating news, he wrote the Dark Lady. That meant impotence. Another doctor proposed burning it out with an electric needle, and gave a slightly less bleak prognosis: at best, partial impotence. "What woman could endure me—save as a companion?" he grieved. He put off the operation, took medicine, and visited a top urologist, who was, he told

Lengel, "famous for his success with mental and nervous cases." The treatment cleared up the blockage, making unnecessary the operation he feared.

While waiting and worrying, Dreiser corresponded with Harriet about renting Iroki; he was also trying to subdivide the property and sell a fifteen-acre parcel, including the cabins and the swimming pool. And he was dickering for a publisher. The $10,000 in unearned advances from Simon & Schuster preyed on him. He complained to Lengel that the publisher had dumped his backlist books at low remainder prices to avoid paying him royalties. He had telephoned Leon Shimkin, an S & S executive, about it, and Shimkin, in Dreiser's recollection, told him that it was all a "mistake." Dreiser told Alfred Mendel, editor at Longmans, Green, that S & S could have liquidated his debt long ago if they had kept his titles in print, but because of "their determination to extract the next novel from me" they preferred "to hold this debt over me as a club."

But to friends he offered another reason: his publishers were punishing him for his allegedly anti-Semitic opinions and were bent on "taking me off the market entirely." He found it very significant that Arthur Pell's former secretary was now working for Simon & Schuster. He failed to realize that there was no plot by his publishers to suppress him. The reading public had forgotten him.

In December Shimkin wrote him regarding the publisher's share of a reprint fee, of which Dreiser wanted to keep the entire amount. "It is our feeling," Shimkin said, "that if we are to be your publisher and can look forward to the privilege of publishing your books, as was called for by our contract, we would be entirely happy to overlook the contractual details and accept your suggestion to send the entire fee."

Dreiser replied that "since Horace Liveright died I have never had a publisher." He accused S & S of failing to live up to its obligation to promote his back titles. "It is my personality and reputation alone that is keeping this and my other books alive and selling—through old book stores—and will so keep them alive and selling, but not because of anything that Simon and Schuster has done in connection with them. For it so happens I am not a dead author." With those words, he severed his ties to Simon & Schuster.

As he wrote to the Dark Lady regarding *their* relationship, which, finally, was over. "If a thing is truly dead it is dead and it will not come to life, that I know. . . . I still care for you and always will, I think."

Helen might have taken some spiteful satisfaction in Dreiser's being the rejected one, but she was no longer worrying about her rival in the East. She had one in California: Elizabeth Coakley, the actor Patrick Kearney's sister, who had become Dreiser's unofficial driver. One can see the suspicion forming in her diary, in odd items such as "T. came home late" and "Teddie out with the car." That September, amid an enervating heat wave in southern California, with temperatures as high as 107°, she noted that she had planned to attend a speech he was giving, "but interference prevented. In other words Miss Kearney and car racket. She has moved up since May 2—my birthday when she called for a job in Glendale."

After an evening at the Goodmans' during which Dreiser insulted her, Helen complained, "I wonder where equity starts for him. Surely not at home. Equity he talks and lectures & writes so much but does not practice. Mormanism [sic] is rank capitalism—a certain form of slavery. Profitable too. Like any other form of slavery linked with the capitalist side of life." He always said he believed in fifty-fifty, but where was her fifty?

On September 1 she wrote: "War declared by Germany on Poland."

Dreiser thought it unreal at first. "All are playing a game," he wrote Bruce Crawford. "Each wants a share of the pot. How to get it without fighting a *big fight*. A little fight. Even a hundred thousand killed (say Poles) won't hurt the big boys."

Ruth Kennell, his political conscience on Russia, expressed the standard view of many on the left that after the "treachery and hypocrisy of Chamberlain and Daladier" in selling out Czechoslovakia at Munich, Stalin had no choice. "I'm ready to defend the Soviet-German pact and the Soviet march into Poland as a realistic foreign policy," she wrote him.

Dreiser replied that he didn't know what to make of the situation in Europe. He did not trust Hitler after Spain, but he despised the leaders of Britain and France. He concluded: "If Russia is not to sweep Europe soon, I would prefer to see a strong German state to the rotten financial dictatorship now holding in France and England and Hungary and the Balkans and elsewhere."

In his mind, France, England, Belgium, and the Netherlands were all corrupt capitalist states exploiting the masses, and he welcomed the deposal of their governments, if not by the masses then presumably by Hitler.

He may also have subconsciously seen the war as a reprise of the 1914 conflict. He wrote Richard Duffy, his old friend from his earliest days in New York, that the "nightmare of inequity" of the Treaty of Versailles had spawned the present conflict. "I know that many on both sides—the English, the French, the Italians, we Americans, see only evil in the German wish (greed, if you choose) for a place in the sun." But he remembered how the victorious powers, even Japan, had aggrandized German territory, and how the United States had been "robbed and insulted into the bargain" by its allies.

He began speaking out against social injustice in the United States. California was controlled by the corporations, he wrote Kennell; labor didn't stand a chance. The jobless were sleeping in movie houses. "I talk all the time—violently—and write. But one voice! One person!"

In June of 1939 an agent of the Federal Bureau of Investigation called at Dreiser's house in Hollywood. According to Bureau files, the visit involved a "registration matter" pertaining to the American League for Peace and Democracy, which had cosponsored Dreiser's Paris trip in 1938. The agent reported that Dreiser told him what he had done and said in Paris, of his trip to Barcelona, his activities on behalf of Spanish relief (enabling him to drop the names of Monsignor Ryan, Rufus Jones, and President Roosevelt). At the conclusion, according to the agent's report: "Mr. DREISER stated that he is not a Communist and has never engaged in any Communistic activities and has never been a member of any group which was engaged in radical activities, but he stated that it is well known that he has always been a liberal in all his thoughts and actions."

On New Year's Day 1940, like thousands of other Californians, Dreiser and Helen watched the Pasadena Rose Parade. Did he notice the svelter Helen, twenty pounds lighter after months of dieting? Dreiser's vitality was at a low ebb, and a few weeks later, after a siege of flu and neuritis, he had what the doctors termed a minor heart attack, confining him to bed for nearly six weeks. To friends Helen downplayed the seriousness of the attack, lest a prospective publisher find him a bad risk.

Undoubtedly, worry and depression contributed to his general debility. Fortunately, the medicine he needed arrived in time. The *Sister Carrie* deal was closed on February 12 by Otvos, and Dreiser's health immediately began to improve. The price was $40,000, and RKO paid a binder of $3000. A sizable chunk of the movie money was committed to paying off debts, including $5000 to Jug. (According to Helen, Jug offered Dreiser a divorce if he would give her $10,000, but he refused.) With this financial breathing space, his spirits improved; by April he was back at his desk.

In June came a summons to battle. "Do you feel keenly enough to keep the country out of war to write a book of 70–100,000 words?" Lengel asked him. Dreiser was interested but pointed out that the war might be over before a book came out. Paris had fallen and France was about to surrender; British troops had their backs to the Channel at Dunkirk. Dreiser predicted that "by August 15 Germany will have shot up England sufficiently to make her see the light regardless of what aid we can bring to bear." The publisher believed the book could be rushed out in time if copy was in by September 1. Lengel suggested that Dreiser hire editorial help. The terms were: $1000 on signing, $2000 on delivery of the manuscript, and $2000 on publication.

The publisher was Veritas Press, a small house specializing in scientific and philosophical books, which was run by Oskar Piest, a German émigré. Piest proposed as a working title "Keep Out, America" or "Let's Be Pro-American." The thesis of the book should be that America not sacrifice its freedom and constitutional ideals by becoming embroiled in a European war.

While discussions on the purpose and tenor of the book were transpiring, Dreiser pushed ahead on the research and blocked out some chapters. As editorial assistant he hired Cedric Belfrage, a young English novelist who was trying to survive in Hollywood by writing for movie magazines. Belfrage had read and admired Dreiser's novels but was unaware that he was living in Hollywood. His first impression was of a lonely old man, a forgotten writer living in a small apartment surrounded by people who had no inkling of who he was. He also discovered that Dreiser had some odd ideas, which Belfrage wasn't sure were on the right or the left. He seemed anti-Semitic, always talking about how Liveright had cheated him, and pro-Hitler, regarding the Führer as a kind of Autobahn populist who stood up to big business and finance. Politically he was a "man in a fog groping around, looking for scapegoats."

Belfrage soon discovered that Dreiser was good for about two hours of work in the morning. Then they would walk to Schwab's Drugstore, where the older man would buy a half-pint of whiskey. They would stroll back along Sunset Boulevard, Dreiser "elephantine, lumbering," Belfrage thinking, "Here I am with this great man and no one knows who he is." Once they were back in Dreiser's bedroom, which served as his study, he would pour himself a drink, taking it straight, no ice. The alcohol would affect him almost immediately, and soon he couldn't talk intelligibly. "It was pitiful to see how he crumpled up. He couldn't hold it."

Belfrage later said, "He couldn't have possibly written the book by himself, so in fact I wrote the book." A few of the chapters have a distinct Dreiser flavor, but most of the writing is not in his style and lacks his familiar phraseology and sentence structure. There are occasional Anglicisms he would never have used—e.g., "up a gum tree" and "like a Girl Guides' Field Day." Still, the book surely reflected what Dreiser wanted to say, his outline, his data, except in places where Belfrage steered him away from his more extreme obsessions, as Belfrage saw them. Either Dreiser or Belfrage coined a key term, "the International of Privilege," to convey the idea of an interlocking directorate of financial and business leaders, including Germans, conspiring against the common people to profit from the war.

On September 9 Dreiser sent the final chapter to Piest. Lengel's reaction arrived ten days later: "Considering the fact that the book was designed to show the futility of America getting into the war and to show that our interests lie in developing our own national identity, you have wandered pretty much afield at times and the book indicates that you believe our salvation rests in communism rather than in the development of democracy within the frame-work of the Constitution."

Dreiser explained his position: the Constitution should guarantee economic as well as political rights. America has "wandered so far from the ideals of the Constitution that we can't be said to have real democracy—rather the rule of a financial Oligarchy." These were the points he wanted to make in the book, and he believed they accorded with Piest's outline.

Piest had a personal problem: he had applied for citizenship and evidently feared that he would be accused of communist sympathies. Dreiser made some revisions in line with Piest's criticisms and assured the publisher that he had kept the Constitution and the Declaration of Independence on his desk. Piest seemed satisfied and sent the book to press. But on October 24, while Dreiser was reading galleys, the publisher wired that rumors were being spread by a competitor that he was part of the covert Nazi propaganda effort in America. The charge was untrue of course, but he feared the gossip would stigmatize Dreiser, and he thought it best that someone else publish the book, which in fact was both anti-Hitler and anti–British imperialism.

Piest and Lengel quickly arranged for Modern Age Books, a radical house, to take over. David Zablodowsky, of Modern Age, asked for some cuts, primarily material critical of the Red Cross. Dreiser stubbornly reinserted the material in the galleys. Still, Modern Age was enthusiastic, and Lengel predicted that it might take over his other books.

In December the printer balked, citing a number of potentially libelous statements. Some of their examples were farfetched, suggesting that the political content was also cause for concern. Zablodowsky wrote Dreiser, "We . . . are determined to publish your book and your message, on the ground that a man of your stature has a right to be heard, no matter what he wishes to say." However, he begged Dreiser to excise potentially libelous material. Also, his salesmen reported bookstore resistance to Dreiser's title "Is America Worth Saving?"—too negative. He suggested instead "Is Peace Worth Saving?" And after submitting fifteen new titles, Dreiser agreed to the more positive "America Is Worth Saving."

But he wrote Lengel to complain about all the delays and wondered if the book would ever be published. The libel problems turned out to be minor. The main bone of contention was the Red Cross material, which he finally agreed to drop. He authorized Frederick Field, secretary of American Peace Mobilization and an attorney (not to mention a Vanderbilt heir), to make any necessary cuts. He wanted the book out: "I hate, in this instance most of all, to be once more suppressed."

Then Dreiser demanded ironclad assurances that Piest would pay him the rest of the money. Wearily Lengel forged separate contracts between Dreiser and Piest and Dreiser and Modern Age. Once the book was safely in port, he addressed to Dreiser one of his rare reproaches: "at all times my efforts have been directed solely in *your* behalf—a fact which seems not to have impressed you."

America Is Worth Saving was published in January. *Time* brushed it off as "a spiteful, wretchedly written tract by great, aging Theodore Dreiser . . . who lives in Hollywood, lectures to California's women's clubs." (Dreiser had spoken to the Beverly Hills Junior League.) Less ideological critics found that Dreiser's book made some good points, however intemperate his style and inaccurate some of his facts. (He is at times oddly prescient—predicting the inevitability of the decline of the British Empire and the importance of the splitting of the atom.) But they were put off by his anti-British rhetoric, such as calling England "this black widow of the nations" and characterizing the war as between "Hitlerdum and Hitlerdee." Even recent CP apostates like Granville Hicks, caught in a seismic ideological shift, could not swallow Dreiser's contention that British imperialism was as bad as Hitlerian fascism.

He had failed to recognize that Nazism threatened the destruction of the Constitution he kept on his desk. History, the most merciless critic of all, would give his book its worst review.

In December, while driving on North Kings Road in Hollywood, Dreiser and Helen spied an attractive white stucco Spanish colonial house with a red-tiled roof and a For Sale sign in front. It was situated on a quiet street lined with oak trees and had a large yard with a pond in back. They bought it immediately.

In January three vans containing all their furniture from Iroki and Dreiser's books and papers arrived from the East. The northern wing of the L-shaped structure became Dreiser's quarters, with a bedroom, bath, and study. A storeroom was eventually constructed in the garage for his papers, boxes and boxes of letters, clippings, and manuscripts. The study had a door opening into the garden in back, where he would sometimes work at a card table.

Having finished *America Is Worth Saving,* Dreiser was feeling "healthy and fairly cheerful," he told Masters. "He got his strength back all of a sudden," Helen reported to Alyse Powys, whose husband, Llewelyn Powys, had tragically died in December 1939. (His brother John's affliction, bleeding ulcers, had killed him, not tuberculosis.) "He is trying to take care of himself. He works like a Trojan."

Reinvigorated, Dreiser took to the stump in January. He spoke at an American Peace Mobilization rally in Los Angeles, looking "flushed" and "leonine," according to *People's World,* and had the audience of 3000 roaring with laughter at jokes about FDR (whom he was "down on" for Lend-Lease aid to Britain) picnicking with the King and Queen at Hyde Park: "Damned if I don't think the man has lost his mind. He's delighted when a queen comes over and eats a hot dog with him. I think we're worth more than that—they can't buy us off with a hot dog." At the end of February he flew to New York City for a speech to the American Council of Soviet Relations. Marguerite Tjader Harris found him "full of tumult, argument, very much on the offensive about his book, his opinions." She had never seen him "more violent in speech and action and flaunting opposition with almost diabolic glee." He was full of himself, and once more bubbling over with save-the-world schemes, which may have explained his good health.

But his speech at the banquet was a fiasco. He had no prepared text and grew morose as he listened to a parade of speakers who droned on about Soviet-American friendship. Out of nervousness he did not touch his food, and kept drinking one highball after another. After three hours, in a tipsy state, he heaved himself up to the lectern and began talking about how the press lied about communism. Then his emotions welled up and he segued into an emotional dirge about the poor and wretched of the earth, recalling mining towns in Wales and London slums, breaking into sobs at times. Finally the Reverend John A. Kingsbury, chairman of the Council, seized him during a burst of applause and led him off the platform.

The next day he spoke soberly to the League of American Writers. The novelist Richard Wright, who had been inspired by *An American Tragedy* in writing his own novel *Native Son,* was moved by Dreiser's plea to young writers to fight for social justice. Then, at a mass meeting in Newark, he told the audience, "After all is said, it is the People who run the world. . . . Or should. Henry Ford, and all our big corporations are nothing without the people." He warned them that the big corporations were trying to steal their liberties: "Realize what they are trying to do and remember that when you want to YOU CAN DO IT!" And then he waved briefly and lumbered off, to thunderous applause. Later, he had a rendezvous with the Dark Lady, but the experience convinced her, at least, that the affair was over.

In an interview with Robert van Gelder of *The New York Times Book Review* he made an exhortation not frequently heard in the pages of the *Times:* "I'll tell you, if we don't have a revolution here with America modeling itself on Russia then Americans aren't Americans any more."

While in the city he consulted with Stanley M. Moffat, the attorney handling negotiations to wind up his contract with Simon & Schuster. The sticking point was the amount of his debt to the house, which the publisher estimated at over $10,000, and Dreiser at $8000. He also lunched with Earle Balch, editor-in-chief of G. P. Putnam's Sons, who was definitely interested in taking over his books but would make no commitment until Dreiser had extricated himself from his present publishers.

A piece of good news arrived from Hollywood: the musical version of "My Brother Paul," to be titled *My Gal Sal,* had been sold to Twentieth Century–Fox. The price was in the neighborhood of $35,000, which included the rights to Paul's songs, the money to be split among the brothers and sisters. Only Theodore, Ed, Mame, and Sylvia remained of the ten children born to Sarah and John Paul Dreiser in Indiana.

Early in the morning of June 22, 300 German divisions crossed the Russo-Polish frontier in Hitler's long-awaited Operation Barbarossa. Dreiser, who had supported the Nazi-Soviet Nonaggression Pact, was furious at this perfidy. His first public comment on the invasion, for *The New Masses,* was almost incoherent, as though spat out in blind fury. It was, he said, planned from the very beginning by the "Money International" and its servants England, Germany, France, the United States.

On July 14, in a calmer mood, he dispatched a statement to the Union of Soviet Writers. "Nothing in the history of mankind . . . not even the senseless, barbaric devastation and massacre" by the great scourges of the past, such as Genghis Khan, Tamerlane, Attila, Napoleon, Alexander, could compare with the evil of Hitler's invasion. While he could not forget "Hitler's primary and quite respectable struggle to restore the German people, once they had been struck down by their capitalistic trade rivals of 1914–1918," the dictator's successes had gone to his head and he was pursuing "a dream of Empire for Empire's sake." But Dreiser could not resist adding, "I mistrust England as much as I mistrust Hitler. . . ." He predicted that if Russia defeated Hitler, England would resume its old game of seeking to undermine Russia. Those opinions were stricken from the statement when it appeared in the Soviet Union.

England was now Russia's ally, but he would not budge from his Anglophobia, even when it alienated a man he considered one of his dearest friends, Otto Kyllmann. After receiving a copy of *America Is Worth Saving*, Kyllmann wrote Dreiser in July that at a time when German bombs were killing Londoners, his book was "a stab in the back." Kyllmann supposed that, under the New Order, "you will be happy and prosperous and either work under a Gauleiter or be one yourself."

Shaken, Dreiser replied, "I cannot tell you how much your two letters . . . touched me." He wished most earnestly that Hitler "might be seized and shot or executed tonight." He was not against the English people, only the English aristocracy and financiers, who "ignored and bled 500 million natives in the Empire."

Dreiser's distinction between the English people and their lords and masters was swept away by the bombs raining down on the just and the unjust alike in London. His friend Marguerite Tjader Harris turned down an anti-British diatribe he submitted to *Direction* for fear of adverse reaction. Dreiser's timing was execrable: slamming the British, who had stood alone against Hitler while his "pet," Russia, had remained aloof.

Yet his Anglophobia was no worse than that of many Irish-Americans or isolationists or the Chicago *Tribune* editorial page. And his opposition to fighting a war to save the British Empire was shared in theory by most liberals, including Norman Thomas and FDR privately. After Hitler attacked Russia, Dreiser refused to allow the isolationist America First Committee to distribute offprints of an anti-British chapter from *America Is Worth Saving*. He told the committee he was pro-Russian and not pro-Hitler, and did not wish to be associated with it in any way.

As the news from the Eastern Front became more grim, Dreiser issued passionate statements of support. An ideal dear to him was being brutalized, and he felt humble before the inspiring resistance of the Red Army, which at the eleventh hour had stalled the Nazi advance outside Moscow.

Yet when the Soviet writers union asked him to endorse some Slavophile propaganda, presumably as part of a Moscow campaign to stir up ethnic groups outside the Soviet Union, he demurred. Such chauvinism was wrong, he said, far from the battle; communism should stand for a fair deal for all peoples of the world. "As long as they are against fascism or any other kind of brutality and intolerance, they are on the progressive side. But if you isolate the Slav, it might lead to an evil as bad as to isolate the Aryan. I think these lines should disappear and a new kind of brotherhood and understanding be allowed to be born into the world."

At home, he found few forums to address. When a group in Indianapolis asked him to speak, he accepted on the conditions that he could criticize England for not doing enough to help the Soviet Union and that the proceeds of the meeting go to Soviet relief. The sponsors acceded to his terms, and he departed in mid-November, after a row with Helen, probably related to Elizabeth Coakley.

The meeting, which drew a respectable crowd of 500 in that conservative city, went off without incident. Introduced by Fowler Harper, a professor at Indiana University Law School, Dreiser gave his usual pitch, and no one brought out the tar and feathers. In Washington, however, the ever-vigilant Representative Martin Dies was outraged by the spectacle of pro-Soviet propaganda being spread in the heartland of America, and he later threatened to call Harper before his committee for a grilling. Dreiser wrote Ruth Kennell, "I think Dies has given up on me because I always emphasize our free Press, Radio, Movies. Also Mr. Dies' right to have his say so, whether paid for by the corporations or not."

From Indianapolis he traveled to New York to meet with Balch. Putnam offered him a contract, which he characterized to Helen as "not very good but maybe the best I can get." The good news was that Moffat had liberated him from Simon & Schuster, at a price of $8500. He returned to Helen in Portland in a conciliatory mood. "I can't stand ruling by others," he wrote her, "and so we clash often so uselessly it seems to me since nothing is gained by it. We go on as before." He was trying to do better. In September she had undergone a hysterectomy to correct a chronic gynecological problem. She had complained to Fabri of poor health for about a year. Her nerves were bad; she was "too sensitive a variety of person for the force that played on me." She had tried to find "*some sort* of relief. But T. never really realized it. He can't. He is too powerful—too ambitious—too self-centered. But that is genius. And my fate." And his too.

She came through the operation in good shape, returning home after about two weeks. Dreiser and Pearl, the maid, were there to greet her, and she cooed in her diary, "I *love* my home with Teddie *so* much and I love *him* so much." But a fortnight later she wrote: "T. out at 4 with Coakley to dinner etc. etc."

On December 7, 1941, the Japanese attack on Pearl Harbor wrote finis to the Great Debate. In the immediate aftermath, rumors of enemy bombers in home skies and invasion fleets offshore flickered up and down the West Coast. The Japanese attack had the effect of drawing him closer to his country. He told the *Daily Worker* that Americans "ought to be willing . . . to serve the officials of this government to produce a united front . . . we have a country that is democratic in spirit, and once its dream of real democracy is made effective, it may actually democratize the whole world."

When Louise Campbell wrote him of her worries about being killed by a bomb and her depressed state of mind, he comforted her. America was in for "storm & stress, but it certainly has had a long run of ease, peace and plenty—so much so that it has grown cocky, indolent, self-pleasuring and inequitably indifferent to the needs of its own underprivileged." He closed on a note being sounded in homes everywhere: ". . . we're all in this together & instead of spending time brooding on who's going to get killed first we'd better be figuring out how to kill some of our enemies first."

CHAPTER 36

The Avocado Tree

> I am not an "isolationist" in the sense that people define this
> slogan any more than I am a 'communist' in the sense that
> the *word* is interpreted by the American people as meaning
> something dark and mysterious and antiAmerican and this
> and that.
>
> —Dreiser to Hortense N. Dillon (1942)

D reiser had joked to Louise that he had some "defense work" on his desk—probably *The Bulwark*. In a schedule he furnished Lengel, he had placed the novel second on his agenda. But Lengel and Balch insisted he begin with it. Dreiser acquiesced, adding, "It is far enough along to finish it in the time that I said," that is, by fall 1942.

In reality, *The Bulwark* was an even more problematical novel for him now than when he had abandoned it to work on *An American Tragedy*. He must reconcile the four different versions of the novel that he had on hand, all written prior to 1920. And his conception of the central character, the father Solon Barnes, had changed. But one scene at least remained the same. He had written it before he even started the novel to test whether he could do justice to the tragedy inherent in the material. That is the scene in which Solon steals downstairs late at night to view the body of his son Stewart, who has been charged with murder and, rather than face his parents, commits suicide in jail. In that confrontation was buried the autobiographical seed of the novel—Dreiser's long-repressed need for his father's approval. The suicide of Stewart was his own symbolic suicide, a cry for love and a reproach, and a turning upon himself of his hostility toward John Paul Dreiser.

Although in April he reported to Mencken that he was "doing quite well" with the book, he saw now that much writing lay ahead. He confessed to Lengel that the novel would not be ready for some time. "It is a very intimate and touchy problem in connection with religious family life—and, like The [sic] American Tragedy I find it difficult." He offered to repay the advance if it would ease Balch's mind.

Putnam had announced *The Bulwark* in its catalogue and set a deadline of September 1. This unnerved Dreiser. "You understand it is a long book and not an easy one to write," he told Balch, "something on the order of *The Financier* or *The 'Genius.'* " Still, he assured Balch that he was working every day.

Typically, he confided hints of his state of mind to a woman friend, Sylvia Bradshaw,* an American living in Toronto and working in a war plant. Bradshaw had been drawn to Dreiser's novels several years before and, on a whim, decided to send him a Christmas card in 1941. He immediately launched one of his epistolary flirtations, which received a sympathetic response. They had unhappy marriages in common, and her grandmother was a Quaker, so Dreiser queried her about ordinary life among the Friends sixty or seventy years ago, when the novel, as it now stood, was set. He was specifically interested in "arresting incidents of one kind or another connected with the average human attempt to live up to a religious or moral ideal," the "amusing results of spiritual striving" when one fails in the attempt.

He betrays a nervously frivolous view of *The Bulwark*. A part of him was uncomfortable with good gray Quakers. Then too, he felt that seeming too religious would interfere with his campaign to arrange a tryst with Bradshaw. He proposed "a relationship that will comfort both of us for years and make life less difficult for us to bear."

The war was another distraction. Dreiser was anxious to do his part. On his personal home front, the war of *Sister Carrie* went on. Two Broadway writers failed to lick the script problems. Dreiser began to believe it would never be made. Hurstwood's end was just "too dark" for Hollywood. The light and entertaining *My Gal Sal,* however, presented no problems. It sailed through production and was released in June. Dreiser was actually proud of it, calling it "nostalgic but a better movie than they usually make."

He let on that he wrote the original script, but that was not quite true. At most, he worked over a treatment that Helen had composed from a draft by Esther McCoy, but this story was tossed into the wastebasket, and three

---

*A fictitious name.

studio hands concocted the shooting script. The film was almost entirely fantasy, beginning with the casting of Victor Mature, a beefcake male lead, as the corpulent Paul, and glamorous Rita Hayworth as Sal, who is not the Evansville madam Sallie Walker, who inspired Paul's song, but a musical-comedy star. There are glimpses of the Dreiser family in the opening scenes; in one a tearful Theodore says goodbye to Paul before he runs away. After that, any relationship to characters living or dead is coincidental. It was a typical "Gay 90s" musical, a genre popular in the 1940s. How Dreiser could say that Twentieth Century–Fox had done well by his story is difficult to imagine. Perhaps, after the years of futile attempts to sell a movie, he was relieved to have his name connected with something—and a commercially successful picture at that. Al Manuel, a Hollywood agent who discussed with Dreiser three scripts he had written with Elizabeth Coakley (one designed as a vehicle for the popular skating star Sonja Henie), got the impression that Dreiser longed to write a *Saturday Evening Post* story.

Meanwhile he had arranged a rendezvous with Miss Bradshaw. Abandoning plans for a romantic interlude at Niagara Falls, they agreed that she should travel to Los Angeles in July, and he sent her train fare. They spent eleven days together that he later called "the sweetest, lovingest days of my life." Sylvia was no young thing; she was forty—intelligent, pleasant, attractive, though no beauty. But she instinctively gave him the mothering, adoration, and sensual warmth he hungered for. He compared her to the heroine of "The Darling," his favorite Chekhov story. The heroine personified his ideal woman, sacrificially loving one man after another, a maternal figure.

"It was paradise for both of us for we got along so well," Sylvia recalled. "We were much alike in many ways." She shared his fascination with the occult, and later had telepathic visitations by him, including one after his death. Almost fifty years later she remembered sitting in the car with him at the beach; hulking, sausage-shaped barrage balloons loomed in the sky, and barbed wire and machine-gun emplacements lined the shore. "He liked to talk on and on . . . and I loved to listen." Sometimes he would watch her swim. Exercise was out for him; he was physically incapable of walking even short distances. That July was hot in Los Angeles, so when not at the beach they spent most of the day in their air-conditioned room at the Mayfair Hotel, going for drives at night.

When it came time to leave, she wept uncontrollably. "I could have preferred dying, the day I was to leave. All the way back to Toronto, I was miserable."

The idyll with Sylvia would have an untoward effect. In August he received an invitation from the Toronto Forum to speak on the necessity for an

Allied invasion of Europe to relieve the German pressure on Russia. Like most on the left, Dreiser strongly advocated such a second front. He was still sore at England, he wrote Louise Campbell. "Its sole aim is to save the British Empire with its sacred *clawses*. . . . So I'm out to go to jail before I'm through."

Seeing Sylvia again, all expenses paid, was his primary motive for the trip. The fee was only $200, plus $225 for travel and expenses (he had sent Miss Bradshaw $170 to cover the same journey). Another incentive was a tentative speaking engagement in Indiana for September 26—five days after his talk in Canada.

He had no qualms about carrying an anti-British message into a British dominion, and in a letter to Sylvia he jocularly wondered why he had been asked, "for I plan to roast the English beef as I always do. If they want to take me to the border afterwards and throw me out into the night, that's their business."

When Dreiser arrived in Toronto early on Sunday, September 20, there were no signs of potential trouble. His talk had been well advertised, and the *Telegram* hailed him as a "massive figure in American literature" and "this honest quiet writer." Sylvia met him and they went to his room. That night he had dinner with reporters and spoke of his reverence for "an immaterial force that is shaping the world and everything in it."

Realizing that their visitor was "box-office in Toronto," as the *Telegram* had written, Forum officials postponed the speech until September 22 so that a bigger crowd might be assembled. According to Dreiser, the Forum asked him to participate in another press conference on the morning of the twenty-first to stir up additional publicity. He agreed and met with a motley collection of reporters, including two from the gossip sheets *Flash* and *Hush*, a radio interviewer, and Margaret Aiken of the *Evening Telegram*. Bradshaw and Sir Charles G. D. Roberts, a Canadian novelist whom Dreiser had known in his Village days, were also present.

The reporters were well aware of his distaste for England, particularly Aiken, a niece of press magnate Lord Beaverbrook and a fervent Anglophile. Her paper was Tory in politics and had recently published some dismissive editorials about a second-front rally in the city sponsored by two leftist trade unions. Her hostile questions stunned Dreiser, who later said, "She seemed like a nice girl." He no doubt noticed that she was also an attractive one, which caused him to lower his guard. As he remembered it, he began outlining the ideas in his speech, as he had done the night before, only to be interrupted by sharp questions about his past statements on England and the second front. Under fire, he became defensive and lost his temper.

Her story generated front-page headlines in the afternoon edition: "ABUSE FOR BRITAIN DREISER'S CONTRIBUTION TO ANGLO-U.S. UNITY." Her account was just as tendentious. The lead sentence identified Dreiser as an "American author of German parentage." She quoted him as saying, "Should Russia go down to defeat I hope the Germans invade England. I would rather see Germans in England than those damn, aristocratic, horse-riding snobs there now." He scored the "unbelievable gall and brass of the English," who had received lavish aid from the United States but had done nothing to help the Russians. He accused Churchill of not opening a second front because he was "afraid the communists will rule the world."

Dreiser's remarks were extremely impolitic, and Aiken did everything possible to make him look like a Nazi sympathizer, stressing his German background, his stern German father, his supposed admiration for Charles Lindbergh and the isolationist cause, and portraying him as a Red. Even when Dreiser insisted that he was anti-Hitler, she sniffed, "He also claims to hate Hitler—and most of his 'hymn of hate' was directed against Hitler's most formidable enemy, Britain."

After Aiken's version hit the streets, the telephone lines at the offices of local and national authorities in the city were jammed with calls from angry Canadians demanding that the speech be prohibited and Dreiser be arrested and either deported or interned. In urgent session the city council adopted a resolution calling on the mayor to meet with the commissioners of police and ask them "to take such action as is necessary to prohibit Mr. Theodore Dreiser from addressing any public meeting in this city. . . ." This was done and the commissioners banned the meeting, fearing violence, they said. The federal minister of justice issued an order forbidding Dreiser to make any speech in Canada or even to issue a statement. Canada's minister for external affairs advised the American embassy in Ottawa that if a Canadian had said what Dreiser did he would have been clapped into jail. The American consul in Toronto made a report directly to the secretary of state, assessing the potential damage to U.S.-Canadian relations.

Following the fatal press conference, Sylvia, worried about Dreiser's health (he had a severe cold), took charge. They had lunch and did some sightseeing until the afternoon papers appeared. When they saw the *Telegram*'s headline, they agreed that they must leave the city. She remembered that the Detroit train stopped briefly at a station in the western part of the city and decided to catch it there. The central station had several flights of stairs, and she did not think he could make the descent to the platform.

They returned to the hotel, hurriedly packed, and caught a taxi, arriving only a few minutes before train time. No warrant for his arrest had been issued, but the Royal Canadian Mounted Police kept track of their movements.

Before fleeing, Dreiser took telephone calls from two Canadian reporters and told them that he had been misquoted and misinterpreted. In a long-distance interview with the New York liberal paper *PM*, he said that he did not remember saying he would rather see Germans in England than the snobs now in charge, but admitted he had said, "I would be perfectly happy to see the Germans remove the 15 per cent that is holding down the English people." When his other quotes were read to him, he agreed they were more or less accurate, but he denied that he was, as Aiken reported, an admirer of Lindbergh. That had been "before Pearl Harbor." Now, of course, he was no isolationist: "I want Germany defeated, in self-defense and to save the heroic Russian people."

The train ride was uneventful and no one tried to stop them. They got off in Port Huron, Michigan. Sylvia, who had trained as a nurse, feared he might develop pneumonia—his cold had spread to his chest, and he was having difficulty breathing—so they holed up in a hotel room for three days. But the Port Huron *Times-Herald* was tipped off about his presence by a hotel employee, who recognized him even though he signed the register "T. H. Dresser and wife." A reporter and a photographer camped out in the room next to his. First they tried to telephone him, but Sylvia coolly told them they had the wrong number. Was Theodore Dreiser in town? She would love to meet him.

The reporters knew he was in the hotel, and when Sylvia emerged they confronted her. She persuaded them to retire to their adjoining room, and once they were inside slammed the door and turned the key they had left in the lock. While they were immobilized, she and Dreiser checked out of the hotel. She went off to purchase train tickets, telling him to meet her on a certain corner, but became lost. As he anxiously waited for her, the liberated reporter-photographer team found him and asked for a comment. Dreiser groused that he didn't give a damn about what the Canadian press said about him and asked caustically what the reporter thought of the "Canadian ideal of free speech." The photographer snapped his picture, which ran under the headline SECOND AMERICAN TRAGEDY.

Finally Sylvia rejoined him and they escaped to Detroit, remaining there two nights. Dreiser then caught a bus for Indianapolis, where he stayed with friends until he felt up to making the long train journey to Los Angeles. His cold was worse, and he had laryngitis and was coughing painfully. His friends relayed to the *Star* his version of what had really happened in Canada: "I didn't say and I didn't mean that I hoped England would be defeated by Hitler." He said the British were still fighting "the sitzkrieg they declared on Germany three years ago." If Russia was defeated, "we'll have 20 years of uphill slogging before the war is over." People who thought he was pro-Nazi "can get that out of their systems." After a few days of recuperation, he boarded a train and spent the entire trip in his berth, greasing his chest with Mentholatum and subsisting on beer and a pound of nuts that a reporter bought for him.

A few editorial writers criticized him for jeopardizing Allied unity. The Writers War Board, a group formed to turn out propaganda for the government on a voluntary basis, issued a statement signed by its president, Rex

Stout, and several others, including Pearl Buck, expressing regret that "an American writer of Mr. Dreiser's eminence should thus insult and offend our allies." And in a crueler cut, it observed: "Our enemies would pay him well for his disservice to our country's cause."

In his public reply, Dreiser charged that the board had, "without troubling to investigate the facts concerning my remarks made about England's titled class, proceeded to ally me with Hitler and against the allies." He reiterated that his remarks were directed at the British aristocracy; he did not want "to see Hitler rule the English people as a whole." America's true allies were the "great masses of India, Russia, China and the common people of England," not the titled snobs. He asked Pearl Buck how she could sign such a document after all she had written about "the brutal rule by the British Tories of the colonial peoples of the Far East."

Later Pearl Buck (the third American Nobel Laureate to say Dreiser deserved the award in her stead) wrote him that the statement of the Writers War Board had been issued without her knowledge. Although she did not agree with what he had reportedly said in Toronto, "I still believe in free speech." In his statement Dreiser had asked for an apology, but she declined, telling him, "I think your stature is too great to take this matter as seriously as you are doing." Dreiser agreed, writing her on November 19, "I am sick of the entire affair." The final indignity was a letter from Norman Cowan, the Forum's program director, demanding a refund of the traveling expenses advanced him.

Even before Toronto, the FBI's file on Dreiser had graduated to a full dossier, a "Custodial Detention" card listing his left-wing affiliations. This had been compiled in November 1941, under a Bureau program to detain enemy aliens and "subversives" in a national emergency. Dreiser made the list as a communist, though there was not a single report that he belonged to the Party. Indeed, the Bureau usually identified him as a sympathizer or an "intellectual Communist." Following his Toronto speech, his "dangerousness classification" was upgraded to "A-1." (This index was the Bureau's creation, and the following year Attorney General Francis Biddle ordered that it be dropped because it had no legal standing and served no legitimate purpose.)

An agent from the Detroit field office was assigned to the case. He reported that Dreiser had stayed in a hotel with a woman not his wife, and Washington conceived the idea of prosecuting him for transporting a woman for immoral purposes under the White Slave Traffic Act. Detroit was ordered to look into the matter further, although a high Bureau official admitted that "Dreiser is 71 years of age and the possibility of his having had natural relations with [Sylvia Bradshaw] seems unlikely." Then the U.S.

Attorney in Detroit said that if the Bureau would present him the facts he would bring a Mann Act prosecution. But the attorney general later instructed Director Hoover to drop the investigation.

Although the Mann Act prosecution died a well-deserved death, the Bureau continued to track Dreiser. One informant charged he had an immoral relationship with a woman in New York who worked for the government and was in a position to feed him classified information. (She was the Dark Lady.) In a "Memorandum for the Director," D. M. Ladd added, "The Bureau, of course, has an extensive file on Dreiser and he has been known to have been in communication with officials of the U.S.S.R. . . ." In an earlier letter Hoover had pointed out to the attorney general that "allegations to the effect that Dreiser has consorted with women have been called to the Bureau's attention." With Dreiser it was a close question whether the FBI was more interested in his consorting with women or his "subversive" activities.

Although he knew nothing of the Bureau's interest in his sex life, in early 1942 he wrote George Seldes, publisher of *In Fact*, that he suspected his books were on the FBI's "black list." He asked Seldes to locate a copy of said list (apparently there was none). He grew more cautious in his public utterances, and when radical groups and publications used his name without his permission he protested more vehemently than in the past. On one such occasion he remonstrated with Marguerite Harris that he objected to "being pushed to the front as a leading and even violent Communist. . . ." Rewriting history a bit, he said, "I have avoided (always) joining the Party on the ground that it is better to be an independent American campaigner for the social equities that would, if emphasized here, bring the equivalent of Communism here and actually gain a swifter support for all of them, rather than a prolonged & delaying quarrel over a name."

He was unaware that by 1943 the FBI was monitoring his communications to and from Russia, including cables, through the Office of Censorship, a wartime agency that inspected foreign mail. His correspondence with Sylvia Bradshaw in Canada was sometimes opened.

Other than providing grist for J. Edgar Hoover's gossip mill, the Toronto trip may have had a positive result. Helen writes that the incident "with its accompanying notoriety had taken its toll in spite of his well developed immunity to criticism." He vowed to cut down on his speaking and finish his book.

In fact he was in an unsettled mood and asked Sylvia to send him a "strength wave—something that would inspire me in connection with my book. It's hard to work when youre troubled in your mind about love & desire & financial complications." He urged her to move to Los Angeles, where there were plenty of high-paying jobs. She was reluctant; like others before her, she didn't want to share him with Helen. He told her what he had told them—that he owed Helen something and could not just throw her out. Once he came into some money he would pay her off.

His letters to Bradshaw show affection and gratitude for her pluck and her care for him in Canada. In one he describes a flaw in his nature that he had never admitted before: "I'm in the main a bad egg—selfish, self centered, interested in large problems which concern the welfare of millions but fails [sic] to take into consideration the poor failure at [my] door-step. And that is very bad. I can see it clearly—the Lone Wolf complex. And yet I love & respect those who, like you, do look after the individual as well as the mass."

He would also write Sylvia: "Life, apart from love and desire and satiation in the arms of the beloved, is scarcely worth the living. And it is because of that so often I think of death as a door to rest or peace—the end of strain and disappointment."

On October 1, 1942, Sara White Dreiser had passed through the door to rest or peace. She died in Missouri of what her niece called "a complication of illnesses." The funeral was held at the Methodist Church in Mexico, Missouri. The minister read a statement Jug had requested, that she and Theodore had been separated but not divorced. It was her life's triumph to cling to his name until it could be carved in the stone that marks her grave in the little cemetery near Montgomery City, next to her father and mother. Etched on Archibald Herndon White's stone are the words "A True Patriarch"—the title of the story Dreiser wrote about Jug's father forty years previously. He never commented on her death. She was someone he had known long ago.

How goes *The Bulwark*? Mencken asked Dreiser, seeking news and trying to revive their flagging correspondence. Dreiser replied he was on chapter 34 and promised "it will come through." He was supposed to be finishing the first third of the book to submit to Balch; instead, he wrote Sylvia that he had been hard at work on his tax return and outlining a script for *The "Genius."*

Financial worries had him by the throat again, though surely they weren't as serious as he made them seem (the main setback was that the buyer for the Iroki property had canceled). He announced to Sylvia he was trying to sell an idea for a movie (an adaptation of *The "Genius"*). Then he inexplicably agreed to write an article for the *Writers Digest Yearbook,* though the fee was only $75. He proposed to describe "his general stand as to world politics." It would not be a defense of the position he took in Canada, Helen explained to A. M. Mathieu, assistant editor; rather, "a kind of résumé of the whole situation that led to that stand."

The essay contained Dreiser's familiar criticisms of England and praise of the Soviet Union; he closed with a peroration, "stop the fight, stop the

destruction. Send the men behind the guns back to the fields and the laboratories, and let's welcome the new day." He was hardly calling for the Allies
to lay down their arms, yet incredibly that was how *Writers Digest* interpreted his words. Mathieu promptly submitted the article to the Office of
Censorship, which had the power to forbid the export of magazines, movies,
or books containing material that was considered harmful to the war effort.
In the case of Dreiser's article, the office provided an advance ruling that the
article contained "Propaganda detrimental to the war efforts of the United
States or the United Nations" and material "whose dissemination might
directly or indirectly bring aid and comfort to the enemy or interfere with
the war effort. . . ." If the *Yearbook* were banned overseas, the publisher
would lose money.

Mathieu gratuitously added a second reason: Dreiser's appeal for an end
to the fighting was Nazi propaganda. Although Mathieu wouldn't go so far
as to accuse Dreiser of being a "conscious instrument" of the Reich, "it is
impossible to say that this manuscript is not an unconscious instrument of
this Nazi propaganda for peace." To publish it "would be treason. I cannot
see it any other way except treason."

An outraged Helen warned the editor not to be so "glib throwing
accusations of treason around." Mr. Dreiser, she said, didn't need the $75 and
hadn't written for such a small amount in years. Mathieu brushed aside
Helen's letter, telling her that *he* knew what Dreiser meant when he said
"stop the fighting." It wasn't like Dreiser to let these aspersions pass without
a murmur. But coming a few months after the experience in Toronto, the
charges apparently stunned him into silence.

Despite his optimistic words to Mencken about his progress on *The Bulwark*,
he wrote Sylvia that he felt a sense of failure. His trouble was psychological.
His niece Vera Dreiser thought that he was "identifying his own father with
the character in his trials and tribulations. He was also suffering from self-
identification, which happened with all his writing." This self-identification
confused him as to who he was or should be. Solon was hard to live in, and
with; Dreiser could hardly claim to emulate the Quaker's morality in his
own life, yet he could no longer view him with the distancing irony of his
original conception.

To Sylvia he praised George Fox and John Woolman as "two authors
of the loveliest and most truthful Journals ever written—these and the
Autobiography of Jean Jacques Rousseau." Quakerism, he told her, is "the
most beautiful religion in the world . . . the only honest self-sacrificial
religion." But its discipline is so hard to live up to. *"It is so exacting. So
difficult. And yet I love it so."* He speaks of wanting to meet her in Detroit
but is sure John Woolman wouldn't approve. Quaker discipline represented

the order and control he missed in his life *("I love it so")*. This desire for order (for peace), in himself, in the universe, clashed with the creative, sensual, anarchic side of his nature. Marguerite Tjader Harris once wrote, "The Satyr in him was as strong as the Saint." Now, immersed in Quakerism, he was torn between the saint—Solon—and the satyr in himself.

In response to his pleas, Bradshaw agreed to come for an indefinite stay. She found a small apartment on North Hayworth, and Dreiser visited her there. She obtained a job at the Los Angeles *Times* in the classified department to support herself. The work was hard, the wartime hours long.

Sylvia's presence did not inspire him to work on the novel, however. She recalled that he quizzed her about her Quaker forebears but otherwise did not discuss it. In August Helen's mother suffered a stroke. With Helen's tacit approval, Sylvia moved in with Theodore at the Kings Road house for a few weeks. Someone must take care of him while Helen went to Oregon. But Sylvia knew it was a temporary arrangement. Since Jug's death, Helen was fiercely determined to marry Dreiser. "She carried a gun of some kind," Sylvia recalled. "I didn't want to be involved in any shooting accidents. Helen wasn't fooling as to marriage."

Although he urged her to stay, Sylvia decided to return to Canada. "I had to look ahead a little," she explained, "and I knew that Theodore did not look after himself too well and no one else did. If anything happened to him, L.A. had no attraction for me." Although in a letter to her he mentions her "fiery jealousy" and her constant threats to leave, her memory was, "We never quarreled. Never! Helen was the problem."

Shortly after Sylvia withdrew from the field, Dreiser wrote Helen in Portland that he had decided to drop *The Bulwark* and take up the third volume of his autobiography instead. But surely he realized that finding a new publisher was no easy matter. And his general mood was not conducive to starting another book. In September he told Sylvia that he had developed a case of "nerves" which evoked "a sense of dread or fear in regard to myself. . . . Suddenly the ability to write . . . to go on with *The Bulwark* or in fact anything in the way of work that is before me is up the chimney." He could only lie down and worry about what would happen if he didn't finish the novel and his script.

Stanley Moffat had written Helen that the entire relationship with Putnam depended on his finishing *The Bulwark*, and he warned that the company might lose interest or even bring a breach of contract suit. She agreed that he must finish the novel. Dreiser had been making good progress on it, she said, but now his mood was not right and he was "not a well man." It would be "cruel and wicked" to bring a suit against a man his age; he would gladly refund the $1000. Moffat met with Balch and reported that the latter was willing "to let the situation go along just as it stands in the hope that the book will ultimately be produced." The thought of a suit was "the farthest thing from Putnam's minds."

Helen's offer to refund the money suggests they were not facing the poorhouse, but Dreiser continued to cast about for low-paying magazine projects, turning to his favorite outlet, *Esquire,* for which he conceived a series of articles called "Unworthy Characters." The idea derived from his frustration at trying to write an inspirational piece for the *Reader's Digest*'s "Most Unforgettable Character" series. The subjects of *his* series, he wrote Arnold Gingrich, the editor, would be black sheep—"men and women—young and old—who are mostly their own, not the public's worst enemies and who frequently serve to amuse one or another of us." Gingrich bought the idea, and Dreiser recruited Sylvia and Louise Campbell to contribute some of the sketches, which would appear under his name. He would also take two-thirds of the $300 fee for each. It was his byline, after all, that the magazine was buying, he explained. His ghosts didn't object.

In early November Dreiser wrote Sylvia that he had come down with chills and a fever because he had been so worried about *The Bulwark* and "got tired struggling over an essay, 'My Creator.' " The essay had come to him while he was spading around an avocado tree in the garden. It was a beautiful and flourishing tree, he wrote, its roots extending down some twelve feet into the earth, its "smooth and shiny leaves—graceful as a warrior's shield is graceful," bearing in November a dark-green fruit. The tree was a symbol of all created things, "an illustration of the supreme genius of this creative force that so overawes me. . . ." The design and beauty and intelligible purpose "of this so carefully engineered and regulated universe—this amazing process called living"—were the abundant tokens of an intelligent, benign mind at work. Contemplating its handiwork, he was

> moved not only to awe but to reverence for the Creator . . . concerning whom—his presence in all things from worm to star to thought—I meditate constantly even though it be, as I see it, that my import to this, my Creator, can be but as nothing, or less, if that were possible.
>
> Yet awe I have. And, at long last, profound reverence for so amazing and esthetic and wondrous a process that may truly have been, and for all that I know, may yet continue to be forever and forever. An esthetic and wondrous process of which I might pray—and do—to remain the infinitesimal part of that same that I now am.

The thought had long been in his mind, but it needed to be clothed in the foliage of words. He was a writer, not a philosopher; he needed the image, the metaphor, of belief.

. . .

In December came the news that Edgar Lee Masters had been discovered ill and penniless in his room in New York's Chelsea Hotel. A sculptor friend found him and took him to Bellevue Hospital, where, due to wartime crowding, he was given a bed in the hall. Alice Davis, his long-time companion, bowed out of his life, and his wife, the young, capable Ellen Masters, from whom he had been estranged for years and who was now a teacher, strode in and took over his care. Financial help arrived from the Authors League and the Carnegie Fund, as well as checks from Mencken and other friends. He was transferred to a hospital room and was soon recovering.

Dreiser was luckier than Masters. Out of Russia came a miracle, even as the Red Army was mopping up the remnants of the Wehrmacht at Stalingrad. Having heard that some American authors were receiving royalty payments, whereas he had received little on an edition of his books published in 1940, he wrote Stalin demanding equity. Two months later his bank notified him that a sum had been transferred to his account. He read the figure as $3.46 and wondered why they bothered him with such a petty amount. But his eyesight was dimming. Helen looked at the figure: it was $34,600. A call to the bank verified that it had come from the Soviet government: payment in full for royalties due. Dreiser's face lit up.

"I refuse to worry any more," he said. "This will carry me through to the end."

CHAPTER **37**   *Closing the Accounts*

> Dreiser came to New York to accept a prize from the
> American Academy of Arts and Letters. I didn't come to
> see him, for I simply couldn't endure any such transaction.
> . . . For him to now take a cash prize from them seems to
> me to be intolerable. I think I'd rather starve first.
> —Mencken to James T. Farrell (1944)

In early January Dreiser received another piece of news, a letter from Walter Damrosch, the conductor and president of the National Academy of Arts and Letters, informing him that he had been chosen to receive the Award of Merit, bestowed every five years and carrying with it a gold medal and a $1000 prize. He accepted but wrote Damrosch that his health and the state of his affairs might preclude his accepting in person.

He was worried about an unexplained loss of weight, his good eye was failing, and he had a new complaint—an allergic rash that had broken out after he applied some mercury ointment to a small pimple. It would plague him for six months. He consulted Dr. Mencken, who advised that the quacks knew nothing about allergies; he had tried about twenty different cures for hay fever over the past forty years and not one worked. He added, indirectly referring to his own troubles as a result of a minor stroke: "In all this world there is nothing more unpleasant than the situation of a literary gent who finds writing difficult or impossible."

Mencken! How could Dreiser tell him that he had decided to accept an honor from their old foe, the Academy, symbol of the literary establishment? (Neither may have known that Sinclair Lewis had led the fight by younger members to give the award to Dreiser.) Almost sheepishly, Dreiser wrote that he planned to be in New York in May, for reasons he would explain later. But he couldn't evade Mencken. "I can only deplore the fact that you are having any truck with that gang. . . . If they have actually offered you a hand-out, I hope you invite them to stick it up their rain-spouts," he said.

The Code of the von Menckens was, Never forget, never forgive, but Dreiser had grown philosophical about those old battles. When James T. Farrell complained that the Philistines had objected to a novel of his, Dreiser advised him to cheer up: "You will outlive them."

But he truly needed Mencken's emotional support for the ordeal and apologetically invited him to the dinner Damrosch was giving after the ceremonies on May 19. He would feel "forlorn, deluded, even impostor like" if Mencken didn't come but would consider himself "justly reproved" if Mencken refused. The latter would not bend his principles: "Unhappily I can't join you at the orgies. . . . Some of the chief members of that preposterous organization made brave efforts to stab you in the back in 1916, and I am not disposed to forget it."

Dreiser expected this rebuke, though he really could see nothing wrong with accepting $1000 and a free trip to New York; he planned to ease his conscience by padding his travel expenses. Helen had planned to accompany him and parley with a possible buyer of Iroki, whom Moffat had located. But she had to go to Portland and nurse her mother in February, leaving Dreiser on his own. He wrote Sylvia: "I feel sort of abandoned and inadequate and generally forsaken. . . . Solitude—silence,—want of companionship is about the worst thing that can befall anyone." He was not thinking of suicide, he assured her, but "if loneliness is to be one's affliction or punishment for this or that kind of defect—well—give me death."

Well aware of how lost he was when on his own, Helen alerted Ralph Fabri to look after him in New York, making sure he ate regular meals. Swallowing her jealousy, she also enlisted Marguerite Tjader Harris, who replied, "You know *I love him more than almost anyone* on earth. I'm always so glad that he has you, to be with him. I don't think anyone has ever understood or loved him as you have, and do . . . so you know you can depend on me to take the best care of him. . . ." Helen had no choice; her mother was seriously ill. Besides, she was about to play her trump card, which would eliminate all her rivals.

Marguerite met his train and took him to his favorite hotel, the Commodore, near Grand Central Station. He was so much thinner, almost gaunt-looking. She made a remark about God bringing him here safely, and he announced, "Well, I believe in God, now—a Creative force."

Also greeting him was Margaret Carson, a bright, attractive young woman who was handling publicity for the awards ceremony. Dreiser was entranced by her and told Marguerite, "My that was a smart girl. It's really these women who should run the world nowadays. The men ought to retire." Carson later discovered that after a few drinks he became flirtatious and tried to embrace her.

He wired Mencken, urging him to come to New York for a session. The latter replied that an "extraordinary amount of tedious business" had fallen on him, and he was in a "somewhat shaky state physically." He held out the vague hope that he might make it for a brief get-together. When Dreiser received this, he merely shook his head, "Good old Menck." He understood that he was being reproved and accepted the verdict.

There was too much pressing business for Dreiser to brood about Mencken's absence. His sister Mame had written him before he left that she was ill. She was now in Kew Gardens Hospital; cancer of the bladder was suspected and a later operation confirmed the preliminary diagnosis. Dreiser reported to Helen that Mame had only $200 in the bank for funeral expenses; her share of the *My Gal Sal* money was almost gone. Dreiser suggested that the six heirs assign an equal share of their next royalty payments from Paul's songs to Mame's funeral.

The visit to the hospital was an emotional experience. He was surprised to find Ed and Mai and Vera there when he arrived. Mame cried when she saw Theodore. She fretted about the expense, and asked if she might go home to die. He kissed her, held her hand, and told her everything would be taken care of. Mame said, "You've always been so good to me. I can never repay you." She urged him to get to know Ed's daughter Vera—"there are so few of us left."

He had lunch with Earle Balch at the Century Club; Richard Duffy, who had volunteered to work up a prospectus for a collected edition, outlined his plan. But the Putnam editor said he could not spend any more money on Dreiser since he was already in too deep. A Dreiser novel would sell itself and create demand for his other works. Dreiser wearily agreed to the familiar condition. Balch had not been enthusiastic about the new chapters of *The Bulwark* Dreiser had sent him in May 1943; they consisted largely of background on the characters and did not advance the story. After a long lunch, Dreiser returned to the hotel a bit worse for liquor.

Meeting no encouragement from other publishers he saw, Dreiser began to lose heart. He was like Willy Loman, dragging a sample case of old books from one publisher to another. They were more or less polite; they knew who he was (or had been), but with wartime paper shortages the idea of a complete set was out of the question.

Dreiser told Robert Elias that he felt like Kipling, who said that one day his genius had abandoned him. He saw his new agent, Jacques Chambrun, who advised him to stop being obsessed with the old novels: write something new—some short stories. Dreiser said he had written lots of them. Weren't they still good? Was what he had achieved nothing? Here in this noisy, confusing, changing city, old men were consigned to the ash heap unless they kept up with the literary procession.

One admirer remained steadfast—Will Lengel, now editor of *True Confessions.* Lengel encouraged him to do articles for the magazine and they agreed on a schedule, beginning with a piece called "Dear Mr. Dreiser." The Great American Novelist in *True Confessions?* Lengel thought privately that Dreiser's mind was failing. Fabri agreed. The latter had taken Dreiser to visit a couple he knew, and the next day Dreiser had completely forgotten about it. Once, at Fabri's studio, he and Marguerite engaged in a public display of affection, which disgusted Fabri, a close friend of Helen's. Dreiser, he decided, feared death and was desperately clinging to youth.

James T. Farrell called at the Commodore and got the impression that Dreiser "was closing out the accounts of an entire past." In appearance he had become an old man since Farrell last saw him at the Democratic convention in 1936. But he seemed mentally alert and quizzed the younger man about the new writers. Were they any good? What were they writing about? He said he had recently read Charles Jackson's *The Lost Weekend,* a harrowing tale of an alcoholic's bender, and simply did not get it. "What kind of subject is that? For years I've been burying relatives who drank themselves to death."

He himself had avoided the alcoholic's fate, but as he had told Mencken about whiskey, "I love and need it so." He carried a half pint of cheap rye in his pocket and would take a nip whenever he felt bored or tired. "I don't know what's the matter with me," he would tell Marguerite. "I guess a little whiskey will fix me up." He would gulp down vitamin pills, almost absentmindedly. He could not adjust to the fact that he was nearly seventy-three and slowing down.

On May 19 he taxied to the rambling brick building that housed the National Institute of Arts and Letters on 155th Street. He had prepared an acceptance speech, on a pet idea of his, which seemed suitable for this august gathering—the creation of a cabinet-level secretary of the arts. In a letter to Arthur Ficke in March he explained that helping artists who were impoverished in their old age (Masters came immediately to mind) would be one of the functions a Department of the Arts might perform.

He submitted a short statement in advance, but someone at the Academy, the Institute's parent body, told him that the speech raised controversial issues and must be reviewed. Since there was no time for such a proceeding, he was requested not to deliver the speech. So he told Marguerite. However, Felicia Geffen Van Veen, Damrosch's assistant, had no recollection of anyone's asking Dreiser not to give the speech. Nor did she think there was any practice of reviewing the nominees' speeches. She remembered he came to the ceremony with the speech in his pocket; Marguerite said he told her he might speak out after all.

With Edgar Lee Masters beside him for moral support, he watched the sedate procession of academicians in black gowns to the stage. There were four honorees—Dreiser, Willa Cather, S. S. McClure, and Paul Robeson. Cather responded to National Institute president Arthur Train's fond introduction with some gracious remarks. The eighty-nine-year-old McClure, now a recluse and living off donations from friends and relatives, received an Award of Merit for his achievements as editor of *McClure's* in recognizing new talent and creating a new form of journalism. Cather rushed to embrace the man for whom she worked as managing editor in the 1900s.

Then it was Dreiser's turn. Whereas Train had introduced the preceding winners as old friends, he was presented by Professor Chauncey B. Tinker as a kind of literary fossil. In a speech many thought condescending, Tinker said Dreiser was chosen as a pioneer and leading exponent of the naturalistic school. But he made it clear that the views of said school, and certainly of its chief exponent, were definitely not those of the Academy, which "is neither conservative nor radical. . . . It sponsors no school and has no programme." Its sole aim was to honor ability in whatever guise it appeared. Why, if this were the eighteenth century, he went on, it might have honored Voltaire, thus evoking another heretic. Some of those present may also have been reminded of Voltaire's famous dictum—particularly the part about disagreeing with what you say.

Undampened by Tinker's remarks, the audience applauded warmly as Dreiser rose and walked to the podium. To Marguerite he looked like a caged lion. He retreated into his own dignity, turning his back on the audience to bow and accept the medal from Damrosch. His speech remained in his pocket as he mumbled a few words of thanks. He probably hadn't the heart to say more after the equivocal tribute from Professor Tinker.

Afterward there was a reception and tea. Dreiser stood apart with a group of friends who had come to support him, including Marguerite, Robert Elias, and Ellen Masters. Robeson, whom Dreiser had known since the 1920s, came over to offer some friendly words, as did Farrell and Louis Untermeyer. The latter recalled, "You had a feeling that he was quite alone and isolated there. I think he felt that he was there somewhat by sufferance."

His group proceeded to Masters' apartment in the East Sixties, where several drinks restored their spirits. When it came time to go to Damrosch's for dinner, Dreiser said to Marguerite, "Get me out of it, if you can." He felt he was not wanted; perhaps, too, this was a gesture to Mencken.

He spent several evenings with Masters, who was visibly slowed but receiving devoted care from his wife, the kind of brisk, take-charge young woman

Dreiser liked (needed). At Lüchow's the headwaiter recognized them and seated them at their favorite table near the orchestra, which did not strike up "Nearer My God to Thee" as Mencken once predicted. (How they must have missed him!) Hearing Dreiser mildly complain that the music was not as romantic as it used to be, the headwaiter spoke to the conductor, who played a round of Gypsy airs. Over *wurst* and beer they reminisced about their past escapades and the women they had pursued. They agreed they were paying for those excesses of the flesh, but it was too late now. Masters read a letter from Jack Powys, which spoke of "we three who are closer than lovers with exactly the same amount of reverence and affection."

Also entertaining him was his niece Vera, now a practicing psychologist. Vera was intensely curious about her famous uncle, to whom she had hardly spoken since she was a teenager. One evening she accompanied him to see Robeson in *Othello.* After the performance, they went backstage to invite the actor out for a bite, but he told them that no restaurant in the theater district would serve him because of his race, so they would have to go to the Village. Dreiser was too tired to make the journey.

Vera had become concerned about his health and talked him into getting a physical checkup. The physician could find nothing seriously wrong for a man his age and routinely advised him to cut down on alcohol, avoid spicy foods, and take vitamins. He also discovered some abscessed teeth and suggested they be removed because the infection was draining his vitality. Dreiser grumbled about "this damned medical nonsense."

The next day Vera took him for lunch and a drive in Fort Tryon Park. He asked her, "How would you like me as a patient?" She told him it would be too difficult a job. She recognized the symptoms of hero-worship in herself and felt an affection for him that was not sexual. They talked of his many women and he confessed, "I've been in love a thousand times . . . or maybe never at all. . . . most likely never at all. . . ." She asked him, "Is that why you had so much hostility toward women?" This took him aback and he changed the subject. She asked him if he believed in God. He said, "not only do I believe in God, but I will go into any scientific laboratory and prove it to you."

The following weekend he visited Ed and Mai at their large home in Far Rockaway, Queens. The brothers spent most of the afternoon reminiscing about their childhood. Ed, still trim and fit, looked fifteen years younger than Theodore, though he was only two years his junior. When Ed sang an old German folk song about leaving the gates of the city, which their father used to sing to them, the memory of it came back in a rush to Theodore, bringing tears to his eyes. He spoke sympathetically of John Paul Dreiser.

He thought it amazing the way Mai and Ed still held hands after forty years of marriage. Sitting in that comfortable home with a brother he loved, he perceived the void in his life, Vera thought, the lack of a stable home and a family.

The next day they visited Mame, who was sinking rapidly. One by one they slipped in to say goodbye. Outside the hospital they gathered for a moment. Ed had to go to work, and as he was about to leave, Theodore kissed him on the cheek and said, "Long life, Ed." They embraced silently and Ed strode off to the subway, tears in his eyes.

Driving back to Manhattan, Dreiser suggested to Vera that she come to California and help him with the novel. He needed someone with her intelligence and energy. When she told him she had a baby daughter and a career and could not possibly leave, he shrugged and said, "If you really wanted to, you'd arrange it."

On another day he paid a farewell visit to Iroki, which Helen, working by long-distance phone, had sold for $22,000. He and Marguerite wandered about, taking a last look at the big house, now empty and desolate-looking. The stone mushrooms leaned at odd angles and the grass on the lawn was tall and unkempt. In a window Dreiser found a dead starling, its beak impaled in the mesh of the screen. He carefully extracted it, smoothed its iridescent feathers, and laid it on the ground, as though laying to rest a dead dream that had once fluttered about this place.

And then came a request from the Office of War Information to make two broadcasts, one to the people of America and the other to the people of Germany, to be beamed on the eve of the Allied invasion of Europe. This assignment was the best tonic of the whole trip. He sat before the microphone, speaking the words in a husky voice:

> I have just come across the country . . . this great America of ours . . . and I wish you could have been with me. You would have seen, as I did, in railway stations, or trains, in hotels, or the streets . . . an amazing display of youthful vigor, enthusiasm, youthful yet manly love of country. . . . I see millions of the finest type of fighting men, who seek nothing as much as the day and hour when they can try their young strength, their American vitality and brains, their American alertness and inventiveness, against the Nazi brutes, whom they do not fear but whom they abhor, as do all Americans.

He went back a few days later to speak to the enemy. Identifying himself as the son of a German-born father who had left his native land to escape Prussian militarism, he called on the German people to recover their past greatness, which had produced statesmen, scientists, and artists, and to help bring a new era of justice in the world. He closed, "Just as a tryout, let's have a few hundred years of the brotherhood of man."

And then a farewell cocktail party for all the New York friends who had rallied around him during his stay. Edwin Seaver, Marguerite's co-editor on *Direction*, was there; Charles Scribner, still talking about publishing a Dreiser set; Dorothy Norman, a columnist for the New York *Post*, who later wrote, "[Dreiser] has never lost his passionate interest in all movements, all work that reaches out to enrich life"; William Gropper, the artist; Isidore Schneider, literary editor of *Soviet Russia Today*, for which he had written an article; George Seldes; Richard Wright; Elias; and various wives and children. Wright found Dreiser refreshingly humble, unlike most writers: "If you asked him a question, he would say a little something in reply; and later, a little more, and perhaps later, still more—as if any idea was enough to start some deep emotional, psychological movement in him."

As people were making motions to depart, Dreiser received a telephone call informing him that Mame had died. He lay down awhile in the darkened bedroom and then came out to say his farewells.

And then more interviews with Elias, whom he liked now. He almost came to tears as he recounted the old story about his suicidal thoughts in Brooklyn in 1903 and how a boisterous canal-boatman had saved him. The story had become a kind of personal myth; he had faced the ultimate choice and opted for life—or rather fate had made him do so. It was a strange and wonderful fact: most of us choose to live. They discussed the U.S. Communist Party's recent meeting in New York City, at which it had dissolved and reconstituted itself as the Communist Political Association. This represented a triumph for Earl Browder's Teheran Doctrine, calling for cooperation with capitalism in the postwar era. Dreiser generally approved the Party's new course, though he seemed, as usual, poorly informed about the inner maneuverings—unaware, for example, that William Z. Foster had opposed aspects of the policy. To Dreiser, the Browder line represented a vindication of his advocacy of a communist movement in the American grain that did not preach "a lot of Marxism nobody understands."

But Dreiser was less interested in politics than in his future as a writer. He confessed to Elias that he was depressed. Elias, seconded by Marguerite, urged him to finish *The Bulwark*. Dreiser agreed: he always said that work was the only cure for a low mental state. Turning to Marguerite, he said, "If you will come to California and help me, I think I can do it." Marguerite agreed to come—but only with Helen's permission.

And then Mame's funeral. She looked beautiful in death, the lines of suffering smoothed from her face. Dreiser was moved by the young minister's reading of the traditional funeral service. "What beautiful words," he told Marguerite. "He reminded me of Aloysha Karamazov."

On June 5 he boarded a train for the West. But his destination was not Los Angeles; it was the town of Stevenson, Washington, where Helen awaited him. Stevenson was noted for its spectacular scenery and its quick marriages. Dreiser had at last agreed to marry Helen, after some diplomatic interventions by Helen's sister, Myrtle (herself engaged to Chester Butcher, a rancher), and surprisingly, by Mai, who had come to accept their unconventional union and who now thought it only fitting that they seal it.

What Dreiser really thought about this step can only be guessed, since he did not discuss his plans in New York. But he seems to have done it to please Helen—a gesture of atonement, putting a legal seal on their long relationship. That bout of loneliness earlier in the spring had reminded him of his need for her care. He had seen what Ellen Masters had done for Edgar, and even joked about how he was lucky to have his "lawful wedded wife" looking after him. Bradshaw seemed no longer interested, and he wrote her later that, although his feelings toward her were the same, he could not bring himself "to break up the practical relationship here." Helen's hold over him was too strong. She provided a well-run home where he could store his books and papers; she was someone he could depend on to look after him and perform the routine secretarial chores.

Although he was going to his wedding, he yearned for Marguerite in New York. Aboard the train he wrote her that he missed her "dynamic affectionate force"; she had doubled his strength and energy "as though you in your youth had completely blended with me to produce a new youth in me—a received personality." He was "truly lonely" and lamented "Lord Lord! how am I to make out now?"

After a wearying three-day journey, he arrived at six in the morning. Later they took a walk and then sat on a "wishing bench." He gave Helen his medal from the Academy, telling her it belonged to her as much as it did to him.

The ceremony was performed by a justice of the peace, with only Helen and Dreiser, Myrtle and her fiancé present. To avoid newspaper attention, Dreiser signed the register with his baptismal first name, Herman. Helen wanted no publicity, since it might remind the world of their twenty-five-year unsanctioned liaison. She had sometimes passed as Helen Dreiser, though she rarely used "Mrs. Theodore Dreiser," feeling he would resent it. Now the title was legally hers. Soon after the ceremony she proudly wrote it at the top of a letter to Fabri.

In keeping with Helen's wishes, and probably his own, Dreiser told few friends about the wedding. He made no mention of it in a conciliatory letter he wrote Mencken. The Academy affair had been a "dreary demonstration," he reported. He was sorry they hadn't had a session, but could understand the other's reasons. Mencken said he too regretted they hadn't met, though he did not apologize. He made it clear he would speak no more about the issue that had divided them, and took care to extend his condolences for Mame's death. Later he wrote, "I am sorry indeed that we are living so far apart." Dreiser did not respond, and wrote Masters, "I think Mencken is off of me for life" because he had accepted the award.

He was kinder to Helen now, but looked forward to Marguerite's arrival. They had been close in New York, and she had also served as hostess, typist, companion, schedule keeper, morale booster. He expected her to help him finish both the novel and the philosophy. The details of *The Bulwark* were clear in his mind, he wrote her, and he "could easily outline the successive chapters or structure and when that was done paint in the various scenes— their respective colors and emotional qualities."

Although he had Helen, he needed an opposing feminine magnetic pole to draw forth the erotic energy that still fitfully drove his creativity. Vera diagnosed oedipal longings in him, "the force that had drawn him to all women." He was also "borrowing strength" from women "to enhance his own security." In Vera's case she recognized the transference of patient to analyst; she had become the "supporting, maternal surrogate which was the image sought by him in a love relationship."

Marguerite formally requested Helen's permission to come. Helen warned her about wartime conditions in Los Angeles—the housing shortage, the necessity of a car, gasoline rationing. Although both spoke in the most high-minded way, a hint of potential rivalry broke through. Marguerite assured Helen that she would be strictly business, a euphemism for avoiding an amorous entanglement. "I'm sure there'll be no discord between us," Helen replied. "Surely we are beyond that." And she went on: "I know you love Teddie dearly. . . . Perhaps I love him more like you love Hilary [her son]. It's that kind of love. Once I allowed myself to worship him. But that was corrected by a realization that came through difficult years, that it was wrong. . . . It is very bad to worship any human being be it man, child or woman. . . . It is so characteristic of a woman to worship. But it's not the way." The words showed a hard-won maturity. She told Marguerite she would be welcome.

Probably with an eye to Helen's reading over his shoulder, Marguerite wrote him a stiff business letter setting ground rules for their collaboration. Resenting her "dictatorial tone," he replied angrily, and she sent a more affectionate letter. He explained, "I took it that you were drawn to me and that if we decided to try to work together on The Bulwark it would not necessarily follow that a Trappistic self-restraint on my part should reign, seeing that I know full well that no such program governs in your case or ever has." He had already offered to pay her transportation, and later they signed an agreement giving her 10 percent of the returns from the novel or any other projects she worked on.

In August she and Hilary drove out in an old convertible. They arrived in time for the celebration of Dreiser's seventy-third birthday on the twenty-seventh. He hated such occasions, so Helen disguised the event as a kind of party for *The Bulwark,* complete with a cake in the shape of a book on a revolving stand that played "Happy Birthday." The guest list grew to sixty people. Along with friends from the old days, like Lillian and Mark Goodman, Clare Kummer and her daughter Marjorie, the Tobeys, and Masters' daughter Marcia and *her* daughter, there were the new recruits to his Hollywood set: Clifford Odets and spouse, the Al Manuels, the A. Dorian Otvoses, the Russian consul Ivan Boutnikoff, their neighbors the Wards (she was the actress Jane Wyatt), Dr. Chang, the Chinese consul, and family, and Will and Ariel Durant, among others.

Dreiser looked fresh and dapper in a cream-colored suit, and Helen glowed with some of her old radiance in her white hostess dress. It was an odd assortment of people. Clare and Lill played songs they had composed long ago, which no one remembered. A pupil of Lill's sang Dreiser's favorite air, "Jeannie with the Light Brown Hair." The Chinese consul's daughter played Grieg's Piano Concerto. The men hunted for some hard stuff, which they knew Dreiser kept in his desk, rather than go on with Helen's famous orange punch. "It was one of our most successful parties," Helen summed up, "and the last one of any size."

Marguerite and Hilary settled into temporary accommodations in a motel. The housing shortage was fierce, but they eventually secured a tiny three-room house located in a cul-de-sac near Cahuenga Boulevard.

The Putnam contract had been weighing on Dreiser's mind, and he decided to refund the advance. With that obligation lifted and Marguerite to edit and type his various drafts, his mind was eased. But much remained to be done. Helen says he quoted frequently from the Bible at this time, and one line recurred while he worked on the novel: ". . . this night thy soul shall be required of thee."

CHAPTER **38**   *The Bulwark*

> Nature, machine-like, works definitely and heartlessly, if in
> the main beautifully. Hence if, we, as individuals, do not
> make this dream of a God or what he stands for to us, real,
> in our thoughts and deeds—then He is not real or true.
> —Dreiser (1934)

Dreiser had only one deadline now, the time remaining to him. Their workday began at ten, when Marguerite picked him up and drove him to the little house on Cadet Court. He would be carrying a stack of manuscript or a bundle wrapped in twine or stuck in a decaying brown envelope—material he had excavated from his files and decided was usable. "This is the stuff on Isobel," he would say. "This is about Stewart at school." Once he brought an unusually thick sheaf of pages. "Fifty thousand words more. Now this will send you back to Connecticut!" Piles of manuscripts littered her tiny living room until she dragged in her steamer trunk to serve as a filing case.

They read through the four extant typescripts and decided that two were worth salvaging. One dealt with the various family members and the other recounted Solon's business career. The latter was too detailed, so it was cut drastically and merged with the family version. They cannibalized from a third manuscript, which had been too severely cut but which carried Stewart's story further than the other two. These three scripts were merged into a working draft, to which more cutting and fleshing out and rewriting was done.

In this fashion—and probably Marguerite did much of the stitching together—they built up the novel on the foundation of the thirty introductory chapters he had written in 1942–1943 and submitted to Balch. After rereading them in the light of his more recent work, Dreiser was appalled that he had parted with them. Now, with Marguerite's help, he would be able to compress them.

Marguerite worked a double shift, going over the manuscripts by day and editing and typing the reorganized material at night. When the pages had been spliced into a coherent narrative, they made a diagram of the story, showing where each character stood and what remained to be written, and from this Dreiser prepared a fourteen-page outline for submission to a publisher. Al Manuel, now with the Goldstone Agency in Hollywood, had interested Doubleday in the manuscript but Dreiser did not want to sign a contract until he had completed the book.

His uncertain health slowed their progress. In October he wrote Sylvia that he was "too weak and nervously shaken to work," and that he was "doctoring and—or vitamining." He told Masters he was continually tired and "laying off of work of any kind and as much as possible." His doctor had diagnosed a thyroid condition of an unspecified nature and prescribed medication. That complaint would have contributed to his lethargy and weight loss.

During a visit in September, Vera thought he looked weary and ill. He was almost childishly dependent on Helen, who mothered him in the good-humoredly dictatorial way of a nurse long accustomed to the crotchets of her charge. Once she and Vera went out shopping and stayed away longer than planned. When they returned he was pulling at his hair and almost screamed: "Where were you? I was going to call the police in another few minutes. I was worried sick!" Helen merely laughed and walked off. She represented, Vera now realized, "the one person he could depend upon to be there when he needed her," and when she wasn't he became distraught. Another time, while he and Vera were standing in the driveway waiting for Helen to get the car, he muttered, "Strange girl!" as though he were seeing her for the first time.

Once when he and Vera were alone he pulled her to him and tried to kiss her. She broke away but later thought she had been "cruel" and that he had not been making a sexual advance but seeking affection and reassurance from her.

She diagnosed sagging self-esteem. Once when she wished to see some movie people about several songs she had written, his name gained her immediate entrée. When she told him this, "He could not believe that anyone was really interested. He had to be reassured constantly, by word, by deed."

In fact, he was regarded as a sort of literary monument in a town where reputations were planted in shifting sands. His parties drew many admirers, most of them displaced New York intellectuals of the liberal-left persuasion. One guest recalled, "You always felt as if they were going to collect for something." Folk singers Woody Guthrie and Pete Seeger had sung ballads in his living room. Charlie Chaplin performed impromptu sketches that made Dreiser laugh until the tears streamed down his face. In 1945 Paul Robeson came to tea, and he and Dreiser talked intently about the problems of Negroes. Dreiser proposed an article on the subject. When Robeson had to leave for a performance, Dreiser asked him to sing one song. Robeson leaned against the living-room table and boomed out a stirring "Ol' Man River."

Dreiser had become less vocal on political issues and was content to listen to others, occasionally interjecting a cogent question. This was in marked contrast to his bellicosity as little as two years before—as Helen's cousin Harold Dies discovered. A lieutenant in the Army transportation corps, he had traveled in the Far East on merchant ships, and after a trip to India spent a leave with Dreiser and Helen. Dreiser was initially wary of Harold because he was also a cousin of the Red-baiting Representative Martin Dies. He sternly asked the young man if he shared the Red-hunter's views. When Harold assured him he didn't, Dreiser relaxed and began quizzing him about India. But in a discussion of Russia, when Harold remarked that there seemed to be inequality under communism, Dreiser became so apoplectic that Helen intervened, fearing he might have a heart attack.

As he became more engrossed in the novel, his social life tapered off. On Sundays Helen took him to one of the churches in the area, in keeping with her project of helping him find spiritual peace. They attended a Christian Science church for a while, but he preferred the Mt. Hollywood Congregational Church, whose pastor, the Reverend Alan Hunter, was a liberal in politics as well as theology. The ritual at his church featured a period of individual meditation, which may have made it seem to Dreiser more Quakerly and nonsectarian. On Good Friday he insisted on attending an evening service at the Congregational Church, and when they emerged under a starry sky and palm trees, a setting Hunter had compared to the Holy Land, he said little but seemed profoundly moved.

In January he ran into a block on the novel and was laid up by a cold that led to a severe depression. "He could be so difficult at times," Marguerite recalled of her charge, "so sunk in a negative mood that death, and all sorts of disasters seemed actually lurking around him, as if he were deliberately drawing them to himself." He had reached the stage in the narrative where the rebellious Etta, encouraged by her freethinking friend Volida, runs away to the University of Wisconsin. (Volida, who exhibits mannish traits and wants to study medicine, is a discreet shadow of her prototype, the lesbian doctor who had seduced Anna Tatum.) One night he dreamed of Solon in a hotel room in Madison; indeed he *was* Solon. It was a break-through; he had achieved the needed identification with the character and could move ahead with the story.

By March he had reached the point in the narrative where Stewart, joyriding with his friends, is involved in the death of a girl, an incident inspired by a case Dreiser had read about some thirty years ago. When he dictated a description of the scene in which Stewart decides to plunge the knife into his chest rather than face his father and mother, he became the boy. At the point where the press trumpets the family's disgrace, he suddenly stopped. "That's enough," he sighed, emotionally drained. This was "the works."

Without Marguerite's energy to draw upon, the book would have been impossible for him. She roused him in the morning and gently pushed him through the day. She lavished encouragement and at times physical affection on him. His virility was waning, but age hadn't diminished his need for physical love, even if it consisted of her sitting in his lap or simply hugging him. He needed this physical touching.

Marguerite "believed that she had a special 'spiritual' relationship with Dreiser, that they were communicating on a 'higher' level," a friend recalled. If he was just a medium for a higher power, as he always contended, then it followed that she was a medium for him. She was mentally attuned to the rhythms of his prose and became so mesmerized by his voice that even his awkward locutions seemed right to her.

And she provided the sympathetic ear he needed to overcome his inhibitions about writing a religious story, for she had recently embarked on a spiritual search of her own. But she strongly denied exercising a Svengali-like influence over him. As she wrote Robert Elias at the time, "I do know that the ideas, and all the ideas . . . expressed in the *Bulwark*, are his own, and not planted by me, or anyone. . . . we were close in what we both believed, especially about that universal element of Love, flowing from God and through all created things."

By March they were approaching the last chapters. On fine days he would work on the patio. He might suddenly eject a phrase or describe a scene so fluently that she would grab her pencil and copy the words down on a box lid or whatever paper was handy. Now in relatively good health and feeling the story carrying him along to the ending he had imagined thirty years ago, he was as happy as he had ever been. He loved to sit on the patio and hum to himself (a sign of serenity) or watch the antics of Hilary's guinea pigs, which ran loose in the garden.

But although Marguerite was an ideal midwife, she was no editor. Inevitably, he thought of Louise Campbell and wrote her that he would be finished within a month. Could she take over the manuscript? "For you are, as you know,—a swell editor," he cajoled, "the best I have ever known and I'll feel troubled if you find yourself unable to edit."

It took him a month longer than he had anticipated, but the final scenes contained the novel's most moving passages, written in simple, Biblical prose. He spoke the phrases to Marguerite as if they had been patiently waiting, fully formed, all these years. Solon had become a Jobian figure, battered by the world. Having resigned from the bank where he was treasurer in protest against financial chicanery, and mourning Stewart, he is haunted by a sense of failure. His children have all but abandoned Quakerism and no longer care about him.

At this point Dreiser gave Solon words hard-earned in his own quest for meaning. One day Solon walks in the garden and observes a glittering green fly feeding on an insect. In a reversal of the squid and lobster scene of *The Financier,* Dreiser uses this encounter to demonstrate Solon's vision of the unity of all creation; cruelty and strife are but transitory shifts as Nature ceaselessly seeks a balance between opposing forces in the equation inevitable. Solon studies the flowers and the grass, as Dreiser had done in "My Creator," and concludes, "Surely there must be a Creative Divinity, and so a purpose, behind all this variety and beauty and tragedy of life." Later he encounters a puff adder and, as Dreiser had done at Iroki, assures it that he means no harm. As the snake crawls across his shoe, Solon realizes that the creature understood his loving intent and was no longer afraid. Similarly, God must feel good intent—love—toward all things. All creatures are part of the design of creation, of God: "How would it understand me, and I it, if we were not both part of Himself?" This rigidly pious man now worries that he was not forgiving enough with his children, and tells his daughter that he has learned charity and "the need of love toward all created things."

Hearing of Stewart's suicide, blaming her own rebellion for inspiring Stewart, and regretting the lies she told her parents, Etta returns to ask her father's forgiveness and to take care of him. One morning while shaving he looks in the mirror and asks her, "Daughter, what has become of that poor old man who was dying of cancer?" What old man? she asks him. "Why . . . why . . . that poor old man whose son killed himself." Solon's words carried a faint echo of an ironic comment Dreiser made to Esther McCoy about being forgotten: "Is that man still alive? Why doesn't he die?"

While reading to the dying Solon from Woolman's *Journal,* Etta comes to understand her father's faith. She grows more spiritual. At Solon's funeral, her brother Orville, now a stolid, conservative businessman, asks her how she can weep when it was she who started all the family's troubles with her rebellion. She tells him, "Oh, I am not crying for myself—or for Father—I am crying *for life.*" In an outline of the novel, written nearly thirty years before, Dreiser had anticipated this scene: "Orville's request to Etta not to cry, and her answer." (And even before that, he had written in his European Diary, "I fancy my tears are for the whole world. . . .") No one is blameworthy, all life is a tragedy of desire. All traces of individual strivings are immersed in the solvent of universal tears. Etta and Stewart, like so many of Dreiser's earlier characters, craved a fuller life—the former of intellectual freedom, the latter (so like Dreiser in his youth) of women and the color and excitement of the city. But in the end Stewart kills himself, and Etta reconciles with her father and finds peace: "In this love and unity with all nature, as she now sensed, there was nothing fitful or changing or disappointing— nothing that glowed one minute and was gone the next. This love was rather as constant as nature itself, everywhere the same, in sunshine or in darkness, the filtered splendor of the dawn, the seeded beauty of the night. It was an intimate relation to the very heart of being."

Carrie had been led by beauty, forever in pursuit "of that radiance which tints the distant hilltops of the world," but was fated to find neither "surfeit nor content." Now Dreiser had reached the last hilltop. He was, perhaps, content.

All that remained was for Marguerite to type the final version. This provoked a minor clash with Helen because Dreiser had promised that she could type the chapters that made up Part I—the chapters on family history and Solon's boyhood that they had worked on before Marguerite came upon the scene. When Helen saw how severely this section had been cut, she felt betrayed and blamed Marguerite. But Dreiser managed to convince her that the deletions were necessary, and she completed the job.

He sent a copy of the script to Campbell, who read it with growing dismay. She found herself out of sympathy with the talk about God and the Inner Light. She thought the novel inferior work, poorly written, and it espoused values that contradicted Dreiser's entire career. She gently conveyed her opinion to him, and it awakened his own doubts. "While I am not sure that all you say is correct," he wrote her, "I will have to go over it and see how much I agree, and what I can do." He instructed her to hold on to the manuscript because he might want her to cut it. Then he asked James T. Farrell to read it and advise him.

Louise's impression was that he had taken it away from Marguerite: "He was obviously dissatisfied with it, though she wasn't. . . ." Marguerite had her own explanation: "He has had a reaction," she told Elias, "a certain fear, perhaps of becoming 'too' religious, caused by—what? I will not attempt to say." Shortly after finishing the novel, he and Helen visited the Tobeys, Esther McCoy and her husband, Berkeley, at their cottage in Ensenada, and he was so full of his hero and discoursed so constantly on God, or rather his idea of a Creator, that Berkeley, an irreverent old socialist, began singing hymns, and they all joined in (save Dreiser, who hadn't learned any in his Catholic boyhood). Esther thought that Dreiser had immersed himself so deeply in Solon Barnes that he had assumed his religious beliefs. In time, he would have freed himself from the character.

Marguerite suspected that Helen was behind his fear of seeming too religious. But Helen, pagan though she was, had no opposition to the religious passages, and indeed had written Marguerite, "The Bulwark . . . is a beautiful book. It is full of poetry, philosophy and a lot of truth. He is using many quotations from the bible and this truth & beauty takes hold of one. It is, to me, almost hypnotic, especially now in this crazy world. And, working on it, has the power of absorbing one so that the rest seems more or less unimportant."

Helen was more concerned about Dreiser's reputation and his well-being. Not long after he had sent Louise the manuscript, Helen urged her to look for weak spots with "a *critical eye*." She went on, "When the Tragedy was in the making, I was absolutely sure about the outcome of it. I can't say that I feel that same absolute confidence in this book. And it worries me." Better the novel not be published than for it to fail. An adverse critical reaction would be too painful for Dreiser to bear.

Dreiser was also worried. He knew that his first novel since the *Tragedy* would draw much critical attention, and that, given his age, the book would be taken as a kind of summing up. He did not want to be seen as having embraced religion, like the old radical Heywood Broun, who had converted to Catholicism on his deathbed. He and Mencken often joked about Broun as though challenging each other not to weaken in the end.

Dreiser had not embraced Quakerism. It's clear that in the final chapters Solon is more a mouthpiece for Dreiser's views than those of the Society of Friends. The revelations the author granted him stemmed from his own experience. Indeed, Rufus Jones later criticized *The Bulwark* on the ground that Dreiser "never gets inside of this Quaker family or of a Quaker Meeting, and his characters remain too much like constructed frames for presenting the author's theories."

Dreiser also used the Quaker Book of Discipline as a critique of modern capitalism. Its precepts embody the egalitarian virtues of an earlier, more pastoral era, before the rise of the Robber Barons and the trusts. Solon's are the standards of the ethical small businessman, contrasted with the excesses of monopoly capitalism. In his final delirium he cries out, "The banks! The poor and the banks!" The language is Populism rather than Quakerism. Solon's principles are "too high for these days," remarks one of the bank's new directors. (They have been misappropriating depositors' money.) Dreiser also brings in government, in the form of the Federal bank examiner, a New Deal regulator out of the 1930s, rather than the 1920s in which the scene is set. Dreiser used the Book of Discipline to reflect his political views, which had changed from what they were when he wrote his early drafts. Then he had conceived the Quaker rules of conduct as a narrow, outmoded guide to frugality. (His reading of the Talmud aboard the *Normandie* may have contributed to his new—and of course highly personal—interpretation.)

Dreiser describes not Quakerism but a nonsectarian religion in *The Bulwark*. He uses John Woolman's *Journal* as his vehicle. Speaking for the author, Etta says, "Here was no narrow morality, no religion limited by society or creed, but rather, in the words of Woolman, 'a principle placed in the human mind, which in different places and ages had different names; it is, however, pure and proceeds from God. It is deep and inward, confined to no forms of religion, nor excluded from any.' " That was Dreiser's view of "pure religion and undefiled," a direct, unmediated perception of God, of beauty and unconditional love at the center of all things.

The Book of Discipline also represented a kind of paradigm of personal rectitude, as we have seen, though one Dreiser could not easily live up to. Marguerite Harris, who knew his emotional anarchy firsthand, sensed a schism in his nature: "I believe that his fundamental conflict, throughout his life, has been his natural belief—in God, the supernatural, psychic law— whatever you want to call it, and his unwillingness to accept obligation or responsibility in connection with this belief, as applying to his personal life," she wrote Elias in 1945.

He rebelled against discipline that was imposed by unquestioned dogmatic authority—the authority his father had represented. Solon still retains vestiges of the father figure that served as a model for him in the earlier version of the novel. In being humbled by tragedy he learns that discipline is not an end in itself; it must be tempered by mercy. He realizes that he had not been understanding enough with Stewart, as the Reverend McMillan was not with Clyde Griffiths, as Dreiser believed his father had not been with his children. When Etta asks her father for his forgiveness, he tells her that it was not for him to judge her; only God can judge and forgive.

Despite Louise's dissent, there was good news from Doubleday; it wanted to publish the novel. But associate editor Donald B. Elder insisted that it be cut. Dreiser replied that he preferred to do his own trimming first (or rather have Louise do it, subject to his approval), but he was heartened by the news and regained some of his old energy. Soon he was outlining short stories to Marguerite, and an idea for a series of articles on why men leave their wives. (Vicarious release from the fidelity of Solon and Benecia?)

But first he wanted to tackle *The Stoic*, and so they took out that much worked-over manuscript. Marguerite found the writing slick and mechanical—someone else's style not his (this was the version Anna Tatum had edited). The business scenes didn't come to life. Also, she thought the scenario he had written was too rigid and schematic—a potted biography. Her impression was that he was chiefly interested in winding up the book, not reworking it. Marguerite offered to help him with the philosophy instead, but he was bent on finishing the novel, sensing that his time was growing short.

Marguerite had to return to Connecticut in June, and although she offered to extend her stay a few weeks, he did not press her. He was tired, and Helen urged him to take a vacation. Helen probably played a role in Marguerite's banishment. She suspected a triangle forming and resented the other woman's literary influence over him. She reasserted her dominance and took him off to her mother's in Portland, where he was very bored and sat in the yard every day at a card table, working on *The Stoic*. After Marguerite left, he wrote her wistfully, "So my golden girl is gone!"

He was anxiously awaiting Farrell's reactions to his novel, for he respected the younger man's judgment. In June Farrell delivered his verdict, which was positive. Sensing that Louise's objections had been partly to the old-fashioned style, he telephoned her and she confirmed this. He also discovered that she had most disliked those scenes in the final chapters describing Solon's spiritual revelations. Farrell had liked them best; he had years before recognized Dreiser's mystical streak in *Hey, Rub-a-Dub-Dub!*

Meanwhile a complication was brewing. Dreiser had given Marguerite a letter to the Doubleday Company authorizing her to look over the manuscript and to inspect the galleys when they were completed. Upon her return, she called on Donald Elder, who told her he liked the novel but described Campbell's and Farrell's reactions. Marguerite now felt fiercely possessive toward the book and resented the outsiders. She asked Dreiser what was going on. To avert her wrath, he downplayed their roles. Farrell, he said, "seemed to feel that it had some minor errors or inconsistencies which he wanted to correct. . . ." Louise had called the book "a strong piece of work likely to do better than I think," but had suggested "a few corrections." He only wished Marguerite were there to help him discuss their suggestions, which were really trivial.

In fact, he had already authorized Louise to cut the manuscript within Farrell's guidelines of preserving style and religious material. She had forwarded to him the first sixty pages and he had approved her work. He instructed her to continue her editing "in the same spirit." In another letter he warns her that if Mrs. Harris should come to see her, not to be disturbed.

Dreiser was indecisive but inclined to entrust the book to Campbell and Farrell. Anticipating that Marguerite would try to interfere, he had written Elder on August 10 that Louise was preparing "a revised version for me based on suggestions made by James T. Farrell and myself. This might result in a much improved script, in which case I prefer this be the one to use,—after I have approved it, of course."

Torn between his longing for Marguerite to return to Hollywood and his dependence on peace with Helen, he seems to have psychologically collapsed. On August 14 he wrote Marguerite that he wasn't feeling well—"decidedly lethargic"—and needed an "action program—something constructive that will stir me to labor. If I did not feel so sickish—so lethargic I could think something out." He left it to her to decide whether to return. And then, two weeks later, a shakily scrawled note arrived:

> Double, Double, Toil and Trouble
> Fire burn and cauldron bubble.
> I run and fret and worry. I had your understanding letter days ago, but as for an agreeable Solution for you and for me?—*not so easy*. Worry, jealousy. Discord. The feeling of injustice—unfairness. A sense of unjustified scheming and plotting. And eventually *for some one*—retribution. And because of all this the difficulty of creative labor.

The "some one" was surely Helen. Dreiser had observed her hiding a letter and suspected she was reading his mail. Perhaps she opened an affectionate missive from Marguerite, realized for the first time how close the collaborators had grown, and put her foot down. Whatever "unjustified scheming" she was doing involved *The Bulwark;* Marguerite suspected that Helen was trying to purge her influence.

In September Marguerite returned to California. As soon as he had a chance, Dreiser led her into the garden, where they could talk privately. He told her that Helen was helping him finish *The Stoic* and resented her being there. The upshot was that they couldn't work together until the novel was finished. Marguerite said it might be best if she went home, but he gave her such a beseeching look that she agreed to stay.

On August 31 Dreiser sent Elder the "authorized" *Bulwark* manuscript and asked him to use it as a guide in his own editing. Although Louise had very reluctantly agreed to cut it, she had done her best, working to a tight deadline. She sensed that Dreiser was under a strain—desperately trying to finish. She said later that she did a "considerable amount of rewriting of parts of *The Bulwark,*" and, as was her practice, she retyped the manuscript.

And then in another twist in the convoluted history of *The Bulwark,* Elder wrote Dreiser, "Frankly I feel that Mrs. Campbell's revision has damaged the manuscript. . . ." She had cut too much, he said, made the style too slick. He thought her work had distorted the book, and that the pace of the narrative should be slower "so that the reader can assimilate the many details which are so important to the total picture." Elder felt a strong obligation to preserve Dreiser's style.

Confused and weary, Dreiser authorized Elder to use his own judgment. The latter attacked the manuscript with considerable vigor. Actually, he accepted some of Campbell's revisions or substituted his own (better) versions, and sometimes went beyond her proposed cuts. All in all, he compressed the book considerably, excising many of the tedious introductory clauses that Dreiser so favored, simplifying his prolixity, speeding up the narrative. Most of the changes were improvements, resulting in a simpler, plainer style. To be sure, many of Dreiser's old-fashioned locutions still stand, so it cannot be said that Elder (or Campbell) modernized the book in the way Farrell advised against.

While much of the editing was helpful, indeed improved the book's style and readability, religious and philosophical passages were jettisoned. Esther McCoy felt that the stylistic improvements removed Dreiser's personality: "Dreiser was reduced to good clear English in *The Bulwark* and it lost much of its relation to him." Marguerite was incensed by the streamlining of those convoluted sentences she had heard him dictate with such deep emotion, in his tired but musical voice. And she suspected censorship of the religious passages by Helen.

Of course she did not see what they had done until much later. Her last chance to look at the book was when the proofs arrived in September. She telephoned Dreiser and asked if she might help him read them, but Helen wanted no more of her involvement. Receiving an ambiguous reply from him, Harris jumped in her car and drove to North Kings Road. There followed a wrenching scene. Marguerite insisted that she and Dreiser read the proofs at her place. Helen refused and, as Marguerite told Elias, she "was almost driven out, while he stood looking, strangely helpless. . . ." Helen's version of the confrontation in *My Life with Dreiser* has him siding with *her*, though one suspects she was rewriting history to claim a final victory.

The fight was more than a clash between two jealous women. Each was doing what she thought was best for *him*, and for the book. Helen may have been jealous of Dreiser's involvement with Marguerite, but she believed, with considerable justice, that he trusted Louise and Farrell more than he did Marguerite to edit the script. Marguerite may have been in love with Dreiser, but she was also jealous of the version in which she had invested so much of herself. And indeed, with the strength and energy of her own body and spirit, she had literally pulled him back to life as he was sinking into the fatal torpor and lassitude that settles on old people when they have given up.

Dreiser was so torn between the two women that he was rendered helpless. As Marguerite left, driven out by Helen's implacable hostility, he could only mumble to her at the door that he would call her after looking over the galleys. All the women, all the triangles he had known! And now the final one, forming over a book.

The galleys were returned with scarcely a mark on them. Dreiser apparently did not notice the cuts that had been made—or was too tired to care. In his accompanying letter to Elder, he praised the editor for an excellent job, adding, "I am glad to see that you did incorporate some of Mrs. Campbell's ideas . . . but I do not know why she cut so much. It isn't quite like her, as I remember her work."

CHAPTER 39

Equation Inevitable

> And why, since you know what is here to be the merest
> wisp or rumor . . . of that totality, do you cling so fearfully,
> desperately to it when outside of this little stage play,
> rounded by a sleep, is all reality—the ultimate essence or
> base of it all?
>
> —*Notes on Life* (1974)

In the last months he seemed to friends more at peace. Robert Elias saw him in September and found him "obviously tired and in the home stretch." Sometimes his mind was sharp, but at other times it would drift into a fog. His memory of recent events was capricious.

Helen arranged a small party on his seventy-fourth birthday, a quiet affair under a pall cast by the recent death of his agent A. Dorian Otvos. Dreiser had grown fond of the playful Otvos—one of those precious people who made him laugh—and spoke movingly at the funeral.

In September his favorite sister, Sylvia, died. Now only Ed and Theodore were left—and possibly Al, of whom he had lost track. With a heightened consciousness of his dwindling time, his actions took the form of valedictories. The most notable was his decision to join the Communist Party in July. John Howard Lawson said that Dreiser was worried about the postwar world and feared continuing conflict. He had written of this to Louise: "the world seems so topsy-turvy that I mentally feel distrait most of the time. . . . I wonder how this world mess is to end for us. We are so mixed in everything . . . that I fear sometimes that we'll be warring for years with this country & that."

He feared a wave of postwar reaction in which the ruling capitalists would, as he wrote Wendell L. Willkie "wait and see if opportunity might not favor them with the Hitlerian method of crushing labor." He was drawn to the internationalist vision in Willkie's hugely popular book *One World*. But he also noted that Willkie had not raised the problem of the "common man," whose century then–Vice President Wallace had proclaimed it was. He asked the former GOP candidate and Wall Street lawyer how he proposed to make the "ruling five per cent that still controls ninety-five per cent of the wealth and power of the world" give a fairer share to the impoverished multitudes.

A meeting with Mme Chiang Kai-shek, wife of the Chinese Nationalist leader, at a reception at the Chinese consulate in Los Angeles prompted him to question her husband's intention to import U.S.-style capitalism. He pointed to the injustices in America under this system and advocated "some social form of Government,—not necessarily Communism—but something near it" for China. He told her, underlining it for emphasis: *"The progressive forces of the world are the ascending forces. And the ascending forces in the world today are made up of the common man."*

But when the Soviet dictator had sixteen Polish underground leaders arrested in furtherance of his design to impose a communist government in violation of the Yalta agreement, Dreiser sent him a telegram of unprecedented, if mild, protest: URGE CLARIFICATION POLISH QUESTION AS AMERICAN CAPITALIST REACTION IS CREATING MOST UNFORTUNATE MISUNDERSTANDING. OUR TWO GREAT NATIONS SHOULD GROW IN FRIENDSHIP. PLEASE DEAL WITH OUR AMERICANS GENTLY. JUST NOW IT IS SO IMPORTANT. He advocated socialism, but in a form that was indigenous to each nation; he did not imagine it being imposed by the Red Army.

In an essay called "Interdependence," written in September, a month after the end of the terrible war, he said that only cooperation among the masses could prevent the destruction of civilization (he had in mind, presumably, the atomic bombs that were dropped on Hiroshima and Nagasaki in August 1945). But he took care to explain that by "mass" he meant the individuals composing it. "As soon as one begins to think of the other side as a mass or a crowd, the human link seems to go." He believed now that small actions by myriad individuals could cumulatively make a difference. He expressed this idea in a poem called (after Tolstoy) "What to Do":

A small town editor writes the truth about profit and starvation.
And one knocks at a broken door and when it opens hands in a loaf of bread.
And one, step by step, all day long walks to this laborer
*   and that saying united we stand, divided we fall*

And one, the workers' friend, says Vote, Speak, for you are
the Government, by you the leaders rise and fall. . . .

Joining the Party was consistent with those sentiments. And the CP was now hospitable to his application. It had been rocked by an ideological upheaval resulting in the deposition of Earl Browder by a faction, led by William Z. Foster, opposing cooperation with the capitalists. No doubt the Party was eager to exploit the publicity of Dreiser's affiliation at this turning point in its history. But there is no reason to question John Howard Lawson's opinion that the decision was Dreiser's alone. He was not pressured or bamboozled into the ranks. Lawson and Dan James, a Hollywood writer and Party organizer, approached him about joining.

Apparently Dreiser was not an easy convert. But as Lawson recalled, "He felt that the Socialist solution was the ultimate solution and he wanted to go on record about this." Also, there was his long-submerged need to belong. Hy Kraft theorized that "he embraced the Communist party as a last political rite in order to die as a member in good standing of some section of American society." Some said the influence of James, who labored with him, and the example of Berkeley Tobey (who later left the Party, disillusioned) were critical; ironically, both men were brought up in wealthy families, which may have impressed Dreiser.

Using the language of religious conversion to describe Dreiser's decision is somewhat misleading, however. True, he was, in his own way, trying to put himself "right" with the world. And there was a quasi-religious element in his approval of communism. He considered the Russian leaders to be spiritual men—austere, selflessly dedicated to serving the people. (And he called Foster a "saint.") "What the world needs is more spiritual character," he told Elias. And he had compared the ideals of communism to the "white Christ" who Dostoevsky prophesied would come out of Russia and redeem the world.

But Esther McCoy said, "His radical views were all political." She added, "I think he was frightened of death. But he did not turn to religion in the end. He died as he lived, seeking to extract all the juice from life." Ruth Kennell said that Dreiser always considered communism a scientific plan for achieving economic equity.

Another way of putting it is that Dreiser saw no conflict between religion and the ideals of communism, just as he saw none between undogmatic religion and science. He regarded communism as a practical social program, but like the Populists of his youth, he invoked Christ's Sermon on the Mount to express its ideals. He was an enthusiastic reader of the books of Dean Hewlett Johnson, the Archbishop of Canterbury, who professed to find a kinship between communism and Christianity.

He was also saying, though less clearly, that communism *should* have a spiritual basis, without which it is mechanical and inhuman. The principles of communism, he believed, were ultimately those of Christ, and thus the leaders of the world's only communist country were "spiritual" because they were communists—which, as history attests, did not follow at all.

He also told Elias that while he approved of the U.S. Communist Party's program, "the details of the party line" were irrelevant to his decision to join. When Elias asked him if he would bow to Party discipline, he replied that he would speak his mind freely "and if they didn't like it they could throw him out." That resolution was shortly tested. When some local functionaries learned of Dreiser's plan to attend a dinner sponsored by a peace group of which Will Durant was chairman, they urged him not to go, calling the sponsoring group "charlatans." Dreiser rejected their advice. "Durant has been my friend for years," he informed them.

Finally it should be said that Dreiser didn't join the Party in more than a formal sense. One could say he lent it his name as he had sometimes done in the 1930s. The announcement, which was probably written by Lawson or some other Party members, reads like a CP press release rather than a personal statement by Dreiser of his convictions. Prominent mention was made of the Party's early opposition to fascism and its members who had patriotically served in the war. The criticism of Red-baiting certainly accorded with Dreiser's statement in the 1940s, making the point that the Party had a legitimate role to play in the democratic dialogue.

Few of his friends were surprised by the gesture. Mencken wrote him, "I have been thinking of you as a comrade since the beginning of the second holy war against sin." He meant that he had considered Dreiser a communist since Germany invaded Russia. They had "had it out" regarding Dreiser's political views in 1943, when Mencken asked him, "What, precisely, are your ideas about the current crusade to save humanity?" Dreiser replied, probably to Mencken's discomfiture, "Personally, I do not know what can save humanity, unless it is the amazing Creative force which has brought 'humanity,' along with its entire environment into being." He digressed to his contemplation of suicide in 1903, his experiences as Butterick editor-in-chief, his disillusionment with the rich, his affection for the "common man." And then he gets to the heart of the matter:

> You see, Mencken, unlike yourself, I am biased. I was born poor. For a time, in November and December, once, I went without shoes. I saw my beloved mother suffer from want—even worry and wring her hands in misery. And for that reason, perhaps—let it be what it will—I, regardless of whom or what, am for a social system that can and will do better than that for its members—those who try, however, humbly,—and more, *wish to learn how* to help themselves, but are none-the-less defeated by the trickeries of a set of vain-glorious dunces, who actually believe that money—*however come by*—the privilege of buying this and that—distinguishes them above all others of the very social system which has permit-

ted them to be and to trick these others out of the money that makes them so great. . . .

As for the Communist System—as I saw it in Russia in 1927 and '28—I am for it—hide and hoof.

There was much more in the letter, including praise and love for Mencken and gratitude for his battles on Dreiser's behalf. And from Mencken, vociferous dissent as to the loveliness of the communist system and the rectitude of Comrade Stalin; and a reminder that he had not exactly been born rich—he had supported himself since the age of sixteen. Paradoxically, over the ideological gulf between them flowed the warmest sentiments in several years, as a result of Dreiser's expressions of love.

Resigned to Dreiser's radicalism, Mencken was more worried about a deathbed conversion and issued a humorous warning: "In case you are now approached by a Jesuit or Trappist, perhaps disguised as a Jewish rabbi or a Wall Street customers' man, be on your guard. Remember Heywood Broun. If you are fetched I win $2."

Dreiser's answer was a joke—a Catholic indulgence card on which he wrote, "Here's another device for reducing your stay down below. It's going to be hot down there and those hundreds of days off will be welcome I'm sure." It was a signal he had not succumbed.

Mencken's private opinion, later voiced to James T. Farrell, was that "Dreiser was led into the Marxist corral" by Helen. But he goes on to lay the blame on a familiar complaint—Dreiser's gullibility: "I always predicted that if he lived long enough he'd leap back upon the bosom of the holy church."

There is no evidence that Helen played a part in Dreiser's conversion, though she might have encouraged it as a way of helping him to achieve serenity. In Marguerite Harris's opinion, however, Helen wanted him in the Party to counteract Harris's religious influence on him while they were working together on *The Bulwark*. As Harris put it to Elias,

> Toward the end, her attitude was not jealousy because I interfered in any way with their personal life, but it was a kind of literary jealousy, because we had been able to work together on the *Bulwark*, & I do believe she wanted to sabotage that work, for reasons of pride, or even because of a certain anti-spiritual attitude which flared up in her, & also made her anxious to push Dreiser into a Communist position, which he had never wished to take. . . .

Marguerite's suspicion that Helen wanted to sabotage *The Bulwark* became an obsession with her; she hoped that one day the original manuscript—the *true* text—would be published. A jealous Helen had tried to vanquish her influence by changing *The Bulwark*, pushing him into the CP, and intruding yoga into *The Stoic*.

It is true that Helen was a devotee of yoga, Christian Science, and various *outré* California sects, and was anti organized religion, taking after Dreiser. But she was not "anti-spiritual." She was first of all anti-Marguerite. But that does not mean she inveigled Dreiser into joining the Communist Party as an elaborate act of revenge. She hadn't the power. His political views were his own, and she echoed them but would not have been able to push him into taking such an important step.

Marguerite's idea that Helen influenced *The Stoic* is more plausible, since the final chapters are full of yoga. It may be that he sought to placate her—a sort of granting of equal time to her beliefs to counteract Marguerite. And the book was a kind of final bequest to her—a way of providing for her financially. But the words in those chapters represent his sentiments.

When Dreiser took up the novel in June, it was two-thirds done. Seated in his yellow-winged rocking chair, he dictated to Helen at the typewriter. Day after day, the routine was the same: he would rise about 8:30, bathe and shave and put on a coat and tie and come into the kitchen and pour himself a small drink. After breakfast they would work until one or so and have a light lunch. Then they might go out for a drive, often taking dinner at a restaurant. Evenings were spent quietly at home, Helen typing up the day's work and Dreiser reading and editing the already typed manuscript. "It was incredible the way he persisted in his job," she writes of this period; "in fact it was all he wanted to do with the exception of an occasional diversion."

They drew closer during this time, and she writes, almost too glowingly for credibility, "If a woman ever experienced a complete renewal of her love life combined with a new depth of spirit, I had that joy." He flooded her with tenderness and praised her for things she had done for him long ago, trying to make it up to her. And she on her part hovered over him. A friend said she "kept putting an invisible shawl about his shoulders."

But there were episodes Helen doesn't talk about. A bender that ended up in a fancy Hollywood brothel; episodes of senile dementia. At 3:00 A.M. one morning she found him prowling about the house in a distraught state. He told her he was looking for Helen. When she assured him she was Helen, he replied, "Everyone thinks she's Helen." The delusion sometimes lasted for days. Once Marguerite discovered him lying on a couch, his eyes gleaming, his hands hot and feverish. "I don't know where Helen is," he told her. "There was a strange person here this morning. Maybe you can find out for me." Marguerite assured him that Helen, who was out, would return. That pacified him, and when she did come back he recognized her. Marguerite consulted a psychiatrist, who told her that at Dreiser's age there was little to be done, and it was best not to upset him by challenging his hallucinations or whatever they were. Rest and quiet were what he needed.

His visions strikingly symbolized his essentially ambivalent relationship with Helen. He feared that she had abandoned him but also denied her presence, as though he were wishing her away (indeed, Marguerite thought he feared Helen). And so it had been for a long time: she was always there, even when he was away with another woman, and when he was with her he dreamed of another woman. With the other women, he would make a Freudian slip and call them "Helen." In his present mental haze, the subconscious impulsion behind such slips was blown up into a delusion that Helen was not Helen—and that other women thought they were Helen. Now only Helen was left and she was all women.

In late October Dreiser wrote Farrell that he had finished *The Stoic;* as soon as it was typed he would send it to him. He did not do so until early December. The last two chapters had caused him some difficulties. He had no trouble describing Cowperwood's death, his fortune fought over by lawyers, business rivals, and tax collectors, and all the planned memorials to his name—the hospital, the art museum—never built.

But the problem of what happens to Berenice remained. Here too reality had suggested a possible outcome—a trip to India, like her prototype, Emilie Grigsby, to study Eastern philosophy. But reality also suggested Emilie's quest was a failure, which would have pointed to an ironic ending. But Dreiser had himself made a mental pilgrimage to the East; he had saluted the contributions to philosophy of Hinduism and Buddhism in an essay, "The Dawn Is in the East." And so he could not resist sending Berenice to India, a "God-seeking, spirit-loving land." There she encounters a guru, who instantly divines her purpose and accepts her as a disciple. She learns the various techniques and precepts of yoga. The chapter describing her spiritual education reads like a mixture of Vedic writings and Dreiserian philosophy, which is appropriate since the former had influenced the latter.

After four years, Berenice's spiritual education is complete, and she returns to America and founds a charity hospital with some of the money Cowperwood left her. She trains as a nurse, then takes charge of the children's ward. Her special fondness for some blind children was probably inspired by Dreiser's own visits to a Hollywood orphanage for such children. She comes to a deeper understanding of Cowperwood, realizing "that his worship and constant search for beauty in every form and especially in the form of a woman was nothing more than a search for the Divine design behind all forms—the face of the Brahman shining through." Thus did Dreiser reconcile his own lifelong pursuit of the feminine as a quest for beauty. The manuscript ended with an almost perfunctory essay on the relativity of good and evil, intended as a coda to the trilogy.

Seeking confirmation of the authenticity of his treatment of yoga, he and Helen visited Swami Prabhavananda, head of the Vedanta center in Los Angeles. The holy man described the visit to Alan Hunter: "It was she who did the talking. She wanted to know if they were right in their expression of the Vedanta teachings. I told them I could not tell this, unless I saw the manuscript myself. This they did not have with them. Mr. Dreiser said nothing at all."

If the story is true (it originated with Marguerite), Dreiser was at this point beyond caring. But inaccuracy is not the problem with the chapters on Berenice's conversion. The ideas are not integrated into the narrative; they are not dramatized in terms of character. It might have indeed made an interesting conclusion to relate the spiritual quest of this once frivolous and calculating woman, but Dreiser does not tell that story. Instead, he provides a copybook of wise sayings, their self-evident truth assumed to be sufficient to explain Berenice's acceptance of them.

That Dreiser had doubts about the ending is shown by a letter to Farrell, written on December 14: "Would you prefer, personally, to see the chapters on yoga come out of the book? If so, what would be your idea of a logical ending?" Farrell suggested that the passages about yoga be recast to show Berenice's feelings and reactions and "the ironic inadequacy of her efforts." He was also unhappy with the essay about good and evil, regarding it as too sketchy to serve as the finale of this great trilogy. Dreiser replied equably, "You are dead right about the last chapter in regard to Berenice," and said he intended to rewrite it. "As to the essay on Good and Evil," he went on, "well that is something that can be discussed at length, and there is plenty of time for that."

But there was no longer plenty of time.

In early December he, Marguerite, and Helen attended a production of *The Dybbuk* by a little theater group. The play, with its story of demonic possession, disturbed him. Perhaps he was reminded of apparitions he had seen, both recently and in the past. His interest in the occult seems to have revived, including spiritualism, which after all these years he still regarded as proof of the immortality of the soul, as the series in *The Delineator*, "Are the Dead Alive?" had argued. Marguerite recalled, "He had a growing belief that the spirit lives on after death, in some mysterious way, a part of the force of Creation." Sometimes he thought, as he told Masters, that our minds live on after the body dies, observing, thinking, experiencing.

His interest in the visible world seemed to recede in direct proportion to his preoccupation with an unseen one. He still spoke out feebly for social justice and fretted about the postwar world. In his Christmas message to Mencken he scrawled a few lines of comment on the store-bought card (as he always did—his way of personalizing them), which showed Santa snoozing before the fire. He hoped Mencken was finding similar peace. "And now if it only weren't for those accursed uranium . . . bombs how well off you would and should be."

He and Helen attended a wedding. A photograph taken for the occasion—the last one of him—shows a very ill and tired man. On Christmas Eve he visited Elizabeth Coakley, spending most of the day watching her children decorate their Christmas tree, listening to Elizabeth play the harp. He encouraged her to write a book about her life; he was always urging women friends to write their stories to which he had listened with such warm sympathy. She drove him home in a freezing rain. When they arrived at his door, he said, "Oh how I dread to leave you. I am the loneliest man in the world." He spoke of "paying off" Helen—as he had to so many women in the past. Had he ever really meant it?

On December 27 he worked on the next-to-last chapter of *The Stoic*. The earlier yoga chapters he let stand; the job of revising them in line with Farrell's criticisms was beyond his powers. He continued until five o'-clock, and then they drove to the beach and watched a brilliant Technicolor California sunset, all flame and crimson and gold, the most beautiful Helen had ever seen. He suggested they buy hot dogs for dinner from a stand on the boardwalk. They chatted with the jovial vendor, who told them he supported his wife and five children on what he made from his business. On the way home they talked of how some people could be happy with so little.

He said he was tired and intended to turn in. Helen retyped the chapter he had dictated that day, and when she finished at around 9:00 P.M. she looked in on him. She was disturbed by his appearance; his skin had a glossy look and his face was pale. She said she would show him the script in the morning, but he insisted, "*No,* read it right now!" So she read it to him, and he seemed pleased. Later she turned on the radio so he could listen to the ten o'clock news. He complained of kidney pains and she brought him a heat lamp. After a half hour he felt better and turned out the light.

At 2:45 A.M. she awakened to see him standing in her room in his dressing gown. "Helen," he said, "I have an *intense* pain!" The urgency in his voice made her quickly get up, but he crumpled to the floor before she could reach him. He was in agony, and the cliché of so many World War II movies occurred to Helen: "This is it." She did not want to leave him even to go to the phone. Frantically she piled up pillows and blankets under him and tried to administer a teaspoon of brandy, but his teeth were clenched. His physician, Dr. Hirshfeld, was out, but his assistant, Dr. Chier, came within ten minutes. Helen and the doctor took Dreiser's arms and helped him to his room; he collapsed on the way but they managed to get him in bed and the doctor gave him a shot of morphine. Dreiser told him, "A pain like that could kill a person."

It was a heart attack, a massive one, and Dr. Chier thought Dreiser's chances of recovery were slim. Lillian and Mark Goodman had arrived and stayed with Helen through the night. The next day Dreiser was placed in an oxygen tent and a male nurse brought in.

While driving home from her job with an architect, Esther McCoy remembered she had two books by Theodor Reik and James T. Farrell which Dreiser had asked her to report on, so she decided to drop them off. Helen answered the door and told her that Teddy had had a heart attack. Esther went into his bedroom and found him under the oxygen tent looking "very gray." She noticed how his long eyelashes made him look childishly vulnerable. She asked him how he was. "Bum," he said.

Helen hovered over him, making him comfortable, and Esther walked through his study into the living room, noticing with sudden clarity the familiar talismans on his rosewood desk, the Chinese fisherman, the American Indian, the kewpie doll. There was the high-backed ducal chair he had sat in during parties at the Rodin Studios and now wrote in. She had a feeling that he would never sit in the chair again.

Helen asked Esther to spend the night with her, so Esther went home to get her things. The day had been hot and humid when she arrived, but now a fresh wind was blowing up. A fog rolled in, blurring the Christmas lights on the houses and then blanketing the street lamps. Soon it was so thick she could barely see the road and had to follow the white center line. She recalled Dreiser's idea of death as a fog that slowly, silently blurs the contours of reality, until the world is obliterated.

Meanwhile, Dr. Hirshfeld arrived and examined Dreiser. He seemed better and might pull through. When Helen went into his room, he was lucid. Suddenly he said, "Kiss me, Helen," and she did—on the side of his lips, just as she had in a dream a few weeks before. She kissed him again, and he said, "You look beautiful."

A little later, while Helen was resting, she heard the nurse talking on the telephone in an urgent voice. Dreiser's breathing was shallower; the doctor must come at once. Helen hurried to him. He seemed to be asleep. She held his hand; it was icy. He exhaled once, and then stopped breathing. She could not believe he had gone. The spirit slipped free and the atoms and protons that composed him began the final dissolution that would return all that had been Theodore Dreiser to the primal source, the ultimate matter-energy. The doctor arrived to pronounce him dead at 6:50 P.M.

As he had foretold, Helen was there at the end to close his eyes.

Esther and Berkeley Tobey were first to hear the news. When they arrived, Helen seemed in control of herself. She called the funeral home and the attendants arrived. They placed the corpse on a gurney and wheeled it toward the door. At that moment Marguerite Harris burst into the room and threw herself on the body. The attendants tried to remove her, but she insisted that she go with Dreiser to the funeral home. Helen, who had been quietly watching, said, "Let her go." Esther could not help thinking that Helen, who had shared him with so many women, was now generously sharing him in death. Helen recalled her feelings as the men took him away: "The biggest and best part of my life went through the door with him. I simply crumbled."

The next day Helen was strong enough to go to Forest Lawn to select a lot, explaining that Dreiser had told her he wanted to be buried there. She purchased a site "along a ridge, open to the sky, the sun & moon," she wrote Elias. "There are stately pines, like sentinels all about. . . . It's a heavenly spot." And then she selected "a beautiful dark rich red hardwood mahogany casket lined with a beautiful shade of velvet" and commissioned the sculptor Edgardo Simone to make a death mask and a cast of his right hand.

A gravediggers' strike delayed the burial, allowing time for differences over how the funeral should be conducted to fester. There were two factions, the religious camp and the progressive camp. Marguerite, who belonged to the former, arranged, with Helen's permission, for the Reverend Hunter to preside. The progressives, led by Lawson and James, lobbied for a political statement. Helen's main wish was that Charlie Chaplin read one of Dreiser's poems at the end of the service. She was leery of the CP representatives turning the service into a political rally. On the night before the funeral she was about to discuss it with them, when Marguerite arrived and shouted angrily that no communist officials should speak.

At this usurpation by her rival, Helen forgot that she felt the same way and began berating Marguerite. The two women seemed locked in a contest for Dreiser's soul. Helen had earlier pretended a reconciliation, but now her jealousy spewed forth. She threatened to cancel Dr. Hunter's appearance and then ordered Marguerite out of the house.

Somehow the arrangements were completed. Helen wanted a great man's funeral. He belonged to the world now—he who had never belonged to her, or to anyone. Pallbearers were selected from a cross-section of Dreiser's friends. Upton Sinclair, however, declined because, he explained, he and Dreiser were merely acquaintances, causing Helen to burst into tears. "We went several times a year, at their invitation! He and Teddie had the warmest of relations!"

On January 3, 1946, more than a week after Dreiser's death, the obsequies were held at Forest Lawn. Helen had been distraught that morning. She kept running to the window and saying that Marguerite was outside in a car "spying" on her. Vera could see no one, but Helen would not believe her. Finally Vera got her dressed and with Esther they rode in one of the limousines to the Church of the Recessional. On the way Esther began crying, and Vera efficiently produced a flask of water, a little cup and a pill. It was a cold day, and Helen wore the new fur jacket that Vera had urged her to buy, rather than the borrowed coat she planned to use.

The services represented a carefully scripted compromise between the two factions, a kind of stiff tableau with politics and church receiving equal time in eulogies by John Howard Lawson and the Reverend Alan Hunter. Marguerite called it "a farce or at least a tragic dividing of, & clashing of forces. . . ." But in that sense the ceremony truthfully reflected two contending forces in Dreiser's life. All that was lacking was a veiled woman from out of the past flinging herself on the coffin. As it was, several former lovers were present, but Helen was gracious to them. There was none of the spontaneous human drama that Dreiser loved, none of the moving extemporaneous tributes such as he sometimes delivered over the bier of a friend.

Lawson's talk—or lecture—was a scholarly summation of Dreiser's literary career, relating his works to American society, emphasizing the social consciousness and the desire for equity that ran through all his books. He reminded the mourners that Dreiser's decision to become a member of the Communist Party was the logical consequence of his life and work, and warned that fascism was abroad in the land. Then Charlie Chaplin read a poem from *Moods*, "The Road I Came," which would be engraved on Dreiser's tombstone. Esther had preferred Emerson's "The Red Slayer," with its affirmation of the triumph of the spirit over death. Chaplin intoned the lines in his mellifluous voice:

> *Oh, what is this*
> *That knows the road I came?*

Next, Dr. Hunter, looking somewhat ill at ease, as though he was there on sufferance. He quoted from *The Bulwark*, John Woolman, and George Fox. He did not claim Dreiser for any church—nor could he; he suggested only that the deceased had struggled against the "image of life as a mere machine." He quoted, as Dreiser's most "characteristic cry," the Biblical words, "Lord, I believe, help Thou my unbelief." He closed with a prayer.

Through it all, Dreiser lay in his coffin with what Helen called an "indescribable expression of peace" on his strong countenance. Possibly the tranquillity was cosmetic, a tribute to the embalmer's art, begging the more important question: Had he, before the end, found the answers? Had a truce been achieved among the warring elements within him, those eager, contending desires for love, wealth, power, equity, beauty, God? In his last years he had sought to escape the lonely torment of selfhood and immerse himself in a larger whole, to find some unified-field theory of science and religion that would redeem the pain of life. He searched for a constancy of love from outside himself that would assuage the chilling loneliness of the ego in a bleak universe.

But this faith of his last years—if indeed he had found it to his satisfaction—was grafted on earlier, deeper roots, the belief in a universe governed by chaos, life preying on life. That faith he could never have entirely renounced, because it had been formed and fed by his observations of life, the sensory data of experience, and the "laws" of science as revealed by Darwin and Spencer.

But always he retained that tantalizing conception of an Unknowable behind the veil of appearance. As a child at Communion, hearing that the Spirit was in the bread and wine, he had cried "Give me God!" It was a hunger that was never appeased; in the end, like other desires of the flesh, it wearily surrendered itself to a philosophical monogamy, a metaphysical fidelity, to a single Creator.

The sea is ever dancing or raging, he had written in the Epilogue of *The Titan.* At best a temporary balance is struck between belief and unbelief: And in the end, Equation Inevitable, a final balance, the cessation of all striving. "Nirvana! Nirvana! The ultimate, still, equation."

Envoy

From Baltimore Mencken did what he could for Helen, progressing from "Dear Mrs. Dreiser" to "Dear Helen," advising her on publishing affairs, writing an introduction for the reissue of *An American Tragedy* by the World Publishing Company, which did not, however, undertake the complete set that had been Dreiser's dream. Mencken had been one of the first she notified, ending the telegram with her special grace: "He loved you." That same day, among the mail at 1524 Hollins Street was a letter Mencken sent the previous day. He had forgotten to put a stamp on it, and to his relief it was returned. It was the usual chaff, but no longer appropriate. He had closed, "I trust you are in ruddy health and good spirits. As for me, I grind away at dull tasks and hope for a club-house ticket in Heaven."

He quickly sent Helen a more suitable message: "He was lucky to have you. . . . It is hard to think of his work as ended. What a man he was." And later: "Theodore's death leaves me feeling as if my whole world had blown up . . . there was a time when he was my captain in a war that will never end, and we had a swell time together. No other man had a greater influence on my youth."

Helen pulled out of her depression and devoted herself to disposing of Dreiser's literary remains (the bulk of his papers went to the University of Pennsylvania, but she sent the manuscript of *Dawn* to Indiana University), helping prepare a collection of his short stories, and writing her memoirs, *My Life with Dreiser*. Although in her refined way she suppresses many unpleasant memories, she is surprisingly candid about the love affairs which had made life with Dreiser at times hell. She dedicated the book "To the unknown women in the life of Theodore Dreiser, who devoted themselves unselfishly to the beauty of his intellect and its artistic unfoldment."

She eventually sold the house at 1015 North Kings Road and moved in with her sister Myrtle on a ranch in Washington. Her health was not good, and in time she had a stroke, and then another one that completely incapacitated her. She lay in a special large crib, plump and rouged like a large doll, living out her days. She died in 1957.

. . .

At his death, Dreiser's estate was valued in excess of $100,000, not counting the gold coins stuffed in a strongbox, which the government allowed Helen to redeem. *The Bulwark* sold well, earning over $40,000 in royalties.

When the novel appeared, most reviewers took the occasion to sum up Dreiser's career, and most acclaimed him as a major force in American letters. The novel itself received mixed notices, with much speculation on whether the old materialist had embraced religion at the end. *The Stoic,* published the following year, had been completed by Helen from his notes; the final chapter, however, consists of Dreiser's outline of what he intended to write. The essay on good and evil was dropped. The book was widely judged a tired performance, though some Dreiser loyalists felt in it faint tremors of the old power.

Neither novel was up to the great works that assured that his name would endure—*Sister Carrie, Jennie Gerhardt, The Financier, An American Tragedy.* But neither was a meretricious performance, and *The Bulwark* surely belongs in the second rank. Although it lacked the documentation, the brooding fatalism, the poignancy of desire trapped in the cage of convention, the sweep of his best work, *The Bulwark* was more than the scenario for a Dreiser novel that some held it to be. The form was what Dreiser had struggled for thirty years to find. The book had the simplicity of folk art and a quaint period flavor, like a hand-embroidered sampler hung in a farm kitchen. Some critics took it as Dreiser's reconciliation with his father; but it is the father who forgives the son.

To the end, Dreiser made no compromises with popular taste, and wrote as honestly, if not as well, as he always had. But his search for philosophical answers and his advocacy of social change had carried him beyond the novel to a more urgent vision of science and politics. His style and his fictional imagination could not keep up with his speculations. The mysteries of character, the ironies of fate, and the hidden workings of the social system ceased to interest him, at a time when the social system's failure dominated literary consciousness. In the end he had moved beyond the passions that drove his characters and novels, beyond the gropings of individuals toward a higher realm of meaning; he had stepped out from behind the scrim of fiction and confronted the great questions directly.

He had an enormous influence on American literature during the first quarter of the century—and for a time he *was* American literature, the only writer worth talking about in the same breath with the European masters. Out of his passions, contradictions, and sufferings, he wrenched the art that was his salvation from the hungers and depressions that racked him. It was no wonder that he elevated the creative principle to a godhead and encouraged by word and example truthful expression in others. If one were to identify the central, unifying theme of his contradiction-riddled life it was that he was totally subsumed in the role of author. Like many novelists, he was a congeries of different selves, from Hurstwood and Carrie to Cowperwood and Clyde. Moreover, he saw himself and all human beings as characters in the great, shapeless novel of life manipulated by the Author/Creator behind the veil.

He was the most "American" of novelists. His hungry curiosity probed the nooks and crannies of the national life, as he sought to perform what he saw as his mission—understanding a large, youthful, dynamic country that had no deep roots in the past and that was in a perpetual state of change and becoming. He retained a deep compassion for the voiceless mass of individuals in this land; their tawdry dreams and desires had for him the beauty of prayers.

His journey ended, ironically, in Hollywood, a factory town of dreams, beneath the expensive soil of Forest Lawn. He had frequently written of the lure of illusion and how it betrays the seeker. But art and beauty and love were themselves illusions. Or were they? In the end, he discovered, perhaps, that they were part of the greater Reality.

Acknowledgments

As books are wont to do, the second volume of this biography took longer than anticipated. It would never have been completed at all without the generosity of *The Nation* magazine. Thanks again for the gift of time to Victor Navasky, editor, and Arthur Carter, publisher. At G. P. Putnam's, my editor, Faith Sale, bore the brunt of my dilatory ways and meted out appropriate measures of nagging and encouragement. Fred Sawyer copy-edited with skill a difficult manuscript. For home front services beyond the call of duty, Anthea and Jenifer Lingeman are herewith awarded another oak leaf cluster on the Order of Family Merit.

In Volume I of this biography, I acknowledged my intellectual debt to a number of Dreiser scholars, whose names I will not repeat here. And I must express my deep gratitude to the people who related their recollections of Dreiser, shared with me their research, permitted me to quote from letters, or aided me in other ways. To list them alphabetically:

Sam Abbott, Cedric Belfrage, Alfred P. Bingham, Craig Brandon, "Sylvia Bradshaw," Margaret Carson, Dr. Francis X. Claps, Beatrice Cole, Harold Dies, Vera Dreiser, Yvette Eastman, Robert H. Elias, Clifton Fadiman, Vincent Fitzpatrick, Franklin Folsom, Louise Graham, Shari Handlin, Hilary Harris, Harriet B. Hubbard, Clara C. Jaeger, Ernest Kroll, Herman Liveright, Hazel L. Mack, Ellen C. Masters, Ken McCormick, Esther McCoy, Thomas P. Riggio, Mrs. Dwight Robinson, Felicia Van Veen, Gupton and Grace Vogt, James L. W. West III.

Many of Dreiser's contemporaries have passed on, but fortunately I was able to draw on three excellent biographies whose authors did talk to them: Dorothy Dudley, Robert H. Elias, and W. A. Swanberg. In addition I was able to consult the material Mr. Elias deposited at the Cornell University Library, and notes that Mr. Swanberg deeded to the Dreiser Collection at the University of Pennsylvania. This material included interviews with people no longer alive, and I have cited them in the Chapter Notes.

Gary Giddins kindly lent me copies of financial records and correspondence belonging to Arthur Pell. Ken Silverstein efficiently tracked down many obscure publications. Michelle Galen, then of the Nation Institute, filed numerous Freedom of Information Act requests in my behalf. (I cannot thank the Federal Bureau of Investigation for the excessively censored files it grudgingly produced, however; and I must observe that the investigation of Dreiser that produced those files was disgraceful and a waste of taxpayers' money.) And Shirley Sulat typed several chapters on short order.

The staffs of the libraries holding papers relevant to Dreiser were unfailingly cooperative. First and foremost, my gratitude to Daniel Traister, Kathleen Reed, and Nancy Shawcross at the Dreiser Collection, University of Pennsylvania. Thanks also to Cathy Henderson at the Harry Ransom Humanities Research Center, University of Texas at Austin. Other libraries that provided access to Dreiser materials: the Lilly Library, Indiana University; Rare Book and Manuscript Library, Columbia University; the Manuscripts and Archives Division of the New York Public Library; the Mencken Collection at the Enoch Pratt Free Library, Baltimore; the Robert H. Elias Collection, Cornell University Library; Theodore Dreiser Collection (#6220), Clifton Waller Barrett Library, Manuscripts Division, Special Collections Department, University of Virginia; the University of Rochester Library; the University Library, University of Illinois at Urbana-Champaign; and the New York Society Library. Unless otherwise noted, all papers cited in the Chapter Notes are located at the University of Pennsylvania. Libraries are cited by the following abbreviations:

> ColU—Columbia University Library, New York City
> CorU—Cornell University Library, Ithaca, New York
> EPFL—Enoch Pratt Free Library, Baltimore
> EU—Emory University Library, Atlanta, Georgia
> IndU—Lilly Library, Indiana University, Bloomington, Indiana
> NYPL—New York Public Library, New York City
> THL—Emeline Fairbanks Library, Terre Haute, Indiana
> UIll—University of Illinois at Urbana-Champaign
> UP—University of Pennsylvania, Philadelphia
> URo—University of Rochester Library, Rochester, New York
> UTex—Harry Ransom Humanities Research Center, The University of Texas at Austin
> UVa—University of Virginia Library.

For permission to quote unpublished Dreiser material I thank the Trustees of the University of Pennsylvania and Daniel Traister, Assistant Director of Libraries for Special Collections. Permission to publish extracts from the Mencken letters has been granted by the Enoch Pratt Free Library in accordance with the terms of the will of H. L. Mencken.

I am indebted to the following for photographs:

Theodore Dreiser Collection, Department of Special Collections, Van Pelt Library, University of Pennsylvania, for the following photographs: Dreiser, Grant Richards and Sir Hugh Lane; Estelle Bloom Kubitz; Helen Richardson in 1920; Dreiser in 1920; Helen and Dreiser in Hollywood, 1921;

Helen in black lace dress; Dreiser correcting typescript; first page of holograph of *An American Tragedy;* Dreiser in Russia; Dreiser in the 1920s; Iroki scenes; Dreiser, Edgar Lee Masters and Harriet Bissell; *Jennie Gerhardt* film still; Dreiser addressing peace conference; Dreiser at Harris's mansion; Dreiser and Robeson; Dreiser and Helen in Hollywood in the 1940s; snapshot of Marguerite Tjader Harris; last photograph of Dreiser.

Alfred A. Knopf for photograph of H. L. Mencken.

The National Portrait Gallery, Smithsonian Institution, for photograph of bust of Dreiser by Onorio Ruotolo.

Los Angeles *Herald-Examiner* for photograph of Dreiser and George Douglas.

Emory University Library and Vera Dreiser for photographs of Theodore and Vera Dreiser and profile of Dreiser.

Clara Clark Jaeger for photograph of herself.

Sylvia Bradshaw for photograph of herself.

Notes

For frequently cited works only the author's name is used after the first identification, or author's name and short title of the book in the case of an author of two or more frequently cited books. All page references with communications between Dreiser and Mencken are from Thomas P. Riggio, ed., Dreiser-Mencken Letters.

Chapter 1.

"Are you writing" Quoted in Donald Pizer, ed., *Theodore Dreiser: A Selection of Uncollected Prose*, 164.

"the idea of" "Concerning Us All," *Delineator*, Jan. 1908.

an astonishing 43,000 Note in Dreiser Manuscripts II (IndU).

"a fashion sheet" Arthur S. Hoffman to Elias, Jan. 10, 1945 (CorU).

"You probably know" TD to HLM, 12.

"What homes have" Undated clipping.

"G. W. had the ideas" "Memoirs of Edward B. Emory," 1948, box 1, folder 7, Butterick Company Archives.

"the child that" "Concerning Us All," *Delineator*, Nov. 1907.

"One must live" William C. Lengel, "The 'Genius' Himself, *Esquire*, Sept. 1938.

"partly finished" Quoted in Pizer, *Uncollected Prose*, 164, 163.

"I don't want" Grant Richards to TD, Dec. 6, 1905 (UIll).

"keen pleasure" GR to TD, March 6, 1908 (UIll).

"better drop" TD to GR, March 14, 1908 (UIll).

"All I can say" GR to TD, March 31, 1908 (UIll).

"a very simple person" Quoted in Dorothy Dudley, *Dreiser and the Land of the Free*, 225.

"The label gives" Quoted in Lengel.

Ludwig Lewisohn "An American Memory," Alfred Kazin and Charles Shapiro, eds., *The Stature of Theodore Dreiser*, 17.

Upton Sinclair had written TD, "The Epic Sinclair," *Esquire*, Dec. 1934.

"Can you make" William Rickey to TD, April 21, 1910.

Dodge admitted BWD to TD, July 15, 1913.

a new board BWD to TD, Oct. 1910.

"have some fun" TD to HLM, July 11, 1909, 26.

"in with both feet" HLM to TD, [after July 11, 1909], 26.

"tainted fiction" "a big catholic" TD to HLM, Aug. 8, 1909, 29.

Mencken's first HLM to TD, [before Aug. 9, 1909], 29; TD to HLM, Aug. 9, 1909, 31.

"I am getting along" HLM to TD, March 7, 1909, 22.

"Need three funny" TD to HLM (telegram), Oct. 15, 1909, ibid., 36.

"with the confidence" Quoted in Isaac Goldberg, *The Man Mencken*, 379.

"Schopenhauer" TD to HLM, Dec. 16, 1909, 42.

"In memory of" Quoted in Robert H. Elias, *Letters of Theodore Dreiser*, I, 97.

"The truth is" TD to HLM, Nov. 2, 1909, 37.

"Back of all" *Delineator*, Nov. 1907.

"with the rank" Quoted in Douglas C. Stenerson, *H. L. Mencken: Iconoclast from Baltimore*, 125.

"I feel a sense" TD to HLM, Feb. 20, 1910, 45.

"Nothing could equal" *"Genius,"* 522.

"Theo wants" Thelma Cudlipp Whitman, "October's Child" (unpublished MS), with W. A. Swanberg Papers.

"Do you like" "Then he kissed" Ibid.

"your soft little" TD to Cudlipp, Elias, *Letters*, I, 107.

"dwarfed his capacity" Vera Dreiser, *My Uncle Theodore*, 103.

"I wish you" Jug to TD, Sept. 6, 1907.

One spouse Genevieve Myers to Emily, March 12, 1947.

"In case a man" "Concerning Us All," *Delineator*, Oct. 1907.

"had no confidence" McKee to Elias, March 1, 1950.

perambulator dream Clara Jaeger, *Philadelphia Rebel*, 76.

"He must have hypnotized" Quoted in W. A. Swanberg, *Dreiser*, 134.

"I NEED you" TD to TC, Oct. 7, 1910. Elias, *Letters*, I, 108.

"Mrs. Dreiser was quite" TD to HLM, July 28, 1910, 50.

Chapter 2.

"Here was all" *"Genius,"* 666–67.

"Though the young" Hoffman to Elias, Jan. 19, 1945.

increased circulation Dudley, 223–24.

"Butterick . . . was" Hoffman to Elias, Jan. 19, 1945 (CorU).

"the working arrangements" TD to Erman Ridgway, Sept. 8, 1910 (IndU).

"Are the Dead" See *Delineator*, Oct. 1908.

"have raised a storm" "Still We think We Are Justified," *Delineator*, Dec. 1908.

"Our editor" Wilder to Charles W. Taylor Jr., Boston *Globe*, Nov. 13, 1908 (IndU).

"the spirit" "You and the Editor," *Delineator*, Dec. 1908.

"might delight" "to modify" TD to Duffield, Aug. 7, 1910 (UIll).

"I do not consider" TD to Rider, Oct. 11, 1910.

"I have just" Undated memo.

"Nothing's up" TD to HLM, Oct. 11, 1910, 52.

endlessly folding Lengel, *Esquire*, Sept. 1938.

acquiring an interest Edwin Wildman to TD, Oct. 24, 1910.

"not at all anxious" "You are worth" TD to Cudlipp, Oct. 3, 1910, Elias, *Letters*, I, 105–6.

"even a mere" "Oh, Honeypot" Ibid., 108–9.

"had counted on me" Whitman, "October's Child."

"I'm sorry" Quoted in Dudley, 231.

"It was pathetic" Quoted in F. O. Matthiessen, *Dreiser*, 107–8.

Chapter 3.

"I have just" TD to HLM, Feb. 24, 1911, 63.

"Little by little" McKee to Elias, March 23, 1949 (CorU).

"about the biggest" Lewis letter quoted in Mark Schorer, *Sinclair Lewis*, 179.

"fortunate enough" Hitchcock to TD, Nov. 11, 1910.

"establishes a standard" Rosenthal to TD, Jan. 25, 1911.

"I am convinced" TD to Rider, Elias, *Letters*, I, 110.

"I seize every" HLM to TD, March 14, 1911, 65.

"There are some" TD to Holly, March 9, 1911.

"I sometimes think" TD to HLM, March 10, 1911, 65.

"I had better" TD to Richards, June 26, 1911 (UIll).

visit to Sloan Van Wyck Brooks, *John Sloan: A Painter's Life*, 188–89.

"a dignified American" TD to GR, June 26, 1911 (UIll).

"They were nervous" Ibid.

"the 3d book" TD to HLM, April 17, 1911, 67.

"They may not" TD to GR, June 26, 1911 (IUll).

"I have just finished" HLM to TD, April 23, 1911, 68.

"as grim" TD to HLM, April 28, 1911, 71.

"You write like" Huneker to TD, [May] 4, 1911.

"rosy dawn" Phillips to TD, Oct. 1911[?].

"You don't know" TD to Lengel, [1912] (Col U).

"I understand" *Jennie Gerhardt* TS (UVa). James L. W. West to author, Sept. 8, 1987.

"I couldn't" *Jennie*, 164–65.

Trites Quoted in Richards to TD, April 15, 1912.

"If anyone" HLM to TD, April 23, 1911, 69.

"Why you should" Hitchcock to TD, May 5, 1911.

"put back pages" Hitchcock to TD, July 14, 1911.

"during the ruddiest" *Jennie* TS, ch. VI, 79 (U Va).

"there was scarcely" Ibid., 81.

"irritated me" HLM to TD, Nov. 9, 1911, 81.

". . . the Harpers cut" HLM to Wilson, Oct. 25, 1911. In Guy Forgue, ed., *Letters of H. L. Mencken*, 18.

"carefully edited" TD to Huneker, May 5, 1911.

"We can congratulate" Hitchcock to Holly, Sept. 5, 1911.

"practically gathered" TD to HLM, Aug. 8, 1911, 73.

"marked for cutting" TD to HLM, Sept. 4, 1911, 76.

"the best American" In Jack Salzman, ed., *Theodore Dreiser: The Critical Reception*, 62.

"but don't let" TD to Mrs. Dell, Oct. 17, 1911.

"must be due to" Salzman, 65, 67.

"with power" "Is a woman" Ibid., 58, 59.

"is a long" Ibid., 92.

"rather unpleasant" Carbon, Duneka to Mabie, Oct. 6, 1911 (Morgan Lib.).

"reverential" "very winning" Mabie to Duneka, Oct. 11, 1911 (Morgan Lib.).

Dreiser was unhappy TD to Duneka, Oct. 17, 1911.

"It looks to me" TD to HLM, [ca. Nov. 1, 1911], 80.

"Dreiser simply" HLM to Ernest Boyd, Aug. 20, 1925. Forgue, 281.

Chapter 4.

"Sunday Nov. 5th" "Autobiographical Attack on Grant Richards," [ca. 1911] (UVa).

their comfortable lifestyle Rembrandt Realty Co. to TD, June 5, 1911; "Autobiographical Attack."

"He's gone around" Quoted in Swanberg, 151. WAS sets this incident earlier, but I assume TD was visiting Lillian Rosenthal.

"I think I know" European Diary, Dec. 31, 1911.

"There is no question" Sylvia Kishima to TD, n.d.

"If only some" *Jennie*, 396.

"great power to make" Jug to TD, April 19, 1926.

"was not helpful" Leigh to TD, Nov. 8, 1911.

"What do you think" Dell told Swanberg, May 19, 1963.

"I have a" TD to HLM, Nov. 11, 1911, 82.

"I hope if you" TD to Richards, Nov. 4, 1911 (UIll)

He was broke "Autobiographical Attack."

"risky" "difficult fellow" Richards, *Author Hunting*, 179.

"other propositions" Quoted in Duneka to TD, Nov. 14, 1911.

"bluff" "A Traveler at Forty," TS, ch. III.

"Strictly between" TD to HLM, Nov. 11, 1911, 82.

"the fact that" Duneka to TD, Nov. 14, 1911.

"that stretch" Quoted in Pizer, *Uncollected Prose*, 188–89.

"love its" "Autobiographical Attack."

"the American" Baldwin Macy, "New York Letter," New York *Evening Post*, Nov. 24, 1911.

"Greek Arcadian" European Diary, Dec. 30, 1911.

"gold-braided boy" Richards to TD, Dec. 8, 1911.

"We made last" Richards to TD, Dec. 6, 1911 (UIll).

"No publisher" *Author Hunting*, 228.

"The prostitute" TD to HLM, Nov. 8, 1912, 105.

"luck with Thelma" Ibid. Dec. 30, 1911.

"Defeated them all" Ibid. Jan. 5, 1912.

"If I were" Ibid., Jan. 5, 1912.

"With one foot" Richards, *Caviare*, 49.

Mme de Villiers Diary, Jan. 17.

news from Duneka Duneka to TD, Jan. 16, 1912.

"If I were you" TD to Richards, Jan. 16, 1912.

"Tush" Richards to TD, Jan. 28, 1912.

"39" "Rentier" Card with diary.

"eighth-rate city" TD to Richards, Feb. 12.

"Christianity" Diary, Feb. 9.

"race of" Quoted in Pizer, *Uncollected Prose*, 197.

"come together" Diary, Feb. 15.

affairs in America TD to Duneka, March 9, Feb. 20, 1912.

"I may go back" TD to Richards, Feb. 25, 1912.

"disloyal . . ." "I've been" Richards to TD, March 19, 1912.

"Such things" Richards to TD, March 14, 1912.

"trembling" "Not that" Duneka to TD, Feb. 19, 1912.

"No more Europe" TD to Richards, Feb. 28, 1912.

"glad . . . that you" Richards to TD, March 14, 1912.

"If the Century" TD to Richards, Feb. 21, 1912.

"Theodor" "dear old" Diary March 12.

"If there is" Ibid., March 13.

Mme Culp Ibid., March 15.

"the great fact" Ibid., March 20.

"genius" Ibid.

"I fancy my" Ibid., March 22.

"that America" Ibid., April 4.

"a true advocate" Ibid.

"find myself" Ibid.

"Teutonic" *"returning"* Ibid., April 17, 20.

"Youth is gone" Ibid., April 20.

"America today" Markham clipping with diary, April 24.

Chapter 5.

"Like a wolf" *Financier,* 495.

"I cannot grant" "I tho't" Jug to TD, March 14, 1912.

"so nice to me" Jug to TD, Dec. 19, 1911.

"—and *slept*" Jug to TD, Jan. 16, 1912.

breaks between volumes TD to Richards, May 26, 1912.

"are civil" Ibid.

"I have preferred" Ibid.

"I am profoundly" TD to Richards, May 4, 1912.

"One day you" Richards to TD, June 7, 1912.

"For heaven" TD to HLM, May [June] 7, 1912, 95.

Dreiser's research See Philip Gerber, "Dreiser's Financier: A Genesis," *Journal of Modern Literature,* March 1971.

"your young couple" Coates to TD, April 19, July 10, July 18, 1912.

"later in the history" *Financier,* 31.

"It was seldom" Quoted in Shelley Fisher Fishkin, *From Fact to Fiction,* 99.

"He was not worse" Quoted in Gerber, "The Financier Himself: Dreiser and C. T. Yerkes," *Proceedings of the Modern Language Association,* Jan. 1973. My account of Dreiser and Yerkes is drawn largely from Gerber's articles. See also Gerber, "The Alabaster Protégé," *American Literature,* May 1971.

"Whatever I do" Quoted in Pizer, *Novels of TD,* 326, n.27.

"Jennie's temperament" Quoted in Pizer, *Uncollected Prose,* 194.

Jay Cooke Gerber, "Dreiser's Debt to *Jay Cooke,*" *Library Chronicle,* Winter 1972.

"How was life" *Financier,* 5.

"A Lesson" *Tom Watson's Magazine,* Jan. 1906. In Pizer, *Uncollected Prose,* 161ff.

"Our Red Slayer" In *Color of a Great City,* 133.

Spilky *Dawn,* 46–47.

"A real man" *Financier,* 44.

"The strong man" Quoted in Gerber, "Financier Himself."

"Morality and ethics" European Diary, March 13, 1912.

"Wealth does not buy" Quoted in "Financier Himself."

"were like wondrous" Quoted in Pizer, *Novels of TD,* 172.

"We who feel" TD to Howells, May 17, 1910 (IndU).

"I want to" Hitchcock to TD, June 13, 1912.

Hitchcock had another worry Hitchcock to TD, July 2 and 3, 1912.

"the rumor" Hitchcock to TD, June 6, 1912.

"It looks to be" TD to HLM, Aug. 28, 1912, 97.

"Let me have" HLM to TD, Aug. 30, 1912, 97.

"No better picture" HLM to TD, Oct. 6, 1912, 99.

"I am glad" TD to HLM, [after Oct. 5, 1912], 101.

"got drunk on" HLM to Wilson, Dec. 10, 1912. Forgue, 28.

"the girl's initiation" HLM to TD, Oct. 6.

"You always see" TD to HLM, [after Oct. 6, 1912], 102.

"Do you really" TD to Richards, July 7, 1912.

"did not care" TD to Richards, July 24, 1912 (UTex).

"My poor friend" Richards to TD, Aug. 8, 1912.

"There's something" Quoted in Richards, *Author Hunting,* 205.

"Quite deliberately" TD to Richards, Dec. 16, 1912.

"After some" *Author Hunting,* 205.

"I would give anything" Quoted in Dudley, 284.

"unexpurgated" "clear" Doty to Richards, Dec. 5, 1912 (UTex).

"a go between" Richards to Doty, Dec. 12, 1912 (UTex).

"What you have" Doty to Richards, Oct. 16, 1912 (UTex).

"take his book" Doty to Richards, n.d. (UTex).

"You are gaining" HLM to TD, Aug. 1, 1913, 122.

"the more important" Quoted in Salzman, 102.

"Dreiser is a real" HLM to Wright, Nov. 12, 1913. Forgue, 34.

"I have had" *Financier* (1927 edition), 499.

"We live in" *Financier* (1912 edition), 250.

took time off TD to Paul Reynolds, Nov. 11, 1912.

"master and no master" *Financier* (1927 edition), 503.

"I didn't know" Lengel, *Esquire*, Sept. 1938.

lived together *American Diaries 1902–1926*, 207–8.

Chapter 6.

"Chicago is my love" Quoted in Pizer, *Uncollected Prose*, 193.

"The poetry" Quoted in Dale Kramer, *Chicago Renaissance*, 148.

"consistent and" Fuller to TD, Nov. 4, 1911.

"Do you like" Garland to TD, Jan. 13, 1913.

"Oh, no" TD to Edgar Lee Masters, March 7, 1940. Elias, *Letters*, III, 874.

"The horse" ELM to TD, July 11, 1914.

"like a botanist" John Cowper Powys, *Autobiography*, 554.

"You, whom I" Quoted in Fanny Butcher, *Many Lives, One Love*, 47.

invited Barry TD to Elizabeth Barry, April 17, 1913.

"half-baked entry" Kramer, 196–97

"He needs me" Dell told Swanberg, May 19, 1963.

"gave herself" *American Diaries*, 207.

"radical" "the real thing" TD to HLM, Feb. 17, 1913, 115.

"going to place" Ibid.

"I have drawn" TD to Leigh, Feb. 19, 24, 1913.

"certain delicate conditions" Hitchcock to Holly, Oct. 17, 1912.

"badly written" Dell to TD, [April] 1913.

"would do more" Lengel to TD, March 31, 1913 (ColU).

"could not possibly" Quoted in Swanberg, 167.

"You know I" "The whole" TD to Lengel, April 14, 1913 (ColU).

lost manuscript TD to HLM, [before July 18] 1913, 122.

fifty-two chapters Markham to TD, May 20, 1913.

travel book See TD to HLM, Aug. 9, 1913, 123.

publisher badgering him Duneka to TD, Dec. 10, 1913.

"relatively concise" Hitchcock to TD, March 6, 1913.

"the forbearance" Sutphen to TD, May 29, 1914.

"The country is" Quoted in Dudley, 292.

"because it is" Tatum, unpublished article on TD.

yearning letters Markham to TD, Feb. 18, 1913.

"I suppose when" Dell told Swanberg, May 19, 1963.

"Miss Kirah Markham" Quoted in Swanberg, 169.

"strictly sober" Dodge to TD, Feb. 12, 1913.

"that I could" Dodge to TD, March 20, 1913.

"If he takes" HLM to TD, March 24, 1913, 120.

"a physical exercise" Dodge to TD, Dec. 28, 1913.

"bureaucratic &" TD to Cosgrave, before July 18, 1913, Elias, *Letters*, I, 154.

"will give me" TD to HLM, 124.

Chapter 7.

"After I am" TD to HLM, Nov. 18, 1913, 127.

"I think true" *Traveler at Forty* TS, LXIV.

"objected" TD to HLM, Nov. 18, 1913, 126.

"invidious comparisons" Richards, *Author Hunting*, 185.

"illicit relations" Quoted in Lars Ahnebrink, "Garland and Dreiser: An Abortive Friendship," *Midwest Journal*, Winter 1955–56.

"Back to Alexander" European Diary, March 26, 1912.

"Occasionally I" Ibid.

"It is so" Ibid.

"I'm cutting" Doty to Johnson, n.d. (NYPL).

"it would be" Doty to Richards, July 21, 1913 (UTex).

"between the devil" Ibid.

"much liked" Ellsworth to Richards, July 3, 1913 (UTex).

"Mr. Dreiser thinks" "meant to tell" Ellsworth to Richards, Aug. 5, 1913 (UTex).

"The damn book" Doty to Richards, July 21, 1913 (UTex).

"dragging in tempo" "an effect" HLM to TD, Nov. 16, 1913, 125.

"the last half" TD to HLM, Nov. 18, 1912, 126.

"For heaven" [after Nov. 16, 1913], 127.

"He is an agnostic" HLM to TD, Nov. 16, 1912, 125.

"For myself" *Traveler*, 4.

"I acknowledge" Ibid., 6.

"made people" Quoted in Salzman, 163.

"In due time" *Traveler*, 207.

"We can have" Quoted in Salzman, 163.

"Look, this" Quoted in Swanberg, 192.

"one last look" Quoted in Salzman, 192.

"in marriage" *Traveler*, 498.

"intellectual" "will guarantee" Ibid., 500.

"An orphan" Chicago *Examiner*, Jan. 13, 1913.

"I am an" Philadelphia *Press*, April 26, 1913.

"went no further" Quoted in Matthew J. Bruccoli, *The Fortunes of Mitchell Kennerley*, 74.

"Be careful" Quoted in William Manchester, *H. L. Mencken: Disturber of the Peace*, 92.

"I am in rotten" HLM to TD, Jan. 11, 1914, 130.

"What is" TD to HLM, Jan. 14, 1914, 130.

"Do you suppose" TD to HLM, Jan. 8, 1914, 129.

"For several years" Quoted in Phillip Gerber, "The Alabaster Protégé."

"I believe" Quoted in Swanberg, 168.

"Certainly you'll" HLM to TD, Jan. 11, 1914, 130.

Chapter 8.

"My Dear Mencken" TD to HLM, March 6, 1914, 132.

"An eternal pox" HLM to TD, March 18, 1914, 134.

"young, smug" *Titan*, 206.

"tall, melancholy" Ibid., 226.

"Fighting Yerkes" "Imagine them" Quoted in Gerber, "Financier Himself."

"We do not" Ibid.

"the realism is" TD to HLM, March 6, 1914, 132.

"hard, cold" TD to Alfred A. Knopf, March 13, 1914.

"If this were" TD to HLM, March 6, 1914, 132.

"The Harpers" HLM to TD, March 6, 1914, 132.

"He is a" Tatum to TD, March 11, 1914.

"Oh, Dodo" Ibid.

"a far more" Ibid.

"commercial possibility" TD to Knopf, March 13, 1914.

"the leading" Quoted in Riggio, 137, fn.1.

"abnormal &" TD to HLM, March 25, 1914.

staggering Ben Hecht, *A Child of the Century*, 205.

"A big city" Quoted in Swanberg, 172.

"a terrible thing" Ibid.

"I've got it" Ibid.

"a new philosophic" TD to HLM, March 16, 1914, 133.

"proud" Quoted in Riggio, 137, fn.2.

"Too much truth" Tatum to TD, March 18, 1914.

"immigrant vulgarian" Quoted in Kramer, *Chicago Renaissance* 140.

"If you will" TD to HLM, March 31, 1914, 138–39.

Jones asked Dreiser TD, "The Titan in England," unpublished TS.

written to Masters TD to ELM, June 11, 1914.

"There is not" HLM to TD, March 23, 1914, 135.

"The book of" TD to Knopf, March 3, 1914.

"The story is" Quoted in Salzman, 189.

"a satyr" "no more" Ibid., 188, 189, 176.

"The book tells" Ibid., 202.

overworked words solecisms Ibid., 187, 177.

"a balance must" Ibid., 551.

Chapter 9.

"Only youth and enthusiasm" Unpublished MS, "Greenwich Village."
"Don't give" TD to HLM, April 5, 1914, 140.
He called it *American Diaries*, 448.
"an absolutely" New York *Sun*, Sept. 28, 1912.
"to discard" Quoted in Robert H. Elias, *Theodore Dreiser: Apostle of Nature*, 175.
"a great" HLM to TD, March 27, 1914, 138.
"the people" Quoted in Salzman, 179.
"Bouncing around" TD to Knopf, April 24, 1914.
"All authors" TD to Fort, May 12, 1914. Elias, *Letters*, I, 167.
"the Spoon River" ELM to TD, June 11, July 11, 1914.
"blinding poignancy" TD to Hecht, May 20, 1914.
"try to edit" TD to HLM, June 22, 1914, 144.
"I have many" TD to HLM, June 22, 1914, 144.
One of Dreiser's schemes TD, "Myself and the Movies," *Esquire*, July 1943.
Broadway waters Welch to TD, April 8, 1914.
"The winter of" Orrick Johns, *Time of Our Lives*, 217.
TD's studio Estelle Kubitz told Swanberg, Dec. 12, 1962; Ralph Fabri to Swanberg, Dec. 23, 1962.
one upright piano TD to Ettinge, April 1921.
Jug would stand Markham told Swanberg, Dec. 12, 1962. TD used this in the "Aglaia" episode in his serial *This Madness*.
Louis Untermeyer LU told Swanberg, Nov. 11, 1962.
"Genius?" "Greenwich Village."
"Underneath my" TD to HLM, July 29, 1914, 147.
"I am not turning" Ibid.
"blaze out" HLM to TD, Aug. 11, 1914, 149.
"heroin, Pilsner" Ibid.
"We simply" HLM to TD, Aug. 17, 1914, 151.
"In Paris" Quoted in Manchester, *H. L. Mencken*, 111.

"bombarded daily" HLM to Sedgwick, Oct. 10, 1914, in Forgue, 52.
"The Lost Phoebe" Welch to TD, Aug. 21, 1914.
"fine stuff" HLM to TD, Aug. 29, 1914, 153.
"from one or two" TD to HLM, Aug. 22, 1914, 152.
"the place of" HLM to TD, Nov. 8, 1914, 164.
"Nathan is so full" Ibid., Oct. 13, 1914, 160.
Ray Long TD to HLM, Oct. 13, 1914, 160; Welch to TD, Sept. 1, 1914.
"We are in" HLM to TD, Oct. 17, 1914, 163.
"I may talk" TD to Richards, Feb. 12, 1912.
"under-described" HLM to TD, Dec. 9, 1914, 168.
"friendly row" HLM to TD, Sept. 5, 1925, 536.
"But that's what" HLM told Elias, Nov. 2, 1944. HLM in New York *World-Telegram & Sun*, March 25, 1946.
Dell's cuts Floyd Dell, *Homecoming*, 269. Dell told Swanberg, May 19, 1963.
"the kind of woman" TD to John Golden, June 17, 1938. Elias, *Letters*, III, 796.
separation contract Undated copy at UP.
"the madame" Markham to TD, Feb. 16, 1915.
"emotional steamroller" Swanberg, 181–82.
"that it has shown" HLM to TD, April 6, 1915, 193.
"Under you and Nathan" TD to HLM, April 20, 1915, 194.
"Represents a compromise" HLM to TD, April 22, 1915, 196.
"I sometimes think" TD to HLM, April 26, 1915, 198.
"For far less" HLM to TD, April 29, 1915.
"I have no hope" Quoted in Dudley, 334.
"epileptic enthusiasms" Mordell to TD, Dec. 2, 1914.
through Elias Rosenthal Rosenthal to TD, Sept. 5, 1914.
"Important: Molineux" Quoted in Lehan, *Theodore Dreiser*, 144.
"keen passion" "The Rake," unpublished MS.

Chapter 10.

"Don't despair" TD to HLM, March 25, 1914, 137.
"parlor socialists" Undated clipping,

"The First Anthology Night of the Season."
"His teeth stuck" Edgar Lee Masters, *After Spoon River*, 367.

"How would you" "A Hoosier Holiday" Diary.

"Sophocles and" Ibid., Aug. 6, 1915.

"O ye deathward" Dell, *Homecoming*, 269.

"40 miles" *AHH* Diary, Aug. 11.

"the blue hills" Ibid., Aug. 12.

"somewhere down" *A Hoosier Holiday*, 304.

"Life is not" *AHH* Diary, Aug. 23.

"a blazing hot" *Ibid.*

"New life" Ibid., Aug. 26.

"smug and" Ibid., Aug. 17.

"America is so" Ibid., Aug. 14.

"The 'Genius' " is as Quoted in Salzman, 242–43.

"the greatest" Ibid., 212.

"American prose-epic" Ibid., 226.

"subterranean current" Ibid., 234–35.

"What Mr. Dreiser" Ibid., 234.

"a procession" "literary Caliban" "an abnormal" "contemptible cur" "drummer" Ibid., 249, 252, 226, 243, 224.

"the book" "We hope" Ibid., 220, 226.

"I have not" Ibid., 243.

"In the case of" *Nation*, Dec. 2, 1915. Reprinted in Kazin and Shapiro, *Stature of TD*, 70–80.

"a masterly" HLM to TD, Dec. 8, 1915, 211.

"rot" "animal" Quoted in Elias, *Letters*, I, 204, fn.26.

"These moonbeam" TD to Hersey, Dec. 19, 1915. Ibid., 205.

"Each of us" Quoted in Swanberg, 176.

"out of mystic" Quoted in Dudley, 382.

"The market price" HLM to TD, Jan. 21, 1916, 216.

"horrible things" TD to HLM, Feb. 4, 1916, 217.

Mencken eventually HLM to TD, Feb. 18, 1916, 222.

Lo, the earth *Moods: Cadenced and Declaimed*, 225.

travel journal *American Diaries 1902–1926*, 117ff.

"What brooding" Ibid., 120.

"thin, anemic" Ibid., 128.

"Very lonely" Ibid., 132.

"SWEETHEART" Ibid., 133.

"I despise" "See how I" Ibid., 133, 134.

"In a fine" Ibid., 143.

"Wishes for" Ibid., 144.

"My spiritual" Ibid.

"apparently not" TD to HLM, Feb. 14, 1916, 221.

"convention" Ibid., March 11, 1916, 225.

Chapter 11.

"The exact" TD to HLM, July 29, 1916, 247.

"still a moral" Quoted in Carl Bode, *H. L. Mencken*, 100.

"in their efforts" N.Y. Society for the Suppression of Vice, *45th Annual Report 1918*, 14 (NYPL).

"quite Teutonic" Quoted in Riggio, 236, fn. 1.

"typically and" HLM to TD, June 6, 1916, 235.

"He shows" Riggio, 780.

"one of the" TD to HLM, [before June 19, 1916], 236.

"If it ever" Ibid., TD to HLM, June 24, 1916, 239.

"relatives and" "A Hoosier Holiday" MS, chs. LII, XLI.

"The book is" HLM to TD, June 26, 1916, 240.

"very unwise" Ibid., June 28, 1916, 241.

"lewd, obscene" TD to HLM, July 7, 1916, 242.

"The essential" Quoted in Dudley, 358.

"In passing" TD to HLM, July 27, 1916, 244.

"Information filed" Copy in box 89, UP.

"She stood" "his sex" "great" "naked model" *"Genius,"* 20, 44, 51, 55.

"After all" HLM to TD, July 28, 1916, 245.

go to jail TD to HLM, July 29, 1916, 246.

to telephone him HLM to TD, Aug. 3, 1916, 248.

"A fight" TD to HLM, Aug. 4, 1916, 249–50.

"A man accused" HLM to TD, Aug. 4, 1916, 251.

"compromise on" Ibid., Aug. 5, 1916, 251.

three passages TD to HLM, Aug. 10, 1916, 254.

"a few thousand" HLM to TD, Aug. 5, 1916, 252.

"Money will be" TD to HLM, Aug. 8, 1916, 252.

"I may break" HLM to TD, Aug. 5, 252; TD to HLM, Aug. 8, 1916, 252.

"down" TD to HLM, Aug. 10, 1916, 254.

"intellectual harem" Markham to TD, March 29, 1916.

"If I could" TD to Markham, May 10, 1916.

"You want me" *Newspaper Days*, holograph MS, ch. XXV.

Estelle Kubitz Autobiographical MS (NYPL).

"A public protest" HLM to Hersey, Aug. 9, 1916. Quoted in Elias, *Theodore Dreiser*, 199.

"A band of" Hersey's notes, box 89.

"lewd, licentious" Quoted in Elias, *Letters*, I, 226, fn.26.

"Some of us" Riggio, 802–3.

"to stand" TD to HLM, Aug. 8, 1916, 252.

He, Jones TD to Ficke, Sept. 21, 1916.

"tinpot revolutionaries" HLM to TD, Sept. 5, 1916, 264.

"a fearful ass" HLM to Boyd, Sept. 6, 1916. Quoted in Forgue, 90.

"Despite our" HLM to TD, Oct. 6, 1916, 266.

"dictatorial tone" TD to HLM, Oct. 9, 1916, 268.

"professional" HLM to TD, Oct. 10, 1916, 268–69.

"a shrewd" Garland to Schuler, Oct. 2, 1916. Quoted in Ahnebrink.

"I think any" Quoted in Dudley, 366.

"a general offensive" HLM to TD, Nov. 14, 1916, 274.

"carefully designed" Nov. 24, 1916, 275.

"I have no" Quoted in Dudley, 358.

"the most overrated" Benét to HLM, Nov. 22, 1916.

"beyond that" Frost to HLM, Dec. 16, 1916.

"Nothing would" Lowell to HLM, Sept. 18, 1916.

"poor old" Quoted in Louis Oldani, "Two Unpublished Pound Letters: Pound's Aid to Dreiser," *Library Chronicle*, Spring 1977.

"Authors taken" Sumner to Harvey, Sept. 19, 1916.

"through the story" Sumner to Keating, Nov. 22, 1916.

"a mighty tough" TD to HLM, Nov. 4, 1916, 271.

"at your" Jones to TD, Oct. 26, 1916.

"to let his" Quoted in Dudley, 353–54.

In a letter to Mencken JJJ to HLM, Oct. 31, 1916 (NYPL).

"by Monday" "arrested" TD to HLM, Dec. 13, 1916, 280.

owed his publisher Royalty statement, Oct. 16, 1916.

"One German" *A Hoosier Holiday*, 180.

"the high tide" Quoted in Salzman, 279.

"worse than" Ibid., 285.

"Never—" Ibid., 282.

"an ill-bred" Ibid., 296.

"In symphonies" *AHH*, 18.

"men were free" Ibid., 513. In MS the book concludes: "Of dreams and the memory of them is life compounded. But now it is no more."

Chapter 12.

"We are to have" *Hey, Rub-a-Dub-Dub!*, 281.

"You fill me" HLM to TD, Dec. 20, 1916, 285.

"the greatest" Quoted in Vrest Orton, 42.

"distinctly wrong" TD to HLM, Nov. 4, 1916, 273.

"That Dreiser" Quoted in Salzman, 352.

Leo Frank Ibid., 351. In his diary for *A Hoosier Holiday*, Aug. 26, 1915, TD mentions discussing the case with his companions.

Ben Hecht, See *A Child of the Century*, 152.

sterilized Paul Gormley to Vera Dreiser, Dec. 12, 1965.

"Life and the" Quoted in Elias, *Theodore Dreiser*, 181.

"the sexual" *Hey, Rub*, 138.

"a fire" "an all but" Ibid., 141.

"only the fit" Quoted in Pizer, *Uncollected Prose*, 227.

"the one thing" TD to HLM, Dec. 13, 1916, 280.

"not only because" HLM to TD, [Dec. 16, 1916], 281.

"weak pervert" TD to HLM, Dec. 18, 1916, 283.

"I wonder" Ibid., 284.

"As for the" HLM to TD, Dec. 20, 1916, 285.

"cheap pornography" HLM to Huebsch, March 16, 1918. In Bode, *New Mencken Letters*, 83.

"great" TD to HLM, Dec. 21, 1916, 286.

"Take the advice" HLM to TD, [Dec. 20, 1916], 285.

"In all matters" Quoted in Sara Mayfield, *The Constant Circle*, 167.

"You are the" HLM to TD, Dec. 23, 1916, 290.

"In the face" TD to HLM, Dec. 25, 1916, 291.

"has strayed into" *Hey, Rub*, 275.

"the worst" Ibid., 284.

"Life is to be" Ibid.

Chapter 13.

"I feel" *American Diaries*, 176.

"Dreiser is" HLM to Boyd, [1918] (NYPL).

Guido Bruno See Riggio, 293, fn.1.

"Prussianism" Quoted in Mark Sullivan, *Over Here*, 468.

"I am for" Quoted in Max Eastman, *Love and Revolution*, 35.

volunteer as midwives HLM to TD, [April 1917], 298.

Prefaces turned down Yewdale to TD, June 28, 1917.

"the touching" TD to HLM, May 2, 1917, 299.

"to artistic" Auerbach brief, *TD v. John Lane Company*, 45.

"deprave or corrupt" Ibid., 39.

"have been continuously" Card at UP. Quoted in Walker Gilmer, *Horace Liveright*, 14.

Jones's board TD to HLM, Oct. 25, 1917, 310; Jones to TD, Nov. 19, 1917.

$200 in February Jones to TD, Feb. 16, 1917.

"of the friendliest" TD to HLM, May 24, 1917, 302.

"Little Bill" *Am. Diaries*, 149.

"Tension of" Ibid.

"live in somebody" Kubitz to Marion Bloom, [Sept. 12] (NYPL).

"Why in hell" HLM to Kubitz, April 17, 1917 (NYPL).

"I advocate" *Am. Diaries*, 190.

"I am fond" Ibid., 156.

"I would like" Quoted, ibid., 193.

"I seem to have" in Campbell to TD, Feb. 26, 1917.

"we fall to" *Am. Diaries*, 158.

"thirsting for" Ibid., 203.

"You talk" Ibid., 210.

"her driving" Ibid., 196.

"I must give up" Ibid., 176.

"oh, so down" Quoted in Swanberg, 211.

"What's the good" *Am. Diaries*, 185.

"sad, beautiful" Ibid., 214.

"I have so" Ibid., 176.

"Money, success" Ibid., 200.

Dreiser placed work Hutchins Hapgood, *A Victorian in the Modern World*, 266.

"between rounds" *Am. Diaries*, 193.

"the story" Ibid., 232.

"I suppose" TD to Baker, Feb. 15, 1917.

"if I've thought" TD to Baker, July 23, 1917.

"not so much" TD to Frank, July 1, 1917.

"If you fall" HLM to Kubitz, July 20, 1917 (NYPL).

"I've worked and" Unpublished MS, July 10, 1917 (NYPL).

Chapter 14.

"As for Dreiser" HLM to Boyd, [1918]. In Forgue, 113.

"a mass of" *American Diaries*, 181.

"but there" See Riggio, 786.

"slapstick" "represent really" TD to Huebsch, March 10, 1918. Elias, *Letters*, I, 250–51.

"Mr. Mencken" Quoted in Manchester, *H. L. Mencken*, 122.

"Why ask" Ibid., 127.

"Am rather" *Am. Diaries*, 108.

"The Lost Phoebe" See Don Graham, "Pyschological Veracity in 'The Lost Phoebe': Dreiser's Revisions," *Studies in American Fiction*, Spring 1978.

Irwin Granich Karsner to TD, Jan. 15, Jan. 16, 1918.

Lower East Side Mike Gold, *Mike Gold Reader*, 161–62.

"It is the best" Quoted in Dudley, 395.

"I don't believe" Quoted in George Jean Nathan, *Intimate Notebooks of George Jean Nathan*, 52.

"That apartment" *Am. Diaries*, 233.

"ridiculously small" Horace Liveright to TD, Sept. 7, 1917.

"a mighty" Liveright to TD, June 4, 1918.

a proofreader Liveright to TD, June 24, 1918.

"sold all" Liveright to TD, Aug. 7, 1918.

"you have" Liveright to TD, June 24, 1918.

Swanberg added Swanberg, 226.

"Once again" Doty to TD, Sept. 6, 1918.

"too complicated" Roberts to TD, [1918].

"comes clearly" Quoted in Swanberg, 220–21.

"one of" "Perhaps . . ." "We like" Quoted in Swanberg, 226.

"trusts" "America" Unpublished MS, "Rural America in Wartime."

"as a member" Harvey to TD, Aug. 24, 1917.

"the menace" Harvey to TD, Apr. 19, 1919.

"Good" *Am. Diaries*, 202.

"The United" Karsner, "Theodore Dreiser," *New York Call*, March 2, 1918.

"In what other lands" Quoted in Richard Lehan, *Theodore Dreiser*, 133.

"Marx, the" *Hey, Rub*, 95.

"They are" *Am. Diaries*, 184.

"The present" Ibid.

"Germans singing" Ibid., 183.

"I hope" Ibid., 196.

"We walked" Quoted in Kazin and Shapiro, *Stature of TD*, 19–20.

"full of some" HLM to Boyd, [1917] (NYPL).

"idiotic petulance" HLM to Boyd, [Fall 1917], Forgue, 111.

"He is doing" Ibid., April 20, 1918. Forgue, 120.

"He still" HLM to George Sterling, March 10, 1918. In Bode, *New Mencken Letters*, 85.

"He has gone" HLM to Louis Untermeyer, Aug. 21, 1918. Forgue, 127.

"All I propose" HLM to B. W. Huebsch, Aug. 16, 1918. Bode, 84–85.

"It goes" HLM to Kubitz, March 14, 1918 (NYPL).

"I am overly" TD to Huebsch, March 10, 1918. Elias, *Letters*, I, 250.

"a serious" HLM to TD, June 20, 1918, 312.

"awful stuff" HLM to Boyd, May 27, 1918 (NYPL).

"I still avoid" Ibid., June 29, 1918 (NYPL).

"door-mat" "one roll" HLM to Kubitz, Jan. 23, 1918 (NYPL).

"old Warsaw" "the Warsaw" "that ancient" HLM to Kublitz, ibid., and Oct. 19, 1918 (NYPL).

"awful stuff" "tried" HLM to Boyd, Sept. 4, 1918 (NYPL).

"succumbed to" HLM to TD, Nov. 25 [1918], 318.

"What angel" HLM to [TD], Dec. 25, 1918, 320.

On opening night *Am. Diaries*, 228.

The Weavers Ibid., 254.

Liveright thought $500 Liveright to TD, Dec. 10, 1918, Feb. 11, 1919.

"it might get" cost him his job Kline to TD, [April 9, 1919].

"any delays" Jones to TD, Sept. 20, 1918.

"out of the" Liveright to TD, Nov. 26, 1918; Jones to Liveright, Nov. 25, 1918.

He could point See Jones to TD, Feb. 16, 1917.

Jones countered Ibid., Sept. 20, 1918.

Liveright's lawyer Liveright to TD, Nov. 17, 1918.

"Why in hell" HLM to TD, Feb. 1, 1919, 335.

"I have the" "Personally" TD to HLM, Feb. 3, 1919, 335–36.

Chapter 15.

"[Freud] reminded" TD, "Remarks," *Psychoanalytic Review*, July 1931. In Pizer, *Uncollected Prose*, 263.

"Cries and" *American Diaries*, 209.

Society for See TD to Gaylord Yost, July 5, 1918.

Hersey Hersey to TD, March 15, 1919.

Mencken suggested name HLM to TD, March 29, 1919, 341.

Yewdale protested Yewdale to TD, March 29, 1919.

Mencken's Declaration HLM to TD, May 7, 1919, 340.

fine writing Dudley, 384–85.

Orpet case Gillette Richesen See Ellen Moers, *Two Dreisers*, 190–99.

"All truth" "The Right to Kill," in Pizer, 226.

Aleister Crowley Burton Rascoe, "Burn This," New York *Daily News* [n.d.].

"that strange" "Self" "Dawn," holograph MS (IndU) *Dawn*, 23.

"At that time" "Remarks," Pizer, 263.

Brill assured him See Moers, 265.

"If you do" *Am. Diaries*, 105.

"compelling the body" In Pizer, 221.

"ever at work" Ibid., 223.

"Just below" TD to A. A. Brill, Dec. 20, 1918.

asked Mencken TD to HLM, April 9, 1919, 344.

"on account of" Loeb to TD, June 3, 1919.

"the appeal of" TD to Brill, Jan. 20, 1919.

"Let me hear" HLM to TD, May 14, 1919, 350.

"I think all" HLM to Kubitz, May 20, 1919 (NYPL).

"I truly don't" Smith to TD, June 22, 1919.

"some important" John Cowper Powys, *Autobiography*, 554.

"monied class" Huntington *Press*, June 18, 1919.

"An old ache" "Life" *Am. Diaries*, 261.

"dreadful dreams" Ibid.

"an errant mind" Quoted in Pizer, *Novels of TD*, 206.

"Dreiser, I hear" HLM to Boyd, July 19, 1919. In Forgue, 152.

"practically giving" TD to HLM, Aug. 13, 1919, 353.

"state definitely" TD to Jones, Aug. 8, 1919.

"without making" Jones to TD, Sept. 9, 1919.

"pathological drama" Quoted in Salzman, 366.

"blown religion" "were being" Berenice Sidelsky, "Labor Union of Authors?" Brooklyn *Eagle*, Nov. 11, 1919.

"We live, not" HLM to Untermeyer, Nov. 25, 1919. Forgue, 117.

"to stay away" "She has" *Am. Diaries*, 217.

"Feel very" Ibid., 216.

"And love" "To a Wood Dove," *Moods: Cadenced and Declaimed*, 41.

"in the gutter" "Jealousy" *Am. Diaries*, 234.

"Amazing feeling" Ibid., 249.

"phase of her" Ibid., 255.

"I feel sorry" Ibid., 256.

"worried about" "I was possessed" "mental" Ibid., 277–78.

"The close" Freud, *Interpretation of Dreams*, 429.

"one with" *Am. Diaries*, 277.

"This day" Ibid., 278.

Chapter 16.

"We whisper" *American Diaries*, 284.

"lymphatic sensuality" "strident" "age" "only good" "youth" Ibid., 278.

"but my interest" Ibid., 281.

"a new chapter" Ibid., 282.

Helen's life Ibid., 318–19, 339, 353; Helen Dreiser, *My Life with Dreiser*, 315–26.

"We were like" Helen, *Life*, 31.

"a fear of" Ibid., 28.

"Her beauty" *Am. Diaries*, 291.

"she is as insane" Ibid., 284.

"The constant" Ibid., 285.

"The place is" TD to HLM, 369.

"pure hoakum" *Am. Diaries*, 308.

"The Long, Long Trail" Ibid., 294, n.24.

"Life seems" Ibid., 299.

"an adequate" TD to Lewin, [after May 24, 1920].

"It would be" HLM to Kubitz, Jan. 1, 1920 (NYPL).

"More idling" *Am. Diaries*, 294.

"the most infernally" Ibid., 313.

"Babes Cute" Ibid., 295.

"the most coaxing" Ibid., 291.

"From 10 to" Ibid., 304.

"We stage" Ibid., 315.

"Teddie caught" Helen, *Life*, 40.

" 'I'll never' " "The Promise" Quoted in Helen to Ralph Fabri, May 11, 1939.

"financial relations" Liveright to TD, Sept. 10, Oct. 4, 1920.

Anna Tatum suit *Am. Diaries*, 314.

"Society & what" Ibid., 290.

Frank Richardson Ibid., 321. Frank to Helen, n.d.

"When I watch" TD to Johnson, July 29, 1920.

"She is too" *Am. Diaries*, 312.

"wild desperation" Ibid., 313.

"confused and" Ibid.

"Greatly wrought" Ibid., 326.

"Helen gets" "This sex" Ibid., 327

"youth & beauty" Ibid.

"I am depressed" Ibid., 309.

"terrible hard" Ibid., 310.

"new version" Ibid.

"but frankly" Liveright to TD, June 28, 1920.

"The Bulwark" TD to HLM, Aug. 13, 1920, 382.

"In the morning" *Am. Diaries*, 336–37.

"supplied the" Helen, *Life*, 37.

"sensitive" TD to Edward Smith, Dec. 12, 1930. Elias, *Letters*, I, 308.

"envying the rich" *Newspaper Days*, 376.

"The average" Quoted in Shelley Fisher Fishkin, *From Fact to Fiction*, 105.

"that across" *Sister Carrie*, 115–16.

"I planned" MS, "American Tragedies."

"the young" "a more attractive" TD, "I Find the Real American Tragedy," *Mystery Magazine*, Feb.–June, 1935. Reprinted in *Resources for American Literary Studies*, Spring 1972.

wrote to Ward Ward to TD, Sept. 7, 1920, which refers to TD to Ward, Aug. 13, 1920.

"Dusk of a summer" Holograph MS, *An American Tragedy*.

Gillette testified See New York *World*, Nov. 29, 1906. For a full account of Gillette's life see Craig Brandon, *Murder in the Adirondacks*, to which I am deeply indebted.

Chapter 17.

"I am and have" TD to HLM, Sept. 20, 1920.

"a great hit" *American Diaries*, 338.

wrote Douglas TD to Douglas, Oct. 7, 1920.

He told Sterling TD to Sterling, Oct. 2, Oct. 8, 1920.

"the injustice" "the rank" *Am. Diaries,* 337.

YOUR TELEGRAM Ibid., 344.

"It is so" Helen to TD, [Oct. 19, 1920], 345.

"Get drunk" *Am. Diaries,* 344–45.

"Nightly I was" TD to HLM, Oct. 25, 1920, 403.

"my cool grey" Sterling to Helen, Sept. 22, 1922.

"in transports" *Am. Diaries,* 347.

"the power of" "he would" Quoted in Dudley, 406.

"I accept wholly" TD to Newbegin, June 4, 1921. Elias, *Letters,* I, 369.

"Religion is a" "My next" TD to Smith, Jan. 10, 1921. Ibid., 337–38.

"deep psychic wound" Holograph MS *of An American Tragedy.* Reprinted in *Esquire,* Oct. 1958.

"by some psychic" Ibid.

"via love or" Quoted in Lehan, *Theodore Dreiser,* 157.

"mines" Ibid., 156.

Asa Conklin See *Dawn,* 469.

"revising" it *Am. Diaries,* 351, 381.

"Everyone is waiting" Liveright to TD, June 28, 1920.

"another source" "our leading" Ibid., July 8, 1920.

"I could have done" HLM to TD, Dec. 11, 1920, 416.

"quietly and" TD to HLM, Aug. 27, 1920, 384.

"We simply must" Liveright to TD, Nov. 22, 1920.

"The truth is" TD to Liveright, Dec. 3, 1920. Elias, *Letters,* 310.

"catch novel" TD to Llewelyn Powys, July 9, 1921, ibid., 372.

"PLEASE ASK LENGEL" Liveright to TD (telegram), Dec. 21, 1920.

"Where you are" TD to Liveright, Dec. 21, 1920.

"after all you" Liveright to TD, Jan. 6, 1921.

"splendid work" "The present" "one with some" Briggs to TD, Jan. 4, 1921.

"Advance" "you are bound" HLM to TD, Sept. 18, 1920, 393.

"I can safely" TD to Smith, Dec. 26, 1920. Elias, *Letters,* 326.

"My Confidence" Liveright to TD, Sept. 18, 1920.

Mea Culpa Am. Diaries, 369, n. 137. The surviving MS shows the narrator to be a middle-aged man reminiscing about his life. His father owned a glove factory and he will come into $250,000 at the age of fifty-five (a strange age to come into a legacy). Dreiser has trouble establishing the hero's position on the social scale; for example, the character speaks both of emulating the wealthier youths in town and impressing the girls in his father's factory with his money and fine clothes. He seems to have no occupation, explaining that his love of beauty and pleasure have been a "deterrent to any material advance on my part." There are hints of rivalry with his brother and great admiration for another youth, suggesting that *Mea Culpa* was another try at the novel about a murderer.

asked Louise Campbell TD to Campbell, Feb. 16, 1921. Elias, *Letters,* 351.

"As I understand" Liveright to TD, Oct. 8, 1922.

"It's almost humiliating" Liveright to TD, June 15, 1921.

"are muddle-brained" TD to Le Berthon, Jan. 8, 1921. Elias, *Letters,* 387.

demanding a guarantee Cook to TD (telegram), Oct. 12, 1921.

subsequent letter Smith to TD, Dec. 8, 1921.

"with only three" Kenton to TD, Dec. 30, 1921.

"Am wishing for" *Am. Diaries,* 388.

"his mother's temperament" Helen Dreiser, *My Life With Dreiser,* 49.

"Whispering" *Am. Diaries,* 378.

"How divine" Llewelyn Powys to TD, n.d.

"Get a little" *Am. Diaries,* 369.

"Hold me" Ibid., 387.

Mencken dispatched HLM to TD, March 16, 1922, 464–65.

"The Dodd people" TD to HLM, March 22, 1922, 466.

Mencken assured him HLM to TD, April 22, 1922, 468.

"more daring" TD to Hume, April 18, 1922. Elias, *Letters,* II, 396.

"on the sex side" Hume to TD, May 9, 1922.

subsequent letter Hume to TD, June 7, 1922.

"succeeded in putting" Quoted in Hume to TD, May 23, 1922.

Dodd wanted Hume to TD, June 7, 1922.

Dreiser forwarded TD to HLM, May 22, 1922, 473.

"It will be" HLM to Kubitz, May 26, 1922 (NYPL).

Mencken persuaded Sumner HLM to TD, June 1, 1922, 473.

Dreiser was willing TD to HLM, June 8, 1922, 474–75.

"was done for" TD to HLM, June 24, 1922.

"tickled to death" Liveright to TD, July 22, 1922.

"ought to be read" Quoted in Salzman, 409.

"that mad scramble" Ibid., 421.

"Before we realized" Helen, *Life*, 63.

"How long" HLM to TD, Nov. 15, 1921, 453.

"So you would" TD to HLM, Nov. 23, 1921, 453.

scathing letter Kubitz to TD, Dec. 12, 1921.

"In the matter" TD to Lengel, Elias, *Letters*, I, 341.

Ditrichstein *Am. Diaries*, 386, 388, TD to Margaret Johnson, May 16, 1922.

"Bad news from" *Am. Diaries*, 394.

"The days go by" Ibid., 384.

"I want to be" Quoted in Dudley, 442.

"rub Sumner" See Liveright to TD, Sept. 1, 1922.

"I longed" Helen, *Life*, 63–64.

Chapter 18.

"And what did you" New York *World*, Nov. 29, 1906.

"immense, congested" TD to Johnson, Jan. 8, 1923.

"acted very decently" HLM to TD, Oct. 28, 1922, 479.

"He must not" Dodd to Hume, Dec. 13, 1922.

intemperate letter See Hume to TD, Dec. 20, 1922.

contract with Liveright "Memorandum of Agreement," Jan. 19, 1923.

Liveright had a knack See Gilmer, *Liveright*, for an account of the publisher's career.

"Helen packing" "Helen begins" "What will" *American Diaries*, 396.

"dad's sweetheart" Quoted in Gilmer, 79.

"to advance" Quoted in Elias, *Letters*, II, 408.

Dreiser wrote Beach TD to Beach, May 5, 1923. Ibid.

"as much time" Quoted in Elias, 410.

"received no further" "give her" TD to Burgess, [between May 19 and June 2, 1923], ibid., 415, 416.

"a critic in" HLM to TD, May 31, 1923, 493.

"In 'The Bulwark' " HLM to TD, March 20, 1923, 488.

"as an institution" Liveright to TD, Aug. 2, 1923.

"a lousy 3,000" Ibid., Aug. 7, 1923.

"In spite of your" Ibid., March 27, 1923.

"real results" "I am going" Ibid., Aug. 2, 1923.

"more varied" TD, *Color of a Great City*, v.

"our dream" Helen, *Life*, 66.

"Thousand and One Nights" Quoted in Moers, *Two Dreisers*, 268. Moers explores the influence of Brill and the *Arabian Nights* at some length.

reread in 1918 *Am. Diaries*, 153, 172, 198, 199.

"phantastic dreamers" Quoted in Moers, 269.

"quite old" "very positive" *Am. Diaries*, 396–97.

"an isolated spot" Helen, *Life*, 84.

Dreiser records *Am. Diaries*, 401.

"Maybe Teddie will" Helen, *Life*, 85.

"beautiful, simple" *Am. Diaries,*, 402.

George Ward's widow See Craig Brandon, *Murder in the Adirondacks*, 341.

"oily" letter TD to Sally Kusell, July 29, 1923.

"Confidentially, I am" HLM to TD, July 28, 1923, 407.

"You may attack" HLM to TD, Aug. 2, 1923, 498.

"my little Yankee" TD to Kusell, July 29, Aug. 4, 1923.

"The trouble with" TD to Kusell, Aug. 4, 1923.

"and that in the face" TD to Kusell, Aug. 13, 1923.

"Ordinarily, I" Helen, *Life*, 88.

"I walked the streets" Ibid., 89.

"Six naked women" *Am. Diaries*, 402.

"glad to be back" Ibid., 406.

"Realism is not" Rose C. Feld, "Mr. Dreiser Passes Judgment on American Literature," *Book Review*, Dec. 23, 1923.

"is thinking more" TD to HLM, May 12, 1924, 516. The writer referred to was Thomas Craven, author of *Paint*.

"Like a kite" TD to Karsner, Feb. 12, 1923.

"are interested in but" TD to Charles Boni Jr., in New York *Globe*, Feb. 14, 1921.

vaguely located in the 1920s See Pizer, *Novels of TD*, 217.

"A heavy taboo" Robert S. and Helen Merrell Lynd, *Middletown*, 112.

Chapter 19.

"But by this time" New York *World*, Nov. 18, 1906.

"settle in a" TD to Helen, Feb. 23, 1924.

"troublesome" waves TD to Helen, March 24.

"I know you think" TD to Helen, April 21.

"If this seeing people" TD to Helen, April 23.

"They think it is" TD to Helen, March 24.

"I boast not" TD to Helen, March 26.

He was lucky TD to Helen, April 4.

working hard TD to Helen, April 6.

"fixed & struggling" TD to Helen, June 26.

"unholy task" "I might as well" Ibid.

"When the book" TD to Helen, June 18.

"surer now than I" Ibid.

"the top of the range" TD to Helen, May 3.

"It is too intricate" TD to Helen, April 16.

"I'm to where the factory" TD to Helen, June 18.

"spiritually alone" TD to Helen, June 26.

"My body appears" TD to Helen, July 16.

"He might begin" TD to Helen, April 12.

"The new book" Liveright to TD, April 2.

"Griffith, An American" Liveright to TD, April 23.

"Ewing" or "Warner" Liveright to TD, May 6.

"Orion" "who were misled" "The Love Cast" TD to Helen, May 23; April 27.

"I call it" Quoted in Claude Bowers, *My Life*, 156.

Louise Campbell See Campbell, *Letters to Louise*, 14–22.

"Magdalene [sic]" "When I invite" Ibid., 410, 408.

"not to moon around" "She was one" Quoted in Dudley, 467–68.

Gallery of Women as a substitute TD to Helen, July 28.

"I may have" TD to Helen, Aug. 4. Quoted in Helen, *Life*, 99.

"If I promise" Ibid., Sept. 26.

"on a pedestal" "Perhaps" "Since when" TD to Helen, June 17, 1924.

"young Krog" TD to Helen, Nov. 17.

"Well," he kept "sharp and accusing" Helen, *Life*, 106.

Chapter 20.

"HE SWAM AWAY" New York *World*, Dec. 1, 1906.

"He tried to place" Ibid., 126.

"Sex and beer parties" TD to HLM, [before April 14, 1924], 532.

"Do you ever get" Quoted in Bowers, "Author of 'The Genius' and 'The Titan' Celebrated in World of Letters," undated clipping.

"There is the old" Quoted in Bowers, *My Life*, 157.

"Finally revised and cut" Quoted in Pizer, *Novels of TD*, 230.

"heavy and brooding" Quoted in Bruce Kellner, *Carl Van Vechten and the Irreverent Decades*, 201.

"that life is largely" Quoted in Kellner, 167.

"the first flashing" *An American Tragedy*, I, 300.

"the very substance" Ibid., II, 48–49.

"His was a dual" Helen, *Life*, 216.

"those veiled mysterious" Marguerite Tjader, *Dreiser: A New Dimension*, 33.

"confides his dilemma" Philip Emerson Wood, "An Interview with Theodore Dreiser in which He Discusses Errant Youth," Philadelphia *Public Ledger*, undated clipping.

"in endless space" "a huge" *AAT*, II, 74.

"distorted and fulgurous" Ibid., 76.

"chemic revulsion" Ibid., 77.

"a palsy" Ibid., 76.

passive voice See Shelley Fisher Fishkin, *From Fact to Fiction*, 130–33.

"And yet fearing" *AAT*, II, 77.

"that last frantic" Ibid., 79.

Dreiser's forbidden wish For comments on TD's Oedipal conflicts see Robert Forrey, "Theodore Dreiser: Oedipus Redivivus," *Modern Fiction Studies*, Autumn 1977; and Richard B. Hovey and Ruth S. Ralph, "Dreiser's *The 'Genius'*: Structure and Motivation," *Hartford Studies in Literature*, Number 2, 1970. In the latter the authors write, "Witla cannot resolve his wife's dual role: she is both lover and mother, playmate-sinner and jailer-punisher."

"He expected" Quoted in Brandon, *Murder*, 182.

"Well, I will end" New York *World*, Nov. 29, 1906.

"well made and cunningly" Quoted in Brandon, *Murder*, 232.

"wasn't good for business" NY *World*, Nov. 20, 1906.

"This book will be" TD to Campbell, Jan. 9, 1925. In Elias, *Letters*, II, 433.

Chapter 21.

"When I was leaving" Quoted in Brandon, *Murder in the Adirondacks*, 290.

"the last five or six" Smith to TD, June 3, 1925.

increase royalty Smith to TD, July 23, 1925.

cash-flow problems See Gilmer, *Liveright*, 101–3.

Smith begged Smith to TD, Aug. 17, 1925.

"easier waters" HLM to TD, Sept. 5, 1925, 537.

"the old eternal triangle" *Chains*, 134.

accused of plagiarizing See Morris Ernst and William Seagle, *Obscenity and the Censor*. See Brandon, *Murder*, 347.

"COURT IN TEARS" New York *World*, Nov. 20, 1906.

changing the wording For example, he renders the passage quoted as follows:

I have been bidding goodbye to some places to-day. There are so many nooks, dear, and all of them so dear to me. I have lived here all my life, you know. First, there was the spring-house with its great masses of green moss, and in passing it I said good by to it, for I won't be coming to it soon again—maybe never. And then the old apple tree where we had our play-house years ago—Emily and Tom and Gifford and I. Then the "Believe," a cute little house in the orchard where we sometimes played. (*An American Tragedy*, II, 254–55)

"A case of the" Ibid., 274.

"not without sorrow" "His last" Ibid., 383.

"a kind of inferno" Ibid., 360.

"a reflection of the" Quoted in Philip Emerson Wood, "An Interview with Theodore Dreiser in which He Discusses Errant Youth," Philadelphia *Public Ledger*, undated clipping.

"God has heard" *AAT*, II, 289.

"Now it was here" Ibid., 405.

"eye magnetism" Marguerite Tjader Harris and John J. McAleer, eds., *Notes on Life*, 336.

"his eyes fixed nervously" *AAT*, II, 406.

"an earnest, child-heart" *Color*, 282.

"not the Execution room" TD to HLM, Nov. 14, 1925, 544. A year earlier Dreiser obtained permission to witness an execution, but the condemned men were reprieved. See Edward Smith to TD, Sept. 15, 17, 1924.

Cain replied See HLM to TD, Nov. 21, 1925, 545.

"THIS PUTS ME" HLM to TD, Nov. 28, 1925 (telegram), 546.

"THE WORLD LIES" TD to HLM, Nov. 28, 1925 (telegram), 547.

"Dreiser Interviews" "a strangely" "One opened" New York *World*, Nov. 30, 1925.

"my imagination" TD to HLM, Dec. 3, 1925, 547.

He did add Galley 244, *AAT*, ch. XXIX.

"For Theodore Dreiser" Quoted in Riggio, 549, n. 2.

inserts some language Galley 164, *AAT*.

"What the hell" Quoted in Gilmer, *Liveright*, 135.

"You'd almost feel" Campbell told Swanberg, June 21, 1962.

" 'The dark days' " Helen, *Life*, 113.

Chapter 22.

"Your writer," "The Bubble of Success," unpublished MS (UVa).

"glorious Saturday" Kusell to TD, Dec. 9, 1925.

"Here wealth builds" Ibid., 434.

"The state is" TD to HLM, 550.

"personally inscribed" TD to HLM, Jan. 14, 1926, 550.

"Dear Heinrich" Quoted in Riggio, 550, n. 3.

"My poor mother" HLM to TD, Jan. 20, 1926.

"These things are" TD to HLM, Feb. 2, 1926, 552.

"all but sick" TD to T. R. Smith, Feb. 14, 1926 [misdated?].

"Letters such as" TD to McCord, Feb. 2, 1926.

"to avoid a deluge" TD to Ficke, Jan. 14, 1926.

"THE REVIEWS" Smith to TD (telegram), Jan. 9, 1926.

"It seems to have" TD to Lengel, Feb. 15, 1926.

"detachment" "complete and" "romantic glozing" "that earlier" Quoted in Salzman, 444.

"Well, it looks" Helen, *Life,* 120.

"the biggest" Ibid., 447.

"The appearance" Ibid., 462.

" 'An American' " Ibid., 471.

"the Mount Everest" Ibid., 473.

"the best novel" Ibid., 474.

"[An] American" Ibid., Quoted in Dudley, 450.

"as solid" Quoted in Salzman, 445.

"He has fortified" Ibid., 460.

"Oh, it is" Ibid., 437.

"the author" Ibid., 446.

"a tacit record" Ibid., 455.

"mixing slang" Ibid., 484.

"He uses language" Ibid., 486.

"a colossal derelict" Ibid., 487.

"despite his looks" *An American Tragedy,* II, 332.

"social importance" Ibid., 330.

"I never once" Quoted in Wood, "Interview With TD," Philadelphia *Public Ledger,* undated clipping.

Chapter 23.

"Now we waited" "Search-Light" [Waldo Frank], *Time Exposures,* 160–61.

"I'm honestly" Liveright to TD, March 8, 1926.

"You know of course" Ibid.

"it's extremely" Ibid.

"if courageously treated" Quinn Martin, "The Magic Lantern: A Book that Would Make a Great Film," New York *World,* March 7, 1926.

stirred up interest See Dudley Nichols, "An American Comedy," NY *World,* March 11, 1926.

Lasky See Jesse Lasky, with Don Weldon, *I Blow My Own Horn.* See also Neil Gabler, *An Empire of Their Own,* 203.

"they're making" TD to Campbell, March 17, 1926. Elias, *Letters,* II, 443.

"absolute loyalty" Liveright to TD, March 26, 1926.

"delaying tactics" Lasky, *Horn,* 203.

American Tragedy negotiations See TD to Liveright, March 23, 1926. Elias, *Letters,* II, 442–46; Liveright to TD, March 26, 1926; Lasky, ibid., 222.

"The way it is" TD statement, June 10, 1931.

"got everything" Liveright to TD, March 26, 1926.

"will be the most" Clipping at UP.

"I have taken" HLM to TD, Jan. 28, 1926, 552.

"shapeless and forbidding" "Is Freudianism" "What is" " 'An American' " Quoted in Salzman, 476–78.

writing in his diary See Charles A. Fecher, ed., *The Diary of H. L. Mencken,* 21–22.

"As for your" TD to HLM, Feb. 8, 1926, 554.

"That boss of yours" Quoted in Charles Angoff, *H. L. Mencken: A Portrait from Memory,* 101.

"Poor old Dreiser" HLM to Van Doren, May 22, 1928. In Forgue, 309.

"The trouble between" TD to Kusell, Feb. 13, 1926.

"You are" "a definite" "I felt" Helen, *Life,* 125–26. Helen does not name the other woman.

"I just sold" TD to Lengel, March 27, 1926.

"If you see him" "Search-Light," 163.

"I am opulent" J. C. Powys to Vera Dreiser, Nov. 1959.

"a special case" J. C. Powys *Autobiography,* 575.

"comparable to no" Winder to TD, Feb. 23, 1927.

"mist [sic] of a" Claire Windsor to TD, April 18, 1926.

"wonderful good fortune" Jug to TD, March 31, 1926; TD to Jug, [April] 1926. Swanberg, 309.

"and did everything" "tentatively" "in order" TD to Malone, carbon of memo, n.d.

he agreed Agreement dated June 1, 1926.

entertained feelers TD to Windsor, April 18, 1926.

"because of a special" TD to Holmes Book Co., April 27, 1926.

kept two sets See Fecher, *Diary of H. L. Mencken,* 87–88.

"except for you" TD to Pell, March 19, 1930. (Courtesty of Gary Giddins)

"a fine thing" Liveright to TD, June 1, 1926.

"from assessments" Memorandum of agreement, June 2, 1926.

"What I am still" Quoted in Nathan, *Intimate Notebooks,* 46.

"felt a strange" "too drastic" Helen, *Life,* 137. See Dr. Renate Schmidt-von Bardelben, "Dreiser on the European Continent," *Dreiser Newsletter,* Fall 1971.

Balzac's house Victor Llona, "Sightseeing in Paris with Theodore Dreiser," *Yale Review,* Spring 1987.

"My own private" Anderson to Burton Emmett, Oct. 4, 1926. In Charles E. Modlin, ed., *Sherwood Anderson: Selected Letters*, 86.

Only Arthur Pell Friede to TD, Dec. 8, 1926.

Rodin Studios Helen, *Life*, 140.

"if it's not the book" Friede to TD, July 20, 1926,

"The poor boy!" Quoted in Donald Friede, *Mechanical Angel*, 43.

Chapter 24.

"I was beginning" Helen, *Life*, 200.

"an almost reverential" Campbell, *Letters to Louise*, 38.

"a helpless male" Ibid.

"Helen will be" Ibid. Dreiser said this to several people.

"No, . . . I see no one" Quoted in Bowers, 164.

"Moving" TD, "Is American Restlessness. . . ." New York *American*, April 10, 1927.

"endowed with ample" "Fools for Love," NY *American*, May 22, 1927.

He, of course, had a strongbox List of stocks in Arthur Pell papers (courtesy of Gary Giddins).

"American Tragedy Brings" New York *Sunday Journal*, May 22, 1927.

Another paper "The Town in Review," New York *Morning Telegraph*, undated clipping.

"American author" Clipping, [Sept. 1929].

"Was Clyde Griffiths" Undated publicity release.

"It was too late" Interview with Zoe Buckley, clipping, March 10, 1928 (CorU).

"dissolved in tears" Quoted in Kellner, *Carl Van Vechten*, 230.

"Your hands run" Helen, *Life*, 143.

"I felt myself physically" Ibid., 144.

"tomb" "his terrible" "short" Helen to Fabri, May 22, 1939.

"a constructive" "Do as you please" Helen, *Life*, 146.

"most evil &" Helen to Fabri, May 22, 1929.

"An impregnable door" Helen, *Life*, 149.

"the distinct sensation" Ibid., 152.

"interests me enormously" TD to Helen, June 5, 1924.

"The peace of that" Russia Diary, Oct. 15, 1927.

"the real, unofficial Russia" Helen, *Life*, 165–66.

Sacco-Vanzetti Liveright to TD, Aug. 24, 1927.

"theories about life" TD to Dinamov, Jan. 5, 1927.

"Who me" Diary, Oct. 11, 1927.

Chapter 25.

"This enormous giant" Russia Diary, Nov. 7, 1927.

"play with B———" Ibid., Oct. 15.

"more passionate" Ibid., Oct. 18.

"am conscience-stricken" Ibid., Oct. 13.

"in spite of" Ibid., Oct. 18.

"I will kneel" Ibid., Oct. 26.

"psychopathic novel" Ibid.

"its theory" Ibid., Oct. 28.

"but I'll be better" TD to Campbell, Oct. 28, 1927. Elias, *Letters*, II, 463.

"as though the matter" Diary, Oct. 28.

"very bad" enlargement "I am not" Ibid., Oct. 29.

"Like a cast away" Ibid.

"an armed dictatorship" TD to McCoy, postcard, n.d.

"the only difference" TD to Helen, n.d.

"flaccid and buttery" "dubious" Diary, Nov. 5.

he told Ruth how lonely Ibid.

"Russian lackey as" Quoted in Ruth Epperson Kennell, *Dreiser and the Soviet Union*, 23.

"since we are already" Diary, Nov. 6.

"I think—if only" Ibid., Nov. 7.

"drab affair" "making overtures" "DT———" Ibid.

"with being facetiously" "sympathetic" Quoted in Vincent Sheean, *Dorothy and Red*, 6.

"delightfully vigorous &" "an elderly man" Diary, Nov. 11.

"You behaved" Ibid.

"The important thing" Quoted in Kennell, 35.

"the greatest writer" Dinamov to TD, Dec. 10, 1926.

"Pennsylvania mining" Diary, Nov. 13.

"Why of course" Ibid., Nov. 16.

"And possibly such" Ibid.

"like a speech" "uplifter" "only through" Ibid.

somewhat disillusioned Marie Seton, *Sergei M. Eisenstein*, 21.

"good as chronicles" Quoted in Kennell, 41.

"I have been treated" Diary, Nov. 15.

"restfulness" Ibid., Nov. 18.

"Russia will never be" Quoted in Kennell, 80.

"take away the spirit" Ibid., 84.

"gets good wages" Ibid., 86.

"any form of tyranny" Bukharin interview Quotes from Kennell, 73–79, and Diary, Dec. 5.

"I choke as I enter" TD, "Dreiser Looks at Russia," New York *World*, March 21, 1928.

"There is no Death" TD to the Booths, Nov. 23, 1927. Elias, *Letters*, II, 465.

"It would be easy" Diary, Nov. 27, 1928.

"They did it for" Quoted, ibid.

"impatient at the still" Quoted in Mark Schorer, *Sinclair Lewis*, 496–97.

"that a nation" Diary, Nov. 27.

"final battle" Ibid., Dec. 7.

"about this Soviet thing" Diary, Dec. 19.

"In America our task" Ibid (TD's hand).

"He is a terrible" Quoted in Kennell, 200.

"His smart light-gray" Ibid., 184.

"I made him a long speech" Ibid., Jan. 10.

"Personally, I am" Quoted in Kennell, 312.

"indifference to proper" Ibid., 313.

"But TD, they haven't" Ibid., 199, 313–14.

"There is too much" Ibid., 314–15.

"SOVIET PLAN TO FAIL" Oakland *Tribune*, n.d.

"THEODORE DREISER FINDS" Chicago *Tribune*, Feb. 6, 1928.

"it seemed as if" Diary, Jan. 14, 1928.

Chapter 26.

"Russia has a dream" TD, interview, New York Paris *Herald*, Oct. 27, 1927.

"I have been digging" TD to Kennell, July 20, 1928.

"Come out into the" Ibid., Jan. 17, 1928.

"In America . . . the rich" Quoted in Kennell, *Soviet Union*, 214.

"I wasn't a Communist" "No Red Bread Line, Says Dreiser," New York *Evening Post*, Feb. 22, 1928.

Russia was no utopia "Dreiser Back from Russia," unidentified clip, Feb. 22, 1928.

"Trotsky and some of" "Dreiser Sure Soviets Will Change World," clipping, n.d.

"is a big man" "Dreiser Home, Sees Soviet Arms Gaining," New York *Times*, Feb. 22, 1928.

"Nowhere in Russia" NY *Evening Post*, Feb. 22, 1928.

"I cannot understand" NY *Times*, Feb. 22, 1928. Quoted in Kennell, 213.

"Unless artists" Ibid., 214.

"I decided that" TD to Kennell, Feb. 24, 1928.

"The Ideals of Washington" Quoted in Kennell, 214.

"unemployment is Russia's" Simon Strunsky, "About Books," *New York Times Book Review*, March 4, 1928.

"Russia will not let" Letter, "Mr. Dreiser Excepts," *New York Times*, March 15, 1928.

"pursuit of the ideal" New York *World*, March 18, 1928.

"which seeks to eliminate" "there are sex murders" *World*, March 19.

"plays that glorify" *World*, March 24.

"the endless outpour" "which does not" *World*, March 25.

"rumors of secret trials" "Is Edison" "semi-religious" *World*, March 27.

"Mr. Darwin" "that fascinating" *World*, March 28.

"[Under communism], this collective" *World*, March 22.

syndicate wanted to publish TD to Kennell, Sept. 5, 1928.

"the G.P.U. stuff" TD to Campbell, June 21, 1928. Elias, *Letters*, II, 468. See also TD to Kennell, Aug. 18, 1928; Swanberg, *Dreiser*, 343; Kennell, *Soviet Union*, 220–22.

"direct, undogmatized gaze" TD to Kennell, July 20, 1928.

"the fairy land" TD to the Booths, July 16, 1928. Elias, *Letters*, II, 471.

"He has that rare" *Collecting Net*, July 21, 1928.

"all mechanists & in" TD to Booths, July 7, 1928. Elias, *Letters*, II, 469–70.

"Some are agnostics" Ibid., July 16, 1928; Ibid., 471.

"Does Ernita" Kennell to TD, June 9, 1928.

"Some of the bits" TD to Kennell, Aug. 18, 1928.

"a hodgepodge" Kennell, *Soviet Union*, 220.

"I have been so" "a possible situation" TD to Kennell, Sept. 5, 1928.

"little youthful stuff" TD to Campbell, Aug. 31, 1928. Elias, *Letters*, 472–73.

"As for trying" Goldman to TD, July 1, 1929.

letter to Gov. Young TD to C. C. Young, Nov. 15, 1928. Elias, *Letters*, II, 482.

"a hall boy" TD to Bliven, Sept. 14, 1928.

"I have read" "You have" Thelma Cudlipp, "October's Child," unpublished MS. Swanberg notes.

"You—/I." "The Muffled Oar," *Nation*, Feb. 27, 1929.

he wrote Beatrice TD to B. Booth, Sept. 25, 1928.

he could talk of nothing See Claude Bowers, *My Life*, 167; William E. Woodward, *The Gift of Life*, 315; Swanberg, 341.

"a wholly lunatic" Quoted in Swanberg, 341.

"the ruthless suppression" TD to Gold, Sept. 19, 1928. Elias, *Letters*, II, 474.

"Life is so difficult" Quoted in Swanberg, 348.

"He was highly critical" "just brood" Van Kralick to Swanberg, Dec. 2, 1962. Beatrice Cole told Lingeman.

"Life is to me" Bookman, Sept. 1928.

"I never read" Cole told Lingeman, Nov. 11, 1986.

"I wonder when he gave" New York *Evening Post*, Nov. 14, 1928.

"She took three" TD to Kennell, Dec. 12, 1928.

"There are the N.E.P." NY *Evening Post*, Feb. 22, 1928.

"The old beast" Quoted in Marion K. Sanders, *Dorothy Thompson*, 146.

"have been distinctly" Cane to Hays, Nov. 26, 1928.

Vincent Sheean thought Sheean, *Dorothy and Red*, 148.

"That I may have" Quoted in Sanders, 146.

"I have good lawyers" TD to Kennell, Dec. 2, 1928.

"both ladies seem" Harry Hansen, New York *World*, Dec. 13, 1928.

"the impression is abroad" Quoted in Salzman, 552–53.

Chapter 27.

"But in the interim" TD "This Madness: Aglaia," *Cosmopolitan*, Feb. 1929.

Harper's Simon & Schuster TD to Lengel, Oct. 19, 1928.

"That in consideration" Van Dresser memorandum.

"fine bit of imagining" TD to Liveright, Feb. 24, 1929.

"bag and baggage" TD to Kyllmann, Feb. 12, 1929.

"deal is off" TD to Kraft, April 14, 1929. See also Hy Kraft, *On My Way to the Theater*, 70–73; Marguerite Tjader, *Theodore Dreiser: A New Dimension*, 14–17; Louise Campbell, *Letters to Louise*, 60–62.

"A story like this" Quoted in Arthur Garfield Hays, *City Lawyer*, 238.

"Well, perhaps where" Quoted in Gilmore, *Horace Liveright*, 171.

"I have stated" TD to Bowers, May 27, 1929. Elias, *Letters*, *II*, 490.

"today we are faced" *Theatre Guild Magazine*, May 1929.

"You people may not" *Cosmopolitan*, June 1929.

"pseudobiography" "false conception" Kennell to TD, March 10, 1929.

"suitable to the censorship" TD to Knight, May 13, 1929. Elias, *Letters*, II, 489.

"I let my hand" Cuts shown on copy of TS of "This Madness."

"an introduction" "In regard" TD to Knight, May 13, 1929.

"Why were they" Yvette Eastman told Lingeman, July 1983.

"My truest friend" Kusell to TD, Feb. 13, 1929.

"He turned to look" Harris, *Dimension*, 1.

"the urgency of the moment" "Dreiser simply" Ibid., 10.

"He would come and" Mrs. K. S. Clark told Swanberg, Oct. 16, 1963.

"I just had a fight" Fabri, Diary, Oct. 25, 1929 (WAS papers, UP).

"He must be fixing" Ibid., Oct. 28, 1929.

paper fortune of $400,000 TD on Dale Carnegie radio show, Sept. 11, 1934.

list of his holdings Arthur Pell Papers (courtesy of Gary Giddins).

"a terrible flop" Friede to Swanberg, Jan. 11, 1963.

"Success does not attend" Quoted in Salzman, 568.

Estelle Kubitz main source She also wrote *Am. Diaries*, 155, n. 20; Kubitz to TD, May 15, 1922.

"a strong compelling" *Gallery of Women*, 257.

"His portrait corresponds" Max Eastman, *Love and Revolution*, 184. See also *Am. Diaries*, 349.

Kennell and "Ernita" Kennell to TD, May 28, 1929.

Estelle Kubitz had told him *Am. Diaries*, 247–48.

"Dinamov as intermediary" Kennell to Dinamov, Feb. 7, 1938.

"indestructable American" TD to Kennell, March 1930.

"bad-good girl" Ibid., 220.

"Kraft, I'm going" Kraft, *Theater*, 67.

Chapter 28.

"I say this country" Statement on arrest of communists in Atlanta [Oct.? 1930].

"natural-born traders" Quoted in Swanberg, 351.

"horrible life" Symon Gould to Elias, Dec. 19, 1949 (CorU).

"One always finds" Nathan, *Intimate Notebooks*, 47.

wired . . . Hummel TD to Hummel (telegram), April 1, 1930.

"a bunch of bugaboos" "Money is the" Albuquerque *Journal*, April 19, 1930.

"just fool dogmatic bunk" "boot out" "the defective" Quoted in Swanberg, *Dreiser*, 362.

"farce" For thirty years Ibid.

"Sadness [comes]" "Art is" Sayre notes, April 18, 1930.

"I appear to be" Quoted in Harris, *Dimension*, 41–42.

"so densely scarred" Dr. Lemon to TD, June 3, 1930.

"DREISER NOW REDISCOVERS" "gold swimming pools" New York *World-Telegram*, July 9, 1930.

"This doesn't hurt" Quoted in Gilmer, *Liveright*, 230.

"Was this money" Ibid., 231.

"Whoever said I was" Quoted in H. L. Mencken's Diary (MS), Nov. 25, 1930 (EPFL).

Kay Sayre go through the manuscript Memo, TD to Sayre.

"a frame-up" Undated statement. See Pass to TD, Oct. 6, 1930.

"a chestnut" "indifference" Undated statement.

"stirred up great interest" Liveright to Pell (telegram), Aug. 13, 1930 (Courtesy of Gary Giddins).

Eisenstein and Liveright Eisenstein, *Immoral Memories*, 156.

"the story about the guy" Quoted in Leon Harris, *Upton Sinclair*, 281.

"tragic course" Eisenstein, *Film Form and the Film Sense*, 96.

"But the machinery" Quoted in Seton, *Eisenstein*, 179.

"Kill—Kill!" "Ending" Ibid., 180.

"the thought of sin" Scenario of *An American Tragedy*, in Ivor Montagu, *With Eisenstein in Hollywood*, 339.

"purblind" "My son" "The mother's" Ibid.

"Is Clyde Griffiths" Eisenstein, *Film Form*, 96.

"there are many questions" Quoted in Seton, 184.

"terminated by mutual" Quoted in Seton, 186.

"Gentlemen, it is" Quoted in Montagu, 120.

"Grim realism" Quoted in Seton, 186.

"several champions" "Dreiser Is Favored to Win Nobel Prize," *New York Times*, Oct. 9, 1930.

Lewis and Nobel Prize Mark Schorer, *Sinclair Lewis*, 546–47.

"almost suicidal" Quoted in Swanberg, 368.

"I cannot imagine" TD to Madeleine Boyd, Nov. 7, 1930. Elias, *Letters*, II, 508.

"very depressing" Anderson to Burton Emmett, in Modlin, ed., *Sherwood Anderson: Selected Letters*, 128.

"Do you intend" TD to Liveright, Oct. 27, 1930.

Sackin reported Sackin to TD, Dec. 18, 1930.

He refused TD to Sackin (telegram), Dec. 19, 1930.

Zukor begged Josef von Sternberg Von Sternberg, *Fun in a Chinese Laundry*, 46.

Chapter 29.

"I have a literary" Quoted in Harris, *Dimension*, 53.

"Although I know" TD to North, Jan. 17, 1931.

"to assure you have" Light to *Daily Worker*, May 1930. "The American Press and Political Prisoners," *Daily Worker*, May 19, 1930.

Nation article Van Doren to TD, Oct. 30, 1930.

research in Passaic *Tragic America*, 14–27.

"I eliminated the sociological" Von Sternberg, *Chinese Laundry*, 47.

"comments, advice" Contract, Jan. 2, 1931.

Dreiser and Kraft in Hollywood Hy

Kraft, "Dreiser's War on Hollywood," *The Screen Writer*, March 1946; Kraft, *Theater*, 77–82.

Paramount suit TD to Lasky, March 17, 1931. Elias, *Letters*, II, 522; Lasky to TD, June 3, 1931; Elias, 522, n. 12; Hays and Hume to Lasky, June 26, 1931; Swanberg, 377.

"In the preparation" Quoted in Elias, *Letters*, II, 562, n. 23.

"I feel, in a way" Quoted in Elias, *Theodore Dreiser*, 249.

Von Sternberg movie version of *AAT* Of all the new scenes Kraft and TD suggested, only seven were used. These included hints of Clyde's home life and his mother's strictness; the joyride resulting in the death of the child; Clyde's subsequent flight and shots of him riding the rails, washing dishes, getting a job as a bellhop. To show the influence of the Green-Davidson hotel in awakening Clyde's dreams of riches, a segment was added in which a wealthy young woman hands him a large tip. When her mother chastises her for giving him so much money, the girl says, "I liked his looks. . . . I wonder what a boy of his kind is doing in this kind of work." This bit of exposition served more to give credibility to Clyde's romance with Sondra than to define his shift of values. In the next scene, a maid, obviously Clyde's girlfriend, accuses him of "getting high hat." He snaps, "I'm not going to be a bellhop all my life." Enter: *Ambition*. Cut to roadhouse and clinging, tipsy couples, jazz, etc.

When Clyde flees after the little girl is killed, his mother prays for his safety and asks forgiveness: "We have always been so terribly poor. We've never been able to give him the happiness, the simple joys and pleasures that should come to every boy." The speech seems mere pious words rather than an explanation of Clyde's character. At the end of the film there is an added scene in the county jail immediately after Clyde's conviction. When his mother assures him that she believes he is innocent, he confesses, "But I'm not—not really." He tells her he swam away because he wanted Roberta to die. He wanted to tell the jury this but couldn't; he was too ashamed. His confession is intended to be taken literally, to emphasize his guilt. His mother is shocked and tells him it was not his fault: "We never gave you the right start. We brought you up among ugly, evil surroundings, and while we were trying to save the souls of others we were letting you go astray." Clyde chokes up: "Mother are they really going to ——?" She tells him to be brave and face his punishment like a man. Then she looks heavenward and says, "I know that somehow, somewhere, you'll be given the right start." See TD to Edwin Wilson, Oct. 22, 1931; TD to Campbell, Aug. 4, 1921. Elias, *Letters*, II, 562.

"the matter of political" Letter dated April 9, 1931. See TD to Pass, May 5, May 12, 1921.

"almost everyone" Malcolm Cowley, *Dream of the Golden Mountain*, 57.

"The time is ripe" Ibid. Quoted in Louis Adamic, *My America*, 110.

"Dreiser's own great" Ibid.

"the real, practical head" Light to Monohan, May 20, 1931.

"definitely aimed" Quoted in Elias, *Theodore Dreiser*, 252.

Foster urged Dreiser Pass to TD, June 12, 1931.

"Watch out" Pittsburgh *Press*, June 25, 1931.

"from each person" "Miners Slaves in Strike Zone Writes Dreiser," New York *World*, June 26, 1931.

"to put a quietus" "Dreiser Assails A.F. of L.," New York *Sun*, June 26, 1931.

William Green to TD, July 1, 1931. Elias, *Letters*, II, 537–42.

Dreiser's rebuttal TD to Green, July 17, 1931. Ibid., 542–61.

"a class instrument" Quoted in Lehan, *Theodore Dreiser*, 183.

"The latest phase" Helen, *Life*, 213–14.

"I've had a hell" TD to Campbell, Aug. 5, 1931. Elias, *Letters*, II, 561.

"How *Dawn* could have" Mame to Markel, n.d. (THL).

"one of the most" Quoted in Salzman, 590.

"looked as if" Campbell, *Letters to Louise*, 43.

"There was no architect" TD to Roberts, July 14, 1936.

"her child" Harriet B. Hubbard to Lingeman, March 20, 1989.

"When you get money" "Dreiser, 60, Glad He's Rich," *New York Times*, Aug. 27, 1931.

Chapter 30.

"to take sides" "The Titan," *New Masses*, Sept. 1931.

T.R. Smith wrote Smith to TD, July 10, 1931.

Kay Sayre chief ghostwriter L. V. Heilbrunn told Elias.

tendered their regrets Undated memo, Sayre to TD.

"representative Americans" Lester Cohen, "Theodore Dreiser: A Personal Memoir," *Discovery* 4, 1954.

"personally responsible" "Dreiser and Group Go to Harlan County," Lawenceburg [Kentucky] *News*, Nov. 4, 1931.

The governor responded "Troops Will Go to Harlan During Probe." Undated clipping.

"snake doctors" Quoted in Irving Bernstein, *The Lean Years*, 380.

"her neatly tailored" John Dos Passos, *The Best Times*, 228.

"doing what came" McCoy to Swanberg, March 4, 1963.

"Well they grow 'em" Quoted in *Harlan Miners Speak*, 101.

"faces out of" "the lilt of Elizabethan" Dos Passos, 228.

"there was a sort" Quoted in Daniel Aaron, *Writers on the Left*, 179.

"The gun thugs" *Harlan Miners Speak*, 206.

"with a sort of reverence" "I don't keer" Quoted in Cohen, 114, 115.

"I thought you were" Quoted, ibid.

"a war feeling" *Harlan Miners*, 229.

"that if you stood" Ibid., 292.

"where the workers are" "Dreiser Eats Beans at Miners Kitchen," *New York Times*, Nov. 7, 1931.

"highly reputable citizens" "capitalize" "dupe" "Dreiser Faces Arrest; Charges of Misconduct," Richmond *Times-Dispatch*, Nov. 10, 1931.

"The first thing" "Dreiser Says Judge Evades Mine Issue," *New York Times*, Nov. 12, 1931.

next surfaced in Norfolk "Dreiser Refuses to Pose or Talk," Norfolk, Va., *Pilot*, Nov. 12, 1931. See Helen, *Life*, 225.

"Something will have to" "I'll tell you" "Mr. Dreiser Speaks His Mind," New York *Evening Post*, Nov. 13, 1932.

"to commit criminal" "Dreiser Group Opens Attack on Extradition," New York *Herald-Tribune*, Nov. 17, 1932.

"sneering tone" Quoted in Aaron, *Writers*, 179.

The lawyer wired Cameron to TD, Nov. 20, 1931.

"This is a speak-easy" "Dreiser Absent As 3,000 Await Talk on Miners," New York *Herald-Tribune*, Dec. 7, 1931.

"It is both funny" Quoted in Eastman, *Love and Revolution*, 537.

"You are the first" TD to Eastman, Nov. 20, 1931. Later, Eastman noted on this letter: "I know upon the most intimate possible authority that he was not at the time impotent." Eastman had married Yvette Szekely (IndU).

"The charges against me" "Dreiser Bans Quiz of Girl Companion." Undated clipping.

"For the past year" "Harlan County Faces," *Fortune*, Feb. 1932.

"in a pine box" Quoted in Klehr, *Heyday*, 46.

"the defeated mine-owners" Quoted in Bernstein, *Turbulent Years*, 45.

"they wouldn't take me" Cohen, "Theodore Dreiser."

"I have been told" "Theodore Dreiser Explains His Political Views," New York *Herald-Tribune*, Dec. 22, 1931.

"There was no question" Swanberg, 393. See also Elias interview of Browder, Aug. 16, 1947, in which Browder gives somewhat different reasons for refusing Dreiser.

"the rank and file" TD to Bailey, May 18, 1931. Elias, *Letters*, II, 531.

"that the leaders" Helen, *Life*, 234. See also Helen to Elias, Aug. 20, 1947 (CorU).

"the poor dumbbells" Harriet Bissell Hubbard to Lingeman, Feb. 23, 1989.

"I would do anything" Quoted in Dudley, 478.

"in the youngsters" Quoted, ibid, 477.

"A revolutionary situation" Quoted in Aaron, *Writers*, 311.

"a very profound" Quoted in Elias, *Letters*, II, 473.

"the human race" TD to Gold, Sept. 19, 1928, Ibid., 474.

"When I take part" TD to Elias, April 17, 1937 (CorU).

Chapter 31.

"As for my Communism" TD to Evelyn Scott, Oct. 28, 1932.

"is for itself" *Crawford's Weekly*, Jan. 2, 1932. *New Masses*, Jan. 1932.

"Stalin uses the same" Transcript in Joseph Brainen, "Human Nature in a Crucible," *Jewish Standard*, Sept. 30, 1932.

"much of the matter" T. R. Smith to TD, Nov. 13, 1931.

"we think you stand" Hays to Liveright Inc., Nov. 11, 1931.

"stood on a soapbox" Genevieve Myers to Emily, March 12, 1947.

Stuart Chase claimed Quoted in Salzman, 632.

Edmund Wilson review Salzman, 641.

"the liberal fallacy" Ibid., 647–48.

"It is entirely understood" Browder to TD, Oct. 20, 1931.

"as blind and uncouth" Salzman, 641.

"*for the masses*" *Tragic America*, 413 (italics in original).

"guarantee official" Ibid., 414.

"I would recommend" *Tragic America*, galley 121.

"Only in this case" *Tragic America*, 419.

"saw no lack of" Ibid.

"Communism as technically" TD to C. E. Yost, April 6, 1932.

to ask Esther McCoy Sebree to TD, March 10, 1933; TD to McCoy, March 20, 1933.

"too colorless" TD to Pass, June 16, 1932.

"then most certainly" TD to Pass, July 5, 1932.

resigned as chairman TD to Levy, Jan. 19, 1932.

American delegation to the World Congress Against War See memo, Light to TD [June 1932]. She complains of this organization listing him as chairman and tells him, "if they make any false moves or crazy statements, its up to you to explain and prove, and all the rest. And you don't even know what they're saying." A handwritten note by Dreiser on this memo reads, "You should stop in at their office & ask to be shown all correspondence. I object to this free stuff & and prefer to resign."

Light appealed to Light to Weinstone, Oct. 3, 1932.

"now, of course" Light to TD, undated memo.

"has always felt" Light to Jacobsen, Dec. 21, 1932.

"I've had to eliminate" TD to Dinamov, Oct. 11, 1932.

"I could find nothing" Light to TD, memo, Oct. 1932.

"would still align" TD to Levy, April 11, 1932.

"Among the Communists" TD to Tom Mooney, April 11, 1932. Mooney Papers, Bancroft Library, Harvard University.

"dangerous anarchist" "If you" Quoted in Orrick Johns, *Time of Our Lives*, 329.

"Clara, Clara" Quoted in Clara Clark Jaeger, *Philadelphia Rebel*, 68.

"an open door" Ibid., 71.

"for a famous novelist" Ibid., 81.

"If I can get it" TD to Campbell, July 21, 1932. *Letters to Louise*, 78.

"do some trading" TD to Campbell, July 31, 1932. Ibid., 79.

"which means 7/8 of" TD to Campbell, July 8, 1932. Ibid., 78.

He was thinking of moving TD to Campbell, Sept. 13, 1932. Ibid., 81.

"The Seventh Commandment" *Liberty*, April 2, 1932.

sent to the Bureau TD's FBI file, received April 7, 1932.

instructed Hume TD to Hume, March 19, 1932. See Helen to Elias, Feb. 8, 1946 (CorU).

"She keeps up a strong" TD to Campbell, April 15, 1932. Elias, *Letters*, II, 585.

He must economize TD to Campbell, July 23, 1932. Ibid., 591.

"I am sick of" TD to Campbell, Ibid.

"writing or just living" TD to Helen, May 15, 1932.

"in a month or so" TD to McCoy, June 9, 1932.

"turn away from" Dudley to TD, July 14, 1931.

"conditions as they are" TD to Dudley, April 7, 1932 (URo).

"Intelligently or unintelligently" *Stoic*, 4.

"the best chance" Quoted in Philip Gerber, "Dreiser's Financier," *Journal of Modern Lit.*, March 1971.

"trickery he had" *Stoic*, 15.

"In his heart" Ibid., 40.

"I am not that man" Quoted in Swanberg, 395.

"sklaved" "it will have" TD to Campbell, July 31, 1932. *Letters to Louise*, 79.

In another letter TD to Campbell, n.d. Ibid., 80.

"Things come about" Lengel to TD, Aug. 12, 1933 (ColU).

Kyllmann warned of libel Kyllmann to TD, Sept. 27, 1932.

He later told Claude Bowers *My Life*, 172.

"You will always find" TD to Nathan, Sept. 19, 1932. Elias, *Letters*, II, 604.

"Can you by some" TD to J. C. Powys, Sept. 20, 1932.

"WE MUST BE KIDDING" TD to Nathan (telegram), Sept. 22, 1932.

"only when and if" *American Spectator*, Nov. 1932.

"I do not think" TD to Nathan, Jan. 7, 1933.

"I cannot get" TD to Hammerstand, Jan. 7, 1933.

"It could be enormous" TD to Kraft, Sept. 29, 1932.

"High drama" Ibid.

"I was set up" Clara Clark Jaeger to Lingeman, March 26, 1989.

"an incredibly rich" Tatum to TD, Oct. 23, 1932.

"almost uniformly opposed" TD to Tatum, March 7, 1933.

"I am still in" TD to Fischler, May 15, 1933 (IndU).

"YOU ARE NOT" TD to Kraft (telegram), May 18, 1933 (UIll).

Schulberg had riled See New York *Daily News*, March 20, 1933.

"previewed beautifully" Schulberg to TD, June 2, 1933.

"kikey" Kraft, *Theater*, 102.

"Just as I feared" TD to Fischler, July 5, 1934 (UIll).

Liveright bankruptcy Light to Hume, May 7, 1933; A. H. Gross memo, May 31, 1933; TD to Hume, Sept. 19, 1933; Gilmer, *Liveright*, 234; "Dreiser in Court Action," *New York Times*, Nov. 11, 1939.

"dreadfully worried" TD to Hume, July 10, 1934.

"Heaving sunlit fields" TD to Ficke, July 14, 1933. Elias, *Letters*, II, 635.

"a man must learn" Quoted in Gladys Brown Ficke to Swanberg, Sept. 26, 1963.

Chapter 32.

"What I cannot" TD to Eastman, June 14, 1933. Elias, *Letters*, II, 633.

"altogether too successful" *American Spectator*, Sept. 1933.

Blum Blum's papers in New York City include rambling notes complaining about Dreiser's treatment of him and arguing with Dreiser's attitude toward Jews.

"If you listen to Jews" TD to Hapgood, Oct. 10, 1933. Elias, *Letters*, II, 651.

"I am supposedly barbarous" TD to Hapgood, Dec. 28, 1933. Elias, *Letters*, II, 662–63.

"the Zionist movement" Ibid.

rendered their decision Hume to TD, Sept. 22, 1934. TD to Briggs, Sept. 21, 1934.

"It is an outpouring" Schuster to TD, Oct. 26, 1934. Elias, *Letters*, II, 721, n. 10.

"a publisher who speaks" TD to Schuster, Oct. 26, 1934.

"I now find certain" TD to Nathan, Oct. 7, 1933. Elias, *Letters*, II, 645.

"direct social arguments" TD to Dos Passos, June 14, 1933. Ibid., 631.

"Of course there were" "Theodore Dreiser to Quit Spectator," New York *World Telegram*, Jan. 12, 1934.

"I am seriously" HLM to TD, Nov. 21, 1934, 564.

"white flags in hand" TD to HLM, Nov. 24, 1934, 565.

"recent portrait" HLM to TD, Nov. 29, 1934, 566.

rendezvous on December 4 Fecher, *Diary of H. L. Mencken*, 73–74.

"Canby's letter offers" HLM to TD, Jan. 3, 1935, 571.

"Whatever the nature" TD to Eastman, May 26, 1933.

Bingham-Muste merger TD to Eastman,

Feb. 26, 1934. Bingham told Lingeman in 1990 that he couldn't recall this episode.

"Personally I despair" TD to Crawford, Jan. 15, 1935. Elias, *Letters*, II, 716.

"between the Jewish" "Dreiser Denies He Is Anti-Semitic," *New Masses*, April 30, 1935.

"I am an individual" Quoted, ibid.

"Is Dreiser Anti-Semitic?" *Nation*, April 17, 1935.

"all reports to the contrary" TD to Brill, May 18, May 30, 1935.

"In spite of my" TD to Fischler, May 30, 1935 (IndU).

not a scintilla of anti-Semitism TD to Heller, May 25, 1938.

"take whatever steps" Statement to H. L. Lack, March 13, 1934.

"every known service" TD to Cherniavsky, July 6, 1934. Elias, *Letters*, II, 679.

asked Dinamov TD to Dinamov, Aug. 22, 1935.

"very confusing" *Modern Monthly*, March 1937.

Duranty See "The Riddle of Russia," *New Republic*, July 14, 1937.

"lend support to" Quoted in Eugene Lyon, *Red Decade*, 253.

"by the sheer weight" Ibid., 247.

Calvin Bridges came Harriet B. Hubbard told Lingeman.

"What has become of Sergei?" Quoted in Kennell, *Soviet Union*, 258.

"Well I was strong" Quoted in Aaron, *Writers*, 352; Theodore Dreiser and John Dos Passos, "A Conversation," *Direction*, Jan. 1938.

"is a very minor" TD to Scott, June 17, 1938. Elias, *Letters*, III, 799–800.

"What Russia has plus" TD to Crawford, Sept. 13, 1939. Ibid., 846.

Chapter 33.

"The mystery of life" TD, "What I Believe," Pizer, *Uncollected Prose*, 245.

"I've written novels" Quoted in Marguerite Tjader and John J. McAleer, eds., *Notes on Life*, vii.

"very dubious" TD to Simon, Feb. 5, 1935. Elias, *Letters*, II, 721.

"to express an individual" TD to Sulamith Ish-Kishor, Feb. 14, 1935. Elias, 728.

"Will it make much" TD to Simon, Jan. 21, 1936.

"deeply disappointed" Simon to TD, Feb. 14, 1936.

"No doubt, today" TS dated June 15, 1936. Other quotes are from this MS, which bears corrections in TD's hand. In the published version, Dreiser says, "I never said that as a race . . . I wholly disliked and distrusted [Jews]." He cut from the manuscript a phrase reading, ". . . as a race, I frankly dislike and distrust them."

"My personal friendship" TD to Simon, July 24, 1936.

"What I am really" TD to Anderson, Jan. 2, 1936. Elias, *Letters*, III, 761.

"He was searching" Tjader, *Dimension*, 68.

"Does life have" "Blessed" "I ask" "You have" "Chaos," TS, Sept. 23, 1932.

"God, how is one" TD to "the Dark Lady," Aug. 1938.

"I am the loneliest" Examples of this statement: Vera Dreiser, *My Uncle Theodore*, 192; also Elizabeth Coakley, quoted in Swanberg, 520; Yvette Eastman told Lingeman; Esherick told Swanberg, June 25, 1962.

"utter sense" Quoted in Swanberg, 182.

"He was . . . suffering" Kraft, *Theater*, 103.

"There was a sad" Eastman told Lingeman, May 21, 1982.

"He always seems" Jaeger, *Rebel*, 107, 106.

"an orphan feeling" Cohen told Swanberg, Oct. 3, 1962.

"Life is a stepmother" McCoy to Lingeman, Feb. 24, 1987.

"some great elemental" "vast schemes" *Hey, Rub*, 23–24.

William James Elias, *Theodore Dreiser*, 287.

"*completely* understanding" TD to Douglas, Jan. 11, 1935. Elias, *Letters*, II, 712.

"a mechanism" TD, "You the Phantom," *Esquire*, Nov. 1934. Pizer, *Uncollected Prose*, 288.

"a considerable period" TD to Douglas, Jan. 11, 1935. Elias, *Letters*, II, 712.

"between matter and energy" TD to Flexner, June 1, 1935. Ibid., 745.

"two phases" Ibid.

"saying over and over" TD to Douglas, Jan. 28, 1936. Ibid., 769. See also Helen, *Life*, 249.

"There is a taste" Quoted in Helen, *Life*, 253.

Piscator *American Tragedy* TD to Campbell, Oct. 26, 1935.

"Drama with a pointer" "It was schematic" Harold Clurman, *Fervent Years*, 174.

"I am slowly but surely" TD to Douglas, Dec. 27, 1935 (UTex).

"a great old man" Harriet B. Hubbard to Lingeman, Feb. 23, 1989.

"Perhaps we spent" Ibid.

"GEORGE'S DEATH HURTS" TD to McCord (telegram), Feb. 11, 1936.

"You will never" Von Sabern to TD, Feb. 14, 1936.

"he lost heart" Mrs. Douglas to TD, Feb. 16, 1936.

"manifestations of some" TD, *Notes on Life*, 72.

"I care for her" TD to McCoy, June 22, 1936.

"If you want a fine" TD to C. E. Yost, Feb. 11, 1936.

"It stopped" Tjader, *Dimension*, 73.

"I feel unhappy about" TD to Helen, Aug. 26, 1936.

Jug's trip around the world Jug to "All," Sept. 18, 1934 (courtesy of Gupton and Grace Vogt).

Liveright suit outcome "Book Peddling and Surrealism Are Two of Issues in Dreiser Suit," New York *American*, April 19, 1937; "Dreiser Ordered to Pay Royalties," June 30, 1937.

"a terrible one" Helen to Fabri, Oct. 27, 1937.

"When you see him" Quoted in Swanberg, 445.

"That's good enough" Quoted in Tjader, *Dimension*, 80.

"conscience is God" TD, "The Tithe of the Lord," *Esquire*, 1938.

"notion of the writer" Anderson to TD, Jan. 12, 1936. Elias, *Letters*, III, 768.

"dull, lifeless" TD to Anderson, Jan. 28, 1936. Ibid., 769.

"very few novels" TD to HLM, Jan. 2, 1937, 620.

"not only because of" TD to HLM, Aug. 9, 1936, 608.

"Literature cannot grow" TD to Fischler, March 31, 1939 (IndU).

"first rate pessimist" TD to Saroyan, March 7, 1936.

"At no time throughout" Breen to Warner Bros., Oct. 11, 1937. See Lengel to TD, Oct. 30, 1937.

"full of labor talk" Golden to TD, Feb. 2, 1938.

"The plan of the play" TD to Golden, June 17, 1938. Ibid., 796.

"I am in the midst" TD to Helen, Dec. 7, 1937.

"I have the new book" TD to Scribner, [after Jan. 10, 1938].

Chapter 34.

"I went on down" TD to McCord, Aug. 18, 1938.

"to be filled in" TD to Fabri, May 15, 1938.

"Last Sunday wires" TD to Yvette Szekely, July 1938. Quoted in Aaron, *Writers*, 444, n. 15.

"Folsom recalled" Folsom told Lingeman, Jan. 9, 1990.

"I think we'll pay" Quoted in Kennell, *Soviet Union*, 257.

talked with Dos Passos Harriet B. Hubbard told Lingeman.

"a floating candy box" TD to Bissell, July 15, 1938. Elias, *Letters*, III, 801.

"a small intense Jew" Ibid.

"And now I see" Ibid.

"families" "parlor" TD to Bissell, July 20, 1938. Elias, *Letters*, III, 804–5.

"I talked to Bonnet" TD to Crawford, Sept. 13, 1939. Ibid., 846.

"Don't go!" Quoted in Helen, *Life*, 260.

"very strong" "such as" "to avoid" "Americans Favor U.S. Action to End Bombing of Civilians, Dreiser Says," Paris *Herald-Tribune*, July 24, 1938.

"My blue devils" TD to Bissell, July 26, 1938. Elias, *Letters*, III, 808.

"I felt war immediately" TD, "Barcelona in August," *Direction*, Nov. 1938.

"dangerous atmosphere" TD to Bissell, Aug. 2, 1938. Elias, *Letters*, II, 809.

"I never worked harder" TD to Bissell, Aug. 8, 1938. Elias, *Letters*, III, 811.

"Folsom, we've got" Folsom told Lingeman, Jan. 9, 1990.

"France, Spain" TD to Bissell, Aug. 5, 1938. Ibid., 810.

"Their courage" TD to Bissell, Aug. 2, 1938. Ibid., 809.

"As you know" TD to Rufus M. Jones, Dec. 1, 1938.

"the enormous value" TD to Roosevelt, Jan. 5, 1939. See Helen, *Life*, 262.

Dreiser and Thoreau See D. B. Graham, "Dreiser and Thoreau: An Early Influence," *Dreiser Newsletter*, Spring 1976.

"supreme regulating" TD, *Living Thoughts of Thoreau*. In Pizer, *Uncollected Prose*, 306.

"in the mechanical sense" Ibid., 308.

"tapping some marvelous" Ibid., 309–10.

"gone abroad for" TD to Helen, Dec. 7, 1937.

"it was lovely" TD to Helen, Dec. 19.

"he should be using" Helen to Fabri, July 6, 1938.

"that he really cares" Helen to Fabri, Aug. 31.

"Am I demonstrating" Helen's diary, Aug. 2.

"I stand before you" Quoted in Helen to Fabri, July 22.

"It is a diary" Helen's diary, April 29.

"The friendship" Ibid., Sept. 20.

"I have hung on" Helen to Fabri, July 6.

"I am moving out" TD to HLM, Nov. 8, 1938.

"How long" HLM to TD, Nov. 9, 1938, 629.

"I am not planning" TD to HLM, Nov. 10, 1938, 630.

"George Douglas and I" Ibid.

"Odd, don't come tonight" Quoted in Bruce Crawford, "Theodore Dreiser: Letter-Writing Citizen," *South Atlantic Quarterly*, April 1954.

"As the antique order" Quoted in Tjader, *Dimension*, 82–83.

"for reasons" "You do not" TD to Folsom, Dec. 19, 1938.

Chapter 35.

"Mentally, I am alone" TD to "Dark Lady," [1938].

"All who come here" TD to Masters, April 12, 1939.

"Living with you" TD to Dark Lady, [1938].

"I am the judge" Ibid.

"come to a clarifying" Ibid.

"I am hanging" Masters to TD, Jan. 1, 1939.

"wild ideas" Lawson told Swanberg, Oct. 16, 1963.

"Well, if three" TD to Bissell, Dec. 30, 1938.

"on the rebound" Confidential source.

Lord, lord TD to Dark Lady, [1938].

"Let no destructive" Helen's diary, Jan. 1, 1939.

"He won't let anyone" Helen to Fabri, Feb. 3, 1939.

"He strikes me as" TD to Bissell, Dec. 16, 1938.

they were charmed Tjader, *Dimension*, 165.

"nature or God" TD to Thompson, Jan. 18, 1939. Elias, *Letters*, III, 833–34.

"Up until I was" Quoted in Friedrich.

"I look at all" TD to Dark Lady, [1938].

"I hang over" TD to Bissell, July 5, 1939.

"They think it can't" "Awake Get Ready for War, Dreiser Admonishes U.S.," Salt Lake City *Telegraph*, Jan. 20, 1939.

"the motion picture" Clipping with TD to Fischler, March 6, 1939 (IndU).

"face the music" TD to Bissell, May 6, 1939.

"even selling does not" TD to Masters, Aug. 30, 1939.

"This is a selfish" TD to Stoddart, June 22, 1939.

"I have had the help" Quoted in Helen, *Life*, 267–68.

"and at the end" Helen to Fabri, May 11, 1939.

his symptoms Dr. F. X. Claps told Lingeman.

"What woman could" TD to Dark Lady, 1939.

"famous for his success" TD to Lengel, Aug. 4, 1939.

"mistake" TD to Shimkin, Dec. 21, 1939. Elias, *Letters*, III, 861.

"their determination" TD to Mendel, Nov. 20, 1939.

"taking me off" TD to Lengel, Aug. 4, 1939.

no plot Clifton Fadiman to Lingeman, May 4, 1989.

"It is our feeling" Shimkin to TD, Dec. 15, 1939.

"since Horace Liveright" TD to Shimkin, Dec. 21, 1939. Elias, *Letters*, III, 859.

"It is my personality" "For it so" Ibid., 860.

"If a thing" TD to Dark Lady, [1939].

"but interference" Helen's diary, Sept. 17, 1939.

"I wonder where" Ibid., Sept. 22.

"War declared" Ibid., Sept. 1.

"All are playing" TD to Crawford, Sept. 13, 1939. Elias, *Letters*, III, 845–46.

"treachery and hypocrisy" "I'm ready" Kennell to TD, Sept. 20, 1939.

"If Russia is not" Quoted in Kennell, *Soviet Union*, 273.

"nightmare of inequity" TD to Duffy, Nov. 5, 1939. Elias, *Letters*, III, 852.

"I talk all" Quoted in Kennell, *Soviet Union*, 275.

"registration matter" "Mr. DREISER" Bureau File 100–34431, June 7, 1943.

twenty pounds lighter Helen's diary, Dec. 26, 1939.

Dreiser's health . . . began to improve Ibid., Feb. 12, 1940. See Helen, *Life*, 275.

"Do you feel keenly" Lengel to TD, June 4, 1940.

"by August 15" TD to Lengel, [after June 19, 1940].

Lengel suggested Lengel to TD, July 6, 1940.

"A man in a fog" Belfrage told Lingeman, July 13, 1982.

"Considering the fact" Lengel to TD, Sept. 19, 1940.

"wandered so far" TD to Lengel, Sept. 24, 1940. Elias, *Letters*, III, 901.

the publisher wired Piest to TD (telegram), Oct. 24, 1940.

asked for some cuts Zabladowsky to TD, Oct. 29, 1940.

"We . . . are determined" Zabladowsky to TD, Dec. 6.

"I hate, in this" TD to Field, Dec. 18, 1940. Elias, *Letters*, III, 914, n. 53.

"at all times" Lengel to TD, Jan. 3, 1941.

"a spiteful, wretchedly" Quoted in Salzman, 652.

"healthy and fairly" TD to Masters, Jan. 5, 1941.

"He got his strength" Helen to Powys, Dec. 6, 1940.

"Damned If I don't" Quoted in "3,000 in Biggest L.A. Peace Rally," *People's World*, Jan. 15, 1941.

"full of tumult" Tjader, *Dimension*, 113–14.

"After all is said" Quoted, ibid., 122.

"I'll tell you" Robert van Gelder, "An Interview With Theodore Dreiser," *New York Times Book Review*, March 10, 1941.

"Money International" TD to North (telegram), [after June 26, 1941].

"Nothing in the history" TD to Fadeyev, July 14, 1941.

Those opinions were stricken Translation of published statement in Kennell, *Soviet Union*, 293–94.

"a stab in the back" Kyllmann to TD, July 23. Elias, *Letters*, III, 932.

"I cannot tell" TD to Kyllmann, Aug. 12, 1941. Ibid., 934–37.

America First Committee TD to Shoemaker, Aug. 1, 1941.

"As long as they" TD to Fadeyev, Dec. 19, 1941. Elias, *Letters*, III, 945.

"I think Dies" Quoted in Kennell, 294.

"not very good" "I can't stand" TD to Helen, Dec. 2, 1941.

"too sensitive a variety" Helen to Fabri, Jan. 21, 1941.

"I *love* my home" Helen's diary, Oct. 7, 1941.

"T. out at 4" Ibid., Oct. 19.

"ought to be willing" TD to *Daily Worker*, Dec. 12, 1941.

"storm & stress" TD to Campbell, Dec. 31, 1941. Elias, *Letters*, III, 946–48.

Chapter 36.

"I am not" TD to Dillon, Oct. 20, 1942.

"It is far enough" TD to Lengel, Nov. 13, 1942. Elias, *Letters*, III, 944.

"doing quite well" TD to HLM, April 2, 1942, 671.

"It is a very intimate" TD to Lengel, July 1, 1942.

"You understand" TD to Balch, May 1, 1942.

he assured Balch TD to Balch, Aug. 11.

"arresting incidents" "a relationship" TD to Bradshaw, April 2, 1942.

"nostalgic but a better" TD to McCord, June 15, 1942.

"the sweetest, lovingest" TD to Bradshaw, n.d.

"It was paradise" "He liked" Bradshaw told Lingeman, 1987.

"I could have" Bradshaw told Lingeman, April 26, 1987.

"Its sole aim" TD to Campbell, July 23, 1942. Elias, *Letters*, III, 963.

"for I plan" TD to Bradshaw, Sept. 13, 1942.

"massive figure" Quoted in Joseph Griffin, "Theodore Dreiser Visits Toronto," *Canadian Review of American Studies*, Spring 1983.

"box-office in Toronto" Ibid.

the Forum asked him TD to Cowan, Oct. 22, 1942.

"She seemed like" Bradshaw told Lingeman, 1987.

"ABUSE FOR BRITAIN" "Should Russia" Quoted in Griffin.

"to take such action" Ibid.

The American consul Moffat to Secretary of State, Sept. 24, 1942. FBI file.

account of Dreiser's flight Bradshaw told Lingeman. See also Moffat to Secretary of State.

calls from two Canadian reporters In Griffin.

PM **interview** George McIntyre, "PM Interviews Dreiser to Learn What He Said in *That* Interview," *PM*, Sept. 22, 1942.

TD in Port Huron Bradshaw told Lingeman. FBI memo, Nov. 11, 1942.

"Canadian ideal" "Novelist Dreiser Dodges Interview with Reporters," Port Huron *Times-Herald*, Sept. 24, 1942.

"I didn't say" Dreiser Tells Friends Here of Speech for Audience in Toronto," Indianapolis *Star*, Oct. 4, 1942.

"an American writer" Quoted in Griffin.

"Our enemies" Quoted in Elias, *Letters*, III, 973, n. 20.

"without troubling" Quoted in Helen, *Life*, 203–4.

"I still believe" "I think" Buck to TD, Quoted in Griffin.

"I am sick" TD to Buck, Nov. 19, 1942. Quoted, Ibid.

"Custodial Detention" FBI file.

"dangerousness classification" Special Agent report, Dec. 2, 1942.

"Dreiser is 71" Ugo Carusi to Hoover, Jan. 22, 1943. FBI files. See also Hood to director, March 24, 1943; Hoover to SAC, Los Angeles, April 30, 1943; memo for the director from Ladd, Jan. 7, 1943; agent report from Louisville, Jan. 12, 1943.

immoral relationship "The Bureau" Ladd to director, Jan. 4, 1943.

"allegations" Hoover memo to the attorney general, Jan. 21, 1943.

"black list" TD to Seldes, Jan. 9, 1942.

"being pushed" TD to Harris, June 12, 1941. Elias, *Letters*, III, 928.

FBI was monitoring Hoover to SAC, Los Angeles, Jan. 14, 1943. Office of Censorship document, Aug. 7, 1943.

"with its accompanying" Helen, *Life*, 287.

"I'm in the main" TD to Bradshaw, Nov. 19, 1942.

"a complication of illnesses" Grace Vogt to Elias, July 12, 1945. Elias Papers (CorU).

"A True Patriarch" Lingeman's visit.

Jug's funeral Louise Graham (niece) told Lingeman, Nov. 1985.

"it will come through" TD to HLM, March 8, 1943, 685.

purchaser for Iroki TD to Delattre, Nov. 5, 1942.

"his general stand" "a kind of résumé" Helen to Mathieu, Jan. 27, 1943.

"stop the fight" Unpublished MS.

"Propaganda detrimental" "conscious instrument" "would be treason" Mathieu to TD, Feb. 22, 1943.

"glib throwing" Helen to Mathieu, Feb. 28, 1943.

"identifying his own" Vera Dreiser, *My Uncle Theodore*, 208.

"two authors" TD to Bradshaw, Feb. 3, 1943.

"The Satyr in him" Tjader, *Dimension*, 205.

Sylvia in Los Angeles Bradshaw told Lingeman, 1987.

"She carried a gun" "I didn't want" Bradshaw told Lingeman, ibid.

"nerves" "sense of" TD to Bradshaw, Sept. 2, 1943.

"not a well man" "cruel" Helen to Moffat, Sept. 24, 1943. See Moffat to Helen, Sept. 22, 1943.

"the farthest thing" Moffat to Helen, Sept. 28, 1943.

"men and women" TD to Gingrich, Oct. 29, 1943.

"got tired" TD to Bradshaw, Nov. 1943.

"smooth and shiny" "an illustration" "of this" "moved not only" "My Creator," unpublished MS. Pizer, *Uncollected Prose*, 326–29.

Masters found ill See Hilary Masters, *Last Stands*, 166–68. Also HLM *Diary*, 297, which says, contrary to Masters' book, that Mencken did donate money to his father.

"I refuse to worry" Quoted in Helen, *Life*, 294.

Chapter 37.

"Dreiser came to New York" HLM to Farrell, June 5, 1944. Forgue, 481.

He accepted TD to Damrosch, Jan. 10, 1944. Elias, *Letters*, III, 1001–2.

"In all this world" HLM to TD, Feb. 3, 1944, 706.

"I can only deplore" HLM to TD, March 27, 1944, 708.

"You will outlive" TD to Farrell, Nov. 5, 1943. Elias, *Letters*, III, 990.

"forlorn, deluded" "justly reproved" TD to HLM, May 5, 1944, 710–12

"Unhappily I can't" HLM to TD, May 9, 1944, 712.

"I feel sort of" TD to Bradshaw, Feb. 19, 1944.

"You know *I love*" Harris to Helen, April 17, 1944.

"Well, I believe" Quoted in Tjader, *Dimension*, 126.

"My that was" Ibid. Margaret Carson told Lingeman, Nov. 13, 1986.

"extraordinary amount" HLM to TD, May 15, 1944, 713.

"Good old Menck" Tjader, 126.

"You've always been" Vera Dreiser, *Uncle*, 178.

lunch with Balch TD to Helen, May 19, 1944.

"a bit worse" Tjader, 128.

disgusted Fabri Fabri to Swanberg, Dec. 23, 1962.

"was closing out" Farrell, *Reflections at 50*, 127.

"What kind of subject" Ibid., 126.

"I don't know" Tjader, 128–29.

letter to Ficke TD to Ficke, March 14, 1944.

Van Veen Felicia Van Veen told Lingeman, Dec. 3, 1986.

Academy ceremony Elias, *Theodore Dreiser*, 293–95; Swanberg, 499–500; Tjader, 130–32.

"You had a feeling" Quoted in Swanberg, 500.

"Get me out" Quoted in Tjader, 132.

"we three" Quoted in Tjader, 133.

"this damned medical" Quoted in Vera, *Uncle*, 182.

"How would you like" Ibid.

"I've been in love" Ibid., 185.

"Is that why" Ibid., 184.

"not only do I" Ibid., 184–85.

"Long life, Ed" Ibid., 189.

"I have just come" *Direction*, Summer 1944.

"Just as a tryout" Quoted in Tjader, 136.

"[Dreiser] has never lost" Quoted in Tjader, 128.

"a lot of Marxism" TD told Elias, June 3, 1944.

"If you will come" Quoted in Tjader, 143.

"to break up the" TD to Bradshaw, Sept. 1, 1944.

"dynamic affectionate" TD to Tjader, June 12, 1944.

"dreary demonstration" TD to HLM, June 28, 1944, 713.

"I am sorry" HLM to TD, Nov. 7, 1944, 715.

"could easily outline" TD to Harris, June 15, 1944.

"the force that had" Vera, *Uncle*, 197.

"I'm sure there'll be" Helen to Harris, June 26, 1944.

"dictatorial tone" TD to Harris, June 27, 1944 (UTex).

"I took it" TD to Harris, July 5, 1944 (UTex).

"It was one of" Helen, *Life*, 301. See also

McCoy, "Dreiser's Last Party," Los Angeles *Times*, Aug. 21, 1977.

". . . this night thy soul" Helen, *Life*, 303.

Chapter 38.

"Nature, machine-like" Enc., TD to Fabri, July 12, 1934.

"This is the stuff" Tjader, *Dimension*, 156.

"too weak and nervously" TD to Bradshaw, Oct. 2, 1944.

"doctoring—and or vitamining" TD to Masters, Oct. 4, 1944.

"Where were you?" Quoted in Vera Dreiser, *Uncle*, 202.

"the one person" Ibid., 206.

tried to kiss her Ibid., 204.

"He could not believe" Ibid., 201.

"You always felt" Friede to Swanberg, Jan. 11, 1963.

Dreiser was initially wary Dies to Lingeman, April 28, 1987.

"He could be" Tjader, 169.

Dreiser's dream Ibid., 169.

"That's enough" Ibid., 182.

Marguerite "believed" Hubbard to Lingeman, April 24, 1989.

"I do know" Harris to Elias, [1945] (CorU).

"For you are" TD to Campbell, March 4, 1945. Elias, *Letters*, III, 1016.

"Surely there must be" *Bulwark*, 317.

"How would it understand" Ibid., 319.

"Is that man" Quoted in Esther McCoy, unpublished MS.

"Oh, I am not crying" *Bulwark*, 337.

"Orville's request" *Bulwark* notes, box 120.

"In this love" *Bulwark*, 331.

"While I am not sure" TD to Campbell, May 21, 1945. See Campbell, *Letters to Louise*, 116ff.

"He was obviously dissatisfied" Campbell to Mr. Dudding, Oct. 20, 1965, box 120.

"He has had a reaction" Harris to Elias, [1945] (CorU).

visited the Tobeys McCoy to Lingeman, Feb. 7, 1987.

"The Bulwark . . . is a" Helen to Harris, June 6, 1944.

"When the Tragedy was" Helen to Campbell, May 9, 1945.

"never gets inside" Quoted in Elizabeth Gray Vining, *Friend of Life*, 29. See also Carroll T. Brown, "Dreiser's *Bulwark* and Philadelphia Quakerism," *Bulletin of Friends Historical Association*, Autumn 1946.

"The banks! The banks!" *Bulwark*, 333.

"too high for these" Ibid., 305.

"Here was no narrow" Ibid., 328.

"I believe that his" Harris to Elias, [1945] (CorU).

"So my golden girl" TD to Harris, June 24, 1945 (UTex).

Farrell delivered his verdict Farrell, *Reflections*, 136–38. For excerpts from Farrell's letter, as well as from other correspondence on the novel, see Jack Salzman, "The Curious History of Dreiser's *The Bulwark*," *Yearbook of American Biographical and Textual Studies*, 1973.

had given Marguerite TD to Doubleday, June 21, 1945.

"seemed to feel" TD to Harris, July 28, 1945 (UTex).

"in the same spirit" TD to Campbell, July 27, 1945.

In another letter TD to Campbell, Aug. 1945.

"a revised version" TD to Elder, Aug. 10, 1945. Elias, *Letters*, III, 1023.

"decidedly lethargic" TD to Harris, Aug. 14, 1945 (UTex).

"Double, Double" TD to Harris, Aug. 25, 1945 (UTex).

Dreiser sent Elder the "authorized" TD to Elder, Aug. 31, 1945. Elias, *Letters*, III, 1027.

"considerable amount of rewriting" Campbell, *Letters to Louise*, 120.

"Frankly, I feel that" Elder to TD, Sept. 20, 1945.

Dreiser authorized Elder TD to Elder (telegram), Sept. 22, 1945.

Elder's editing of *The Bulwark* For example, Dreiser wrote "Interiorally, the old house. . . ." Louise made this "The house itself was. . . ." In Elder's final version the sentence reads, "Inside, the old house was. . . ." (Campbell MS, box 125, p. 24. *Bulwark*, p. 11.) Dreiser wrote, "Yet because of the fact that he felt himself unattractive to girls he would never at that date, or later, have ventured to think that any attractive girl was interested in him" (MS pp. 59–66). Louise left the sentence alone. Elder made it: "Yet feeling himself to be unattractive to girls, he did not venture to think that she would be interested in him" (*Bulwark*, 32).

Marguerite Tjader Harris, in "Dreiser's Style," TS, box 384E, describes other cuts. For example, part of Solon's prayer while viewing Stewart's body in the parlor was deleted. The phrase "palely flaring candle" was changed to "a single candle in his hand, its flame wavering palely. . . ." This observation about Etta after

Stewart's death was cut: "She had not learned that beauty of spirit must hang upon a cross—"

For still another account of the writing of *The Bulwark,* see Jack Salzman, "The Curious History of Dreiser's *The Bulwark."* Salzman essentially accepts Elder's assurances, in a letter to him (Dec. 10, 1961), that he restored much of what Campbell had cut: "Working from the original version and the revised one, I produced a third, in which the book was cut, the plot simplified and a lot of subplot cut out, much earlier dialogue and some Dreiserian soliloquies restored."

My own conclusions, admittedly tentative, are that Elder did more editing than his letter indicates. I compared the published book with the MS identified by Marguerite Tjader Harris as "Original typed version—with editorial changes marked by Louise Campbell." This manuscript was checked by Dreiser in April 1945 (before it was sent to Louise), Harris says. She adds, "Any, and all other corrections were made by some one else, supposedly, Louise Campbell." However, Salzman is correct in observing that there was still another MS. This was Elder's "third" version, the setting MS. It comprises two kinds of paper, onionskin and heavier bond. A note identifies the "light paper [i.e., onionskin]" as the Campbell version and the bond paper as Elder's. Apparently, then, this setting MS is Elder's reconciliation of his version with Campbell's. The latter—the onionskin—is probably a carbon copy of the retyped MS. Apparently Campbell made her suggested editorial changes on a part of a copy of TD's TS (the one mentioned by Harris, above) and sent it to him for his approval. He looked over her changes and, in his letter of June 27, 1945, gave her his approval to proceed with the editing. As was her custom, she then retyped the MS with her changes incorporated. Elder worked with this script or a copy of it.

Regarding the galleys, Salzman writes that another hand, not TD's, made some corrections. This would be after TD had seen them but before the final version was set. According to Carroll T. Brown, in "Dreiser's *Bulwark* and Philadelphia Quakerism," the galleys were sent to Richmond Miller for verification of the Quaker references, and he made some changes. Some of the changes visible on the proofs are for style or to restore words dropped by the printer, and so are by the proofreader. But others seem to be Miller's (for example, "church" is changed to "meeting-house"). Also, the Farmers and Traders Bank, the name of an actual bank in Philadelphia, was changed in the proof stage to Traders and Builders Bank, at Dreiser's suggestion, after Elder warned him of the possibility of a libel suit (Elder to TD [telegram, n.d.]; TD to Elder [telegram], Nov. 8, 1945) (CorU).

"was almost driven out" Harris to Elias, Jan. 7, 1946 (CorU).

"I am glad to see" TD to Elder, Dec. 22, 1945.

Chapter 39.

"And why, since you" TD, *Notes,* 318.

"obviously tired" Quoted in Swanberg, 517.

"I sincerely hope" TD to Campbell, July 15, 1944. Elias, *Letters,* III, 1010.

"wait and see" TD to Willkie, June 28, 1944. Ibid., 1005. Willkie invited Dreiser to call him the next time he was in New York City. (Willkie to TD, July 12, 1944) (IndU).

"some social form" TD to Mme Chiang, July 3, 1944. Ibid., 1005, 1008, 1009.

"URGE CLARIFICATION" TD to Stalin (telegram), May 18, 1945.

"As soon as one" Quoted in Elias, *Theodore Dreiser,* 302.

"A small town editor" Ibid., 303–4.

"He felt that the" Lawson told Swanberg, Oct. 16, 1963.

"he embraced the Communist party" Kraft, *Theater,* 103.

"What the world needs" Quoted in Swanberg, 518.

"His radical views" McCoy to Lingeman, Feb. 7, 1987.

"the details of the party line" Quoted in Swanberg, 517.

"Durant has been" McCoy to Swanberg, March 5, 1963.

"I have been thinking" HLM to TD, Sept. 11, 1945, 719.

"You see, Mencken" TD to HLM, March 27, 1943, 688–90.

"Here's another device" TD to HLM, [Dec. 1945], 719.

"Dreiser was led" HLM to Farrell, June 12, 1946. Forgue, 498–99.

"Toward the end" Harris to Elias, Nov. 13, 1956 (CorU).

"It was incredible" Helen, *Life,* 307.

"kept putting an invisible" Friede to Swanberg, Jan. 11, 1963.

"Everyone thinks she's" Quoted in Swanberg, 517.

"I don't know where" Quoted in Tjader, *Dimension*, 221.

"God-seeking, spirit-loving" *Stoic*, 314.

"that his worship" Ibid., 327.

"It was she who" Quoted in Tjader, 230–31.

"Would you prefer" TD to Farrell. Quoted in Swanberg, 580, n. 18.

"You are dead right" TD to Farrell, Dec. 24, 1945. Elias, *Letters*, III, 1035.

"He had a growing" Quoted in Tjader, 233.

"And now if" TD to HLM, [Dec. 1945], 719.

"Oh how I dread" Quoted in Richard Dowell, "Dreiser and Kathleen Mavourneen," *Dreiser Newsletter*, Fall 1977.

"No, read it" Helen to Elias, Feb. 7, 1946 (CorU).

"Helen, I have" "This is it" "A pain" Ibid.

"very gray" "Bum" Esther McCoy, "The Death of Dreiser," *Grand Street*, Winter 1988.

"Kiss me, Helen" Helen to Elias, Feb. 7, 1946 (CorU).

"Let her go" Quoted in McCoy, "Death of Dreiser."

"The biggest and best" Helen, *Life*, 317.

"along a ridge" "a beautiful" Helen to Elias, Feb. 7, 1946 (CorU).

Marguerite arrived and shouted Helen to Elias, Feb. 8, 1946 (CorU).

She threatened to cancel Harris to Elias, Jan. 7, 1946 (CorU).

"We went several times" Quoted in McCoy, unpublished MS.

"spying" on her Vera Dreiser, *Uncle*, 238.

"a farce or at least" Harris to Elias, Jan. 7, 1946 (CorU).

"indescribable expression" Helen, *Life*, 321.

Envoy

"He loved you" Helen to HLM, Dec. 29, 1945.

"I trust you are" HLM to TD, Dec. 27, 1945, 720.

"He was lucky" HLM to Helen, Dec. 29, 1945. Riggio, 723.

"Theodore's death" HLM to Helen, Dec. 30, 1945. Riggio, 723–24.

lay in a special large crib William Targ, *Indecent Pleasures*, 73.

Bibliography

Aaron, Daniel. *Writers on the Left.* New York: Oxford University Press, 1947.

Adamic, Louis. *My America.* New York: Harper & Row, 1938.

Angoff, Charles. *H. L. Mencken: A Portrait From Memory.* New York: Thomas Yoseloff, 1956.

Arkright, Frank. *The ABCs of Technocracy.* New York: Harper & Brothers, 1933.

Bernstein, Irving. *The Lean Years.* New York: Da Capo Press, 1960.

————. *Turbulent Years.* Boston: Houghton Mifflin, 1970.

Bode, Carl. *Mencken.* Carbondale and Edwardsville: Southern Illinois University Press, 1969.

————, ed. *The New Mencken Letters.* New York: Dial Press, 1977.

Bourne, Randolph. *The History of a Literary Radical & Other Papers.* New York: S. A. Russell, 1956.

————. *The Radical Will: Randolph Bourne, Selected Writings, 1911, 1918.* Olaf Hansen, ed. New York: Urizen Books, 1977.

Bowers, Claude. *My Life.* New York: Simon & Schuster, 1962.

Brandon, Craig. *Murder in the Adirondacks.* Utica, N.Y.: North Country Books, 1986.

Brill, A. A. *Psychoanalysis, Its Theory and Practical Applications.* Philadelphia: W. B. Saunders, 1914.

Brooks, Van Wyck. *John Sloan: A Painter's Life.* New York: E. P. Dutton, 1955.

Bruccoli, Matthew J. *The Fortunes of Mitchell Kennerley, Bookman.* New York: Harcourt Brace Jovanovich, 1986.

Butcher, Fanny. *Many Lives—One Love.* New York: Harper & Row, 1972.

Callard, D. A. *Pretty Good for a Woman: The Enigmas of Evelyn Scott.* London: Jonathan Cape, 1985.

Campbell, Louise. *Letters from Louise.* Philadelphia: University of Pennsylvania Press, 1959.

Cerf, Bennett. *At Random.* New York: Random House, 1977.

Clurman, Harold. *The Fervent Years.* New York: Alfred A. Knopf, 1945.

Cowley, Malcolm. *The Dream of the Golden Mountain.* New York: Penguin Books, 1981.

Croy, Homer. *Country Cured.* New York: Harper & Brothers, 1943.

Dell, Floyd. *Homecoming.* New York: Farrar & Rinehart, 1933.

Dos Passos, John. *The Best Times.* New York: Signet Books, 1968.

Dreiser, Helen. *My Life With Dreiser.* Cleveland and New York: World Publishing Company, 1951.

Dreiser, Theodore. *America Is Worth Saving.* New York: Modern Age Books, 1941.

————. *An American Tragedy.* 2 volumes. New York: Boni and Liveright, 1925.

————. *The Bulwark.* Garden City, N.Y.: Doubleday & Co., 1946.

————. *Chains.* London: Constable & Co., 1928.

————. *The Color of a Great City.* New York: Boni and Liveright, 1923.

————. *Dawn.* New York: Horace Liveright, 1931.

————. *Dreiser Looks at Russia.* New York: Horace Liveright, 1928.

————. *The Financier.* New York: Harper & Brothers, 1912.

————. *The Financier.* Revised edition. New York: Thomas Y. Crowell, 1974.

————. *Free and Other Stories.* New York: The Modern Library, 1925.

————. *The Hand of the Potter.* New York: Boni and Liveright, 1918.

————. *A Hoosier Holiday.* New York: John Lane Company, 1916.

———. *A Gallery of Women.* 2 volumes. New York: Horace Liveright, 1929.

———. *The "Genius."* New York: Boni and Liveright, 1923.

———. *Hey, Rub-a-Dub-Dub!* London: Constable & Co., 1931.

———. *Jennie Gerhardt.* Garden City, N.Y.: Garden City Publishing Company, n.d.

———. *Moods: Cadenced and Declaimed.* London: Constable & Company, 1929.

———. *Newspaper Days.* New York: Beekman Publishers, 1974.

———. *Notes on Life.* Marguerite Tjader and John J. McAleer, eds. University, Ala.: University of Alabama Press, 1974.

———. *Sister Carrie.* Pennsylvania Edition. John C. Berkey, Alice M. Winters, James L. W. West III, and Neda M. Westlake, eds. Philadelphia: University of Pennsylvania Press, 1981.

———. *The Stoic.* New York: New American Library, 1981.

———. *The Titan.* New York: Thomas Y. Crowell Company, 1974.

———. *Tragic America.* New York: Horace Liveright, 1931.

———. *Twelve Men.* New York: Boni and Liveright, 1919.

Dreiser, Vera, with Howard Brett. *My Uncle Theodore.* New York: Nash Publishing, 1976.

Dudley, Dorothy. *Dreiser and the Land of the Free.* New York: The Beechurst Press, 1959.

Eastman, Max. *Love and Revolution.* New York: Random House, 1964.

Eisenstein, Sergei. *Film Form and the Film Sense.* New York: Meridian Books, 1957.

———. *Immoral Memories.* Trans. by Herbert Marshall. Boston: Houghton Mifflin, 1983.

Elias, Robert H. *Theodore Dreiser: Apostle of Nature.* Emended Edition. Ithaca, N.Y.: Cornell University Press, 1970.

———. ed. *Letters of Theodore Dreiser.* 3 volumes. Philadelphia: University of Pennsylvania Press, 1959.

Exman, Eugene. *The House of Harper.* New York: Harper & Row, 1967.

Farrell, James T. *Reflections at Fifty.* New York: Vanguard Press, 1954.

Fecher, Charles A., ed. *The Diary of H. L. Mencken.* New York: Alfred A. Knopf, 1990.

Fishkin, Shelley Fisher. *From Fact to Fiction.* New York: Oxford University Press, 1985.

Forgue, Guy, ed. *Letters of H. L. Mencken.* Boston: Northeastern University Press, 1981.

Fowler, Gene. *Beau James.* New York: The Viking Press, 1949.

Freeman, Joseph. *An American Testament.* New York: Farrar and Rinehart, 1936.

Friede, Donald. *The Mechanical Angel.* New York: Alfred A. Knopf, 1948.

Gabler, Neal. *An Empire of Their Own.* New York: Crown Publishers, 1988.

Gilmer, Walker. *Horace Liveright.* New York: David Lewis, 1970.

Gold, Mike. *The Mike Gold Reader,* Samuel Sillen, ed. New York: International Publishers, 1954.

Goldberg, Isaac. *The Man Mencken.* New York: Simon & Schuster, 1925.

Griffin, Joseph. *The Small Canvas.* Rutherford, N.J.: Fairleigh Dickinson University Press, 1985.

Hapgood, Hutchins. *A Victorian in the Modern World.* New York: Harcourt, Brace and Company, 1939.

Harris, Leon, A. *Upton Sinclair: American Rebel.* New York: Thomas Crowell, 1975.

Hays, Arthur Garfield. *City Lawyer.* New York: Simon & Schuster, 1942.

Hecht, Ben. *A Child of the Century.* New York: Simon & Schuster, 1954.

Hurst, Fannie. *Anatomy of Me.* New York: Doubleday, 1958.

Isserman, Maurice. *Which Side Were You On?* Middletown, Conn.: Wesleyan University Press, 1982.

Jaeger, Clara. *Philadelphia Rebel.* Richmond, Virginia: Grosvenor, 1988.

Johns, Orrick. *Time of Our Lives.* New York: Stackpole Sons, 1937.

Jones, Howard Mumford, and Rideout, Walter B., eds. *Letters of Sherwood Anderson.* Boston: Little, Brown, 1969.

Kazin, Alfred, and Shapiro, Charles, eds. *The Stature of Theodore Dreiser.* Bloomington: Indiana University Press, 1965.

Kellner, Bruce. *Carl Van Vechten and the Irreverent Decades.* Norman: University of Oklahoma Press, 1968.

Kennell, Ruth Epperson. *Dreiser and the Soviet Union.* New York: International Publishers, 1969.

Klehr, Harvey. *The Heyday of American Communism.* New York: Basic Books, 1984.

Kraft, Hy. *On My Way to the Theater.* New York: Macmillan, 1971.

Kramer, Dale. *Chicago Renaissance.* New York: Appleton-Century, 1966.

Lasky, Jesse, with Weldon, Don. *I Blow My Own Horn.* Boston: Houghton Mifflin, 1963.

Lehan, Richard. *Theodore Dreiser: His World and His Novels.* Carbondale and Edwardsville: Southern Illinois University Press, 1969.

Lewisohn, Ludwig. *Up Stream.* New York: Modern Library, 1926.

———. *Mid-Channel.* New York: Blue Ribbon Books, 1929.

———. *Expression in America.* New York: Harper & Brothers, 1932.

Loeb, Jacques. *The Mechanistic Conception of Life*. Cambridge, Mass.: Harvard University Press, Belknap Press, 1964.

Ludington, Townsend. *John Dos Passos*. New York: E. P. Dutton, 1980.

Lyons, Eugene. *The Red Decade*. Indianapolis: Bobbs Merrill, 1941.

Manchester, William. *H. L. Mencken: Disturber of the Peace*. New York: Collier Books, 1962.

Masters, Edgar Lee. *Across Spoon River*. New York: Farrar & Rinehart, 1936.

Masters, Hilary. *Last Stands*. Boston: David R. Godine, 1982.

Matthiessen, F. O. *Theodore Dreiser*. New York: William Sloane, 1951.

Mayfield, Sara. *The Constant Circle*. New York: Delacorte, 1968.

Modlin, Charles, ed. *Sherwood Anderson: Selected Letters*. Knoxville: University of Tennessee Press, 1984.

Moers, Ellen. *Two Dreisers*. New York: Viking Press, 1969.

Montagu, Ivor. *With Eisenstein in Hollywood*. New York: International Publishers, 1969.

Nathan, George Jean. *The Intimate Notebooks of George Jean Nathan*. New York: Alfred A. Knopf, 1932.

——— et al., eds. *The American Spectator Yearbook*. New York: Stokes, 1934.

National Committee for the Defense of Political Prisoners. *Harlan Miners Speak*. New York: Harcourt, Brace, 1932.

Odets, Clifford. *The Time Is Ripe*. New York: Grove Press, 1988.

Orton, Vrest. *Dreiseriana: A Book About His Books*. New York: Haskell House, 1973.

Pizer, Donald. *The Novels of Theodore Dreiser*. Minneapolis: University of Minnesota Press, 1976.

———. ed. *Theodore Dreiser: A Selection of Uncollected Prose*. Detroit: Wayne State University Press, 1977.

Powys, John Cowper. *Autobiography*. London: Macdonald, 1967.

Powys, Llewelyn. *The Verdict of Bridlegoose*. New York: Harcourt Brace, 1926.

Rascoe, Burton. *Theodore Dreiser*. New York: Robert M. McBride, 1925.

———. *Before I Forget*. New York: Literary Guild, 1937.

———. *But We Were Interrupted*. New York: Doubleday, 1947.

Ravitz, Abe C. *David Graham Phillips*. New York: Twayne, 1966.

Richards, Grant. *Author Hunting by an Old Literary Sportsman*. New York: Coward-McCann, 1934.

Riggio, Thomas P. ed. *Theodore Dreiser: The American Diaries 1902–1906*. Philadelphia: University of Pennsylvania Press, 1982.

———. ed. *Dreiser-Mencken Letters*. 2 volumes. Philadelphia: University of Pennsylvania Press, 1986.

Salzman, Jack, ed. *Theodore Dreiser: The Critical Reception*. New York: David Lewis, 1972.

Sanders, Marion K. *Dorothy Thompson: A Legend in Her Time*. Boston: Houghton Mifflin, 1973.

Search-Light [Waldo Frank], *Time Exposures*. New York: Boni & Liveright, 1926.

Schorer, Mark. *Sinclair Lewis: An American Life*. New York: McGraw-Hill, 1961.

Seton, Marie. *Sergei M. Eisenstein*. New York: A. A. Wynn, n.d.

Sheean, Vincent. *Dorothy and Red*. Boston: Houghton Mifflin, 1963.

Stenerson, Douglas C. *H. L. Mencken: Iconoclast from Baltimore*. Chicago: University of Chicago Press, 1971.

Swanberg, W. A. *Dreiser*. New York: Scribner, 1965.

Targ, William. *Indecent Pleasures*. New York: Macmillan, 1975.

Tjader, Marguerite. *Dreiser: A New Dimension*. Norwalk, Conn.: Silvermine Publishers, 1965.

Towne, Charles Hanson. *Adventures in Editing*. New York: D. Appleton and Company, 1926.

———. *So Far So Good*. New York: Julian Messner, 1945.

Vining, Elizabeth Gray. *Friend of Life*. Philadelphia: J. B. Lippincott, 1958.

Von Sternberg, Josef. *Fun in a Chinese Laundry*. New York: Macmillan, 1965.

Index